# Lecture Notes in Computer Science 4103

*Commenced Publication in 1973*
Founding and Former Series Editors:
Gerhard Goos, Juris Hartmanis, and Jan van Leeuwen

Johann Eder   Schahram Dustdar (Eds.)

# Business Process Management Workshops

BPM 2006 International Workshops
BPD, BPI, ENEI, GPWW, DPM, semantics4ws
Vienna, Austria, September 4-7, 2006
Proceedings

 Springer

Volume Editors

Johann Eder
University of Vienna, Department of Knowledge and Business Engineering
Rathausstr. 19/9, 1010 Vienna, Austria
E-mail: johann.eder@univie.ac.at

Schahram Dustdar
Vienna University of Technology, Information Systems Institute
Argentinierstrasse 8/184-1, 1040 Wien, Austria
E-mail: dustdar@infosys.tuwien.ac.at

Library of Congress Control Number: 2006931935

CR Subject Classification (1998): H.3.5, H.4.1, H.5.3, K.4.3, K.4.4, K.6, J.1

LNCS Sublibrary: SL 3 – Information Systems and Application, incl. Internet/Web and HCI

| ISSN | 0302-9743 |
|---|---|
| ISBN-10 | 3-540-38444-8 Springer Berlin Heidelberg New York |
| ISBN-13 | 978-3-540-38444-1 Springer Berlin Heidelberg New York |

Springer is a part of Springer Science+Business Media

springer.com

© Springer-Verlag Berlin Heidelberg 2006
Printed in Germany

Typesetting: Camera-ready by author, data conversion by Scientific Publishing Services, Chennai, India
Printed on acid-free paper    SPIN: 11837862    06/3142    5 4 3 2 1 0

# Preface

BPM 2006 was the fourth in a conference series that provides a forum for researchers and practitioners in all areas of business process management. In conjunction with BPM 2006, a series of workshops were held. They were meant to facilitate the exchange of ideas and experiences between active researchers, and to stimulate discussions on new and emerging topics in line with the conference topics. We see the workshops as a necessary extension to the main conference.

BPM has established itself rapidly as a high quality conference with a highly competitive selection process. The following workshops were approved and accepted for inclusion in the BPM 2006 program:

- BPD 2006 – 2nd International Workshop on Business Process Design
- BPI 2006 – 2nd International Workshop on Business Process Intelligence
- ENEI 2006 – 2nd International Workshop on Enterprise and Networked Enterprises Interoperability
- GPWW 2006 – 2nd International Workshop on Grid and Peer-to-Peer based Workflows
- DPM 2006 – International Workshop on Dynamic Process Management
- semantics4ws 2006 – Advances in Semantics for Web Services

The program of each of these workshops was developed by a separate dedicated organization team and program committee. In summary the respective calls for papers attracted a total of 94 submissions out of which 40 papers were selected for presentation and are included in this volume.

The organization of these workshops was made possible by the voluntary dedicated efforts of many individuals. We thank all the workshop organizers, the members of the program committees and the additional reviewers for their excellent service to the community. We thank the authors for submitting papers to these workshops. And last but not least we thank Marek Lehmann for the careful compilation of this volume.

June 2006

Johann Eder
Schahram Dustdar

# Organization

BPM 2006 was organized by the VitaLab, Distributed Systems Group, Institute of Information Systems, Vienna University of Technology.

## Executive Committee

General Chair:     Schahram Dustdar (Vienna Univ. of Technology, Austria)

Program Co-chairs:     Schahram Dustdar (Vienna Univ. of Technology, Austria)
José Fiadeiro (Univ. of Leicester, UK)
Amit P. Sheth (LSDIS lab, Univ. of Georgia, and Semagix, Inc., USA)

Industrial Chair:     Frank Leymann (Univ. of Stuttgart, Germany)

Workshop Chair:     Johann Eder (Univ. of Vienna, Austria)

Demo Chair:     Jan Mendling (Vienna Univ. of Economics and Business Administration)

Local Organization:     Florian Rosenberg, Chair (Vienna Univ. of Technology, Austria)
Martin Vasko (Vienna Univ. of Technology, Austria)
Eva Nedoma (Vienna Univ. of Technology, Austria)
Gudrun Ott (Vienna Univ. of Technology, Austria)
Margret Steinbuch (Vienna Univ. of Technology, Austria)

## Sponsoring Institutions

We acknowledge the support of the following companies and institutions:
Ultimus, Austrian Computer Society, Stadt Wien, University of Vienna, TU Wien

# Table of Contents

## Workshop on Business Process Design (BPD 2006)

## Workshop on Business Process Intelligence (BPI 2006)

## Workshop on Dynamic Process Management (DPM 2006)

# Workshop on Enterprise and Networked Enterprises Interoperability (ENEI 2006)

## Session 1: Enterprise Systems Interoperability Issues

## Session 2: Model-Based Approach for Enterprise Interoperability

## Session 3: Ontology-Based Approach for Enterprise Interoperability

## Workshop on Grid and Peer-to-Peer Based Workflows (GPWW 2006)

## Advances in Semantics for Web Services (semantics4ws 2006)

# Workshop on Business Process Design (BPD 2006)

# Workshop on Business Process Design
# (BPD 2006)
# Preface

Business Process Management (BPM) remains of high popularity as a paradigm for the evaluation and design of organizational and IT systems as well as an increasingly attractive domain for academic research. There are definite signs of maturity in the operationalization and value generation of process-based management approaches and communities of practice (e.g., BPMG.org), and events like the annual Business Process Management conference contribute to a fast growing body of knowledge on BPM.

However, it is surprising to note that the actual process of process management still remains largely unstructured. Unlike other areas such as Project Management (e.g., PMBOK) or Software Engineering (e.g., Spiral Model, RUP), the Business Process Management community lacks a well-accepted and empirically evaluated procedure model. This is even more disturbing as "process" is the core focus of BPM.

On the one hand, a high number of idiosyncratic methodologies have been developed in-house or are distributed as vendorized packages by consulting companies. Furthermore, related concepts such as Six Sigma are often used in practice as the main reference point for the design of BPM initiatives. On the other hand, the academic community tends to focus its attention on the intellectually stimulating parts of the business process lifecycle such as issues related to modeling and executing business processes. The core challenge of a BPM initiative, generating improved, more compliant or entire new business processes, however, seems to remain based on the ATAMO principle ("and then a miracle occurs").

The aim of this Second Workshop on Business Process Design was to continue the discussion initiated at last year's event and to further nurture the development of a body of knowledge on the disciplined, well-understood and appropriately evaluated design of business processes.

The Call for Papers for this workshop attracted 12 high quality international submissions. Within a rigorous process, in which each paper was reviewed by at least two experts, we selected 7 papers for inclusion in this workshop.

We are very grateful to the efforts of all authors related to writing, revising and presenting their papers. Finally, we appreciate the indispensable support of the members of the Program Committee who provided excellent feedback and valuable directions.

June 2006

Tom Davenport
Selma Mansar
Hajo Reijers
Michael Rosemann
(Editors)

# Workshop Organization

## Co-chairs

Tom Davenport
School of Executive Education
Babson College at Wellesley
Babson Park, MA 02457-0310
USA

Selma Limam Mansar
College of Business Sciences
Zayed University
P.O. BOX 19282, Dubai
U.A.E.

Hajo Reijers
Department of Technology Management
Eindhoven University of Technology
5600 MB, Pav.D14, Eindhoven
The Netherlands

Michael Rosemann
BPM Research Group
Queensland University of Technology
126 Margaret Street, Brisbane Qld 4000
Australia

## Workshop Program Committee

Wil van der Aalst (The Netherlands)
Wasana Bandara (Australia)
Hyerim Bae (Korea)
Injun Choi (Korea)
Leonid Churilov (Australia)
Eric Deakins (New Zealand)
Peter Green (Australia)
Lilia Gzara (France)
Kees van Hee (The Netherlands)
Monique Jansen-Vullers
    (The Netherlands)

Peter Kueng (Switzerland)
Jan Mendling (Austria)
Trevor Naidoo (USA)
Stephan Poelmans (Belgium)
Brad Power (USA)
Manfred Reichert (The Netherlands)
Andrew Spanyi (USA)
Robert van der Toorn
    (The Netherlands)
Roger Tregear (Australia)
Michael zur Muehlen (USA)

# Designing Compliant Business Processes with Obligations and Permissions

Stijn Goedertier and Jan Vanthienen

Department of Decision Sciences & Information Management,
Katholieke Universiteit Leuven, Belgium
`myFirstName.myLastName@econ.kuleuven.be`

**Abstract.** The sequence and timing constraints on the activities in business processes are an important aspect of business process compliance. To date, these constraints are most often implicitly transcribed into control-flow-based process models. This implicit representation of constraints, however, complicates the verification, validation and reuse in business process design. In this paper, we investigate the use of temporal deontic assignments on activities as a means to declaratively capture the control-flow semantics that reside in business regulations and business policies. In particular, we introduce PENELOPE, a language to express temporal rules about the obligations and permissions in a business interaction, and an algorithm to generate compliant sequence-flow-based process models that can be used in business process design.

## 1 Motivation and Methodology

Nowadays there is an increased pressure on companies to guarantee compliance of their business processes with business policy, the whole of internally defined business constraints, and business regulations, the whole of externally imposed business constraints. The obligation to guarantee compliance, whether imposed by management, customers, governments or financial markets, is often the main driver for business process automation. The downside to automating business processes, however, is that ill-conceived automation can make business processes more difficult to adapt to ever changing business policies and regulations. As such, automated business processes risk to become in time an impediment to compliance, rather than a enabler. Consequently, reconciling compliance and flexibility is a major concern in business process design.

Companies often only implicitly think about business policy and regulations when they design business processes and pay little attention to avoid hard-coding policies and regulations directly in control-flow based process models. What is lacking is a more declarative approach in business process design in which business policy and regulations are made explicit in terms of definitions and constraints. The sequence and timing constraints on the activities in business processes, known as control flow, are an important aspect of compliance. In a software-release process, for instance, a new version may only be put in production after it has been tested and approved. Similarly, in an order-to-cash

J. Eder, S. Dustdar et al. (Eds.): BPM 2006 Workshops, LNCS 4103, pp. 5–14, 2006.

process, an order may only be shipped by the dispatching office after it has been accepted by a salesperson. Designers often think implicitly about these kinds of permissions and obligations when modeling the control-flow perspective of business processes.

In this paper we show how the logic behind the obligations and permissions can be made explicit in the form of temporal deontic assignments that can be (re)used in business process design. To verify and validate such a set of deontic assignments, we show how to generate a compliant control-flow-based process model from it. The generated process model is not intended for process execution, but can rather be used by the process designer for verification and validation. Moreover, the generated process model allows the designer to identify the decision points and all possible violations of obligations, i.e. exceptions, that can occur.

The remainder of this article is structured as follows. In section 2 we discus the relevant literature on the use of constraints in obtaining business process compliance and flexibility. In section 3, we formally introduce PENELOPE (**P**rocess **EN**tailment from the **EL**icitation of **O**bligations and **PE**rmissions), a language to express temporal deontic assignments. Next, we discuss some issues in the verification and validation of temporal deontic assignments. Finally, in section 5 we define and illustrate the algorithm to generate control-flow based process models from a rule set of obligations and permissions.

## 2    Related Work

Recently, there is an increased pressure by governments and financial markets on companies to guarantee compliance with corporate governance regulations. Frameworks such as ITIL and COBIT lay down control objectives for specific processes in an IT organization. The Sarbanes-Oxley Act imposes the design of internal controls to prevent fraud for the whole company in general and for the IT organization in particular. Our work focusses on the use of business rules in designing compliant business processes. Different categories of business rules can be used to declaratively specify the control-flow (sequence and timing of activities), data (data validation and requirements) and resource perspectives (task allocation and data access rights) on business processes [1]. In this paper we focus on obtaining a compliant ordering and timing of activities. The subject of compliance, however, is broader than these control flow concerns and comprises issues like the introduction of control steps, separation of duties, the four-eyes principle...

Business process languages such as UML Activity Diagrams, BPMN, Event-Process-Chains, etc. are most often based on the control-flow paradigm, and define an explicit order relation between the activities in the process. These order relations even occur in the case handling paradigm, in which a *preferred* or *normal* control-flow is defined between activities [2]. What is lacking is a declarative approach that makes the partial order relations due to legal requirements more explicit. Bons et al. [3] identify this need to incorporate the legal state into the model of a trade procedure. To this end, the authors propose to annotate the states in Petri nets with a description of the deontic state. Regulations can be specified between the business partners in a business collaboration (between external agents). In this context regulations are called business protocols [4] or business contracts. Several authors describe a language for intelligent agents to reason about contract state [5] [6] [7] [8]. The objective of this paper differs in that it does not consider the execution-time monitoring of business contracts, but rather considers the impact of sequence and timing constraints on business process design. The issue of compliance is of course also relevant during the diagnosis phase of the BPM life-cycle, in which a conformance check between the sequence and timing constraints and the logged process instances could be possible [9].

## 3    The PENELOPE Language

Deontic logic is a logic for representing and reasoning about deontic concepts such as obligation, permission, prohibition and waived obligation. Various axiomatizations of deontic logic have been proposed with considerable extensions to Føllesdal and Hilpinen's Standard Deontic logic (SDL) [10]. Broersen et al. use CTL [11] to express the notion of deadline obligations [12]. Several authors have built a Deontic Logic [5] [6] [7] using the Event Calculus formalism, for which Shanahan provides suitable axiomatizations [13]. In these works deontic properties are represented as fluents, such that it is possible to represent and reason about the effects of activities on the obligations and permissions of actors. Table 1 enumerates some of the deontic fluents and axioms we use to represent temporal deontic assignments.

PENELOPE is different from existing languages mainly because it is designed with a purpose to generate compliant control-flow-based process models from a rule set of permissions and obligations. In order to distinguish necessity from possibility in business policy and regulations, the language considers the deontic modalities of obligation, conditional commitment and permission, whereas other languages only consider commitments and conditional commitments [6] [7]. PENELOPE does not consider prohibition or waived obligation. Prohibition is assumed, however, if neither permission nor obligation can be derived. The exclusion of prohibition and waiver prevents a lot of anomalies [14]. Some implementations of Deontic logic interpret deontic assignments as the obligation to bring about a certain proposition, others see it as the obligation to perform a certain activity. Because PENELOPE aims at entailing process models from deontic assignments, activities rather than propositions are the object of deontic assignments. This also allows us to model compound activities such as $Xor(AcceptOrder, RejectOrder)$. Unlike other languages, PENELOPE allows to explicitly define deadlines on the performance of activities in terms of the performance of previous activities. When an agent performs an obligation or permission within due time, the permission or obligation ceases to exist. This is expressed in axioms 1 and 2. Conversely, not performing an obligation within due date leads to a violation, as described in axiom 3. Business policies or regulations might provide so-called reparation, or contrary-to-duty, obligations to deal with violations [8]. Because we want to capture the semantics of both external regulations and internal business policy, we need to express deontic assignments to both external and internal agents involved in a business interaction. Internal agents in business policies are subordinate to the external agent they represent. Activities performed by an internal agent resort in the same deontic fluents as if they were performed by the representative external agent.

**Table 1.** Some deontic properties of PENELOPE [14]

| term | meaning |
| --- | --- |
| $Xor(\alpha_1, \alpha_2)$ | compound activity $alpha_1$ XOR $alpha_2$ |
| $Or(\alpha_1, \alpha_2)$ | compound activity $alpha_1$ OR $alpha_2$ |
| $And(\alpha_1, \alpha_2)$ | compound activity $alpha_1$ AND $alpha_2$ |
| $Oblig(\pi, \alpha, \delta)$ | partner $\pi$ must do activity $\alpha$ by due date $\delta$ |
| $Perm(\pi, \alpha, \delta)$ | partner $\pi$ can do activity $\alpha$ prior to due date $\delta$ |
| $CC(\pi, \alpha_1, \delta_1, \alpha_2, \delta_2)$ | partner $\pi$ must do activity $\alpha_2$ by due date $\delta_2$ after activity $\alpha_1$ is performed prior to due date $\delta_1$ |

(1) $Terminates(\alpha, Oblig(\pi, \alpha, \delta), \tau) \leftarrow \tau \leq \delta$
(2) $Terminates(\alpha, Perm(\pi, \alpha, \delta), \tau) \leftarrow \tau \leq \delta$
(3) $Happens(Violation(Oblig(\pi, \alpha, \delta)), \delta) \leftarrow$
$\qquad HoldsAt((Oblig(\pi, \alpha, \delta)), \delta) \wedge \smallfrown Happens(\alpha, \delta)$
(4) $Initiates(\alpha_1, Oblig(\pi, \alpha_2, \delta_2), \tau) \leftarrow$
$\qquad \tau \leq \delta_1 \wedge HoldsAt(CC(\pi, \alpha_1, \delta_1, \alpha_2, \delta_2)), \tau)$
(5) $Terminates(\alpha_1, CC(\pi, \alpha_1, \delta_1, \alpha_2, \delta_2), \tau) \leftarrow \tau \leq \delta_1$

We give an example to demonstrate the intuition behind PENELOPE. In an order-to-cash business process the external roles of Buyer and Seller may be distinguished. A seller can have, among others, the internal roles of Sales, and Dispatch. In addition, the following externally visible activity types could exist: PlaceOrder, AcceptOrder, RejectOrder, Pay and Ship. For these roles and activities a number of temporal deontic assignments are displayed in Table 2. Assignments 1 to 4 categorize the external business regulation payment-after-shipment, specifying that payment takes place after shipment. Assignment 5, however, is an internal business policy, specifying that no order may be shipped without previously being accepted. These permissions and obligations impose partial order constraints on the activities in a business processes. This set of deontic assignments leads to the process model for both seller and buyer that is displayed in Fig. 1.

## 4   Verifying and Validating Temporal Constraints

Temporal deontic assignments lay down the rules of interaction either between business partners or among the internal agents of a business partner in particular. Because temporal deontic assignments are the starting point for the design of

**Table 2.** Payment-after-shipment

| natural and formal expression |
| --- |
| (1) Initially the buyer has the permission to place an order. $Initially_p(Perm(Buyer, PlaceOrder(Buyer, Seller)))$ |
| (2) When the seller accepts the order, the seller is committed to pay the seller, one time unit after the seller ships. $Initiates(AcceptOrder(Seller, Buyer), CC(Buyer, Ship(Seller, Buyer), \delta_s, Pay(Buyer, Seller), \delta_s + 1), \tau)$ |
| (3) When the buyer places an order, the seller must either accept or reject it within one time period $Initiates(PlaceOrder(Buyer, Seller), Oblig(Seller, Xor(Accept(Seller, Buyer), Reject(Seller, Buyer)), \tau + 1), \tau)$ |
| (4) When the seller accepts the order, the seller must ship within two time units. $Initiates(Accept(Buyer, Seller), Oblig(Seller, Ship(Seller, Buyer), \tau + 2), \tau)$ |
| (5) Only when sales accepts the order, dispatch may ship the order $Initiates(Accept(Sales, Buyer), Perm(Dispatch, Ship(Dispatch, Buyer), \delta), \tau)$ |

a business' private business processes they must be verified and validated. The rich semantics and the availability of efficient reasoning procedures present new opportunities for verification and validation. Without going into detail, we can highlight deadlock, livelock, deontic conflict, temporal conflict and trust conflict verification issues.

In a business interaction each legal scenario must lead to **termination**, a state in which no obligations or permissions exist. In a **deadlocks** situation, no permissible performance can carry the business interaction forward such that a new state of permissions, obligations and conditional commitments exist. Such a scenario might consist of two business partners having conditional commitments towards each other, but the conditional performance to turn at least one of these conditions into a base-level obligation is not permitted. For example, the buyer has made the conditional commitment to pay upon delivery, whereas the seller has made the conditional commitment to deliver upon payment. In a **livelock** situation, the protocol state is trapped in an infinite loop. Notice that it is not the occurrence of a loop that defines the livelock, but the occurrence of loops without a permissible performance that leads to a deontic state outside the loop.

**Deontic conflicts** arise when there are protocol states in which a business partner has both the permission and the prohibition to a performance or when he has both an obligation and obligation waiver to a performance. Note, however, that it is not possible to have deontic conflicts in PENELOPE, because it does not make use of prohibition and waiver modalities. **Temporal conflicts** occur when two deontic assignments at the same time initiate and terminate a permission, obligation or conditional commitment. In a business interaction **trust conflicts** can also occur. This happens when a business interaction puts the business in a position were it has direct obligations towards non-trusted business partners that involve sensitive activities such as payment or the shipment of goods, that are not neutralized by preceding performances of the opposite party.

# 5    Generating State Space and Control Flow

In this section we introduce an algorithm do generate the state space of a set
of temporal deontic assignments. This state space can be used for verification
of the above mentioned anomalies. In addition, this state space can be mapped
to control-flow-based process models for each of the business partners in the
interaction. Generated process models are not intended for process execution,
but can rather be used by the process designer for validation and allow to identify
the decision points and possible violations of obligations that can occur.

To generate the process model for a role in a business interaction, one must
analyze the temporal obligations and permissions that hold at certain points
in time, given certain narratives of activity performances $N$. To this end, the
expressions below define sets of obligations $O(\tau)$ and permissions $P(\tau)$ that hold
at state $\tau$, sets of obligations $Od(\delta)$ and permissions $Pd(\delta)$ that are due at state
$\delta$ and a set of violations without reparation $VWR(\tau)$ that happen at state $\tau$.
Notice that a narrative of activity performances $N$ is implicitly assumed in each
of these expressions.

$$O(\tau) = \{\alpha : HoldsAt(Oblig(\pi, \alpha, \delta), \tau)\} \tag{1}$$

$$P(\tau) = \{\alpha : HoldsAt(Perm(\pi, \alpha, \delta), \tau)\} \tag{2}$$

$$Od(\delta) = \{\alpha : HoldsAt(Oblig(\pi, \alpha, \delta), \delta)\} \tag{3}$$

$$Pd(\delta) = \{\alpha : HoldsAt(Perm(\pi, \alpha, \delta), \delta)\} \tag{4}$$

$$VWR(\tau) = \{\alpha : Happens(violation(Oblig(\pi, \alpha, \delta)), \tau),$$
$$\neg\exists Initiates(violation(Oblig(\pi, \alpha, \delta)), o, \tau)\} \tag{5}$$

A state $\tau$ in our state space corresponds to a set of obligations $O(\tau)$, permissions $P(\tau)$ and conditional commitments $CC(\tau)$ that hold this state. State
transitions are defined differently in PENELOPE than in the commitment space
defined by Yolum [15]. In PENELOPE a business interaction can move from a
state $\tau_1$ to a state $\tau_2$ if there exists a narrative $N$ of permissible performances,
between states $\tau_1$ and $\tau_2$, such that the performance of the activities makes the
same deontic fluents hold at state $\tau_2$ that are contained by state $\tau_2$. Under the
assumption that no cycles can occur in the interaction, the state space can be
represented as a directed acyclic graph. To efficiently enumerate a state space
beyond a state $\tau$, it suffices to perform all different combinations of permissible
performances that are due at the earliest due date of the obligations and permissions that hold in state $\tau$. Figure 2 enumerates the state space of the deontic
assignments of the order-to-cash business process in Table 2. A state $\tau$ is an
end state if no obligations or permissions hold at $\tau$ or if there exist violations
without reparation.

$$endState(\tau) \Leftrightarrow O(\tau) \cup P(\tau) = \emptyset \vee VWR(\tau) \neq \emptyset \tag{6}$$

Temporal deontic assignments to internal and external agents in a business
interaction impose *partial* order constraints on the activities that are carried
out. The problem of generation the control-flow for a particular role in a set of

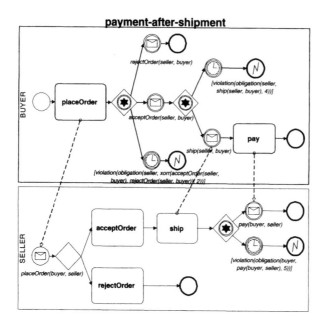

**Fig. 1.** Two process models generated by PENELOPE

temporal deontic assignments can either be *under specified*, *even specified* or *over specified*. A problem is under specified if no unique sequence flow can be entailed. For even and over specified problems, a unique sequence flow can be derived, provided that the deontic assignments contain no anomalies such as livelocks, deadlocks or contradictions. Given rules 1 to 4 in the example of Table 2, the generation problem is even specified. Adding rule 5 makes the problem over specified, but introduces no contradictions.

We have implemented the PENELOPE language in CLP(fd). In addition we have constructed an algorithm in Prolog to generate a proprietary XML file with the BPMN process model for all external roles in a set of deontic assignments. From this XML file a Microsoft Visio Add-in was written to draw the generated model. We have chosen the BPMN because its visualizations allow us to model external events and exceptions in control-flow. We make use of well-understood and general control flow constructs such as sequence, XOR-split, AND-split, etc. However, due to lack of space and because the process model is intended to facilitate validation for the process designer, we do not clearly formulate the process modeling language used.

The algorithm, of which a summary in pseudo-code is provided below, progressively enumerates all states in the state space and draws the BPMN model for role $\pi$. Whenever during state transitions the role $\pi$ performs activities, this is modeled as a task. Whenever another role performs an activity of which $\pi$ is a recipient, this is modeled as a message event. The drawing logic of the algorithm is represented by a large number of IF-THEN rules. In the algorithm the obligations and permissions of role $\pi$ that are due at state $\delta$ are contained by

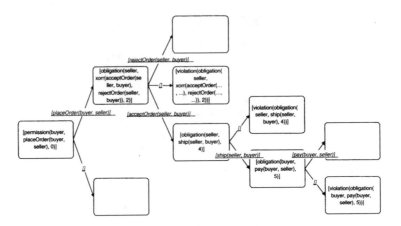

**Fig. 2.** The state space of the example deontic assignments

the sets $Od(\pi, \delta)$ and $Pd(\pi, \delta)$. A generated process model for a particular role $\pi$ must not violate the obligations for which no violation is allowed. Therefore, whenever the set $PO(\pi, \delta)$ contains obligations to fulfil, these are drawn as tasks in BPMN. By way of precaution, a generated process model for a particular role $\pi$ must foresee the possibility that other business partners violate obligations. For instance, when a buyer places an order, he must foresee never to receive a rejection or acceptance from the seller. Violations of obligations can only be detected if the due dates on obligations are timed during process enactment. This is represented in the BPMN model using intermediate timeout events. The obligations and permissions towards role $\pi$ due at time $\delta$ are contained in the sets $OTP(\pi, \delta)$ and $PTM(\pi, \delta)$. In a state in which a violation occurs for which no reparation exists, an error end event is drawn. Notice that process design can only identify exceptions, it is up to the process modeler to properly deal with them. In some cases, the deontic conflicts between business partners might be resolved through human interaction.

1   $PO(\pi, \delta) = \{\alpha : HoldsAt(Oblig(\pi, \alpha, \delta), \delta)\}$
2   $PP(\pi, \delta) = \{\alpha : HoldsAt(Perm(\pi, \alpha, \delta), \delta)\}$
3   $OTP(\pi, \delta) = \{\alpha : HoldsAt(Oblig(\phi, \alpha, \delta), \delta), recipient(\alpha) = \pi\}$
4   $PTP(\pi, \delta) = \{\alpha : HoldsAt(Perm(\phi, \alpha, \delta), \delta), recipient(\alpha) = \pi\}$
5   $OO(\pi, \delta) = \{\alpha : HoldsAt(Oblig(\phi, \alpha, \delta), \delta), \phi \neq \pi\}$
6   $OP(\pi, \delta) = \{\alpha : HoldsAt(Perm(\phi, \alpha, \delta), \delta), \phi \neq \pi\}$
7   **drawControlFlow**$(\pi, \tau)$
8   **if** $\neg endState(S(\tau))$ **then**
9     $\delta \leftarrow earliestDueDate(\tau)$
10    **if** $\{\alpha : \alpha \in PO(\pi, \delta), atomic(\alpha)\} \neq \emptyset$ **then** draw tasks in sequence
11    **if** $\{and(\alpha_1, \alpha_2) : and(\alpha_1, \alpha_2) \in PO(\pi, \delta)\} \neq \emptyset$ **then** draw tasks in parallel
12    **if** $\exists xor(\alpha_1, \alpha_2) \in PO(\pi, \delta)$ **or** $PP(\pi, \delta) \neq \emptyset$ **then** draw XOR gateway
13    $ACs \leftarrow allCombinations(OO(\pi, \delta) \cup OP(\pi, \delta) \cup PP(\pi, \delta))$
14    **forall** $AC \in ACs$
15      $As \leftarrow AC \cup PO(\pi, \delta)$

16      **if** $\exists \alpha : \alpha \in As, \alpha \in xor(\alpha_1, \alpha_2), xor(\alpha_1, \alpha_2) \in PO(\pi, \delta)$ **then** draw task $\alpha$
17      **if** $\exists \alpha : \alpha \in As, atomic(\alpha), \alpha \in PP(\pi, \delta)$ **then** draw (start event and) task $\alpha$
18      **if** $\exists \alpha : \alpha \in As, \alpha \in xor(\alpha_1, \alpha_2), xor(\alpha_1, \alpha_2) \in PP(\pi, \delta)$
19          **then** draw (start event and) task $\alpha$
20      **if** $\exists \alpha_1, \alpha_2 : \alpha_1 \in As, \alpha_2 \in As, and(\alpha_1, \alpha_2) \in PP(\pi, \delta)$
21          **then** draw (start event and) tasks $\alpha_1, \alpha_2$ in parallel
22      **if** $OTP(\pi, \delta) \cup PTP(\pi, \delta) \neq \emptyset$ **then** (draw event gateway)
23      **if** $\exists \alpha : \alpha \in OTP(\pi, \delta), \alpha \in As$ **then** draw start/intermediate event $\alpha$
24      **if** $\exists \alpha : \alpha \in OTP(\pi, \delta), \alpha \notin As$ **then** draw intermediate timeout event $\alpha$
25      **if** $\exists \alpha : \alpha \in PTP(\pi, \delta), \alpha \in As$ **then** draw start/intermediate event $\alpha$
26      perform activities $As$
27      drawControlFlow$(\pi, \delta)$
28      revoke activities $As$
29      **end forall**
30  **else**
31      **if** $\{\nu : \nu \in VTM(\pi, \delta)\} \neq \emptyset$ **then** draw error end event
32      **if** $\neg\exists\nu : \nu \in VTM(\pi, \delta)$ **then** (draw end event)
33  **end if**

# 6   Conclusion

The sequence and timing constraints on the activities in business processes are an important aspect of compliance. In this paper, we present an approach that declaratively captures these constraints, with the purpose of (re)using them in business process design. Rather than modeling precedence relations for one business partner in a particular process, PENELOPE focuses on what *can* or *must* be done at certain points in time, by *all* business partners, in order to achieve their business goals, without considering one business process model in particular.

The third party perspective on the modeling of sequence and timing constraints makes it possible for external deontic assignments to be shared among process designers of different organizations. In addition, deontic assignments are autonomous units of business logic that hold in general rather than for one particular business process. A such, changes to sequence and timing aspects in business policy and regulations can be translated into temporal deontic assignments that potentially constrain multiple business process models. The generation of individual process models from temporal deontic assignments is not intended as a means for process execution, but to be used by the process designer for verification and validation. Moreover, this explicit generation of control flow can be used to identify the *freedom of choice* that is left by the sequence and timing constraints. It is up to the designer of the process to decide whether this freedom of choice is to be filled in at design-time or at runtime. In addition, the automatic generation of control flow contains an enumeration of all possible violations of obligations by other agents that allows the process designer to anticipate exceptions in current business process design.

# References

1. Goedertier, S., Vanthienen, J.: Compliant and Flexible Business Processes with Business Rules. In: CAiSE'06 Workshop BPMDS'06, Proceedings. (2006) forthcoming.
2. Reijers, H.A., Rigter, J.H.M., van der Aalst, W.M.P.: The case handling case. Int. J. Cooperative Inf. Syst. **12**(3) (2003) 365–391
3. Bons, R.W.H., Lee, R.M., Wagenaar, R.W., Wrigley, C.D.: Modelling interorganizational trade using documentary petri nets. In: HICSS (3). (1995) 189–198
4. Bussler, C.: The role of B2B protocols in inter-enterprise process execution. In: TES '01: Proceedings of the Second International Workshop on Technologies for E-Services, London, UK, Springer-Verlag (2001) 16–29
5. Marín, R.H., Sartor, G.: Time and norms: a formalisation in the event-calculus. In: ICAIL '99: Proceedings of the 7th international conference on Artificial intelligence and law, New York, NY, USA, ACM Press (1999) 90–99
6. Yolum, P., Singh, M.P.: Reasoning about commitments in the event calculus: An approach for specifying and executing protocols. Annals of Mathematics and Artificial Intelligence **42**(1-3) (2004) 227–253
7. Knottenbelt, J., Clark, K.: An architecture for contract-based communicating agents. In: Proceedings of the 2nd Europ. Workshop on Multi-Agent Sys. (2004)
8. Governatori, G.: Representing business contracts in *uleml*. Int. J. Cooperative Inf. Syst. **14**(2-3) (2005) 181–216
9. van der Aalst, W.M.P., van Dongen, B.F., Herbst, J., Maruster, L., Schimm, G., Weijters, A.J.M.M.: Workflow mining: A survey of issues and approaches. Data Knowl. Eng. **47**(2) (2003) 237–267
10. Føllesdal, D., Hilpinen, R.: Deontic logic: An introduction. In Hilpinen, R., ed.: Deontic Logic: Introductory and Systematic Readings. D. Reidel Publishing Company, Dordrecht (1971) 1–35
11. Clarke, E.M., Grumberg, O., Long, D.E.: Verification tools for finite-state concurrent systems. In de Bakker, J.W., de Roever, W.P., Rozenberg, G., eds.: REX School/Symposium. Volume 803 of LNCS., Springer (1993) 124–175
12. Broersen, J., Dignum, F., Dignum, V., Meyer, J.J.C.: Designing a deontic logic of deadlines. In Lomuscio, A., Nute, D., eds.: DEON. Volume 3065 of LNCS., Springer (2004) 43–56
13. Shanahan, M.: Solving the frame problem: a mathematical investigation of the common sense law of inertia. MIT Press, Cambridge, MA, USA (1997)
14. Goedertier, S., Vanthienen, J.: Business Rules for Compliant Business Process Models. In: Proceeding of the 9th International Conference on Business Information Systems (BIS 2006). Volume P-85 of LNI., GI (2006)
15. Yolum, P.: Towards design tools for protocol development. In: AAMAS '05, New York, NY, USA, ACM Press (2005) 99–105

# Design Methods for Collaborative Emergent Processes

Igor Hawryszkiewycz

Department of Information systems
University of Technology, Sydney
igorh@it.uts.edu.au

**Abstract.** Organizations are often faced with managing a variety of processes. These range from predefined to emergent. There has been very little work on supporting emergent processes many of which are founded on collaboration between process workers. A variety of technologies are available to support collaboration. However, people in most business processes still use the basic technologies such as e-mail or intranet information portals and do not fully realize the advantages provided by emerging technologies. This paper describes a method for extending collaboration beyond simple exchanges and into collaborative work process support.

**Keywords:** Situation analysis, Collaboration, Knowledge Sharing.

## 1 Introduction

Business processes now range from predefined to emergent processes as shown in Figure 1 using dataflow diagrams. Each circle in Figure 1 represents an activity. A directed line between two circles shows how one activity follows another. One extreme are predefined processes where steps follow a predefined sequence. At the other extreme are emergent processes where the sequence of steps can change, as can the actions taken in each step. In addition it is also often possible to create unanticipated tasks. This often happens in planning or design. New ideas may come up depending on the situation. Each idea may be evaluated using a prespecified procedure or may require a new task to be introduced.

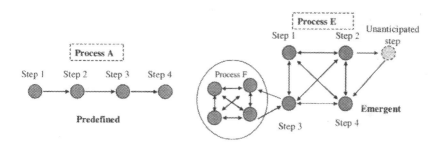

**Fig. 1.** Predefined and emergent processes

J. Eder, S. Dustdar et al. (Eds.): BPM 2006 Workshops, LNCS 4103, pp. 15 – 24, 2006.
© Springer-Verlag Berlin Heidelberg 2006

This paper concentrates on design for emergent processes. There are a large number of different kinds of emergent processes. These include:

- the capture of best practices [1] through sharing of knowledge,
- joint design of documents or other artifacts, or
- responding to a continually changing situation.

Although emergent processes differ, their most common characteristic is that they are collaborative in nature. As a result, their design must go beyond supporting defined process flows and functions. Design must also consider other factors especially culture, policy, process, and management of an organization, and its goals. Design must also consider various enables to foster team work and collaboration. These factors themselves may change as the process emerges and consequently any process support system must change with the process. Hence any design process is multi-dimensional and dynamic.

There are also a number of alternatives for supporting collaboration. These include:

- A laizzes-faire approach where users choose technologies to meet local transient goals,
- Adopting organizational wide infrastructure is developed with processes in place for knowledge management [2].
- Providing a technical and information infrastructure that can be adapted by users themselves for their particular situation, but which is integrated with the organizations services.

This paper concentrates on the latter and ways that infrastructure can be adapted to emergence as the situation changes, or the last of the above kinds of emergent process. The paper will first describe the emergent process in more detail and then address ways to support activities as the process emerges.

## 2 Modeling Emergent Processes

Figure 2 illustrates typical activities in an emergent process. Figure 2 illustrates the activities by clouded shapes. Roles involved in the activities are represented by circles and information by disks. These activities defined by Jacobs [3] for emergency systems but are generally applicable to any evolving situation. A similar example can be found in most planning situations. The activities illustrated in Figure 2 are:

Identifying a situation, where first indications of an emerging situation, such as client loss, become apparent and require responsible people to be informed. This includes both external roles that report on the situation as well as internal roles that distribute such information to people in effected units.

Situation assessment, which requires quick interchanges of information between a variety of assessor roles to define the scale and nature of the situation, and identify organizational units that must respond to the situation.

Course of action generation, by unit managers identifying response action and resource requirements, and use organizational directories to identify tasks needed to respond to the situation and identify responsibilities for these tasks.

Course of action selection, which selects a plan and assigns tasks to business units. The kind of roles envisaged here are coordinator roles as well as task leaders and members.

Execution Planning, where business units are assigned tasks and task leaders, and team members assigned to carry out the tasks, and

Execution, where the task leaders and members carry out their designated tasks, including coordination between business units.

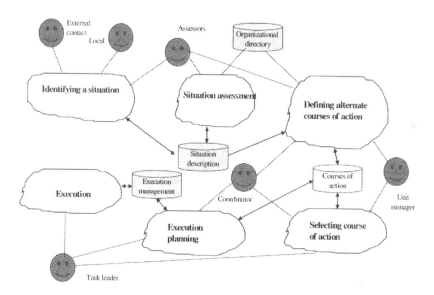

**Fig. 2.** Activities in a typical situation

Apart from emergency situations, such a process is also common in other applications characterized by changing situations. For example [4] describes a process for strategic planning in the World Health organization. Here situation assessment is the collection of data from many regions which is then assessed and alternate courses of action suggested. These may be directing medical supplies or clearing a swamp. Each of the activities includes a number of roles, with designated responsibilities. These roles can coordinate tasks in the activities or who use their knowledge and information to initiate new actions. People with the necessary qualification must be assigned to each role. Process management now takes place more through assignment of responsibilities and setting up relationships.

## 3 Defining the Dimensions in the Multi-dimensional Design Process

Design of collaborative systems to support emergent processes is not a precise science as it is dependent on many qualitative factors including organizational culture, community practices and structure and the purpose of the collaboration. The design method must first identify and classify these factors before suggesting ways to provide technology support. The design dimensions are illustrated in Figure 3.

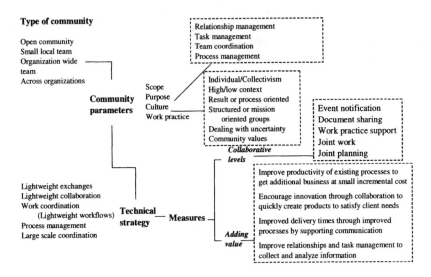

**Fig. 3.** The Design Dimensions

Each dimension here itself is in itself and subject of study. For example culture has been described by Hofstede [5] in parameters that include power distance, individualism/collectivism, uncertainty avoidance, and context. Details of these can be found in the literature. The paper concentrates technical strategies suggested in this paper are:

Lightweight exchange primarily concerns exchange of messages between loosely connected individuals. It usually supports an environment where people stay in touch and share their responsibility but have no particular goal to achieve some outcome.

Lightweight coordination now includes the need to proceed to some outcome, although the outcome is decided as the process proceeds. Hence we now require ways to set up tasks, create new tasks, and assign responsibilities for them.

Work Coordination where the goal is more specific and usually requires the setting up of a plan and monitoring progress. The plan can be easily changed although the goal is usually remains the same.

Process management, where goals are now precisely defined and processes strictly followed.

The idea of lightweight exchange and collaboration was introduced by Whittaker [6] to illustrate the kinds of technologies needed to establish and maintain productive relationships. Lightweight collaboration goes further where the communication exchange leads to some expected result as for example in [7] where a flexible workflow was developed for review processes in digital libraries. Lightweight in this sense means low entry barrier, flexible and web-based.

# 4 Choosing and Implementing Technologies

Technologies must be chosen to add business value to the organization. Technology is not seen as a solution on its own but it requires other enablers to achieve desired levels of collaboration [8]. Figure 4 illustrates the top-level approach to design. Here we define the required business value and match it to collaboration level and then define the required enablers. These enablers together with the collaboration level provide the guidelines for choosing the technical strategy. We now define the collaboration level followed together with the required enablers.

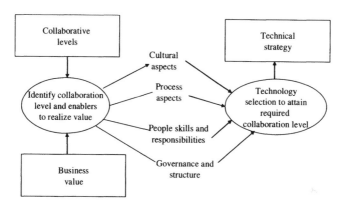

**Fig. 4.** Design Choice Process

## 4.1 Measures

Measures are here considered to be those that specifically support creation of business value. Collaboration is defined in terms of levels. Usually collaboration starts with event notification, which simply concerns notifying people of changes that can impact on their work. Then document sharing is added to ensure that people are provided with information needed to carry out their responsibilities. Subsequent levels are more complex as they require more intense interaction to coordinate activities. Work process support, requires a precise definition of the way that collaboration takes place. It includes the definition of responsibilities of identified roles. The specific rules may define the expertise needed to define a solution, the risk assessment, budgetary evaluation, legal aspects and so on. The structure of documents may also be specifically defined. Joint work goes further in that many of the activities may be carried out synchronously thus reducing completion time. Joint goal setting is where involved units together plan and agree on their work processes. This level often requires support for asynchronous work as goal setting often includes resolving many imprecisely defined alternatives.

**Table 1.** Levels of Collaboration and Related Enablers

| Collaboration Level | Knowledge requirements |
|---|---|
| Collaboration level 1 - Event notification, where roles are informed of any changes that effect the roles | People responsibilities in the organization and their expertise and availability to direct alerts. |
| Collaboration level 2 - Document Sharing, where documents are distributed between responsible roles. Typical example is the capture of best practices. | Building of trust. Reward systems for participation.                     Information requirements of different roles. Facilitate learning about practices. |
| Collaboration level 3 - Work process support, which often defines monitoring levels of activity and sending reminders to collaborators. Results in quicker completion of complex tasks. | Defined team structures and responsibilities for identified situations. Define required people skills. Provide coordination mechanisms. |
| Collaboration level 4 - Joint work where users work together in a synchronous manner. Adds to the quality of work outcomes. | Standards defining quality outcomes. |
| Collaboration level 5 - Joint goal setting where people jointly decide how they will work together. Minimizes resources needed to reach business objectives. | Organizational strategy and mission. Definition of clear governance rules. |

In summary collaboration levels 1 are essential in identifying a situation, whereas level 3 is needed to facilitate assessment and defining courses of action while selecting courses of action and execution will need higher levels.

## 5    Choosing the Technical Strategy

The emphasis on culture and organizational issues requires emphasis on user analysis [9] in order to make an initial strategic choice. Figure 4 provides guideline that can be used to make an initial strategy choice. It shows that the technical strategies themselves overlap and indicates how some cultural factors can influence the initial choice. As an example small groups working primarily as individuals in a large context where results are defined in general terms would probably select lightweight exchange. As the emphasis changes towards emphasis on results, then lightweight collaboration may be introduced.

Our goal is to provide an infrastructure on which groups can easily set up collaboration spaces. The idea is to provide a guideline for an initial choice and perhaps an open template to realize the choice. All that will be left then is to decide on integrating specific preferred technologies into the collaboration space.

Figure 4 simply provides a guideline to make an initial choice. For example, the round circles on Figure 4 show the assessment of different perspectives for planning.

The tendency of the circles to be close to the left of the diagram suggests lightweight exchange or collaboration as the solution. The crosses show a similar assessment for emergency response. In this case a better starting point would be lightweight workflows. These are workflows that can be easily changed as is obvious in an emergency situation.

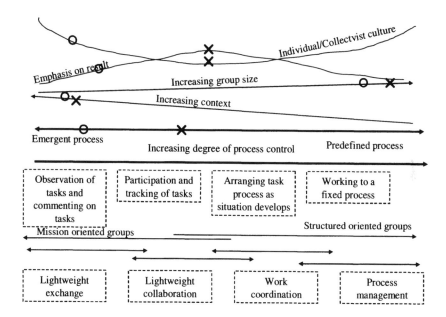

**Fig. 5.** Guidelines for choosing the technical strategy

One important factor is that different strategies may be needed at different parts of the emergent process shown in Figure 2 and any supporting system must support system evolution. For example:

Identifying a situation requires lightweight exchange, as here it is not clear what specific information is needed and people often work as individuals and closely follows the proposal of Whittaker [6],

Situation assessment may be more lightweight collaboration,

Defining alternate courses of action is usually a lightweight collaborative process or possibly work coordination if there is some urgency

Selecting a course may introduce more controls and move to work process support as in many cases the selected course must be approved by a number of people.

Execution often follows a predefined process, which may be agreed upon during course of action selection.

The support thus changes as we proceed through the process starting with emphasis on exchanges and completing with well defined processes.

## 5.1  Choosing the Technology

Figure 5 illustrates the kinds of technologies needed for the different technical strategies. Usually such progress requires adoption of increasingly leading edge technologies such as for example shared whiteboards, workspaces or video interactions. Most business practices primarily using current practices such as e-mail, portals or in some cases discussion systems and rely on individuals to adopt technologies to suit their personal preferences. Extending to collaboration and work practice support requires the introduction of new technologies and often training to ensure consistent use.

The choice is often left to users with the organization providing the infrastructure for making this choice and process integration.

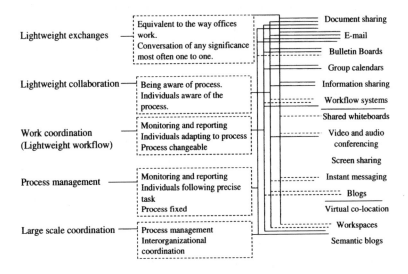

**Fig. 6.** Choosing technologies

One approach to support collaboration is through groupware technology. Groupware implementation will require gradual introduction of technologies as the process emerges. An example is shown using our LiveNet system where there is an initial workspace that contains the communication technologies for exchange of information about a new competitor. Progressing to formulating a response requires some lightweight collaboration and new technologies are added for this purpose. This includes a plan that shows the collaboration activities, the assignment of responsibilities and a calendar. Activities may include suggesting new ideas and following them up. The new technologies enable people to keep track of the activities carried out be other team members, ensure they follow up and contribute to these activities to formulate a timely response.

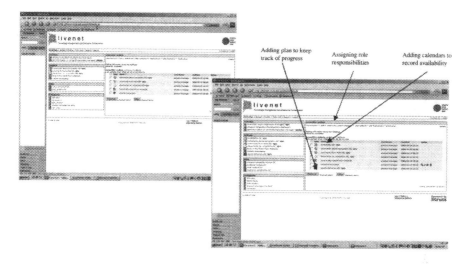

**Fig. 7.** Progression between strategies – from exchange to collaboration

# 6  Summary

This paper developed a framework for assessing levels of collaboration and improving collaboration in situations that require the collection and analysis of information and using this to respond to the situation.

# References

[1]  Artail, H. (2006): "Application of KM measures to the impact of a specialized groupware system on corporate productivity and operations" Information and Management, 2006, Elsevier Press.

[2]  Hansen, M.T., Nohria, N. and Tierney, T. (1999): "Whats your Strategy for Managing Knowledge" Harvard Business Review, March-April, 1999, pp. 106-116.

[3]  Jacobs, J.L., Dorneich, C.P. and Jones, P.M. (1998): "Activity Representation and Management for Crisis Action Planning" IEEE International Conference on Systems, Management and Cybernetics, October 1998, pp. 961-966.

[4]  Hawryszkiewycz, I.T. (1997): "A Framework for Strategic Planning for Communications Support" *Proceedings of The inaugural Conference of Informatics in Multinational Enterprises*, Washington, October, 1997, pp. 141-151.

[5]  Hofstede, G. (1980): Culture's Consequences: International Differences in Work-related values" Sage, Beverly Hills, California.

[6]  Whittaker, S., Swanson, J., Kucan, J. and Sidner, C. (1999): "Telenotes: Managing lightweight interactions in the desktop"

[7]  Anderson, K.M., Anderson, A., Wadhwani, w., Bartolo, L. (2003): "Metis: A lightweight, Flexible, and Web-based Workflow Services for Digital Libraries" Proceedings 3$^{rd}$. ACM/IEEE conference on digital libraries, May 2003, pp. 98-109.

[8] Adenfelt, M. Lagenstrom, K. (2006): "Enabling knowledge creation and sharing in transnational projects" International Journal of Project Management 24, 2006, pp. 191-198. Elsevier Press.

[9] Zhang, J., Patel, V., Johnson, K., Smith, J. (2002): "Designing Human Centered Distributed Information Systems, IEEE Intelligent Systems, September/October, 2002, pp. 42-47.

[10] Livenet: http://livenet4.it.uts.edu.au

# Process Design Strategies to Address Breadth and Depth Complexity

Michael Soanes

Department of Information Technology, University of Technology, Sydney, Australia
Michael.G.Soanes@uts.edu.au

**Abstract.** There is a growing focus on achieving competitive advantage through the dynamic reconfiguration of the value chain. It is advocated that as a result of conceptual and technology convergence, BPM is now ready to be the enabler of this dynamic reconfiguration capability. Business processing is increasing in complexity. It is proposed that there are two dimensions to complexity: breadth complexity (the range of activity types within a process) and depth complexity (the abstraction levels of process logic within a process). Current process design strategies tend to specialise in specific breadth/depth complexity combinations. Given individual processes can span multiple breadth/depth segments, this specialisation strategy can result in multiple process design strategies and toolsets within the one process. This will prevent true business process dynamic reconfiguration. A number of conceptual and technology developments need to be further evaluated with the objective being an integrated consistent process design strategy across all breadth and depth complexity segments.

**Keywords:** Process design methodologies, process design tools.

## 1 Introduction

Dynamic reconfiguration of the value chain is gaining momentum as a new competitive advantage. Gartner Group [1] has labeled this trend "business process fusion" and defines it as "the transformation of business activities that is achieved by integrating previously autonomous business processes to create a new scope of management capabilities." Gartner Group [2] says that through a new operating and management focus on enterprise wide processes and technology integration, business process fusion will enable an enterprise to increase its agility and improve efficiency.

There is a recent trend to advocate the revitalization of business process management (BPM) as a key enabler for business process fusion based upon the convergence of conceptual and technology trends. This paper will provide an overview of the conceptual and technical evolution of BPM as the background to understanding the convergence required to achieve business process fusion.

The complexity of the business processing environment is increasing with greater variability in content and the sequence of activities within business processes. Cokins

J. Eder, S. Dustdar et al. (Eds.): BPM 2006 Workshops, LNCS 4103, pp. 25–34, 2006.
© Springer-Verlag Berlin Heidelberg 2006

[3] claims that over the last few decades, competition has forced organisations to increase their range of products / services as well as their support for more distribution channels. Introducing greater variation and diversity results in increasing business process complexity. This paper will identify two dimensions to business process complexity: breadth and depth. It will then justify the need for a consistent process design approach that addresses both the breadth and depth complexity dimensions.

Conceptual and technology developments will then be identified that should be evaluated as potentially contributing to achieve a consistent process design approach across the breadth/depth combinations.

## 2  BPM Conceptual Evolution

Porter's [4] introduction of the value chain concept advocated the importance of managing business processes within and across organisations. Martin [5] further advocated the concept of value stream integration at the technology level through integration of application silos.

Davenport's [6] concept of "Process Innovation" and Hammer and Champy's [7] concept of "Business Reengineering" evolved into "Business Process Reengineering (BPR)." Hammer and Champy defined BPR as the "fundamental reconsideration of and radical redesign of organizational processes, in order to achieve drastic improvement of current performance in cost, service and speed." By the mid-1990's, BPR had gained the reputation of being a nice way of saying "downsizing." According to Hammer, lack of sustained management commitment and leadership, unrealistic scope and expectations, and resistance to change prompted management to abandon the concept of BPR.

Another significant development related to business process management is the quality movement. Ehrlich [8] describes the evolution of the quality movement from Statistical Process Control (SPC), to Total Quality Management (TQM), to Kaizen and to the most recent incarnation as Six Sigma. Ehrlich defines Six Sigma as a disciplined data driven approach of continually improving process quality and productivity through reducing the amount of variation in process, leading to consistent and predictable output. Although Six Sigma is a total business improvement methodology, process analysis and design is a fundamental component of that strategy.

The emergence of e-commerce has moved the focus of business process improvement from intra-organisational to inter-organisational. Hammer [9] states that because cross - company processes are not coordinated, a vast number of activities end up being duplicated. Hammer says streamlining cross company processes is the next great frontier for reducing costs, enhancing quality and speeding operations.

Smith and Fingar [10] define a third wave of BPM which they call "the break-through that redefines competitive advantage for the next fifty years". They define the first wave as the scientific management principles of the 1920's. The second wave as the past decade or so focus on fixed static process design within ERP systems and other off the shelf packaged systems. They imply the third wave is the enabler for business users to dynamically change process configurations. The comment by Smith and Fingar "BPM doesn't speed up applications development; it eliminates the need for it." highlights a risk in seeing BPM as a concept independent of the total business application architecture.

Thus conceptually, BPM is being held up as the new enabler of competitive advantage through dynamic management and reconfiguration of the value chain and that its time has come through the convergence of multiple technology trends. As described above, Gartner Group has labeled this trend business process fusion. The risk at this point in the BPM revitalisation debate is that it is more conceptual with the lack of a strong technology grounding of how this will be achieved.

## 3  BPM Technology Evolution

To appreciate the opportunity provided by technology convergence as advocated by the business process fusion concept, it is necessary to review the evolution of multiple threads of BPM related technologies.

Zur Muehlen [11] defines a history of process automation technology. He describes the research into office automation between 1975 and 1985 as the ancestor of BPM. Commercial exploitation of workflow technology began in the early 1980's with a document imaging routing bias that evolved into what is known as production workflow. In parallel, enhanced email systems enabled the introduction of process map based routing of email messages that evolved as part of the groupware focus. During the 1990's Enterprise Resource Planning (ERP) emerged as a key enabler for integrating application silos. ERP packages such as SAP developed their own BPM capabilities which were embedded and integrated into the package. At the same time enterprise application integration (EAI) became a driver for integrating disparate application systems on different platforms. EAI tools developed their own mechanism for defining the sequencing of messages between applications. In recent times e-commerce has identified the need to sequence messages between organisations resulting in the development of standards and tools focused on inter-organisation business processing. One outcome is an architecture called the Service Oriented Architecture (SOA) based upon the concept of abstracting and encapsulating services that are then sequenced to achieve business processing requirements.

Thus from a technology perspective, there have been multiple threads of BPM evolving that the business process fusion concept suggests are now ready to converge.

## 4  Business Process Breadth Complexity

A common categorisation of BPM is from the viewpoint of the support required for different process types. For example, Gartner Group [12] classifies BPM as:

administrative and task support (Visual BPM); team process support tools (Collaborative BPM); application specific (Preconfigured BPM); integration focused BPM (a.k.a. EAI) and application independent (Pure-play BPM).

It is proposed that to understand the process design requirements of a specific process, it is more appropriate to classify the types of activities the process consists of. Furthermore, analyzing activities by frequency of the activity and the predictability of the occurrence of the activity in relationship to other activities, there are three broad activity types. Firstly, production activities are regular and predictable activities that occur within a repeatable process. Secondly, project activities are infrequent activities that occur within the context of a plannable set of activities to achieve an outcome. Thirdly, ad-hoc activities are infrequent activities that have no predictability in their occurrence in relationship to other activities. This activity classification scheme is more of a continuum as reflected in the following:

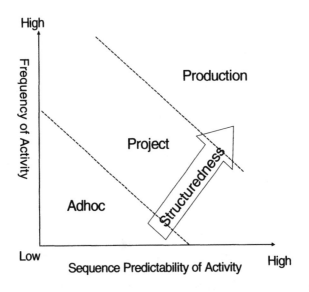

**Fig. 1.** Continuum of activity types based upon frequency vs sequence predictability

In practice, all processes have a mixture of activity types. Even highly structured production processes have exception sub flows that are unstructured and may require a customized set of activities (in effect a mini project) to deal with the exception requirements of a specific process instance. Adams, Edmond and ter Hofstede [13] state that "even for highly structured work practices (such as banking or air traffic control), it remains difficult (if not impossible) to successfully capture all work activities, and in particular all of the task sequences possible."

Correspondingly, specific roles performed by human actors within organisations participate simultaneously in many processes and result in executing multiple types of activities. Specific roles may have a predominance of a particular activity type (e.g. an insurance administrator would predominantly perform production activities). However many roles have a mixture of all activity types.

Due to the current situation of different tools been used for different process types (e.g. production workflow for production processes, project management tools for projects, groupware for administrative processes etc) and the fact that specific roles perform a mixture of processes results in the need for the role to understand and use multiple toolsets. Disparate toolsets create natural silos which need to be integrated by the human participant performing translation and transferal in real time of the syntax and semantics of one business process type to another business process type based upon the business value chain of the company. This can easily introduce human errors which can be propagated throughout the value chain.

This paper defines "business process breadth complexity" as the continuum of structuredness of activities (ranging from production to ad-hoc). The inherent intermixing of different activity types within the one process combined with multi-tasking across multiple processes at the one time, results in the need for human participants to switch between tools depending on the activity type.

## 5  Breadth Complexity Strategies

Two separate developments are relevant to consider in relation to addressing business process breadth complexity.

Analysing systems from a top down holistic perspective has evolved into complexity theory that defines organizations and its processes / activities as complex adaptive systems consisting of cooperative participants that communicate via messages. Vidal, Buhler and Stahl [14] describe in relation to leveraging web services that there are two extremes of flexibility. They define static workflow enactment as the classical approach of prescriptively having to define the workflow of service enactments in advance. They define Darpa Agent Markup Language (DAML) with its dynamic web service composition as the extreme end of flexibility. They define a multi-agent workflow based approach as the mid point of workflow definition flexibility.

Multi-agent based workflow approaches are advocated as the approach to manage emergent processes. Debenham[15] defines emergent processes as having tasks that are typically not predefined and emerge as the process develops. He goes onto say that emergent processes are business processes but they are different to production workflows that are routine in nature.

The breadth complexity concept advocated in this paper proposes that even production processes have exception handling requirements that more resemble emergent process characteristics. Consequently using different process design and management approaches based upon categorising the requirements as production or emergent would result in the need for two process management strategies within the same process. Consequently the multi agent based workflow approach needs to be considered as a possible approach to cover the full spectrum of breadth complexity.

Analysing human activities from a bottom up perspective has been the domain of cognitive psychology (a.k.a. activity theory). Such concepts as Human Computer Interaction (HCI) have resulted from this focus. A more relevant development is the Computer Supported Collaborative Work (CSCW) focus. Harrison – Broninski [16] has further developed these ideas and has labeled it "Human Interaction Management" which he calls "a complete theory of collaborative human work and its management." Amongst many principles, one key principle is that humans do not sequence their activities in a procedural, prescriptive way: "people do what they feel to be appropriate at the time, not what someone decided in advance they will do every time." Harrison – Broninski states that a system that implements human interaction management needs to implement supportive rather than prescriptive activity management. This paper proposes that Harrison – Broninski's "Human Interaction Management" concepts warrants further consideration in addressing requirements of business process breadth complexity.

## 6  Business Process Depth Complexity

VCOR [17] and SCOR[18] are two prominent process classification frameworks that attempt to provide a standardised classification of processes across the total value chain of an organization (for both primary and support activities). They provide very similar models (although different terminology) for defining the depth of business processes within an organisation. VCOR defines a five level pyramid of depth complexity including strategic processes, tactical processes, operational processes, activities and actions. It provides suggested process designs down to level three. SCOR defines a six level hierarchy of process types, process categories, process elements, tasks, activities and detailed steps. SCOR provides suggested process designs to level three and states that below level three, each element is described by classical hierarchical process decomposition.

The key observation from the comparison of these two models is the arbitrary cutoff of what is defined as a process and what are activities or tasks. Every level is in effect a process decomposition until you have an atomic action that is trivial to further decompose. Although VCOR and SCOR have fixed levels, in reality individual processes would vary in the depth of decomposition they require based upon their depth complexity.

Erl [19] defines that a key design issue within SOA is what is called service interface level abstraction. Erl says that services are abstracted to be black boxes. Varying the level of the service abstraction will vary what of the implementation details are public (and therefore reusable) and what is hidden. Erl says the primary driver of the abstraction level the service is pitched at, is the reuse potential.

VCOR have defined a Federated Enterprise Reference Architecture (FERA) that maps the VCOR business process framework to a SOA model as the direct technology implementation. Although the mapping is very comprehensive, fundamentally an activity within VCOR is a service within SOA.

One of the technology enablers advocated for a revitalization of BPM is the role BPM could play as the orchestration of services within SOA to facilitate complete business processes. Inferring the dynamic redefinition of process logic within a BPM strategy provides the business with greater agility to adjust to changing circumstances. The process rules of the services itself are encapsulated and private to the service.

From the above it is proposed that there are three observations. Firstly, the differentiation between what is a process and what is an activity is quite arbitrary (in effect an activity is still a process that can be decomposed). Secondly, the abstraction of what depth a service is defined within SOA is variable depending on reuse objectives. Thirdly, the BPM/SOA integration approach is based upon different strategies for process rules managed by BPM and process rules private to the service.

Correlating these three observations results in the reality that there will be two different approaches for defining process rules (a BPM repository and a service definition repository). What depth of process rules will exist in each repository will vary from process to process based upon service reuse design objectives. This will mean that the agility of individual processes will vary dependent on that process's categorisation of process logic between the two repositories.

This paper proposes that BPM cannot be considered as a separate component for process definition logic and that in effect there needs to a consistent process logic definition strategy across the entire business process depth complexity.

## 7 Depth Complexity Strategies

Independent of BPM developments, a further conceptual and technology stream commonly called "the business rules approach" (Ross[20]) has been evolving. In general the business rules approach is about an organised approach to defining and implementing business rules. The definition approach typically involves a declarative definition of atomic rules. Although Ross does not define the implementation of the rules definition, many advocates propose a business rules engine is required to execute the rules (eg Chisholm [21]). Similar to BPM, the business rules approach's objective is to provide ease of business logic maintenance to support business agility objectives.

There has been recent discussion regarding the overlap between the BPM approach to process rules management and the general business rules management strategy within the business rules approach. Lienhard and Kunzi [22] propose that a BPM strategy combined with process based web services can address the total business rules approach and that a separate tool such as a business rules engine is not required.

Enix [23] identify that BPM and the business rules approach have developed independently and analyse approaches to integrating the two. They conclude by stating that a fully integrated environment requires the fusing of business rules, business processes and an extensible object model.

The basic tenet of this paper is that a common design approach and tool should be used across the depth complexity. Whether BPM process definition approaches are extended to process rules within services or whether the general business rules definition strategy of the business rules approach is applied across the full spectrum of process rules (both exterior and interior to a service) requires further evaluation.

## 8   Breadth / Depth Quadrants

Combining the breadth and depth complexity dimensions results in the following quadrants:

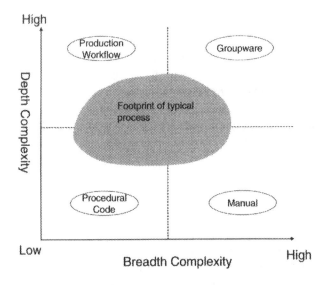

**Fig. 2.** Potential mapping of process definition approaches to the breadth/depth quadrants

To illustrate the mapping of process definition approaches to the breadth/depth quadrants, a simple real world business process example will be used that has a footprint that includes aspects of all quadrants. An insurance claim is received that is captured in the production workflow system and routed to a claims officer. The claims officer while reviewing the claim suspects potential fraud. They need to refer it to an investigator. Although the initial routing of the claim to the investigator may occur within the production workflow system, it is most likely that the ongoing interactions are highly unpredictable and most likely will occur via email. Finally it is identified that some of the items on the claim will be paid and others will be declined. The claims officer accesses the claims transaction processing system to process the accepted items. The claims systems has a number of functions and screens required to enter the claim details. The claims system has pre designed the flow that should be followed. For the rejected items, a manual letter is generated.

There is process logic throughout this example that has been implemented in multiple repositories. There is the initial high depth level, highly structured routing of the claim to the claims officer and investigator that is ideally suited for production workflow tools. There is the high depth level, unstructured interactions occurring in the email system to implement the fraud investigations (which is in effect a mini project). Then there is the low depth level, highly structured flow of functions and screens embedded as procedural code in the claims system. Finally there is the manual low depth, unstructured process knowledge the claims officer applies to handle the fraud rejection items.

One could argue that a specialist production workflow system could address all of the process flow requirements. However it was the goal of the above breadth and depth complexity discussions to illustrate that there may be the need to reevaluate alternate process design approaches that are better suited to addressing all four breadth/depth quadrants. A strategy of multiple repositories as described in the above example will hinder business agility.

# 9 Conclusion

The convergence of conceptual and technology trends provides the opportunity for BPM to be leveraged as a key enabler of business process fusion. To ensure that this opportunity is not added to the list of many technology silver bullets, there is a need to clearly identify what trends need to be combined to achieve the correct conceptual framework and technology underpinning.

Process design strategies are one critical conceptual and technology enabler. They must provide an integrated solution to address both the breadth complexity of business processes and the depth complexity of business processes.

Current process design strategies tend to specialise their focus on one segment of the breadth and depth complexity continuum resulting in different strategies and toolsets to deal with each segment. Given that individual processes can have a combination of breadth / depth segment complexities, this often results in multiple strategies and toolsets within individual processes. This reduces the opportunity for dynamic process change and business agility.

Further research is required to review the opportunity to leverage the complex adaptive systems developments (and their current application to emergent processes) and the "human interaction management" developments as enablers of an integrated process design strategy to address breadth complexity. Further research is required to review the opportunity to leverage the business rules approach as an enabler of a common process logic definition strategy across the spectrum of depth complexity.

Failing to address a consistent approach to the breadth and depth complexity of business processes will limit the ability to achieve business process fusion.

# References

1. Simon Hayward, Gartner Group. Business Process Fusion: Enabling the Real-Time Enterprise. 16th October 2003.
2. Mark McDonald and Andy Rowsell-Jones, Gartner Group. Agility and Efficiency: Business Process Fusion. April 2004.
3. Gary Cokins. Activity-Based Cost Management – An Executive's Guide. 2001.
4. Michael E Porter. Competitive Advantage 1985.
5. James Martin. The Great Transition 1995.
6. Tom Davenport. Process Innovation Reengineering Work through Information Technology. 1992.
7. Michael Hammer and James Champy. Reengineering the Corporation: A Manifesto for Business Revolution. 1993.
8. Betsi Harris Ehrlich. Transactional Six Sigma and Lean Servicing. 2002.
9. Michael Hammer. The Super Efficient Company. Harvard Business Review Sept. 2001.
10. Howard Smith and Peter Fingar. Business Process Management the third wave. 2003.
11. Michael zur Muehlen. Workflow-based Process Controlling. 2004.
12. J. Sinar, T. Bell Gartner Group. A BPM Taxonomy:Creating Clarity in a confusing market. May 2003.
13. Michael Adams, David Edmond and Arthur H. M. ter Hofstede. The Application of Activity Theory to Dynamic Workflow Adaption Issues. 7th Pacific Conference on Information Systems July 2003.
14. Vidal Vidal, Paul Buhler and Christian Stahl. Multi-Agent Systems with Workflows IEEE Internet Computing January/February 2004 (Vol 8 No 1 pages 76-82).
15. John Debenham. A Multi-Agent System for Emergent Process Management in proceedings Nineteenth International Conference on Knowledge Based Systems and Applied Artificial Intelligence ES-99: Applications and Innovations in Expert Systems VII, Cambridge UK, December 1999, pp51-62.
16. Keith Harrison-Broninski. Human Interactions – the heart and soul of business process management. 2005.
17. Value Chain Group VCOR model at www.value-chain.org.
18. Supply Chain Council SCOR model at www.supply-chain.org.
19. Thomas Erl. Business Analysis and SOA Parts 1-6. Tech-Target. March – June 2006.
20. Ronald G. Ross. Principles of the Business Rules Approach. 2003.
21. Malcolm Chisholm. How to Build a Business Rules Engine. October 2003.
22. Heinz Lienhard and Urs Martin Kunzi. Workflow and Business Rules – a common approach. In Workflow Handbook 2005.
23. Enix Consulting Limited. Business Rules are from Mars and Processes from Venus at www.enix.co.uk.

# Improving Business Process Models with Reference Models in Business-Driven Development

Jochen M. Küster, Jana Koehler, and Ksenia Ryndina

IBM Zurich Research Laboratory
8803 Rüschlikon, Switzerland

**Abstract.** Reference models capture best-practice solutions for a specific industry such as retail, banking, or insurance. The models usually cover the whole range of solution components such as product models, business rules, data models, and service models. Over the past years, *business process reference models* have gained increasing attention. *Process merging* is a technique that brings together several process models to create a new process model. In this paper, we introduce process merging for a scenario which focuses on the improvement of an existing AS-IS business process by using a reference process model. We describe an approach that enables a business architect to establish *correspondences* between two process models in a systematic way and show how these correspondences define concrete *refactoring operations* that serve to improve the AS-IS model.

**Keywords:** Reference models, process merging.
**Category:** Industry paper.

## 1 Introduction

Over the past years, the role of business processes has been continously growing. The need to sense, analyze and respond more effectively to continuously changing market conditions and risks is the main driver behind this development. As a consequence, greater flexibility is required from business models and the supporting IT architecture. In order to meet this requirement, companies begin to eliminate "line of business" silos and move towards networked models. At the business level, composable business processes are key, while at the IT level, Web services [18] and the adoption of a Service-Oriented Architecture [5] are at the core of the new technologies.

The field of business process modeling has a long standing tradition. Recently, new requirements and opportunities have been identified, which result from the need to directly derive the IT solution from a business process model. Business-driven development (BDD) [11] is a methodology for developing IT solutions that directly satisfy business requirements and needs. BDD begins with the business strategy and requirements and takes them through an execution framework that is standardized, well understood, and that can be executed repeatedly and successfully [11]. Business process models are an essential means in BDD to create a link between the business needs and the IT implementations.

Modeling the processes of an enterprise is a time-consuming and methodologically challenging task. It is therefore not surprising that *reference models* have been developed that capture processes and data at an abstract level. Reference models describe the best practices of an industry and are also often aligned with emerging industry-specific

J. Eder, S. Dustdar et al. (Eds.): BPM 2006 Workshops, LNCS 4103, pp. 35–44, 2006.

and cross-industry standards. Many examples of reference models exist, see [7] for an overview. An example of an industry-specific reference model is IBM's Insurance Application Architecture [9], which has been developed with the assistance of more than 40 leading international insurance companies, while [2] provides a process classification framework for cross-industry relevant business processes.

Using reference models in BDD has several advantages. First, they significantly speed up the design of business process models by providing reusable and high quality content. Secondly, reference models lead to better and optimized process designs as they have been developed over a longer period and usually capture the business insight of more than one industry player. Thirdly, the reference model content usually bridges the business and the IT domain. For example, business process models can be linked with predefined interface definition models and Web service models.

There are two main different scenarios, which make use of reference models. On the one hand, there is the approach of *reference model customization*, which starts from a process model that is equipped with configuration options and configures this model to the needs of an enterprise, see for example the work described in [3, 4, 14, 13, 16]. In this scenario, a reference model provides the starting point of the configuration process. This reference model is adapted to the needs of the customer e.g., by refining system roles, by adding and removing business activities in the process, by setting the values of process attributes, or by applying configuration patterns.

On the other hand, there is the increasingly important scenario of *process merging*. In this scenario, two or more process models have to be brought together in order to create an improved business process. One scenario for process merging is the improvement of an existing process model (AS-IS model) by a reference model where some parts of the existing model should be preserved and others should be replaced. Process merging is also required when companies become subject to acquisitions and mergers. In such situations, processes have to be aligned at the business and IT level, however, differences also have to be identified and preserved if appropriate.

Process merging differs from process configuration in the way that it usually requires to preserve certain parts of the AS-IS process model and the underlying IT systems. Therefore, a pure configuration of the reference model is not possible as this would not consider the existing business processes sufficiently enough. Process merging has similarities to model composition [8] but needs to be tailored to the characteristics of process models. A key technique for process merging is the ability to establish *correspondences* between the elements contained in two business processes. These correspondences allow to clearly identify related parts of process models and provide the basis for systematic process merging.

The paper is organized as follows: Section 2 briefly reviews *business-driven development* and discusses why *process merging* is becoming increasingly important. It also introduces two process models as an example for process merging. In Section 3, we introduce the two main steps of our method: the comparison of process models to establish *correspondences* and the derivation of a TO-BE model using *refactoring operations* driven by the correspondences. Correspondences are introduced in detail in Section 4, while the derivation of refactoring operations is covered in Section 5. We conclude with an outlook on next steps in Section 6.

## 2   Process Merging and the Role of Reference Models

Business-driven development provides a model-driven approach to business-IT alignment. We distinguish between *analysis* and *design models* of business processes [10]—a distinction which is also made in object-oriented modeling. An analysis model describes what the process is doing. It shows the initial partitioning of the process into subprocesses and activities with the main flow of control and, optionally, of data. It completely abstracts from IT-related aspects, but can be used for simulation and discussion with business analysts. A design model contains a refined partitioning of the process that reflects existing application systems and shows an IT-based flow of data and control and it describes how the process is realized using hardware, software, and people.

In business-driven development, we distinguish between *vertical* and *horizontal* scenarios of process merging. Horizontal scenarios involve the merging of process models at the same level of abstraction and usually in the same modeling notation whereas vertical scenarios involve models at different levels of abstraction, e.g., merging an analysis and a design model. Another vertical example scenario is the merging of a business process model and its underlying implementation, e.g., given in the Business Process Execution Language, BPEL [6], when either the process model or the BPEL have been modified and changes need to be identified.

A particular scenario that we are going to investigate in this paper is the merging of an AS-IS process model with a reference business process model with the goal to improve the AS-IS process and to capture this improvement in a TO-BE process model. This process improvement scenario is presented as a purely horizontal, analysis-level scenario. However, we would like to point out that this is only capturing the initial process improvement phase. In realistic BDD, business requirements flow downwards from the analysis model to the design model, while IT requirements flow upwards from the design model to the analysis model. This means, while improving an AS-IS process with a reference model, it can happen that certain improvement steps are inhibited by the underlying IT infrastructure. Furthermore, design-level decisions also have to be reflected in the improvement scenario when a *migration plan* has to be derived showing how the AS-IS process is migrated to the TO-BE process at the IT level. Due to space restrictions, we cannot discuss these vertical merging elements.

We present our example analysis models in the notation of IBM's WebSphere Business Modeler [1], which is based on UML 2.0 activity diagrams [12]. In these models, we distinguish *task* and *subprocess* elements. While tasks capture the atomic, not further dividable activities in the business process models, subprocesses can be further refined into more subprocesses and tasks. Control and data flow edges can connect tasks and subprocesses. The control and data flow can be split or merged using control nodes such as *decision, fork, merge,* and *join*. Process start and end points are depicted by *start* and *end nodes*.

Figure 1 introduces a simplified AS-IS process to handle an insurance claim submitted by a customer. The process model shows five subprocesses and two decisions. In this analysis model, we completely abstract from data flow and show the basic process structure and control flow only. In the *Check Requirements* subprocess, the claim requirements are first checked against the customer's insurance policy. If insufficient

information was provided by the customer, this information needs to be obtained first
and thus the process cycles back to the initial state. If sufficient information is available,
the subprocess *Make Accept-Reject Decision* makes an accept-reject decision about the
claim. Depending on the outcome of this decision, a payment is made by the insurance
or the claim is rejected.

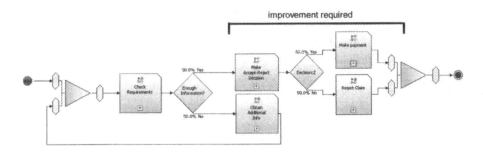

**Fig. 1.** AS-IS model of the claim handling process

Figure 2 shows a simplified reference model for the claim-handling process. We assume that this reference process has been selected, because of its better separation of
the recording of the claim from its validation and the subsequent settlement process,
which is much better worked out than the currently used payment process. This reference model therefore fits our anticipated improvement goal, which aims at improving
the compliance of the current AS-IS process with new legal requirements. In order to
meet these requirements, a more fine-grained process has to be developed, showing the
detailed steps of making a payment to a customer.

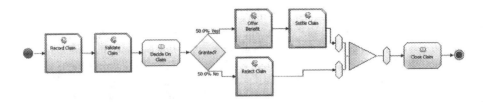

**Fig. 2.** Reference model for the claim handling process

## 3   Overview of Improvement Approach

An existing business process model can be improved under a diverse set of criteria, including *functional* aspects as well as *non-functional* aspects such as the cost it imposes
while being run in an enterprise. The functional aspect of a business process model
is determined by its tasks as well as their overall organization. For example, a business process can support *Claim Validation* functionality by including tasks that perform
claim validation. Our improvement approach concentrates on these functional aspects,
leaving out data flow and non-functional aspects.

Improvement can either be performed in a *revolutionary* or *conservative* approach. In the revolutionary approach, the reference model is taken as the initial TO-BE model. This TO-BE model is iteratively customized by integrating parts of the AS-IS model. As the IT legacy is disconnected of the initial TO-BE model with this approach, monitoring and evaluating intermediate results on the IT level is usually not possible.

In the conservative approach, the AS-IS model is taken as the initial TO-BE model. This initial TO-BE model is then adapted by considering tasks and subprocesses in the reference model. Changes introduced in the TO-BE model can be propagated to the IT-level immediately and an incremental approach can be adopted with regards to IT-level changes. This leads to the ability to monitor intermediate results by implementing inter-mediate process models and thereby reduces the risk of process migration. We favor the conservative approach and assume for the following discussion that the AS-IS model is taken as an initial TO-BE model. Figure 3 illustrates the main steps of our approach:

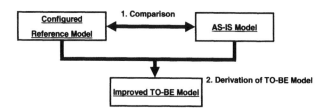

**Fig. 3.** Main steps of the approach

– *Comparison of AS-IS and Reference Model*: The first step is a detailed comparison of the AS-IS and reference model to detect similarities and differences, with re-gards to tasks, subprocesses and their organization. The comparison can be focused on improvement areas or extended to the complete models in order to perform a detailed analysis. In the first case, business goals lead to the identification of im-provement areas. In the latter, a form of delta analysis [17] is used to identify those parts (hot spots) of the AS-IS model that should be improved by integrating parts of the reference model. A migration plan can be elaborated that clearly determines milestones for the envisioned improvement.
– *Derivation of TO-BE Model*: The AS-IS model is taken as the initial TO-BE model. This model is iteratively improved by refactoring operations: task contents are adapted, additional tasks and subprocesses are introduced or removed, the hier-archical structure is reorganized and the control flow is adjusted.

Optionally, the first step can be preceded by a process configuration step (e. g. [3, 4]). This involves configuring a configurable process model to the needs of the current do-main.

The output of the approach is a TO-BE model that has been improved by integrating tasks and subprocesses of the reference model. The relationships of each AS-IS task or AS-IS subprocess with regards to the reference model are clearly defined.

In the next sections, we will discuss our solution to the problem of comparing process models and methods for derivation of an improved TO-BE model from the initial TO-BE model.

## 4   Comparison of AS-IS Model and Reference Model

This section introduces a systematic approach for a comparison between the AS-IS model and the reference model. In principle, two process models can be compared along different criteria, for example, tasks and subprocesses used, ordering of tasks and subprocesses by control flow as well as data used within processes.

In this section, we focus on comparison of tasks and subprocesses used in the processes without taking into account detailed control flow. As tasks represent the atomic unit of behavior, a relation on the task and subprocess level is a prerequisite for control flow or data flow comparison which is beyond the scope of this paper.

In order to visualize task and subprocess relations, we use a *tree structural view* which is a tree constructed of modeling elements of the business process model: The tree contains as root the process name node and each level $i$ of the tree contains all activities of the process model with depth $i$. Tree edges represent hierarchical relationships of the process model, e.g., , if a subprocess contains a task, then the tree contains an edge from the subprocess to the task.

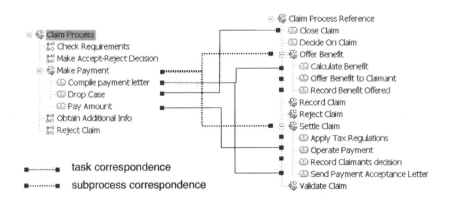

**Fig. 4.** Correspondences for the claim-handling scenario

In Figure 4, two tree structural views are shown. On the left, the structural view of the AS-IS claim handling process is displayed, showing the details of the *Make Payment* subprocess. On the right, the reference claim process is displayed.

When comparing business processes, one can find tasks that model the same business activity. The goal of a detailed comparison is to find all these *correspondences* between tasks of AS-IS and reference models and also to identify those tasks that do not have corresponding tasks. The idea is that a task has a correspondence to another task if they represent the same functionality. Typically, establishing correspondences requires a reference model expert and the business architect who designed the AS-IS model. Together, they have to review every task in the AS-IS and reference models, discuss the task content and establish correspondences manually. Optionally, correspondences can be established automatically if similarity of task content can be identified automatically e.g. by using automated semantic matching (see e.g. [15]). We identify the following types of task correspondences:

- *1-to-1*: One AS-IS task has a direct correspondence with a reference task.
- *1-to-0*: The AS-IS element does not have a corresponding reference task.
- *1-to-many*: The AS-IS task has several corresponding tasks in the reference model.
- *many-to-1*: Several AS-IS tasks have one corresponding task in the reference model.
- *0-to-1*: The reference task has no corresponding AS-IS task.

In Figure 4, we show task correspondences for our example, focusing on the tasks of the *Make Payment* subprocess:

- *Drop Case* has a 1-to-1 correspondence to *Close Claim* in the reference process,
- *Pay Amount* has a 1-to-1 correspondence to *Operate Payment*,
- *Compile Payment letter* has a 1-to-many correspondence to *Calculate Benefit* and *Send Payment Acceptance letter*,
- reference tasks *Offer Benefit to Claimant*, *Record Benefit Offered*, *Apply Tax Regulations* and *Record Claimants decision* have no corresponding AS-IS tasks.

Tasks that are in a correspondence relation can be compared with respect to their content which represents an even finer degree of comparison. Given two tasks, the *content* can either be *equal*, *inclusive* or *overlapping*. Note that the content of tasks has to be compared with respect to their semantics. A pure naming comparison is not enough.

After task correspondences have been established, subprocess correspondences can be automatically derived: The basic idea is to relate those subprocesses to each other that contain related tasks. Subprocess correspondences can be used to identify those subprocesses that have identical or overlapping behavior. In our example, the AS-IS *Make Payment* subprocess has a 1-to-many correspondence to the reference *Offer Benefit* and *Settle Claim* subprocesses. Details of the algorithm to derive subprocess correspondences are beyond the scope of this paper.

If two process models are captured on different abstraction levels, it can happen that a subprocess in the AS-IS model only has a single task as its counterpart in the reference model and vice versa. We assume that subprocess correspondences also include these types of correspondences between an AS-IS subprocess and one or more reference tasks.

In general, if there are many 0-to-1 correspondences, this means that the reference model contains functionality that is currently not included in the AS-IS model. On the contrary, 1-to-0 correspondences either show that the AS-IS model is very specific or that the reference model may not be suitable. A large number of many-to-1 and 1-to-many correspondences hints at a mismatch with regards to the abstraction levels at which the two models are captured.

Correspondences allow the definition of various quantifiable degrees of similarity between processes. For example, one can calculate a functionality gap between the two processes by dividing the reference tasks having 0-to-1 correspondence by the overall number of reference tasks. The example shows a 57% gap in the area of *Make Payment* because 4 of the total 7 tasks of the reference model have 0-to-1 correspondences.

The correspondences provide the basis for the derivation of the improved TO-BE model, which is discussed in the following section.

## 5   Derivation of Improved TO-BE Model

The objective of this step is to create a TO-BE model that takes into account the results of the mapping between the AS-IS model and the reference model. This TO-BE model represents an improved version of the AS-IS model by incorporating parts of the reference model. The more parts are incorporated into the initial TO-BE model, the closer will the resulting TO-BE model be to the best practice. The fewer changes are made, the closer will the resulting TO-BE model be to the existing AS-IS model. The ideal amount of changes is different for each customer situation and is found by also considering IT legacy constraints.

Based on the task and subprocess correspondences, we can identify the following refactoring operations that can be applied to the initial TO-BE model:

- 0-to-1 correspondence: addition of reference task or reference subprocess,
- 1-to-0 correspondence: removal of AS-IS task or subprocess,
- 1-to-many correspondence: splitting of AS-IS task or subprocess,
- many-to-1 correspondence: merging of AS-IS task or subprocess,
- correspondence between task and subprocess: conversion of tasks to subprocesses and vice versa,
- correspondence between elements with different depth $i$: changes in the hierarchy such as moving a task from one subprocess to another one.

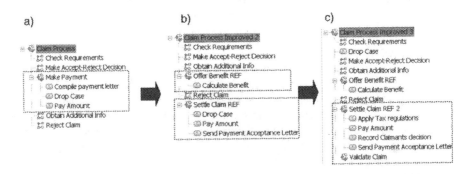

**Fig. 5.** Evolution of the TO-BE model

Figure 5 shows the application of these refactoring operations to the example. In the first step, it is decided to split the *Make Payment* subprocess into two subprocesses,*Offer Benefit REF* and *Settle Claim REF*, because the *Make Payment* subprocess is the area where improvement of the process is required. The contained tasks are split according to their correspondences, e.g., *Pay Amount* is placed into the *Settle Claim REF* subprocess. The *Compile Payment Letter* task is split (note the 1-to-many correspondence in Figure 4) and replaced by the *Calculate Benefit* and *Send Payment Acceptance Letter* tasks, leading to the result shown in Figure 5 b).

In the second step, the *Apply Tax Regulations* and the *Record Claimants decision* tasks are added to the *Settle Claim REF* subprocess (note the 0-to-1 correspondences in

Figure 4). Further, the *Drop Case* task is moved into its parent process, because it has a 1-to-1 correspondence to the *Close Claim* task in the reference model. It is decided to integrate the *Validate Claim* subprocess into the TO-BE model because *Validate Claim* represents a functionality that is not at all represented in the AS-IS model. This leads to an improved TO-BE model shown in Figure 5 c).

In a last step, all control flows between new and existing tasks and subprocesses are manually adjusted. Each subprocess or task that has been modified needs to be examined and the control flow needs to be reconnected because subprocesses or tasks cannot automatically be integrated into an existing control flow. Figure 6 a) shows the *Settle Claim* subprocess of the TO-BE model after the previously described refactoring operations, with unconnected control flow. The right order of the tasks has to be determined by adding control edges between the tasks, leading to the result shown in Figure 6 b). The resulting TO-BE model models the payment on a fine-grained level and therefore fulfills the original improvement goal.

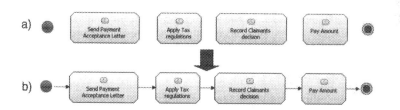

**Fig. 6.** Establishing the control flow in the *SettleClaim* subprocess of the TO-BE model

# 6  Conclusion

Within business-driven development, process merging allows the systematic integration of different processes to create a new business process. One scenario is the improvement of an existing business process by integrating parts of reference models.

In this paper, we propose a *process merging* approach that allows the detailed comparison of two process models and systematic derivation of an improved TO-BE model. Our approach has a number of benefits: The correspondences between tasks and subprocesses can be used to clearly capture the degree of alignment and to identify the hot spots of the AS-IS model that need to be improved. Concrete refactoring operations are determined by the correspondences and can be executed semi-automatically. As the refactoring operations can be recorded, process model improvement can be made reproducible, which can be a major cost reduction effort if new versions of the reference model have to be customized for the same company or if improvement proceeds over a longer time period.

One important area of future work is tool support for refactoring process models with the capability of change tracking. Further future work includes the elaboration of the concept of migration plans and the integration with a bottom-up approach that takes into account existing legacy applications.

# References

1. IBM WebSphere Business Modeler.    http:///www-306.ibm.com/software/integration/ wbimodeler/.
2. Process Classification Framework.    http://www.apqc.org/portal/apqc/ksn/PCF_Complete _May_5_2004.pdf, 2004.
3. J. Becker, P. Delfmann, A. Dreiling, R. Knackstedt, and D. Kuropka. Configurative Process Modeling - Outlining an Approach to Increased Business Process Model Usability. In *Proceedings of the 2004 Information Resources Management Association Conference. New Orleans.*, pages 615–619, 2004.
4. A. Dreiling, M. Rosemann, W. van der Aalst, W. Sadiq, and S. Khan. Model-Driven Process Configuration of Enterprise Systems. In S. Eckert O.K. Ferstl, E.J. Sinz and T. Isselhorst, editors, *Wirtschaftsinformatik 2005*, pages 687–706. Physica-Verlag, 2005.
5. T. Erl. *Service-Oriented Architecture: Concept, Technology, and Design*. Prentice Hall, 2005.
6. T. Andrews et al. Business Process Execution Language for Web Services. http://www. ibm.com/developerworks/webservices/library/ws-bpel, 2002.
7. P. Fettke, P. Loos, and J. Zwicker. Business Process Reference Models: Survey and Classification. In Christoph Bussler and Armin Haller, editors, *Business Process Management Workshops, BPM 2005 International Workshops, BPI, BPD, ENEI, BPRM, WSCOBPM, BPS, Nancy, France, September 5, 2005, Revised Selected Papers*, volume 3812, pages 469–483, 2006.
8. M. Gervais, K. Engel, D. Kolovos, D. Touzet, Y. Shaham-Gafni, R. Paige, and J. Aagedal. MODELWARE Delivery 1.5 Model Composition: Definition of Model Composition Properties. http://www.modelware-ist.org/.
9. IBM Insurance Application Architecture. http://www.ibm.com/industries/financialservices/ iaa.
10. J. Koehler, R. Hauser, J. Küster, K. Ryndina, J. Vanhatalo, and M. Wahler. The Role of Visual Modeleling and Model Transformations in Business-Driven Development. In *Proceedings of the 5th International Workshop on Graph Transformations and Visual Modeling Techniques*, pages 1–12, 2006.
11. T. Mitra. Business-driven development. IBM developerWorks article, http://www.ibm.com/ developerworks/webservices/library/ws-bdd, IBM, 2005.
12. Object Management Group (OMG). *UML 2.0 Superstructure Final Adopted Specification. OMG document pts/03-08-02*, August 2003.
13. J. Recker, M. Rosemann, W. M. P. van der Aalst, and J. Mendling. On the Syntax of Reference Model Configuration - Transforming the C-EPC into Lawful EPC Models. In *Business Process Management Workshops, BPM 2005 International Workshops, BPI, BPD, ENEI, BPRM, WSCOBPM, BPS, Nancy, France, September 5, 2005, Revised Selected Papers*, pages 497–511, 2005.
14. M. Rosemann and W. van der Aalst. A Configuarable Reference Modeling Language. *Information Systems*, 2006. To appear.
15. T. Syeda-Mahmood, G. Shah, R. Akkiraju, A. Ivan, and R. Goodwin. Searching Service Repositories by Combining Semantic and Ontological Matching. In *2005 IEEE International Conference on Web Services (ICWS 2005), 11-15 July 2005, Orlando, FL, USA*, pages 13–20. IEEE Computer Society, 2005.
16. O. Thomas, O. Adam, and P. Loos. Using Reference Models for Business Process Improvement: A Fuzzy Paradigm Approach. In *9th International Conference on Business Information Systems (BIS 2006), Klagenfurt, Austria, May 31-June 2, 2006*. To appear.
17. W. van der Aalst. Business Alignment: Using Process Mining as a Tool for Delta Analysis and Conformance Testing. *Requirements Engineering Journal*, 2006. to appear.
18. O. Zimmermann, M. Tomlinson, and S. Peuser. *Perspectives on Web Services - Applying SOAP, WSDL and UDDI to real-world projects*. Springer, 2003.

# ERP Reference Process Models:
# From Generic to Specific

Avi Wasser, Maya Lincoln, and Reuven Karni

Center for Dynamic Enterprise Modeling
The William Davidson Faculty for Industrial Engineering and Management
Technion, Israel Institute of Technology
Mount Carmel, Haifa 32000, Israel
http://iew3.technion.ac.il/Lab/Dynam/
{awasser, mayal}@technion.ac.il,
rkarni@ie.technion.ac.il

**Abstract.** Generic reference models are based on the assumption of similarity between enterprises - either cross industrial or within a given sector. The research describes a validated reference metamodel, based on an empirical study of enterprises from various industrial sectors. Drawing on the metamodel, we suggest a methodology and tools for the design and generation of individualized business process models.

**Keywords:** industry blueprints, reference models, case studies and experiments.

## 1 Introduction

Modern enterprise operations and management are firmly based upon the principle of functionality and business processes supported by an enterprise-wide integrated IT infrastructure. Management focus has shifted to integrating and managing the process-centered enterprise – i.e. the chain of activities whose final aim is the "production of a specified output for a particular customer or market" [1] using tools such as Business Process Management (BPM) and Enterprise Resource Planning (ERP) [2]. These tools form the basis for enterprise activity design, operations, change and improvement.

The current main thrust of business process management research has focused on the study of structural frameworks and IT related execution patterns [6] putting little emphasis on the content layer that is supposed to populate these frameworks. "Real life" business process models, which contain practical content objects, have been somewhat disregarded except in illustrative examples. Few scientific publications have addressed the topic of designing business process content [9],[11],[10], opting to develop theories, empirical studies and supporting tools. The lack of suggestions for standard structure, terminology and tools for the process content layer has restricted the development of "reference modeling content science", leaving it mostly to vendors and commercial organizations [8].

J. Eder, S. Dustdar et al. (Eds.): BPM 2006 Workshops, LNCS 4103, pp. 45–54, 2006.
© Springer-Verlag Berlin Heidelberg 2006

Presumably, professionals have developed business process repositories on the basis of experience accumulated through analyzing business activity and implementing IT systems in a variety of industries. This has led to a paradigm whereby these content frameworks are presented as generic – i.e. typical for an industrial sector (e.g. SAP's "aerospace industry" business solutions [5] or Oracle's "retail solutions" [12]). However, the existence of numerous "generic" reference models (or "best practices"), that vary significantly between ERP vendors, even for a given sector, indicates a lack of scientific systematization in developing such content models and raises the question as to whether these models actually constitute generic validated prototypes [6]. Another concern is the generation of individualized process models - conventionally based on customization of sectorial models. This approach overlooks the fact that sectorial classifications reflect the end-product of the enterprise, rather than its modus operandi [13].

Aiming to confront these concerns, the objective of this research is to: (1) demonstrate a generic, validated business process metamodel (2) suggest a structured methodology for the construction of enterprise-specific business process models based on the operational characteristics of the implementing organization.

After a review of related work (section 2), we present the validated metamodel (section 3), and a methodology for the design and generation of enterprise-specific process models (section 4). Section 5 includes conclusions and directions for future work.

## 2   Application of Reference Process Models

### 2.1   Commercial Reference Models

Commercial reference process models are usually developed by vendors such as SAP [5] and Oracle [4]; by system integrators such as EDS [16], IBM BCS (Business Consulting Services) [17], and Accenture [18]; and by BPM specific companies such as Staffware[20], Pegasystems [19], FileNet [21] and others.

ERP vendor reference process models include, for example, SAP's industry and cross-industry Business Solution Maps [5], Lawson-Intentia's ERM (Enterprise Reference Models) [14], and Oracle's OBM (Oracle Business Models) library [4]. In the SAP business solution maps, the top level "solution map" for an industrial sector presents names and descriptions of the high level functionalities for that industry (about 7), and the corresponding main processes (about 7) for each major process. From these categorizations vendors and integrators develop a suite of processes, reflecting what an enterprise does, or needs to do, in order to achieve its objectives [15].

These models are based on the assumption of significant similarity between enterprises that operate within a certain industry. Oracle corporation for example, offers process flows that cover 19 industrial branches [4]; SAP offers Business Solutions for 24 industrial branches [5]; and other ERP/SCM/CRM vendors similarly base their business process models on a finite set of predefined business processes, that comprise "industry-specific" reference models.

In summary, research into commercial business process models has introduced the following concepts: (a) the idea of generic reference industry-related business process models (featuring industrial-sector or output genericity); (b) the idea that a specific enterprise process model is a sub-set of a generic reference business process model. The current research elaborates these concepts in the following ways: (a) suggesting a generic business process metamodel (functional or operational genericity); (b) applying quantitative statistical methods in validating the genericity of the reference process metamodel; (c) suggesting a structured method for generating derived individualized process models.

## 2.2  Derivation of Individualized Process Models

While academia has devised novel notions regarding model-driven structural process configuration of enterprise systems [24],[25], the prevailing practitioner procedure for generating individualized process models content is a top-down customization of generic sectorial models. When a vendor, integrator or BPM specialist approaches, say, two enterprises x, y within a certain industrial branch "α" (such as manufacturing, utilities, chemicals, healthcare, consumer goods products) both enterprises are first presented with an identical reference process model. The next stage would be a top-down customization of the reference model, by eliminating unnecessary functionalities or processes, so that it would best fit the needs of the enterprise (Fig. 1).

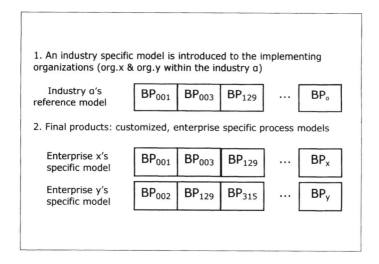

**Fig. 1.** Reference based content modeling: state of the art

This approach overlooks the fact that sectorial classifications reflect the end-product of the enterprise, rather than its modus operandi. Hence, focusing on *what* the enterprise produces (or supplies), instead of *how* this production is carried out, can be misleading and may result in inappropriate business process models [6]. For example, an enterprise from the manufacturing sector may be based on fabrication processes – or assembly processes; or mass-production processes – or customized production processes. In each case the "production" and "logistics" functionalities are very different. A single "manufacturing" model would probably not cover all cases.

This research suggests an alternative approach for generating individualized process models, based on the correlation between the operational characteristics of the organization and a set of corresponding business processes.

## 3   Constructing a Validated Generic Metamodel

The current metamodel encompasses a hierarchy of over 2,000 processes gleaned from a survey of the content models published by SAP and Oracle, and further field surveys and student projects. These resulted in a sample of 101 enterprises from a wide range of industrial sectors. Top-level operational classifications were developed in two stages: a first partition into business-oriented functionalities and industry-oriented functionalities; and a further subdivision into basic and support functionalities on the one hand, and goods and services on the other. Thus processes are divided into five operational classes: (a) business functionalities: (1) basic business processes, (2) business support processes; (b) industrial functionalities: (3) basic manufacturing processes, (4) manufacturing support processes, (5) service processes. This top-level categorization is then decomposed into two further levels, following the lead of the breakdown presented in the Oracle business solution maps: each business process is subsumed under a main process; and each main process is subsumed under a major process.

Two attributes were considered necessary if the metamodel was to be regarded as meaningful at the major process (high) level:

- The set of major processes could be reproduced by performing clustering on the set of all main (lower level) processes over all enterprises (*separability*)
- Implementation of a major process implied implementation of all or most of the main processes it comprises (*genericity*)

Our analysis was carried out in two directions: bottom-up and top-down. First, all business processes were linked (a) to some main process and (b) to those industries in the sample in which they were found to be implemented. Then, clustering [22] was used to find significant groupings of main processes, based on the implementation findings. The clusters or groupings were found to correspond to a high degree with the 29 major processes empirically determined during metamodel construction by studying upper-level functionalities in the SAP and Oracle models and from conventional division of organizations into functional departments. It was found that (a) the probability is high that industries are significantly associated with the same number and content of clusters corresponding to the number of main processes in each class; and (b) the degree of separation between clusters is almost absolute. Thus the major processes can be considered separable (i.e. no overlapping of main processes within major processes). This completed the bottom-up partitioning of processes at the major, main and operational levels. For example: Major: "procurement"; main: "procurement order"; basic: "authorization of procurement order".

As a first step to proving functional genericity, it was noted that the average probabilities of an enterprise implementing all the main processes within the five classes were: (a) business functionalities: (1) basic business processes (91%), (2) business support processes (59%); (b) industrial functionalities: (3) basic manufacturing processes (40%), (4) manufacturing support processes (51%), (5) service processes (59%). Thus, even at this level, the basic business processes can be considered common to almost all enterprises – i.e. functionally generic.

As a second step – top-down analysis – a major process was considered generic, at one of three levels, according to the following measure of "genericity":

- Strong genericity: all enterprises that implement the major process implement all of its requisite main processes – i.e. that a significant number of basic processes within the major-main hierarchy are implemented. This level was attained by all basic business processes, all business support processes (except "Information Service Management"), "Configuration Management", all manufacturing support processes, and all service processes.
- Intermediate genericity: the probability that a main process will be implemented in an enterprise, if the major process is implemented, is not less than 90% (i.e. 90% of the enterprises studied implemented the process). This level was attained by "Information Service Management" (91%) and "Product Engineering" (93%).
- Weak genericity: the probability that a main process will be implemented in an enterprise, if the major process is implemented, is not less than 65%. This level was achieved by "Research and Development" (76%) and "Production/ Operations" (65%).
- No genericity: the probability that a main process will be implemented in an enterprise, if the major process is implemented, is less than 65%. No major process exhibited this level of genericity.

Thus almost all the major processes show appreciable separability and genericity; and so are meaningful in general. These findings also enable two significant conclusions to be drawn: (a) an enterprise model can be constructed by a separable and additive set of business processes; (b) if an enterprise implements a major process, it most likely implements the corresponding main processes.

The metamodel thus possesses the following important properties:

- It encompasses 29 major processes, 169 main processes and some 2,000 processes.
- Its major processes are separable and generic, so that any derived model is composed of an *additive* set of major and main processes.
- Most business functionalities are common to all enterprises.
- Enterprises are differentiated mainly by their industrial functionalities – the degree to which each of the manufacturing and service sub-classes are implemented.

These properties enable us to utilize the metamodel in a systematic way for the design of individualized business process models.

# 4   Generating Individualized Process Models

This research elaborates a method that was presented in [6] as a possible solution to the above mentioned concerns. Instead of determining *what* organizations are producing and then tagging them according to their industrial classification, we determine in a general and then detailed way *how* organizations are operating, so that they are expressed by their operational characteristics. In order to establish an enterprise-specific business process suite, we analyze the existing or planned functionalities in the enterprise and create an enterprise-specific model. Each main process constitutes a generic building block, and incorporates a set of possible business processes exclusive to that main process. This course of action enables the construction of an "individualized" organizational model which itemizes the specific business processes of a given organization. The top-down approach is appropriate for two reasons. (a) Functional characterization of a specific enterprise is performed incrementally: first, major processes are analyzed; then, main processes, and finally basic business processes. (b) We apply the principle of separability (a particular business process is classified under one main process only; a specific main process is classified under one major process only) and additivity (as the major processes are separable, a model is formed from a conjunction of major processes, and thus main processes, and thus business processes).

## 4.1   Determining the Operational Classification of an Enterprise

Lincoln and Karni [15] proposed a general typological representation of enterprises, that overcame the necessity to distinguish between production and service industries, seeing that both types of activity occur in most organizations. Their typology characterizes industrial functionality by two codes: M(*) and S(*). M(*) defines goods production functionality (oriented along product development through manufacture) , whilst S(*) defines service provision functionality (oriented towards the proximity between the provider and customer. The scale of functionalities ranges from "pure goods production" (M(4)) through "pure service provision" (S(4)) (Table 1).

This presentation implies that an enterprise implementing "full production" functionality (R&D, product engineering, configuration management and production), with no service functionality, would be coded as M(1+2+3+4)S(0).

An enterprise implementing "full service" functionality (front office, contact office, mobile office and remote office), with no goods functionality, would be coded as M(0)S(1+2+3+4). All other enterprises can be characterized within this spectrum in accordance with their tendency to be oriented towards manufacturing or service. For example: a ticket sales office that is a "pure" service enterprise would be coded as M(0)S(1+2+3+4) (sales of tickets via the web, through agents in the field, via a call center, and person-to-person at the enterprise offices). A software company oriented both towards creating software and providing services would be coded as M(2+3+4)S(2+3) (development of customized software reusing modules; providing a help desk in the field and through a call center).

**Table 1.** The primary functional typology

| Operational Characteristic | Code |
|---|---|
| Production/operations (MtS) | M(4) |
| Configuration management (AtO) | M(3) |
| Product engineering (EtO) | M(2) |
| Research and development (DtO) | M(1) |
| No significant goods production | M(0) |
| No significant service provision | S(0) |
| Remote office service (web/vending) | S(1) |
| Mobile office service (field) | S(2) |
| Contact office service (call center) | S(3) |
| Front office service (provider) | S(4) |

## 4.2 Generation of Individualized Business Process Content Models

The procedure for generating an individual business process model is as follows, based upon the major-main-basic hierarchical tree within the metamodel:

a) Using a comprehensive questionnaire, identify the general operational characteristics of the enterprise (as described in section 4.1).
b) From the metamodel, select the major processes constituting the top-level operational characteristics of the enterprise.
c) Automatically generate a reduced model, encompassing only those major processes selected and incorporating all the main processes in the sub-trees below the major processes.
d) From this model, select the main processes constituting the second-level operational characteristics of the enterprise.
e) Automatically generate a further reduced model, encompassing only those major and main processes selected and incorporating all basic processes in the sub-trees below the main processes.
f) Using a general threshold probability given by the enterprise, automatically retrieve those business processes, for each main process in the condensed capstone, having a probability equal to or greater than the threshold value.
g) Automatically generate the initial model (all process levels) for the enterprise.
h) Fine tune the model – usually at the process (low) level – to ensure that all relevant processes have been included, and unnecessary processes eliminated. This may require some time, as the various "key users" in the enterprise become involved at this stage. However, they begin from the specific enterprise model as an initial input, rather than a generalized vendor offering. This focuses attention on the enterprise functionality, and can greatly shorten the time to reach agreement on the final model.

A summary of the steps is described in Fig. 2.

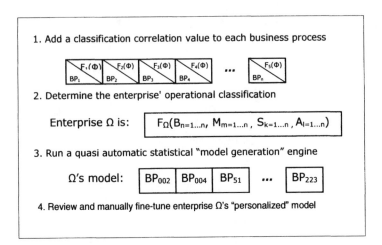

**Fig. 2.** Generating the enterprise specific model

For example, a confectionery manufacturer produces and markets a range of mass-produced candies for sale at the entrances to a chain of supermarkets. From the questionnaire we learn that its operations are characterized by make-to-stock production, a call center for customer orders, a fleet of refrigerated vans for distribution to the outlets, and refilling of candy vending machines outside the premises of each outlet. According to the categorization of operational characteristics (Table 1), the enterprise would be classified as M(3+4)S(1+2+3): managing the candy mix and distributing customer orders; and receiving the orders and maintaining vending machines. The corresponding set of industrial processes can be retrieved top-down from the business process repository, and, as a consequence of the additive property of the process clusters, the operational modules can be easily combined to rapidly establish the confectionery manufacturer's business process model. The next stage would be the fine-tuning of the model by the manufacturer. This model is then process as the launch pad for the blueprinting stages of the ERP project. This generation process has been carried out in several organizations in Israel, and has been found to be highly effective.

# 5 Conclusion

The business functionality and process aspects of ERP have, to a large extent, been overshadowed by IT perspectives of ERP software and vendor industry-based perspectives of functional commonality. However, business process modeling and design is distinctly different from information system process modeling [3], and a specific enterprise does not necessarily conform to the paradigm proposed for the sector under which it is classified. From a business viewpoint, it is implicit that the process approach is applicable to almost any industry or enterprise – at least at the nominal level (naming functions and processes). However, the correct process suite for a particular enterprise can only be assembled by careful consideration of operational characteristics;

if this is done correctly many classical customization problems can be avoided. Our investigation has demonstrated the tenability of this assertion, and has shown that such models can serve as rich tools for understanding enterprise functionality in general, and, specifically, those classed as business, manufacturing or service. It has been demonstrated that the method described in this paper significantly facilitates the design and construction of individualized process models, starting from the questionnaire, through focused model generation, and the fine tuning of the generated model. Each step has been found to contribute significantly to that following, so that a minimum of extraneous processes, at all levels, needs to be taken into account for elimination. The challenge for further research is to improve the predictive capabilities of the model (top-down stepwise generation) first by extending the metamodel representation level, and next by increasing the accuracy of the correlation between operational characteristics and corresponding business processes incorporated into the model.

# References

[1] Davenport, T., Process Innovation: Reengineering Work through Information Technology, Harvard Business Press, 1993.
[2] Hatten, K. J. and Rosenthal, S. R., "Managing the Process-Centered Enterprise", Long Range Planning, 32 (3), 1999, pp. 293-310.
[3] Gulledge, T. R., Simon, G. and Sommer, R. A., "Using ARIS to Manage SAP Interoperability", in Scheer, A.-W., Jost, W., Abolhassan, F., and Kirchmer, M. (Editors), Business Process Excellence: ARIS in Practice, Springer-Verlag, 2002, pp. 87-108.
[4] Oracle. Business Models (OBM), http://www.oracle.com/consulting/offerings/implementation/methods_tools/, 2004.
[5] SAP. Business Maps and Solution Composer, http://www.sap.com/solutions/businessmaps/composer/, 2004.
[6] Avi Wasser, Maya Lincoln, Reuven Karni: Accelerated Enterprise Process Modeling Through a Formalized Functional Typology. BPM2005: 446-451.
[7] Wil M. P. van der Aalst, Arthur H. M. ter Hofstede: YAWL: yet another workflow language. Inf. Syst. 30(4): 245-275 (2005)
[8] Fettke, P.; Loos, P.; Zwicker, J.: Business Process Reference Models - Survey and Classification. In: Kindler, E.; Nottgens, M.: Business Process Reference Models – BPRM: 1-15 (2005).
[9] Chrysanthos Dellarocas, Mark Klein: A Knowledge-Based Approach for Designing Robust Business Processes. Business Process Management 2000: 50-65
[10] A. Bernstein. Process Recombination: An Ontology Based Approach for Business Process Re-Design. SAP Design Guild, Vol. 7, October 2003.
[11] Malone, T. W., Crowston, K. G., & Herman, G. (Eds.) Organizing Business Knowledge: The MIT Process Handbook. Cambridge, MA: MIT Press, 2003.
[12] www.oracle.com/industries/retail/index.html
[13] B. Light, The maintenance implications of the customization of ERP software, J. Software Maintenance: Res. Practice 13 (2001) 415–429.
[14] Intentia. Enterprise Reference Models, http://www.intentia.com/WCW.nsf/pub/tools_index, 2004.
[15] M. Lincoln, Karni R. A Generic Business Function Framework for Industrial Enterprises. CD Proceedings of 17th ICPR Conference, Blacksburg, VA, USA, October 2003.

[16] EDS. EDS web-site, URL=www.eds.com, 2005.

[17] IBM. IBM web-site. URL=ww1.ibm.com/services/us/bcs/html/bcs_index.html?trac=L1, 2005.

[18] Accenture. Accenture web-site. URL=www.accenture.com/, 2005.

[19] Pegasystems. Pegasystems web-site. URL=www.pegasystems.com, 2005.

[20] Staffware. Staffware web-site. URL=www.staffware.com, 2005.

[21] Filenet. Filenet web-site. URL=www.filenet.com, 2005.

[22] SPSS, SPSS User Guide to Software Version 9, SPSS Institute, 2006.

[23] Mathias Weske, Wil M. P. van der Aalst, H. M. W. (Eric) Verbeek: Advances in business process management. Data Knowl. Eng. 50(1): 1-8 (2004)

[24] J. Recker, M. Rosemann, W.M.P. van der Aalst, and J. Mendling. On the Syntax of Reference Model Configuration: Transforming the C-EPC into Lawful EPC Models. BPM Center Report BPM-05-21,

[25] Recker, J., Mendling, J., van der Aalst, W.M.P., Rosemann, M.: Model-driven Enterprise Systems Configuration. In: Dubois, E., Pohl, K. (eds.): Advanced Information Systems Engineering - CAiSE 2006. Lecture Notes in Computer Science, Vol. 4001. Springer, Luxembourg, Grand-Duchy of Luxembourg (2006) 369-383

# Business Process Design by View Integration

Jan Mendling[1] and Carlo Simon[2]

[1] Vienna University of Economics and Business Administration
Augasse 2-6, 1090 Vienna, Austria
jan.mendling@wu-wien.ac.at
[2] University of Koblenz-Landau, Germany
simon@uni-koblenz.de

**Abstract.** Even though the design of business processes most often has to consolidate the knowledge of several process stakeholders, this fact is utilized only to a limited extent by existing modeling methodologies. We address this shortcoming in this paper by building an analogy between database schema design by view integration on the one hand and process modeling on the other hand. In particular, we specify a method for business process design by view integration starting from two views of a process as input. We identify formal semantic relationships between elements of the two process views which are then used to calculate the integrated process model applying the merge operator. Finally, the integrated model is optimized using reduction rules. A case study with two EPC business process models from the SAP reference model demonstrates the applicability of our approach.

## 1 Introduction

Business process design and in particular the design of business process models that capture real-world process semantics is a difficult task. While work procedures that are executed by one person are easy to document, business processes often span several departments of a company and include several activities performed by different persons. This implies a considerable complexity of the design task and calls for a structured approach. In this paper, we build on insight from database design theory, in particular view integration. View integration is a classical technique for database schema design. The idea is to identify the different views on the data of every person that is supposed to work with the database. Each person is interviewed and her view is documented in a separate so-called input schema. Then, the matching parts of the input schemas are identified. Based on these matches, the integrated schema is derived as a merge of the input schemas.

For so far, this technique has attracted only little attention in the context of business process modeling, basically, due to two reasons. First, the conceptual difference of process models and data models hinders a direct application of database schema integration for process design. An approach is needed that is analogous to data schema integration, but which addresses the specific nature of business process models, i.e., control flow defined between activities. Second,

J. Eder, S. Dustdar et al. (Eds.): BPM 2006 Workshops, LNCS 4103, pp. 55–64, 2006.
© Springer-Verlag Berlin Heidelberg 2006

dedicated techniques for behavior integration have been defined for Petri nets (cf. [12,16,17]), but not for conceptual languages such as EPCs. As EPCs are frequently used in process modeling practice (see e.g. the SAP reference model [4,7]) and EPCs offer OR-joins which cannot be mapped to Petri nets without loosing readability, there is a more general approach needed.

The contribution of this paper is threefold. First, we identify semantic relationships between activities of different business process models. Second, we define a merge operator for EPCs that takes as input two EPCs and semantic relationships between their activities to calculate an integrated EPC. Third, we propose a set of restructuring rules in order to arrive at an integrated EPC that does not include unnecessary structure. The availability of view integration techniques for conceptual business process modeling languages provides several advantages for business process design. If a business process designer conducts interviews with process stakeholders, she can document each view in an input EPC and use a merge operation to integrate them. This is less prone to errors and more time efficient than building an integrated model manually. Furthermore, this procedure provides traceability: changes to the input EPCs can be studied with respect to their impact on the resulting integrated process model. If all interviews would be directly documented in one process model, the individual views are lost. Beyond that, our approach can also support a merger scenario where business process models of two companies with overlapping semantics have to be integrated into one repository.

Following this line of argumentation, the remainder of this paper is structured as follows: in Section 2 we give a definition of EPCs and an overview of our integration approach. Furthermore, we introduce semantic relationships between activities of different business process models, we define the merge operator for EPCs, and we identify restructuring rules. In Section 3, we apply this integration technique to two EPC business process models from the SAP reference model. The example models have the same name and share several activities. Section 4 gives an overview of related research before Section 5 concludes the paper.

## 2   Preliminaries

In this section, we first introduce Event-driven Process Chain (EPC) as a business process modeling language (Sect. 2.1). The subsequent sections introduce the steps of our integration approach, i.e. definition of semantic relationships (Sect. 2.2), the merge operator (Sect. 2.3), and restructuring rules (Sect. 2.4).

### 2.1   Event-Driven Process Chains (EPCs)

Event-driven Process Chain (EPC) is a business process modeling language representing temporal and logical dependencies between activities of a process [6]. EPCs offer *function type* elements to capture activities of a process, *event type* elements which describe pre- and post-conditions of functions, and three kinds of *connector types* including *and*, *or*, and *xor*. Control flow arcs are used to link these elements. Connectors have either multiple incoming and one outgoing arcs (join connectors) or one incoming and multiple outgoing arcs (split connectors). As a syntax rule, functions and events alternate but may be separated by connectors. For more details on EPCs, we refer to [8,9]. Formally, the structure of EPC models is defined as follows:

**Notation 1 (Predecessor and Successor Nodes).** Let $(N, A)$ be a directed graph consisting of a set of *nodes* $N$ and a relation $A \subseteq N \times N$ defining the set of *directed arcs* between the nodes of $N$. For each node $n \in N$, we define the set of its *predecessor nodes* $\bullet n := \{x \in N | (x, n) \in A\}$, and the set of *successor nodes* $n \bullet := \{x \in N | (n, x) \in A\}$.

**Definition 1 (EPC).** An $EPC = (E, F, C, l, A)$ is a directed graph consisting of three pairwise disjoint sets of nodes $E$ called *events*, $F$ called *functions*, and $C$ called *connectors*, a mapping $l : C \to \{and, or, xor\}$ specifying the connectors' types, and a binary relation $A \subseteq (E \cup F \cup C) \times (E \cup F \cup C)$ of the directed arcs between these nodes defining the intended control flow of the $EPC$ such that

- $|\bullet e| \leq 1$ and $|e \bullet| \leq 1$ for each $e \in E$.
- $|\bullet f| = 1$ and $|f \bullet| = 1$ for each $f \in F$.
- Either $|\bullet c| = 1$ and $|c \bullet| > 1$ or $|\bullet c| > 1$ and $|c \bullet| = 1$ for each $c \in C$.

Figure 1 illustrates this definition showing two EPCs. Both describe similar processes of how a customer inquiry about products is received, processed, and how a quotation is created from the inquiry. The left EPC is taken from the Project Management branch of the SAP reference model and it is called *Customer Inquiry and Quotation Processing*. The second process EPC stems from the Sales and Distribution branch and its name is *Customer Inquiry*. The processes share two events and one function indicated by equal names. In the following, we elaborate how these two process models can be integrated.

## 2.2   Semantic Relationships

In the following, we define two kinds of semantic relationships between functions and events of two distinct EPCs, namely equivalence and sequence.

**Definition 2 (Equivalence).** Let $EPC_1 = (E_1, F_1, C_1, l_1, A_1)$ and $EPC_2 = (E_2, F_2, C_2, l_2, A_2)$ be two EPCs and $Eq \subseteq (E \times E) \cup (F \times F)$ a binary relation.

- If $e_1 \in E_1$ and $e_2 \in E_2$ describe the same real-world events, we write $(e_1, e_2) \in Eq$.
- If $f_1 \in F_1$ and $f_2 \in F_2$ describe the same real-world functions, we write $(f_1, f_2) \in Eq$.

**Definition 3 (Sequence).** Let $EPC_1$ and $EPC_2$ be two EPCs and $Seq \subseteq (E \times F) \cup (F \times E)$ a binary relation.

- If $e_1 \in E_1$ is always followed by $f_2 \in F_2$, we write $(e_1, f_2) \in Seq$.
- If $f_1 \in F_1$ is always followed by $e_2 \in E_2$, we write $(f_1, e_2) \in Seq$.

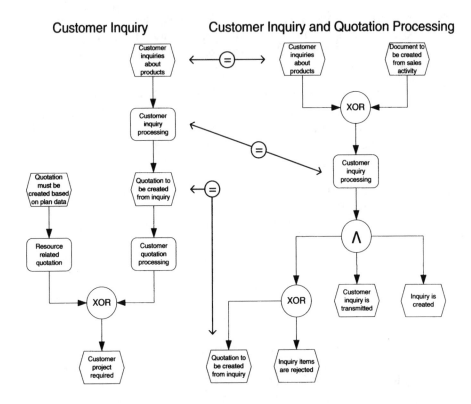

**Fig. 1.** *Customer Inquiry* and *Customer Inquiry and Quotation Processing* EPCs

WhenIf two views on the same business process have been documented as two EPC business process models, the business process designer has to identify semantic relationships in terms of equivalence and sequence between functions and events of the different models. Figure 1 might suggest that functions and events with similar labels are equivalent. Please note that EPC nodes can be also equivalent when syntactically different labels are used (analogous to synonyms) and that syntactically equivalent labels might relate to different business functions of another context (analogous to homonyms).

## 2.3   Merge Operator

The merge operator introduced in this section is novel. It takes two EPC views of the same business process plus a set of identified semantic relationships as input and produces an integrated EPC. As a first step, the integrated EPC includes all elements of the two input EPCs. Then, each pair of nodes $(n_1, n_2)$ which describe the same real-world events or functions, i.e. $(n_1, n_2) \in Eq$, is merged into a single node and the former input and output arcs are joined and split with *and*-connectors, respectively. Finally, for each pair of nodes in the sequence relationship, an *and*-split is inserted after the predecessor node, followed by an arc to a new *and*-join before the successor node.

**Definition 4 (Integrated EPC).** Let $EPC_1$ and $EPC_2$ be two EPCs. The integrated EPC $EPC_i := (E_i, F_i, C_i, l_i, A_i)$ is defined in five consecutive steps as follows:

1. Basically, the elements of $EPC_1$ and $EPC_2$ are combined in a single diagram:

$$E_i := E_1 \cup E_2$$
$$F_i := F_1 \cup F_2$$
$$C_i := C_1 \cup C_2$$
$$l_i := l_1 \cup l_2$$
$$A_i := A_1 \cup A_2$$

2. Each pair $(e_1, e_2) \in Eq$ of event elements which describe the same real-world events is fused into a single event. The former incoming and outgoing control flow arcs are synchronized with the aid of two new connectors $c_{split}$ and $c_{join}$:

$$E_i := E_i \setminus \{e_2\}$$
$$C_i := C_i \cup \{c_{split}, c_{join}\}$$
$$l_i := l_i \cup \{(c_{split}, and), (c_{join}, and)\}$$
$$A_i := A_i \setminus \{(x_1, e_1), (x_2, e_2), (e_1, y_1), (e_2, y_2)\} \cup$$
$$\{(x_1, c_{join}), (x_2, c_{join}), (c_{join}, e_1), (e_1, c_{split}), (c_{split}, y_1), (c_{split}, y_2)\}$$

3. For each $(f_1, f_2) \in Eq$ of function elements which describe the same real-world functions is fused into a single event. The former incoming and outgoing control flow arcs are synchronized with the aid of two new connectors $c_{split}$ and $c_{join}$:

$$F_i := F_i \setminus \{f_2\}$$
$$C_i := C_i \cup \{c_{split}, c_{join}\}$$
$$l_i := l_i \cup \{(c_{split}, and), (c_{join}, and)\}$$
$$A_i := A_i \setminus \{(x_1, f_1), (x_2, f_2), (f_1, y_1), (f_2, y_2)\} \cup$$
$$\{(x_1, c_{join}), (x_2, c_{join}), (c_{join}, f_1), (f_1, c_{split}), (c_{split}, y_1), (c_{split}, y_2)\}$$

4. For each $(e_1, f_2) \in Seq$ of an event that is always followed by a function, two new connectors $c_{split}$ and $c_{join}$ are added and the arc from the new split after the event to the new join before the function makes the control flow explicit:

$$C_i := C_i \cup \{c_{split}, c_{join}\}$$
$$l_i := l_i \cup \{(c_{split}, and), (c_{join}, and)\}$$
$$A_i := A_i \setminus \{(e_1, y_1), (x_2, f_2)\} \cup$$
$$\{(e_1, c_{split}), (c_{split}, y_1), (c_{split}, c_{join}), (c_{join}, f_2), (x_2, c_{join})\}$$

5. For each $(f_1, e_2) \in Seq$ of a function that is always followed by an event, two new connectors $c_{split}$ and $c_{join}$ are added and the arc from the new split

after the function to the new join before the event makes the control flow explicit:

$$C_i := C_i \cup \{c_{split}, c_{join}\}$$
$$l_i := l_i \cup \{(c_{split}, and), (c_{join}, and)\}$$
$$A_i := A_i \setminus \{(f_1, y_1), (x_2, e_2)\} \cup$$
$$\{(f_1, c_{split}), (c_{split}, y_1), (c_{split}, c_{join}), (c_{join}, e_2), (x_2, c_{join})\}$$

## 2.4  Restructuring Rules

Deriving the integrated EPC according to Definition 4 may result in unnecessary structure of the process graph. In particular, we identify two reduction rules:

**Definition 5 (Reduction Rules).** Let $EPC = (E, F, C, l, A)$ be an (integrated) EPC. The following reduction rules can be applied without affecting the control flow in terms of the order of functions and events:

1. If there is a path $(c_1, p_1, \ldots, p_n, c_2)$ with $P = \{p_1, \ldots, p_n\} \in (E \cup F \cup C)$ and $(c_1, c_2) \in A$, then $A := A \setminus \{(c_1, c_2)\}$
2. If $c \in C \wedge |c\bullet| = |\bullet c| = 1$, then $A := A \setminus \{(x, c), (c, y)\} \cup \{(x, y)\}$ and $C := C \setminus \{c\}$.

The first rule eliminates redundant arcs between two connectors that represent control flow which is implicitly captured by an alternative path between these connectors. The second rule eliminates connectors that have only one input and one output arc. Such unnecessary connectors can result from applying the first reduction rule. Please note that the first rule can change the execution semantics of the EPC: if there is an *xor*-split or an *or*-split in the path between the *and*-split and the *and*-join, the *and*-join can run into a deadlock. As such a potential deadlock is introduced in the integration step, we argue that it should be eliminated using the first rule.

# 3   Application to the SAP Reference Model

In order to demonstrate the applicability of our process view integration approach, we use two EPC process models from the SAP reference model [4,7], namely the two processes *Customer Inquiry and Quotation Processing* and *Customer Inquiry* that were presented in Figure 1.

In Section 2, we have identified semantic equivalence relationships between the events *Customer inquiries about products* and *Quotation to be created* and the function *Customer inquiry processing* that appear in both input EPCs. Figure 2 shows the integrated EPC model after applying the merge operator. For each pair of equivalent functions and events, the respective *and*-joins and -splits are inserted following Definition 4. The first and the second pair of *and*-split and -join can be reduced according to the reduction rules of Definition 5. The restructured EPC model is given in Figure 3.

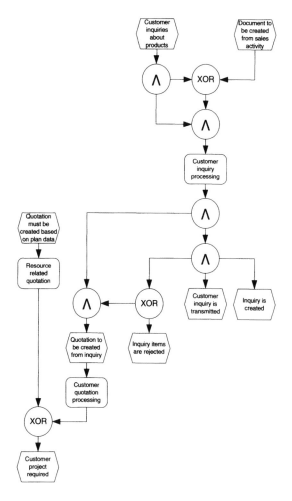

**Fig. 2.** Integrated EPC for *Customer Inquiry and Quotation Processing*

# 4   Related Research

There is extensive work in the database community on view integration and schema integration. Batini et al. [3] provide a comparative analysis of schema integration methodologies. They distinguish the schema integration activities of preintegration, comparing, conforming, merging, and restructuring. In our paper, we focus on comparing, merging, and restructuring EPCs. There are several contributions that focus on specific aspects of schema integration. Rahm and Bernstein provide a survey on how matches across different schemas can be identified automatically [13]. Rizopoulos and McBrien discuss the application of the hypergraph data model (HDM) with a wide set of semantic relationships for merging data schemas [14]. For a comprehensive integration method and a detailed overview of work on schema integration see [15].

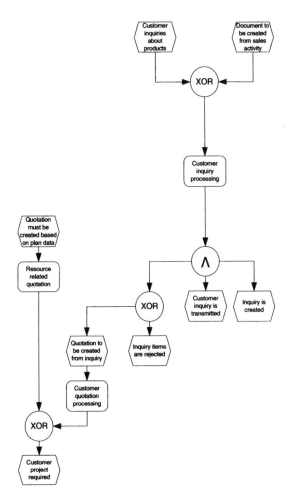

**Fig. 3.** Restructured EPC for *Customer Inquiry and Quotation Processing*

The heterogeneity of business process modeling languages is a notorious problem both for theory and practice [10]. Formalizing the metamodel of such a language as a schema makes schema integration applicable for process modeling language consolidation. In [11], the authors point to the problem of different control flow representations (graph-based versus block-oriented) as a specific source of heterogeneity. In [5] an integration process for business process metamodels is presented that is able to cope with such control flow heterogeneity.

There has been some work on joining and merging business process models with Petri net based formalisms. The integration of EPC models is conducted here in analogy with central concepts of the Semantic Process Language (SPL) [16,17]. In this language, formulas called modules can be formulated to specify process sets over elementary processes (in which an action occurs or is being forbidden) using operators for sequence building, alternatives, concurrency and synchronization, iteration, and negation. Canonical building rules take modules as input and generate Module nets, i.e. Petri nets with explicit *start* and *goal* transitions. Processes of such a Module net are firing sequences which reproduce the empty initial marking. Per definition, they are also processes of the module from which the Module net was generated.

In principle, applying the *and*-operator of SPL (for concurrency and synchronization) yields the intersection of the process sets of the participating modules concerning common actions. For Module net implementations, all transitions interpreted by the same elementary process are fused into a single one. Also *start* and *goal* transitions are synchronized in order to enforce the co-execution of the entire processes. Finally, all contradicting elementary processes (in which an action occurs in one operand and is forbidden within the other) are prohibited from occurring together (or even synchronously) in a process by additional conflict places - a rule which is of no importance for our approach here since EPCs do not support prohibition.

Comparable work is reported in [12]. Calculating merges and joins of process models can also be related to problems and solutions on determining inheritance relationships between process models [2,1]. Still, the mentioned approaches have not yet been adopted for conceptual languages such as EPCs as we propose in our approach.

## 5   Contributions and Limitations

In this paper we have presented an approach to business process design by view integration. In particular, we have formalized semantic relationships between elements of different process models, we have specified a merge operator to integrate input process models, and have identified reduction rules to simplify the integrated process model. Furthermore, we have applied this approach to an example of two EPC business process models from the SAP reference model to demonstrate the applicability of our approach. It has to be mentioned that the approach, although defined for EPCs, can be adopted for other process modeling languages. In future work, we aim to provide tool support for the merging of EPC business process models.

## References

1. Wil M. P. van der Aalst. Inheritance of business processes: A journey visiting four notorious problems. In Hartmut Ehrig, Wolfgang Reisig, Grzegorz Rozenberg, and Herbert Weber, editors, *Petri Net Technology for Communication-Based Systems - Advances in Petri Nets*, volume 2472 of *Lecture Notes in Computer Science*, pages 383–408. Springer, 2003.
2. T. Basten. *In Terms of Nets: System Design with Petri Nets and Process Algebra*. PhD thesis, Eindhoven University of Technology, The Netherlands, December 1998.
3. C. Batini, M. Lenzerini, and S. B. Navathe. A Comparative Analysis of Methodologies for Database Schema Integration. *ACM Computing Surveys*, 18(4):323–364, December 1986.

4. Thomas Curran, Gerhard Keller, and Andrew Ladd. *SAP R/3 Business Blueprint: Understanding the Business Process Reference Model.* Enterprise Resource Planning Series. Prentice Hall PTR, Upper Saddle River, 1997.
5. T. Hornung, A. Koschmider, and J. Mendling. Integration of heterogeneous BPM Schemas: The Case of XPDL and BPEL. Technical Report JM-2006-03-10, Vienna University of Economics and Business Administration, 2006.
6. G. Keller, M. Nüttgens, and A. W. Scheer. Semantische Prozessmodellierung auf der Grundlage "Ereignisgesteuerter Prozessketten (EPK)". Heft 89, Institut für Wirtschaftsinformatik, Saarbrücken, Germany, 1992.
7. G. Keller and T. Teufel. *SAP(R) R/3 Process Oriented Implementation: Iterative Process Prototyping.* Addison-Wesley, 1998.
8. E. Kindler. On the semantics of EPCs: Resolving the vicious circle. In J. Desel and B. Pernici and M. Weske, editor, *Business Process Management, 2nd International Conference, BPM 2004*, volume 3080 of *Lecture Notes in Computer Science*, pages 82–97, 2004.
9. Jan Mendling and Markus Nüttgens. EPC Markup Language (EPML) - An XML-Based Interchange Format for Event-Driven Process Chains (EPC). *Information Systems and e-Business Management*, 4, 2006.
10. Jan Mendling, Markus Nüttgens, and Gustaf Neumann. A Comparison of XML Interchange Formats for Business Process Modelling. In F. Feltz, A. Oberweis, and B. Otjacques, editors, *Proceedings of EMISA 2004 - Information Systems in E-Business and E-Government*, volume 56 of *Lecture Notes in Informatics*, 2004.
11. Jan Mendling, Cristian Pérez de Laborda, and Uwe Zdun. Towards an Integrated BPM Schema: Control Flow Heterogeneity of PNML and BPEL4WS. In K.-D. Althoff, A. Dengel, R. Bergmann, M. Nick, and T. Roth-Berghofer, editors, *Post-Proceedings of the 3rd Conference Professional Knowledge Management (WM 2005)*, volume 3782 of *Lecture Notes in Artificial Intelligence*, pages 570–579. Springer Verlag, 2005.
12. Günter Preuner, Stefan Conrad, and Michael Schrefl. View integration of behavior in object-oriented databases. *Data Knowl. Eng.*, 36(2):153–183, 2001.
13. E. Rahm and P. A. Bernstein. A survey of approaches to automatic schema matching. *VLDB Journal*, 10(4):334–350, 2001.
14. Nikolaos Rizopoulos and Peter McBrien. A general approach to the generation of conceptual model transformations. In Oscar Pastor and João Falcão e Cunha, editors, *Advanced Information Systems Engineering, 17th International Conference, CAiSE 2005, Porto, Portugal, June 13-17, 2005, Proceedings*, volume 3520 of *Lecture Notes in Computer Science*, pages 326–341. Springer, 2005.
15. Ingo Schmitt and Gunter Saake. A comprehensive database schema integration method based on the theory of formal concepts. *Acta Inf.*, 41(7-8):475–524, 2005.
16. Carlo Simon. *A Logic of Actions and Its Application to the Development of Programmable Controllers.* PhD thesis, University of Koblenz-Landau, Department of Computer Science, Germany, May 2002.
17. Carlo Simon. Incremental Development of Business Process Models. In Jörg Desel and Ullrich Frank, editors, *Proceedings of the Workshop Enterprise Modelling and Information Systems Architectures*, volume 75 of *Lecture Notes in Informatics*, pages 222–235, Klagenfurt, Austria, October 2005. German Informatics Society.

# An Approximate Analysis of Expected Cycle Time in Business Process Execution

Byung-Hyun Ha[1], Hajo A. Reijers[2], Joonsoo Bae[3], and Hyerim Bae[1,*]

[1] Dept. of Industrial Engineering, Pusan National Univ.,
San 30, Jangjeon-dong, Geumjeong-gu, Pusan, 609-735, Korea
{bhha, hrbae}@pusan.ac.kr
[2] Dept. of Technology Management, Eindhoven Univ.,
P.O. Box 513, 5600 MB, Eindhoven, The Netherlands
h.a.reijers@tm.tue.nl
[3] Dept. of Industrial & Sys. Eng., Chonbuk National Univ.,
664-14, Duckjin-dong, Duckjin-gu, Jeonju, Jeonbuk, 561-756, Korea
jsbae@chonbuk.ac.kr

**Abstract.** The accurate prediction of business process performance during its design phase can facilitate the assessment of existing processes and the generation of alternatives. In this paper, an approximation method to estimate the cycle time of a business process is introduced. First, we propose a process execution scheme, with which Business Process Management Systems (BPMS) can control the execution of processes. Second, an approximation method for analyzing its cycle time, based on queueing theory, is presented. We consider agents as queueing servers with multi-class customers and predict the response time of the agents. The cycle time of the whole process is calculated using the expected response time and process structure, taking into account parallel process execution. Finally, the results from the analytical approximation are validated against those of a simulation. This analysis can be used to obtain an optimal process execution plan.

## 1 Introduction

To secure advantage in today's competitive and customer-oriented business environments, it is necessary to maintain the effectiveness of business processes. Efficient management in rendering business processes effective is a key element of competitiveness. Business Process Management Systems (BPMS) were introduced in an effort to manage business processes efficiently. BPMS is an information system for designing, administering, and improving intra/inter-organizational business processes. As a result, BPMS has become a core engine for integrating enterprise information systems in a process-oriented way [11]. One of the most important reasons for employing BPMS is that it can be a sound basis for improving business processes. Integral to this end is performance analysis.

---

* Corresponding author.

J. Eder, S. Dustdar et al. (Eds.): BPM 2006 Workshops, LNCS 4103, pp. 65–74, 2006.

A performance index of a business process can be determined according to customers, internal processes, suppliers, finance, and employees [13]. We consider as our performance index cycle time, which has commonly been used to define the period of time between the receipt of an order from a customer and the completion of the order. Since business processes managed by BPMSs are very dynamic, complete information is rarely known before executing them. Hence, if cycle time can be predicted at process design time, it can facilitate the assessment and streamlining of existing process as well as the outlining of new processes. In this paper, a queueing model for estimating the cycle time of business processes is introduced.

Employing stochastic models as analytic models for business processes has been researched in numerous ways for various purposes. Early research has examined the assertion that queuing theory can be used to redesign business processes [2,10]. Narahari *et al.* have analyzed the cycle time of the New Product Development (NPD) process by modeling an organization's departments as queueing servers, and proposed several ways to reduce cycle time by means of queueing theory and a simulation method [7]. Son and Kim have suggested a capacity planning scheme to satisfy due dates by modeling tasks of business processes as queueing servers [12]. Another extensively researched model based on a well-defined theoretical foundation is Stochastic Workflow Net (SWN), the results of which can be used to analyze the performance of business processes and to plan agent capacity, among other ends [1,9]. However, in most of the previous studies it was presumed that the capacity of the agents is *infinite* and that an agent is dedicated to only a single task. These assumptions can hinder a more accurate description and analysis of business processes, which is the main motivation for us to devise a more realistic approach.

## 2 Models for Business Process Analysis

Process models used by commercial BPMSs usually include detailed information on the automatic execution of the processes involved. However, since the purpose of our research is to analyze process efficiency, it might not be necessary to consider all business information, e.g. business rules. Therefore, we provide, as required to analyze processes, a simplified process model. Our model includes three aspects of process information: process structure, resource capacity, and statistical information. The following is a definition of a process model.

**Definition 1 (Process Model).** A *process model* is defined as a tuple $\langle T, SB, L, A, \mu, rp, pe, \Phi \rangle$ which is characterized as follows:

   i) $T$ is a set of *tasks*.
   ii) $SB = \langle B_S, B_R, B_P, s_o \rangle$ is a tuple of blocks, where $B_S$, $B_R$, $B_P$, and $s_o$ are a set of *sequence blocks*, a set of *repeat blocks*, a set of *parallel blocks*, and an *outmost sequence block*, respectively. Each block can be nested, that is, a block can include tasks and internal blocks as its members.
   iii) $L \subset \cup \{B \times B \mid B \in B_S \cup B_R\}$ is a set of *links*.
   iv) $A$ is a set of *agents*.
   v) $\mu : T \times A \rightarrow R^+ \cup \{0\}$ is a function of *average service rate*.

vi) $rp : B_R \to R^+$ is a function of *repeat probability*.

vii) $pe : \cup\{2^p \mid p \in P\} \to R^+ \cup \{0\}$ is a function of *parallel execution probability*, where $pe_\varnothing = 0$.

viii) $\Phi$ is *customer arrival rate*.

A sample process is represented in Fig. 1 (a), which illustrates an 'Internet loan process.' After a customer requests a loan, a clerk first checks the loan application. Then, two tasks, 'History Review' and 'Credit Inquiry,' are executed simultaneously if their respective preconditions are met. The probability of each task's execution is marked on a split arrow. Taking the results of these tasks into account, the task 'Loan Grant' is executed next. Note that this appraisal may lead to a repeated execution of the history review and credit inquiry tasks.

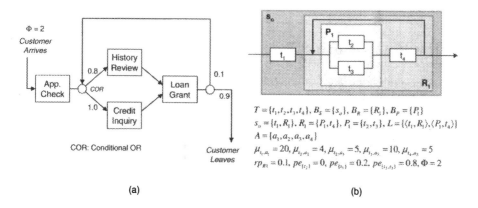

(a)                                              (b)

**Fig. 1.** A simple process model (a) a sample process (b) a process model

The sample process can be mapped onto our process model as shown in Fig. 1 (b). All tasks establish a task set, $T$, and also defined are sets of blocks ($B_S$, $B_P$, and $B_R$), links ($L$), and agents ($A$). Block execution probabilities for parallel and repeat blocks are derived from the task execution probabilities of the original process. For example, the probability that both $t_2$ and $t_3$ will execute ($pe_{\{t_2,t_3\}}$) is 0.8, because $t_3$ is always executed and $t_2$ is executed with probability of 0.8. In this sample process, customers arrive every 2 time units on the average, that is, $\Phi=2$. For an agent $a$ and a task $t$, a positive value for average service rate $\mu_{t,a}$ indicates the average number of $t$ that can be performed by $a$ per unit time. Otherwise, $\mu_{t,a}$ equals zero. This kind of statistical information can be estimated by domain experts in the design phase or just collected from the execution history of the business process as registered by the BPMS.

To analyze the cycle time of a business process based on the model above, we first introduce the execution frequency of each task. An *expected execution frequency* of $b$, denoted by $f_b$, is the frequency of performing block $b$ while a business process is executed. The expected execution frequencies of blocks are recursively calculated using the following equation:

$$f_{s_o} = 1,$$
$$f_s = f_S \qquad \forall s \in S \text{ where } S \in B_S,$$
$$f_r = f_R/(1 - rp_R) \qquad \forall r \in R \text{ where } R \in B_R, \qquad (1)$$
$$f_p = \sum_{B \in \{S \in 2^P | p \in S\}} pe_B \cdot f_p \quad \forall p \in P \text{ where } P \in B_P.$$

In the sample process depicted in Fig. 1, the expected execution frequencies of the tasks, $\langle f_{t_1}, f_{t_2}, f_{t_3}, f_{t_4} \rangle$ are determined to be $\langle 1, 8/9, 10/9, 10/9 \rangle$.

In addition, the notation below is employed to simplify the formulas in the following sections. The shorthands represent a set of tasks that can be performed by agent $a$ and a set of agents who can perform task $t$, respectively:

$$T_a := \{t \mid \mu_{t,a} > 0\}, \quad A_t := \{t \mid \mu_{t,a} > 0\}. \qquad (2)$$

## 3 Queueing Analysis of Process Execution

In this section, a method of executing business processes is presented and the main ideas behind the performance analysis of business processes using queuing theory are illustrated. When tasks are required to be performed, a BPMS assigns them to agents by putting them into worklists. The performance of process execution depends on the method of managing worklists and the order of performing tasks in worklists [5]. In this paper, we consider a work environment in which each agent has his own worklist.

When a business process is executed in such an environment, the cycle time depends on the ability of the agent who performs a task. In the process execution phase, a task is assigned to a specific agent with predefined probability as defined below.

**Definition 2 (Task Assignment Probability).** A *task assignment probability* of task $t$ assigned to agent $a$, denoted by $p_{t,a}$, is the probability that agent $a$ is selected to perform task $t$ in business process execution, where $\mu_{t,a} > 0$.

In the process execution phase, we apply the following rules: i) when a task is to be assigned, it is assigned to a specific worklist of an agent using the predefined task assignment probability $(p_{t,a})$, and ii) each agent performs the tasks in his worklist using the First-In-First-Out (FIFO) dispatching rule.

To analyze business processes using queueing theory, agents are modeled as queueing servers, which are called *agent servers*. A queueing network can be built by connecting the agent servers. The jobs arriving at an agent server are the tasks assigned to the worklist of the corresponding agent.

The *task arrival rate* of $t$ $(\lambda_t)$ is the average number of occurrences of task $t$ per time unit when the business process is continuously visited by customers. Similarly, $\lambda_{t,a}$ and $\lambda_{\bullet a}$ are defined as the *task arrival rate* of task $t$ assigned to agent $a$ and the *task arrival rate* assigned to agent $a$ regardless of task type, respectively. The task assignment probabilities can be calculated as follows:

$$\lambda_t = \Phi \cdot f_t, \quad \lambda_{t,a} = p_{t,a} \cdot \lambda_t, \quad \lambda_{\bullet a} = \sum_{t \in T_a} \lambda_{t,a},$$

(3)

and the utilization rate of agent $a$ ($ld_a$) is derived as [4]:

$$ld_a = \sum_{t \in T_a} \frac{\lambda_{t,a}}{\mu_{t,a}} = \sum_{t \in T_a} \frac{\lambda_t p_{t,a}}{\mu_{t,a}} = \Phi \sum_{t \in T_a} \frac{f_t p_{t,a}}{\mu_{t,a}}.$$

(4)

The response time (cycle time) of an agent can be obtained by analyzing the corresponding agent server. Let $ST_{t,a}$ and $ST_a$ be the random variables (RV) denoting the service time of agent $a$ for task $t$ and the service time of agent $a$ regardless of task type, respectively. (Note that $E[ST_{t,a}]$ is $\mu_{t,a}$.) Because $ST_{t,a}$ can be assumed to be independent of each other, the moments of $ST_a$ are derived as follows:

$$E[ST_a^n] = \sum_{t \in T_a} \frac{\lambda_{t,a}}{\lambda_{\bullet a}} E[ST_{t,a}^n].$$

(5)

Let $CT_a$ be the RV denoting the cycle time of an agent $a$. Recall that in this research, an agent handles tasks in a worklist with the FIFO rule. And jobs can be assumed to arrive at agent servers according to the Poisson process [12]. Hence, the moments of the cycle time can be derived as follows [4]:

$$E[CT_a] = \frac{\lambda_{\bullet a} E[ST_a^2]}{2(1 - ld_a)} + \frac{ld_a}{\lambda_{\bullet a}}, \quad E[CT_a^2] = \frac{\lambda_{\bullet a} E[ST_a^3]}{3(1 - ld_a)} + \frac{\lambda_{\bullet a}^2 E[ST_a^2]^2}{2(1 - ld_a)^2} + \frac{E[ST_a^2]}{(1 - ld_a)}.$$

(6)

The cycle times of agents are independent of each other and tasks are assigned to agents with predefined task assignment probabilities ($p_{t,a}$) regardless of their arrival order. Therefore, the moments of the cycle time $CT_t$ of task t are expected to be:

$$E[CT_t] = \sum_{a \in A_t} p_{t,a} \cdot E[CT_a], \quad E[CT_t^2] = \sum_{a \in A_t} p_{t,a} \cdot E[CT_a^2].$$

(7)

# 4 Estimating Cycle Time

The expected cycle time of each block is derived using those of its internal blocks, and the cycle time of a process is that of the outmost block $s_o$. In other words, the cycle time of the whole process is recursively calculated from the innermost blocks, that is, the tasks. The results of this section are based mainly on queueing theory and, thus, on the assumption of a steady state system.

**Sequence blocks.** The cycle times of internal blocks that structure a sequence block are not independent of each other. In other words, if one of the internal blocks has a long cycle time, there is also a very high probability of other blocks in the same sequence having a long cycle time. This kind of dependency can be modeled using the coefficient of correlation. Commonly, the coefficient of correlation varies with the structure of the queueing network and the server utilization rate [3]. However, we fix the coefficient of correlation of sequence blocks ($\rho_s$) as 0.5, based on comprehensive experiments, and assume that only adjacent blocks are correlated.

Let $CT_S$ be the RV denoting the cycle time of sequence block $S$; then it is straightforward to obtain the mean and variance of the cycle time:

$$E[CT_S] = \sum_{b \in S} E[CT_b],$$

$$Var[CT_S] = \sum_{b \in S} Var[CT_b] + \sum_{\langle b_1, b_2 \rangle \in L \cap S^2} 2\rho_s \sqrt{Var[CT_{b_1}]Var[CT_{b_2}]}.$$

(8)

**Repeat blocks.** The number of executions of a repeat block $R$ depends on its repeat probability $rp_R$. Let $CT_R$ and $CT_{R,1}$ be the RV denoting the cycle time of repeat block $R$ and the cycle time of $R$ when it is executed only once, respectively. Then,

$$CT_R = CT_{R,1} + rp_R CT_{R,1} + rp_R^2 CT_{R,1} + \cdots,$$

(9)

and the statistics for $CT_{R,1}$ are not different from those of the sequence block.

As in the sequential case, the cycle times from the repeated execution of a block are not independent of each other. We also fixed the coefficient of correlation of the repeated execution ($\rho_r$) at 0.4. Note that the coefficient of correlation of repeat blocks is different from that of sequence block. That is, the former represents inter-block dependency, while the latter represents the dependency of adjacent inner blocks. The mean and variance of the cycle time of repeat blocks are derived as follows:

$$E[CT_R] = E[CT_{R,1}]/(1 - rp_R),$$

$$Var[CT_R] = \sum_{i=1}^{\infty} rp_R^{2(i-1)} Var[CT_{R,1}] + 2\sum_{i=1}^{\infty} rp_R^{2i-1} \rho_r \sqrt{Var[CT_{R,1}]Var[CT_{R,1}]}$$

(10)

$$= (1 + 2\rho_r rp_R)Var[CT_{R,1}]/(1 - rp_R^2).$$

**Parallel blocks.** The cycle time of a parallel execution is the maximum of the cycle times of inner blocks. Given that in general it is not easy to obtain accurate performance measures of parallel blocks, we employ an approximation method for Fork-Join Queue [8] and adapt it to business processes.

Let $CT_P$ and $PT_B$ be the RV's denoting the cycle time of parallel block $P$ and the cycle time of inner blocks $B \subset P$ when every block in $B$ is executed, respectively. Then, the mean and variance of block $P$ (with the coefficient of correlation $\rho_p = 0.5$) are given by:

$$E[CT_P] = \sum_{B \in 2^P} pe_B E[PT_B],$$

$$Var[CT_P] = \sum_{B \in 2^P} pe_B^2 Var[PT_B] + \sum_{\substack{\langle B_1, B_2 \rangle \in 2^P \times 2^P, \\ B_1 \neq B_2}} 2\rho_P pe_{B_1} pe_{B_2} \sqrt{Var[PT_{B_1}]Var[PT_{B_2}]},$$

(11)

where $E[PT_\varnothing] = Var[PT_\varnothing] = 0$.

The cycle time of the inner blocks is approximated using a generalized exponential distribution [8]. Let $CT_b$ and $AT_b$ be the RV denoting the cycle time of inner block $b \in B$ and its approximated cycle time using a generalized exponential distribution, respectively. When $E[CT_b]^2 > Var[CT_b]$, the cumulative distribution function of $AT_b$ is given by:

$$F_{AT_b}(x) = 1 - e^{-(x-d_b)/m_b} \quad x \geq d_b$$

$$= 0 \qquad \text{otherwise, where } m_b = \sqrt{Var[CT_b]}, d_b = E[CT_b] - m_b. \qquad (12)$$

Note that the mean and variance of $AT_b$ and $CT_b$ are the same. If the cycle times of the inner blocks are assumed to be independent of each other, the cumulative distribution function of $PT_B$ is approximated as follows:

$$F_{PT_B}(x) = \Pr[PT_B \leq x] = \Pr[CT_b \leq x, \forall b \in B] = \prod_{b \in B} \Pr[CT_b \leq x]$$

$$\cong \prod_{b \in B} F_{AT_b}(x) = \prod_{b \in B} 1 - e^{-(x-d_b)/m_b}, \qquad \text{where } x \geq \max_{b \in B}\{d_b\}. \qquad (13)$$

As a result, the first and second moments of $PT_B$ are approximated as follows,

$$E[PT_B] \cong d + \sum_{A \in 2^B \setminus \{\emptyset\}} (-1)^{|A|-1} k_A \exp\left(\sum_{b \in A} -\frac{d-d_b}{m_b}\right),$$

$$E[PT_B^2] \cong d^2 + 2 \sum_{A \in 2^B \setminus \{\emptyset\}} (-1)^{|A|-1} k_A (d+k_A) \exp\left(\sum_{b \in A} -\frac{d-d_b}{m_b}\right), \qquad (14)$$

where

$$d = \max_{b \in B}\{d_b\}, \quad k_A = \prod_{b \in A} m_b \Big/ \sum_{b \in A} \prod_{c \in A \setminus \{b\}} m_c. \qquad (15)$$

## 5  Experimental Results

To validate the accuracy of our method, the analytical results for predicting process cycle time were compared with simulation results. In this validation, we used random processes of which the structure and the parameters are randomly determined by a computer.

Each random process is created with the number of tasks and the number of agents as input data. First, the average service rate of each task is determined using uniform distributions, and service rates of agents were randomly generated based on the average service rate of the task. The service times for tasks were assumed to have gamma distributions with the shape parameter $\alpha = 2$, an assumption to be known as generally applicable in practice [6]. The simulation was set to prevent any single agent doing more than 10 tasks on the average. Generation of the process structure started from the outmost sequence block, and then the type of inner structure was determined randomly. The numbers of tasks, repeat blocks, and parallel blocks in a sequence or repeat block were respectively set to be 10, 2 and 3 on the average. Task assignment probabilities were generated at random too, and task arrival rates that allow a maximum workload of agents of 50, 60, 70, 80 and 90 % were used for our simulation.

Fig. 2 illustrates a sample random process, and the experimental results of the cycle time approximation. Fig. 2 (a) shows that the sample process consists of 12 tasks, 3 parallel blocks, and a repeat block. Five agents participate in the execution of the

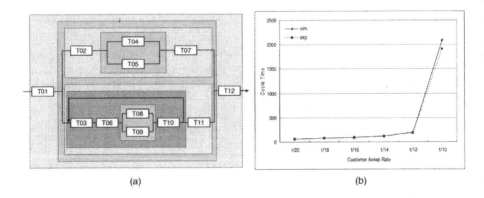

(a)                                    (b)

**Fig. 2.** A sample process for experiments. (a) A random process model. (b) Comparison between the analytical and simulation results.

process. With customer arrival rates varying from 1/20 to 1/10, simulation results were compared with the cycle times calculated by our method. From the result in Fig. 2 (b), it can be seen that the estimation was quite satisfactory across all customer arrival rates.

**Table 1.** Summary of experiment results with # of business processes[*], ME (Mean Error) in %[**], and MSE (Mean Squared Error) in %[***]

| # of agents | # of tasks | | | | | | | | | | |
|---|---|---|---|---|---|---|---|---|---|---|---|
| | 20 | 30 | 40 | 50 | 60 | 70 | 80 | 90 | 100 | 110 | 120 |
| **10** | 249[*] | 248 | 249 | 249 | 246 | 245 | 251 | 271 | 271 | 271 | 271 |
| | 6.84[**] | 6.82 | 6.89 | 6.22 | 6.61 | 7.50 | 8.11 | 8.19 | 7.88 | 7.60 | 8.58 |
| | 66.80[***] | 63.34 | 69.35 | 52.60 | 57.34 | 75.23 | 91.36 | 90.26 | 84.22 | 78.88 | 92.97 |
| **20** | 263 | 264 | 264 | 261 | 260 | 262 | 262 | 251 | 251 | 251 | 251 |
| | 3.78 | 4.64 | 4.75 | 5.82 | 5.14 | 5.66 | 6.06 | 5.71 | 6.09 | 5.67 | 5.83 |
| | 23.07 | 33.37 | 35.52 | 54.58 | 38.69 | 46.60 | 54.60 | 47.69 | 60.70 | 49.17 | 51.15 |
| **30** | 261 | 259 | 259 | 273 | 272 | 251 | 251 | 251 | | | |
| | 3.86 | 3.30 | 4.21 | 4.19 | 4.51 | 4.29 | 4.85 | 4.81 | | | |
| | 22.61 | 16.10 | 26.56 | 25.53 | 32.27 | 28.35 | 39.93 | 32.44 | | | |
| **40** | 251 | 251 | 251 | 251 | 251 | 251 | 251 | 251 | | | |
| | 2.68 | 3.45 | 3.50 | 3.66 | 3.65 | 3.93 | 4.28 | 3.99 | | | |
| | 13.00 | 21.04 | 22.36 | 20.92 | 19.91 | 24.18 | 27.33 | 28.64 | | | |
| **50** | 251 | 251 | 251 | 251 | 251 | 251 | 251 | | | | |
| | 3.13 | 2.90 | 3.22 | 3.41 | 3.76 | 3.78 | 4.17 | | | | |
| | 15.09 | 14.77 | 15.79 | 17.39 | 23.66 | 21.55 | 28.88 | | | | |

11,503 iterations of the experiments were conducted for the random processes with varying numbers of agents (from 10 to 50) and numbers of tasks (from 20 to 120). The experimental results show that the total mean error is 5.08 (%) and the mean squared error is 41.42 (%). The results are summarized in Table 1.

In Table 1, the second row of each cell shows the percentage of time difference between the predicted cycle time and the simulation result. The results show that our prediction of the cycle time is within a 10% error on average. It can be seen that the error generally increases as the number of tasks increases, but the trend is not so significant. This fact implies that complex process structures can cause an estimation error. At the same time, the error decreases as the number of agents increases. This is because an increased number of agents likely reduces the variance in the cycle times of tasks.

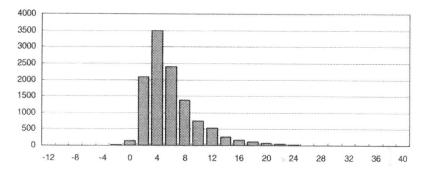

**Fig. 3.** The histogram of errors in %

Fig. 3, which depicts the overall distribution of error, shows that the variance of error is not so large.

## 6  Conclusions

In this paper, we provide an approximate analysis of the average cycle time of business processes. For this purpose we first considered a process execution scheme assuming BPMS to control the execution of the processes. Under this execution scheme, an agent is assumed to have an individual worklist and the BPMS assigns tasks to the worklists. An approximation method for the setting of the individual worklist was devised to analyze the cycle time. The method is based on queueing theory, and we considered agents as queueing servers with multi-class customers in order to predict the response time of the agents. The cycle time of the whole process was calculated using the expected response time and process structure, taking into account parallel process execution. We conducted simulation experiments to verify the effectiveness of our approach, and showed that our method can predict cycle time with acceptable accuracy. We expect that the prediction of business process performance in the design phase can facilitate the assessment of existing processes and help to recommend the generation of new designs.

With respect to further research, since we can evaluate a process with respect to its cycle time, it might be possible to find, under the process execution scheme introduced in this paper, execution rules that minimize the cycle time. Though mathematical solutions are often difficult, a meta-heuristic approach to this problem can be very effective.

## Acknowledgements

This work was supported by the Regional Research Centers Program (Research Center for Logistics Information Technology), granted by the Korean Ministry of Education & Human Resources Development.

## References

1. van der Aalst, W., van Hee, K., Houben, G.: Modelling and analysing workflow using a petri-net based approach. In: Proceedings of the Second Workshop on Computer-Supported Cooperative Work, Petri Nets and Related Formalisms. (1994)
2. Buzacott, J.A.: Commonalities in reengineered business processes: models and issues. Management Science 42(5) (1996) 768–782
3. Daduna, H., Szekli, R.: On the correlation of sojourn times in open networks of exponential multiserver queues. Queueing Systems 34(1-4) (2000) 169–181
4. Gross, D., Harris, C.: Fundamentals of Queueing Theory. John Wiley & Sons, New York (1998)
5. Ha, B.H., Bae, J., Park, Y.T., Kang, S.H.: Development of process execution rules for workload balancing on agents. Data & Knowledge Engineering 56(1) (2006) 64–84
6. Law, A.M., Kelton, W.D.: Simulation Modeling and Analysis. Third edn. McGraw-Hill, Boston, MA (2000)
7. Narahari, Y., Viswanadham, N., Kumar, K.V.: Lead time modeling and acceleration of product design and development. IEEE Transaction on Robotics and Automation 15(5) (1999) 882–896
8. Rajaraman, B., Morgan, T.W.: Approximate analysis of the average delay in parallel program execution. In: Proceeding of the Twenty-Sixth Hawaii International Conference on System Sciences, Hawaii (1993) 584–593
9. Reijers, H.A.: Design and Control of Workflow Processes. Springer-Verlag (2003)
10. Seidmann, A., Sundararajan, A.: The effects of task and information asymmetry on business process redesign. International Journal of Production Economics 50(2-3) (1997) 117–128
11. Smith, H., Fingar, P.: Business Process Management: The Third Wave. Meghan-Kiffer, Tampa (2003)
12. Son, J., Kim, M.: Improving the performance of time-constrained workflow processing. Journal of Systems and Software 58(3) (2001) 211–219
13. Wesner J.W., Hiatt, J.M., Trimble, D.C.: Winning With Quality: Applying Quality Principles in Product Development. Addison-Wesley, Reading, MA (1995)

# Workshop on Business Process Intelligence (BPI 2006)

# Workshop on Business Process Intelligence (BPI 2006)
# Preface

Surviving in today's competitive market demands that enterprises improve the efficiency of their business processes not only by their automation, as they have done for years, but also by gaining intelligence about such processes to get reduced costs and higher performance. Business Process Intelligence (BPI) is an emerging, interdisciplinary area that aims at developing models, techniques and tools to improve different aspects of how business processes are modeled and conducted. BPI is not only the application of Business Intelligence techniques to business processes but it also integrates contributions from other research areas like BAM (Business Activity Monitoring), BOM (Business Operations Management), BPM (Business Performance Management), and others.

Following the success of the first BPI workshop, held in Nancy on September 5, 2005, this second workshop intended to bridge across the various research areas that are related to BPI. At the same time the workshop was an opportunity to continue consolidating this area and building a multidisciplinary community.

The workshop BPI 2006 consisted of a keynote talk on "Process Mining: Practical Experiences and a Reality Check", seven contributed papers that were selected by the program committee for presentation at the workshop, and a panel on "Business Process Intelligence and Business Intelligence: Differences and Convergences".

In his keynote talk, Wil van der Aalst gave an overview of the various process mining techniques that have been developed in the last 10 years, and discussed the many perspectives of viewing process mining: from the reverse engineering of code and the monitoring of embedded systems to cross-organizational workflows and health-care processes. The goal was to promote a discussion on the challenges that need to be addressed to improve the applicability of process mining.

The seven papers cover some of the main topics addressed by BPI. In particular, the paper "Process Mining and Petri Net Synthesis" by E. Kindler, V. Rubin and W. Schäfer, deals with the topic of *process discovery*, which refers to the analysis of enterprise operations in order to derive the process models that these operations obey. A contribution to this topic is also given by the industrial paper "A Generic Import Framework for Process Event Logs" by C.W. Günther and W.M.P. van der Aalst, which illustrates a framework for acquiring log data from a Process-Aware Information System. The topic of *intelligent process analysis* (analysis of business process execution to discover interesting correlations) is addressed by the paper "Process Mining by Measuring Process Block Similarity" by J. Bae, J. Caverlee, L. Liu, B. Rouse, and H. Yan, which presents an approach for measuring the similarity between two process models.

Another topic relevant to BPI, *exception handling*, is dealt with by the paper "Improving Exception Handling by Discovering Change Dependencies in Adaptive Process Management Systems" by B. Weber, W. Wild, M. Lauer and M. Reichert. A novel topic of process modeling and reasoning is covered by the paper "Process Representation and Reasoning Using a Logic Formalism with Object-Oriented Features" by A. Gualtieri, T. Dell'Armi and N. Leone. The topic of *business process measurement* is analyzed by the survey paper "A Discourse on Complexity of Process Models" by J. Cardoso, J. Mendling, G. Neumann and H.A. Reijers, which focuses on the problem of defining complexity metrics for business processes. Finally, the position paper "Measuring Performance in the Retail Industry" by G. Marketos and Y. Theodoridis deals with the application of BPI in the context of the retail industry by suitably exploiting the RFID technology.

The panel discussed convergences between Business Intelligence (BI) and Business Process Intelligence: how techniques of BI can be effectively applied to add intelligence to the analysis of processes? The panel also intended to evidence differences between the two areas, as BPI is not just an application of BI, but it is a multidisciplinary area.

## Acknowledgments

We wish to express a special word of thanks to the Program Committee members (Francesco Archetti, Boualem Benatallah, Fabio Casati, Jonathan E. Cook, Peter Dadam, Saso Dzeroski, Fosca Giannotti, Mati Golani, Gianluigi Greco, Dimitrios Georgakopoulos, Joachim Herbst, Shlomit S. Pinter, Michael Rosemann, Wil van der Aalst, Mathias Weske, Michael zur Muhlen) for providing their technical expertise in reviewing the submitted papers and their valuable support to create an interesting program. We are particularly grateful to the keynote speaker, Wil van der Aalst, for his interesting keynote talk and, more generally, for his pioneering contribution to the area of BPI. We also thank all the authors of the accepted papers for sharing their work and experiences in this workshop. Finally, we want to express our sincere appreciation to the BPM 2006 Workshops Chair, Johann Eder, for his support in the organization of the workshops and the proceedings.

June 2006

Malu Castellanos
Domenico Saccà
Ton Weijters
(Editors)

# Workshop Organization

## Executive Committee

Organizers and PC Chairs        Malu Castellanos, Hewlett-Packard Labs, USA
                                Domenico Saccà, University of Calabria, Italy
                                Ton Weijters, Eindhoven University
                                    of Technology, The Netherlands

Publication and Coord. Chairs   Antonella Guzzo, ICAR-CNR, Italy
                                Ana Karla A. de Medeiros, Eindhoven
                                    University of Technology, The Netherlands

## Program Committee

Francesco Archetti (University of Milan Bicocca, Italy)
Boualem Benatallah (University of New South Wales, Australia)
Fabio Casati (Hewlett-Packard, USA)
Malu Castellanos (Hewlett-Packard Laboratories, USA)
Jonathan E. Cook (New Mexico State University, USA)
Peter Dadam (University of Ulm, Germany)
Saso Dzeroski (Jozef Stefan Institute, Slovenia)
Fosca Giannotti (ISTI-CNR, Italy)
Mati Golani (Ort Braude College, Israel)
Gianluigi Greco (University of Calabria, Italy)
Dimitrios Georgakopoulos (Telcordia Technologies, Austin, USA)
Joachim Herbst (DaimlerChrysler AG, Germany)
Shlomit S. Pinter (IBM Haifa Research Lab, Israel)
Michael Rosemann (Queensland University of Technology, Australia)
Domenico Saccà (University of Calabria, Italy)
Wil Van der Aalst (University of Eindhoven, The Netherlands)
Mathias Weske (Hasso Plattner Institute, University of Potsdam, Germany)
Ton Weijters (Eindhoven University of Technology, The Netherlands)
Michael zur Muhlen (Stevens Institute of Technology, USA)

# A Generic Import Framework
# for Process Event Logs
## Industrial Paper

Christian W. Günther and Wil M.P. van der Aalst

Department of Technology Management, Eindhoven University of Technology
P.O. Box 513, NL-5600 MB, Eindhoven, The Netherlands
{c.w.gunther, w.m.p.v.d.aalst}@tm.tue.nl

**Abstract.** The application of process mining techniques to real-life corporate environments has been of an ad-hoc nature so far, focused on proving the concept. One major reason for this rather slow adoption has been the complicated task of transforming real-life event log data to the MXML format used by advanced process mining tools, such as ProM. In this paper, the ProM Import Framework is presented, which has been designed to bridge this gap and to build a stable foundation for the extraction of event log data from any given PAIS implementation. Its flexible and extensible architecture, adherence to open standards, and open source availability make it a versatile contribution to the general BPI community.

## 1 Introduction

*Process-Aware Information Systems* (PAISs) are a commonplace part of the modern enterprise IT infrastructure, as dedicated process management systems or as workflow management components embedded in larger frameworks, such as Enterprise Resource Planning (ERP) systems.

At this point in time, most *business process monitoring* solutions focus on the performance aspects of process executions, providing statistical data and identifying problematic cases. The area of *Process Mining* [3], in contrast, is based on the *a-posteriori* analysis of process execution event logs. From this information, process mining techniques can derive abstract information about the different perspectives of a process, e.g. control flow, social network, etc.

There exists a great variety of PAIS implementations in field use, of which each one follows a custom manner of specifying, controlling and interpreting business processes. As an example, consider the utter difference in paradigm between a traditional, rigid Workflow Management System (WFMS) like Staffware on the one side, and a flexible case handling [5] system like FLOW*er* [7] on the other. This scale brings with it a corresponding plethora of event log formats, and concepts for their storage and accessibility.

In order to render the design of process mining techniques and tools independent of the target PAIS implementation, the *MXML* event log format has been devised. While this format has been designed to meet the requirements of

J. Eder, S. Dustdar et al. (Eds.): BPM 2006 Workshops, LNCS 4103, pp. 81–92, 2006.

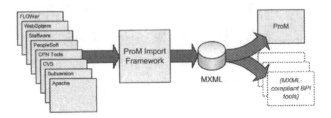

**Fig. 1.** Positioning the ProM Import Framework in the BPI landscape

process mining tools in the best possible way, the conversion from many PAIS's custom formats to MXML is a non-trivial task at best.

This combination of recurring and time-consuming tasks calls for a generic software framework, which allows the implementation of import routines to concentrate on the core tasks which differentiate it from others. Providing a common base for a large number of import routines further enables to leverage the complete product with marginal additional implementation cost, e.g. by providing a common graphical user interface (GUI) within the host application.

The ProM Import Framework addresses these requirements, featuring a flexible and extensible plug-in architecture. Hosted import plug-ins are provided with a set of convenience functionality at no additional implementation cost, thus making the development of these plug-ins efficient and fast.

This paper is organized as follows. Section 2 introduces process mining and the ProM framework, followed by an introduction to the underlying MXML format in Section 3. Section 4 describes requirements, design, architecture, and implementation of the ProM Import Framework. Subsequently, Section 5 gives an overview about target systems for which import plug-ins have already been developed, after which Section 6 draws conclusions.

## 2   Process Mining and ProM

Process-aware information systems, such as WfMS, ERP, CRM and B2B systems, need to be configured based on process models specifying the order in which process steps are to be executed [1]. Creating such models is a complex and time-consuming task for which different approaches exist. The most traditional approach is to analyze and design the processes explicitly, making use of a business process modeling tool. However, this approach has often resulted in discrepancies between the actual business processes and the ones as perceived by designers [3]; therefore, very often, the initial design of a process model is incomplete, subjective, and at a too high level. Instead of starting with an explicit process design, process mining aims at extracting process knowledge from "process execution logs".

Process mining techniques such as the alpha algorithm [4] typically assume that it is possible to sequentially record events such that each event refers to an activity (i.e., a well-defined step in the process) and to a case (i.e., a process instance). Moreover, there are other techniques explicitly using additional information, such as the performer and timestamp of the event, or data elements recorded with the event (e.g., the size of an order).

This information can be used to automatically construct process models, for which various approaches have been devised [6,8,11,12]. For example, the alpha algorithm [4] can construct a Petri net model describing the behavior observed in the log. The Multi-Phase Mining approach [9] can be used to construct an Event-driven Process Chain (EPC) [14] based on similar information. At this point in time there are mature tools such as the ProM framework to construct different types of models based on real process executions [10].

So far, research on process mining has mainly focused on issues related to control flow mining. Different algorithms and advanced mining techniques have been developed and implemented in this context (e.g., making use of inductive learning techniques or genetic algorithms). Tackled problems include concurrency and loop backs in process executions, but also issues related to the handling of noise (e.g., exceptions). Furthermore, some initial work regarding the mining of other model perspectives (e.g., organizational aspects) and data-driven process support systems (e.g., case handling systems) has been conducted [2].

## 3   The MXML Format

The *MXML* format (as in *Mining XML*) is a generic XML-based format suitable for representing and storing event log data. While focusing on the core information necessary to perform process mining, the format reserves generic fields for extra information that is potentially provided by a PAIS.

The structure of an MXML document is depicted in Figure 2, in the format of a UML 2.0 class diagram. The root node of each MXML document is a *WorkflowLog*, representing a log file. Every workflow log can potentially contain

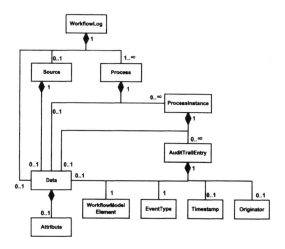

**Fig. 2.** Schema of the MXML format (UML diagram)

one *Source* element, which is used to describe the system the log has been imported from.

A workflow log can contain an arbitrary number of *Processes* as child elements. Each element of type "Process" groups events having occurred during the execution of a specific process definition. The single executions of that process definition are represented by child elements of type *ProcessInstance*. Thus, each process instance represents one specific case in the system.

Finally, process instances each group an arbitrary number of *AuditTrailEntry* child nodes, each describing one specific event in the log. Every audit trail entry must contain at least two child elements: The *WorkflowModelElement* describes the process definition element to which the event refers, e.g. the name of the task that was executed. The second mandatory element is the *EventType*, describing the nature of the event, e.g. whether a task was scheduled, completed, etc. Two further child elements of an audit trail entry are optional, namely the *Timestamp* and the *Originator*. The timestamp holds the exact date and time of when the event has occurred, while the originator identifies the resource, e.g. person, which has triggered the event in the system.

The elements described above provide the basic set of information used by current process mining techniques. To enable the flexible extension of this format with additional information extracted from a PAIS, all mentioned elements (except the child elements of *AuditTrailEntry*) can also have a generic *Data* child element. The data element groups an arbitrary number of *Attributes*, which are key-value pairs of strings.

# 4    The ProM Import Framework

While the ProM tool suite, which is based on interpreting event log data in the MXML format, has matured over the last couple of years, there is still a gap in *actually getting these logs* in the MXML format. Creating event logs in MXML has, in the past, been mostly achieved by artificial means, i.e. simulation, or by ad-hoc solutions which are not applicable to production use.

The *ProM Import Framework* steps in to bridge this gap. Its incentive is, on the one hand, to provide an adequate and convenient means for process mining researchers to actually acquire event logs from real production systems. On the other hand, it gives the owners of processes, i.e. management in organizations relying on PAIS operations, a means for productively applying process mining analysis techniques to their installations.

The following subsection introduces the incentives and high-level goals which have triggered the development of the ProM Import Framework. Section 4.2 derives from these goals a set of prominent design decisions, which form the basis of the system architecture, introduced in Section 4.3.

## 4.1    Goals and Requirements

In order to further progress the field of process mining it is essential to adapt and tailor both present and future techniques towards real-life usage scenarios, such that process mining can evolve into production use. This evolution fundamentally depends on the availability of real-life event log data, as only these can provide the necessary feedback for the development of process mining techniques.

Conversely, the process of actually applying process mining techniques in real world scenarios has to be eased and streamlined significantly. While several successful projects have proved the concept, it is a necessity to improve tool support for the entire process mining procedure from beginning to end.

A practical process mining endeavor is characterized by three, mainly independent, phases: At first, the event log data has to be imported from the source system. Secondly, the log data needs to be analyzed using an appropriate set of process mining techniques. Third and last, the results gained from process mining need thorough and domain-dependent interpretation, to figure out what the results mean in the given context, and what conclusions can be drawn.

The process mining specialist is required in the second and third phase, while the user, or process owner, is involved mainly in the third phase. What makes the first phase stick out is that it is at the moment the one task which can be performed with the least domain and process mining knowledge involved. Therefore, it is the logical next step for the progression of process mining to provide adequate and convenient tool support for the event log extraction phase.

A tool for supporting the event log extraction phase should thus address the following, high-level goals:

- The tool must be relatively *easy to operate*, such that also less qualified personnel can perform the task of event log extraction. This requirement implies, that:
  - By separating a configuration and adjustment phase from the extraction phase, which can potentially run unattended, the whole process can be leveraged and rendered more efficient.
- While ease of use is among the top goals, it must not supersede *flexibility and configurability* of the application. It must be applicable in as great an array of PAIS installations as possible.
- The tool must *provide an extensible and stable platform* for future development.
- It is advisable to *provide the tool on a free basis*, in order to encourage its widespread use and lower potential barriers for user acceptance. Further, *providing the code under an open source license* is expected to attract also external developers to participate. This enables the application to benefit from community feedback and contribution, thereby greatly leveraging the tool and, ultimately, process mining as a whole.

The subsequent subsection introduces the design decisions which were derived from these high-level goals.

## 4.2 Design Decisions

The ProM Import Framework has been developed from scratch, with the fundamental goal to provide a most friendly environment for developing import filters[1]. Consequently, a strong focus has been on extensibility and stability of the design, while including as much functionality as possible in the framework itself.

This emphasis has led to six crucial design choices, which have served as the cornerstone for developing the architecture of the system:

1. **Extensibility:** The design must incorporate a strict separation between general framework code and extension components. An additional requirement is to shift as much application logic as possible into the core framework, to prevent code duplication and to ease the development of extensions.
2. **Anonymization of log information:** The framework shall enable users to anonymize sensitive information contained in event logs in a transparent and convenient manner, thereby providing a means to protect the log owner's intellectual property.
3. **Flexible log-writing pipeline:** A logical *log-writing pipeline* shall be implemented, allowing to transparently chain a random number of log data-altering algorithms between event extraction and final storage.
4. **Decoupled configuration management:** It shall be sufficient for an import routine to specify its configuration options, and their corresponding types. Based on this information, the framework should transparently handle presenting these options to the user and allowing him to change them in a convenient manner.
5. **Decoupled dependencies management:** One further requirement towards the framework is to transparently satisfy all import routines' external requirements, e.g. database connectivity libraries.
6. **Convenient and decoupled user interface:** The application shall be relatively easy to use, i.e. it shall not require the user to have knowledge about process mining internals or the process of importing the event log data.

These design principles, together with the high-level goals presented in Section 4.1, have been used as an imperative in shaping the application's concrete architecture, which is presented in the following subsection.

### 4.3 Architecture

The architecture reflects the design principles stated in Section 4.2, and thus directly supports the high-level goals of Section 4.1. Figure 3 describes the abstract architecture of the framework, identifying the major classes involved and their mutual relationships in form of a UML 2.0 class diagram.

A flexible plug-in architecture satisfies the requirement for extensibility. For every target PAIS implementation, one dedicated import filter is supposed to be implemented as a plug-in. Each import filter plug-in is contained within one dedicated class, derived from the abstract superclass *ImportFilter*. From this base class, every import filter plug-in inherits a set of methods which it can call in its constructor, to notify the system of its configuration options and external

---

[1] The distribution is available at http://promimport.sourceforge.net.

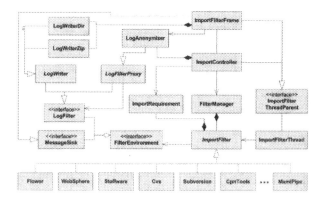

**Fig. 3.** Architecture of the ProM Import Framework, core components (UML diagram)

dependencies. For the actual import routine, the plug-in is passed an object implementing the interface *FilterEnvironment*, connecting the import filter to fundamental framework capabilities during the import procedure.

All elements of the log-writing pipeline implement the *LogFilter* interface, which allows for their flexible arrangement within the pipeline at will. This interface is used in a sequential manner, i.e. it incorporates methods to start and finish log files, processes and process instances, and a method for passing audit trail entries. The final endpoint of the log-writing pipeline is marked by an object derived from the abstract class *LogWriter* providing basic MXML formatting, while actual writing to permanent storage is implemented in LogWriter's subclasses.

Intermediate elements of the log-writing pipeline, such as the *LogAnonymizer*, are derived from the abstract class *LogFilterProxy*, implementing their transparent integration into the pipeline. At this point in time the anonymizer component is the only intermediate pipeline transformer available.

The *FilterManager* groups the set of import filters, provides named access to them, and provides their configuration within the framework for abstract access and modification. The *ImportController*, which incorporates the filter manager, manages the persistency of configuration data for the whole application and transparently manages and satisfies import filters' external requirements.

The class *ImportFilterFrame* implements the main graphical user interface of the application, including basic user interaction logic.

### 4.4 Disk-Buffered Event Sorting

The log writing pipeline in the framework expects process instances to be transmitted one after another, while audit trail entries are supposed to be transmitted in their natural order (i.e., order of occurrence). As not all import routines can expect their events in an ordered fashion, the framework provides the plug-in developer with a simple interface for transmitting unsorted event data, while ensuring that the sorting takes place in a transparent, resource-efficient manner.

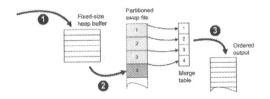

**Fig. 4.** Disk-buffered sorting in the framework

As this concept implies that all audit trail entries of an import session have to be buffered, before the first of them can be written, the process instance buffers are implemented to swap their content partially to disk storage.

This disk-buffered sorting mechanism is described in Figure 4.

1. Every buffer is equipped with a fixed-size buffer residing in heap space. This heap buffer is filled, as new audit trail entries are added to the process instance buffer.
2. When the heap buffer is completely filled with audit trail entries, it needs to be *flushed*. First, the events contained within the heap buffer are sorted using a Quicksort [13] algorithm. Then, all events in the heap buffer are appended to a swap file. Thus, the swap file contains subsequent segments, of which each contains a fixed number of sorted audit trail entries corresponding to one flush operation.
3. After all events have been received, the buffer needs to be emptied into the log writing pipeline in a sorted manner. An array called the *merge table*, with one cell per flush segment in the swap file, is initially filled with the first audit trail entry from each segment. Then, a modified merge sort [15] algorithm picks the first (in terms of logical order) event from the merge table, writes it to the log writing pipeline, and replaces it with the next entry from the respective flush segment in the swap file. This procedure is repeated, until all audit trail entries from the swap file have been loaded and the merge table is empty.

The presented disk-buffered sorting mechanism manages to effectively limit memory usage of the application. At the same time, a performance lag due to disk I/O is minimized by pre-buffering and sorting events in the heap buffer. Note that the algorithm scales well with the degree, in which incoming audit trail entries are already ordered. The less audit trail entries are in wrong order, the faster the initial sorting can be performed.

## 4.5   User Interface

The graphical user interface, which is depicted in Figure 5, is kept rather simple. On the left, an overview list allows the user to pick the import filter plug-in to be used. The upper right part shows general import filter properties, such as name, description, and author. Further, this part includes controls for the import procedure and the log anonymizer component.

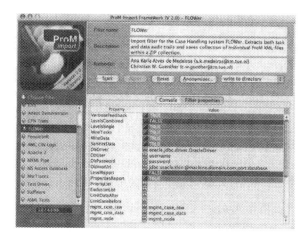

**Fig. 5.** User interface of the ProM Import Framework

The lower right part of the interface can either display a console view, or a configuration pane allowing to modify configuration settings for import filters. When the import procedure is started, the view switches to show the console, which is used to display feedback and error messages to the user.

# 5 Target Systems

The number of target systems, for which import plug-ins have been developed, has been steadily growing and diversifying since the development of the ProM Import Framework began[2]. On the one hand, this development is driven by advances in industry and practice, making ever more real-life PAIS implementations available for process mining research. On the other hand, this research triggers new applications from within, thus extending the field of "interesting" target systems.

In both directions, the flexible and extensible architecture of the ProM Import Framework has allowed developers to quickly implement solid and versatile solutions, taking advantage of the broad set of support functionality and clean user interface which the framework provides. At the time of this writing, there exist import plug-ins for the following target systems:

**FLOWer:** This product is an implementation of the *case handling* paradigm, which represents a very flexible, data-driven approach within the greater family of workflow management systems.

**WebSphere Process Choreographer:** As a part of IBM's WebSphere suite, the Process Choreographer is used to implement high-level business processes, based on the BPEL language.

---

[2] The current distribution of the framework, including all plug-ins, can be downloaded from http://promimport.sourceforge.net.

**Staffware:** A workflow management system in the traditional sense, which has an impressive market coverage.

**PeopleSoft Financials:** Part of the PeopleSoft suite for Enterprise Resource Planning (ERP), this module is concerned with financial administration within an organization.

**CPN Tools:** CPN Tools provides excellent tool support for modelling Colored Petri Nets (CPN), a family of high-level Petri Nets, including a simulation engine for executing models. An extension to CPN tools has been developed, allowing to create synthetic event logs during a model simulation.

**CVS:** The process of distributed software development, as reflected in the commits to a source code repository like CVS, can also be analyzed with techniques from the process mining family.

**Subversion:** The Subversion system addresses fundamental flaws present in CVS, providing change logs that can also be interpreted by means of process mining.

**Apache 2:** As the access logs of web servers, like Apache 2, reveal the identity of users from their IP, the exact time and items requested, it is straightforward to distill process event logs from them.

As diverse as this list may read, it shows the impressive capabilities of the framework in enabling rapid development of import capabilities. The complexity of demanding import filters is significantly reduced by standard functionality offered by the framework. On top of that, the existence of a powerful framework allows for rapid prototyping of event log import capabilities.

Thereby it stimulates and supports experiments with less obvious systems, which may otherwise have been deemed not worth the effort. These can serve as effective and efficient means to evaluate the feasibility and usefulness of an import effort. An excerpt of ad-hoc solutions to import custom data sets, which were rapidly and successfully implemented using the ProM Import Framework, includes:

- Import of event logs describing the process of patient treatments from raw database tables provided by a Dutch hospital.
- Production unit test logs from an international manufacturer of IC chip production equipment.
- Conversion of spreadsheets containing patient treatment processes, from an ambulant care unit in Israel and a large Dutch hospital.
- Versatile and highly configurable import from the WFMS Adept [16], which is known for its rich set of features addressing flexibility.

# 6   Conclusions

The MXML format is the most widely adopted standard for the storage of process event logs in process mining research. This is most notably due to the fact that the ProM framework, providing a wide selection of process mining analysis techniques, relies on MXML for reading event logs.

However, due to a lack of convenient conversion tools, the availability of real-life event logs in MXML format has not been satisfactory so far. On the one hand, this lack of actual logs had a serious impact on the credibility of process mining techniques with respect to real-life applications. On the other hand, these techniques could not be used to analyze and improve industrial processes, and could thus not be put to use in real-life organizations.

In this paper, we have presented the ProM Import Framework, which is effectively bridging this gap. It represents a typical *enabling technology*, connecting formerly separate areas to their mutual benefit. In its current release, this application already features import plug-ins supporting seven process-aware information systems. Most notably, the support for commercial systems like FLOW*er*, WebSphere, and Staffware covers an immense installed base of users. Additional functionality that has been shifted into the framework makes the development of additional import plug-ins a convenient, time-effective task.

We hold this extension to the process mining tool landscape to be crucial with respect to the quality and credibility of process mining research. Real-life event log data often exhibits awkward and strange properties, which are unforeseen on a theoretical level, and which have to be taken into account in order to obtain meaningful results. It is only after process mining techniques have been proven to successfully analyze real-life logs, and thus to benefit businesses in their daily operations, that these techniques can grow into productive tools for business process optimization.

## Acknowledgements

This research is supported by the Technology Foundation STW, applied science division of NWO and the technology programme of the Dutch Ministry of Economic Affairs.

## References

1. W.M.P. van der Aalst and K.M. van Hee. *Workflow Management: Models, Methods, and Systems.* MIT press, Cambridge, MA, 2002.
2. W.M.P. van der Aalst and M. Song. Mining Social Networks: Uncovering Interaction Patterns in Business Processes. In J. Desel, B. Pernici, and M. Weske, editors, *International Conference on Business Process Management (BPM 2004)*, volume 3080 of *Lecture Notes in Computer Science*, pages 244–260. Springer-Verlag, Berlin, 2004.
3. W.M.P. van der Aalst, B.F. van Dongen, J. Herbst, L. Maruster, G. Schimm, and A.J.M.M. Weijters. Workflow Mining: A Survey of Issues and Approaches. *Data and Knowledge Engineering*, 47(2):237–267, 2003.
4. W.M.P. van der Aalst, A.J.M.M. Weijters, and L. Maruster. Workflow Mining: Discovering Process Models from Event Logs. *IEEE Transactions on Knowledge and Data Engineering*, 16(9):1128–1142, 2004.
5. W.M.P. van der Aalst, M. Weske, and D. Grünbauer. Case Handling: A New Paradigm for Business Process Support. *Data and Knowledge Engineering*, 53(2):129–162, 2005.

6. R. Agrawal, D. Gunopulos, and F. Leymann. Mining Process Models from Workflow Logs. In *Sixth International Conference on Extending Database Technology*, pages 469–483, 1998.
7. Pallas Athena. *Case Handling with FLOWer: Beyond workflow*. Pallas Athena BV, Apeldoorn, The Netherlands, 2002.
8. J.E. Cook and A.L. Wolf. Discovering Models of Software Processes from Event-Based Data. *ACM Transactions on Software Engineering and Methodology*, 7(3):215–249, 1998.
9. B.F. van Dongen and W.M.P. van der Aalst. Multi-Phase Process Mining: Building Instance Graphs. In P. Atzeni, W. Chu, H. Lu, S. Zhou, and T.W. Ling, editors, *International Conference on Conceptual Modeling (ER 2004)*, volume 3288 of *Lecture Notes in Computer Science*, pages 362–376. Springer-Verlag, Berlin, 2004.
10. B.F. van Dongen, A.K. de Medeiros, H.M.W. Verbeek, A.J.M.M. Weijters, and W.M.P. van der Aalst. The prom framework: A new era in process mining tool support. In G. Ciardo and P. Darondeau, editors, *Proceedings of the 26th International Conference on Applications and Theory of Petri Nets (ICATPN 2005)*, volume 3536 of *Lecture Notes in Computer Science*, pages 444–454. Springer-Verlag, Berlin, 2005.
11. D. Grigori, F. Casati, M. Castellanos, U. Dayal, M. Sayal, and M.C. Shan. Business process intelligence. *Computers in Industry*, 53(3):321–343, 2004.
12. J. Herbst and D. Karagiannis. An Inductive Approach to the Acquisition and Adaptation of Workflow Models. In M. Ibrahim and B. Drabble, editors, *Proceedings of the IJCAI'99 Workshop on Intelligent Workflow and Process Management: The New Frontier for AI in Business*, pages 52–57, Stockholm, Sweden, August 1999.
13. C.A.R. Hoare. Algorithm 64: Quicksort. *Commun. ACM*, 4(7):321, 1961.
14. G. Keller, M. Nüttgens, and A.W. Scheer. Semantische Processmodellierung auf der Grundlage Ereignisgesteuerter Processketten (EPK). Veröffentlichungen des Instituts für Wirtschaftsinformatik, Heft 89 (in German), University of Saarland, Saarbrücken, 1992.
15. D.E. Knuth. *The Art of Computer Programming*, volume 3: Sorting and Searching. Addison Wesley, Reading, MA, USA, 2 edition, 1998.
16. M. Reichert and P. Dadam. ADEPTflex: Supporting Dynamic Changes of Workflow without Loosing Control. *Journal of Intelligent Information Systems*, 10(2):93–129, 1998.

# Improving Exception Handling by Discovering Change Dependencies in Adaptive Process Management Systems

Barbara Weber[1,*], Werner Wild[2], Markus Lauer[3], and Manfred Reichert[4]

[1] Quality Engineering Research Group, University of Innsbruck, Austria
Barbara.Weber@uibk.ac.at
[2] Evolution Consulting, Innsbruck, Austria
werner.wild@evolution.at
[3] Dept. Databases and Information Systems, University of Ulm, Germany
markus.lauer@uni-ulm.de
[4] Information Systems Group, University of Twente, The Netherlands
m.u.reichert@utwente.nl

**Abstract.** Process-aware information systems should enable the flexible alignment of business processes to new requirements by supporting deviations from the predefined process model at runtime. To facilitate such dynamic process changes we have adopted techniques from case-based reasoning (CBR). In particular, our existing approach allows to capture the semantics of ad-hoc changes, to support their memorization, and to enable their reuse in upcoming exceptional situations. To further improve change reuse this paper presents an approach for discovering dependencies between ad-hoc modifications from change history. Based on this information better user assistance can be provided when dynamic process changes have to be made.

## 1 Introduction

Due to frequent changes in its business environment an enterprise must be able to flexibly and continuously align its information systems (IS) and its business processes. Enterprise IS therefore must provide for flexible process support while still enforcing some degree of control [1]. In particular, there is an essential requirement for maintaining a close "fit" between real-world business processes and the workflows as supported by the IS, their current generation is known as Process-Aware Information Systems (PAIS) [2].

Recently, significant efforts have been undertaken to make PAIS more flexible and several approaches for *adaptive* process management have emerged [1,3,4]. The underlying idea is to enable (dynamic) changes of different process aspects (e.g., control flow, organizational, functional, and informational perspectives) and at different process levels (e.g., instance and type level). In particular, authorized users must be able to deviate from the pre-defined process model as needed, i.e., ad-hoc changes (e.g., to add or shift activities) of individual process

---

* Part of this research was funded by a grant from the Tiroler Wissenschaftsfond.

J. Eder, S. Dustdar et al. (Eds.): BPM 2006 Workshops, LNCS 4103, pp. 93–104, 2006.

instances must be possible at runtime to deal with exceptional or changing situations. For example, during a medical treatment process the patient's current medication may have to be changed due to an allergic reaction, i.e., the process instance representing this treatment procedure must be dynamically adapted.

To facilitate exception handling we have adopted techniques from *case-based resoning* (CBR) [5,6,7]. This allows us to capture contextual knowledge about ad-hoc changes and to assist actors in reusing it. For this we apply an interactive variant of CBR (i.e., *conversational CBR* [8]), describe ad-hoc changes as *cases* and memorize them in a *case base CB*. In its simplest form a case covers a single change operation (e.g., insertion of a process activity). However, cases may contain several (semantically) related change operations as well. For example, in a medical treatment process a magnet resonance tomography (MRT) may have to be skipped for a patient with cardiac pacemaker, instead, another imaging procedure (e.g., computer tomography) might have to be applied. Our objective is to support reuse of such complex changes in similar situations to enable actors to operate at a higher semantical level and to relieve them from specifying the change from scratch each time.

Since ad-hoc changes are often applied in exceptional situations, we cannot expect that semantically related adaptations are always conducted at the same time, i.e., they are not always added as a single case to the PAIS. This happens when end users are rather inexperienced and do not think through all consequences, when changes to the same instance are performed by different actors or when these dependencies are not known when adding a case. Over time, the PAIS may end up with several inter-related cases which are frequently applied in combination with each other. By discovering such inter-case dependencies and by considering this knowledge in the context of change reuse we provide for better user assistance. When reusing a certain case the PAIS can suggest users to apply dependent cases as well. To further improve this approach, cases which always co-occur shall be merged and the CB should be refactored accordingly.

Section 2 summarizes background information needed for the understanding of our approach. In Section 3 we introduce the notion of co-occuring cases. Based on this, in Section 4 we sketch how actors can be assisted in reusing inter-dependent changes and in refactoring a CB by merging cases. Section 5 discusses related work and Section 6 concludes with a summary and outlook.

## 2   Supporting Change Reuse Through CBR

This section covers backgrounds needed for the understanding of this paper. First, we introduce basic notions related to process management. Second, we discuss how CBR is used in our approach for capturing the semantics of ad-hoc changes, for memorizing these changes, and for reusing them in similar situations.

### 2.1   Basic Notions

For each supported business process a corresponding *process type T* exists. It can be related with one or more process schemes representing different versions of the process. Each *process schema* $S$ is described in a graph-like fashion, and comprises a set of *activities* and *control connectors* between them. Based on a schema $S$ new *process instances* can be created and executed accordingly. For example, in instance $I_1$ in Fig. 1 activities A and C are completed whereas activity B is activated (i.e., its work items are offered to users in their worklists).

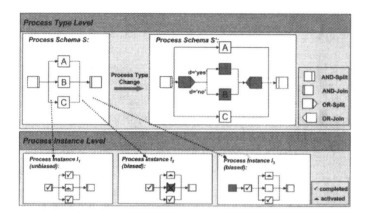

**Fig. 1.** Process Type and Process Instance

To deal with exceptional situations at the instance level, users must deviate from the pre-modeled schema (e.g., by deleting activities) [1,5,9]. *Ad-hoc changes* are instance-specific and do not affect the *execution schema* of any other running process instances. In Fig. 1, instance $I_2$ has undergone an individual modification (i.e., the dynamic deletion of activity B). Thus the execution schema of $I_2$ deviates from its original process schema $S$. Individually modified process instances are called *biased*, unchanged ones are denoted as *unbiased*.

## 2.2   Capturing Semantics of Ad-Hoc Changes with CBR

Our approach uses case-based reasoning (CBR) techniques to capture the semantics of an ad-hoc change, to memorize it and to support its reuse in similar situations (for details see [6,7]). Case-based reasoning (CBR) is a contemporary approach to problem solving and learning [10]. New problems are dealt with by drawing on past experiences – described in cases and stored in case bases – and by adapting their solutions to the new problem situation. For representing a concrete ad-hoc change we use the concept of a *case*, which captures the context of, and the reasons for the respective deviation (cf. Fig. 2). More precisely, a case contains a textual problem description *pd* which briefly summarizes the exceptional situation that led to the ad-hoc deviation. The reasons for the change are described in question-answer (QA) pairs $\{q_1a_1, \ldots, q_na_n\}$ each of which denotes one particular condition (for details see below). The solution part *sol* (i.e., the action list) of a case contains the concrete change operations applied.

The ad-hoc changes covered by a particular case $c$ can be reused, i.e., they can be re-applied to other instances. QA pairs are used to retrieve cases handling similar problems. If an adequate case is found its solution part can be applied to the given process instance. All instances to which case $c$ has been applied to are kept in its instance set $instanceSet_c$. If no similar cases can be found the user adds a new case with the respective change information to the system.

**Definition 1 (Case).** *A case $c$ is a tuple ($pd_c$, $qaSet_c$, $sol_c$, $instanceSet_c$) where*

- *$pd_c$ is a textual problem description*
- *$qaSet_c = \{q_1 a_1, \ldots, q_n a_n\}$ denotes a set of question-answer pairs*
- *$sol_c = \{ op_j \mid op_j = (opType_j, s_j, paramList_j), j = 1, \ldots, k\}$ is the solution part of the case denoting a list of change operations (i.e., the changes that have been applied to one or more process instances)* [1]
- *$instanceSet_c$ is the set of process instances to which case $c$ has been applied*

The question of a QA pair is usually entered as free text, however, to reduce duplicates it can alternatively be selected from a list of already existing questions. The answer can either be free text or a structured answer expression (cf. Fig 2 (a)). Answer expressions allow us to use contextual knowledge already kept in the PAIS (e.g., due to legal requirements), thus avoiding redundant data entry. Questions with answer expressions can be evaluated automatically by retrieving values for their context attributes from existing data in the system (e.g., the medical problems of a patient as stored in his electronic patient record), i.e., they do not have to be answered by users, thus preventing errors and saving time. Free text answers are used when no suitable context attributes are defined within the system or the user is not trained to write answer expressions. For example, the second QA pair in Fig. 2 (a) contains an answer expression using the context attribute *Patient.age*. It can therefore be evaluated automatically. By contrast, the answer in the first QA pair is free text provided by the user.

To be able to reason about the changes applied to a particular process instance $I$ we introduce $caseList_I$ as the list of all cases which have been applied to $I$, in their application order. If an instance $I$ is *biased* its $caseList_I$ is not empty. All cases applied to process instances created from schema version $S$ are stored in a case base $CB_S$ associated with $S$.

**Definition 2 (Case Base).** *A case base $CB_S$ is a tuple ($S$, $\{c_1, \ldots, c_m\}$) where*

- *$S$ denotes the schema version to which the case base is related*
- *$\{c_1, \ldots, c_m\}$ denotes a set of cases (cf. Def. 1)*

When deviations from the pre-defined process schema become necessary the user initiates a case retrieval dialogue (cf. Fig 2 (b)). The system then assists her in finding already stored similar cases (i.e., change scenarios in our context) by presenting a set of questions to be answered in any number and any order. Questions

---

[1] An operation $op_j := (opType_j, s_j, paramList_j)$ (j = 1, ..., k) consists of operation type $opType_j$, subject $s_j$ of the change, and parameter list $paramList_j$.

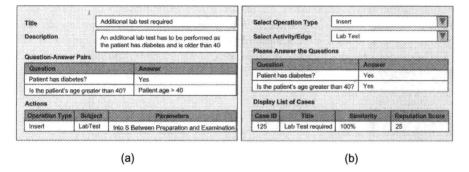

**Fig. 2.** CCBR Dialogs - Adding a New Case (a) and Retrieving Similar Cases (b)

with an answer expression are automatically evaluated by retrieving the values of the respective context attributes from the PAIS without user intervention. Based on this the system then searches for similar cases by calculating the similarity for each case in the case base $CB_S$. Similarity is calculated by dividing the number of correctly answered questions minus the number of incorrectly answered questions by the total number of questions in the case. It then displays the top $n$ ranked cases (ordered by decreasing similarity) as well as related information (e.g., reputation scores). The user then has several options:

1. The user can directly answer any of the remaining unanswered questions (in arbitrary order), similarity is then recalculated and the $n$ most similar cases are displayed to the user.
2. The user can apply a filter to the case base (e.g., by only considering cases whose solution part contains a particular change operation). All cases not matching the filter criteria are removed from the displayed list of cases.
3. The user can decide to review displayed cases in detail.
4. The user can select one of the displayed cases for reuse. The actions specified in the case's solution part are then forwarded to and executed by the PAIS. The instance set of the selected case is adjusted accordingly.

## 3    Inter-case Dependencies

This section first gives a typical example for inter-case dependencies and then introduces the formal notation to be used in this paper.

### 3.1    Motivating Example

Fig. 3 shows the cruciate rupture treatment process for a particular patient. This treatment process had to be modified due to an unanticipated situation. To confirm the suspicion of a cruciate rupture usually an x-ray as well as a magnet resonance tomography (MRT) are performed. However, as this patient has a cardiac pacemaker the radiologist decided to skip the MRT. To still get a reliable diagnosis, the attending physician ordered a computer tomography (CT) instead. Though these two changes are related to each other they were added to the system by different actors at different times. Case $c_1$ was added by the radiologist and resulted in the deletion of the MRT activity. Some time later the attending physician added case $c_{17}$ to insert the CT activity.

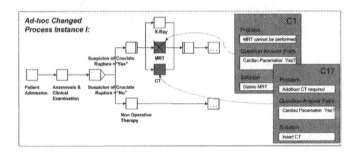

**Fig. 3.** Application Example

Cases applied to the same instance may be independent of, or dependent on each other. In our example the deletion of the MRT activity caused the insertion of the CT activity, i.e., the additional CT compensates the missing MRT. When such inter-case dependencies exist, the reuse of a particular case might necessitate further changes. In our example, reusing case $c_1$ may require the application of case $c_{17}$ as well since an alternative imaging procedure is needed. Discovering such inter-case dependencies is crucial to better assist users when they need to make complex changes to the system.

### 3.2   Co-occuring Cases

Let $CB_S$ be a case base and let $c_1$ and $c_2$ be two cases in $CB_S$. A metrics about inter-case dependencies is the *conditional co-occurence rate* $CoRate(c_2|c_1)$. For a set of process instances this metrics denotes the relative frequency of the application of case $c_2$ on condition that case $c_1$ has been applied too.

**Definition 3 (Conditional Co-Occurrence Rate).** *Let $S$ be a process schema with case base $CB_S$ and let $c_1$, $c_2 \in CB_S$ be two cases. The conditional co-occurence rate $CoRate(c_2|c_1)$ denotes the relative frequency of case $c_2$ on condition that case $c_1$ has already been applied. Formally:*

$$CoRate(c_2|c_1) = \frac{|instanceSet_{c_2} \cap instanceSet_{c_1}|}{|instanceSet_{c_1}|}$$

When a user wants to reuse a case $c \in CB_S$ we present her all other cases $c_k \in CB_S$ with $CoRate(c_k|c)$ exceeding threshold *thres* $\leq 1$. Section 4 describes how we assist actors in reusing inter-dependent changes. In this context cases with *strong co-occurence* are of particular interest.

**Definition 4 (Strong Co-Occurence of Cases).** *Let $S$ be a process schema with case base $CB_S$. Let further $c_1, c_2 \in CB_S$. Then:*

1. *If $CoRate(c_2|c_1) = 1$ holds we denote case $c_2$ as strongly co-occurrent with case $c_1$ (i.e., $c_2$ must only have been applied when $c_1$ has been applied too).*
2. *If $CoRate(c_2|c_1) = CoRate(c_1|c_2) = 1$ holds we denote cases $c_2$ and $c_1$ as being strongly co-occurent with each other (i.e., $c_2$ always occurs when $c_1$ has been applied and vice versa).*

If $c_2$ is strongly co-occurrent with $c_1$ (cf. Def. 4.1), obviously, $instanceSet_{c_1} \subseteq instanceSet_{c_2}$ must hold. Consequently, we obtain $CoRate(c_2|c_1) = 1$ and $CoRate(c_1|c_2) = \frac{|instanceSet_{c_1}|}{|instanceSet_{c_2}|}$. As a special scenario consider two cases $c_1$ and $c_2$ which are strongly co-occurent with each other (cf. Def. 4.2). Trivially, we then obtain $|instanceSet_{c_1}| = |instanceSet_{c_2}|$. If cases $c_1$ and $c_2$ are strongly co-occurent with each other and the total number of co-occurrences exceeds threshold $minOccur \in \mathbb{N}$, the process engineer is notified about the option to merge these inter-dependent cases (cf. Section 4.2).

# 4 Discovering and Utilizing Knowledge About Inter-case Dependencies

To discover co-occurent changes we analyze a process schema's CB. We utilize the obtained knowledge to assist actors in reusing complex changes (cf. Section 4.1) and to support process engineers in refactoring CBs (cf. Section 4.2).

## 4.1 Assisting Actors in Reusing Dependent Cases

When a case $c \in CB_S$ is reused (i.e., $c$ is applied to a process instance $I$) the system displays all cases $cse \in CB_S$ for optional reuse[2] which co-occur with $c$ and for which the co-occurence rate $CoRate(cse|c)$ exceeds a given threshold. This is accomplished by Algorithm 1. First, Algorithm 1 adds case $c$ to the list of cases ($caseList_I$) which have already been applied to instance $I$ (line 3). For each case $cse$ (except for already applied cases to instance $I$), Algorithm 1 then determines the conditional co-occurence rate $CoRate(cse|c)$. This is done by determining the total number of co-occurences between $cse$ and $c$ over all instances of process schema $S$ and by dividing it by the total number of occurences for case $c$ (line 6). Finally, only those cases $c_k$ are displayed (for potential reuse) whose co-occurence rate $CoRate(cse|c)$ exceeds the given threshold $thres$.

For example, consider the scenario depicted in Fig. 4. Assume that the changes represented by case $c_5$ shall be applied to process instance $I_{132}$. According to Algorithm 1 the system adds case $c_5$ to $CaseList_{I132}$ and then determines the conditional co-occurence rate $CoRate(cse|c_5)$ for each case $cse \in CB_s \setminus CaseList_{I132}$ (i.e., $\{c_3, c_{19}\}$) related to any instance from $InstanceSet_{c_5} = \{I_{44}, I_{143}, I_{147}\}$. We

---

[2] Cases which have already been applied to process instance I are not shown.

---

**Algorithm 1.** Display_CoOccurent_Cases

---

1: Input: Case $c$; ProcessInstance $I$; float thres;
2:
3: add case c to $CaseList_I$;
4: Integer TotalOccurenceOfC := $|InstanceSet_c|$;
5: **for all** $cse \in CB_S \setminus CaseList_I$ **do**
6:    $CoOccurenceRate_{cse} := \frac{|instanceSet_c \cap instanceSet_{cse}|}{TotalOccurenceOfC}$;
7:    **if** $CoOccurenceRate_{cse} \geq$ thres **then**
8:       DISPLAY(cse)
9:    **end if**
10: **end for**

---

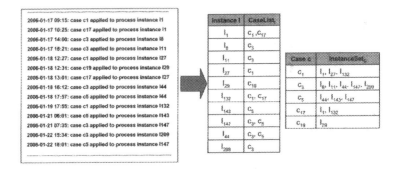

**Fig. 4.** Log File

obtain $CoRate(c_3|c_5) = \frac{2}{3}$ and $CoRate(c_{19}|c_5) = \frac{0}{3}$. For example, if we have chosen $thres = 0.6$ case $c_3$ will be displayed to the users (for optional reuse) when applying $c_5$ to instance $I_{132}$.

When reusing a case a wizard opens and all dependent cases are displayed to the user (cf. Fig. 5). For each dependent case its identifier, title and co-occurrance rate are shown. The co-occurance rate reflects the confidence of the system that the dependent case should be applied too in this particular situation. The user can then optionally reuse any of the displayed cases.

At first glance the described approach seems to be easy to implement. However, when reusing a case and applying its changes it must be guaranteed that the respective process instance still meets certain correctness and consistency constraints. In particular, the pre-conditions for applying the change operations captured by a case must be met when reusing it. As an illustrative example consider the medical treatment process depicted in Fig. 6. Assume that the respective patient complains about pains in his knee. The attending physician therefore orders an additional examination. This change is represented by case $c_{22}$ which captures the insertion of activity Follow-up examination between activities Non Operative Therapy and Documentation and Discharge. Assume further that during the follow-up examination it is found that the patient suffers from a contusion and the physician therefore decides that a puncture has

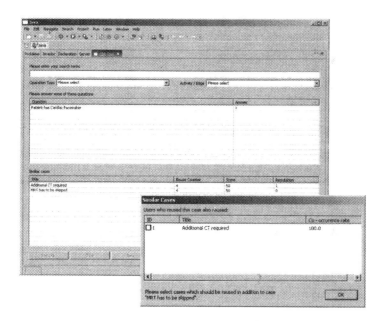

**Fig. 5.** Presenting Dependent Cases to the User

to be performed as well. This change is captured by case $c_{35}$ (subsequent insertion of activity `Puncture` between activities `Follow-up examination` and `Documentation and Discharge`). Note that the definition of the latter change depends on the presence of activity `Follow-up examination` which was introduced by case $c_{22}$. Such dependencies, in turn, could result in parameterization problems or inconsistencies when a user solely wants to reuse case $c_{35}$. Generally, the change framework we use allows us to efficiently detect such undesired situations [11]. In our example, a user who wants to reuse case $c_{35}$ has two options. Either she can apply case $c_{22}$ as well or she may adapt the case by modifying the parameterization of the respective change (e.g., by replacing the position parameter `Follow-up examination` with `Non Operative Therapy`).

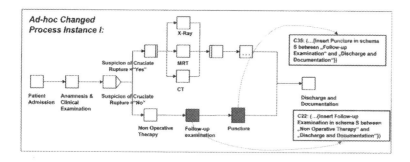

**Fig. 6.** System Supported Conflict Resolution

## 4.2   Refactoring Case Bases by Merging Cases

In order to increase problem solving efficiency we can compress the case base by merging strongly co-occurent cases. For this scenario, consider the reuse of a case $c$ and its application to a particular process instance. Whenever such an event occurs, it triggers an analysis of the case base. More precisely, it is checked whether the reused case is strongly co-occurent with other cases. If so, the knowledge engineer is notified accordingly and may then decide to merge respective cases. Note that in this scenario we can restrict the analysis (i.e., the comparison of case $c$ with other cases) to those cases belonging to the case list $caseList_I$, as only cases within that list can be strongly co-occurent with case $c$. Algorithm 2 is applied to detect cases which strongly co-occur with each other (cf. Def. 4). For the sake of readability we treat this algorithm separately from Algorithm 1, however, for a practical implementation they can easily be merged.

---

**Algorithm 2.** Notify_About_Strongly_CoOccurent_Cases

---

1: Input: Case $c$; ProcessInstance $I$; int minOccur;
2:
3:  Add $I$ to $instanceSet_c$;
4:  **for all** $cse \in CaseList_I$ **do**
5:     **if** $instanceSet_{cse} = instanceSet_c$ **then**
6:        **if** $|instanceSet_c| \geq minOccur$ **then**
7:           NOTIFY(c, cse)
8:        **end if**
9:     **end if**
10: **end for**

---

Again consider the example from from Fig. 4. Assume that case $c_{17}$ is applied to instance $I_{27}$. Instance $I_{27}$ is then added to the instance set of case $c_{17}$. Further, Algorithm 2 (with, e.g., $minOccur = 3$) identifies case $c_1$ as being strongly co-occurent with case $c_{17}$. Consequently, the process engineer is notified that $c_1$ and $c_{17}$ are strongly co-occurent which each other and thus could merge these two cases. In this situation a new case $c'$ can be created in $CB_S$ and the original cases are deactivated[3], i.e., a refactoring of the case base takes place. The problem descriptions and QA pairs related to the two cases have to be manually merged by the process engineer; the corresponding solution parts, in turn, can be automatically merged by unifying the change operations of the original cases in the correct order. Different optimizations for purging the resulting operation sets can be applied in this context. However, this is beyond the scope of this paper. In addition, the schema-specific case base $CB_S$ can be regularly searched for any strongly co-occurent cases by applying Algorithm 3.

---

[3] For traceability reasons respective cases are not deleted, but only deactivated.

---

**Algorithm 3.** Scan_For_Strongly_CoOccurent_Cases

---

1: Input: Case Base $CB_S$; int minOccur;
2:
3: $CB = CB_S$
4: **while** $CB \neq \emptyset$ **do**
5:    take arbitrary case $cse$ from $CB$
6:    $CB = CB \setminus \{cse\}$
7:    **for all** $case \in CB$ **do**
8:       **if** $instanceSet_{case} = instanceSet_{cse}$ **then**
9:          **if** $|instanceSet_{case}| \geq minOccur$ **then**
10:             NOTIFY(case, cse)
11:          **end if**
12:       **end if**
13:    **end for**
14: **end while**

---

## 5   Related Work

Similar to our approach process mining aims at extracting process knowledge from log data. So far, focus of mining techniques has been on the extraction of process models from execution logs [12,13,14]. For example, the alpha algorithm can be used to construct a Petri net model describing the behavior observed in the log. Similarly, the Multi-Phase Mining approach can be used to construct event-driven process chains from logs. Recent approaches also use event-based data for mining model perspectives other than control flow (e.g., process performance [15]). Mature tools like the ProM framework allow constructing different types of models from real process executions. However, process mining research has not yet addressed applying minig techniques to change logs.

The necessity to support the user in exceptional situations has been addressed by adaptive process management technology [1,9,16]. ADEPT [1], for instance, supports the user in defining (syntactically) correct process changes during runtime. For example, when an activity is deleted at the process instance level, the system might suggest the deletion of data dependent activities as well. However, ADEPT does not consider semantical dependencies between changes yet.

Complementary to this paper [17] covers quality aspects relevant when applying CBR for the memorization and the reuse of ad-hoc modifications and the deriviation of process type changes. While [17] broadly deals with quality issues and aims at increasing the performance of the CBR system by increasing problem solving efficiency, CB competence and solution quality, this paper addresses how user assistance can be improved through mining inter-case dependencies.

## 6   Summary and Outlook

We have proposed an approach to improve exception handling in adaptive process management systems through discovering and utilizing knowledge about dependencies between ad-hoc modifications. Actors are assisted in reusing previously applied ad-hoc changes by presenting related modifications to them as well. In addition, knowledge about inter-case dependencies is used to improve the quality of the CB (i.e., the collection of retrievable and reusable ad-hoc changes) and to increase problem solving efficiency. Ongoing work includes the evaluation of our prototype in a real world scenario. Future work will investigate how the reuse of ad-hoc modifications can be further improved. For example, a particular case representing an ad-hoc modification might not directly be applicable, but may require some adaptation (e.g., the parameterization of change operations may have to be adapted). Finally, we aim to use more of the semantics captured in our approach, e.g., to be able to reason about "similarity" of changes.

# References

1. Reichert, M., Dadam, P.: ADEPT$_{flex}$ – supporting dynamic changes of workflows without losing control. JIIS **10** (1998) 93–129
2. Dumas, M., ter Hofstede, A., van der Aalst, W., eds. In: Process Aware Information Systems. Wiley Publishing (2005)
3. Jørgensen, H.D.: Interactive Process Models. PhD thesis, Norwegian University of Science and Technology, Trondheim, Norway (2004)
4. Rinderle, S., Reichert, M., Dadam, P.: Correctness criteria for dynamic changes in workflow systems – a survey. Data and Knowledge Engineering **50** (2004) 9–34
5. Weber, B., Wild, W., Breu, R.: CBRFlow: Enabling adaptive workflow management through conversational case-based reasoning. In: ECCBR'04, Madrid (2004) 434–448
6. Weber, B., Rinderle, S., Wild, W., Reichert, M.: CCBR–driven business process evolution. In: ICCBR'05, Chicago (2005) 610–624
7. Rinderle, S., Weber, B., Reichert, M., Wild, W.: Integrating process learning and process evolution - a semantics based approach. In: BPM 2005. (2005) 252–267
8. Aha, D.W., Muñoz-Avila, H.: Introduction: Interactive case-based reasoning. Applied Intelligence **14** (2001) 7–8
9. Luo, Z., Sheth, A., Kochut, K., Miller, J.: Exception handling in workflow systems. Applied Intelligence **13** (2000) 125–147
10. Kolodner, J.L.: Case-Based Reasoning. Morgan Kaufmann (1993)
11. Rinderle, S.: Schema Evolution in Process Management Systems. PhD thesis, University of Ulm (2004)
12. v.d. Aalst, W., van Dongen, B., Herbst, J., Maruster, L., Schimm, G., Weijters, A.: Workflow mining: A survey of issues and approaches. Data and Knowledge Engineering **27** (2003) 237–267
13. Golani, M., Pinter, S.S.: Generating a process model from a process audit log. In: Proc. BPM'03, Eindhoven (2003) 136–151
14. van Dongen, B., van der Aalst, W.: Multi-phase process mining: Building instance graphs. In: Conceptual Modeling - ER 2004. LNCS 3288, Berlin (2004) 362–376
15. van der Aalst, W., Song, M.: Mining social networks. uncovering interaction patterns in business processes. In: Proc. BPM'04, Potsdam, Germany (2004) 244–260
16. Weske, M.: Workflow management systems: Formal foundation, conceptual design, implementation aspects. University of Münster, Germany (2000) Habil Thesis.
17. Weber, B., Reichert, M., Wild, W.: Case-base maintenance for ccbr-based process evolution. In: ECCBR'06. (2006)

# Process Mining and Petri Net Synthesis

Ekkart Kindler, Vladimir Rubin, and Wilhelm Schäfer

Software Engineering Group, University of Paderborn,
Warburger Str. 100, D-33098 Paderborn, Germany
{kindler, vroubine, wilhelm}@uni-paderborn.de

**Abstract.** The theory of regions and the algorithms for synthesizing a Petri net model from a transition system, which are based on this theory, have interesting practical applications – in particular in the design of electronic circuits. In this paper, we show that this theory can be also applied for mining the underlying process from the user interactions with a document management system. To this end, we combine an algorithm that we called activity mining with such Petri net synthesis algorithms. We present the basic idea of this approach, show some first results, and compare them with classical process mining techniques. The main benefit is that, in combination, the activity mining algorithm and the synthesis algorithms do not need a log of the activities, which is not available when the processes are supported by a document management system only.

## 1 Introduction

Today, there is a bunch of techniques that help to automatically come up with process models from a sequence of activities that are executed in an enterprise [1]. Typically, such sequences come from the log of a workflow management system or some standard software which is used for executing these processes. There are many different algorithms and methods that help to obtain faithful process models; some techniques come up with an initial model quite fast and the process models are incrementally improved by new observations [2]. All these techniques can be summarized by the term *process mining*.

Our interest in process mining came from the area of software engineering. Software engineering processes are often not well-documented, though good engineers have the processes in their minds. In the Capability Maturity Model (CMM), this *level of maturity* of a software company is called *repeatable* [3]. Therefore, we looked for methods for automatically mining these process models from the observed work. The main source for observing the work of software engineers are the logs of the version management systems and document management systems that are used in the development process. The problem, however, is that these systems are aware of documents only and not of the underlying activities. Basically, they see the creation, modification, and checkin of documents, but they are not aware of the activities and to which activity these events belong to. Therefore, the standard mining algorithms do not work; we must identify the activities from the event logs of the document management systems before: we call this *activity mining*. By activity mining, we get more information on the

J. Eder, S. Dustdar et al. (Eds.): BPM 2006 Workshops, LNCS 4103, pp. 105–116, 2006.

process than just a sequence of activities. In order to exploit this information, we developed an algorithm for obtaining the process models [4].

Having a closer look to the results of activity mining algorithms revealed that we could easily obtain a transition system for the underlying processes, where the transitions are the activities of the processes. So, basically, deriving a process model from the result of the activity mining algorithm means deriving a Petri net from a transition system, which is a well-known area of Petri net theory called *Petri net synthesis*. It was established by the seminal paper by Ehrenfeucht and Rozenberg [5] on *regions* and later extended and elaborated by other authors [6,7,8]. In this paper, we show that our activity mining algorithm in combination with the tool Petrify [9] can be used for faithfully mining process models from logs of document management systems and version management systems. The focus of this paper is on the use of synthesis algorithm; for details on the activity mining algorithms, we refer to [4].

## 2   Related Work

There is much research in the area of *process mining* [1]. People from different research domains, such as software process engineering, software configuration management, workflow management, and data mining are interested in deriving the behavioural models from the audit trails of the standard software.

The first application of "process mining" to the *workflow domain* was presented by Agrawal et al. in 1998 [10]. The approach of Herbst and Karagiannis [11] uses machine learning techniques for acquisition and adaptation of workflow models. The seminal work in the area of process mining was presented by van der Aalst et al. [12,13]. In this work, the causality relations between activities in logs are introduced and the $\alpha$-mining algorithm for discovering workflow models is defined. The research in the area of *software process mining* started in the mid 90ties with new approaches to the grammar inference problem proposed by Cook and Wolf [14]. The other work from the software domain is in the area of mining from software repositories [15]. Our approach [4] aims at combining software process mining with mining from software repositories; it derives a software process from the logs of software configuration management systems.

Another research area, which is discussed in this paper, is the area of *Petri net synthesis* and the *theory of regions*. The seminal paper in this area was written by Ehrenfeucht and Rozenberg [5]. It answered a long open question in Petri net theory: how to obtain a Petri net model from a transition system. Further research in this area came up with synthesis algorithms for elementary net systems [7] and even proved some promising complexity results for bounded place/transition systems [6].

First ideas of combining process mining and process synthesis were already mentioned in the process mining domain [13,16]. In this paper, we make the next step, we present an algorithm that enables us using the Petri net synthesis tool Petrify [9] for process mining.

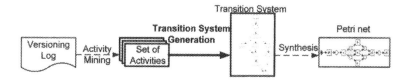

**Fig. 1.** Mining and Synthesis Schema

# 3 Mining and Synthesis

In this section, we present the overall approach; it combines our mining algorithms with Petri net synthesis algorithms in order to discover process models from *versioning logs* of document management systems.

The overall scheme of this approach is presented in Fig. 1. It starts with a versioning log as an input; by means of our *activity mining* algorithm, we derive a set of activities from the log. Using the set of activities, we do *transition system generation*. From the transition system, we derive a Petri net with the help of the *synthesis algorithm*. In this paper, we briefly discuss our activity mining algorithm; however, the focus of this paper is on the transition system generation, the use of the synthesis algorithm and the process models that can be obtained by it.

## 3.1 Transition System Generation from Versioning Logs

In this section, we deal with the versioning logs and present the transition system generation algorithm.

**Initial Input and Activity Mining.** Here, we briefly discuss our activity mining algorithm and the structure of the input it needs. This input information is versioning logs of different document management systems, such as Software Configuration Management (SCM) systems, Product Data Management (PDM) systems and other configuration and version management systems.

An example of a *versioning log* is shown in Table 1. The log contains data on the documents and timestamps of their commits to the system along with data on users and log comments. The versioning log consists of execution logs (in our example, they are separated by double lines), the structure of which can be derived using additional information, not discussed in this paper. These *execution logs* contain information about the instances of the process. Our small example was inspired by the software change process [17]; for this process, there are different executions, in which different documents are committed in different order starting with the "design" and finishing with the "review". We group execution logs into clusters. A *cluster* is a set of execution logs, which contains identical sets of documents. For example, the first two execution logs make up a cluster, because they both contain "design", "code", "testPlan" and "review" documents; the third execution log forms another cluster.

From the information about the execution logs and their clusters, the documents and the order of their commits to the system, we derive a set of activities

**Table 1.** Versioning Log

| Document | Date | Author | Comment |
|---|---|---|---|
| design | 01.01.05 14:30 | de | status: initial |
| code | 01.01.05 15:00 | dev | status: generated |
| testPlan | 05.01.05 10:00 | qa | status: initial |
| review | 07.01.05 11:00 | se | status: pending |
| design | 01.02.05 11:00 | de | status: initial |
| testPlan | 15.02.05 17:00 | qa | status: initial |
| code | 20.02.05 09:00 | dev | status: generated |
| review | 28.02.05 18:45 | se | status: pending |
| design | 01.02.05 11:00 | de | status: initial |
| verificationResults | 15.02.05 17:00 | se | status: initial |
| code | 20.02.05 09:00 | dev | status: generated |
| review | 28.02.05 18:45 | se | status: pending |

with the help of the *activity mining* algorithm (for details, see [4]). The resulting set is shown in Table 2. Since we have only information about the documents, we adopt a *document-oriented view* on the activities: they are defined by the input and the output documents[1]. The output documents are derived from the logs straightforwardly; the challenge of activity mining is deriving the inputs, because this information is not represented explicitly. The input contains all the documents that precede the output document in all the execution logs. For each activity, we have also shown the clusters from which it was derived; i.e. "1" means the cluster with the first two execution logs, "2" is the cluster with the third one. For example, activity 1 has $s0$ as input, *design* as output and can be derived from clusters 1 or 2.

In general, let us assume, there are $n$ clusters and each cluster is given a unique identifier from the set $C = \{1, \ldots, n\}$. For every subset $cl \subseteq C$, there is a set $D_{cl}$, which contains the intersection of sets of documents that belong to each execution log of this $cl$: $D_{cl} = \bigcap_{e \in cl} D_e$. So, each activity is a tuple $(I, O, cl)$, where $cl$ is a set of clusters from which this activity was derived; I and O are the sets of input and output documents resp. In a formal notation, a set of activities is defined the following way:

$$A \subseteq \{(I, O, cl) | I \subset D_{cl}, O \subset D_{cl}, cl \subseteq C\} \tag{1}$$

For each tuple, we define a "." notation, which gives the concrete field value by its name. E.g. for activity $a_1 = (\{s0\}, \{design\}, \{1, 2\})$, we have $a_1.I = \{s0\}$, $a_1.O = \{design\}$ and $a_1.cl = \{1, 2\}$.

---

[1] For technical reason, we include a document "s0" to the input of every activity except 0 and also add two additional activities that produce "e0"; it is done for making the process start and the process end explicit.

**Table 2.** Set of Activities

| Number | Input | Output | Clusters |
|---|---|---|---|
| 0 | | s0 | 1, 2 |
| 1 | s0 | design | 1, 2 |
| 2 | s0, design | code | 1 |
| 3 | s0, design, verificationResults | code | 2 |
| 4 | s0, design | testPlan | 1 |
| 5 | s0, design | verificationResults | 2 |
| 6 | s0, design, code, testPlan | review | 1 |
| 7 | s0, design, code, verificationResults | review | 2 |
| 8 | s0, design, code, testPlan, review | e0 | 1 |
| 9 | s0, design, code, verificationResults, review | e0 | 2 |

**Transition System Generation.** Different clusters, described in the previous section, correspond to different sets of documents and represent an alternative behaviour, whereas from one cluster we can derive concurrent behaviour. For example, activities $4$ and $5$ in Table 2 belong to different clusters, their output documents "testPlan" and "verificationResults" belong to the document sets of different clusters respectively. Thus, after creating the "design", there is an *alternative* either to produce a "testPlan" or to obtain "verificationResults". But the activities $2$ and $4$ belong to the same cluster, thus, after the "design", it is possible both to produce "code" and then a "testPlan" or first a "testPlan" and then "code", i.e. they are *concurrent*.

The main goal of the *transition system generation* algorithm is generating a labelled transition system using a set of activities and modelling the alternatives and the concurrency in it. The transition system consists of states, events and a transition relation between states, which are labelled with events. In our context, a *state* is a set of activities, which represents the history of the process, i.e. it contains the activities that were executed. All the activities of the state must occur in the same cluster. For example, the system is in a state $s_1 = \{0, 1, 2\}$ when activities 0, 1 and 2 have been executed and, thus, documents "s0", "design" and "code" have been produced. An *event* is a document produced by an activity enabled in a state. An activity is *enabled* in a state if it does not belong to the state but belongs to the same cluster as the state's activities; and the set of the documents produced by the state's activities includes the input set of the enabled activity. For example, activity 4 is enabled in state $s_1$, because it does not belong to the state, but it belongs to the same cluster as activities 0, 1 and 2; and it needs the documents "s0" and "design" as an input, these documents are a subset of the document set produced by $s_1$. So, when activity 4 is executed in the state $s_1$, it produces a document "testPlan" and the system goes to a new state $s_2 = \{0, 1, 2, 4\}$. Thus, there is a *transition* between states $s_1$ and $s_2$ and it is labelled with "testPlan". The resulting *transition system* is shown in Fig. 2; for better readability, the states' names do not contain the activities but the names of the produced documents, e.g. $s_1$ is called "s_s0_design" and $s_2$ – "s_design_s0_testPlan" respectively.

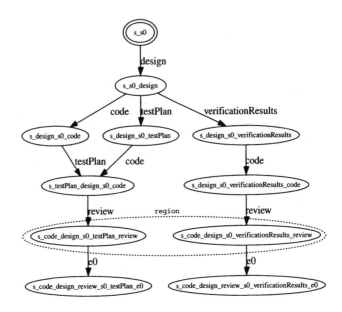

**Fig. 2.** Generated Transition System

Formally, a transition system is a tuple $TS = (S, E, T, s_0)$, where $S$ is a set of states, $E$ is a set of events, $T \subseteq S \times E \times S$ is transition relation and $s_0 \in S$ is an initial state. In our case, a state $s \in S$ is a subset of activities, i.e. $s \subseteq A$, where $A$ is defined in (1). The initial state $s_0 = \{(\{\}, \{s0\}, C)\}$ contains the activity, which produces "s0" and belongs to all clusters. There is a transition $s \xrightarrow{e} s'$ between two states, if there is an activity $a \in A$ such that $(a = s' \setminus s) \wedge (a.O = e)$ and for all $b \in s : a.cl \subseteq b.cl$, i.e. it belongs to the same cluster as the activities in $s$ and $a.I \subseteq \bigcup_{b \in s} b.O$, i.e. it is enabled in $s$.

We implemented these formal definitions as a set of clauses in SWI-Prolog [18]. As output, our algorithm generates a file with the transition system. This file is accepted by a synthesis tool, see Sect. 3.2, and can be automatically visualized as shown in Fig. 2.

## 3.2 Petri Net Synthesis

In this section, we describe the last step of our mining and synthesis approach: synthesis of a Petri Net from a mined transition system. We use the tool *Petrify* [9] for it.

Petrify, given a finite transition system, synthesizes a Petri net with a reachability graph that is *bisimilar* to the transition system. The synthesis algorithm is based on the *theory of regions* and was described in the work of Cortadella et al. [19]. Petrify uses labelled Petri nets and, thus, supports synthesis from arbitrary transition systems. It supports different methods for minimizing the Petri nets and for improving the efficiency of the synthesis algorithm. Here, we do not go into the details of the synthesis algorithm, but give the essential idea and motivate the relevance of it for the process mining area.

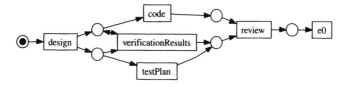

**Fig. 3.** Synthesized Petri Net

A *region* is a set of states to which all transitions with the same labels have the same relations: either they enter this set, or they exit this set or they do not cross this set. For example, in the transition system in Fig. 2, the set of states

$$\{ \quad s\_code\_design\_s0\_testPlan\_review,$$
$$s\_code\_design\_s0\_verification Results\_review \quad \}$$

is a region, because all transitions with a label "review" enter this set and all transitions with a label "e0" exit it. Petrify discovers a complete set of minimal regions for the given transition system and then removes the redundant ones. A region corresponds to a *place* in the synthesized Petri Net; so, Petrify tries to minimize the number of places and to make the Petri net understandable. For example, the synthesized Petri net is shown in Fig. 3. A place between Petri net transitions "review" and "e0" corresponds to the set of states, shown above. In the transition system, different transitions correspond to the same event. An event in the transition system corresponds to a Petri net *transition*. For example, for the event "review" there is a transition with the identical name. There is an arc between a transition and a place in the Petri net, if the corresponding transition in the transition system enters or exits the corresponding region.

In the context of process mining, the generated Petri net represents the control aspect of the process and models concurrency and alternatives, which were initially hidden in the logs. The transitions represent the activities. Since we have a document-oriented view on the activities, the execution of every activity results in committing a document to the document management system. By now, activities are named by the names of the committed documents, for example, activity "code" results in committing the document "code" to the system.

Since Petrify supports label splitting, it allows us to synthesize Petri nets under different optimization criteria and belonging to different classes, such as pure, free-choice, etc. Practically, for big projects, for complex Petri nets, we can generate pure or free-choice versions of them, which can be better understandable by managers and process engineers and, therefore, serve communication purposes in the company. For example, for the Petri net shown in Fig. 3, we can generate a "pure" analog of it, see Fig. 4.

### 3.3   Other Applications – Activity Logs

Along with applying our algorithms to the area of process mining from the versioning logs, we have also dealt with the *activity logs* as a standard input for

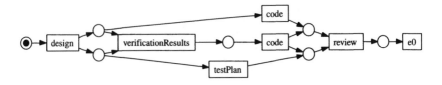

**Fig. 4.** Synthesized Pure Petri Net

**Table 3.** Activity Log

| Execution 1 | Execution 2 | Execution 3 |
|---|---|---|
| s0 | s0 | s0 |
| doDesign | doDesign | doDesign |
| writeCode | planTest | verify |
| planTest | writeCode | writeCode |
| doReview | doReview | doReview |
| e0 | e0 | e0 |

the most of classical mining approaches [13,14]. These logs are usually obtained from the workflow management systems or some standard software which is used for executing the processes in the company. For activity logs, we have deliberately chosen an example, which is very similar to the one given for verioning logs in the previous part of this section; it was done to motivate the generality of the mining and synthesis approach and to improve the readability of the paper. Actually, the algorithms for dealing with the versioning logs and for dealing with the activity logs are absolutely different and one can not be replaced by the other.

An example of the activity log (event log, as it is often called in literature) is shown in Table 3. It consists of process executions, which represent process instances (cases); in our example, we have three instances of the process. Every instance contains a set of activities and an order of their execution. For example, in the first instance, activities are executed in the following order: "doDesign", "writeCode", "planTest" and then "doReview". We add activity "s0" to the beginning of every log and activity "e0" to the end of every log to make the process start and the process end explicit.

From the activity log, without any preprocessing steps, we can generate a transition system. In this case, a *state* is again a set of activities. An *event* is an activity enabled in a state. An activity is enabled in a state when there is a process execution, where the activity is executed after the set of the activities of the state. For example, the system is in a state $s_1 = \{s0, doDesign\}$, when activities $s_0$ and *doDesign* have been executed. Since in the "Execution 1", an activity "writeCode" is executed after the activities of the state $s_1$, an event "writeCode" can occur in this state. When the activity is executed, the system comes to a state $s_2 = \{s0, doDesign, writeCode\}$; so, there is a transition between the states $s_1$ and $s_2$. The resulting transition system is shown in Fig. 5. The Petrify synthesis algorithm generates a Petri net from it, see Fig. 6.

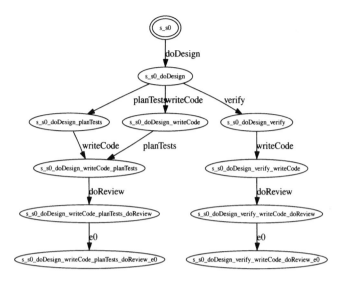

**Fig. 5.** Generated Transition System

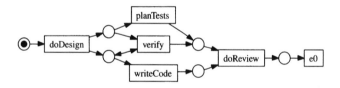

**Fig. 6.** Synthesized Petri Net

In a formal notation, there is a transition $s \xrightarrow{a} s'$ between two states, where $s = \{a_1, \ldots, a_{i-1}\}$, $a = a_i$, $s' = \{a_1, \ldots, a_i\}$ and $a_1, \ldots, a_i$ are activities, if and only if there is a following execution $a_1, \ldots, a_{i-1}, a_i, \ldots$.

### 3.4  Implementation and Evaluation

In this section, we show the first steps and directions for the evaluation of the presented algorithms. For making a small ad-hoc comparison with the existing process mining approaches, we have used ProM and the $\alpha$-algorithm [13] for generating a Petri net from the log presented in Table 3. As a result, we have got the Petri net shown in Fig. 7. The algorithms provide different results, but, for example, for our small activity log, the synthesized Petri net has no deadlocks and it models all the process executions from the activity log, whereas the model obtained with ProM reaches a deadlock situation after executing activities "doDesign" and "planTests" and, thus, does not model the "Execution 2".

This shows that our algorithm gives a better result for at least one example. But there are other benefits: First, we are capable of dealing with different sources of information: versioning logs and activity logs. Second, our approach is

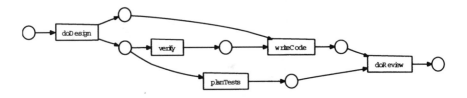

**Fig. 7.** Petri Net generated by ProM

**Table 4.** Execution Times

| # of Executions | 3 | 5 | 7 | 10 |
|---|---|---|---|---|
| **Average # of Documents in Execution** | 4 | 5 | 6 | 10 |
| **Execution Time (msec)** | 941 | 1157 | 2307 | 9994 |

flexible and extensible, because improving the initial algorithms (they work with versioning logs) for dealing with the activity logs resulted in: 1) removing clustering and activity mining parts, which are specific and necessary for versioning logs; 2) slightly changing the transition system generation part[2]. In general, the Petri net synthesis approach assumes having complete transition system with all possible transitions, which is not always a realistic case; but, for the versioning logs, the activity mining algorithm has to cope with the defects of the input data and the transition system generation algorithm remains the same.

Our algorithms were implemented in Prolog, which gives a certain flexibility of the solution and simplifies the capabilities of experimenting with it and expanding it. We have made several experiments with the algorithms. For these experiments, the logs were generated artificially but they are based on our experience on real examples. The execution times of all the algorithms (mining, transition system generation and synthesis) are shown in Table 4. The execution time depends on the number of executions (execution log) and the average number of documents in the execution. The columns in the table correspond to the experiments; the time needed for constructing a Petri net from 10 logs with 10 documents in each log is less then 10 seconds, which is a rather promising result, since this is an example in the size of a realistic log.

In this section, we have presented the first steps towards combining the mining and the synthesis approaches for discovering process models from both versioning logs and activity logs. Though, the approach is not fully worked out and evaluated yet, we can already see its benefits even for the given simple examples.

## 4   Conclusion and Future Work

In this paper, we have presented *mining and synthesis* algorithms, which derive a Petri net model of a business process from a versioning log of a document

---

[2] Now, the ProM community has done their own implementation of some regions algorithms, which is available as a "Region miner" plugin for ProM.

management system. This way, we have opened a new application area for mining without activity logs. We have also shown an extension of our approach, which can deal with activity logs of workflow management systems. The approach uses the well-developed and practically-applicable theory of "Petri net synthesis" for solving a vital problem of process mining. In order to do it, we have developed a *transition system generation* algorithm, which is the main focus of the paper.

The algorithms which were presented in this paper can deal with concurrency and alternatives in the process models. By now, we are not dealing with iterations. Detecting iterations in the versioning logs is a very important domain-specific and company-specific problem. We will deal with this problem in our future research, even though this problem appears rather seldom, if the conventions of using the document management system are introduced and fulfilled in the company. Another relevant domain-specific problem is identifying the activities and naming them meaningfully. Both issues belong to the part on activity mining. In the future, we will improve the activity mining algorithm and, possibly, use the interaction with the user for solving these problems. However, activity mining is not the focus of this paper; as soon as it is improved, the transition system generation algorithm has only to be slightly changed for introducing iterations and activities' identifiers to the transition systems.

Much work has to be done in applying the mining and synthesis algorithms to different document management systems in different application areas and making practical evaluation of them both in the area of business process management and software process engineering. Since our approach is also relevant to the area of mining the activity logs, in the future, we should also compare it to the existing approaches in this area. This paper aims at making the first step from the well-developed theory of Petri net synthesis to the practically relevant research domain of process mining.

# References

1. van der Aalst, W., van Dongena, B.F., Herbst, J., Marustera, L., Schimm, G., Weijters, A.J.M.M.: Workflow mining: A survey of issues and approaches. Data & Knowledge Engineering **47** (2003) 237–267
2. Kindler, E., Rubin, V., Schäfer, W.: Incremental Workflow mining based on Document Versioning Information. In Li, M., Boehm, B., Osterweil, L.J., eds.: Proc. of the Software Process Workshop 2005, Beijing, China. Volume 3840 of LNCS., Springer (2005) 287–301
3. Humphrey, W.S.: Managing the software process. Addison-Wesley Longman Publishing Co., Inc., Boston, MA, USA (1989)
4. Kindler, E., Rubin, V., Schäfer, W.: Activity mining for discovering software process models. In Biel, B., Book, M., Gruhn, V., eds.: Proc. of the Software Engineering 2006 Conference, Leipzig, Germany. Volume P-79 of LNI., Gesellschaft für Informatik (2006) 175–180
5. Ehrenfeucht, A., Rozenberg, G.: Partial (Set) 2-Structures. Part I: Basic Notions and the Representation Problem. Acta Informatica **27** (1989) 315–342
6. Badouel, E., Bernardinello, L., Darondeau, P.: Polynomial algorithms for the synthesis of bounded nets. In: TAPSOFT. (1995) 364–378

7. Desel, J., Reisig, W.: The synthesis problem of Petri nets. Acta Inf. **33** (1996) 297–315
8. Badouel, E., Darondeau, P.: Theory of regions. In: Lectures on Petri Nets I: Basic Models, Advances in Petri Nets, the volumes are based on the Advanced Course on Petri Nets, London, UK, Springer-Verlag (1998) 529–586
9. Cortadella, J., Kishinevsky, M., Kondratyev, A., Lavagno, L., Yakovlev, A.: Petrify: a tool for manipulating concurrent specifications and synthesis of asynchronous controllers. IEICE Transactions on Information and Systems **E80-D** (1997) 315–325
10. Agrawal, R., Gunopulos, D., Leymann, F.: Mining Process Models from Workflow Logs. In: Proceedings of the 6th International Conference on Extending Database Technology, Springer-Verlag (1998) 469–483
11. Herbst, J., Karagiannis, D.: An Inductive approach to the Acquisition and Adaptation of Workflow Models. citeseer.ist.psu.edu/herbst99inductive.html (1999)
12. Weijters, A., van der Aalst, W.: Workflow Mining: Discovering Workflow Models from Event-Based Data. In Dousson, C., Höppner, F., Quiniou, R., eds.: Proceedings of the ECAI Workshop on Knowledge Discovery and Spatial Data. (2002) 78–84
13. van der Aalst, W., Weijters, T., Maruster, L.: Workflow mining: Discovering process models from event logs. IEEE Transactions on Knowledge and Data Engineering **16** (2004) 1128–1142
14. Cook, J.E., Wolf, A.L.: Discovering Models of Software Processes from Event-Based Data. ACM Trans. Softw. Eng. Methodol. **7** (1998) 215–249
15. MSR 2005 International Workshop on Mining Software Repositories. In: ICSE '05: Proceedings of the 27th international conference on Software engineering, New York, NY, USA, ACM Press (2005)
16. Herbst, J.: Ein induktiver Ansatz zur Akquisition und Adaption von Workflow-Modellen. PhD thesis, Universität Ulm (2001)
17. Kellner, M.I., Felier, P.H., Finkelstein, A., Katayama, T., Osterweil, L., Penedo, M., Rombach, H.: ISPW-6 Software Process Example. In: Proceedings of the First International Conference on the Software Process, Redondo Beach, CA, USA, IEEE Computer Society Press (1991) 176–186
18. Wielemaker, J.: An overview of the SWI-Prolog programming environment. In Mesnard, F., Serebenik, A., eds.: Proceedings of the 13th International Workshop on Logic Programming Environments, Heverlee, Belgium, Katholieke Universiteit Leuven (2003) 1–16 CW 371.
19. Cortadella, J., Kishinevsky, M., Lavagno, L., Yakovlev, A.: Deriving Petri nets from finite transition systems. IEEE Transactions on Computers **47** (1998) 859–882

# A Discourse on Complexity of Process Models
## (Survey Paper)

J. Cardoso[1], J. Mendling[2], G. Neumann[2], and H.A. Reijers[3]

[1] University of Madeira
9000-390 Funchal, Portugal
jcardoso@uma.pt
[2] Vienna University of Economics and Business Administration
Augasse 2-6, 1090 Vienna, Austria
{jan.mendling, neumann}@wu-wien.ac.at
[3] Eindhoven University of Technology
P.O. Box 513, 5600 MB Eindhoven, The Netherlands
h.a.reijers@tm.tue.nl

**Abstract.** Complexity has undesirable effects on, among others, the correctness, maintainability, and understandability of business process models. Yet, measuring complexity of business process models is a rather new area of research with only a small number of contributions. In this paper, we survey findings from neighboring disciplines on how complexity can be measured. In particular, we gather insight from software engineering, cognitive science, and graph theory, and discuss in how far analogous metrics can be defined on business process models.

## 1 Introduction

Since business process management has become an accepted concept for the implementation and integration of large-scale information systems, there is an increasing need for insight into how errors can be avoided, how maintenance can be facilitated, or how the quality of the processes can be improved. In this context, there is some evidence that complexity is a determinant of error probability of a business process [18]. As process complexity and its measurement is a rather new field in business process management, there is only a limited understanding of how far existing knowledge of complexity e.g. for the software engineering domain can be adopted.

The complexity of a software program comes in three 'flavors': computational complexity, psychological complexity, and representational complexity [26]. The most important is psychological complexity, which encompasses programmer characteristics, product/documentation complexity and problem complexity. Obviously, the latter aspect, the complexity of the problem itself, cannot be controlled in developing software. It is therefore frequently dismissed from consideration in the software engineering literature. It seems sensible to do the same for analyzing the complexity of process models. However, the issue remains that complex processes will require more complex process models. Therefore, for

J. Eder, S. Dustdar et al. (Eds.): BPM 2006 Workshops, LNCS 4103, pp. 117–128, 2006.

the development of process model complexity it seems worthwhile to evaluate complexity measures as *relative* to the underlying process complexity.

Existing theoretical approaches to formulate 'complexity metrics' for software include the use of information theory from signal processing (e.g. [10]) and communication theory (e.g. [24]), as well as approaches based on analogues with graph theory (e.g. [15]) and lattice theory (e.g. [11]). Approaches taking the cognitive sciences as starting point have resulted, for example, in Bastani's complexity model [4]. An overview of some 50 different software complexity metrics is provided in Table 1 in [5].

In this paper, we contribute to a better understanding of business process model complexity. In particular, we provide a theoretical survey of complexity considerations and metrics in the fields of software engineering, cognitive science, and graph theory and we relate them to business process modelling. A further empirical investigation might ultimately lead to establishing a complexity theory of business process models. Following this line of argumentation, the rest of the paper is structured as follows. Section 2 discusses complexity metrics for software and their applicability for business process models. After a general introduction to the discipline, we define analogous metrics to the Line-of-Code, McCabe's Cyclomatic Complexity called Control-Flow Complexity, Halstead Complexity Metric, and Information Flow Complexity as defined by Henry and Kafura. Section 3 relates findings from cognitive science to measuring complexity in software engineering. In Section 4 graph theoretical measures are considered as potential complexity metrics for business process models. Section 5 closes the paper and gives an outlook on future research with a focus on how the process complexity metrics can be validated.

## 2   Complexity in Business Processes

### 2.1   Software Metrics

Over the last 30 years many measures have been proposed by researchers to analyze software complexity, understandability, and maintenance. Metrics were designed to analyze software such as imperative, procedural, and object-oriented programs. Software measurement is concerned with deriving a numeric value for an attribute of a software product, i.e. a measurement is a mapping from the empirical world to the formal world. From the several software metrics available we are particularly interested in studying complexity metrics and find out how they can be used to evaluate the complexity of business processes.

Software metrics are often used to give a quantitative indication of a program's complexity. However, it is not to be confused with computational complexity measures (cf. $O(n)$-Notation), whose aim is to compare the performance of algorithms. Software metrics have been found to be useful in reducing software maintenance costs by assigning a numeric value to reflect the ease or difficulty with which a program module may be understood.

There are hundreds of software complexity measures that have been described and published by many researchers. For example, the most basic complexity measure, the number of lines of code (LOC), simply counts the lines of executable code, data declarations, comments, and so on. While this measure is extremely simple, it has been shown to be very useful and correlates well with the number of errors in programs.

## 2.2 The Analogy Between Software and Business Processes

While traditional software metrics were designed to be applied to programs written in languages such as C++, Java, FORTRAN, etc, we believe that they can be revised and adapted to analyze and study business processes characteristics, such as complexity, understandability, and maintenance. We based our intuition on the fact that there is a strong analogy between programs and business processes, as argued before in e.g. [23,9]. Business process languages aim to enable programming in the large. The concepts of programming in the large and programming in the small distinguish between two aspects of writing the type of long-running asynchronous processes that one typically sees in business processes. Programming in the large emphasis is on partitioning the work into modules whose interactions are precisely specified and can refer to programming code that represents the high-level state transition logic of a business process (typically using splits and joins). This state transition logic included information such as when to wait for messages from incoming transitions, when to activate outgoing transitions, and when to compensate for failed activities, etc.

A business process, possibly modeled with a language such as BPEL [2], can be seen as a traditional software program that has been partitioned into modules or functions (i.e. activities) that take in a group of inputs and provide some output. Module interactions are precisely specified using predefine logic operators such as sequence, XOR-splits, OR-splits, and AND-splits. There is a mapping that can be established between software programs constructs and business processes. Functions, procedures, or modules are mapped to activities. Two sequential software statements (i.e. instructions or functions) can be mapped to two sequential process activities. A 'switch' statement can be mapped to a XOR-split. In programs, threads can be used to model concurrency and can be mapped to AND-splits. Finally, the conditional creation of threads using a sequence of 'if-then' statements can be mapped to an OR-split.

## 2.3 Business Process Metrics

We believe that the future for process metrics lies in using relatively simple metrics to build tools that will assist process analysts and designer in making design decisions. Furthermore, because business processes are a high-level notion made up of many different elements (splits, joins, resources, data, activities, etc.), there can never be a single measure of process complexity. The same conclusion has been reached in software engineering. Nagappan et al. [20] point out that there is no single set of complexity metrics that could act as a universally best defect predictor for software programs. For this reason several process metrics can be designed to analyze business processes. For example, Cardoso [8] identifies four main types of complexity metrics for processes: activity complexity, control-flow complexity, data-flow complexity, and resource complexity.

The following sections describe several approaches to adapt known software metrics proposed by researches worldwide to business processes analysis. Having established that there is a mapping from traditional programming languages and business processes; we will study and adapt some of the most well known and widely used source code metric, i.e. number of lines of code (LOC) [13], McCabe cyclomatic complexity [15,16], Halstead's software science measures [10], and Henry and Kafura [12] information flow metric.

## 2.4   Adapting the LOC Metric

One of the earliest and fundamental measures based on the analysis of software code is based on the basic count of the number of Lines of Code (LOC) of a program. Despite being widely criticized as a measure of complexity, it continues to have widespread popularity mainly due to its simplicity [3]. The basis of the LOC measure is that program length can be used as a predictor of program characteristics such as errors occurrences, reliability, and ease of maintenance.

If we view a process activity as a statement of a software program, we can derive a very simple metric (metric *M1*) that merely counts the number of activities (*NOA*) in a business process. It should be noticed that the *NOA* metric characterizes only one specific view of size, namely length, it takes no account of functionality or complexity. Also, bad process design may cause an excessive number of activities. Compared to the original LOC metric, the *NOA* is not language-dependent and it is easier for users to understand.

*M1: NOA* = Number of activities in a process

Another adaptation of the LOC metric is to view not only activities as program statements, but to also take into account process control-flow elements (i.e. control structures). Control-flow elements affect the execution sequence of activities. This statements are different since they are executed for their effect and do not have values. Two types of metrics can be designed depending on the structured of process.

On the one hand, we can consider that processes are well-structured [1]. When processes are well-structured we can simply count the control structures corresponding to splits, since it is explicitly known that a corresponding join exits. Please note that the structure of well-structured processes is analogue to software programs. In computer programming, a statement block is a section of code which is grouped together, much like a paragraph; such blocks consist of one or more statements. For example, in a C statement blocks are enclosed by braces { and }. In Pascal, blocks are denoted by **begin** and **end** statements. Having these characteristics in mind we design our second metric (*M2*) which counts the activities and control-flow elements of a process:

*M2: NOAC* = Number of activities and control-flow elements in a process

On the other hand, we also have to consider that some languages allow the construction of processes that are not well-structured. As we have already mentioned, examples of such languages include EPC and Workflow nets. In these modeling languages, splits do not have to match a corresponding join. These processes are generally more difficult to understand and result often in design errors. For processes that are not well-structured we can design a third metric (*M3*) which counts the number of activities and the number of splits and joins of a process.

*M3: NOAJS* = Number of activities, joins, and splits in a process

In EPC models, we would count the number of activities, XOR-joins and -splits, OR-joins and -splits, and AND-joins and -splits to calculate *NOAJS*.

## 2.5  Adapting McCabe's Cyclomatic Complexity

An early measure, proposed by McCabe [15], views program complexity related to the number of control paths through a program module. McCabe derived a software complexity measure from graph theory using the definition of the cyclomatic number which corresponds to the number of linearly independent paths in a program. It is intended to be independent of language and language format [17]. This measure provides a single number that can be compared to the complexity of other programs.

Since its development, McCabe's cyclomatic complexity (*MCC*) has been one of the most widely accepted software metrics and has been applied to tens of millions of lines of code in both the Department of Defense (DoD) and commercial applications. The resulting base of empirical knowledge has allowed software developers to calibrate measurements of their own software and arrive at some understanding of its complexity. McCabe's cyclomatic complexity is an indication of a program module's control-flow complexity and has been found to be a reliable indicator of complexity in large software projects [25]. Considering the number of control paths through the program, a 10-line program with 10 assignment statements is easier to understand than a 10-line program with 10 if-then statements.

*MCC* is defined for each module to be $e - n + 2$, where $e$ and $n$ are the number of edges and nodes in the control flow graph, respectively. Control flow graphs describe the logic structure of software modules. The nodes represent computational statements or expressions, and the edges represent transfer of control between nodes. Each possible execution path of a software module has a corresponding path from the entry to the exit node of the module's control flow graph. For example, in Figure 1, the *MCC* of the control flow graph for the Java code described is $14 - 11 + 2 = 5$.

## 2.6  The CFC Metric

In our previous work [6,7] we have designed a process complexity metric that borrows some ideas from McCabe's cyclomatic complexity. Our objective was to

| Node | Statement |
|------|-----------|
| (1) | `while(x<100){` |
| (2) | `   if (a[x] % 2 == 0) {` |
| (3) | `       parity =  0;` |
|     | `   }` |
|     | `   else {` |
| (4) | `       parity =  1;` |
| (5) | `   }` |
| (6) | `   switch(parity){` |
|     | `       case 0:` |
| (7) | `           println( "a[" + i + "] is even");` |
|     | `       case 1:` |
| (8) | `           println( "a[" + i + "] is odd");` |
|     | `       default:` |
| (9) | `           println( "Unexpected error");` |
|     | `   }` |
| (10) | `   x++;` |
|     | `}` |
| (11) | `p = true;` |

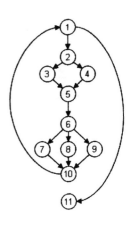

**Fig. 1.** of a Java program and its corresponding flowgraph

develop a metric that could be used in the same way as the MCC metric but to evaluate processes' complexity.

One of the first important observations that can be made from the MCC control flow graph, shown in Figure 1, is that this graph is extremely similar to a process. One major difference is that the nodes of a MCC control flow graph have identical semantics, while process nodes (i.e., activities) can have different semantics (e.g., AND-splits, XOR-splits, OR-joins, etc). Our approach has tackled this major difference.

The metric that we have previously developed and tested, called Control-flow Complexity (CFC) metric, was based on the analysis of XOR-splits, OR-splits, and AND-splits control-flow elements. The main idea behind the metric was to evaluate the number of mental states that have to be considered when a designer is developing a process. Splits introduce the notion of mental states in processes. When a split (XOR, OR, or AND) is introduced in a process, the business process designer has to mentally create a map or structure that accounts for the number of states that can be reached from the split. The notion of mental state is important since there are theories [19] suggesting that complexity beyond a certain point defeats the human mind's ability to perform accurate symbolic manipulations, and hence results in error.

Mathematically, the control-flow complexity metric is additive, thus it is very easy to calculate the complexity of a process, by simply adding the CFC of all split constructs. The control-flow complexity was calculated as follows, where $P$ is a process and $a$ an activity.

$$CFC(P) = \sum_{a \in P,a \text{ isa } xor-split} CFC_{XOR}(a)$$

$$+ \sum_{a \in P,a \text{ isa } or-split} CFC_{OR}(a) + \sum_{a \in P,a \text{ isa } and-split} CFC_{AND}(a)$$

The $CFC_{XOR} - split$, $CFC_{OR} - split$, and $CFC_{AND} - split$ functions is calculated as follows:

- $CFC_{XOR} - split(a) = fan - out(a)$. The control-flow complexity of XOR-splits is determined by the number of branches that can be taken.
- $CFC_{OR} - split(a) = 2^{fan-out(a)} - 1$. The control-flow complexity of OR-splits is determined by the number of states that may arise from the execution of an OR-split construct.
- $CFC_{AND} - split(a) = 1$. For an AND-split, the complexity is simply 1.

The higher the value of $CFC_{XOR} - split$, $CFC_{OR} - split$, and $CFC_{AND} - split$, the more complex is a process design, since developer has to handle all the states between control-flow constructs (splits) and their associated outgoing transitions and activities. Each formula to calculate the complexity of a split construct is based on the number of states that follow the construct. CFC analysis seeks to evaluate complexity without direct execution of processes.

The advantages of the CFC metric is that it can be used as a maintenance and quality metric, it gives the relative complexity of process designs, and it is easy to apply. Disadvantages of the CFC metric include the inability to measure data complexity, only control-flow complexity is measured. Additionally, the same weight is placed on nested and non-nested loops. However, deeply nested conditional structures are harder to understand than non-nested structures.

## 2.7 Adapting the Halstead Complexity Metric

The measures of Halstead [10] are the best known and most thoroughly studied composite measure of software complexity. The measures were developed as a means of determining a quantitative measure of complexity based on a program comprehension as a function of program operands (variables and constants) and operators (arithmetic operators and keywords which alter program control-flow). Halstead's metrics comprise a set of primitive measures (n1, n2, N1, and N2) that may be derived from the source code:

- n1 = number of unique operators (if, while, =, ECHO, etc);
- n2 = number of unique operands (variables or constants);
- N1 = total number of operator occurrences;
- N2 = total number of operand occurrences.

In our work, we suggest to map business process elements to the set of primitive measures proposed by Halstead. For example, n1 is the number of unique activities, splits and joins, and control-flow elements (such as sequence, switch, while, etc. in BPEL) of a business process. While the variable n2 is the number of unique data variables that are manipulated by the process and its activities. N1 and N2 can be easily derived directly from n1 and n2. With these primitive measures we introduce the notion of Halstead-based Process Complexity ($HPC$) measures for estimating process length, volume, and difficulty. These measures are based on Halstead measures and are calculates as follows:

- Process Length: N = n1*log2(n1) + n2*log2(n2)
- Process Volume: V = (N1+N2)*log2(n1+n2)
- Process Difficulty: D = (n1/2)*(N2/n2)

By the means of the presented mapping we can design an additional measure for processes based on the original measurement proposed by Halstead, including the process level, effort to implement, time to implement, and number of delivered bugs. We do not formalize these measurements since they require calibration that can only be done with empirical experiments.

Using *HPC* measures for processes has several advantages. The measures do not require in-depth analysis of process structures, they can predict rate of errors and maintenance effort, they are simple to calculate, and they can be used for most process modelling languages.

## 2.8    Adapting the Information Flow Metric by Henry and Kafura

Henry and Kafura [12] proposed a metric based on the impact of the information flow in a program' structure. The technique suggests identifying the number of calls to a module (i.e. the flows of local information entering: fan-in) and identifying the number of calls from a module (i.e. the flows of local information leaving: fan-out). The complexity of a procedure (*PC*) is defined as:

$$PC = \text{Length} * (\text{Fan-in} * \text{Fan-out})^2$$

The value of the variable length can be obtained by applying the lines of code or alternatively the McCabe's cyclomatic complexity metric. The procedure complexities are used to establish module complexities. A module with respect to a data structure DS consists of those procedures which either directly update DS or directly retrieve information from DS. As it can be seen, the measure is sensitive to the decomposition of the program into procedures and functions, on the size and the flow of information into procedures and out of procedures.

Henry and Kafura metric can be adapted to evaluate the complexity of processes in the following way. To calculate the length of an activity we need first to identify if activities are seen as black boxes or white boxes by the business process management system. If activities are black boxes then only their interface is known. Therefore, it is not possible to calculate the length of an activity. In this situation we assume the length to be 1. If activities are white boxes then the length of an activity is based on knowledge of its source code. In this situation, the length can be calculated using traditional software engineering metrics that have been previously presented, namely the LOC and *MCC*.

The fan-in and fan-out can be mapped directly to the inputs and outputs of activities. Activities are invoked when their inputs (fan-in) are available and the activities are scheduled for execution. When an activity completes its execution, its output data is transferred to the activities connected to it through transitions. We propose a metric called interface complexity (*IC*) of an activity which is defined as:

$IC$ = Length * (number of inputs * number of ouputs)$^2$

The advantages of the IC metric are that it takes into account data-driven processes and it can be calculated prior to coding, during the design stage. The drawbacks of the metric are that it can give complexity values of zero if an activity has no external interactions. This typically only happens with the end activities of a process. This means the, for example, EPC processes with a large percentage of end activities will have a low complexity.

## 3   Cognitive Science on Software Complexity

Most approaches in the software engineering domain take certain characteristics of software as a starting point and attempt to define what effect they might have on the difficulty of the various programmer tasks (e.g. maintaining, testing and understanding code). In [5], it is argued that it is much more useful to analyse the processes involved in programmer tasks first, as well as the parameters which govern those efforts: ".. one should start with the symptoms of complexity, which are all manifested in the mind, and attempt to understand the processes which produce such symptoms". Using results from cognitive sciences, e.g. the division of the mind into short-term and long-term memory, and the mental processes involved with programming known as "chunking" and "tracing", Cant et al. come up with a set of tentative complexity metrics for software programs [5].

A similar approach for determining the complexity of a process model would be to determine meaningful process model "chunks", which can be captured as a single section in the short-term memory. One could think of constructions like a (short) sequence of activities or a control construct like an XOR-split. Each of these "chunks" would have to be characterized by a complexity score. The work in [5] suggests that notably the size of the chunk would be a good estimate. Next, it is necessary to see the control flow through these chunks, as people need to scan the relations between chunks to understand the complete picture. This is referred to as the "tracing" mechanism. In [5], not only the length of the path but also the kind of dependency influences the comprehension of the flow between chunks. For software, for example, Cant et al. state that "a conditional control structure is more complex to understand than a normal sequential section of code". For a process model, this could mean that both (a) the distance between the chunks and (b) a complexity factor for the specific kind of dependency should be used. Unfortunately, the work in [5] rather sets an agenda for complexity metrics than providing exact measures. Therefore, it is far from straightforward to transfer the presented, tentative relations to the process modelling domain.

## 4   Complexity of the Process Graph

Graph theory provides a rich set of graph metrics or graph measures that can be adapted for calculation of the complexity of the process graph. In [14] the coefficient of network complexity (CNC), the complexity index (CI), the restrictiveness estimator (RT), and the number of trees in a graph are discussed as suitable for business process models.

The coefficient of network complexity (CNC) provides a rather simple metric for the complexity of a graph. It can easily be calculated as the number of arcs divided by the number of nodes. In the context of a business process model, the number of arcs has to be divided by the number of activities, joins, and splits. In formal esthetics this coefficient is also considered with the notion of elegance [21].

CNC = number of arcs / (number of activities, joins, and splits)

The complexity index (CI), or reduction complexity is defined as the minimal number of node reductions that reduces the graph to a single node. This measure shares so similarity to the notion of structuredness of a process graph and respective reduction rules. In a BPEL process it can be associated with the number of structured activities. The complexity index of a process graph has to be calculated algorithmically and is not applicable for process models with arbitrary cycles.

Restrictiveness estimator (RT) is an estimator for the number of feasible sequences in a graph. RT requires the reachability matrix $r_{ij}$, i.e. the transitive closure of the adjacency matrix, to be calculated.

$$RT = 2\Sigma r_{ij} - 6(N-1)/(N-2)(N-3)$$

There are further measures in graph theory which demand rather complex computations. The number of trees in a graph requires the tree-generating determinant to be calculated based on the adjacency matrix (see [14]). Measures such as tree width, directed tree width, and directed acyclic graph width are compared in [22]. The latter measures how close a graph is to a directed acyclic graph.

## 5  Contributions and Limitations

In this paper, we have surveyed several contributions from software engineering, cognitive science, and graph theory, and we discussed to what extent analogous metrics and measurements can be defined for business process models. In order to demonstrate that these metrics serves their purpose, we plan to carry out several empirical validations by means of controlled experiments. These experiments will involve more than 100 students from the Eindhoven University of Technology (Netherlands), the Vienna University of Economics and Business Administration (Austria), and the University of Madeira (Portugal). The collected data will be analyzed using statistical methods to verify the degree of correlation between students' perception of the complexity of processes and the proposed metrics. It should be noted that we have already conducted a small experiment that involved 19 graduate students in Computer Science, as part of a research project, and tested if the control-flow complexity of a set of 22 business processes could be predicted using the CFC metric. Analyzing the collected data using statistical methods we have concluded that the CFC metric is highly correlated with the control-flow complexity of processes. This metric can, therefore, be used by business process analysts and process designers to analyze the complexity of processes and, if possible, develop simpler processes.

# References

1. W.M.P. van der Aalst. The Application of Petri Nets to Workflow Management. *The Journal of Circuits, Systems and Computers*, 8(1):21–66, 1998.
2. T. Andrews, F. Curbera, H. Dholakia, Y. Goland, J. Klein, F. Leymann, K. Liu, D. Roller, D. Smith, S. Thatte, I. Trickovic, and S. Weerawarana. Business Process Execution Language for Web Services, Version 1.1. Specification, BEA Systems, IBM Corp., Microsoft Corp., SAP AG, Siebel Systems, 2003.
3. M. Azuma and D. Mole. Software management practice and metrics in the european community and japan: Some results of a survey. *Journal of Systems and Software*, 26(1):5–18, 1994.
4. F. B. Bastani. An approach to measuring program complexity. *COMPSAC '83*, pages 1–8, 1983.
5. S. N. Cant, D. R. Jeffery, and B. Henderson-Sellers. A conceptual model of cognitive complexity of elements of the programming process. *Information and Software Technology*, 37(7).
6. J. Cardoso. Control-flow Complexity Measurement of Processes and Weyuker's Properties. In *6th International Enformatika Conference*, Transactions on Enformatika, Systems Sciences and Engineering, Vol. 8, pages 213–218, 2005.
7. J. Cardoso. *Workflow Handbook 2005*, chapter Evaluating Workflows and Web Process Complexity, pages 284–290. Future Strategies, Inc., Lighthouse Point, FL, USA, 2005.
8. J. Cardoso. Complexity analysis of bpel web processes. *Journal of Software Process: Improvement and Practice*, 2006. to appear.
9. A.S. Guceglioglu and O.W. Demiros. Using Software Quality Characteristics to Measure Business Process Quality. In W.M.P. van der Aalst, B. Benatallah, F. Casati, and F. Curbera, editors, *Business Process Management (BPM 2005)*, volume 3649, pages 374–379. Springer-Verlag, Berlin, 2005.
10. M. H. Halstead. *Elements of Software Science*. Elsevier, Amsterdam, 1987.
11. W. Harrison and K. Magel. A topological analysis of computer programs with less than three binary branches. *ACM SIGPLAN Notices*, april:51–63, 1981.
12. S. Henry and D. Kafura. Software structure metrics based on information-flow. *IEEE Transactions On Software Engineering*, 7(5):510–518, 1981.
13. G. E. Kalb. Counting lines of code, confusions, conclusions, and recommendations. Briefing to the 3rd Annual REVIC User's Group Conference, 1990.
14. Antti M. Latva-Koivisto. Finding a complexity for business process models. Research report, Helsinki University of Technology, February 2001.
15. T. J. McCabe. A complexity measure. *IEEE Transactions on Software Engineering*, 2(4):308–320, 1976.
16. T. J. McCabe and C. W. Butler. Design complexity measurement and testing. *Communications of the ACM*, 32:1415–1425, 1989.

17. T. J. McCabe and A. H. Watson. Software complexity. *Journal of Defence Software Engineering*, 7(12):5–9, 1994. Crosstalk.
18. J. Mendling, M. Moser, G. Neumann, H.M.W. Verbeek, and B.F. van Dongen W.M.P. van der Aalst. A Quantitative Analysis of Faulty EPCs in the SAP Reference Model. BPM Center Report BPM-06-08, Eindhoven University of Technology, Eindhoven, 2006.
19. G. Miller. The magical number seven, plus or minus two: Some limits on our capacity for processing information. *The Psychological Review*, 1956.
20. Nachiappan Nagappan, Thomas Ball, and Andreas Zeller. Mining metrics to predict component failures. In *Proceedings of the 28th International Conference on Software Engineering*, Shanghai, China, 2006.
21. G. Neumann. *Metaprogrammierung und Prolog*. Addison-Wesley, December 1988.
22. Jan Obdrzalek. Dag-width: connectivity measure for directed graphs. In *Symposium on Discrete Algorithms*, pages 814–821. ACM Press, 2006.
23. H.A. Reijers and Irene T.P. Vanderfeesten. Cohesion and Coupling Metrics for Workflow Process Design. In J. Desel, B. Pernici, and M. Weske, editors, *Business Process Management (BPM 2004)*, volume 3080, pages 290–305. Springer-Verlag, Berlin, 2004.
24. M. Shepperd. Early life-cycle metrics and software quality models. *Information and Software Technology*, 32(4):311–316, 1990.
25. W. Ward. Software defect prevention using mccabe's complexity metric. *Hewlett Packard Journal*, 40(2):64–69, 1989.
26. H. Zuse. *Software Complexity: Measures and Methods*. Walter de Gruyter and Co, New Jersey, 1991.

# Measuring Performance in the Retail Industry
## (Position Paper)

Gerasimos Marketos and Yannis Theodoridis

Department of Informatics, University of Piraeus,
80 Karaoli-Dimitriou St., GR-18534 Piraeus, Greece
{marketos, ytheod}@unipi.gr
http://isl.cs.unipi.gr/db

**Abstract.** Bearing in mind the changeable and complicated needs of business environment, in this paper we examine the necessity of evolution in the traditional decision support techniques. Our aim is to intensify the need for integrated performance measurement and management, as a way to ameliorate the existing tools for decision making, which are currently based on historical data. Because of the nature of challenges and trends in the retail industry, it is considered to be an appropriate application scenario. In addition to that, a framework is proposed and a case study is described as a proof of our claim.

**Keywords:** Performance management, business intelligence, retailing.

## 1 Introduction

Business Intelligence (BI) developed a few years ago as a set of applications and technologies for gathering, storing, analyzing, and providing access to corporate data to aid in decision making. BI includes, among others, decision support systems (DSS), statistical analysis, information visualization, data warehousing (DW) and online analytical processing (OLAP), and data mining (DM).

Turban and Aronson [16] argue that the decisions are taken at three levels: strategic, tactical and operational. The differences among them are related with the time scale that every decision demands and with the nature of them as well. The top management is responsible for the strategic planning of their organizations, middle managers make tactical decisions following the plans of top management and finally operational managers are responsible for the daily activity of the organization.

Obviously, performers at each level need different kind of information. The top management wants to see the "big picture" of the company situation. They usually prefer dashboards, consisting of Key Performance Indicators (KPIs), which show the trends of the organization. Middle managers want to have access in advanced, dynamic reports. They prefer aggregated instead of raw data, thus OLAP cubes and patterns extracted from data mining models look very useful for them. Operational managers need more real-time information. In fact, traditional BI can not serve them because it focuses on historical business data and thus it fits in better with strategic and tactical decision making (figure 1).

J. Eder, S. Dustdar et al. (Eds.): BPM 2006 Workshops, LNCS 4103, pp. 129–140, 2006.

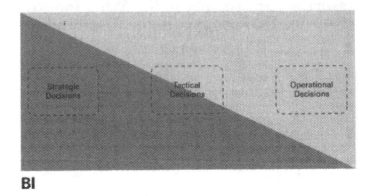

**Fig. 1.** Traditional BI coverage of decision making levels [15].

The above prove that modern organizations need something more than BI. Furthermore, the need for process-oriented organizations having efficient business processes that cut across organizational boundaries, raise the need for a more complete management of organizational performance. Focus on operational data is required because performance can not be measured only by trying to find patterns on historical business data. Strategic and tactical decisions are still critical, but without efficient operational decisions the real time and process oriented enterprise can not be realized.

The target is clear: decision makers, independently of level, should have the right information on the right time in order to serve efficiently and effectively the customer-centric processes in which they participate. This paper proposes a realization of the above target and its application in the retail industry.

The rest of the paper is organized as follows. In Section 2, we outline the challenges of the retail industry. In Section 3 we survey the proposed approaches for measuring and managing performance. Sections 4 and 5 present a framework for measuring performance on the retail industry and an application in a case study, respectively. Conclusions and hints for further work are drawn in Section 6.

## 2  Trends and Challenges in the Retail Industry

Retailing serves the selling of goods and services to consumers for personal or household consumption. A classification of the retail industry divisions can be found in [14]: groceries, apparel, electronics, drugstores, books/music, mail-order, mixed assortments and others. Retailers are at the end of the supply chain, which may consist of various suppliers, importers, manufacturers, wholesalers and distributors, and thus they interact directly with the consumer. To serve this purpose, the majority of technological advances are quickly applied in this sector so as to facilitate trade. Data management, supply chain management and marketing strategies, among others, are combined to this aim.

From a data management perspective, the emerging trends create many opportunities for delivering more value but they also bring problems that should be faced. Radio Frequency Identification (RFID) is a new challenging technology that is coming into sight, replacing traditional barcodes. Although the adoption of this technology has raised a lot of controversy, its importance has been recognized and thus a further discussion about RFID significance is beyond the scope of this paper. Furthermore, we choose to focus on how data produced by RFID tags can be transformed into knowledge, and not on the management of the huge volume of data being researched by data streams community. What RFID can give us is:

a. **Sequence of purchase:** It is possible to know in which order people buy things. In fact, we know the exact time of putting an item in the basket. Extracting such patterns, retailers may decide, for instance, to change the position of some items in the store in order to facilitate (or not) people in the store.

b. **Positive/ negative preferences:** It is possible to have answers on questions such as: Are there customers that, after taking an item, change their mind and put it back on the shelf? Is there a specific pattern behind this behaviour? How much time do customers need to decide about the selection or not of a product?

c. **Routes of customers:** By placing RFID labels on the baskets, it is possible to track the movement of customers inside the store. Thus, by placing an Indoor Positioning System (IPS), customers could be informed based on their interests and their location.

As far as *supply management* is concerned, it gives retailers a competitive advantage. The collected shopping data can be transformed to valuable information and shared throughout retailers' supply chain networks of suppliers, factories and distribution centers to predict trends on product demand for controlling inventories and stocks.

For marketing purposes, *personalized and real time offers* is a critical tool to realize the necessary customer-centricity. Customers should feel that retailers know and meet efficiently their needs. RFID technology and IPSs can provide the necessary infrastructure for collecting data and providing useful information. The issue here is how to interpret the raw data to shopping information that is valuable for each customer. Several papers have been proposed for predicting shopping lists [6] and building shopping assistants [5] but they do not take into consideration the latest technological advances and they are only based on analyzing historical data. Prediction of shopping lists can be considered as a special case of recommendation techniques which are overviewed in [2].

The above challenges show that retailers need something more than BI for supporting strategic and tactical decisions. A more complete solution is required in the retail environment in order for performance management to integrate business processes and historical data.

## 3 Performance Measurement and Management

Performance management is a challenging issue due to three core reasons [11]: (a) goals and objectives against which we measure companies' performance are exponentially increasing, (b) external unstructured data and events have to be encompassed and, finally, (c) acting in a timely and effective manner on the resulted imperatives is required.

The recent years, several researchers have presented their suggestions about BI evolution in order to serve performance measurement and management. We present them in order to show their common characteristics and find the set of operations that best fit in the retail industry.

In [3], performance management is concerned in terms of process execution monitoring and analysis. Authors consider that simple reports off the process execution database and OLAP-style analysis are not adequate. Business Process Intelligence is proposed as a way to explain process behavior and to predict problems in process executions by applying "process mining" algorithms. An overview of issues and approaches on workflow mining can be found in [1].

**Analysts**

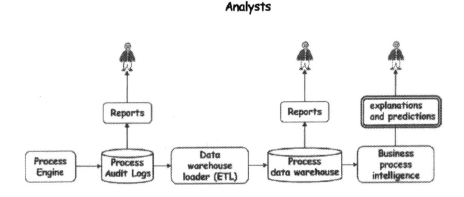

**Fig. 2.** Different approaches to business process analysis and management [3]

In [13], a Corporate Performance Measurement System is proposed by integrating business process performance information into a traditional data warehouse. The DW is built using operational data coming from the workflow log which provides very detailed information on the history of process instances. In fact, it is the same approach as the process data warehouse to appear in figure 2.

In [9], Business Performance Management is considered as a set of processes for optimizing performance by encouraging process effectiveness as well as efficient use of financial, human, and material resources. The main idea behind this proposal is that DW is not enough to this end since its technology is neither suitable for the grain nor for the freshness of the collected information, that should quickly flow throughout the different levels of the company.

Operational BI, Enterprise Decision Management [15], Business Activity Monitoring and Business Operations Management are other usually mentioned terms to describe the ideas presented in this section. In table 1, the differences from traditional BI are referred.

In the section that follows, we propose a framework as an application of the above mentioned and not a different approach. We try to intensify the need to evolve the traditional systems so as to satisfy the emerging needs in business environment.

**Table 1.** Traditional BI versus the performance management approach [15]

|  | **Traditional BI** | **The performance management approach** |
|---|---|---|
| *Focus* | Improve strategy development through insight into trends and performance | Improve strategy execution through automating decisions |
| *Activity* | After transaction | During transaction |
| *Key methodologies* | Data analysis, OLAP, reporting and query tools, data warehousing | Traditional methodologies plus KPIs, dashboards, business rules engines |
| *Workflow* | Offline, disconnected from business processes | Embedded in operational processes and systems |
| *Analytics* | Summarize past performance, group behavior, trends | Continuously measuring and managing performance |

## 4   A Framework for the Retail Industry

In this section, we present the architecture of a framework for measuring and managing performance in the retail industry (figure 3). Combining traditional BI techniques with the technologies presented in section 3, we can have a complete solution for dealing with the challenges and trends outlined in section 2.

Our framework consists of a number of modules. In the following paragraphs, a reasonable sequence of the stages of the proposed framework is described, from the raw data to the final output. In particular:

a. **Source data:** Apart from shopping data and workflow logs, other data streams can be also input in the system. For instance, data collected from RFID tags include useful information that should be analyzed, although it is not necessary to be archived in the operational database. For a survey in data stream management see [8].

b. **Integration manager:** The role of this module is to manage the above heterogeneous data sources and to feed the appropriate analytics. Likewise, it guarantees that the feeding process happens on the right time for each analytic: ETL tools can be fed once a day as OLAP-style analysis focus on historical data while Activity Monitoring components need real time data.

c. **OLAP Cubes:** ETL tools transform raw data into aggregated information providing thus data warehousing capabilities. Instead of providing only OLAP-style analysis on shopping data (business data warehouse), the proposed architecture includes data warehouses for both business and process execution data.

d. **Activity monitoring:** This module deals with real time information. It updates and controls KPIs and triggers Business Rules Manager for verifying that corporate rules are satisfied. KPIs can be also verified for satisfying predefined Business Rules (BRs). Most Business Process Management (BPM) suites support process monitoring.

e. **Data mining engine:** DM engine consists of a set of algorithms and techniques for identifying patterns on data. Customer segmentation, correlations between products and prediction of product demand are typical tasks that can be applied on shopping data. We consider as important to include special process mining algorithms that are applied on workflow logs, for predicting critical situations and discovering interesting correlations. Applying mining techniques on real time information (sequence of purchase, routes of purchase) is also a challenging issue and an active research area [7].

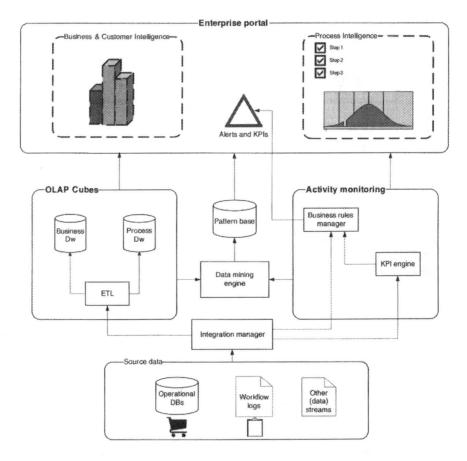

**Fig. 3.** The proposed architecture

f. **Pattern base:** A Pattern Base Management System (PBMS) provides pattern management functionality as a Database Management System (DBMS) does for data. Patterns are extracted from various data sources applying the data mining algorithms and techniques included in the data mining engine. Our framework proposes the integration of the pattern base with the data warehouses and the operational databases. Thus, data can be viewed from three quite different but useful perspectives: raw data (operational databases), aggregated data (data warehouses), and analyzed data-extracted knowledge (pattern base). Pattern management is an active research area in which various approaches have been introduced [4], [12].

g. **Enterprise portal:** This is the output (portal) of the proposed system. It includes a role-based architecture which provides users in various positions with the appropriate information. For instance, operational managers may be interested in process intelligence reports while tactical decision makers may find useful the business and customer intelligence reports. Generally speaking, users will be able to build their own dashboards by subscribing to the services the role based systems has allocated to them.

# 5  Applying Our Framework: A Case Study

In the following paragraphs, we outline the application of our framework addressing design issues. In particular, we present the data sources involved, the data warehouses (cubes) built for OLAP purposes, and some indicative KPIs and BRs materialized to address top management needs.

## 5.1  Data Sources

The operational database includes tables for storing customer demographics and details about their transactions. Each transaction takes place in a specific store and embodies details of the products that were purchased by the customer. The system may also include details about the supplier of each product. A sample diagram is depicted in figure 4.

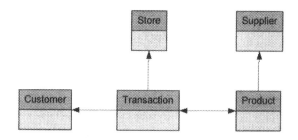

**Fig. 4.** A sample E-R diagram for operational data

In figure 4, the relationships between the core entities of the system are represented. As it is shown, a transaction takes place in a specific store and a single customer participates in it. Namely, a transaction represents a customer's basket and may consist of one or more products (purchased in the same basket). Moreover, the supplier of each product (and other information regarding supplying processes) is recorded.

As far as the workflow logs are concerned, the simplest format is presented in table 2 where only the execution time of each activity (step) is recorded. Workflow logs are tightly related both to the workflow engine that is used to manage business processes and to the nature of them. Typical business processes in the retail industry are orders to suppliers and distribution centers.

**Table 2.** A sample workflow log

| Process_Instance | Activity | Timestamp |
|---|---|---|
| Order supplies of product A | Send order | 1/4/2006 21:05:14 |
| Order supplies of product A | Receive products | 3/4/2006 10:15:04 |
| Order supplies of product A | Inventory products | 3/4/2006 12:55:09 |

## 5.2 OLAP Cubes

We have proposed the coexistence of business and process data warehouse for providing OLAP-style analysis to business and process data. In figure 5, we present the dimensions of a business data warehouse. Apart from geography, product category and time dimensions, we have included a number of customer hierarchies (age, sex, profession, marital status, education level and number of children). Measures are related to quantities and values of products. Figure 5 presents only some of them and takes into consideration the case of private label products that the retailer may sell.

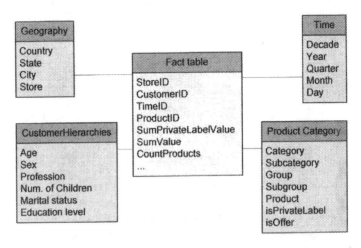

**Fig. 5.** A sample data warehouse for business data

Furthermore, in figure 6, a general case process warehouse is presented. The data warehouse depends on retailer's organizational structure and needs, and thus the proposed schema cannot be suitable at every case. We consider that processes and activities can be classified according to their types. For instance, both human-triggered and automatic activities should be considered. Geographical hierarchy provides analysis capabilities in many different levels. Suppliers dimension classifies them to various types according to the nature of products they provide.

The defined performance measures should help in analyzing raw process execution data in a multidimensional way. Interesting measures are the total execution time and the time lags of each process.

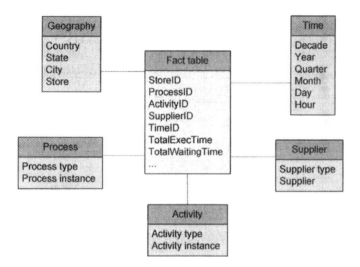

**Fig. 6.** A sample data warehouse for process data

In both cubes classic OLAP operations can be applied. We illustrate the benefits obtained by such an approach with two examples of operations supported by our proposed business and process data warehouses and OLAP technologies:

**a.** A user may ask to view the average value of private label products in baskets in the past quarter, over Athens, and, moreover, he/she can easily view the same information for specific stores in Athens (more detailed view, formally a *drill-down* operation) or over Greece (more summarized view, formally a *roll-up* operation).

**b.** Similarly, the total waiting time for processes of a specific process type, over Athens, in the past quarter may be requested. The user can also easily view the same information both for each month of the selected quarter and also for the whole year.

Further to roll-up and drill-down operations described above, typical data cube operations include *slice* and *dice*, for selecting parts of a data cube by imposing conditions on a single or multiple cube dimensions, respectively and *pivot*, which provides the user with alternative presentations of the cube.

### 5.3 Activity Monitoring

As already mentioned, BPM suites support process monitoring consisting of BRs and measured by KPIs. We argue that this can be generalized to include monitoring of business related activities. Tables 3 and 4 present some interesting KPIs and BRs that could be continuously calculated and checked respectively. Violation of BRs could trigger alerts in the enterprise portal for assuring human attention.

**Table 3.** Sample Key Performance Indicators

| KPI | Target value |
|---|---|
| Average waiting time for check out | 5 sec. per product |
| Average value of customer baskets | 20 € (weekdays) 50 € (weekends) |
| Average value of private-label products in customer baskets | 30% |
| Average weekly sales per state | 500K € |

**Table 4.** Sample Business Rules

| BR | Expression |
|---|---|
| Waiting time for check out | ≤ 20 min. |
| Execution time for process type: "Order dairy products" | ≤ 1 day |

KPIs provide instant and continuous view of the running activities. However, the target values are based on past experience. In other words, the definition of target values for complex KPIs can be assisted by using multidimensional analysis (OLAP) and the aggregated information stored in the two data warehouses (business and process cubes). Furthermore, it is useful to define BRs on KPIs ensuring alerting if target values are violated.

## 5.4  Pattern Base

The execution of data mining models results in patterns that are stored in a PBMS. Pattern management issues such us update, merging, comparing, querying, evaluation etc. are active research problems but a detailed discussion about them is beyond the scope of this paper. Frequent itemsets (FIs), association rules and clusters extracted from warehouse data are typical examples of patterns.

FIs represent sets of products that are often purchased together (e.g. {milk, bread, frozen food}) while association rules introduce correlation between items (e.g. {bread, frozen food} ⇒ {milk}). Quite more interesting is the discovery of the temporal sequence of purchasing in such itemsets (e.g. milk, then bread, then frozen food). On the other hand, clustering algorithms could result in clusters showing correlations between demographics and shopping preferences. For example a profile of shoppers (women, aged 30-35) appears to have a specific preference (buy dairy twice a week) and so on.

We illustrate the benefits obtained by such an approach with two examples of queries supported by the pattern base:

**a.** A user may request to view demographic details about a specific cluster of customers, for instance: costumers who visit any store once a week and buy private label products valued 0-5 euros, and the value of their baskets in total is between 20-30 euros.

**b.** A user may have the information that milk is in high demand in a specific store and he/she requires knowing what products are purchased supplementary to milk in order to check their supplies. The proposed pattern base can provide a list of these products which are associated with milk, and moreover, to give a hierarchical order of their association with milk combined with information about stores supplies.

## 6 Conclusions – Further Work

Taking into account current challenges and trends in the demanding and complicated area of the retail industry, it is evident that decision making analysis should be based on real time information and not only on historical data, as the traditional methods have used so far. In this paper, we propose a framework for extending traditional BI to an integrated environment for measuring and managing performance. As it was highlighted in [10] the importance of measurement in controlling, managing and improving the processes is vital. The framework consists of several modules that enable both business and process intelligence capabilities. It includes tools so as to give the proper information on the right time to each decision making level.

Our research is at early stage; future steps include the evaluation and incorporation of process mining algorithms in the data mining engine and the development of a prototype following the proposed architecture. The application of our framework in other industries could also be a task for future work.

**Acknowledgements.** Research supported by the General Secretariat for Research and Technology of the Greek Ministry of Development under a PENED'2003 grant.

## References

[1] van der Aalst, W.M.P., van Dongen, B.F., Herbst, J., Maruster, L., Schimm, G., Weijters, A.J.M.M.: Workflow mining: a survey of issues and approaches, Data & Knowledge Engineering 47 (2003) 237-267

[2] Adomavicius, G., Sankaranarayanan, R., Sen, S., Tuzhilin A.: Incorporating contextual information in recommender systems using a multidimensional approach. ACM Transactions on Information Systems 23 (2005) 103–145

[3] Castellanos, M., Casati, F., Dayal, U., Shan, M.C.: A Comprehensive and Automated Approach to Intelligent Business Processes Execution Analysis. Int. J. Distributed and Parallel Databases 16 (2004) 239-273

[4] Catania, B., Maddalena, A.: Flexible Pattern Management within PSYCHO. Proc. PaRMa'06, Munich, Germany (2006)

[5] Cumby, C., Fano, A., Ghani, R., Krema, M.: Building Intelligent Shopping Assistants Using Individual Consumer Models. Proc. IUI'05, San Diego, CA, USA (2005)

[6] Cumby, C., Fano, A., Ghani, R., Krema, M.: Predicting Customer Shopping Lists from Point of Sale Purchase Data. Proc. KDD '04, Seattle, WA, USA (2004)

[7] Gaber, M.M., Zaslavsky, A., Krishnaswamy, S.: Mining Data Streams: a review. ACM SIGMOD Record 34 (2005) 18-26

[8] Golab, L., Ozsu, M.T.: Issues in Data Stream Management. ACM SIGMOD Record 32 (2003) 5-14

[9] Golfarelli, M., Rizzi, S., Cella, I.: Beyond Data Warehousing: What's next in Business Intelligence? Proc. DOLAP'04, Washington, DC, USA (2004)

[10] Harrington, J.H.: Business Process Improvement – The breakthrough strategy for total quality, productivity, and competitiveness. McGraw-Hill, New York, USA (1991)

[11] Keziere, R.: Are we there yet? Three challenges for BPM. Cutter IT Journal 18 (2005)

[12] Kotsifakos, E., Ntoutsi, I., Theodoridis, Y.: Database Support for Data Mining Patterns. Proc. PCI'05, Volos, Greece (2005)

[13] List, B., Machaczek, K.: Towards a Corporate Performance Measurement System. Proc. ACM SAC'04, Nicosia, Cyprus (2004)

[14] Madlberger, M.: Strategies and Business Models in Electronic Retailing: Indications from the U.S. and the UK. Proc. ICEC'04, Delft, Netherlands (2004)

[15] Taylor, J.: Beyond BI: Building intelligence into your operational decisions. Fair Isaac white paper (2005)

[16] Turban E., Aronson J.E.: Decision Support Systems and Intelligent Systems. Prentice Hall (1998)

# Process Mining by Measuring Process Block Similarity

Joonsoo Bae[1], James Caverlee[2], Ling Liu[2], and Hua Yan[2]

[1] Dept of Industrial & Sys. Eng., Chonbuk National Univ., South Korea
jsbae@chonbuk.ac.kr
[2] College of Computing, Georgia Institute of Technology, US
{caverlee, lingliu, huayan}@cc.gatech.edu

**Abstract.** Mining, discovering, and integrating process-oriented services has attracted growing attention in the recent years. Workflow precedence graph and workflow block structures are two important factors for comparing and mining processes based on distance similarity measure. Some existing work has done on comparing workflow designs based on their precedence graphs. However, there lacks of standard distance metrics for comparing workflows that contain complex block structures such as parallel OR, parallel AND. In this paper we present a quantitative approach to modeling and capturing the similarity and dissimilarity between different workflow designs, focusing on similarity and dissimilarity between the block structures of different workflow designs. We derive the distance-based similarity measures by analyzing the workflow block structure of the participating workflow processes in four consecutive phases. We first convert each workflow dependency graph into a block tree by using our block detection algorithm. Second, we transform the block tree into a binary tree to provide a normalized reference structure for distance based similarity analysis. Third, we construct a binary branch vector by encoding the binary tree. Finally, we calculate the distance metric between two binary branch vectors.

## 1 Introduction

Business process management has continued to attract attentions of both academics and industry. With the increasing interest and wide deployment of BPML, we see a growing demand for efficient business process management architectures and technologies that support enterprise transformation [7]. Effective enterprise transformation refers to strategic business agility in terms of how efficiently an enterprise can respond to its competitors and how timely an enterprise can anticipate new opportunities that may arise in the future. In the increasingly globalized economy, enterprises face complex challenges that require rapid and possibly continual transformations. As a result, more and more enterprises are focused on the strategic management of fundamental changes with respect to markets, products, and services [10]. Such transformation typically has a direct impact on the business processes of an enterprise. In addition, the wide spread use of process-centric systems has made it possible to accumulate process definitions and to accelerate the analysis and comprehension of process definitions.

Although business process management systems have been deployed in many industrial engineering fields, research on analysis, mining and integration of business processes are still in its infancy. One of the representative existing studies on process

J. Eder, S. Dustdar et al. (Eds.): BPM 2006 Workshops, LNCS 4103, pp. 141–152, 2006.
© Springer-Verlag Berlin Heidelberg 2006

improvement is workflow mining, which investigates the traces and results of workflow execution, and determines significant information in order to improve the existing workflow processes [2, 3, 7]. However, most of the existing workflow mining research does not provide a quantitative measure to compare and capture the similarity of different workflow designs. The objective of this research is to develop a distance based similarity measure to discover, mine and integration of existing workflow definitions by analysis of workflow dependency graphs.

Workflow precedence graph and workflow block structures are two important factors for comparing and mining business processes based on distance similarity measures. Although some existing work has done in comparing workflow designs based on their precedence graphs [4], there lacks of formal distance metrics for comparing workflows that contain complex block structures such as parallel OR, parallel AND. In this paper, we present a novel process difference analysis method using distance measures between block structures of two business processes. We present a quantitative approach to derive the distance-based similarity measures in four consecutive phases. We first convert each workflow dependency graph into a block tree by using our block detection algorithm. Then, we transform the block tree into a binary tree to provide a normalized reference structure for distance based similarity analysis. In the third phase, we construct a binary branch vector by encoding the binary tree. Finally, we calculate the distance metric between two binary branch vectors. The proposed difference analysis method achieves three distinct goals. First, by analyzing the block structures of process models, we present a quantitative process similarity metric to determine the relative distance between two process designs in terms of their block structure similarity. This similarity analysis facilitates not only the comparison of existing process models with each other, but also provides the flexibility to adapt to changes in existing business workflow processes. Second, the proposed method is quick and flexible, which reduces the cost of both the analysis and design phases of web service processes. Third, the proposed method enables the flexible deployment of process mining, discovery, and integration – all key features that are necessary for effective transformation of an enterprise. We argue that the block structure based distance measure can be effectively combined with a workflow precedence based similarity analysis tool [4] in process mining, process merging, and process clustering, and ultimately it can help to reduce or minimize the costs involved in design, analysis, and evolution of workflow systems.

## 2  Process Definition Model

The business process reference model (process model for short in the rest of the paper) consists of business process definitions and the specification of workflows among the processes with respect to data flow, control flow, and operational views [11]. We define a business process in terms of business activity patterns. An activity pattern consists of objects, messages, message exchange constraints, preconditions and postconditions [12], and is designed to specify the service actions and execution dependencies of the business process. We consider two types of activity patterns – elementary activity patterns and composite activity patterns [1, 5]. An elementary activity pattern is an atomic unit. A composite activity pattern consists of a one or more elementary activity patterns or other composite activity patterns.

We define a business workflow as a collection of business activities connected by data flow and control flow, where each represents a business process. We use data flow among processes to define the data dependencies among processes within a given business workflow. We use control flow to capture the operational structure of the business workflow service, including the process execution ordering, the transactional semantics and dependencies of the workflow.

Formally, each workflow service is specified in terms of process definitions. We can model each process definition using a directed graph, in which the nodes of the graph are activities. The process *dependency graph* captures information about how activities share information and how data flows from one activity to another. Due to the space constraint, in this paper we focus our discussion only on the dependency graph.

**Definition 1 (Dependency Graph, *DG*).** A dependency graph *DG* is defined by a binary tuple <*DN, DE*>, where

- $DN = \{nd_1, nd_2, ..., nd_n\}$ is a finite set of activity nodes.

- $DE = \{e_1, e_2, ..., e_m\}$ is a set of edges. Each edge is of the form $nd_i \rightarrow nd_j$.     ■

Note that in the dependency graph formulation, self-edges are disallowed since edges are intended to denote data flow dependencies between different activities (nodes). Additionally, a dependency graph must be a connected graph. Unconnected nodes and isolated groups of nodes are disallowed in the graph, as isolated nodes or groups of nodes are considered a separate service process in our reference model.

As a real-life example of business process, there are many PIPs (Partner Interface Processes) as defined by RosettaNet[9]. PIPs define business processes between trading partners. PIPs fit into seven Clusters, or groups of core business processes, that represent the backbone of the trading network. Each Cluster is broken down into Segments and within each Segment are individual PIPs. RosettaNet standards provide the infrastructure for integrating business processes with trading partners across the globe, delivering essential value to industries and proven real-world business results. Fig. 1 shows a standard process of procurement order by buyer, which is in Segment 3A(Quote and Order Entry) of Cluster 3(Order Management). This example process has 13 activities and their dependencies.

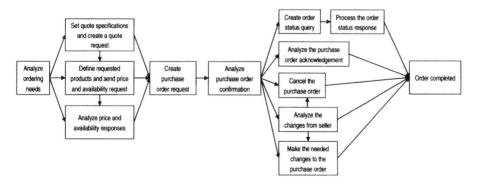

**Fig. 1** A real-life example of business process

Given two workflow processes and their respective dependency graphs, there are numerous ways these two graphs may differ. Typically, it makes more sense to compare only those graphs that have sufficient similarity in terms of their dependency graphs. Consider two extreme cases: one is when the two dependency graphs have the same set of nodes and the other is when there is no common node between two graphs. By assigning 1 for the first case and 0 for the latter case, we define a comparability measure that indicates the ratio of common nodes in two graphs. One way to measure the extent of comparability between two graphs is to use a user-controlled threshold, called $\delta$-Comparability, which is set to be between 0 and 1. Because this value represents the ratio of common nodes over the union of all nodes in two graphs, the larger the value is, the greater degree of comparability between the two graphs. Note that $\delta$ value can not be 0 since $\delta = 0$ means that there is no common node between two graphs, i.e., $DN_1 \cap DN_2 \neq \varnothing$.

**Definition 2 ($\delta$-Comparability of $DG$)**

Let $DG_1 = (DN_1, DE_1)$ and $DG_2 = (DN_2, DE_2)$ be two dependency graphs, and $\delta$ be a user-defined control threshold. We say that $DG_1$ and $DG_2$ are $\delta$-comparable if the condition $\dfrac{|DN_1 \cap DN_2|}{|DN_1 \cup DN_2|} \geq \delta$ holds, where $0 < \delta \leq 1$ ∎

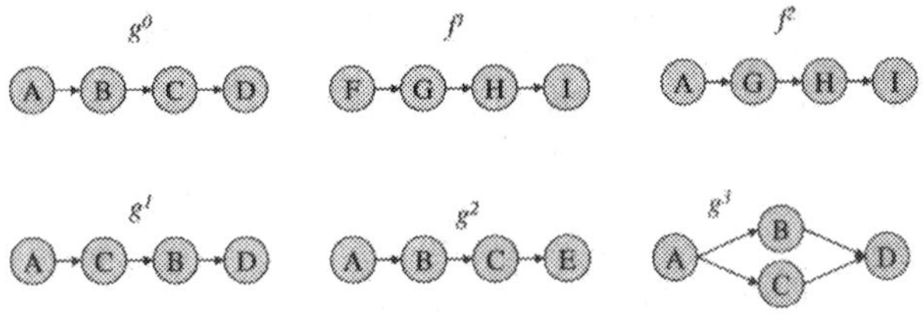

If we apply the $\delta$-Comparability to the example graphs shown in Fig. 2 with $\delta$=0.5, $g^0$ and $f^2$ are not comparable because the number of common nodes is only one but the number of total nodes is 7, that is

**Fig. 2.** Examples of $\delta$-Comparability

$\dfrac{|DN_1 \cap DN_2|}{|DN_1 \cup DN_2|} = \dfrac{1}{7} < 0.5$. On the other hand, $g^0$ and $g^2$ are $\delta$-comparable because there are 3 common nodes and the total number of nodes is 5, thus the two graphs satisfy the $\delta$-comparability condition $\dfrac{|DN_1 \cap DN_2|}{|DN_1 \cup DN_2|} = \dfrac{3}{5} \geq 0.5$.

## 3 Motivating Scenarios

Given the process reference model, we consider two motivating scenarios that benefit from the difference analysis methodology introduced in this paper. Consider a scenario where a company has maintained a warehouse of existing processes used in various business locations. *Process mining*[2, 3]of the process warehouse can help the enterprise to discover interesting associations or classifications among business processes running at different locations or branches of the company.

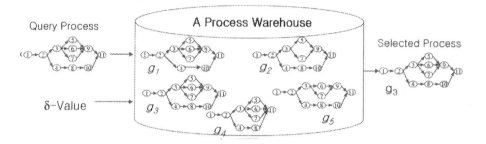

**Fig. 3.** Process mining example

In Fig. 3, we show a process warehouse that contains many types of processes (for example, $g_1$, $g_2$, $g_3$, $g_4$, $g_5$). A typical process mining scenario is the identification of the processes most similar to a baseline process template in the process warehouse. Given a query process and a comparability threshold δ-value, the process mining will identify ($g_3$) as the process that is most similar based on the comparability criterion. It is obvious that the concept of process similarity (or distance) is critical to the effectiveness of process mining.

## 4   Block Structure in Workflow

The first task in block structure based similarity analysis is to identify and extract structural patterns between two business processes. We assume that each business process and their process steps are described in terms of workflow and its activities in a precedence dependency graph. Our similarity comparison algorithm takes two workflow activity dependency graphs that satisfy δ-Comparability criteria as input and produces a block structure-based distance measure. Let's use two derived processes that are variations of procurement order process in Fig. 1. These two processes have 10 activities respectively but have different activities with each other. The first process ($g_{11}$) has $A_6$ but does not have $A_8$, and the second process ($g_{22}$) has $A_8$ but

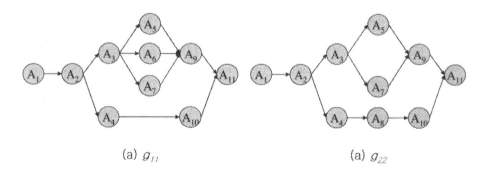

(a) $g_{11}$                           (a) $g_{22}$

**Fig. 4.** Two extended examples of real-life business process in Fig. 1

does not have $A_6$, and vice versa. These two graphs satisfy $\delta$-Comparability as
$$\frac{|DN_1 \cap DN_2|}{|DN_1 \cup DN_2|} = \frac{9}{11} \geq 0.5 \text{ and } \delta = 0.5.$$

## 4.1 Block Types

If we use dependency graph in the process definition, the precedence relationships and existence of activities can be represented well. However, if there are splits in workflow (workflow denoting a parallel relationship), the dependency graph does not include the meaning completely. Thus, we need another representation method to measure parallel relationships. In this section the structure information that can be found in the dependency graph is used to define the distance measure between processes.

Fig. 4 provides an example of a parallel relationship in the process definition, in which there are properties other than precedence relationship. One of other properties is parallel relationship and this parallel relationship comprises the structure of a process by using a nested relationship. In order to compare the structure properties, it is necessary to define how a process is composed of basic structures.

In order to represent the parallel relationship, the concept of block is introduced in this paper. A block is a unit of representation that can minimally specify the behavioral pattern of process flow. The behavioral patterns found in process models are classified into iterative, serial and parallel ones, each of which is illustrated in Fig. 5. Our discussion

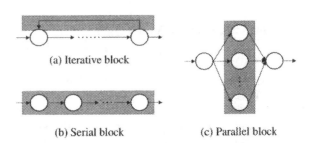

(a) Iterative block

(b) Serial block

(c) Parallel block

**Fig. 5.** Block types

in this paper is confined to such networks that can be built by combining those patterns. In this paper, the iterative block is not dealt with because it has less meaning in similarity of dependency and structure than serial and parallel. A serial pattern is shown in Fig. 5 (b). This pattern is simple in that it involves no iteration and has no split or merge in its task flow. But the serial block is related with the dependency measure which is discussed in the previous section. In this section, the parallel block is investigated in more detail.

A parallel pattern is such a flow that a node splits into two or more branches, the branches proceed in parallel, and merge into a node. Fig. 5 (c) is an illustration of this kind of pattern. The pattern is further subdivided into four types: AND-, XOR-, and SOR-parallel. Although all the parallel patterns are different in terms of their semantics, they have the same graphical structure. This is because the graphical objects of nodes and arcs deal only with the split-and-merge relations of tasks. The semantics distinguishing the parallel patterns are usually specified on the split or merge nodes.

## 4.2  Block Detection Algorithm

Since a component task of a process can be a nested process, the structure relation can be represented as a block structure. So in this paper, a block detection algorithm is used in order to generate blocks in the process and the generated blocks are used in the development of distance measure. The block detection algorithm[5] searches serial block and parallel block alternately and modifies the original network to construct a block tree from a process definition.

In reference [5], the block detection algorithm finds a cycle in the process network but these cycles are not used in the distance measure because the cycle does not affect the structure of a process. After serial blocks and parallel blocks are found alternately, this algorithm finally ends with a single node that means the uppermost block in the block tree. Fig. 6 provides an example of transforming a process network into block structure by using the block detection algorithm. In the example, the cycle block is removed at first, and then serial block, AND-parallel block, serial block, XOR-parallel block and serial block are generated. Since these blocks have hierarchy information, a tree can be made by combining the found blocks.

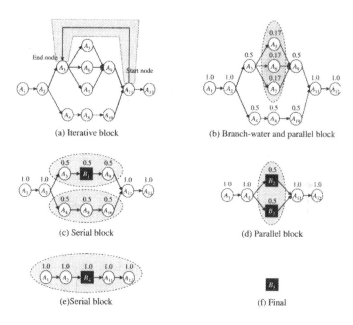

(a) Iterative block

(b) Branch-water and parallel block

(c) Serial block

(d) Parallel block

(e) Serial block

(f) Final

**Fig. 6.** Example of block generation

## Definition 3 (Block Tree)

Let $DG_1 = (DN_1, DE_1)$ be the input and $T=(N, E, Root(T), label)$ be the output of block detection algorithm respectively. The output is called block tree $N$ is a finite set of nodes, which include the $DN_1$ and detected blocks. $E$ is a binary relation on $N$ where each pair $(u,v) \in E$ represents the parent-child relationship between two nodes $u, v \in N$. Node $u$ is the parent of node $v$ and $v$ is one of the child nodes of $u$. Parent is nesting block and children are the nested components of the super block. There exists only one root note, denoted as $Root(T) \in N$, which has no parent. The root node is always serial block. Every other node of the tree has exactly one parent and it can be reached through a path of edges from the root. The nodes which have a common parent $u$ (i.e., all the children of $u$) are siblings. $|T|$ is the number of nodes in tree $T$, or the size of $T$.                                                                                                       ■

The block tree $T_{11}$ in Fig. 7 has a serial block $B_5$ as root node, which has 5 components, $A_1$, $A_2$, $B_4$, $A_{11}$, and $A_{12}$. These 5 components comprise first depth in the tree. Again a parallel block $B_4$ has two components, $B_2$ and $B_3$, which are serial blocks and second depth in the tree. At third depth, a serial block $B_2$ has three components, $A_3$, $B_1$, $A_9$ and a serial block $B_3$ has three components, $A_4$, $A_8$, $A_{10}$. Finally, three components $A_5$, $A_6$, $A_7$ are at the fourth depth as children of a parallel block $B_1$.

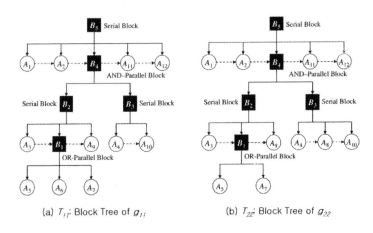

(a) $T_{11}$: Block Tree of $g_{11}$          (b) $T_{22}$: Block Tree of $g_{22}$

**Fig. 7.** Block Trees of Fig. 4

## 5  Structural Similarity in Tree Format

We have seen that block tree has two block types alternating serial and parallel as the depth increases in the previous section. So we can compare two block trees with the same block type (serial or parallel) in the same depth if we start from root node. We can define structural comparison by restricting the comparable depth in both block trees.

**Definition 4 (Structural Comparison by Depth $d$)**
If we have block trees $T_1=(N_1,\ E_1,\ Root(T_1),\ label_1)$, $T_2=(N_2,\ E_2,\ Root(T_2),\ label_2)$, the structural comparison by depth $d$ is the block tree comparison from root node to depth $d$.                                                                                                       ■

The measure of similarity between two trees $T_1$ and $T_2$ has been well studied in combinatorial pattern matching. Most studies use edit distance to measure the dissimilarity between trees (notice that similarity computation is the dual problem of distance computation). [14] Our proposed mapping of tree structures into a numeric vector space is based on the binary tree representation of rooted ordered labeled trees[13]:

**Definition 5 (Binary Tree)**
A binary tree consists of a finite set of nodes. It is:

1. an empty set. Or
2. a structure constructed by a root node, the left subtree and the right subtree of the root. Both subtrees are binary trees, too. ■

There is a natural correspondence between forests and binary trees. The standard algorithm to transform a forest (or a tree) to its corresponding binary tree is through the left-child, right-sibling representation of the forest (tree):

  (i)  Link all the siblings in the tree with edges.
  (ii) Delete all the edges between each node and its children in the tree except those edges which connect it with its first child.

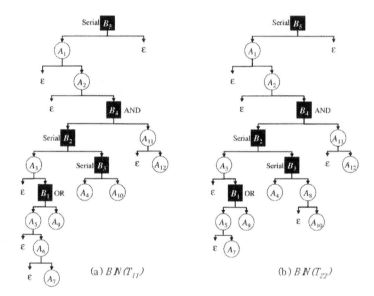

**Fig. 8.** Normalized Binary Tree Representation

Note that the transformation does not change the labels of vertices in the tree. We can transform $T_{11}$ and $T_{22}$ of Fig. 7 into $BIN(T_{11})$ and $BIN(T_{22})$ shown in Fig 8, respectively. The binary tree representation is denoted as $BIN(T) = (N, E_l, E_r, Root(T), label)$ in our paper.

A binary tree corresponding to a forest retains all the structure information of the forest. Particularly, in the binary tree representation, the original parent-child relationships between nodes, except the ones between each inner nodes and its first child, are removed. The removed parent-child relationships are replaced by the link edges between the original siblings. This property makes the transformed binary tree representation appropriate for highlighting the effect of the edit-based operations on original trees.

# 6  A Structural Similarity Measure

The key element of our algorithm is to transform rooted, ordered, labeled trees to a numeric multi-dimensional vector space equipped with the norm L1 distance. The mapping of a tree $T$ to its numeric vector ensures that the features of the vector representation retain the structural information of the original tree. Furthermore, the tree-edit distance can be lower bounded by the L1 distance of the corresponding vectors. In this section, we present the transformation methods to get structural similarity measure.

## 6.1  Vector Representation of Trees

To encode the structural information we normalize the transformed binary tree representation $BIN(T)$ of $T$. In $BIN(T)$, for any node $u$, if $u$ has no right (or left) child, we append a $\varepsilon$ node (i.e., nodes labeled as $\varepsilon$ do not exist in $T$) as $u$'s right (or left) child. Thus we make $T$ a full binary tree in which all the original nodes have two children and all the leaves are labeled as $\varepsilon$ (as in Fig. 8). The normalized binary tree representation is defined as $BIN(T) = (N \cup \{\varepsilon\}, E_l, E_r, Root(BIN(T)), label)$, where $\varepsilon$ denotes the appended nodes as well as their labels. To simplify the notation, in this paper $u \in N$ represents the node as well as its label where no confusion arises. In order to quantify change detection in a binary tree, we define the binary branch on normalized binary trees:

**Definition 6 (Binary Branch)**
Binary branch (or branch for short) is the branch structure of one level in the binary tree. For a tree $T$, $\forall u \in N$ there is a binary branch $BiB(u)$ in $BIN(T)$ such that $BiB(u) = (N_u, E_{u_l}, E_{u_r}, Root(T_u))$, where $N_u = \{u, u_1, u_2\}$ ( $u \in N; u_i \in N \cup \{\varepsilon\}, i = 1, 2$ ), $E_{u_l} = \{\langle u, u_1 \rangle_l\}$, $E_{u_r} = \{\langle u, u_2 \rangle_r\}$ and $Root(T_u) = u$ in the normalized $BIN(T)$. ∎

Assume that the universe of binary branches $BiB()$ of all trees in the dataset composes alphabet $\Gamma$ and the symbols in the alphabet are sorted lexicographically on the string $uu_1u_2$.

**Definition 7 (Binary Branch Vector)**
The binary branch vector $BBV(T)$ of a tree $T$ is a vector $(b_1, b_2, ..., b_{|\Gamma|})$, with each element $b_i$ representing the number of occurrences of the $i^{th}$ binary branch in the tree. $|\Gamma|$ is the size of the binary branch space of the dataset. ∎

We can first build an inverted file for all binary branches, as shown in Fig. 9 (a). An inverted file has two main parts: a vocabulary which stores all distinct values being indexed, and an inverted list for each distinct value which stores the identifiers of the records containing the value. The vocabulary here consists of all existing binary branches in the datasets. The inverted list of each component records the number of occurrences of it in the corresponding trees. The resulting vectors of our transformation for the block trees in Fig. 7 and the normalized binary trees in Fig. 8 are shown in Fig. 9 (b). Based on the vector representation, we define a new distance of the tree structure as the L1 distance between the vector images of two trees:

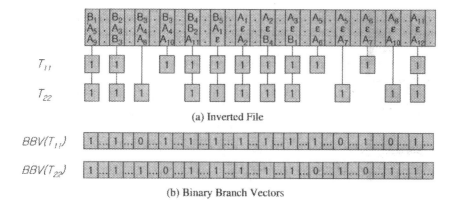

(a) Inverted File

$BBV(T_{11})$

$BBV(T_{22})$

(b) Binary Branch Vectors

**Fig. 9.** Binary Branch Vector Representation

**Definition 8 (Structural Distance)**

Let $BBV(T_1) = (b_1, b_2, ..., b_{|\Gamma|})$, $BBV(T_2) = (b'_1, b'_2, ..., b'_{|\Gamma|})$ be the binary branch vectors of trees $T_1$ and $T_2$ respectively. The structural distance of $T_1$ and $T_2$ is

$$BDist(T_1, T_2) = \sum_{i=1}^{|\Gamma|} |b_i - b'_i| \qquad \blacksquare$$

This structural distance has been proved that the distance properties met in reference [13]. And we can get the structural distance at depth 4 of Fig. 9 is 6.

In order to calculate running time complexity, we consider each step of the algorithm. Since the block detection algorithm depends on the number of node in dependency graph[5], we consider only the tree comparison steps. Assume that the size of the dataset, i.e., the total number of tree data objects, is |D|. For record $T_i$, there are $|T_i|$ nodes in it. To build the vector representation, the whole inverted file has to be scanned once. So the time and space complexities of the whole vector construction algorithm are both $O(\sum_{i=1}^{|D|} |T_i|)$, which means all information of input processes.

# 7   Conclusion and Future Work

We have presented a structural difference analysis methodology between process definitions. Although there can be many difference attributes in process definitions, structural characteristics as well as dependency information are most important factors to discriminate processes. This paper focuses on the structural characteristic as a distance measure. We first convert each workflow dependency graph into block tree by using block detection algorithm. Second, the block tree is transformed into binary tree to make a binary branch. Third, binary branch vector is generated by encoding binary branch. Finally, we calculate the distance metric between the binary branch vectors. The proposed difference analysis method achieves three distinct goals. First, by analyzing the attributes of process models, we can present a quantitative process similarity metric to determine the relative distance between process models. This facilitates not only the comparison of existing process models with each other, but also provides the flexibility to adapt to changes in processes. Second, the proposed method is fast and flexible, which reduces the cost of both the analysis and design phases of complex web service processes. Third, the proposed method enables the flexible deployment of process mining, discovery, and integration. The next research issue is to integrate structural distance into dependency distance in process definition. And we are interested in developing a prototype system that provides efficient implementation of various similarity analysis methods, including the dependency distance and structure distance presented in this paper.

**Acknowledgments.** The first author was supported by the Korea Research Foundation Grant (KRF-2004-003-D00477).

# References

1. W.M.P. van der Aalst, A.H.M. ter Hofstede, B. Kiepuszewski, and A.P. Barros, "Workflow Patterns," Distributed and Parallel Databases, 14(3), pages 5-51, July 2003.
2. W.M.P. van der Aalst, B.F.van Dongen, J. Herbst, L. Maruster, G. Schimm and A.J.M.M. Weijters, "Workflow Mining: A Survey of Issues and Approaches," Data and Knowledge Engineering. 47(2), 237-267, 2003
3. W.M.P. van der Aalst, A.J.M.M. Weijters and L. Maruster, "Workflow Mining: Discovering Process Models from Event Logs," IEEE Transactions on Knowledge and Data Engineering. 16(9), pp. 1128-1142, 2004
4. J. Bae, J. Caverlee, L. Liu, B. Rouse, "Process Mining, Discovery, and Integration using Distance Measures," Technical Report GT-CSS-2006-006, Apr. 2006.
5. J. Bae, H. Bae, S. Kang, Y. Kim, "Automatic control of workflow process using ECA rules," IEEE Trans. on Knowledge and Data Engineering, vol.16, no.8, pp. 1010-1023, 2004.
6. H. Bunke, K. Shearer, "A Graph Distance Metric based on the Maximal Common Subgraph," Pattern Recognition Letters, vol.19, issues 3-4, pp. 255-259, 1998.
7. J.E. Cook and A.L. Wolf, "Software Process Validation: Quantitatively Measuring the Correspondence of a Process to a Model," ACM Transactions on Software Engineering and Methodology, 8(2), pp. 147-176, 1999.
8. K.M. Hammouda, M.S. Kamel, "Efficient Phrase-Based Document Indexing for Web Document Clustering," IEEE Transactions on Knowledge and Data Engineering, vol.16, no.10, pp. 1279-1296, 2004.
9. RosettaNet, http://www.rosettanet.org, RosettaNet Standard (RosettaNet Partner Interface Processes)
10. W. B. Rouse, "A Theory of Enterprise Transformation," Systems Engineering, vol. 8, no. 4, 2005.
11. R. Rush, W.A. Wallace, "Elicitation of knowledge from multiple experts using network inference," IEEE Transactions on Knowledge and Data Engineering, vol. 9, no. 5, pp. 688-698, 1997.
12. WfMC, Workflow Management Coalition Workflow Standard Process Definition Interface -- XML Process Definition Language, Document Number WFMC-TC-1025 Version 1.13, September 7, 2005
13. Yang, R., Kalnis, P, Tung, A., "Similarity Evaluation on Tree-structured Data," ACM SIMOD 2005, June 14-16, 2005, pp. 754-765
14. K. Zhang, D. Shasha, "Simple Fast Algorithms for the Editing Distance between Trees and Related Problems," SIAM Journal of Computing, vol.18, no.6, pp. 1245-1262, 1989.

# Process Representation and Reasoning Using a Logic Formalism with Object-Oriented Features

Andrea Gualtieri[1,2], Tina Dell'Armi[1] and Nicola Leone[3]

[1] Exeura srl, University of Calabria, Rende (CS) 87036, Italy
{gualtieri, dellarmi}@exeura.it
www.exeura.it
[2] DEIS, University of Calabria, Rende (CS) 87036, Italy
[3] Department of Mathematics, University of Calabria, Rende (CS) 87036, Italy
leone@mat.unical.it

**Abstract.** A novel approach to model processes and workflows is presented. It is based on the OntoDLP language, an extension of Disjunctive Logic Programming with object-oriented features. Compared to traditional models, the approach enables knowledge inference on dynamic structures of the process, thanks to the reasoning capabilities of OntoDLP. Moreover, the approach can be also used to redefine and classify existing workflow schemes. Indeed, their execution traces, produced by workflow engines, can be easily imported through the mapping facilities of the underlying metamodel, and eventually organized into taxonomic structures for modeling different execution-patterns.

## 1 Introduction

Process management phases require both definition and analysis of process schemas. A large number of formalisms and approaches have been already proposed to support the design of processes [10] [11]. A cornerstone for characterizing a formalism is the specific metamodel adopted, which is an high level and platform-independent definition of the workflow items which are admitted. Many workflow systems refer an explicit metamodel, others have an implicit one, imposed by the offered features.

Essential requirements in a metamodel are an unambiguous semantics and the capability to express the main elements of a workflow, e.g., according with [12]: decomposition of process in activities; definition of control-flow rules among activities; assignment of activities to execution entities; annotation of input and output elements to each activity.

The implementation of a metamodel item is demanded to specific languages, allowing to define process schemas, each of them establishing a pattern of execution. Every time that a workflow execution runs, a workflow instance is generated, and a workflow log is recorded. By analyzing workflow logs it is possible to modify his own process schema or to generate a new one [13].

The approach proposed in this paper is based on a metamodel allowing for an intuitive graph-oriented representation of processes, based on the explicit definition of node and transition. The metamodel includes a set of constructs

J. Eder, S. Dustdar et al. (Eds.): BPM 2006 Workshops, LNCS 4103, pp. 153–163, 2006.

allowing to abstract workflow solutions adopted by a large number of tools in the open source community. We implement this metamodel by using the OntoDLP language, an extension of Disjunctive Logic Programming (DLP) with object-oriented features. We are able to define classes of processes and activities that can be both composed, to make process schemas, and classified to obtain hierarchical structures. Importantly, thanks to the reasoning capabilities provided by the DLP, we can define logic rules to analyze and automatically classify the traces of processes execution and to infer new knowledge about process-schema structures.

## 2   Process Modeling Overview

A standard formalism to represent processes and workflows does not exist in literature. Several works have proposed a large variety of methods and approaches to represent dynamic knowledge. Traditional ones are connected to the standard language XPDL provided by the Workflow Management Coalition (WfMC)[14]. This family of languages is based on a graph-oriented model, in which transitions are formalized by using arcs between activities. Another formalism, based on the use of Petri Nets models, provides a consistent framework to derive interesting results about structural properties of workflow [17].

An alternative approach derives from the view proposed by the BPML standard language provided by the Business Process Management Initiative (BPMI) [15]. This approach is based on a block-oriented model, in which transition are not explicitly declared: besides specific and customized activity blocks, BPML provides, in fact, specific blocks to define dynamic aspects of the process execution. Every process is defined on a sequence block that contains every activity of the process grouped in a set: to model control flows alternative to the sequence, particular dynamic blocks are placed in specific points of the set. Both XPDL and BPML also support recursive decomposition, transaction and exception handling mechanism [16].

The BPML approach is adopted in the family of formalisms connected to the Business Process Execution Language (BPEL). In particular, BPEL extension like BPEL4WS are oriented to the web services orchestration: in this way every activity of the process can be demanded to a specific web service able to execute it. Another evolution of BPEL is BPELJ, a formalism that enables Java and BPEL to cooperate by allowing sections of Java code, called Java snippets, to be included in BPEL process definitions [18]. Snippets are expressions or small blocks of Java code that can be used for things such as: loop conditions, branching conditions, variable initialization, web service message preparation, logic of business functions.

Also JBoss community provides a formalism to integrate process definition elements and java code. The Java Process Definition Language allows a process definition as a combination of a declaratively specified process graph and, optionally, a set of related java classes [19]. The java classes can then be made available to the jBPM runtime environment, that is the workflow engine integrated or linked by all the open source tools based on JBoss platform. Just for this reason, jBPM is one of the most adopted solution to implement workflow execution. Moreover, JPDL structure allows grouping of nodes based on the super-state construct. From this point of view, JPDL is a promising solution to capture logs of workflow execution provided by a wide number of open source tools and organize them in hierarchies based on properties of super-states.

# 3   A Metamodel for Logic Process Representation

The metamodel adopted in our approach is graph-oriented, so it provides explicit constructs to express node and transition elements. It is derived from JPDL modeling approach just to allow an easy mapping to process traces generated by jBPM workflow engine. As shown in 1, we consider a process as a composition of nodes, events, actions and task.

A task should be associated both to a process or to specific portion of it. As in JPDL, we adopt a "swimlane" item to express a group of tasks that refer an unique assignment. Assignment shall be then associated to many kind of actors, based on particular workflow execution context.

We connect "event" and "action" items to "node" and "transition" respectively, just to express that a transaction executed anywhere should be acknowledged in our context and associated to a specific state of our process schema. About nodes, we distinguish the initial and the ending point of the process, by using "start state" and "end state" respectively. All other nodes are classified as "common nodes". As shown in 2, we assume many kind of common nodes. For example, "fork", "join" and "wait node" are flow control nodes. A "decision node" is a particular node which is associated to a "condition" and to an "handler" that is an entity able to resolve the issue. A task node, should instead be

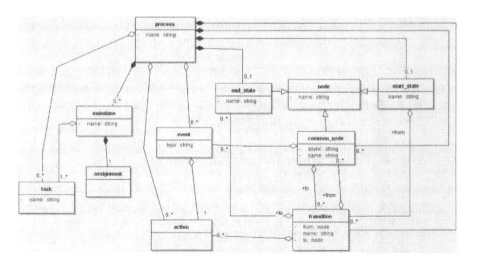

**Fig. 1.** A portion of process metamodel

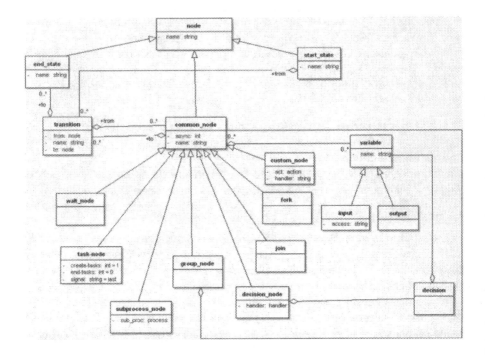

**Fig. 2.** A focus on node constructs

associated to one or more task assigned to an actor. Every common node has also one or more variables that can be used to map input and output elements of the activity.

A particular kind of node is a "subprocess node" that is an activity that refers an external process to the current one. Significantly different is a "group node" that contains a set of activities without any constraint about their composition. By defining specific relations among a "group node" and many common nodes, we are able to express that a particular node is a collection of nodes. We can also use these collections to facilitate the categorization of processes. A group node, in fact, should express a common semantics that results an abstraction of the semantics connected to the single activities. So, for example, a "development" activity should be composed by an "implementation" and a "test" step.

## 4   Process Representation and Reasoning

Our approach is based on the formal representation of processes, according with the metamodel illustrated in the previous section, in the logic-based language OntoDLP. On top of such a representation, we can then specify a number of (OntoDLP) inference rules, which allow us to discover new process properties and capture also dynamic knowledge which is hidden in process schemas.

In this section, we first recall the OntoDLP language for knowledge representation and reasoning. Then, we show some sample reasoning tasks.

## 4.1   OntoDLP: Language Overview

OntoDLP is an extension of Disjunctive Logic Programming (DLP) by object-oriented features. It combines the expressive and deductive power of DLP[1] (capture the complexity class $\Sigma_P^2$) with the facilities of the object-oriented paradigm for a natural and effective real-world knowledge representation and reasoning. In particular, the language includes, besides the concept of **relations**, the object-oriented notions of **classes, objects** (class instances), **object-identity, complex-objects, (multiple) inheritance**, and the concept of modular programming by mean of **reasoning modules**.

In the following, an overview of the language is given by informally describing its most significant features and by giving language use examples for the representation of some of the main concepts related to the workflow domain.

Classes can be declared in OntoDLP by using the keyword `class` followed by the class name and by a comma separated list of attributes. Each attribute is a couple (`attribute-name : attribute-type`). The attribute-type is either a user-defined class, or a built-in class (in order to deal with concrete data types, OntoDLP makes available two built-in classes *string* and *integer*). For instance, a generic process can be represented by declaring the class process with an attribute of type string as follows:

```
class process(name:string).
```

Objects, that is class instances, are declared by asserting new facts. An Instance for the class process, can be declared as follows:

```
#1:process(name:"Web sale order").
```

The string "Web sale order" values the attribute name; while #1 is the *object-identifier (oid)* of this instance (each instance is equipped by a unique oid).

Classes can be organized in a taxonomy by using the *isa* relation. For example, a common_node is a node characterized by a possible asynchronously activation. This class specialization can be represented in OntoDLP, declaring class common_node as an extension of class node with a new attribute asynchronous:

```
class common_node isa {node}
      (asynchronous:string).
```

Instances of the class common_node are declared as usual, by asserting new facts:

```
#2:common_node(name:"Password required",
    asynchronous:"true").
#3:common_node(name:"Registration required",
    asynchronously:"false").
```

Like in common object-oriented languages with inheritance, each instance of a sub-class becomes, automatically, an instance of all super classes (isa relation induces an inclusion relation between classes). In the example, "Passwor required"

---

[1] In the field of logic-based Artificial Intelligence, DLP is widely recognized as a valuable tool for knowledge representation, commonsense reasoning and incomplete-knowledge modeling [1,2,3,4,5,6,7,8].

and "Registration required" are instances of both node and common_node. Moreover, sub-classes inherit attributes from all super-classes. In the example, the common_node class inherits attribute name of class node and declares a new local attribute named asynchronous.

The language provides a built-in most general class named *Object* that is the class of all individuals and is a superclass of all OntoDLP classes.

Also multiple inheritance is supported. Attribute inheritance in OntoDLP follows the strategy adopted in the COMPLEX language, for a formal description refer to [9].

The possibility to specify user-defined classes as attribute types allows for complex objects or nested classes, i.e. objects made of other objects. For example, the class transition, besides the name of type string, is characterized by two attributes of the user-defined type node.

```
class transition(name:string,from:node,to:node).
```

The following declaration of class create_timer includes, besides timer_name and duedate, an attribute of type action, namely, action_to_execute.

```
class action(name:string).
class create_timer isa {action}
  (timer_name:string,duedate:integer,action_to_execute:action).
```

Note that this declaration is "recursive" (both action and create_timer are of type action). An instance of class create_timer can be specified as follows:

```
#4:create_timer(name:"Sell timer creation", timer_name:"Sell timer",
            duedate:30,action_to_execute:#5).
```

where the oid #5 identifies a selling action:

```
#5:action(name:"Sell").
```

Instance arguments can be valued both specifying object identifiers and by using a nested class predicate (complex term) which works like a function. For example, the action to execute is specified by a complex term in the following declaration:

```
#6:create_timer(name:"Auction timer creation",timer_name:"Auction timer",
            duedate:60,action_to_execute:action(name:"Auction").
```

Relations represent relationships among objects. Base relations are declared like classes and tuples are specified (as usual) asserting a set of facts (but tuples are not equipped with an oid). For instance, the base relation contains, and a tuple asserting that the process identified by oid #1 contains the common_node identified by oid #2, can be declared as follows:

```
relation contains(process:process,node:node).
contains(#1,#2).
```

Classes and base relations are, from a data-base point of view, the extensional part of the OntoDLP language. Conversely, derived relation are the intensional (deductive) part of the language and are specified by using reasoning modules. Reasoning modules, like DLP programs, are composed of logic rules and integrity constraints. OntoDLP reasoning modules allow one to exploit the full power of DLP. As an example, consider the following module, encoding the path search problem between two nodes in a process schema.

```
relation path(from:node, to:node).

module(path){
path(from:X,to:Y) :- T:transition(from:X,to:Y).

path(from:X,to:Y) :- T:transition(from:X,to,Z), path(from:Z,to:Y).}
```

## 4.2   Reasoning on Process Schema

A process schema is a definition of a path of execution of activities that can be enacted many times. Every execution of a schema is a process instance in which variables have their value assignment. Before the instances generation, in the process schema are so defined only classes of activities that can admit different enactments in relation to different values assigned to their variables. We represent these classes of activities as specializations of the nodes introduced in the metamodel. In this way, a particular activity belonging to a specific process,

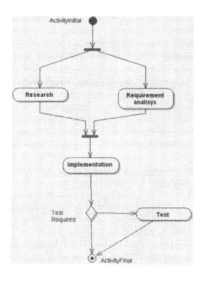

**Fig. 3.** An example of process schema

is modeled as a specialization of one of the classes specifying an "activity node" element of the metamodel. So, for example, "requirement analisys", "research", "implementation" and "test" activities are subclasses of "task node" and may be involved in a "project" element, modeled as a "process" subclass:

```
class project isa {process}.

class research isa {task_node}.

class requirement_analisys isa {task_node}.

class implementation isa {task_node}.

class test isa {task_node}.

relation has_research_task(proj:project, res:research).

relation has_requirement_analysis_task(proj:project,
    req_anal:requirement_analysis).

relation has_implementation_task(proj:project,
    impl:implementation).

relation has_test_task(proj:project, test:test).
```

We can then define a pattern of execution for a "project" type process, by declaring a set of subclasses of the "transition" element associating pairs of activities:

```
class start_fork_transition isa {transition}
    (from:start_state, to:fork).

class research_join_transition isa {transition}
    (from:research, to:join).

class requirement_analisys_join_transition isa {transition}
    (from:requirement_analisys, to:join).

class decision_test_transition isa {transition}
    (from:decision_node, to:test).

class test_end_state_transition isa {transition}
    (from:test, to:end_state).
```

Moreover, similarly to the nodes, also these specific transitions must be associated to the specific "project" element.

In our approach, every instance of a process will generate several logical facts. So, for example, an instance of the above schema for a KMS process is here formalized as follows:

```
#7:process(name:"KMS").

#8:research(name:"KMS research", asynchronous:"true").

#9:requirement_analisys(name:"KMS requirement analisys",
    asynchronous:"true").
```

```
#10:test(name:"KMS test", asynchronous:"true").
```

```
#11:join(name:"join node", asynchronous:"true").
```

```
#12:research_join_transition
    (name:"KMS research-join transition",from:#8, to:#11)
```

```
#13:requirement_analisys_join_transition
    (name:"KMS requirement analisys-join transition",from:#9, to:#11)
```

By performing reasoning on these facts we are able to infer new knowledge on static and dynamic aspect of processes. For example, we can define a rule expressing that every process that involves a "requirement analysis" and an "implementation" activity is "project" type process.

```
P:project(N):- contains(process:P, node:N1),
    contains(process:P,node:N2), N1:requirement_analisys(),
    N2:implementation(), P:process(name:N).
```

This way, the KMS process above defined, will be classified also as instance of "project" class. Adopting recursively this approach, we are able to recognize a "research and development project" as a project that involves also a "research" activity.

```
P:research_development_project(N):- contains(project:P, node:N1),
    N1:research(),P:project(name:N).
```

where class research_development_project is defined as

```
class research_development_project isa {project}.
```

This way we are able to define a hierarchical structure of process schemas. When we start to design a process, we can use this hierarchical structure to find an appropriate schema for modeling a specific context. If we modify this schema, by adding or removing activities, we will be always able to automatically classify new instances, by using specific reasoning rules.

For example, if an ontology or a quality certification system provides a document classification we are able to classify a generic activity that receives as input a "notification" and produces as output a "research deliverable" as a research activity, using the following rule:

```
C:research(name:N, asynchronous:"true"):-
    C:node(name:N).
    has_input(c_node:C, v:variable(name:"notification")),
    has_output(c_node:C, v:variable(name:"research deliverable")).
```

where relations has_input and has_output are defined as follows:

```
relation has_input(c_node:common_node, v:variable).
```

```
relation has_output(c_node:common_node, v:variable).
```

Moreover, also if an activity is not modeled as atomic node, we can discover it in a path of activities that receives a specified input and produces a specified output. For example, we can define a project as a "research and development project" if it contains a research activity and a "development", i.e. a path from a node that receives a "requirement analysis document" to a node that produces a "test report".

```
P:research_development_project(N):- P:process(name:N),
  contains(process:P, node:N1),
  contains(process:P, node:N2),
  contains(process:P, node:N3),
  N1:research(),
  has_input(c_node:N2, v:variable(name:"requirement analysis document")),
  has_output(c_node:N3, v:variable(name:"test report")),
  path(from:N2, to:N3).
```

where, path relation is defined in section 4.1.

This way, we are able to capture also dynamic knowledge that is hidden in process schemas.

## 5   Implementation and Future Works

The approach introduced in this paper has been implemented in OntoDLV system [21], that is an ontology management platform based on OntoDLP language and allowing to create, modify, navigate and query ontologies using a user-friendly visual environment. The metamodel adopted and presented in this work has been defined using the graphical interface and validated by the consistency check offered by the system. The addition of reasoning modules in OntoDLV allows the extraction of new knowledge about process schemas. In fact OntoDLV guarantees inference capabilities thanks to the integration of DLV system, widely recognised as the state of the art in the field of non monotonic reasoning (and disjunctive logic programming). For complexity analysis issues in OntoDLV refer to DLV results, shown in [22].

The long-term goal of this approach is to provide a support in the whole process management life-cycle. Actually, the metamodel has to be integrated in a framework for specifying enterprise models [20]. This way, it is possible to obtain an ontology of organizational processes that should support an architecture of heterogeneous open source tools for enterprise activities, like project planning and monitoring, timesheet compiling and analyzing, document management. Just to be easily mapped on JBoss process framework, widely adopted in open source community, the metamodel is inspired to JPDL formalism. With respect to JPDL and other xml-based languages, the proposed approach is able to use inference rules of DLP. This is particularly useful to link the triggers generated by generic JBoss-based tools to particular process events. Moreover, logic rules make possible to discover semantic dependencies inside process elements: actually, as it is illustrated in this paper, hierarchical structures are set just on the belonging of activities to process schemas; our purpose is to reason and to extract hierarchies also on the behaviour of processes.

The inference rules should be semi-automatically suggested by integrating process mining techniques that examine process instances. Process structures obtained should be useful in the process design phase: using OntoDLV querying we are able to find classes of process either composed by particular activities or associated to specific parameters or actors. A correlated future work regards the definition of techniques to semi-automatically compose a particular process schema as a function of the provided input, the required output and the existing classes of activities.

# References

1. Baral C. and Gelfond M.: Logic Programming and Knowledge Representation, JLP vol 19/20, 73–148 (1994).
2. Lobo J., Minker J. and Rajasekar A.: Foundations of Disjunctive Logic Programming, The MIT Press, Cambridge, Massachusetts (1992).
3. Disjunctive Logic Programming and Disjunctive Databases, 13$^{th}$ IFIP World Computer Congress, Hamburg, Germany (1994).
4. Eiter T., Faber W., Gottlob G., Koch C., Leone N., Mateis C., Pfeifer G. and Scarcello F.: The DLV System, Workshop on Logic-Based Artificial Intelligence, Washington, DC (1999).
5. Gelfond M. and Lifschitz V.: Classical Negation in Logic Programs and Disjunctive Databases, NGC vol 9, 365–385 (1991).
6. Lifschitz V.: Foundations of Logic Programming, Principles of Knowledge Representation, 69–127 (1996).
7. Minker J.:Overview of Disjunctive Logic Programming, AMAI vol 12 1–24 (1994).
8. Baral C.: Knowledge Representation, Reasoning and Declarative Problem Solving, Cambridge University Press (2002).
9. Greco S., Leone N. and Rullo P.: COMPLEX: An Object-Oriented Logic Programming System, IEEETKDE vol 4 (1992).
10. Casati F., Ceri S., Pernici B., and Pozzi G.: Conceptual Modeling of Workflows. In Proc. 14th Object-Oriented and Entity-Relationship Modelling , Gold Coast, Australia, December (1995).
11. Kappel G., Lang P., Rausch-Schott S., and RetschitzeggerW.: Workflow Management Based on Objects, Rules, and Roles. Bulletin of the Technical Committee on Data Engineering, IEEE Computer Society, 18(1), pages 11–18 (1995).
12. Kradolfer M.: A Workflow Metamodel Supporting Dynamic, Reuse-Based Model Evolution, University of Zrich, Ph. D. Thesis
13. Greco G., Guzzo A., Manco G., Sacc D.: Mining and Reasoning on Workflows. IEEE Trans. Knowl. Data Eng. 17(4): 519-534 (2005)
14. Workflow Management Coalition: Terminology and Glossary, Issue 3.0. Document Number WfMC TC-1011 (1999).
15. Arkin A.: Business Process Modeling Language, BPMI.org (2002)
16. Shapiro R.: A comparison of XPDL, BPML and BPEL4WS, Cape Vision (2002).
17. van der Aalst W.M.P., The Application of Petri Nets to Workflow Management. The Journal of Circuits, Systems and Computers, 8(1):21-66 (1998).
18. IBM: Business process execution language web services, version 1.0 (2002)
19. Jboss: jBPM Process Definition Language, version 3.0 (2005)
20. Gualtieri A., Ruffolo M.: An Ontology-Based Framework for Representing Organizational Knowledge, Proceeding of I-Know '05 - 5$^{th}$ International Conference on Knowledge Management, Graz Austria (2005)
21. OntoDLV system, http://www.exeura.it/ontodlv
22. Ricca F., Leone N.: Disjunctive Logic Programming with Types and Objects: The DLV+ System. Journal of Applied Logics Elsevier ISSN: 1570-8683 (to appear); KBS Research Reports INFSYS RR-1843-05-10 Institut fr Informationssysteme Technische Universitt Wien Favoritenstrasse 11 A-1040 Vienna Austria (2006)

# Workshop on Dynamic Process Management (DPM 2006)

# Workshop on Dynamic Process Management (DPM 2006)
## Preface

The agility of an enterprise increasingly depends on its ability to dynamically set up new business processes or to modify existing ones, and to quickly adapt its information systems to these process changes. Companies are therefore developing a growing interest in concepts, technologies and systems that help them to flexibly align their businesses and engineering processes to meet changing needs and to optimize their interactions with customers and business partners.

In this context dynamic process support has become an extensive research topic in areas like business process management, Web service technology and engineering workflows with several specialized aspects. Besides business requirements there are many technical challenges like the correct and efficient support of dynamic workflows (e.g., evolution of workflow specifications and dynamic change propagation, data-driven workflows), the support of autonomic or self-organizing processes, the dynamic selection of best service providers, the dynamic evolution of local processes as well as their involvement in cross-organizational collaborations, or the handling of security and trust issues in dynamic processes. While there has been major progress in some of these areas, dynamic process support is still a vision when looking at more complex scenarios.

The aim of the DPM 2006 workshop, which took place in Vienna on September 4th, was to provide a forum wherein challenges and paradigms for dynamic process management could be debated. The workshop brought together researchers and practitioners from different communities and application domains who share an interest in dynamic process support. We received 10 contributions from which 5 were accepted for the workshop proceedings. Papers were evaluated on the basis of significance, relevance, technical quality and exposition. We hope you will find the papers of this workshop interesting and stimulating.

We would like to acknowledge the support of the workshop program committee. We also thank Johann Eder as workshops chair and Schahram Dustdar as general chair of the BPM 2006 conference.

September 2006

Manfred Reichert
Kunal Verma
Andreas Wombacher
(Editors)

# Workshop Organization

## Organization Committee

**Manfred Reichert**
University of Twente
m.u.reichert@utwente.nl

**Kunal Verma**
The University of Georgia
verma@cs.uga.edu

**Andreas Wombacher**
University of Twente
a.wombacher@utwente.nl

## Program Committee

Wil van der Aalst, The Netherlands
Fabio Casati, USA
Peter Dadam, Germany
Prashant Doshi, USA
Richard Goodwin, USA
Yanbo Han, China
Dimitrios Karagianis, Austria
Akhil Kumar, USA
Olivera Marjanovic, Australia
Michael Maxmillien, USA
Andreas Oberweis, Germany
Marco Pistore, Italy
Hajo Reijers, The Netherlands
Stefanie Rinderle, Germany
Heiko Schuldt, Switzerland
Vlamidir Tosic, Canada
Barbara Weber, Austria
Mathias Weske, Germany
Michal Zaremba, Ireland

## Additional Referees

Paolo Busetta, Linh Thao Ly, Michael Predeschly

# A Declarative Approach for Flexible Business Processes Management

M. Pesic and W.M.P. van der Aalst

Department of Technology Management, Eindhoven University of Technology,
P.O.Box 513, NL-5600 MB, Eindhoven, The Netherlands
m.pesic@tm.tue.nl, w.m.p.v.d.aalst@tm.tue.nl

**Abstract.** Management of dynamic processes in an important issue in
rapidly changing organizations. Workflow management systems are systems that use detailed process models to drive the business processes.
Current business process modelling languages and models are of *imperative* nature – they strictly prescribe how to work. Systems that allow users to maneuver within the process model or even change the
model while working are considered to be the most suitable for dynamic
processes management. However, in many companies it is not realistic
to expect that end-users are able to change their processes. Moreover,
the imperative nature of these languages forces designer to over-specify
processes, which results in frequent changes. We propose a fundamental paradigm shift for flexible process management and propose a more
*declarative* approach. Declarative models specify what should be done
without specifying how it should be done. We propose the *ConDec language* for modelling and enacting dynamic business processes. ConDec is
based on temporal logic rather than some imperative process modelling
language.

**Keywords:** Workflow management, declarative model specification, dynamic workflow, flexibility, temporal logic.

## 1  Introduction

Companies need to adapt to rapid changes in their environment. In order to
maintain agility at a competitive level, business processes are subjected to frequent changes. As software products that are used in companies for automatic
driving of the business processes, workflow management systems (WFMSs) [2,10]
should be able to support the dynamics of business processes.

Workflow management systems are generic information systems which can be
implemented in variety of organizations to manage the flow of work. In traditional WFMSs, every change of such a business process model is a time consuming and complex endeavor. Therefore, these systems are not suitable for rapidly
evolving processes. The rigid nature of today's systems results from the way they
model and enact the business process. A business process model can be seen as
a scheme which defines the 'algorithm' of the process execution. During the execution of the model, the system uses the business process model as a 'recipe'

J. Eder, S. Dustdar et al. (Eds.): BPM 2006 Workshops, LNCS 4103, pp. 169–180, 2006.

to determine the sequence (order) of tasks to be executed. Since the enactment of the model highly depends of the modelling technique and the modelling language, the later two play a determining role in the way the prescribed process can be executed. The weaker this prescription is, the easier it is to deviate from the prescribed process. However, most process models enforce the prescribed procedure without deviations. Flexible WFMSs should allow users to deviate from the prescribed execution path [12]. For example, traditional systems have the reputation to be too rigid because they impose a strictly predefined execution procedure.

The *case-handling* paradigm is usually considered as 'a more flexible approach' [5] because users work with whole cases and can modify to some extent the predefined process model. An example of such a system is FLOWer, which offers the possibility to open or skip work items that are not enabled yet, skip or execute enabled work items and redo executed or skipped items.

Systems for dynamic process management emerge as a necessity to enable dynamic changes in workflow management systems [12,6]. As response on demand for dynamic business process management, a new generation of *adaptive* workflow management systems is developed [20,17,15]. When working with adaptive systems, users can change execution paths (e.g., in ADEPT users can insert, delete or move tasks in process models [17]).

Both in traditional, case-handling and adaptive systems, process models are presented in a process modelling language (e.g., Petri nets [18] ,Pi calculus [16], etc.), which defines the 'algorithm' for the process execution. Based on this algorithm, the system decides about the order of the task execution. Because process modelling languages like Petri nets and Pi calculus precisely prescribe the algorithm to be executed, the resulting models are *imperative*. Although case-handling and adaptive workflow systems allow for deviations/changes of models written in imperative languages, the result remains an imperative model. This can result in many efforts to implement various changes over and over again.

To abandon the imperative nature of contemporary WFMSs, we propose a paradigm shift by using a *declarative* language. In this paper we propose *ConDec* as a declarative language for modelling business processes. Unlike imperative languages, declarative languages specify the "what" without determining of the "how". When working with such a model, the users are driven by the system to produce required results, while the manner in which the results are produced depends on the preferences of users. Figure 1 characterizes the differences between classical imperative languages and ConDec. Figure 1(a) illustrates that ConDec specifies the "what" by starting from all possibilities and using constraints to approximate the desired behavior (outside-to-inside).

Imperative languages start from the inside by explicitly specifying the procedure (the "how") and thus over-specifying the process. To illustrate this, consider the ConDec constraint shown in Figure 1 (b). This constraint implies that the only requirement is that for a given case not both A and B are executed, i.e., it is possible to execute A once or more times as long as B is not executed and vice versa. It is also possible that none of them is executed. In an imperative

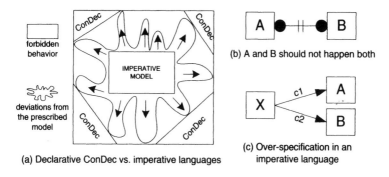

Fig. 1. A shift from imperative to declarative languages

language one tends to *over-specify* this as shown in Figure 1 (c). Unlike Figure 1 (b), now a decision activity is introduced – X. This activity needs to be executed at a particular time and requires rules (e.g. conditions c1 and c2) to make this decision. Moreover, implicitly it is assumed that A or B is executed only once. Hence, there is an over-specification of the original requirement and as a result (1) changes are more likely and (2) people have less choice when using the system.

In this paper we first introduce ConDec, a new language for modelling dynamic business processes (Section 2). In Section 2.1 we show an illustrative example of a ConDec model. Section 2.2 shows how a ConDec model can be enacted by a process management system. Related work is presented in Section 3. Section 4 concludes the paper and proposes future work.

## 2 Declarative Business Process Models

ConDec is a declarative language that can be used to build a wide range of models: from very 'strict' models that define the process in detail to very 'relaxed' models that state only what work should be done, without specifying how it should be done. Taking an optimistic approach, the simplest model to make in ConDec is a model specifying which tasks are possible. Users can execute such a model in their own preference – they can choose which tasks to execute and how many times, and in which order to execute tasks. However, such a simple too-relaxed model can be too 'anarchic' – there are often some rules that should be followed while working. These rules can also be added to a ConDec model - thus making it more rigid if desired. As an 'strict' extreme, a ConDec model can be supplied with such rules, that it behaves as an imperative model during the execution: the process is strictly prescribed and followed.

Initially, a ConDec model consists of a number of tasks, which are the possible tasks that can be executed. The notion of a task is the smallest unit of work, like in any other workflow language. In an extreme case, a model consisting only of tasks can be instantiated and enacted. When working on such a process instance, users would be able to execute whichever tasks in whatever order. The next step in developing a ConDec model is to define the relations between tasks. The notion of relations between tasks in ConDec is considerably different than in a Petri net and other traditional workflow models. Relations between tasks in a Petri net describe the order of execution, i.e, *how* the flow will be executed. We refer to the relations between tasks in ConDec as *constraints*. A constraint represents a policy (or a business rule). At any point in time during the execution of the model, each constraint has a boolean value 'true' or 'false', and this value can change during the execution. If a constraint has the value 'true', the referring policy is fulfilled and vice versa – if a constraint has the value 'false', the policy is violated. At every moment during the execution of a process model, the model is evaluated to be correct or not. The execution of a model is correct at one moment of time if all its constraints have the value 'true' at that moment of time. Since some constraints can evaluate to 'false' at the very beginning of the execution, a constraint which has the value 'false' during the execution is not considered an error. Consider an example of a constraint that specifies that, each execution of task $A$ is eventually followed by task $B$. Initially (before any task is executed), this constraint expression evaluates to *true*. After executing $A$ the constraint evaluates to *false* and this value remains *false* until $B$ is executed. This illustrates that a constraints may be temporarily violated. However, the goal is to end the execution of a ConDec model in a state where all constraints evaluate to *true*.

We use *Linear Temporal Logic* (LTL) [14] for declarative modelling of relations between tasks – constraints. In addition to the basic logical operators, temporal logic includes temporal operators: nexttime ($\bigcirc F$), eventually ($\diamond F$), always ($\square F$), and until ($F \sqcup G$). However, LTL formulas are difficult to read due to the complexity of expressions. Therefore, we define a graphical syntax for some typical constraints that can be encountered in workflows. The combination of this graphical language and the mapping of this graphical language to LTL forms the `declarative` process modelling language - ConDec. We propose ConDec for specification of dynamic processes.

Because LTL expressions can be complex and difficult to create for non-experts, we introduce *constraint templates* for creating constraints. Each template consists of a formula written in LTL and a graphical representation of the formula. An example is the "response constraint" which is denoted by a special arc connecting two activities $A$ and $B$. The semantics of such an arc connecting $A$ and $B$ are given by the LTL expression $\square(A \longrightarrow \diamond B)$, i.e., any execution of $A$ is eventually followed by $B$. Users use graphical representation of the templates to develop constraints in the ConDec model. Every template has an LTL expression of the constraint. It is the LTL expression and not the graphical representation that is used for the enactment (execution) of the model.

We have developed a starting set of more than twenty constraint templates. Constraint templates define various types of dependencies between activities at an abstract level. Once defined, a template can be reused to specify constraints between activities in various ConDec models. It is fairly easy to change, remove and add templates, which makes ConDec an 'open language' that can evolve and be extended according to the demands from different domains. Currently, there are three groups of templates: (1) "existence", (2) "relation", and (3) "negation" templates. Because a template assigns a graphical representation to an LTL formula, we can refer to such a template as a formula. Presentation of all templates is not necessary for the demonstration of the language. For a full description of the developed templates, we refer the reader to the report [4]. Figure 2 shows an illustrative ConDec model consisting of three tasks: A, B, and C. Tasks A and B are tagged with a constraint specifying the number of times the task should be executed. These are the so-called "existence formulas" that specify how many times a task can be executed within one case. Since task C does not have a constraint on the number of executions, it can be executed zero or multiple times (0..*). The arc between A and B is a relation formula and corresponds to the LTL expression for "response" discussed before: $\Box(A \longrightarrow \Diamond B)$. The response constraint is satisfied if task B is executed after task A, but not necessarily as the next task after A. This constraint allows that some other tasks are executed after task A and before task B. The connection between C and A denotes the "co-existence" relation formula: $( \Diamond C \longrightarrow \Diamond A ) \wedge ( \Diamond A \longrightarrow \Diamond C )$. According to this constraint, if C is executed at least once, A is also executed at least once and vice versa. This constraint allows any order of the execution of tasks C and A, and also an arbitrary number of tasks between tasks C and A. Note that it is not easy to provide a classical procedural model (e.g., a Petri net) that allows for all behavior modelled Figure 2.

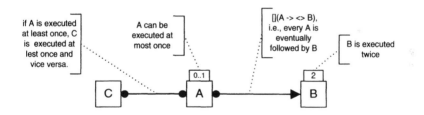

**Fig. 2.** An simple example of a ConDec model

Note that a ConDec model can be developed as an imperative model when using the right constraints. For example, we developed a constraint template "chain succession" [4] that can be used to specify a direct succession between two activities.

We use an illustrative example to explain the concept of declarative languages and advantages of declarative process models. First, we develop a Petri net model of a simple example of on-line book purchasing. Next, we show how to develop a ConDec model for the same example. This will show how ConDec specifies the relations between tasks in a more natural and refined way.

Figure 3 shows a Petri net model of a simple proces for on-line book purchasing. A Petri net consists of *places* (represented by circles) and *transitions* (represented by rectangles). Transitions and places are connected with directed arcs – a transition has its input and output places. Initially, there is a token in the place `start`. A transition is enabled when there is a token in each of its input places. If a transition is enabled, it fires by consuming a token from each of its input places and producing a token in each of its output places. In our example, the transition `order` is enabled and will fire the first by consuming and producing one token. The produced token will enable transitions `accepted` and `declined`. If the order is not accepted, the transition `declined` will fire by consuming a token from the input place and producing a token in its output place – `end`. This process execution would end with the initial order being declined and the book would not be purchased. If the order is accepted, the transition `accepted` fires by consuming one token and producing two. This will result in transitions `receive book` and `receive bill` being enabled. We assume that the book and the bill arrive separately, because it is possible that the book arrives from the shipper and the bill from the bookstore. When the book arrives the transition `receive book` fires, and transition `receive bill` fires when the bill arrives. Only after these two transitions fire and produce tokens in two input places of the transition `pay`, the book will be payed by firing this transition, and thus ending the process of book purchasing.

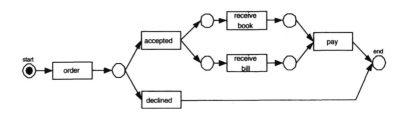

**Fig. 3.** Petri net - Purchasing a book

## 2.1    Declaring a Business Process in ConDec

In this section, we develop a ConDec model for the book purchasing example and explain the concept of constraints using this model. Figure 4 shows a Con-Dec model for the purchasing book example. We first define the same tasks like in the Petri net model in Figure 3. However, instead of defining the relations with Petri net arcs, we create a number of constraints, based on templates presented in [4]. First we develop a number of unary "existence" constraints. These constraints define how many times a task can be executed – the cardinality of a task. The graphical representation of these constraints indicates the cardinality for each task. Task `order` has the "existence" constraint "exactly_1" [4]. This constraint can be seen as the cardinality symbol '1' above the task `order`, and it specifies that this task will be executed exactly once. All other tasks have the "existence" constraint "absence_2" [4]. The graphical representation for this constraint is the cardinality symbol '0..1' and it specifies that the task can execute at most one time. In this example, the book will be ordered exactly once, and this is why the task `order` has the cardinality '1'. The order can be accepted or not. Similarly, the order can be declined or not. This is why these two tasks have the cardinalities '0..1'. The book, the bill and the payment will not be executed more that one time. However, due to the possible declining of the order and errors, it might happen that these tasks do not execute at all. Therefore, tasks receive book, receive bill and pay have cardinality '0..1'.

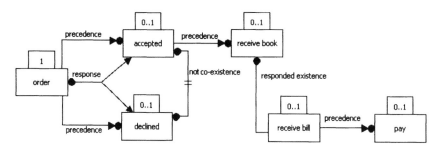

**Fig. 4.** ConDec - Purchasing a book

Next, we define relations between tasks. Several "relation" and "negation" [4] constrains are added to describe dependencies between tasks in the ConDec model in Figure 4. There is a branched response from the task order. It has two branches: one to the task accepted and the other to the task declined. Some binary "relation" and "negation" constraints can be extended with *branches*. The branched response in Figure 4 specifies that, after every execution of order, at least one of the tasks accepted or declined will eventually be executed. However, it is now possible that both tasks are executed, and to prevent this we add the not co-existence constraint between tasks accepted and declined. So far, we have managed to make sure that after the task order only one of the activities accepted and declined will execute in the model. One problem remains to be solved – we have to specify that both tasks accepted and declined can be executed only after the task order was executed. We achieve this by creating two precedence constraints: (1) one between the tasks order and accepted making sure that the task accepted can be executed only after the task order was executed, and (2) one between tasks order and declined makes sure that the task declined can be executed only after the task order was executed.

Further, we specify the relation between the activities accepted and receive book. In the Petri net model we had a strict sequence between these two activities. However, due to some problems or errors in the bookstore it might happen that, although the order was accepted (the task accepted is executed), the book does not arrive (the task receive book is not executed). However, we assume that the book will not arrive before the order was accepted – the constraint precedence between the activities accepted and receive book specifies that the task receive book cannot be executed until the task accepted was executed.

The original Petri net specifies that if the bill arrives also the book will arrive, and vice versa. This may not be always true. The ConDec model in Figure 4 accepts the situation when the bill arrives even without the book being sent. This could happen in the case of an error in the bookstore when a declined order was archived as accepted, and the bill was sent without the shipment of the book. However, we assume that every bookstore that delivers a book, also sends a bill for the book. We specify this with the *responded existence* constraint between the `receive book` task and the `receive bill` task. This constraint forces that if the task `receive book` is executed, then the task `receive bill` must have been executed before or will be executed after the task `receive book`. Thus, if the execution of the task `receive book` exists, then also the execution of the task `receive bill` exists.

The constraint *precedence* between the tasks `receive bill` and `pay` means that the payment will be done after the bill was received. However, after the bill was received the customer does not necessarily pay, like in the Petri net model. It might happen that the received book was not the one that was ordered or it was damaged. In these cases, the customer can decide not to pay the bill. Note that the ConDec model in Figure 4 allows users to pay even before the book has arrived. If the order was accepted, then the book can be received. The bill can be paid as soon as the bill is received, and the bill can be received before the book. This allows for the execution of the model where the book arrives after the received bill had been paid.

Note that in this section we used a Petri net model as a starting point and showed the corresponding ConDec model after some relaxations. For real-life processes we propose *not* to do this. Starting with a classical process model may lead to the introduction of unnecessary constraints that limit users and flexibility. Because of a (potential) large number of different (types of) relations between activities, ConDecmodel can become to complex. Therefore, we recommend a careful selection of a small number of relations (constraints) that are appropriate for the desired ConDec model.

## 2.2   Enacting Declarative Models

While the graphical notation of constraint templates enables a user-friendly interface and masks the underlying formula, the formula written in LTL captures the semantics of the constraint. A 'raw' ConDec model consists of a set of tasks and a number of LTL expressions that should all evaluate to *true* at the end of the model execution. ConDec models can be executed due to the fact that they are based on LTL expressions, and every LTL formula can be translated into an automaton [14,11]. The possibility to translate an LTL expression into an automaton and the algorithms to do so, have been developed for and extensively used in the field of *model checking* [14]. The Spin tool [13] uses an automata theoretic approach for the simulation and exhaustive formal verification of systems, and as a proof approximation system. Spin can verify the correctness of requirements, which are written as LTL formulas, in a system model written in Promela (PROcess MEta LAnguage) [13]. A more detailed explanation about the automata theory and the creation of the Buchi automatons from LTL formulas is out of scope of this article and we refer the interested readers to [13,14].

We can execute a ConDec model [4] by constructing an automaton [11] for each of the LTL expressions or constructing a single automaton for the whole model (i.e., construct an automaton for the conjunction of all LTL expressions). Figure 5 shows a simple ConDec model and the corresponding automaton[1]. This model consists of tasks `curse`, `pray`, and `bless` and the constraint `response` between tasks `curse` and `pray`. With this constraint in the model, when a person curses (p2 is not an accepting state), (s)he should eventually pray after this (p1 is an accepting state). Because there are no "existence" constraints in this model, all three activities can be executed an arbitrary number of times.

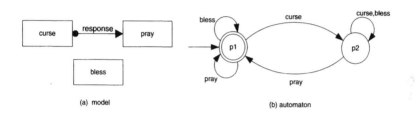

(a) model          (b) automaton

**Fig. 5.** A simple ConDec model

Using automata for the execution of models with constraints allows for the guidance of people, e.g., it is possible to show whether a constraint is in an accepting state or not. Moreover, if the automaton of a constraint is not in an accepting state, it is possible to indicate whether it is still possible to reach an accepting state. This way we can color the constraints *green* (in accepting state), *yellow* (accepting state can still be reached), or *red* (accepting state can not be reached anymore). Using the Buchi automaton some engine could even enforce a constraint.

## 3  Related Work

Although many business processes can be characterized as dynamic processes, traditional rigid WFMSs can not cope with frequent changes. The flexibility of WFMSs can be seen as the ability to change or deviate from the business process and plays an important role in the extend to which such systems can support dynamic processes [12]. The nature of the modelling language itself determines the usability and flexibility of the system [3].

Case-handling systems have the reputation to be more flexible and more appropriate for dynamic business processes [5]. In such systems, users can open a whole case, and work on that case, while in traditional WFMSs, users work with multiple cases. When allowing users to work on whole cases, the system

---

[1] Note that the generated Buchi automaton is a non-deterministic automaton. For simplicity we use a deterministic automaton yielding the same behavior.

has the privilege to allow for much more maneuver in the process (e.g., opening, skipping and re-doing tasks in FLOWer).

The most advanced solution for dynamic processes management is a class of WFMSs that offers the possibility to change the business process model at run-time [20,17,15]. When working with *adaptive* WFMSs, it is possible to change the business process model on the general level (i.e., the change is applied for all business process instances), or on the instance level (i.e., the change is applied only on one instance). Systems like ADEPT [17] develop very complex workflow engines [19] that are able to handle inserting, deleting and moving tasks at run-time.

Declarative properties are used to check whether the model matches the modelled system in [7]. In this approach, causal runs of a Petri net model are generated by means of simulation. Process nets representing causal runs are analyzed with respect to specified properties. The three groups of properties are: facts (the property should *always* hold) [9], causal chains (immediate *causal dependency*) and goals (the property *eventually* holds). While this approach validates Petri net process models, our approach is used to generate and enact the model.

## 4   Conclusions and Future Work

Flexibility of WFMSs is tremendously influenced by their perception of the notion of a business process. In current systems, the model of a business process is seen as an imperative prescription of the procedure that should be followed during work. The present solutions for dynamic process management lie in a flexible execution of the model (i.e., case handling systems such as FLOWer), and in the possibility to change the model during the execution (i.e., adaptive systems such as ADEPT [17]). However, the approach and the model still remain the same: an imperative prescription of *how* the solution should be reached.

ConDec is a declarative language for modelling business processes. It specifies *what* should be done, and users can decide how they will do it. We take an optimistic approach where, in principle, anything is possible. That is, anything is possible unless we specify some *constraints*. Constraints represent policies that should not be violated. In a way, constraints specify what not to do instead of specifying how to work. This leaves a lot of room for the maneuver of users, who can make decisions and work in various ways with the same ConDec model.

Using automata theory and Linear Temporal Logic, ConDec models can be executed by an engine. Developing a system for management of ConDec models brings various challenges. We are currently developing a prototype of such a system. Up to now, we have developed an editor where constraint templates can be defined and used to build a ConDec model. The ConDec model for the purchasing book example is developed in this tool (cf. Figure 6). The next challenge is to develop a complete workflow management system. This system will be used together with the YAWL system (www.yawl-system.com), where the YAWL language [1] deals with the structured workflows at a higher level. Moreover, the system will be linked to our process mining tool ProM [8] (www.processmining.org). This allows for the monitoring of ConDec flexible processes. Actually, ProM already offers an LTL checker for checking the ConDec constraints *after* execution.

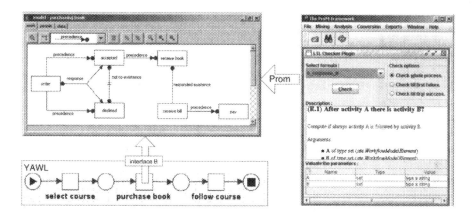

**Fig. 6.** The ConDec system with YAWL and ProM

# References

1. W.M.P. van der Aalst, L. Aldred, M. Dumas, and A.H.M. ter Hofstede. Design and Implementation of the YAWL System. In A. Persson and J. Stirna, editors, *Advanced Information Systems Engineering, Proceedings of the 16th International Conference on Advanced Information Systems Engineering*, volume 3084 of *Lecture Notes in Computer Science*, pages 142–159. Springer-Verlag, Berlin, 2004.
2. W.M.P. van der Aalst and K.M. van Hee. *Workflow Management: Models, Methods, and Systems*. MIT press, Cambridge, MA, 2002.
3. W.M.P. van der Aalst and S. Jablonski. Dealing with Workflow Change: Identification of Issues and Solutions. *International Journal of Computer Systems, Science, and Engineering*, 15(5):267–276, 2000.
4. W.M.P. van der Aalst and M. Pesic. Specifying, discovering, and monitoring service flows: Making web services process-aware. BPM Center Report BPM-06-09, BPM Center, BPMcenter.org, 2006. http://is.tm.tue.nl/staff/wvdaalst/BPMcenter/reports/2006/BPM-06-09.pdf.
5. W.M.P. van der Aalst, M. Weske, and D. Grünbauer. Case Handling: A New Paradigm for Business Process Support. *Data and Knowledge Engineering*, 53(2):129–162, 2005.
6. F. Casati, S. Ceri, B. Pernici, and G. Pozzi. Workflow evolution. In *ER '96: Proceedings of the 15th International Conference on Conceptual Modeling*, pages 438–455. Springer-Verlag, 1996.
7. J. Desel. Validation of process models by construction of process nets. In *Business Process Management, Models, Techniques, and Empirical Studies*, pages 110–128, London, UK, 2000. Springer-Verlag.

8. B. van Dongen, A.K. Alves de Medeiros, H.M.W. Verbeek, A.J.M.M. Weijters, and W.M.P. van der Aalst. The ProM framework: A New Era in Process Mining Tool Support. In G. Ciardo and P. Darondeau, editors, *Application and Theory of Petri Nets 2005*, Lecture Notes in Computer Science, pages 444–454. Springer-Verlag, Berlin, 2005.

9. H. J. Genrich and G. Thieler-Mevissen. The calculus of facts. *Mathematical Foundations of Computer Science 1976*, pages 588–595, 1976.

10. D. Georgakopoulos, M. Hornick, and A. Sheth. An Overview of Workflow Management: From Process Modeling to Workflow Automation Infrastructure. *Distributed and Parallel Databases*, 3:119–153, 1995.

11. R. Gerth, D. Peled, M.Y. Vardi, and P. Wolper. Simple On-The-Fly Automatic Verification of Linear Temporal Logic. In *Proceedings of the Fifteenth IFIP WG6.1 International Symposium on Protocol Specification, Testing and Verification XV*, pages 3–18, London, UK, 1996. Chapman & Hall, Ltd.

12. P. Heinl, S. Horn, S. Jablonski, J. Neeb, K. Stein, and M. Teschke. A comprehensive approach to flexibility in workflow management systems. In *WACC '99: Proceedings of the international joint conference on Work activities coordination and collaboration*, pages 79–88, New York, NY, USA, 1999. ACM Press.

13. G.J. Holzmann. *The SPIN Model Checker: Primer and Reference Manual*. Addison-Wesley, Boston, Massachusetts, USA, 2003.

14. E.M. Clarke Jr., O. Grumberg, and D.A. Peled. *Model Checking*. The MIT Press, Cambridge, Massachusetts and London, UK, 1999.

15. P.J. Kammer, G.A. Bolcer, R.N. Taylor, A.S. Hitomi, and M. Bergman. Techniques for supporting dynamic and adaptive workflow. *Comput. Supported Coop. Work*, 9(3-4):269–292, 2000.

16. R. Milner. *Communicating and Mobile Systems: The Pi-Calculus*. Cambridge University Press, Cambridge, UK, 1999.

17. M. Reichert and P. Dadam. ADEPTflex: Supporting Dynamic Changes of Workflow without Loosing Control. *Journal of Intelligent Information Systems*, 10(2):93–129, 1998.

18. W. Reisig and G. Rozenberg, editors. *Lectures on Petri Nets I: Basic Models*, volume 1491 of *Lecture Notes in Computer Science*. Springer-Verlag, Berlin, 1998.

19. S. Rinderle, M. Reichert, and P. Dadam. Correctness Criteria For Dynamic Changes in Workflow Systems: A Survey. *Data and Knowledge Engineering*, 50(1):9–34, 2004.

20. M. Weske. Formal foundation and conceptual design of dynamic adaptations in a workflow management system. In *HICSS '01: Proceedings of the 34th Annual Hawaii International Conference on System Sciences*, volume 7, page 7051, Washington, DC, USA, 2001. IEEE Computer Society.

# Flexibility of Data-Driven Process Structures*

Dominic Müller[1,2], Manfred Reichert[1], and Joachim Herbst[2]

[1] Information Systems Group, University of Twente, The Netherlands
{d.mueller, m.u.reichert}@ewi.utwente.nl
[2] Dept. REI/ID, DaimlerChrysler AG Research and Technology, Germany
joachim.j.herbst@daimlerchrysler.com

**Abstract.** The coordination of complex process structures is a fundamental task for enterprises, such as in the automotive industry. Usually, such process structures consist of several (sub-)processes whose execution must be coordinated and synchronized. Effecting this manually is both ineffective and error-prone. However, we can benefit from the fact that these processes are correlated with product structures in many application domains, such as product engineering. Specifically, we can utilize the assembly of a complex real object, such as a car consisting of different mechanical, electrical or electronic subcomponents. Each sub-component has related design or testing processes, which have to be executed within an overall process structure according to the product structure. Our goal is to enable product-driven (i.e., data-driven) process modeling, execution and adaptation. We show the necessity of considering the product life cycle and the role of processes, which are triggering state transitions within the product life cycle. This paper discusses important issues related to the design, enactment and change of data-driven process structures. Our considerations are based on several case studies we conducted for engineering processes in the automotive industry.

## 1 Introduction

Industry increasingly demands IT support for the coordination of large and complex process structures, such as production and development processes. Such structures usually comprise numerous single processes with many interdependencies. Though these dependencies are often domain-specific, there exist general patterns. Both development and production processes are often structured according to the product, for example a car or an application software suite. In particular, several single processes have to be executed for every component of the product. Some of The dependencies between the components have to be considered for process coordination. Thus, among other things, the product structure defines the sequence of process executions. The result is a process structure consisting of interconnected single processes according to the assembly of the product. Usually we use the notion of *data-driven process structures* for such patterns.

---

* This work has been funded by *DaimlerChrysler Research and Technology* and has been conducted in the *COREPRO* (*Configuration based Release Processes*) project.

J. Eder, S. Dustdar et al. (Eds.): BPM 2006 Workshops, LNCS 4103, pp. 181–192, 2006.

A real world example for data-driven process structures are development processes in the automotive industry. Release management (RLM), for instance, is an important part of the development process for car electrical systems [1]. RLM covers configuration management, testing and release of all electrical components in a car. Instead of performing RLM processes (e.g., testing) in an isolated fashion and solely at the level of single car components (cf. Fig. 1), there is a great need for coordinated execution and synchronization of the results of all RLM processes related to the different sub-components. That means that the processes for single data objects (in our case representing car components) have to be synchronized. Fig. 1 (Box C) shows an example for such a data-driven process structure.

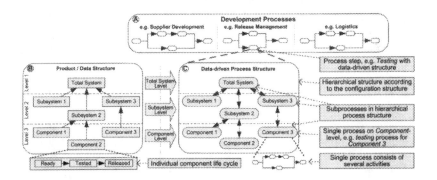

**Fig. 1.** Car development process with a data-driven process structure

Currently, the coordination of such data-driven process structures is mainly done manually due to the lack of suitable concepts for automated management. Except a few approaches [2,3,4,5,6,7], process design and enactment is *activity-driven* in current business process management solutions. Using activity-driven approaches, the connection between data structures and according process structures must be defined manually (i.e., the process structure is modeled according to the data structure). In practice, this leads to inflexible process coordination. In particular, every change of the data structure necessitates a manual change of the process structure. Regarding usability, an engineer is not interested in changing process models if he or she actually wants to change the product structure. Therefore our goal is to automate the generation and maintenance of these process structures during runtime by following a data-driven approach for their design, enactment and change. However, even modeling is difficult tasks. The information provided by the data structure itself (i.e., the dependencies between the components) is insufficient for the generation of data-driven process structures. On the one hand, it does not include the mapping of the components to processes. On the other hand, the data structures do not imply the control flow between the processes of the resulting structures.

The efficient modeling of process structures also necessitates the consideration of domain specific component (i.e., data) states. Possible states are defined by the specific life cycle of the component (cf. Box B in Fig. 1). State transitions are triggered by executing processes. In the RLM, for example, after executing the testing processes, a state transition from *Ready* to *Tested* is triggered. The definition of the dependencies between data states and processes is important information for the generation of data-driven process structures.

In this paper, we present the basics for the management of data-driven process structures. We emphasize the core issues for the separation of data structure and process logic in consideration of data states. Based on this separation, we defined example scenarios for possible runtime adaptations of data-driven process structures. The remainder of this paper is structured as follows. Section 2 describes the modeling of data-driven process structures based on data states while Section 3 describes the enactment of these processes and the role of the data states during execution. Scenarios for flexible process execution are presented in Section 4 and Section 5 discusses the suitability of state-of-the-art approaches for realizing data-driven process structures. The paper concludes with conclusions and an outlook in Section 6.

## 2  Modeling of Data-Driven Process Structures

The idea behind the design and modeling of data-driven process structures is the utilization of data structures as well as data states. Both contribute to creating corresponding process structures and to providing adequate support for their enactment and change. The goal of our data-driven approach is to sustain the separated modeling of data and process *logic*. That enables the independent definition of data and processes by domain experts (cf. Fig. 2). As shown in Fig. 2, generating data-driven process structures integrates data *and* process models. In particular, the definition of *data objects, data states, process templates* and *process states* (Steps 1a to 1d in Fig. 2) constitute prerequisites for the realization of data-driven *process structures*. Data objects and data states are defined by data domain experts and represent (real) components. In this paper, we assume that the content of data objects does not include information necessary for process execution. The *data structure* itself documents the dependencies between single data objects. With regard to data-driven process structures, the most relevant information about a data object is its state. This state describes the current phase of the object within the object life cycle (OLC) and must be defined in Step 2 (cf. Fig. 2). In the RLM example (cf. Section 1), data objects have the different OLC states termed *ready, tested* and *released* (cf. Box B in Fig. 1). Considering the dependencies between data objects, the OLC of a single data object may depend on the life cycle of other data objects. Taking the hierarchical data structure from Box B in Fig. 1, this could mean that a component can be tested only if its sub-components have been successfully tested. Thus, the definition of OLCs depends on the data structure, and it demands the definition of state transitions between single OLCs (cf. Step 3 in Fig. 2).

State transitions within a particular OLC can be realized by the execution of processes which are modifying data objects. The combined application of the OLCs and these processes results in a process structure (cf. Step 4 in Fig. 2).

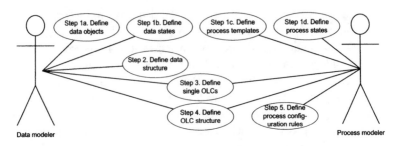

**Fig. 2.** Necessary steps for modeling data-driven process structures

Clearly, this structure depends on the OLC structure (including all single OLC definitions) and thereby on the data structure.

In the following subsections, we describe the necessary steps to realize a data-driven process structure definition. Fig. 3 illustrates the steps described in Fig. 2. The first step consists of the definition of data objects, data states, processes templates and their final states (cf. Boxes 1a-1d in Fig. 3). The second step in modeling data-driven process structures is the definition of the data structure, i.e., the semantic dependencies between data objects (cf. Box 2 in Fig. 3). Generally, these dependencies are hierarchically arranged with every data object having exactly one parent data object. However, these structures often provide many exceptions (e.g., data objects with more than one parent). For the sake of simplicity, we assume the presence of a hierarchical data structure as used, for example, for *bills of material* [8].

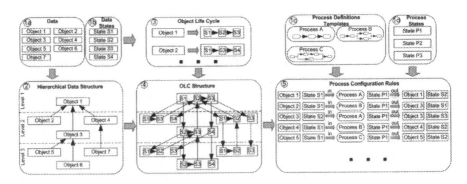

**Fig. 3.** Modeling data-driven process structures according to the steps in Fig. 2

Every data object has its own object life cycle, which describes the states (or stages) an object goes through until reaching the desired final state (cf. Box 3 in Fig. 3). The states are connected by state transitions. Generally, the OLC should not only describe the ideal situation, but also consider exceptional cases (e.g., error states). In addition, OLCs may include hierarchical states, (i.e., with more detailed states). In the RLM, for example, the state *Tested* includes several substates like *Electrical Check* and *Test Drive*. The aspect of OLCs with hierarchical phases is not discussed in this paper.

Defining OLCs for single data objects is only one part of the challenge. When considering data structures and dependencies between data objects, we also have to deal with dependencies between different OLCs. Box 2 in Fig. 3, for example, depicts a hierarchical data structure including data objects organized at three levels. Based on this data structure, an OLC structure must be also modeled by defining state transitions between different OLCs. As a result, we obtain an OLC structure with defined state dependencies between single OLCs of data objects (Box 4 in Fig. 3).

OLC state transitions represent data object modifications. As mentioned earlier, such modifications are accomplished by executing processes. These processes use data objects (in individual states) as input. By executing them, the data objects are modified, and thus their individual states change. These transitions are defined in Box 4 from Fig. 3 in compliance with the OLC structure. As a result, we obtain the *process configuration* describing the structure of the process (cf. Box 5 in Fig. 3). It is used for generating the control flow of the process structure during runtime. As shown in Fig. 3 (Box 5) we have chosen a simple rule-based representation for the process configuration. Every rule defines an OLC state transition which depends on the current OLC state, the process termination state and the OLC state after process execution. The first rule, for example, triggers the execution of *Process A* when *Object 1* reaches *State S1*. If *Process A* terminates in *State P1*, the state of *Object 1* is changed to *S2*.

Process templates may be used within several rules. We have simplified modeling in this paper - in practice the rules have to be enriched by additional constraints (e.g., time constraints) and processes have more input and output parameters.

Based on to the process configuration, the control flow of the process structure is generated. Fig. 4 depicts the control flow of the generated process structure. Note that, in practice, these structures become much more complex due to the fact that data structures include more elements than assumed in our examples, and OLCs may consist of numerous phases in practice [1].

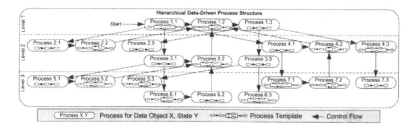

**Fig. 4.** Generated process structure

## 3   Enactment of Data-Driven Process Structures

Typically, data-driven process structures are embedded in larger process environments (e.g., development processes; cf. Box A in Fig. 1) [1]. In our RLM example, the data-driven process structure is part of the total *Release Management* process. The execution order of the single processes is controlled by the process structure according to the OLC structure.

The generated process structure (cf. Fig. 4) implies the execution order of the embedded processes. Note that the coordination of the single processes depends directly on the assigned data object states. In the example from Fig. 4, for instance, some processes depend on more than one input object. The top-level process *P 1.2*, for example, depends on all processes on level 2). We assume an *AND-join* for process synchronization, i.e., the processes of all data objects must terminate before starting execution of Process *P 1.2*.

After instantiation of the process structure, all data objects remain in their initial states until modified by corresponding processes. Fig. 5 shows the impact of executing the generated process in Fig. 4 on data states. In Fig. Fig. 5 we have divided this execution in three phases: A, B and C. The execution order of the state transitions (and thus the related processes) is represented by numbered state transitions. Following this approach, the current state of the whole process structure is represented by the state of the top-level data object.

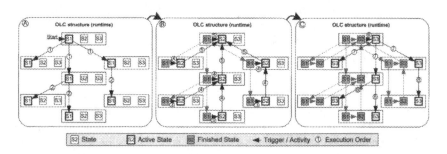

**Fig. 5.** Process execution order illustrated by state transitions (cf. OLC structure in Box 4 of Fig. 3)

In practice, different processes access and modify data objects. For the generation of the data-driven process structure, that means the current OLC state of a data object may have been already changed before process generation or execution. In the example of RLM, a previously executed instance of the testing process may have modified a component and thus have changed the state of the component to *Tested*. Because of the testing process need to be executed only if the component has been changed, it is not necessary to test it again.

The question is whether the predefined state is subsequently used in another process structure or not. Several points have to be considered in this context. First, some data objects may be used in different processes, e.g., testing and release. In this context, the predefined state of the data object must be compatible with the OLC structure of the current process configuration to ensure consistent OLCs (i.e., the current data object state has to be used in the current process configuration). Second, predefined OLC states may lead to an inconsistent OLC structure. Fig. 6 depicts such a situation. Box A shows the OLCs of two data objects (*Object 1* and *2*) with state transitions between them. The predefined state of *Object 2* is *S3* (cf. Box B). Box C shows the problem of an undefined behavior caused by the predefined state: *Object 1* triggers a state transition to *Object 2* and activates a previous state *S3*. Keeping the predefined state leads to an inconsistent state of the OLC structure up to deadlocks (e.g., state transition from state *S2* of *Object 2* to state *S2* of *Object 1*). However, resetting the triggered state makes (the advantages of) the predefined state to be lost and induces the re-execution of processes for this object.

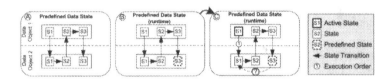

**Fig. 6.** Behavior during runtime with predefined data states

# 4   Adaptation of Data-Driven Process Structures

In practice, data changes (e.g., removing a component from the product structure) and process changes (e.g., changing the order of different testing processes) occur frequently [1]. Flexibility and dynamic adaptation support are therefore not only required at the level of single process executions, but also at the process structure level. An advantage affected by the modeling method presented in Section 2 is the ability to adapt data and processes separately. In addition, the data-driven perspective provides a more intuitive view of changes when compared to solely activity-oriented process structures.

To ensure a consistent OLC structure, the applicability of both data and process changes during runtime depends on the current state of the OLC structure (and the process structure respectively). In the following section, we characterize possible changes (*data structure, object life cycle, object life cycle structure, processes* and *data states*) and discuss the resulting issues and challenges.

## 4.1   Data Structure Changes

Modifying data structures (e.g., by adding or removing data objects) during runtime results in several challenges. After updating the data structure, both the OLC structure and the process configuration must be applied correspondingly. Before modifying a data structure, it must be verified whether this change will lead to a valid result. In hierchical data structures, removing a data object with *child-dependencies* clearly also affects its sub-objects. Whether or not the change is possible or requires further operations depends on the state of the affected OLC structure and on the already triggered state changes. Table 1 gives an overview of the data modification scenarios: (1) adding a data object to the data structure; (2) removing a data object from the data structure; (3) exchanging a data object (and keeping OLC); and (4) moving a data object within the data structure.

**Table 1.** Overview of dynamic data changes

| Scenarios | 1) Add Data Object | 2) Remove Data Object | 3) Exchange of Data Object | 4) Reorder Data Object |
|---|---|---|---|---|
| S1) Total process not started | Ok | Ok[3] | Ok | Ok |
| S2) Total process running, affected data object not running | Ok | Ok[3] | Ok | Ok[2] |
| S3) Total process running, affected object running | - | Ok[3] | Ok[4] | Ok[3,2] |
| S4) Total process running, affected object terminated | - | - | - | - |
| S5) Total process terminated | - | - | - | - |

Ok = change is possible

[1] if no state transition to affected object missed so far
[3] if no state transitions to other objects triggered so far

- = change might lead into inconsistent OLC structure state
[2] if all states in OLC structure stay reachable
[4] Processes for this object have to be restarted

Fig. 7 shows the problems we have to deal with when removing a data object (*Scenario S4* from Table 1). First, all running processes related to this data object must be interrupted and terminated in a semantically correct manner (Box A). Second, state dependencies to other data objects (i.e., control flows between processes) must be removed (Box B). Regarding parent data objects this may imply that certain adaptations have to be carried out to preserve consistency. It may be necessary to reset a previous state of the OLC or adding state transitions to prevent unreachable or inconsistent states. In Fig. 7 (Box C), for example, the current state (S3) of *Object 4* is no longer valid when *Object 7* is removed. The active state of *Object 4* has to be reset to *S2* to prevent inconsistencies. This change also affects other data objects and may necessitate further adaptations of dependent data objects in order to ensure consistent execution of the data-driven process structure. For our example from Fig. 7 this means that the current state (S3) of *Object 1* becomes invalid. However, changing the current state of *Object 1* again results in an inconsistent OLC structure because of further dependencies. The state transitions from state *S3* of *Object 1* to all sub-objects have to be reset. Thus, the whole structure is affected by the initial adaptation.

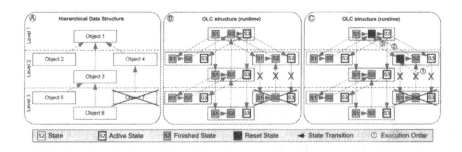

**Fig. 7.** Data structure changes requiring runtime adaptations

## 4.2  Structural Changes of Object Life Cycles

Data structure modifications also affect the OLC structure. For example, adding a new data object may require the insertion of new state transitions to OLCs of dependent data objects as well. Table 2 presents two scenarios for structural changes of OLCs: (1) changes of the OLC structure by itself adding or removing state transitions; and (2) changes of a single OLC.

**Table 2.** Overview dynamic changes of the OLC structure and single OLCs

| Scenarios | 1a) Change OLC Structure (adding transition) | 1b) Change OLC Structure (removing transition) | 2a) Change transitions in Single OLC | 2b) Add or Remove States in Single OLC |
|---|---|---|---|---|
| S1) Total process not started | Ok | Ok[2] | Ok[3] | Ok[2] |
| S2) Total process running; affected data objects not running | Ok | Ok[2] | Ok[2] | Ok[2,3] |
| S3) Total process running; affected objects running | Ok[1] | Ok[1,2] | Ok[1,2] | Ok[2,3] |
| S4) Total process running; affected objects terminated | - | - | - | - |
| S5) Total process terminated | - | - | - | - |

Ok = change is possible    - = change might lead into inconsistent OLC structure state
[1] if start and end state not activated so far  [2] if all states stay reachable  [3] if not state transitions to other data objects affected

Clearly, changes of an OLC structure must be done carefully in order to preserve consistency. Adding or removing state transitions, for example, might lead to inconsistent states for OLC structure as well as to violated dependencies. Fig. 8 (Box A) illustrates the inconsistency that might occur when inserting an additional state transition (cf. Scenario *S4* in Table 2). The activation of the new state transition, as shown in Fig. 8 (Box B), leads to an inconsistent state. One option to deal with this case is to reset the current state of the affected data object. As discussed above, this might again result in an inconsistent OLC structure due to further dependencies.

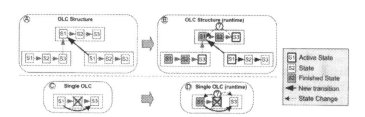

**Fig. 8.** Adding state transition to the OLC structure and changing single OLCs

Another scenario is the change of a single OLC. As an example, consider the removal of a state from a single OLC for optimization reasons (cf. Fig. 8, Box *C*). If state changes for this data object have already occurred, consistent OLC operations need to be ensured. Fig. 8 (Box D) shows the problem when changing OLCs during runtime. State *S2* was removed in the OLC definition. If this state is currently activated, the change leads to an inconsistency. A possible solution to deal with this situation is to reset the state of the data object (which may cause further inconsistent states of the whole OLC structure).

## 4.3   Process Configuration Changes

According to the modeling steps presented in Fig. 2, the changes described in Sections 4.1 and 4.2 affect the process configurations as well (cf. Box 5 in Fig. 3). However, there are other scenarios for process configuration changes (cf. Table 3). If processes are exchanged in the process configuration, for example, the generated process model must be adapted. Due to the fact that processes have no direct dependencies on other processes themselves (these dependencies are defined by the process configuration), processes are simply exchangeable in our approach - if they are not currently executed (Scenario S3).

We also have to consider scenarios for already finished processes (Scenarios S4 and S5). In these states, the exchange of a process makes no sense at first glance. However, the process configuration should be updated, because other reasons may require the re-execution of the process - for example, the external reset of data object states.

**Table 3.** Overview dynamic changes

| Scenarios | 1) Exchange Process in Process Configuration | 2) Change Process Template |
|---|---|---|
| S1) Total process not started | Ok | Ok |
| S2) Total process running; affected process not running | Ok | Ok |
| S3) Total process running, affected process running | - | - |
| S4) Total process running, affected process terminated | Ok | Ok |
| S5) Total process terminated | Ok | Ok |

## 4.4   External State Changes

The external change of data object states is typical for development or manufacturing processes in practice. As example consider a real world failure (e.g., a faulty electrical component) [1] that necessitates a change of the current state of a data object. As discussed earlier, this kind of change may affect the whole OLC structure. Fig. 9 (Box A) shows an example of the external state change of a data object. According to the OLC structure, dependent state transitions must be revoked and OLCs of dependent data objects must be changed. As can be seen from Fig. 9, further data objects have to be involved - even though there is no direct dependency to the initially changed data object. A detailed discussion of this point will be subject of future publications.

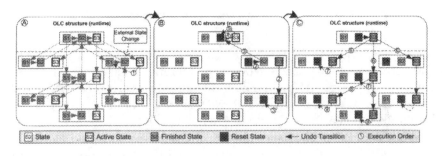

**Fig. 9.** (External) change of a single data object state and its consequences

# 5  Related Work

*Workflow management systems* (WfMS) follow the idea of separating business logic from application code [9]. The resulting workflow specifications can be instantiated and executed during runtime. Several approaches exist for adapting single process instances to handle exceptional situations during runtime [10]. In this paper, we assumed that processes trigger data state transitions. These single processes might be realized as workflows. However, manual mapping of data-driven *structures* to workflow structures leads to inflexible and large workflow models. The result is a mixture of data structure and process logics, which increases complexity for execution and maintenance during runtime and is thus not applicable for data-driven process structures.

*Data-driven approaches*, such as *Case Handling* [2], provide concepts for flexible process execution based on data dependencies. Activities are linked with data items. The execution order of the activities during runtime depends on the availability of data. *Product Driven Case Handling* [3] describes the utilization of the case handling approach for product oriented process design. The idea is to model the process according to product characteristics. The advantage of the case handling approach is the flexible and efficient execution of processes. Case handling does not explicitly consider data states (i.e., domain specific data states), the definition of hierarchical data structures and the automated generation of data-driven process structures.

*Product-driven Workflow Design* defines an analytical method for the product structure based (re-)design of workflows [4]. The idea is to generate a workflow sequence for producing products based on *bills of material* and three design criteria (*quality, costs* and *time*). The goal of this approach is the precise derivation of a process execution sequence according to the product structure. However, we believe that our approach enables a more flexible method for process modeling. In addition, we focus more on the flexible execution of data driven process based on data state dependencies than on optimization criteria.

The idea of *goal-based approaches* [5] is to generate the process based on a specified initial (and final) condition. Therefore, a task ontology with activities - including data input and output - is defined. The necessary task network is generated (e.g., using planning techniques from artificial intelligence) based on the specified output goal. However, this approach does not deal with the special requirements of data-driven process structures based on data states as well as with flexible runtime adaptations.

There are also similarities of our application when compared to domain specific approaches. A project that considers the requirements of the automotive development processes is *WEP* [6]. This approach allows for process definition of both structured and unstructured parts. WEP combines WfMS with the goal-based approach. WEP includes also mechanisms for process synchronization based on *data quality*. However, the WEP does not consider the generation process structures according to a data structure.

*AHEAD* offers dynamic support for (software) development processes [7]. The *CoMa* product model allows for the definition of configurations, i.e., data structures with dependencies between data objects. The *DYNAMITE* activity model enables the flexible execution of corresponding processes. Based on the modeled relationships between data and processes, dynamic task nets are generated. Thus, the approach also separates the data structure from the process structure. However, the relevance of data states as well as relationships between data states are not discussed in this approach.

## 6   Summary and Outlook

The more complex products are the more complex the coordination of related processes becomes. The data-driven generation of these process structures is therefore crucial to their efficient modeling and execution and demands the utilization of data structures. as well as support for process enactment and coordination. The consideration of (product) data life cycles for the definition of data-driven processes is crucial. In this paper, we have discussed the core challenges of data-driven process structures based on a data state oriented view. In addition, we have presented the opportunities of the separation of data and process structures for flexible adaptations during runtime.

Further points, such as data flows in data-driven process structures, concurrently executed processes for one data object (leading to several active states), exception handling (e.g., by using transaction) and the differentiation between changeable and not changeable data states (e.g., physical state *Produced*) as well as applying the approach for a real world process will be subject of further research in this area.

## References

1. Müller, D., Herbst, J., Hammori, M., Reichert, M.: IT support for release management processes in the automotive industry. In: BPM. (2006)
2. Aalst, W., Weske, M., Grünbauer, D.: Case handling: A new paradigm for business process support. DKE **53**(2) (2005) 129–162
3. Aalst, W., Berens, P.J.S.: Beyond workflow management: Product-driven case handling. In: GROUP. (2001) 42–51
4. Reijers, H., Limam, S., Aalst, W.: Product-based workflow design. Management Information Systems **20**(1) (2003) 229–262
5. Mentink, R., Wijnker, T., Lutters, D., Kals, H.: Supporting manufacturing environments. (2002)
6. Beuter, T., Dadam, P., Schneider, P.: The WEP model: Adepquate workflow-management for engineering processes. In: ECEC. (1998)
7. Jäger, D., Schleicher, A., Westfechtel, B.: AHEAD: A graph-based system for modeling and managing development processes. In: AGTIVE. (1999) 325–339
8. Crnkovic, I., Asklund, U., Dahlqvist, A.P.: Implementing and Integrating Product Data Management and Software Configuration Management. Artech House Publishers (2003) ISBN 1-58053-498-8.
9. WFMC: Workflow reference model. Technical report, Workflow Management Coalition, Brussels (1994)
10. Reichert, M., Dadam, P.: ADEPTflex: Supporting dynamic changes of workflow without loosing control. JIIS **10**(2) (1998) 93–129

# Business Rules Segregation for Dynamic Process Management with an Aspect-Oriented Framework

Semih Cetin, N. Ilker Altintas, and Remzi Solmaz

Cybersoft Information Technologies, Ata Plaza 3/3, 34758,
Atasehir, Istanbul, Turkey
{semih.cetin, ilker.altintas, remzi.solmaz}@cs.com.tr
http://www.cybersoft.com.tr/english/index.html

**Abstract.** Almost at every tier of software architecture, business rules crosscut several parts of process management such as workflows, task assignments, and business transactions. Managing business rules on its own hence improves the dynamism of processes in the sense of modeling, implementing, executing, and even maintenance. Moreover, seamless integration with the rest of the picture may offer further dynamism, but this requires smart and reasonably reflective application frameworks for industrial systems. Here, aspect orientation comes to rescue since it mainly aims the separation of crosscutting concerns such as business rules. This paper presents a practical Aspect-Oriented Framework for rule-based business process management where all aspects, facts, rules and rule-sets can be defined and managed dynamically by means of a GUI console. Moreover, this lightweight framework has been implemented in conformance to Adaptive Object Model to facilitate the process dynamism through declarative techniques for design and bytecode engineering for seamless integration.

## 1 Introduction

Business Process Management (BPM) is an emerging technology that organizes the flow of business processes in terms of workflows, rules, and other business entities for improving the efficiency of processes as they are defined, executed, managed and changed without troubles. In this respect, a business process is defined as inclusive and dynamically coordinated set of collaborative/transactional activities [24].

BPM solutions primarily provide the ability to orchestrate and monitor workflows among people and business entities under the supremacy of business rules. Therefore, such solutions are expected to have critical decision points defined and implemented either within a given process or among several processes executed by the workflows. This understanding figures out that business rules are usually tangled in and scattered through today's IT solutions not only within the isolated processes, but also among the workflow-directed processes. Besides, they may occur in different forms like content-based ones at presentation tier for rich clients or workflow-based ones at Web tier for enterprise applications. Therefore, using server-side rule engines may not be sufficient alone to achieve process dynamism against the variety and spreading of business rules.

J. Eder, S. Dustdar et al. (Eds.): BPM 2006 Workshops, LNCS 4103, pp. 193–204, 2006.
© Springer-Verlag Berlin Heidelberg 2006

Aspect orientation is an emerging technology having the first and foremost goal of providing a clear separation and seamless composition of crosscutting concerns such as business rules. This paper introduces such a practical Aspect-Oriented Framework (AOF), "RUMBA ([RU]le-based [M]odel for [B]asic [A]spects)", which provides a declarative environment with a GUI console for rule-based business process modeling. It basically enables the design of any business entity (e.g. person) through the dynamic composition of feature-driven "basic aspects" (e.g. identity as a permanent feature and instructorship as a varying feature used when person is expected to be an instructor). Moreover, every basic aspect such as instructorship may contain other basic aspects, recursively. RUMBA allows the dynamic definition of facts, rules, and rule-sets, too.

In addition to the modeling environment, RUMBA offers a lightweight framework for dynamic integration of business rules with other business processes or business services using "Reflective Aspect", "Reflective Rule" and "Data Face" architectural patterns. These patterns are implemented entirely in Adaptive Object Model (AOM) to dynamically manage basic aspects, facts, rules and rule-sets. Main contribution of the paper is identifying the extensive set of business rules crosscutting the every tier of enterprise application architectures and proposing an AOF to segregate, dynamically manage, and transparently bind these rules to the rest of the picture.

We discuss the existing approaches for business rules segregation towards dynamic process management in the next section. Then comes the taxonomy of business rules crosscutting the architectural tiers of enterprise applications. The paper continues with the design rationale for RUMBA framework and the way it facilitates dynamic process management. Finally, paper ends with the conclusion.

## 2   Existing Approaches for Business Rules Segregation

Managing business rules apart from other business aspects may provide an efficient infrastructure for software flexibility and adaptability, hence, dynamism. Structured development proposed information hiding and modularization principles such as [22]. Introduction of design patterns [13] affected the way to model separation of concerns with a set of patterns (delegate, proxy, visitor, MVC, responsibility chain, etc.) and other object-oriented techniques [5, 11, 12]. Nevertheless, they all have very limited support for process dynamism both for modeling and execution.

Study of recent trends revealed that dynamically modifiable processes and object-oriented views of workflow definitions deserve a "serious attention" from researchers [19]. It is realized by the static hierarchies of class definitions such that once they have been specified and implemented, it would be so hard to modify or adapt dynamically to ever-changing needs of business people. Ever desired dynamic process management cannot acquire such reflexes through static object-oriented hierarchies [26]. Similarly, business processes and other entities must be purified from the crosscutting rules for better process dynamism. This purification requires a dynamic domain model and a declarative environment where actual business processes, associated business entities and controlling business rules can be tailored like Lego toys. Therefore, more dynamic object representation models are required and the commonsense for that is AOM.

AOM[1] is a model that represents classes, attributes, and relationships as metadata. Users change the metadata (object model) to reflect changes in the domain to modify the system's behavior. That is why AOM can be used as a reflective architecture if part of a system such as business rules is constantly changing or if you want to allow users to dynamically configure/extend their system that can lead to "program without programming" [28]. The design of AOM involves three major activities: defining the business entities, rules and relationships; developing an engine for instantiating and manipulating these entities according to their rules in the application; and developing tools for describing these entities, rules and relationships [27]. Thus, reflectivity is an implied concept in AOM, however a generic middleware should be implemented to achieve that reflectivity. Even though separation of business rules from other business entities is not the first-class target of AOM, it can be achieved by implementing proper architectural and/or design patterns with it [2].

Similarly, Aspect-Oriented Programming (AOP) is another approach to be used for business rules segregation [7]. AOP proposes that applications are better structured by separately specifying the various concerns that can be weaved together into a coherent program [10, 17]. These related concerns are grouped as "aspects", and AOP provides appropriate isolation, composition and reuse of the code used to implement them. This is particularly useful when these concerns are crosscutting design decisions that have many objects leading to different places in the code doing the same thing like logging [18]. Even it is pointed out in a recent publication that AOP can be used to separate business rule concerns from other business entities semantically [6]. A group of AOP approaches such as AspectJ [23], Composition Filters [1], HyperJ [16], and DemeterJ [21] exist today. Moreover, several aspect-oriented frameworks[2] like AspectWerkz, Nanning, JAC, Colt, JBossAOP, dynaop, and DynamicAspects are available.

AOM and AOP can be used for segregating the business rules so that rule inference engines or workflow management systems can separately execute them. First, it is our observation that they approach the problem from a single line of insight: AOP intends "functional dynamism" whereas AOM provisions "architectural reflectivity". Second, highly capable rule inference engines like ILOG[3] or JESS[4] and workflow management systems like Staffware[5] are not versatile enough to be used at every tier. For example, they are not suitable for client side rule execution for Rich Internet Applications (RIA) [2, 3] because of high resource needs and lack of dynamic deployment characteristics.

## 3  Taxonomy of Business Rules and Design Rationale for RUMBA

Business rules have received a lot of attention and the main focus has been on the ability to make applications flexible and amenable to change, which is known to be dynamism in general. Both researchers and practitioners are convinced that business

---

[1]  Meta Data and Adaptive Object Model: http://www.adaptiveobjectmodel.com
[2]  Open Source Aspect-Oriented Frameworks in Java: http://java-source.net/
[3]  ILOG Business Rule Management Engine: http://www.ilog.com
[4]  JESS, Te Rule Engine for Java Platform: http://herzberg.ca.sandia.gov/jess/
[5]  Staffware BPM Solutions, Acquired by TIBCO: http://www.staffware.com

rules require explicit treatment for a detailed classification to ensure process agility [4, 9, 15, 20, 25]. The authors present another taxonomy here in Fig. 1 for separation of business rules crosscutting the BPM. This figure specifies the process management as an orthogonal model to architectural tiers of enterprise applications and classifies the business rules again according to this orthogonal model.

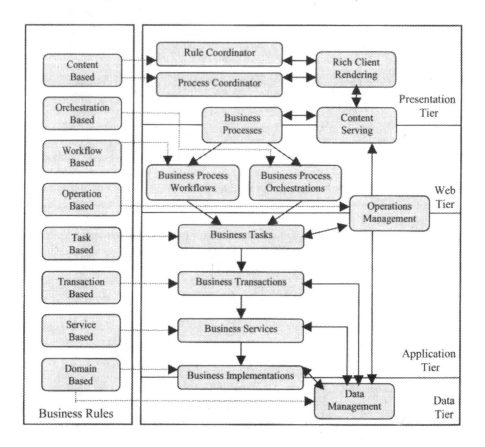

**Fig. 1.** Separation of Business Rules Crosscutting The Process Management Being Orthogonal to Architectural Tiers

## 3.1 The Need for Business Rules Classification

Fig. 1 identifies the general architectural model of BPM where business processes consist of process workflows and process orchestrations. Both process workflows and orchestrations specify how process tasks are structured, but the only difference is that process workflows supervise the flow of user tasks within an organizational process, whereas orchestrations administer the collaboration of internal user tasks with external processes owned by other institutions. In that sense, process orchestrations must have at least one external process task to be accessed with XML-like interfaces.

Business tasks are the internal activities within an organization generated either by the underlying business model or by the users themselves as reminders for their own benefit or in order to delegate work to others. Tasks may contain several independent business transactions as the single and atomic unit of work for a consistent change in the state of a business process. A business transaction may be as short as giving a purchase order or as long as a mortgage (from the initial mortgage application to final satisfaction being sent after the last payment). Business transaction is not the same as data processing transaction, and a single business transaction may contain several data processing transactions encapsulated in business services. Hence, a business service is the combination of business implementations (the set of interrelated data processing transactions) managed by a computational model.

Such an understanding of BPM and applying to enterprise systems like the ones we experienced in banking and insurance domains revealed the categorization of business rules identified in Fig. 2. This taxonomy is performed due to the attributes of business rules such as "complexity" (simple, composite, with backward or forward reasoning), "criticality" (severe, moderate, low), "frequency of change" (high, vibrant, fair, low), "order of execution" (first, last, any order), "type of access" (internal, external, both), or "responsibility" (business, IT, both). For example, domain-based rules have severe criticality since they are the last point for checking data integrity, however content-based ones are not that much critical since they will be double or triple checked through transaction-based and service-based rules at several other tiers.

| Business Rule Category | Complexity | Criticality | Frequency of Change | Order of Execution | Type of Access | Responsibility |
|---|---|---|---|---|---|---|
| Content-based | Simple | Low | Vibrant | Any | Internal | Business |
| Orchestration-based | Simple | Moderate | Low | First | Both | Business |
| Workflow-based | Composite | Moderate | Low | First | Internal | Business |
| Operation-based | Composite | Moderate | High | Any | Internal | IT |
| Task-based | Reasoning | Moderate | Vibrant | Any | Internal | Both |
| Transaction-based | Reasoning | Severe | Fair | Any | Internal | Both |
| Service-based | Reasoning | Severe | Vibrant | Any | Both | Both |
| Domain-based | Reasoning | Severe | Vibrant | First | Internal | Both |

**Fig. 2.** Business Rules Taxonomy

### 3.2  Classification of the Business Rules

Categorizing business rules due to aforementioned attributes facilitates the business rule management issues such as "storage", "caching", "administration" or "execution performance", respectively. We classify the business rules into eight major groups:

- **Content-Based Rules:** control the conditions for variability of rendering platforms such as generating HTML for Web-browsers but WML for mobiles, and include data validation and verification such as checking the age for having driving license. They should be defined once in the system and a proper framework should execute the same business rules both on clients and servers. Whenever such a rule changes, it should be modified once and this update must be automatically reflected to both client-side Rule Coordinator (see Fig. 1) and server-side rule engines. Therefore, a lightweight rule engine that may be used both on clients and servers will simplify the application design. This lightweight engine then executes the identical content-based rules by using the client-side data provided by visual widgets and the server-side data provided by business entities such as process workflows or services even composed of RUMBA basic aspects. In our approach, the content-based rules are categorized into a separate group for having a single point of "administration" and dynamic "caching" of the business rules even on clients. There exist a lot of such rules that can be instantly executed on clients. Otherwise they should be handled on servers that may increase the network traffic unintentionally.

- **Orchestration-Based Rules:** are situations governing the integration of business processes with external ones such as validating the social security ID by means of a Web service from the Social Security Organization to issue credit in a core banking application. It is important to implement orchestration-based rules in an expressible manner such as BPEL[6] or RuleML[7], since both parties should be able to agree on the set of conditions for their business processes to be merged. Hence, business process orchestration engines should be incorporated with a separate rule engine so that exposition/imposition with expressive languages should be fully supported. Moreover, business process orchestration and rule engines must be communicating over a high-speed protocol such as direct method calls instead of slower XML-like interfaces. In our approach, we classify the orchestration-based rules in a separate category to increase the "execution performance" of such type of rules.
- **Workflow-Based Rules:** supervise the workflow of user tasks within a process. A typical example is a set of rules for managing the application to damage repayment in insurance business domain in such a way that when applied to Class-A agencies the repayment is consecutively checked by at least two members of the experts' council whereas when applied to regional office Form-A and Form-B are filled out by an expert. Like content-based rules, workflow-based rules should be able to get executed at server and client sides as connected to process workflow engine.
- **Task-Based Rules:** are circumstances under which the set of business transactions will be executed in coordination. An example to task-based rules is issuing the credit in a core banking application in such a way that if the credit amount is more than 50.000$, then credibility checking through Central Credit Bureau transaction will be executed otherwise direct scoring transaction will be activated. Task-based rules should be executable in conjunction with operation-based rules as well since certain tasks can be assigned to predefined process workflows or orchestrations based on user authorizations, which is an operational concern. Task-based rules may be needed to be inferred with operation-based rules in "backward reasoning", which may complicate the achievement of adaptability and performance.
- **Transaction-Based Rules:** govern the association of related services under certain conditions. A typical example is the forever use of external Web services of Central Credit Bureau if the credit is corporate type, and the use of local credibility services in the case of individual type. Like task-based rules, transaction-based

---

[6] BPEL: http://www.oasis-open.org/committees/tc_home.php?wg_abbrev=wsbpel
[7] RuleML: http://www.ruleml.org/

rules may demand on domain-based rules kept by Data Management (see Fig. 1) that will be executed again in "backward reasoning". For that, keeping simple rules in database queries might be necessary just to get rid of the repetitive definitions of same rules, and this will affect the "storage" and "caching" issues in business rule management.

– **Service-Based Rules:** administer the circumstances for the combinatorial use of business implementations such as selecting the implementation based on quick sort algorithm for limited set of interactive business transactions instead of using the implementations based on "order by" clause of SQL queries for batch transactions. These rules should be executed very fast and the context that should be transferred between rule engine and business implementation should be handled carefully for high volume database queries that may be a concern for "execution performance".

– **Domain-Based Rules:** are the mostly referred and executed rules such as a car is valid to be insured if it is younger than 20 years in insurance domain. They should be executed very fast. Moreover, any change request in domain-based rules should be reflected automatically to business implementation without further compilation and deployment. Thus, "execution performance" and "administration" are of utmost importance.

– **Operation-Based Rules:** manage the operational concerns of an application such as scheduled execution constraints. A typical example is that batch credit due list can only be generated between 01:00 and 06:00 am. Another example is user role determinations in the sense of authorization constraints like a teller cannot execute "customer account update" transaction but branch manager can with the permission granted by central management. They are most likely to change among all, hence the level of dynamism for maintaining operation-based rules and composing with other business aspects without compilation and deployment are of utmost value.

## 4  Dynamic Process Management with RUMBA Framework

RUMBA liberally adopts the vision of a reflective architecture where business rules and other business aspects can be defined dynamically and integrated seamlessly. It uses the term "basic aspect" to facilitate that everything in software modeling can be represented in terms of dynamic features. A basic aspect is a generic container that can host three things: basic and custom data attributes, other aspects as sub-aspects that can yield a very powerful hierarchical and recursively accessible structure, and method implementers having a standard invocation interface. Such a flexible structure allows the modeling of any set of concerns at design time by declaring an aspect having the largest set of attributes, sub-aspects and method implementers.

As an example; a person can be an instructor at university, a father at home and a driver at traffic. In that sense, the same person can be declared in RUMBA to be an aspect to hold the widest set of the following other sub-aspects: "instructorship", "fathership", and "drivership". Supportively, by definition it can hold attributes such as age, sex, name, surname; and methods such as getAge(), getName(), setName(), getSex() to be used generically in any occurrence of the three roles. RUMBA provides a lightweight runtime environment to instantiate a person with "instructorship", "fathership" or "drivership" role by dynamically creating first the common attributes, related methods of being person as well as the desired sub-aspects depending on role type. Whichever role it has been created with, this aspect can be managed with generic access methods like "aspect.invoke("getAge", aspectParams)", or attributes can be accessed as basic Java data types like "aspect.getAttribute("name").toString()". This AOM design unleashes the static dependencies of object hierarchies and provides a closer performance to the Java object access in contrast to the original AOM baseline.

In a clarification, RUMBA synthesizes aspect orientation with AOM for the high performance separation of concerns that can provide a dynamic weaving approach. Unlike classical AOP approaches that has a primary object model together with those crosscutting concerns such as logging and persistence implemented as aspects in "asymmetry", RUMBA presumes that even this primary object model can also be declaratively designed by the GUI console and embodied by underlying framework which is capable of composing all these basic aspects in symmetry [14]. To this end, RUMBA has even extensions to take any custom data type into picture as defined by the user, thanks to the architectural patterns of RUMBA explained below.

## 4.1 Data Face Pattern

RUMBA designers introduced a novel approach to wrap existing data types of Java language in a dynamic manner, provided a way to have custom data types expressed in Java with the AOF, exposed basic and custom data types to RUMBA users, and named this approach as "Data Face" pattern. It is an architectural pattern heavily using bytecode engineering to instantiate derived "face" types from standard "core" types as shown in Fig. 3. RUMBA uses a generic Data type as the base of all basic and custom data types, and other Arguments, Aspect, and RumbaFactory are all using that.

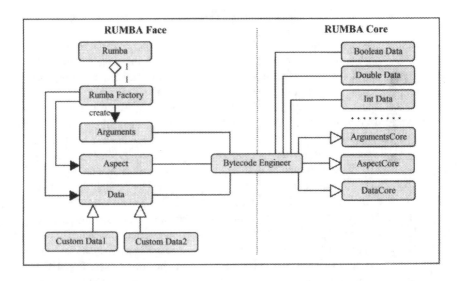

**Fig. 3.** Data Face Pattern

## 4.2  Reflective Aspect Pattern

Reflective Aspect Pattern is another architectural pattern inspired from "Adaptability Aspects Pattern" [8] for providing the reflectivity of basic aspects in terms of design, definition, implementation and maintenance. As shown in Fig. 4, it includes:

- **Generative Aspect Model:** An aspect with reflective properties is nothing than a template definition of adaptive objects complying with AOM structure in RUMBA.
- **Aspect Factory** is a singleton in the core library so that it enables the creation of dynamic aspects at runtime due to the templates kept in Aspect Type Repository.
- **Aspect Type Repository** is composed of set of classes to keep the aspect templates to help Aspect Factory for the instantiation of reflective aspects accordingly. To this end, aspect definition screens will be the front-end of this Central Repository.
- **Aspect (Template) Definition:** Aspect attributes, methods, aspect and sub-aspects and the collaborations with other aspects are all definable with managerial screens.
- **Method Delegator:** Java Method Implementers can be associated with dynamic aspects by means of underlying bytecode engineer.

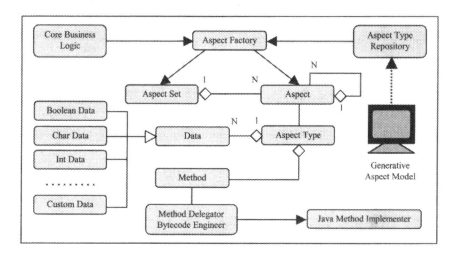

**Fig. 4.** Reflective Aspect Pattern

## 4.3  Reflective Rule Pattern

Similar to Reflective Aspect, we also need a model in which business departments can simply define business rules. Supportively, we propose another meta-model called as Reflective Rule pattern to manage business rules and their relationships with reflective aspects as shown in Fig. 5. "RuleFactory" is the main creator of all rule-related parts. "Rules" contain "Facts" which can be of three types: simple value checks expressions, database lookups and Java method calls. First two are handled dynamically but for the last, an implementer should be associated at runtime through bytecode engineering. "RuleSets" are used to express composite rules. By using the "RuleContext" as the context of pointcuts between rules and basic aspects, any type of rules introduced in Section 3 can be composed into the process management dynamically.

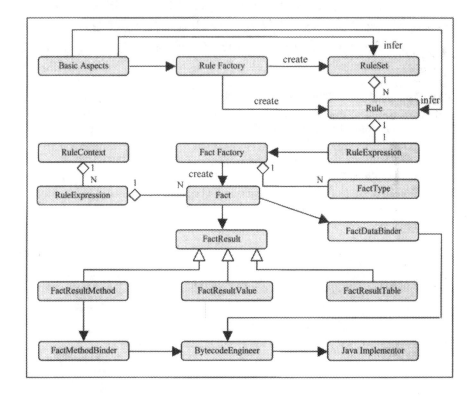

**Fig. 5.** Reflective Rule Pattern

## 4.4 Dynamic Process Management

The logical classification of business rules given in Section 3 aids design to prevent them from crosscutting the process management concerns. However, such a logical design should be able to turn into a physical implementation by a framework that guides the dynamic integration with processes through inherent architectural patterns. RUMBA facilitates the dynamic processes management with:

- **Declarative Environments** to enable the definition of basic aspects, rules and rule-related elements by GUI screens to unleash business people from IT intricacies.
- **Standard Structure for Domain Modeling** to empower IT designers to deal with only simple and easy to model a hierarchical basic elements, that are basic aspects.
- **Seamless Composition of Rules** with a very lightweight framework to associate simple/composite rules with visual widgets at clients and basic aspects at servers.
- **Standard Interfaces** to form pointcut contexts where aspectual data and other rule-related attributes are managed separately through standard Java calls. This will facilitate the integration with process management through standard interfaces, too.

- **Common Use of Rule Contexts** with basic aspects in core functionality and many parts of process management. In contrast to classical approaches, RUMBA enables the sharing of its rule context (it is Java serializable) as is with process engines.
- **Coexistence with Diverse Process Engines** is inherently possible with any sort of business process engine within workflows and orchestrations since it relies on a simple and standard interface; pure Java based rule context having aspects as well.
- **Versatility of Use** on multi-platforms both on servers and clients even including mobiles as long as a JRE 1.4 runtime is provided.
- **Running with RIA Frameworks** is supported by default and any JavaBean can be used for dynamic process management. Currently, it is available on the Aurora RIA [2, 3] framework of Cybersoft, but could be implemented easily on others as well.

## 5  Conclusion

Effective management of business processes in enterprise applications becomes more and more important today. Thus, responding to ever changing business requirements in shorter cycles may put an organization ahead of others in the stiff competition. One way of achieving dynamic process management is the segregation of business rules from other business aspects like business entities and business processes.

In this paper, the authors presented the significance of business rules segregation and to this end, a comprehensive taxonomy of business rules has been introduced to separate business rules crosscutting the process management issues that are orthogonal to the architectural tiers. Such a classification has introduced eight major business rule types that should be modeled separately from the process management.

We also introduced a practical aspect-oriented framework, RUMBA, which has flawless integration with rule-based development concerns by having the visionary perspective for aspect-orientation where every concern of software development can be modeled in terms of basic aspects. Thanks to proper modification of Adaptive Object Model, architectural reflectivity can be achieved without loosing performance, ease of development and maintainability. This practical AOF has been used and proven in the development of new generation Web-based core insurance application for the largest insurance company of Turkey where dynamic process management is of utmost significance stemmed from the nature of insurance business domain.

## References

1. Aksit, M., Tekinerdogan, B.: Aspect-Oriented Programming Using Composition Filters, ECOOP'98 Workshop Reader (1997)
2. Altintas, N. I., Cetin, S.: Integrating a Software Product Line with Rule-Based Business Process Modeling, TEAA: VLDB Workshop, TEAA 2005, LNCS 3888 (2005) 15-28
3. Altintas, N. I., Surav, M., Keskin, O., Cetin, S.: Aurora Software Product Line, Turkish Software Architecture Design Workshop, 2nd National Software Engineering Symposium, Ankara – Turkey, http://trese.cs.utwente.nl/TSAD/Papers/aurora.pdf (2005)
4. Bajec, M., Krisper, M., Rupnik, R.: Using Business Rules Technologies To Bridge The Gap Between Business And Business Applications, Proceedings of the IFIP 16th World Computer Congress (2000) 77-85

5. Buschmann, F. et al: Pattern-Oriented Software Architecture, Volume 1: A System of Patterns, John Wiley & Sons (1996)
6. Cibran, M., D'Hondt, M.: High-Level Specification of Business Rules and Their Crosscutting Connections, AOSD'06 (2006)
7. D'Hondt M.: Hybrid Aspects for Integrating Rule-Based Knowledge and Object-Oriented Functionality, Ph.D. Thesis, Vrije Universiteit, Brussel (2004)
8. Dantas A., Borba P.: Adaptability Aspects: An Architectural Pattern for Structuring Adaptive Applications, SugarLoaf- PLoP'2003, Brazil (2003)
9. Date, C. J.: What Not How: The Business Rules Approach To Application Development, Addison Wesley Longman, Inc. (2000)
10. Elrad, T., Aksit, M., Kiczales, G., Lieberherr, K., Ossher, H.: Discussing Aspects of AOP, Communications of the ACM 44, (2001) 33–38
11. Fayad, M., Schmidt, D., Johnson, R.: Building Application Frameworks: Object-Oriented Foundations of Framework Design, John Wiley & Sons (1999)
12. Fowler, M.: Patterns of Enterprise Application Architecture, Addison-Wesley (2002)
13. Gamma, E. et al: Design Patterns: Elements of Reusable Object-Oriented Software, Addison-Wesley (1994)
14. Harrison, W. H., Ossher, H. L., Tarr, P. L.: Asymmetrically vs. Symmetrically Organized Paradigms for Software Composition, IBM Research Division, RC22685 (2002)
15. Herbst, H.: Business Rules in Systems Analysis: A Meta-Model and Repository System, Information Systems, 21 (2) (1996) 147-166
16. IBM: HyperJ: Multi-Dimensional Separation of Concerns for Java, http://www.research. ibm.com/hyperspace/HyperJ/HyperJ.htm (2001)
17. Kiczales, G.: Aspect-Oriented Programming, ACM Computing Survey, Volume 4: 157 (1996)
18. Kiczales, G., Lamping, J., Mendhekar, A., Maeda, C., Lopes, C. V., Loingtier, J. M., Irwin, J.: Aspect–Oriented Programming, in ECOOP'97, LNCS 1241 (1997) 220–242
19. Mohan, C.: Recent Trends in Workflow Management Products, Standards and Research, Volume 164, http://www.almaden.ibm.com/cs/exotica/wfnato97.ps (1998) 396–409
20. Moriarty, T.: Business Rule Management Facility: System Architect, Intelligent Enterprise, 3 (12) (2000)
21. Northeastern University, College of Computer and Information Science: DemeterJ: Aspect-Oriented Software Development, http://www.ccs.neu.edu/home/lieber/demeter.html (1996)
22. Parnas, D. L.: On the Criteria to be used in Decomposing Systems into Modules, Communications of the ACM, v.15 n.12 (1972) 1053-1058
23. Ramnivas L.: AspectJ in Action, Practical Aspect-Oriented Programming (2003)
24. Smith, H., Fingar, P.: Business Process Management (BPM): The Third Wave, Meghan-Kiffer Press (2003)
25. Struck, D.L.: Business Rule Continuous Requirements Environment, PhD Thesis, Colorado Technical University (1999)
26. Tufekci, O., Cetin, S., Altintas, N. I.: How to Process [Business] Processes, Integrated Design and Process Technology, IDPT-2006, Society for Design and Process Science, http://www.cybersoft.com.tr/free/publications/H2PP.pdf (2006)
27. Yoder J. W., Balaguer, F., Johnson, R.: Adaptive Object Models for Implementing Business Rules, OOPSLA (2001)
28. Yoder J. W., Balaguer F., Johnson R.: Architecture and Design of Adaptive Object Models, Intriguing Technology Presentation at OOPSL '01, ACM SIGPLAN Notices, ACM Press (2001)

# A Dynamic Workflow Management System for Coordination of Cooperative Activities

François Charoy[1], Adnene Guabtni[1], and Miguel Valdes Faura[2]

[1] University Henri Poincaré Nancy 1 - INRIA - LORIA laboratory,
BP 239, F-54506
Vandoeuvre-lès-Nancy Cedex, France
[2] Bull R&D, 1, rue de Provence
38130 Echirolles (France)
Francois.Charoy@loria.fr

**Abstract.** This paper comes back to the problem of coordination of cooperative activities with a Workflow management system. First, we describe the differences that we have noted between business processes and cooperative processes. Then we present a set of requirements for a Workflow management system that aims to support cooperative workflow, and among these requirements are high flexibility and dynamicity. Then we describe how this has been taken into account in the development of the Bonita workflow management system that proposes to remove the idea of process model to work only with process instances that can be derived from each others or that can be composed.
Keywords:Adaptive processes,Cooperative processes,Architectures and tools for dynamic processes.

## 1 Introduction

Using workflow technology to support cooperative activities is an old idea, taking its sources in Office Information Systems. A lot of work has been devoted to this problem during the 90's with the advent of the CSCW field. It must be noted that although automation of business process management and web services composition has gained in visibility and acceptance, its application to coordinate cooperative work is not yet a success. But with the greater acculturation of people to cooperative work over the Internet, the need for better support for coordination if beginning to appear with a greater pressure. A lot of domain, such as e-learning, software development, content management systems, scientific and medical applications, crisis mitigation systems require now better support for coordination and tracking of individual activities.

One of the assumption that has been made some years ago is that workflow and business process modeling could be used, regarding some evolutions, to support the coordination of cooperative activities. A common belief is that the ability to easily change process types or process instances is still considered as an important issue for acceptance of Workflow management System in organisations. In a cooperative environment, this requirement is even more important. Business processes can be considered as stable regarding cooperative

J. Eder, S. Dustdar et al. (Eds.): BPM 2006 Workshops, LNCS 4103, pp. 205–216, 2006.

processes. A business process takes time to be designed and implemented, but this cost is redeemed by the number of its execution and by the expected raise of productivity. Cooperative processes like software development processes are of different nature. They are long lasting processes with a high potential for evolution during their life-time. They are not executed so often. Spending a lot of time to design and implement such a process would be considered as a waste of time.

We consider, following the proponents of ad-hoc workflow for cooperative processes that, defining a complete cooperative process from the beginning with all its details is almost impossible. The process for software development or for technical report production may not be known entirely at their beginning. They may have to be refined during their execution. Our point of view is that a cooperative process will evolve during its execution. Thus, it must be very easy to change during its execution, instance by instance. We try to push this hypothesis to its extreme by not making the difference between model and instance.

To summarize, a Workflow Management System that aims to support cooperative activities must first provide the same kind of support as a WFMS for Business processes i.e. activities, activity dependency management, performer and resources management. It must also be very flexible and allow easy modifications by the users, instance by instance.

In the first part of this paper, we will try to summarize the differences between so-called business processes and cooperative processes. Then we will list the requirements that we want to met. The next part will present the model underlying the Bonita Workflow Management System and how it's flexibility can potentially meet the requirements that we have described.

## 2   Business vs Cooperative Processes

Cooperative and business processes are different in nature. We can identify a number of differences between a WFMS that has to support cooperative process and a WFMS that has to support Business Processes. These differences are the following:

*The number of process models.* In a cooperative environment, the ratio between the number of execution of a process and the number of process definitions is small compared to a business environment. Processes are built from process fragments on a project by project basis. Pushing this assumption to the extreme, all processes in a cooperative environment are different. That means essentially that the participants to a process must be able to design the process.

*The process structure is simpler.* Business process can be relatively complex with many alternatives, compensating activities and the rest. When defining a business process, designer try to consider almost every possible case. Cooperative processes are simpler in general, consisting on sequences of activities executing in loops[1]. We consider that cooperative process are generally the concatenation of successive steps that lead to the production of a final result for the project. It may still happen to find a complex structure inside the steps. However, the organisation of the process itself must be understandable by the participants to the process. Thus it cannot be too complicated.

*The process evolves more often.* A business process is less subject to evolution than a cooperative process. The long duration of a cooperative process encompass in itself the need for change. Changes in the environment or in the goal of the process have more chances to occur. A business process is supposedly shorter and thus less subject to changes during its execution time.

*The process is user driven.* Cooperative processes governs cooperative projects where participants are concerned by a common goal. This is less the case in a classical business process where people are mostly concerned by the task they have to execute. Thus, cooperative workflow management systems should provide their users with a clear view of what has been done, who does what and what remains to be done (even if that is expected to change). A cooperative process is the result of a consensus between its participants.

Althoug these differences are important, we still think that it is possible to adapt workflow models and workflow management systems. in the next part we describe the requirements that are important for such a system.

## 3 Requirements for Cooperative Processes Support System

A system that aims to support explicit cooperative work coordination needs to provide some incentive to its users. Even if there is a feeling for better support for coordination in distributed cooperative project, and even if there is some will to set up clear procedures at the beginning, the use of these procedures and tools to track the activities is most often forgotten as soon as the project begins and the pressure to get results raises. If the users lose the feeling that following the process is useful for them, they stop using it, or use it lazily[1,2].

*Designing the processes.* In a cooperative setting, the plan and the process to follow is generally the result of some consensus after discussions between the members of a team. Decisions are taken and actions to be done are distributed among them. Most of the time, these actions are small processes that have to be refined and connected to the overall group coordination.

For instance, when doing software development, the development plan is decided and then refined. Creating a cooperative process from scratch would be very long and error prone. Most of the time, when starting a cooperative process, even with implicit coordination, people refer to existing process that they have

---

[1] Most design process for instance require several execution of the same activities to reach a given result.

executed before. They try to reuse part of their previous experience in the new project. A cooperative workflow management system must be able to reproduce this behavior by allowing the reuse of fragment of processes that have already been executed.

A cooperative WFMS must provide an efficient library of process instances or fragments that can be easily integrated in a new process (for instance a process for paper reviewing or a process for code release in a software development project).

*Users control the process.* Users participating in a cooperative process should be able to monitor and change the process. Business process are constrained by management and cannot be changed by end-users. This is the contrary in a cooperative process. We consider that the cooperative process is the result of its execution (the process is itself a product of the process). Each user has the ability to add/remove/change activities of the process in which they participate.

*Automation of activities.* The incentive to use a workflow management system is not always clear for user. A lot of experiences have shown that if the users find no benefit using this kind of system they will avoid to use it by any means(see [3] and related works). A cooperative workflow management system should provide some assistance, and some automation for the most repetitive tasks and not just control for the management. It must also be sufficiently integrated to the environment to help the users to find the documentation they need to modify, to publish, retrieve and share these documents, to track what happens to them. If these conditions are fulfilled, there is more chance that users will contribute to the process evolution[2].

In order to reach these goals we have started a project some years ago that has resulted in the development of a Workflow engine called Bonita that has been already used in different settings. The Bonita model was designed with these requirements in mind.

## 4    The Bonita Model

The definition of the model has been done with several constraints in mind. Current standard process models are complex. The definition of a process requires specific skills. They are reserved to specialist and cannot be read by common users. Although we know that the complexity of business process definition may require some expertize, we argue as we have said before that cooperative process need to be managed by their end users.

The definition of the Bonita model is inspired from dynamic languages [4]. It does not separate the model (a class) from its instances (objects). Instances can be directly created from the Bonita API, executed and modified dynamically. A new process can be created either from scratch, by cloning an existing process or by importing a process definition inside an other process. On figure 1, on the

---

[2] Of course this remains to be proved by experiences.

left is a window showing the state of the process for a user, and on the right is the state of the process. This window is also an editor, thus the process can be changed at any time.

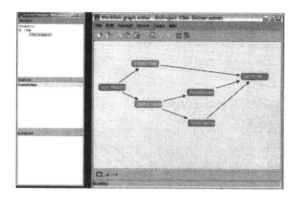

**Fig. 1.** The execution and definition interface

A process describes a set of activities that have to be executed to reach some goal. It has participants that can adopt roles within the process. These roles are used to create the relationship between activities and the user that can execute them. Constraints on the definition of a process are kept minimal to ease its definition by end users. A process is a defined by a set of activities and by dependencies between activities. Dependencies between activities are end/start dependencies, with join conditions and split conditions.

A process is created by a user, the owner of the process. From this point, the process is started. The owner can add activities to the process and dependencies between these activities. A process is started by its owner. It can be terminated automatically when all activities of the process have been terminated, aborted or are dead. It can also be terminated or aborted by a user explicitely.

Activity states are the following : initial, executable, executing, anticipable, anticipating cancelled, aborted, terminated. An activity can be executed as soon as it is created. It is then in the state Executable.

Flexible execution of processes is possible due to the ability to start an activity in advance. This is what we call anticipation. Anticipation which has been already described[5] is a mean to reduce constraints on the execution of cooperative activities. The main idea is that an activity can be executed even when all its activation conditions are not met. But we guarantee that at some time before its termination, they will be met. Thus, at the end of the process execution everything appears to have been executed normally even though some activities have been started before there normal activitation time. The main advantage is that even with strict process definition, flexible execution remains possible. Figure 2 is a case where node1 has been started, node2 and node3 have been started with anticipation and node4 is in a state where it could be started.

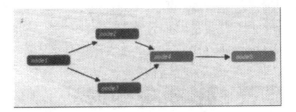

**Fig. 2.** Some activities can be started even when the preceeding ones are not finished

New activities and new dependencies can always be created during the process execution. The only constraints concern the state of activities. It is not possible to change activities and dependencies concerning terminated activities.

The owner of a process can also attach users to the process with specific roles. Users are then participating to the process. They belong to different roles. An activity can only be executed by a user that can take the role specified for the activity.

The workflow engine is able to calculate to do list and executing list for each user participating to a process and to notify users of every change that concerns them.

## 4.1 Process Building Blocks

Of course, defining each new process activity by activity is not a very sound way of working even though we are doing that very often in real life project. The support of the WFMS must appear as valuable and in this case, the risk is that some activities are created at the beginning of the project and no followup occurs. This is often the case with planning tools and can be verified in many open source projects on Sourceforge for instance : a project is created, many tasks and activities are instanciated and assigned and then nothing more happen.

In a cooperative project, the process must be described very easily, based on previous experience. Writing a document as a group has been done many time. If their process require such kind of step, a group of users must be able to find several process fragments that provide a solution for that (plan, edit, review, release or plan, produce, edit, release).

The following example shows different steps in the life of a cooperative project.

**Fig. 3.** The initial process

On figure 3, a small editing process is used to start the production of a document. Several activities are instantiated. Then the process is started and a validation/submit step are added to the process (figure 4).

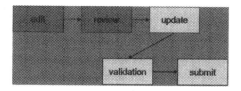

**Fig. 4.** The process is completed with validation/submission

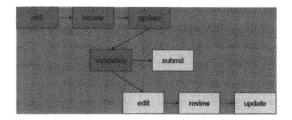

**Fig. 5.** The edition process is reused for a new document

From this result a new document has to be produced. Thus, the editing process is imported again and connected to the validation activity (figure 5).

Process importation and Process cloning are the two main mechanisms that we propose to support this kind of behavior. We follow the path of prototype based language that do not make the difference between classes and instances. Any process instance, running or terminated can be used to instantiate a new process. In this case, activities are reinitialised to their initial state and every properties of the original process are imported in the new one, except users. Thus a process can be build by importing different processes and then by creating dependencies between activities of these fragments. A process can be suspended during this phase. If it is not, state of activities is immediately updated to reflect the new state.

The dynamicity of the model allows this kind of behavior. Dependencies can then be created between existing activities of the process and the imported ones.

### 4.2   Data Flow

A process is not just about coordinating activities. It is also about managing the data that are used by these activities. Our model provides some simple support for process data and has been integrated in a more sophisticated environment for shared data management.

Two kinds of data are directly managed inside a process. Process data and activity data. Process data are properties that can be access and changed by all the activities of a process. Activity data acts as input and output parameters. Each activity has a list of input and output data. These data are represented as properties, with a name, a value and a read/write constraint. Then these data are propagated to the succeeding activities. Conflict may occurs when two properties with the same name are propagated to an activity through an and join node. In this case, we choose to keep the last value for simplcity reasons, but this point need to be consolidated. In cooperative activities, we consider that activities use mostly data from shared workspace (document spaces, source repository) where they commit and checkout data when they need it. For these data, we consider that to each activity, a local workspace is created where the shared data are checked out at the beginning of the activity, and checked in at the end of the activity. Thus conflicts and concurrency problems are managed by the shared repository and depends on its protocol.

## 4.3    Process Correctness

We put very few constraints on the structure of the executing process. This is the cost of dynamicity. Only cycles are detected and forbidden except when they belong to the special iterator construct. A process is always valid. Activities are executable as soon as they meet their start or anticipation condition. A process is considered as terminated when all its activities are dead (not reachable) or terminated. This is a very different approach than the ones that are generally considered in business process management, but we think that flexibility is more important than consistency in this context. As the process is not supposed to be executed a great number of time, consistency problems can be solved when they occur.

## 4.4    Automating Activities

Acceptability of a process control by users depends on the benefits that the users can obtain from the process execution itself. Automation of part of the process is one of these expected benefits. Although many activities in a cooperative workflow are user driven, there are still large part of them that can be automated. Test, compilation, and different kind of supports that can be implemented by services provided by the process execution environment.

In our model, we allow the attachment of scripts that we call hooks to state changes of activities. For instance a script can be associated to the state change from *executable* to *executing* or from *executing* to *terminated* of an activity. When several hooks are associated to the same state change of the same activity, they are all executed in an undefined order. For instance, when a user has finished and editing activity, its workspace can be automatically checked in in a shared repository.

Special kind of activities can be defined as completely automatic. As soon as they become executable, they are executed and all the scripts associated to their state change.

Failure of the execution of a Hook cancel the state change. Thus, hooks can be used to express termination condition on activities. For instance, they can be used to check the status of an activity when the user tries to terminate it. If the check fails, the activity remains in the executing state. Note that state change of activities are atomic and include hook execution. Hook implementation is done in Java or with a script language (BeanShell). Conditions can be expressed using the support provided by the language.

Hooks can be specific to an activity or associated to the process. A hook associated to the process will be executed for a specific event for all activities of the process. This allows to adapt the general behavior of a process.

Of course, hooks can make the definition of a process complex as it requires some programming. Our goal is to provide library of hooks for very generic actions and to provide the ability of using script language to describe simple action. Hook have access to the context of the current activity and they can be used to call WebServices in the scope of the activity execution transaction. Figure 6 is an example of such a hook definition in Java that sends an email when the correct state is reached. This hook is associated with an activity and is executed when the activity is started. The parameters of the hook are objects containing the context of execution, i.e. the activity and the process data.

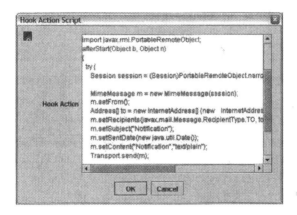

**Fig. 6.** AfterStart hook implementation

Hooks can also be used to modify the current process. We plan to use hooks to generate compensation process when an activity is cancelled or aborted but this is still an ongoing research.

### 4.5 Role Management

Role management is classical. To each process is associated a set of role and activities are associated to roles. User can take role and they can execute activities that are associated to one of their role. Procedure (performer assignements) can also be attached to activities to calculate user assignement.

### 4.6 Awareness

Every event (process change or state change) on a process produces an event that is published in a message queue. Users may register to be notified of these events. They can choose to be notified of every activity termination for a given process. They will receive an email or an instant message. This is a very basic form of awareness. The process edition tool is also kept synchronized with the current state of the process. This is interesting but no so useful as we consider that the pace of execution of a cooperative process is relatively slow, so events will not occur so often.

## 5   The Implementation

The Bonita System (bonita.objectweb.org) is available as Open Source and is actually in use but more for classical business process management than real cooperative one. Its development has started in the LORIA lab and the main support is now provided by Bull R&D. It is implemented on a J2EE Jonas Server and uses the Jabber XMPP protocol for event notifications. Rich Swing clients are maintained up to date with JMS events. A Web interface is also available for an access behind a firewall. Figure 7 provides a view of the Bonita architecture.

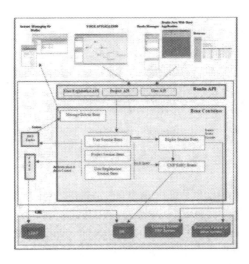

**Fig. 7.** Architecture of Bonita

## 6   Related Work

A lot of work has been devoted to the problem of providing a dynamic of flexible process environment. Some work was devoted to the management of change in processes [6], change in process definition through different techniques [7]. Flexibility and exception handling has also been proposed to manage unexpected situations [8,9]. Other approach like [10] allows for dynamic changes to the process instance but restrictions on the operations that can be applied in order to maintain some consistency. More recent work [11] proposes to combine a classical workflow model with some pocket of flexibility that reduce the constraints on execution. In [12], the authors uses the idea of emergent workflows to allow adaptation of process instances at runtime. It combines planification and workflow management.

A general study on state of the art of correctness criteria for dynamic change in workflow can be found in [13]. The goal of most of this work is to maintain the consistency between the process model and its instances in case of instance or process evolution. All these approaches provide interesting insights on the different kind of flexibility while keeping a correct workflow structure. Our point is that structural consistency is not as important as the ability to build easily dynamic processes that can be controlled by users.

Other works take different directions that are not based on Workflow Management systems. Some years ago, we tried to control process using temporal constraints [14]. In this work, the process was not defined but the state of the system was driven by constraints that forced the system state to go through different stages. The results were interesting but the constraints were difficult to write and to understand for end users. Other work have done in the same direction [15]. Our point of view here is that although rule based systems or constraint based system are interesting, they fail to provide the correct level of support to end users and are hard to maintain. This is why, even with its limitation, the workflow approach is still the best one for us at this time.

## 7    Conclusion and Future Work

With our approach, we have pushed to the extreme the idea of flexibility in workflow management. The process execution is considered as a program execution where the program is written at runtime by its users. Processes are created by hand or by importing or cloning existing processes. Of course, this limit the kind of consistency control that can be done on the process structure, but this allow also quick corrections in case of problems. The only part of the process really known is the one that has already been executed. This requires also to support process definition with library of predefined process fragments that solve generic problems that may occur in cooperative processes (some kind of cooperative process patterns) that need to be defined. It means also that we need to provide more help for users with for instance a greater integration of the process with the user environment. At best the WFMS should be able to guess that the user is working on a given task and even that he has finished to work on it. It should also provide some kind of ubiquitous todo list management system, easily accessible by users. These are some paths that we plan to explore in a near future.

## References

1. Charoy, F., Godart, C., Gregori, N., Hautecouverture, J.C., Jourdain, S.: Co-opera: An environment for teaching and learning internet cooperation. In: IADIS International Conference e-Society 2004, Avila, Espagne. (2004) 323–330
2. Herrmann, T., Hoffmann, M.: The metamorphoses of workflow projects in their early stages. Computer Supported Cooperative Work (CSCW) 14(5) (2005) 399 – 432

3. Suchman, L.A.: Plans and Situated Actions : The Problem of Human-Machine Communication (Learning in Doing: Social, Cognitive & Computational Perspectives). Cambridge University Press (1987)

4. Ungar, D., Chambers, C., Chang, B.W., Holzle, U.: Organizing programs without classes. Lisp and Symbolic Computation **4**(3) (1991)

5. Grigori, D., Charoy, F., Godart, C.: Coo-flow: a process technology to support cooperative processes. International Journal of Software Engineering and Knowledge Engineering - IJSEKE Journal **14(1)** (2004)

6. Ellis, C., Keddara, K., Rozenberg, G.: Dynamic change within workflow systems. In: COCS '95: Proceedings of conference on Organizational computing systems, New York, NY, USA, ACM Press (1995) 10–21

7. Joeris, G., Herzog, O.: Managing evolving workflow specifications. In: Conference on Cooperative Information Systems. (1998) 310–321

8. Hagen, C., Alonso, G.: Flexible exception handling in the OPERA process support system. In: International Conference on Distributed Computing Systems. (1998) 526–533

9. Luo, Z., Sheth, A.P., Kochut, K., Miller, J.A.: Exception handling in workflow systems. Applied Intelligence **13**(2) (2000) 125–147

10. Reichert, M., Dadam, P.: ADEPT flex -supporting dynamic changes of workflows without losing control. Journal of Intelligent Information Systems **10**(2) (1998) 93–129

11. Sadiq, S.W., Orlowska, M.E., Sadiq, W.: Specification and validation of process constraints for flexible workflows. Inf. Syst. **30**(5) (2005) 349–378

12. Bassil, S., Keller, R.K., Kropf, P.G.: A workflow-oriented system architecture for the management of container transportation. In Desel, J., Pernici, B., Weske, M., eds.: Business Process Management. Volume 3080 of Lecture Notes in Computer Science., Springer (2004) 116–131

13. Rinderle, S., Reichert, M., Dadam, P.: Correctness criteria for dynamic changes in workflow systems–a survey. Data & Knowledge Engineering **50**(1) (2004) 9–34

14. Skaf, H., Charoy, F., Godart, C.: A hybrid approach to maintain consistency of cooperative software development activities (1997)

15. Dourish, P., Holmes, J., MacLean, A., Marqvardsen, P., Zbyslaw, A.: Freeflow: mediating between representation and action in workflow systems. In: CSCW '96: Proceedings of the 1996 ACM conference on Computer supported cooperative work, New York, NY, USA, ACM Press (1996) 190–198

# Agile Processes Through Goal- and Context-Oriented Business Process Modeling

Birgit Burmeister[1], Hans-Peter Steiert[2], Thomas Bauer[3], and Hartwig Baumgärtel[4]

[1] DaimlerChrysler Research and Technology, REI/IK, Alt-Moabit 96a, D-10559 Berlin
[2] DaimlerChrysler, ITP/EP, Bela-Barenyi-Str. 1, D-71063 Sindelfingen
[3] DaimlerChrysler Research and Technology, REI/ID, P.O. Box 2360, D-89013 Ulm
[4] University of Applied Sciences Ulm, Prittwitzstr. 10, D-89075 Ulm
{birgit.burmeister, hans-peter.steiert, thomas.tb.bauer}
@daimlerchrysler.com, baumgaertel@hs-ulm.de

**Abstract.** Today's methods for business process modeling like extended event-process-chains only allow the definition of static graph structures. They are not flexible enough for instance to model the change management process of the Mercedes Car Group (MCG) since it requires dynamic selection of process variants, process schema evolution and their (partial) propagation on running workflows, arbitrary dynamic process jumps and changes, etc. We have developed an approach for modeling agile processes based on goals and context rules, which enables the required flexibility. Additionally it is possible to map such a process model to a run-time infrastructure for process execution.

## 1 Introduction

Business processes in today's companies are highly complex, involve many different participants and spawn multiple information systems. Running business processes is no longer possible without support by modern information technology. Moreover, optimizing business processes is crucial for business success of companies. Therefore, the processes have to be continuously improved and have to be flexible enough to deal with the dynamic environment in times of global competition.

Compared to these challenges, the current status of business process management in most companies is disappointing: "Should-be" processes are usually modeled by graphical modeling tools like (in best cases) ARIS or UML, but mostly by simple drawing tools like MS Visio or MS PowerPoint. All of these tools support a very simple mind model behind modeling: processes are seen as long and fixed sequences of activities, which is far away from reality and from the challenges. This leads to the fact that models drawn in such tools are often used only to cover white walls in the offices. The processes really executed in the companies are different from that on the wallpapers, "shadow" processes dominate the "official" ones and IT systems are not understood or inflexible and hence misused by many users.

The reason for inflexibility is that process support within the IT systems is (even today) mostly hard-coded with no explicit representation of the process to be executed

J. Eder, S. Dustdar et al. (Eds.): BPM 2006 Workshops, LNCS 4103, pp. 217–228, 2006.
© Springer-Verlag Berlin Heidelberg 2006

or supported. Hence, process changes are costly, imply the high risk of code modification, and always lag behind reality.

Compared to typical business processes, e.g. in call centers or financial services, managing engineering processes is even more challenging for several reasons: First of all engineering processes are long running tasks. Constructing a car lasts for many years and the next model of a large airliner is the result of nearly a decade of engineering and production planning. During this time period many things change – what has been an up-to-date approach in the beginning may be outdated at the end. Second, engineering processes have to cope with uncertainty because of their mixture of creative tasks, collaborative work and repeating activities. This results in very complex processes with many alternative paths and sections that cannot be planned in advance. Third, some products have become so complex that not all engineering tasks can be performed within one enterprise. Special know how provided by external partners has to be exploited, too. This results in engineering processes which are partly executed by external partners. Managing such processes means to handle external engineering tasks without knowledge about "how" they internally work to provide their service.

Traditionally, business process modeling methods and workflow management systems have been developed based on a mind model of business processes as process chains or task chains. Changes, uncertainty, and hidden processes are seen (and sometimes handled) as exceptions instead as regular events. Hence, support for the special demand of engineering processes is limited [2]. Adequate support for engineering processes in terms of modeling and execution obviously requires a completely new approach for process management that is able to deal with the requirements for flexibility, transparency, and efficiency, both in design and execution phase of the process. A new modeling approach to enable *agile processes* has to

- support the design of huge, complex processes, by using a modular process model but also allowing for an overall picture of the process
- decrease the effort for changing and maintaining the process model and
- allow flexibility and agility not only in process modeling but also in process execution through software systems.

We propose a new modeling and execution approach and illustrate it by means of an engineering change management process in the automotive industry. We implemented a software demonstrator for modeling and process simulation to show the flexible execution of the change management process. We are very optimistic that our results are applicable to other business process domains, as well.

This paper is structured as follows: we start with a short introduction to agent technology in Section 2, since our approach exploits concepts and advantages of this technology. The new modeling approach is introduced in Section 3. Subsequently, we describe the software demonstrator in Section 4, with special emphasize to the real-life use cases modeled and executed with this tool. For productive use, agent technology has to fit into a company's existing IT infrastructure and should be built up based on as much mature of-the-shelf software as possible. Hence, in Section 5 we present how our approach can be mapped to existing products and tools. We conclude the paper with a summary and an outlook to further research and development tasks.

## 2  Using Agent Technology for Enabling Agile Processes

Agent-oriented software technology was first introduced to deal with large-scale, distributed software systems, which are embedded in dynamic environments, and allow for the interaction of different partners. The term "agent" is used as a name for an autonomous software component, which is able to deal with the dynamic environment and may interact with other agents [9]. Typical examples for the application of the technology in the real world are production control [5] and logistics [17].

A specific architecture for agents is the so-called BDI-agent architecture. This architecture is based on a formal theory of human reasoning [3]. Herein an agent is described by its beliefs, i.e. the information an agent has about itself, its environment and possibly other agents; its desires, i.e. motivations of the agents that drive its course of action; and finally its intentions; i.e. the short-term goals that the agent wants to achieve, derived from its desires and external events, to which the agents wants to react. To achieve its goals/intentions an agent has certain plans how the goals can be achieved. A plan consists of certain actions/steps that have to be executed to achieve the corresponding goal.

The BDI architecture was first implemented by [15]. The operational semantics of this implementation is as follows: The activities of an agent can be described as a permanent jump between two different types of actions: on the one hand the execution of basic tasks, which the agent uses to fulfill currently active goals ("execution activity"), and on the other hand the reasoning about the next basic action, which he will execute ("control activity"). Execution activities can be:

- Interactions with the environment, e.g. with a user by creating a window, writing some information to it, asking for an input, reading and interpreting the input and writing the input data to an internal database.
- Sending a message to another agent.
- Waiting for a message from another agent, reading and interpreting the message, and saving the message data.
- Performing some kind of computation, e.g. by executing an external software procedure.
- Manipulating the own data base (belief base) based on incoming sensor information, messages etc.

A control activity results in the choice of an execution activity which will be performed next. For this, the agent introspects its goal base, its set of possible execution activities and its belief base. From the goal base it extracts the goals which are activated and not yet fulfilled. Then it collects all activities which would help to fulfill one of the active goals. Next, it checks which of the activities could be performed as next execution action. That is, it checks if the current context (which is determined by its current belief base) fit to the context the action was designed for. For example, if the agent simulates a traveling salesman which currently travels, but gets tired, and hence activates the goal to have a short break and close his eyes for 5 minutes, it may have several execution actions (or sequences of basic actions): for the case that he travels by train or by aircraft, he immediately may close his eyes. If he travels by car, he needs to look for the next parking, go to there and can then have his break. The different actions are designed for different contexts. The information about the context an action is made for is described by the so called context condition of the action.

The agent has to skip all actions which would fulfill a goal, but only in another context. Among the remaining actions he chooses now the one he will execute next (see Fig. 1). The plan whose condition evaluated to true is then chosen for execution. The single steps of the plan are then executed as defined in the plan.

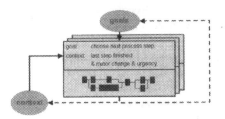

**Fig. 1.** Choosing and Executing of Plans

If there is more than one plan that could be executed in a context, it is possible to attach priorities to plans. In this case, if more than one plan is executable at a time, the plan with the highest priority is chosen for execution. More sophisticated methods to choose from conflicting plans were realized in different implementations of the BDI agent architecture. For example, the plan with the most specific context condition can be chosen, or separate conflict resolution rules can be used to select one plan.

The BDI architecture is well-established agent architecture with several agent tools and applications supporting the architecture, as e.g. JadeX [4]. The ideas of the BDI architecture are also used for business process modeling and management, introduced again by Georgeff and available in the Agentis platform [1].

Based on the ideas of goal-oriented and context-aware execution of agent plans, and of using it for business process modeling and execution, we have enhanced the ideas for a new form of business process modeling.

## 3   Modeling Agile Processes with Goals and Context

Inspired by agent technology and the concept of goal orientation and decomposition the main ideas behind our modeling approach are (i) to have a modular process model that describes the single steps of a process (sub-processes, activities) separate from the goals of the process and the different contexts in which the process can be executed; and (ii) to have different modeling levels, for the different parts of the process model. This modular, goal- and context-based process model can then be executed as an agile process, by considering current goal and context when determining the next step in the process, just as realized in the BDI agent architecture. The agent can be seen as an assistant or guide of the user who is responsible for "driving" a task through the process. Since the agent can perform a lot of routine work for its "boss", it can take over the role of a "process driver" on behalf of the user.

## 3.1  Process Model

A process model in our approach consists of different parts that model the process in different levels of abstraction:

- On the highest level the process is modeled by the goals the process has to fulfill. The goals can be divided into a hierarchy of goals, one goal can be achieved by fulfilling a number of sub-goals; e.g., the main goal of a change management process is to realize a change in the final product. This goal can be achieved by fulfilling several sub-goals, as initiating the change process; gathering the necessary information, deciding on and finally realizing the change (see Fig. 2).

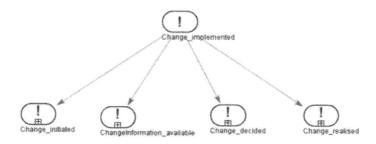

**Fig. 2.** Goal Hierarchy for Change Management

- On the same level the possible contexts of the process have to be defined. The context of a process is described by various context variables and their range of values. These variables model different parameters that influence the flow of the process. Typical context variables in the change management process describe the state of the overall engineering process, the type of the affected product, parameters of the change request, as e.g. number of parts involved, valuation, difficulty, etc.
- The next modeling level contains the process parts (plans, modules) that fulfill the process goals on the lowest level of the goal hierarchy. Each module has an associated "context condition", that describes in which context this module is used to fulfill the corresponding process goal. The context condition refers to context variables and their values for a certain context. Let us look to a change request that has to be assessed regarding certain criteria before a decision is made whether to implement the change or not. In different contexts different assessment criteria are relevant. Fig. 3 shows an example of different modules attached to a goal. A context condition may look like:

```
((Assesment_Relevance-FactorA = TRUE) +
 (ContextVariable = Value)
 ...)
```

- The lowest modeling level contains detailed process models of the modules. These models describe the activities that are executed within the module. These detailed processes can be modeled in any conventional business process modeling notation, e.g. BPMN [13] or UML activity diagrams [14]. Tasks in these models can be either pre-defined tasks, as e.g. data base access, user interaction, and posting of goals, or new basic procedures which have to be specified so that they can later be implemented in a programming language for the execution system.

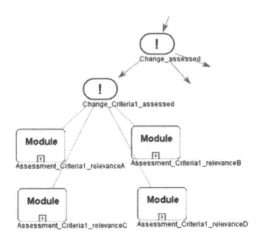

**Fig. 3.** Process modules attached to goals

The different levels of the model correspond to different people in different roles:

- Process analysts, who have a very good understanding of the process but rather small IT know-how, can model the hierarchy of goals and sub-goals, and define which modules can be used to fulfill the goals.
- IT analysts with their good understanding of the process and an intermediate IT know-how can support the process analysts in modeling the goal hierarchy and the process modules. Together these two roles formulate the context conditions of the modules.
- IT consultants (probably of an external consultancy company) have an intermediate understanding of the processes and good IT know-how. Together with the IT analysts they specify the detailed flows of the modules.
- Software developers have only a rough understanding of the process but very good know-how of IT. They write the code for single activities within the detailed process models of the modules.

### 3.2  Evaluation

Prior to the demonstrator implementation (see below) we applied the modeling method to analyze the current system as well as the requirements for a new change management system. In the interviews we conducted with domain experts, software designers, and end users of the current change management system we strictly asked for goals, sub-goals and goal relations of the processes before we talked about task sequences and detailed procedures. Even if the interviews were not a representative sample from a scientific point of view we got some interesting hints about the suitability of our approach in real world projects.

Focus on "What": One source of misunderstanding between domain experts and software designers stems from discussing <u>how</u> the system should behave instead of focusing on <u>what</u> services it should deliver. By this, the domain expert limits the ability of the software designer to find a good solution for his problems. Also, it is very difficult for the software designer to really understand what the needs of the domain experts are. With the goal oriented modeling approach the question to answer is always "What do you want to reach?" By this domain expert and software designer are equal partners in discussing how the goal should be reached. Further it is much clearer what the system is expected to do.

Of course we had to face to some disadvantages, e.g. model review: Not all people involved in requirements analysis are familiar with technology. During our modeling phase those domain experts were guided by a modeling expert. In order to avoid misunderstandings the result needs to be reviewed by the domain experts. While goal-orientation has shown to be a very good tool for guiding people towards new solutions it is not appropriate for review: Most people check the model by applying use cases in order to see "how it works". For this purpose a "bullet-and-arc" representation seems to be more suitable.

As for all concepts there are pros and cons – there is no silver bullet in computer science. But our experience shows that the results from process analysis are much better and justify additional efforts in other development phases.

## 4 Demonstrator

To demonstrate the feasibility of the modeling approach and the flexible execution of agile processes we have implemented a software demonstrator. It shows:

- the modeling of the process model on different levels of abstraction: Different levels of the model can be modeled by people having different roles (see above)
- the automatic, and thus seamless, translation of the process model into an "executable" process model, allowing for easy and fast process improvement
- the flexible execution of processes by achieving the process goals and taking into account the current context of the process.

This demonstrator consists of three components (see Fig. 4):

- A graphical editor, that allows building the process model with goals, context, and modules as described in Section 3. Here we re-used an own universal graphical editor for arbitrary graphs implemented earlier. This tool, called GraphEdit, is based on Java and XML and is designed for maximal modeling flexibility. That is, the meta-models of the graphs have to be specified in a specific XML format which will be read as a configuration file. GraphEdit provides the node and arc types of the meta-model with their parameters for building graphs. The graphs are stored again as XML files. When loading an existing graph model, GraphEdit loads the corresponding meta-model first. To use GraphEdit in our demonstrator we only needed to design a new configuration file, and to create a graphical representation (icon) for the node types. Our meta model contains node types for goals and modules with their context conditions as well as nodes for BPMN like basic processes.
- The process model is then automatically translated into an "executable" process model by an XML-based translator. The process model is stored in an XML-based format (see above). This format is translated into an "executable" process model that can be taken as input for the process engine. In the software demonstrator there

are two different translation components: one translates the goal hierarchy and context ("goal-translator"), another one translates the basic module processes and their context conditions ("plan translator").

The goal translator is able to translate the goal hierarchies and definitions of context variables completely automatically. The plan translator translates process modules that are composed of predefined tasks and certain flow constructs (sequence, alternative and parallel branching). For those tasks within process modules that are not pre-defined the code has to be added to the executable model in this step. The resulting executable process model is now input for the process engine.

- The process engine uses the executable process model to control the execution of single process modules, based on current goals and context as described in Section 2. For the demonstrator we have used the agent tool JadeX as process engine. JadeX is an extension of the widely used agent environment Jade. It extends Jade with a BDI agent architecture [4].

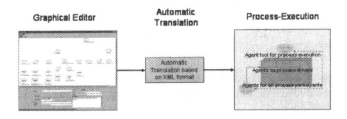

**Fig. 4.** Architecture of Demonstrator for Agile Processes

The demonstrator was applied to the goal- and context-based process model of the engineering change management process of MCG. Different scenarios were tested with the demonstrator, that show how the process can adapt to unplanned events, monitor and react to missing deadlines.

The main advantages of the approach are that it provides a highly modular process model that allows for a flexible and agile adoption of the process, i.e. the process instance is composed of the single modules during process execution. The values of context variables drive the selection of process modules. If a value of a context variable changes during process execution, this will result in the selection of a different process module, than the one, which would have been predicted at the beginning of the process. This resembles an on-line migration to a new process-schema (or even to parts of it). The demonstrator also allows for the reactivation of already fulfilled goals, and thus realizing partial returns to earlier process parts (i.e. dynamic jumps and changes). Finally, a highly parallel execution of modules is possible, since no sequence restrictions are modeled on the goal level.

## 5   IT-Infrastructure for the Execution of Agile Processes

Until now, we have presented an approach for modeling and a software demonstrator for modeling and execution of agile processes. In this section, run-time aspects are considered: An infrastructure for a real-world application at DaimlerChrysler's MCG engineering dept. has to cope with non-functional requirements as very good stability, performance, scalability, etc. Furthermore, it has to fit to the existing IT-infrastructure and products of the strategic IT-partners. Run-time components for process execution additionally always have to fulfill several functional requirements as the storage of the organizational model, actor assignment for activities (e.g. role resolution), worklist management incl. delegation and substitution for tasks, integration of legacy applications, documentation of process execution and user actions, etc.

Workflow products [6, 11] already offer (many of) these functions in order to simplify the implementation of application systems. Their usage is reasonable, therefore, to implement the module processes (see lower part of Fig. 5).

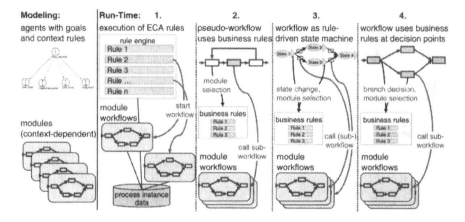

**Fig. 5.** Possible Architectures for Process Execution using the Modeled Context Rules

These modules contain interactive and automatic activities and have a static structure. This allows realizing them with traditional workflow technology using all the features mentioned above. Furthermore, these features are solely required at this level, since the atomic activities (tasks) are completely contained in the module processes.

A drawback of workflow systems is their limited flexibility. In the given scenario, this is a serious problem for the top-level workflow since it has to be modeled using goals and context rules for module selection (cf. left part of Fig. 5). In the following, different architectures are analyzed that enable the execution of such processes and, in addition, fulfill the mentioned functional and non-functional requirements. They differ in the execution style for the top-level workflow (cf. Fig. 5, alternatives 1 to 4).

1. Top-level process control by a rule engine: The modeled context rules can be automatically translated into event-condition-action (ECA) rules that may be executed by a rule engine (e.g. ILog [7]). This enables a very agile top-level process since no graph-oriented process model is used at all. The disadvantages are that this approach will result in a large number of rules, which are difficult to maintain. Additionally, there do not exist products with an integrated (ECA) rule engine and a workflow engine. Two different systems, therefore, have to be coupled, with the consequence that the actions of the rules will call (independent) workflow instances. A context for the whole process does not exist. Process instance data has

to be stored externally and is used by the rule engine and multiple modules (i.e. workflow instance fragments). The workflow engine, therefore, is not able to use workflow internal data in process control (e.g. determining actors of former modules for task assignment). Finally, the coupling of different system types may cause implementation effort and decrease performance and stability.

A variant of this approach is to realize the top-level process control by BDI agents instead of a rule engine. Platforms as Agentis [1] offer support for process execution as well, but for (large) real-world applications the limitations of the corresponding functions are not acceptable. Instead, a production workflow system [11] is required for the control of the module workflows. As discussed above for rule engines, this results in the necessity of coupling two different system types.

2. Top-level as pseudo-workflow: The context of the workflow instance may be kept by using a (top-level) workflow that stores the process instance data and only consists of a loop with a single activity inside. Its task is to call the module sub-workflows. The workflow uses business rules in order to select the modules. There is no necessity for a complete rule engine since the rules are actively called and the actions (sub-workflow calls) are triggered by the workflow. Therefore, a rule component of a today's workflow product, as for instance IBM Process Server [6], is sufficient. The whole application may be realized within one product. This reduces the implementation effort and allows good maintainability. Since the context rules are called continuously and the whole top-level process is controlled by the rules, arbitrary agility may be achieved. Parallel execution of modules can be achieved by starting the modules asynchronously. Since even the synchronization of parallel branches is modeled by the context rules, they guarantee that an activity intended to be executed after a parallelism, in fact, can only be started if these branches are completed.

3. Top-level as state machine: Workflow products as IBM Process Server enable workflow modeling in a state machine style. The goal- and context-oriented model may be automatically translated into a state diagram: The states directly correspond to the modeled goals and the context rules are used to control the state changes and to select module workflows. This allows application implementation within one single product, the context of the process instance is kept, and the modeled goals are even visible at run-time monitoring. The problem with this approach is that a state machine only allows one single active state at one time. Therefore, parallel branches have to be realized at the module level. In the given process almost all activities are executed parallel to others. This would result in a small number of very large modules which have to be realized as traditional workflows. Such a restriction of the agility of process execution is not acceptable.

4. Top-level as traditional workflow: To overcome the restrictions with respect to parallel branches, the top-level process may be realized as workflow that is controlled using traditional workflow technology. Again, context rules are used for the selection of branches and modules, and the whole process control happens within one system. Unfortunately, it is not possible to derive the process graph automatically from the goal-oriented model. Another drawback is the limited flexibility of workflow systems, which typically do not allow arbitrary jumps and dynamic process changes. The rules influence the control flow only at pre-defined points what restricts agility of the process execution. Even flexible workflow approaches

as ADEPT [16] do not offer this kind of agility since there are still based on graph-oriented process models. On the other side, since for each decision point only a few rules are assigned, implementation complexity is reduced and maintainability increases.

The selection of the optimal architecture depends on the concrete requirements of the given process and application scenario. Architecture 1 has several disadvantages which result from the necessary coupling of different systems and the lack of commercially available systems. Architecture 3 may only be used for processes that do not require parallel branches. Since the possibility of parallel execution paths is an important aspect of agility, such processes perhaps do not exist at all. The architecture 4 should be chosen if the offered agility is sufficient, since it maintains the process structure and the workflow products are used as intended. For the given change management process, however, extreme agility is required with the result that architecture 4 may not be used. Therefore, architecture 2 seems most suitable: All the agility enabled by the goal- and context-oriented modeling may be achieved at runtime as well and most features of the workflow system can be used (e.g., user and work-item management). Only workflow actions that depend on the existence of the whole workflow graph (e.g. process visualization) are not useable with the standard realization of the workflow products.

# 7  Discussion, Conclusion, and Outlook

We have presented an approach for business process modeling of agile processes which was inspired by ideas from agent-oriented technology. Our modeling approach, which defines a process model with goals, contexts, and process modules, seems especially suitable for engineering processes. Different roles may model the process on different levels. Process analysts can concentrate on "what" should be achieved by the process; IT analysts and software developers can later define the "how".

Although the coupling of agent technology and business process management is not new, existing approaches [8], [11] focus on agents' communication and cooperation (and mobility) abilities to support the process execution. Single tasks are modeled as services and agents offer and use these services in executing the process. Moreover different types of agents are used for the implementation of a workflow system [10]. Agent communication and cooperation can (and will) enhance our approach for expanding it for the coordination of multiple processes/ agents. For the execution we are investigating several IT-infrastructures as described in section 6.

Up to now we have demonstrated the feasibility of the modeling approach in the area of engineering change management. We have modeled the process and have realized the automatic translation and agent based execution of the process model. Finally, we have investigated different software architectures for the implementation of a new change management system.

We are now in the process of evaluating several potential partners for the implementation of that system. The partners and their chosen architectures and technologies have to enable the required agility by offering the goal-oriented and modular modeling approach and demonstrated agile process execution.

# Acknowledgement

We would like to thank Jürgen Scharpf and the NCM-Team for their support. Special thanks to Christian Wiech for his excellent work in implementing the demonstrator. Finally we would to thank the anonymous reviewers. Due to space limitation we were not able to consider all of their valuable comments. Nevertheless we will take them as inspirations for our future work.

# Literature

1. Agentis Software: Adaptive Enterprise™ Solution Suite. http://www.agentissoftware.com
2. T. Beuter: Workflow-Management für Produktentwicklungsprozesse. Dissertation Universität Ulm. (2002)
3. M. Bratman: Intention, Plans, and Practical Reason. Harvard University Press. (1987)
4. L. Braubach, A. Pokahr, W. Lamersdorf: Jadex: A BDI-Agent System Combining Middleware and Reasoning. In: [18]. (2005)
5. S. Bussmann, N.R. Jennings, M.J. Wooldridge: Multiagent Systems for Manufacturing Control. A Design Methodology. Springer Series on Agent Technology. Springer. (2004)
6. IBM Redbook: Technical Overview of WebSphere Process Server and WebSphere Integration Developer. (2005)
7. ILog Technology. http://www.ilog.com/products/businessrules
8. N.R. Jennings, T.J. Norman, P. Faratin, P. O'Brien, B. Odgers: Autonomous Agents for Business Process Management. In: Int. Journal of Applied Artificial Intelligence 14 (2) 145-189 (2000).
9. N.R. Jennings, M.J. Wooldridge (Eds.): Agent Technology – Foundations, Applications, and Markets. Springer. (1998)
10. G. Joeris: Decentralised and Flexible Workflow Enactment Based on Task Coordination Agents. In Proc. Workshop Agent-Oriented Information Systems (2000)
11. F. Leymann, D. Roller: Production Workflow - Concepts and Techniques. Prentice Hall. (2000)
12. M. Merz, B. Liberman, K. Müller-Jones, W. Lamersdorf: Inter-organisational workflow management with mobile agents in COSM. In: Proc. 1st. Conf. Practical Applications of Intelligent Agents and Multi-Agent Technology (1996)
13. Object Management Group: Business Process Modeling Notation – Specification. (2006)
14. Object Management Group: Unified Modeling Language – Superstructure, Version 2.0. (2005)
15. A.S. Rao, M.P. Georgeff: BDI Agents: From Theory to Practice. In V. Lesser (ed.) Proc. 1st International Conf. on Multi-Agent Systems. MIT-Press. (1995)
16. M. Reichert, P. Dadam: ADEPT$_{flex}$ – Supporting Dynamic Changes of Workflows without Losing Control. Journal of Intelligent Information Systems, Special Issue on Workflow Management Systems 10(2). (1998) 93-129
17. G. Rimassa, M.Calisti, M.E. Kerland: Living Systems™ Technology Suite. In: [18]. (2005)
18. R. Umland, M. Klusch, M. Calisti (eds.): Software Agent-Based Applications, Platforms, and Development Kits. Whitestein Series in Software Agent Technology. Birkhäuser. (2005)

# Workshop on Enterprise and Networked Enterprises Interoperability (ENEI 2006)

# Workshop on Enterprise and Networked Enterprises Interoperability (ENEI 2006) Preface

Following the success of the first workshop, ENEI 2005 (http://www.loria.fr/
~nacer/BPM-ENEI05/ENEI-CfP.html), this second event addressed computer-supported integration and interoperability of enterprise applications and software. Indeed, enterprises are provided with collections of heterogeneous applications and software tools that were neither designed nor developed to favor their interaction and their cooperation.

The problem is more crucial when one considers networked enterprises and enterprise expansion (through, for instance, alliances or mergers). Moreover, interoperability within an enterprise and between enterprises is not limited to data interoperability but should also consider additional levels like applications, business models, process models, enterprise models, and their supporting systems and software.

The workshop was divided into three sessions. The first session shows issues related to enterprise systems interoperability, and more particularly at the manufacturing and shop floor level of enterprises where the product, as seen by enterprises applications, is one of the main information producers and consumers. Interdependence between the subsystems of an enterprise is one of the driving reasons for integrating the enterprise.

The second session is related to model-based approaches for enterprise interoperability. Indeed, while a modeling framework is needed to map semantics between enterprise models, business-to-business collaboration models also require a flexible IT-architecture. Different protocols, such as P2P, may be applied to cooperatively develop business process models for enterprise interoperability.

The last session deals with ontology-based approaches. These approaches may be evaluated within an application for decision making, but also using Web services technology applied to workflow time management algorithms. However, research is in progress to define reference conceptual frameworks to organize ontology knowledge spaces and semantic annotations to augment enterprise models with meaningful meta-data, in order to improve human understanding, machine interoperability, and advanced automatic information management.

It has been a great pleasure to work with the members of the international program committee, who dedicated their valuable effort to reviewing, in time, the submitted papers: we are indebted to all of them as we are indebted to the INTEROP Network of Excellence (FP6 IST-508-011, http://www.interop-noe.org) for its scientific and financial support.

June 2006

Nacer Boudjlida
Hervé Panetto
(Editors)

# Workshop Organization

## Workshop and Program Committee Co-chairs

| | |
|---|---|
| Boudjlida, Nacer | *LORIA UMR 7503, Nancy-University, France* |
| Panetto, Hervé | *CRAN UMR 7039, Nancy-University, CNRS, France* |

## Program Committee

| | |
|---|---|
| Baina, Karim | *ENSIAS, Morrocco* |
| Bellahsène, Zohra | *University of Montpellier, LIRMM, France* |
| Berio, Giuseppe | *University of Turin, Italy* |
| Boudjlida, Nacer | *LORIA UMR 7503, Nancy-University, France* |
| Boufaida, Mahmoud | *University Mentouri, Constantine, Algeria* |
| Carvalho, Joao Alvaro | *University of Minho, Portugal* |
| Castano, Sylvana | *University of Milan, Italy* |
| Chatha, Kamran Ali | *Lahore University of Management Sciences, Pakistan* |
| Chen, Pin | *Defence Science & Technology Organisation, Australia* |
| D'Aquin, Mathieu | *LORIA UMR 7503, Nancy-University, France* |
| Diamantini, Claudia | *Università delle Marche, Italy* |
| Dubois, Eric | *CRP Henri Tudor, Luxembourg* |
| Gruhn, Volker | *University of Leipzig, Germany* |
| Hahn, Axel | *University of Oldenburg, Germany* |
| Jeusfeld, Manfred | *Tilburg University, The Netherlands* |
| Johanson, Paul | *KTH, Sweden* |
| Krogstie, John | *Norwegian Institute of Science and Technology, Norway* |
| Lenzerini, Maurizio | *Università degli Studi di Roma "La Sapienza", Italy* |
| Mezgar, Istvan | *Hungarian Academy of Sciences, Hungary* |
| Molina, Arturo | *Tecnológico de Monterrey, Mexico* |
| Opdahl, Andreas | *L. University of Bergen, Norway* |
| Oquendo, Flavio | *University of South Brittany at Vannes, France* |
| Panetto, Hervé | *CRAN UMR 7039, Nancy-University, CNRS, France* |
| Perrin, Olivier | *LORIA UMR 7503, Nancy-University, France* |
| Petit, Michaël | *University of Namur, Belgium* |
| Tari, Zahir | *RMIT University, Melbourne, Australia* |
| Slimani, Yahya | *FST, University of Tunis, Tunisia* |
| Velardi, Paola | *Università degli Studi di Roma "La Sapienza", Italy* |
| Whitman, Larry | *Wichita State University, USA* |

## Additional Referees

Bergholtz, Maria           *KTH, Sweden*
Elgedawy, Islam            *RMIT University, Melbourne, Australia*
Gooneratne, Nalaka         *RMIT University, Melbourne, Australia*
Jaudoin, Hélène            *ISIMA, France*
Montanelli, Stefano,       *University of Milan, Italy*
Saleem, Khalid             *University of Montpellier, LIRMM, France*
Shazib E., Sheikh          *Lahore University of Management Sciences,*
                           *Pakistan*

# Session 1: Enterprise Systems Interoperability Issues

# Shop Floor Information Management and SOA

Konrad Pfadenhauer[1], Burkhard Kittl[1],
Schahram Dustdar[2], and David Levy[3]

[1] Vienna University of Technology, Institute for Production Engineering,
Karlsplatz 13, 1040 Vienna, Austria
{pfadenhauer, kittl}@mail.ift.tuwien.ac.at
[2] Vienna University of Technology, Information Systems Institute,
Distributed Systems Group, Argentinierstraße 8/184-1, 1040 Vienna, Austria
dustdar@infosys.tuwien.ac.at
[3] University of Sydney, School of Electrical and Information Engineering, Room 327,
Engineering Faculty Building J13, Sydney, NSW, Australia
dlevy@ee.usyd.edu.au

**Abstract.** Service Science is a new term for a new paradigm which aims at the solution of an obvious problem: How to make the increasing fusion of business and IT successful in a dynamically changing and risk adverse environment? This question has to be raised at different levels of abstraction, from macroeconomic viewpoints circulating around qualities of service societies to service oriented architectures of business applications. We worked in an interdisciplinary team consisting of industrial engineers and distributed system experts on the issue of business and IT alignment in a well-defined system, namely the shop-floor domain in discrete production industry. The result of this work is an ANSI/ISA 95 compliant model-driven methodology for manufacturing operations management. This methodology was evaluated by means of the realization of a SOA (Service Oriented Architecture) demo scenario for production operations management.

## 1 Intelligent Manufacturing Information Systems

Discrete manufacturing shop floor information and control flow management is still a challenging task due to the heterogeneity of data structures and information systems (automation components inclusively). The objective of vertical integration from high-level Enterprise Resource Planning (ERP) to the machine level is still unrivalled. Existing solutions led to static process logic coding within monolithic Manufacturing Execution System (MES) utilizing elaborate interfaces for rudimentary integration, lacking the needed flexibility and scalability. This proceeding is not sufficient regarding the requirements of today's dynamic production environments.

Internet based manufacturing, leveraging the latest technologies to achieve distributed information systems, provides new possibilities not only for static, data centric integration of the shop floor into an overall enterprise architecture, but also for full process integration of control and thus field level by means of SOA.

J. Eder, S. Dustdar et al. (Eds.): BPM 2006 Workshops, LNCS 4103, pp. 237–248, 2006.

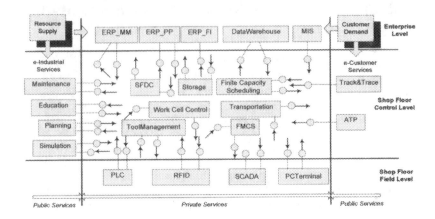

**Fig. 1.** Internal and external service providers at the shop floor control level

We assume that sub-system vendors at the control level (e.g. for tool management or for storage systems) will follow the trend towards service orientation already visible for ERP level modules. More control tasks get transferred to the field level PLCs (Programmable Logic Control) or open PC terminals, where the knowledge is concentrated and reaction times are the shortest. Hence Fig. 1 depicts potential service providers at different levels of the shop floor hierarchy, resulting in a complex distributed architecture which demands for system modelling and process life-cycle management. Public services into and out of the shop floor are next to the outlined vertical, mainly internal integration an issue too. Machine vendors are offering services like online maintenance, education support, planning and optimisation of production and logistics systems or other e-Industrial/tele-services. In our opinion this public, horizontal connectivity is in the short run not as promising as the vertical service integration due to higher coordination demands and security reasons. Recent developments at the machine level (e.g. Radio Frequency Identification) strengthen the call for an intuitive, model-based overview about service distribution and communication networks within the complete architecture.

The aim of this project was to investigate the potential of SOA for information and control flows in the shop floor domain, integrating applications as well as human workers as loosely coupled service providers. A modelling methodology was developed, which brings together system modelling at different levels of abstraction as well as process detailing and implementation at the execution level. Thus by means of existing standards concerning modelling (ANSI/ISA 95, UML (Unified Modeling Language)) as well as implementation technologies (Web Services, UDDI (Universal Description, Discovery and Integration)) Business and IT alignment was established.

The structure of this paper is as follows. We first discuss in Section 2 some manufacturing domain information architecture proposals. In Section 3 we present our model driven service architecture methodology. After that the implementation environment for a demo scenario is outlined in Section 4. Section 5 demonstrates the application of our *MDSA (Model Driven Service Architecture)* methodology by means of the demo scenario. With a conclusion and an outlook at the work to come we will finish this paper.

## 2 Manufacturing Domain Information Architecture Proposals

Enterprise Architecture (EA) research resulted in a number of elaborated architecture proposals with a more general scope (Zachman Framework, PERA (Purdue Enterprise Reference Architecture), GERAM (Generalized Enterprise Reference Architecture and Methodology)) as well as a manufacturing scope (CIMOSA (Computer Integrated Manufacturing Open System Architecture), GRAI Integrated Method). In our opinion these concepts introduce important ideas regarding modelling, modularization and abstraction levels. For instance the basic principles of MDA (Model Driven Architecture) or SOA can all be found in CIMOSA. Regarding modelling techniques applied as well as the assumptions made at the implementation level lack of standardization is the major problem of these architectures. We believe a feasible approach has to take the given techniques and technologies at the execution level into account and embed them into a broader architecture which supports Business and IT alignment. A joined initiative for manufacturing domain object and control flow standardization is ANSI/ISA 95 [2], [3], [4], a proposal derived from PERA. The limited scope, the use of UML and the focus on the higher abstraction levels as with the corresponding information flows makes this a very promising approach which we utilize and extend towards implementation level modelling. Proposals for BPM (Business Process Management) at the implementation level leveraging enterprise application integration, workflow or more recently process markup techniques (BPEL, BPML, XPDL) are promising, but concepts are missing how the integration into an overall platform independent enterprise architecture can be established. For a detailed discussion of state-of-the-art techniques and technologies concerning EA two EU initiatives delivered excellent publications [5], [6]: The aim of INTEROP (Interoperability Research for Networked Enterprise Applications and Software, launched 2004) is the conceptual as well as the technical integration of business by means of reference models. Contrary to our project the inter-enterprise system integration focus is dominant. Nevertheless, the chosen approach of MDA and SOA alignment, together with semantic annotations, shows some similarities to the approach presented in the following. But the INTEROP deliverables remain at a conceptual level, whereas in this work a domain specific real-world implementation proofs the quality of the methodology. Whereas INTEROP is the nucleus mainly of the university research community, ATHENA (Advanced Technologies for interoperability of Heterogeneous Enterprise Networks and their Applications, launched 2004) is an IT industry platform. Although useful but abstract reference models were available from the very beginning, very little relevant information was published how they can be implemented. Lippe et al. [7] demands for a 3-level modelling approach (Business, Technical and Executable Processes) and claim that a process abstraction concept is missing in existing architecture proposals. In their survey on modelling languages they claim that UML does not support business context, but in such a comparison the UML extension mechanism should be considered. All the more, as suitable UML profiles are provided for model driven SOA development (Berre [8]: UML Profile for PIM4SOA; Pondrelli [9]: UML Profiles for Services, Business Objects and Ontologies). In Pondrelli [10] it becomes clear that no new profiles are delivered, but existing proposals (e.g. IBM UML 2.0 Profile for Software Services) are incorporated in a rudimentary methodology.

Berre [8] presents the ATHENA Interoperability Framework. It would have been interesting to get more information about the ATHENA Service Oriented Interoperability Framework or the proposed MPCE Architecture (including Platform Independent Model for SOA (PIM4SOA) & Model Transformations) beyond the description in INTEROP D6.1 [11], but the content published so far is not sufficient for a detailed discussion. In addition, the focus on cross-organizational business processes with a strong emphasis on OMG Meta-Object Facility related model mapping increases the scope which is therefore much broader then the objectives of the single modelling language, intra-organisational approach presented here.

Recently, more emphasis on Service Oriented Analysis and Design (SOAD) can be observed. Arsanjani [12] rediscovers the three model abstraction dimension of reference architecture proposals like CIMOSA when he states that the process of service oriented modelling consists of three phases, namely identification, specification and realization. But he correctly postulates that it can no longer be an exclusively and thus unsuccessful top-down approach of domain decomposition, but a combination of top-down, bottom-up (existing asset analysis) and middle-out (goal-service modelling). For our methodology we adopted the hybrid SOAD modelling approach of Zimmermann et al. [13] who suggests a combination of Object Oriented Analysis and Design, BPM and EA techniques. It is the aim of this work to enrich and unify these fragments towards a comprehensive SOAD approach. Moreover, the methodology has to be validated by means of real-world standards, techniques and applications. Due to the weaknesses of existing solutions, we want to build up a SOA for the shop floor, optimising the trade-off between flexible interconnectivity and network infrastructure complexity. To overcome a situation of vertical, interrupted processes and partly unavailable, partly static accessible functionalities we introduce our concept of a MDSA for the shop floor a combined top-down/bottom-up methodology realized in a tool for user friendly model creation. On a conceptual base, the abstract MDA and SOA concepts are adopted for and enriched with concrete technologies and tools to implement a real-world framework for the shop floor domain.

## 3 Model Driven Service Architecture for the Shop Floor

Our methodological considerations started with the domain dimensions *Business*, *Architecture* and *Application*, each with its own modelling concept. SOAD has to bring those three together. End result should be a platform independent model, which has to be mapped to the actual and potential system assets. Hence it becomes a platform specific model, which will loose some of its *Business* readability as implementation details are added. In Fig. 2 we depict the resulting methodology specifically for the shop floor domain. The before mentioned domain dimensions were replaced by the classical hierarchy levels, namely Enterprise Level, Shop Floor Control Level and Shop Floor Field Level (Fig. 1). In the past the modelling concepts where utilized separately at the levels as shown in the figure.

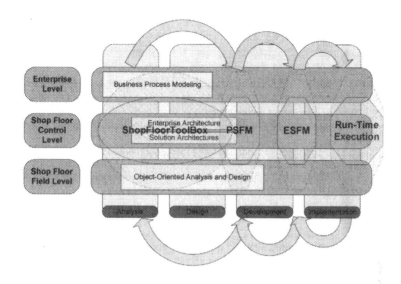

**Fig. 2.** Model Driven Service Architecture for the shop floor

First, fast and easy initial modelling of a given shop floor system has to be supported, focusing on functionality and connectivity of the system as a whole. We achieve this by a generic model collection called *Shop Floor Tool-Box (SFTB)*. The SFTB is an ANSI/ISA 95 compliant tool box which enables fast and standardized modelling of particular shop floor scenarios. The tool consists of an abstract service repository of basic and complex services (what dimension), concrete service providers (who dimension), binding mechanisms and data entities (with dimension). The *PSFM (Particular Shop Floor Model)* at the end of the Design phase can exist at two abstraction levels, platform/computer independent and platform specific. The latter constitutes the *ESFM (Executable Shop Floor Model)*. Whereas the PSFM will consider the actual system specification only roughly (coarse grain functionality distribution), the ESFM must be fully aligned with the assets either already existing or under construction. The PSFM has to support long term platform, infrastructure and service provider decisions through *as-is* and *to-be* comparisons. This high level model has to interact with the ESFM concerning process definition. The latter serves at a tactical level for the (re)design of service flow definitions which are semantically rich enough for executable code generation. Knowledge gained from the PSFM and ESFM should be fed back into the *Shop Floor Tool-Box*, which more and more becomes a valuable knowledge base.

## 4 MDSA Implementation – Assumptions, Technologies and Tools

We already mentioned the different approaches regarding SOAD. We strongly believe that only a combined approach can be successful, matching the given asset structure against high-level requirement business models. Thus we did a comparison of top-down and bottom-up approaches for model driven WS-composition, which led to the result that satisfying technologies enabling stringent methodologies from business oriented system models down to executable service flow definitions hardly exist. Nevertheless, the approaches evolving around UML seemed most promising.

Therefore we implemented a combined *Specification and Representation* approach depicted in Fig 3, with a methodology based on UML 2.0 for high-level use-case and business scenario modelling (system model) resulting in platform independent service collaboration views (modified IBM UML 2.0 Profile for Software Services [14] as Model Representation Language). The *System Model*, which at a low level defines the composition specification, derives its syntax and semantic from a combined meta-model of an ANSI/ISA 95 Profile (leveraging the *Equipment/Functional Hierarchy Model* of Part I and the *Activity Models* of Part III)  and the IBM Profile for Business Modeling [15]. Corresponding templates ease the model management. The repository of assets (service providers, realizing components) as well as other relevant information (data or binding types) are available in the low-level models and are incorporated in the fine-grained flow models (bottom-up). These flow models are the blueprint for the *Composition Model*, in our case BizTalk Orchestration Designer orchestrations. At this stage automated mapping between *Model Representation Language* (UML 2.0 Activity Diagram) and *Executable Composition Language* (XLANG/s) is not included. Other mapping requirements, which would gain importance if different modelling notations shall be integrated, are not relevant due to the limitation of modelling environments (Rational Software Modeler 6.0.1 with profile plug-ins and BizTalk Orchestration Designer 2004).

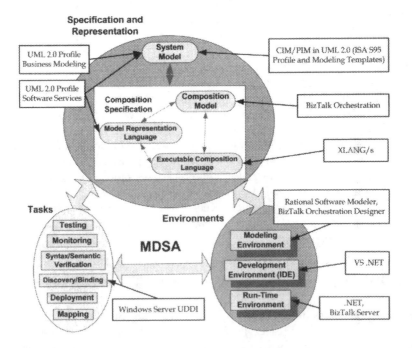

**Fig. 3.** MDSA implementation

We focused on discovery and binding, typically supported by a service broker, which is next to service provider and service requestor the third major role in the basic SOA paradigm. In the demo scenario this role is performed by the UDDI 1.0 compliant Windows Server 2003 UDDI. The Microsoft platform also prevails regarding the Run-Time Environment (.NET 1.1 and BizTalk Server 2004) as well as the Development Environment (Visual Studio .NET 2003).

# 5 MDSA Implementation by Means of a Demo Scenario

Within the modelling framework the complete ANSI/ISA 95 standards can be visualized and used as the guideline for domain modelling. Hence the methodology implementation follows ANSI/ISA 95 Part 1 concerning the general assumptions about hierarchies and functions. The generic *Functional Hierarchy Model* and the *Equipment Hierarchy Model* are the bases for functionality allocation and categorization. The implemented functionality in the demo scenario is part of the *Production Operations Management* grouping within the *Manufacturing Operations Management Model*.

ANSI/ISA 95 models are on the one hand the high-level framework for the SFTB, a collection of models and artefacts ready to be used for modelling projects. Thus the first task was to build an ANSI/ISA 95 UML Meta-Model in our modelling environment. On the other hand this Meta-Model constitutes the UML profile for ANSI/ISA 95, which is used throughout the modelling efforts. Mainly, the purpose of this profile is to keep the relationships to the business related ANSI/ISA 95 models and terminologies especially in low-level diagrams and models alive. Nevertheless, it is important to state that the SFTB is more than an ANSI/ISA 95 Meta-Model. It contains more information at different levels of abstraction and shall grow with every real-world modelling project, which means entities like service providers, data type definitions (OAGIS 9.0 Business Document Objects, OPC XML DA etc.) are continuously fed back into the SFTB.

## 5.1 From SFTB Constructs to Particular Shop Floor Models

For the remainder the Detailed Production Scheduling model shall be used to demonstrate the easy and highly integrated modelling methodology down to executable process specifications. The concept of modularization is important in the SFTB from the very beginning. That is why the use cases are separated from each other (Fig. 4). This gives the modeller the flexibility to first chose the constructs he needs and then integrate them, in the case of use case models through *include* and *extend* relationships or through the replacement of external actors and use cases.

Fig. 4 represents the highest level in the MDSA methodology. The whole Detailed Production Scheduling activity is represented as a *Business Use Case*, interacting with a *Business Actor*, the Production Schedule Provider. Typically, this role is realized by level 4 activities, often an ERP system releasing rough scheduled *Production Schedule*.

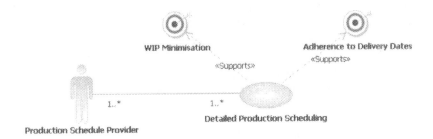

**Fig. 4.** Detailed Production Scheduling use case model

This use case supports two *Business Goals*, WIP Minimization and increased Adherence to Delivery Dates. The definition of goals is a key principle of process orientation, because the achievement of these objectives, refined by means of KPI, determines the effectiveness of the overall process. A control loop like the one presented in this work, has to translate the monitoring results of the operational level into figures representing the business goals. Business Goals are not included in the ANSI/ISA 95 standard and therefore give an example for constructs derived from the SFTB. *Business Collaborations* realize the use case. A centralized view provides the *Detailed Production Scheduling Realization Overview*, a diagram consisting of four diagrams according to the Rational Analysis Model template. However, alternative flow diagrams are optional and of course their number is unlimited. The template suggests using sequence diagrams for basic and alternative flows, but the use of activity diagrams or even non UML diagrams is possible. The first is a class diagram depicting all *Business Workers* and *Business Entities* for this particular realization. At least one dynamic behaviour view completes the basic overview. This is the second compulsory diagram in every Analysis Model.

## 5.2   From Particular to Executable Shop Floor Models

In an iterative process two modelling perspectives evolve, first the top-down derived PIM and secondly the bottom-up originating PSM. Thus the modelling project for a particular scenario can be seen as a central market place, were supply (the actual system configuration plus potential future functionality providers of the repository, part of the constructs of the SFTB) meets demand (the *to-be* system with its processes and goals defined by the business analysts). So far we have determined what *Production Operation Management Activities* we want to implement and modeled the high-level static and dynamic requirement models. Now it is time to have a look at which service providers are available and which roles they can play to realize the postulated system configuration. The service provider models can have two sources, either they are available as low-level constructs in the SFTB, or they are added to the project from the scratch. In either case, the modified IBM Profile for Software Services shall be used. Rational Software Modeler offers a template for this profile, which is used in an extended version for all modelling efforts at the software service level.

The service providers are grouped in a *Service View* perspective. We have already placed emphasis on the fact that the service provider construct is implementation independent. That is to say that the service providers, together with the interfaces respectively operations they realize, can be personnel as well as applications. To give an example: The *Detailed Production Scheduling* activity has an associated service provider role *ScheduingIFProvider* (Fig. 5), which provides for the service flow *scheduleNewOrders* the *IPreactorIF* interface (Fig. 6). This role is assigned to the scheduling software Preactor 9.2 interface extension. Another service provider is *SchedulingProvider*, a role assigned to the Preactor software user. All implementation details will be added in the subsequent step of *Component View* creation. The *Service View*, a component diagram, considers use dependencies as well as realization relationships. A class diagram and a composite structure diagram refine each single service provider component. For instance the *ProductionScheduleCheckProvider Service Provider* consists of two interfaces, stereotyped as *ServiceSpecifications*. Which operations they provide can be explored in the class diagram or in the general *Service View*. Each interface can be accessed at least trough two ports (*Services*), the general type is included in the port name (e.g. scheduleNewOrdersSOAP and scheduleNewOrdersFSO). The detailed type specification (e.g. SOAP-RPC, SOAP-DOC) is included in the documentation and has to be the same as the *Service Channel* binding attribute defined in the *Collaboration View*. This perspective provides a *Composition Overview* and a *Collaboration Overview* diagram. The first, depicted in Fig. 5, shows the relationships between the *Service Partitions*, which are collections of *Service Providers*. It is also shown what roles the partitions fulfil. In our case the partition is compliant with the activities of ANSI/ISA 95 Production Operations Management, thus we find a *Plant1:Scheduling* partition stereotyped *Detailed Production Scheduling*, which realizes the role of a *DetailedProductionScheduleProvider* for other partitions. Partition and UDDI are closely related.

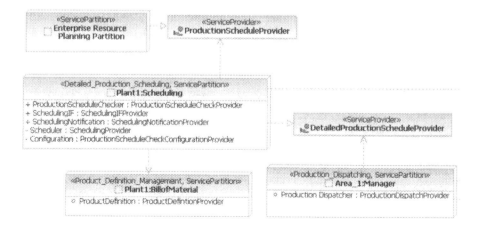

**Fig. 5.** Composition overview of the collaboration view perspective

We decided to map each *Service Partition* to an UDDI provider and every *Service* operation to an UDDI service due to the small number of operations. The UDDI categorization is ANSI/ISA 95 compliant as well, therefore the UDDI provider *Plant1:Scheduling* has the following categorizations assigned and provides all interfaces included in the partition: *Detailed Production Scheduling* (from ANSI/ISA 95 Activity Model categorization schema) and *Site* (from ANSI/ISA 95 Equipment Hierarchy categorization schema). *Service Collaborations* are assigned to ANSI/ISA 95 activities by means of stereotypes and refine the *Business Collaborations* described above. Each collaboration contains a composite structure diagram and at least one diagram for the behaviour view.

Fig. 6 depicts the static composite structure of the *scheduleNewOrders* collaboration. Here we see the participating roles and the provided interfaces (*Service Specifications*). The *Service Channel* stereotype contains the binding information. What we also see is that this collaboration depends on another *Service Collaboration*, namely *createPreactorImportBoM*. This collaboration gets bind by an internal BizTalk call, but offers a WS port (*Service*) as well. For three roles additional information (URL comment) is added. For *ProductDefinition* and *SchedulingIF* the URL points directly to the UDDI window, where detailed information about the actual implementation, e.g. the actual status categorization, is displayed. Those interfaces are statically bound, but *SchedulingNotification* can have a multiplicity greater zero, which means that within the collaboration a lookup for notification subscriptions in the UDDI takes place (*IInquiry* interface). The *DataDefinition* participant represents the XML schema definitions used in this collaboration, which are in this case deployed as .NET DLL at the BizTalk Server.

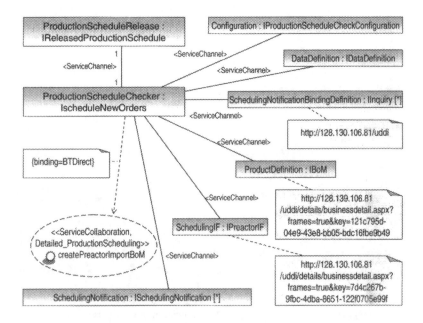

**Fig. 6.** *scheduleNewOrders* collaboration composite structure

The *Configuration* role provides access to the collaboration configuration, which has to be called as a separate BizTalk orchestration (including a business rule call for rules deployed at the BizTalk Business Rule Composer). The wrapping of the business rule call makes the rule platform independent, because the configuration helper orchestration can be published as a WS if necessary. Due to the shortage of space it is not possible to present the activity diagram containing the control flow which is the blueprint for the BizTalk Orchestration, although it remains platform independent in the sense that proprietary actions (e.g. *Transform* shape) are not included. What is added are again URL comments and business rule constraints. In addition, massage types are referenced by name for each object flow.

In the model organization message types and the assigned data types are collected in a *Message View* perspective. To sum it up, this activity model can be reused for different SOA implementation platforms. We have to mention the *Component View* perspective, where the realization of *Service Specifications* by means of components and classes are modelled. This OO abstraction level marks the end point for our methodology from business to enriched but still platform independent models. The mapping to the .NET environment and the BizTalk Orchestration Designer is the final step towards executable flow models.

# 6 Conclusion

The aim of this project was to investigate the potential of SOA in the shop floor domain and we proofed that this concept fulfills the requirements of state of the art intelligent manufacturing information systems. A SOA is flexible enough to realize decentralized control structures where appropriate and to integrate a broad range of service providers in a loosely coupled way. With the proposed MDSA methodology two gaps could be closed, resulting in business and IT alignment. First the gap to the implementation layer, which can be a very heterogeneous one in discrete manufacturing involving sophisticated web applications as well as manual processing tasks. The second gap is the one to the business layer, where business analysts define processes including goal and performance indicator setting. The outcome of this work is an ANSI/ISA 95 compliant model-driven methodology for manufacturing operations management. This methodology was evaluated by means of the realization of a SOA demo scenario for production operations management comprising of two dozens service providers, a central repository and user friendly terminal applications. It was possible to show that the proceeding is consistent enough to provide management capabilities throughout the whole system life-cycle. Moreover, the methodology is flexible enough to embed given shop floor scenarios and components smoothly into the framework with the help of predefined modelling constructs.

The successful participation of IT and domain specialists proofed the feasibility and user friendliness of the proposed methodology. At the implementation level it was interesting to see what restrictions a platform like MS BizTalk dictates in terms of system and not just single flow modelling. Especially the issue of nested flows made some proprietary patterns necessary. Next steps to come are some investigations regarding system dynamics. We would like to know how our approach performs in terms of control loops including flexible system adoption based on monitoring results.

Such a control loop concept must work at different levels of abstraction, providing every level with the right amount and granularity of information. Another focal point will be the interface between platform independent UML 2.0 activity models and the flow models of platform specific implementation environments. At the present stage this requires manual mapping.

# References

1. IBM Research: Cover Story: Are we Ready for "SERVICE"?, Think Tank October 10th, 2005, Translated from Consultation magazine – ThinkTank Media group, accessed from http://researchweb.watson.ibm.com/ssme/20051010_services.shtml at March 15th, 2006
2. ANSI/ISA-95.00.01-2000 Enterprise-Control System Integration Part 1: Models and Terminology, ISA Organization, 2000
3. ANSI/ISA-95.00.02-2001 Enterprise-Control System Integration Part 2: Object Model Attributes, ISA Organization, 2001
4. ANSI/ISA-95.00.03-2005 Enterprise-Control System Integration Part 3: Activity Models of Manufacturing Operations Management, ISA Organization, 2005
5. ATHENA D.A1, Diez, A.B.G.(Document Owner): First Version of State of the Art in Enterprise Modelling Techniques and Technologies to Support Enterprise Interoperability, Deliverable D.A1.1.1, Version 1.0, July 2004
6. INTEROP D4.1: Scientific Integration Conceptual Model and its application in INTEROP, IST-508 011, Version 5.4, November 19th, 2004
7. Lippe S., Greiner U. and Barros A.: A Survey on State of the Art to Facilitate Modelling of Cross-Organisational Business Processes, SAP Research, 2005, accessed at http://www.athena-ip.org on March 24th, 2006
8. Berre A.-J.: Model Driven Interoperability – a standards based approach – and the ATHENA Interoperability Framework, SINTEF, Presentation at eChallenges e-2005, Session Workshop 8°, October 20th, 2005
9. Pondrelli L. (2005a): A MDD Approach to the Development of Interoperable Service Oriented Architectures, Gruppo Formula, Presentation at eChallenges e-2005, Session Workshop 8a, 20th October 2005
10. Pondrelli L. (2005b): An MDD annotation methodology for Semantic Enhanced Service Oriented Architectures, accessed at http://ftp.informatik.rwth-aachen.de/Publications/CEUR-WS/Vol-160/paper27.pdf on March 27th, 2006
11. INTEROP D6.1: Practices, principles and patterns for interoperability, Ed. David Chen, IST-508 011, Final Version 1.0, May 20th, 2005
12. Arsanjani A.: Service-oriented modeling and architecture, IBM developerworks, Nov 11th, 2004; accessed at: http://www-128.ibm.com/developerworks/webservices/library/ws-soa-design1/ on December 12th, 2004
13. Zimmermann O., Krogdahl P. and Gee C.: Elements of Service-Oriented Analysis and Design, IBM developerworks, June 2nd, 2004; accessed at: http://www-128.ibm.com/developerworks/webservices/library/ws-soad1/ on March 7th, 2005
14. Johnston S.: UML 2.0 Profile for Software Services, IBM developerworks, April 13th, 2005; accessed at http://www-128.ibm.com/developerworks/rational/library/05/419_soa/ on May 31st, 2005
15. Johnston S.: Rational UML Profile for business modeling, IBM developerworks June 30th, 2004; accessed at http://www-128.ibm.com/developerworks/rational/library/5167.html on May 31st, 2005

# Product-Driven Enterprise Interoperability for Manufacturing Systems Integration

Michele Dassisti[1], Hervé Panetto[2], and Angela Tursi[1]

[1] Dipartimento di Ingegneria Meccanica e Gestionale, Politecnico di Bari, Italy
m.dassisti@poliba.it,
a.tursi@poliba.it
[2] Centre de Recherche en Automatique de Nancy (CRAN - UMR 7039),
Nancy-University, CNRS, France
Herve.Panetto@cran.uhp-nancy.fr

**Abstract.** The "Babel tower effect", induced by the heterogeneity of applications available in the operation of enterprises brings to a consistent lack of "exchangeability" and risk of semantic loss whenever cooperation has to take place within the same enterprise. Generally speaking, this kind of problem falls within the umbrella of interoperability between local reference information models .This position paper discuss some idea on this field and traces a research roadmap to make enterprise interoperable on the basis of this statement to face interoperability of RIMs by focusing the attention on the product. By applying a transformation between local information models into an **"ontological reference model" centred on the product** it is possible to insure applications interoperability.

**Keywords:** Interoperability, Integration, Product Data Management, Enterprise Model, Ontology.

## 1 Introduction

There are many tools available which cause information overload in the operation of enterprises for several scopes: managerial, production, marketing and so on. This information is characterised by a common problem: the "Babel tower effect" induced by the heterogeneity of applications (such as ERP, SCM, PDM, MES ...), of users and of domains. All this information is strongly influenced mainly by two drivers: the scope (say, criteria) for which this has been collected and used, and the subjectivity induced by each decision maker using it (say interpretation or classification of information).

This situation is due to different information reference models embedded into applications, and thus into a lack of "exchangeability" and a loss of semantics whenever a different use of information is required. This latter kind of problem falls within the umbrella of interoperability problems where, generally speaking, interoperability can be defined as that intrinsic characteristic of a generic entity (organization, system, process, model, ...) allowing its interaction with other entities - to a different

J. Eder, S. Dustdar et al. (Eds.): BPM 2006 Workshops, LNCS 4103, pp. 249–260, 2006.

extent of simplicity - to cooperate for achieving a common goal (second level goal) within a definite interval of time, while pursing its own specific goal (first level goal).

In principle, local reference information models (RIM) embed many classes of information, which responds to specific information classification criteria. Criteria thus define "dimensions", and according to these it is possible to retrieve information whenever required: the heterogeneity of information comes from the specific nature of this classification depending on the two referred drivers. Whenever it is possible to translate these dimensions into, say, neutral dimensions, it would be possible to reach easily a true interoperability between RIMs.

This concept is here translated in practice by referring these RIMs to the common element in all manufacturing operations: the product. The product, which evolves through time (in a diachronic way) along its life cycle, allows thus to define a common reference information model, to support information exchange between the product views and the many applications that refer to them.

The basic assumption of the thesis here sustained is that it is possible in principle to transform local information models (embedded into local applications) to an **"ontological reference model" centred on the product (PCORM)**. In order to insure applications interoperability, the PCORM should be embedded into the product itself; that means information should be deeply linked to the product and possibly recorded into it to be retrieved by applications whenever required.

This position paper presents some idea and traces a research roadmap on this topic, to explore the possibility to make enterprise interoperable on the basis of product-centred information view. The shape of the paper is as follows: section 2 introduces standards and frameworks concerned on information interoperability; section 3 provides the conceptual idea of the paper; section 4 presents some hints for the research roadmap; section 5 summarises the research challenges that have to be faced in the next future and finally in section 6 some general comments are provided.

## 2   Information Interoperability

Enterprises need to focus on their core-competences to improve efficiencies. At the present, the product is perceived again, after the soap-bubble new-economy experiences, the real value of enterprises and a new role is emerging for the whole production process.. In this scenario, the product and production lifecycle and its related management are unavoidably turning to be key aspects, defining a sort of "product centric" or "product-driven" reference point-of-view [1]. The integrated management of all the information regarding the "product" and its manufacturing is one of the related questions. Information interoperability asks for common shared approaches: standardisation and enterprise modelling methodologies are the most advanced tools to this aim.

## 2.1  Standards for Product Data Representation and Exchange

Standardisation initiatives interesting for our purpose are the IEC 62264 set of standards [3] and the ISO 10303 Technical specifications [4], because they are related to Product Data Management at the business and the manufacturing levels of enterprises.

The IEC 62264 set of standards specify a set of reference models for information exchange to facilitate the integration of business applications and manufacturing control applications, within an enterprise. The key aspects for integrating the business applications and the manufacturing operations and control applications are the information structures and exchanges, related to the products, managed by activities, applications, processes, resources, and functions.

Examples of enterprise applications dealing with these exchanges are, at the business levels, ERP (Enterprise Resource Planning) systems or PDM (Product Data Management) systems and, at the manufacturing level, MES (Manufacturing Execution Systems), to name only a few. In particular, MES functions relate production monitoring including materials (raw and finished) and resources (equipment and personnel) traceability information. The International Organization for Standardization (ISO) has been pushing forward the development of standards and models to foster the exchange of information related to goods and services [5]. Efforts like ISO 10303 STEP – Standard for the Exchange of Product model data – deals with the issues of integration and interoperability problem. STEP represents the standard for the computer-interpretable representation of product information and for the exchange of product data. It aims to provide a neutral mechanism capable of describing products throughout their lifecycle. Nowadays, STEP has been recognized as appropriate to help in the integration of manufacturing systems in industries such as automotive, aircraft, shipbuilding, furniture, building and construction, gas and oil.

A significant solution for PDM data exchange is the Unified PDM Schema, which is a basic specification for the exchange of administrative product definition data. It has been created by unifying all PDM data between all existing STEP Application Protocols, such as AP-203, AP-214 and AP-227 and allows the exchange of information that is stored in PDM systems. This information typically forms the metadata for any product. In order to deal with the increasing demands on product models exchange, the standard has specified a set of STEP reusable modules related to PDM. These modules concern all related information attached or describing products technical data such as product structure, configuration control, efficacy, person and organisations, etc. Data integration ensures that the information describing product design, manufacturing and life cycle support is defined only once; STEP data integration eliminates redundancy and the problems caused by redundant information.

## 2.2  Enterprise Modelling Methodologies

Several enterprise modelling methodologies and supporting tools, addressing phases of the enterprise life cycle and various aspects of enterprise modelling, have been developed so far. These methodologies and tools are intended to support business decision-making (such as process visualisation and simulation), enterprise process management, control and monitoring of operational processes (such as workflow) and performance monitoring (such as visualisation of work in progress). Some of the most relevant methodologies and tools are here briefly recalled, highlighting main features and criticalities for the scope of this position paper.

The **ZACHMAN**'s framework [6] is a logical structure for classifying and organising the descriptive representations of an Enterprise. The framework bundle of information consists in representing the design artefacts that constitute the intersection between the roles in the design process It results in a balance between the holistic view and the pragmatic view, in a sort of a framework that results a good classification scheme more oriented to problem solving and planning tasks.

**GERAM** [7], [8] framework encompasses all knowledge needed for enterprise engineering / integration. The completeness of the architecture, which encompasses architectures, methodologies, languages, modelling concepts, models, tools, operation systems for Enterprise Modelling makes this approach a reference for the ISO 15704 standard [20], i.e. an useful guidelines and a way to create a common ontology in the scientific community, more than a specific tool to be used for interoperability.

**GRAI** [9], [10] methodology proposes a modelling framework to support the analysis, design and implementation of an enterprise, referring to two dimensions, based on the systemic approach: functional abstraction and decomposition levels. GIM modelling framework, which is included into the GRAI methodology, introduces the decision dimension/view which is not taken into account in other modelling frameworks: in this sense, it is more decision support oriented.

**ARIS** [11], [12] approach is based on the "multiple views" concept: the objective is to reduce the complexity by dividing the enterprise into individual views, by referring to a number of modelling languages co-ordinated into the Control View. The ARIS architecture forms the framework for the development and optimisation of integrated information systems as well as a description of their implementation by superimposing a structure of interrelations; it is also based on a process-oriented approach [10].

**CIMOSA** [13] is a framework to analyse the requirements of enterprises and translating these into a system which enables and integrates the functions that match the requirements. CIMOSA is neutral in this regard: it addresses concepts and models that are only necessary to model integrated enterprise systems, focusing on process model based enterprise activity control. There is no explicit consideration on interoperability issues in CIMOSA modelling framework. However, CIMOSA can be a contribution for integrated paradigm to establish interoperability (see ISO 14258 [21] and ENV 40003 [22]).

**DoDAF** [14] is one of the most comprehensive enterprise frameworks and provides a good understanding of the stakeholders and users needs. It provides poor contribution to integrated platforms, model-driven design and generation of interoperable solutions. Most all leading Enterprise Architecture vendors are supporting DoDAF, such as METIS Enterprise from Troux Tecnology, System Architect from Popkin, Mega Suite form Mega International, and the other top ten providers.

**TEAF** (Treasury Enterprise Architecture Framework) [14] is another of the most comprehensive enterprise frameworks and gives a good understanding of the stakeholders and users and the minimum of information required to align business and IT. The contribution to integrated platforms, model-driven design and generation of interoperable solutions is poor.

The **AKM** [15] technology and corresponding methodology is based on the concepts of Enterprise Knowledge Spaces, and its four knowledge dimensions:: Approach – Methodology -Infrastructure and Solutions – AMIS. The AKM technology is prone to interoperability, since it implements the layered Enterprise Architecture, and it is prepared for the POPS methodology, for the Enterprise Knowledge Architecture and the Intelligent Infrastructure services.

**ISO 15745** – Open System Application Integration Framework [23] consists of the application integration framework (AIF), which defines generic elements and rules for describing integration models and application interoperability profiles, together with their component profiles (process profiles, information exchange profiles, and resource profiles). It supports the development of interface specifications in the form of application interoperability profiles (AIPs) enabling the selection of suitable resources and the documentation of the "as built" application. A key factor is the concept of interfaces: the interfaces of the resources used to perform the function are configured to work with the corresponding resource interfaces of the other functions, involved in a target manufacturing applications. There is no complete industrial implementation reported so far; furthermore, this approach can work only if various standards used to specify interfaces are interoperable between them.

**MISSION** [16] approach extends the High Level Architecture (HLA) approach [17], [18], [19] includes the modelling aspects which describe how to collect the necessary data for the distributed simulation, specification on how the different simulation models can be coordinated starting from a template library; a simulation manager supports the definition and the interoperability of simulation templates by exchanging objects. Even this interesting solution relies on a top-down specification of objects to be exchanged and the related interfacing information in the federation.

Table 1 summarises the standards and enterprise modelling approaches for interoperability discussed above. Till now, no unified conceptual basis for model-based enterprise engineering -enabling consistency, convergence and interoperability of the various modelling methodologies and supporting tools - has been created so far based on a bottom-up view.

From this brief summary it is evident how all the solutions available so far share the same common *top-down* approach, .relying on the *process-view* approach, which belongs to the static and holistic perception of the enterprise, descending from system theory. To summarise, it is evident how a different conception for the global information reference model is required for cooperation to take place effectively; this justifies the thesis here sustained that the product view may turn to be very interesting, since the product is in some sense "inertial" with respect to the changing cooperation processes and the potential dynamical evolution in time of actors.

**Table 1.** Standards and frameworks comparison

| Standard/ Framework | Interoperability core features | Product view |
|---|---|---|
| IEC 62264 | Information structures and exchanges | Yes |
| ISO 10303 | Representation of product information and exchange of product data | Yes |
| ZACHMAN | Intersection between roles in design process and product abstractions | No |
| GERAM | Components used in all types of enterprise integration processes | No |
| GRAI | Modelling with reference to functional abstraction and decomposition levels | No |
| ARIS | Development and optimisation of integrated information systems | No |
| CIMOSA | Concepts and models strictly necessary to model integrated enterprise systems | No |
| DoDAF | Understanding of the stakeholders and users needs | No |
| TEAF | Information from stakeholders and users alignment in business and IT | No |
| AKM | Layered Enterprise Architecture, POPS methodology, Enterprise Knowledge and Intelligent Infrastructure services | No |
| ISO 15745 | Interfaces | No |
| MISSION | Distributed discrete-event simulation | No |

## 3 Product View for Reference Information Models

It has to be stated firstly that each application adopted for the operation of enterprises uses its own information repository, which serves for its own scopes. Each repository refers to a reference information model (RIM) that specifies the structure of the information treated and its nature. This model embeds several design and management criteria related to the scope of the application to which it is devoted (say subjective part), even though a information is still valid independently of the application itself (say, objective part).

It is thus possible to state that each application retrieves information from its repositories, according to the specific need during its operation: the efficiency of this "information retrieval process (IRP)" is directly dependent on the amount of objective information available. A negative effect results from the subjective part of information, in case this has to be imported from different applications: in this latter case, the translation required might bring to strong loss of information, and thus it may have impact on its significance or pertinence.

Let us imagine that a reference system can be defined for making explicit information concerning the transformations the product has to undergo. This information is always a result of a decisional process made by operators according to their specific scope (*top-down approach*): in this case the information reference system is the operator himself (see $i_{RS}^{1,2,3,\cdots}$ in Fig. 1). The novelty of our idea is to reverse the information reference system (see $i_{RS}^*$ in Fig. 1) by simply making the "product" active part of its transformation process (*bottom-up approach*).

By referring to the "product view" here proposed, it is possible to guarantee a sort of neutrality of the information, thus reducing the risk of subjectivity and consequently the efficiency of the information retrieval process itself.

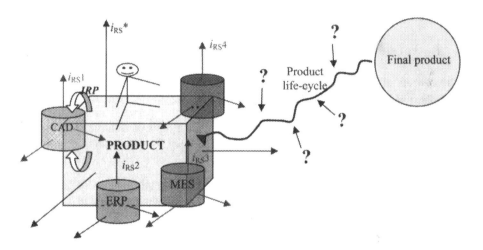

**Fig. 1.** *Product view* representation: $i_{RS}^*$ is the "inertial" reference system centred on product

The efforts devoted to information standardisation, as stated before, is a proof of the need to improve the efficiency of IRP, whether its constraints are in the "top-down" approach, which unavoidably limits its significance to the decision-maker capability of capturing all the relevant aspects of RIM. The product-view approach can be defined, on the contrary, as a "bottom-up" one, where adaptively the product "asks" for information to proceed along its life-cycle (see Fig. 2). This representation is obviously not complete, since features and behavioural rules of the "product" are always designed *a-priori* by the decision maker: it will be a matter of the future research effort to devise if and how it will be possible to allow a pure adaptive mechanism of the class "product", in order to implement a true bottom-up fashion if ever possible.

In order to explain better the product view and the related research challenges, let us imagine a man to "sit on the product" and walk with it during its life-cycle: all the information required to know where to go, which operation to undergo or what kind of information to receive for the next change of state, will turn to have a radically different meaning - and consequently structure - with respect to the classical top-down approach.

Starting from this representation, the first step of the research effort in the development of the product-driven interoperability will be the study of the existing reference information models used by the actual applications concerned with the product life-cycle, to find an unique "product view" representation, that will be the basis to design the structure of the PCORM. For the sake of simplification, one can state that the PCORM will result a meta-model derived from a sort of intersection (or any similar reasonable *logical operation* on models) of the entire specific RIM corresponding to each of the application available in the factory, independently of their objective or subjective nature.

It will be another question of the future research to understand the nature and the contents of this *logical operation* onto the RIMs (or the repositories of information themselves, in case of instantiation in a real application).

## 4  Research on Transformation of Reference Information Models

The concept of interoperability has been widely analyzed, in the last decade, by the research European community (see IDEAS Roadmap, UEML [24], INTEROP NoE [25] and ATHENA IP [26] projects), in a joint effort between industrial world, tertiary industry, suppliers and academic world. On the basis of results reached so far, the fundamental aspects that can be further explored in the development of the interoperability concept are:

✓  the development of synergies between different domains, such as the enterprise modelling, the ontology building and the software architectures and platforms;
✓  the definition and the realisation of methods and tools providing an effective support to the collaboration between experts in the various domains.

A step of the research on product-driven interoperability will be to study the RIMs, embedded into the local applications, such as PDM systems and ERP systems. These applications deal with the product but with different points of view; this has to be done by focusing on the product, tracing its diachronic evolution through time along its life cycle.

Starting from this, the research has to define the transformation operations of local reference information models (RIMs) into an **"ontological reference model" centred on the product (PCORM)**. The idea of this position paper could be inspired to the concept of "schema integration", developed in the Database Management System (DBMS) domain, where various data models (namely, schemas) and architectures are used to design the conceptual structure of databases, which is to design an abstract, global, understandable view of the application.

Batini et al [27] define *schema integration* as "the activity of integrating the schema of existing or proposed databases into a global, unified schema". The contexts in which this concept can be applied are:

✓  the *view integration* (in database design), which produces a global conceptual description of a proposed database,
✓  the *database integration* (in distributed database management), which produces the global schema of a collection of database.

In both contexts, the approach consists in designing an integrated schema (i.e. a conceptual view in the case of *view integration* and a global schema in the case of *database integration*), starting from the single component schema to be integrated (namely: the user views in the *view integration* and the local schema in the *database integration*), with the scope of capturing the meaning of data.

In a similar way, to obtain the "ontological reference model" before mentioned it will be necessary to build an *integrated schema,* containing all the information included in local applications RIMs as necessary (corresponding to the component schemas in the DBMS domain). This "ontological reference model" will be built upon the product, which is the guideline for the design process and to implement information, thus resulting in the bottom up approach.

The framework provided in [27] to face the schema diversity can be a good guideline to suggest a set of steps of the integration process, useful to transform local RIMs into PCORM. Inheriting from the DBMS domain, the integration process can be performed by referring to an ordered mixture of the following activities:

✓ *pre-integration*: it consists of an analysis of local applications RIMs before integration to decide upon some integration policy, what applications to integrate, the order of integration and all additional information relevant to integration;

✓ *comparison of the schemas*: this activity has the scope to determine the correspondences among elements of RIMs and detect possible syntactic or semantics conflicts. Conflicts may rise for several reasons: different perspectives (each application has its own way of modelling the same information), equivalence among constructs of the model (several combinations of constructs can have the same meaning), incompatible design specifications (erroneous choices in inputs to the models integration process). In case common elements may be modelled in different ways, an *inter-schema properties* (i.e. semantic relationships holding between different models) need thus to be recognised;

✓ *conforming the schemas*: an effort is required to solve conflicts, depending on their nature, to make possible merging of various local RIMs;

✓ *merging and restructuring*: once conflicts are eliminated, the RIMs can be superimposed to derive the intermediate "ontological reference model" with an iterative process: at the end of this, the final "ontological reference model" can be derived. It will require a test against the following qualitative criteria:

   o *completeness and correctness*: the ontological reference model must contain all concepts present in any RIM correctly;

   o *minimality*: the concept represented in more than one RIM must be represented only once in the ontological reference model;

   o *understandability*: the ontological reference model should be easy to understand by the designers.

All of the above activities can be performed for building the PCORM, bearing in mind that all the integration activities are strongly influenced by the data model adopted to build the conceptual schemas. As a consequence, these activities might be used only as guidelines or hints for the transformation process of RIMs into the PCORM. Other approaches can be feasible to this aim.

In [28], for example, the integration between PDMs and workflow management systems (which are two integration systems) is suggested using the PDM to store sets of definitions of both the parts and the task that need to be executed on the parts. The PDM acts as the reference database both for the enactment services of the production workflow system and for other systems and manages the Product Breakdown Structure (PBS), the Assembly Breakdown Structure (ABS) and the Work Breakdown Structure (WBS).

In [29], on the other hand, an approach how to link "incompatible" integration systems is suggested, which can represent a valid indication to the research project in exam. The authors introduce a four-layered architecture, which is only a conceptual solution for integration: two partners with the need for co-operation define structural and behavioural patterns of interaction.

All the interaction solutions discussed above are not suitable as a general integration solution for every kind of co-operation between the two or more partners; these can represent a good hint for our research roadmap to devise the transformation operations of local reference information model into the "ontological reference model" centred on the product. Hopefully, an appropriate mix of these can be a good choice to the scope posed for the research.

## 5   Roadmap of Research

Following the premises developed in paragraph 0and 4, herewith we summarise some of the most important research challenges to be faced in the next future for supporting enterprise product-driven interoperability.

The research activities will be centred on the information modelling for the technical management of products and its use for interoperability of the manufacturing applications. These research activities will tend to build on the concept of interoperability based on product view, to be used diffusely in manufacturing cycle, starting from the ideation phase up to the product use.

The methodologies to be used may refer to the design mechanisms of computer science engineering – such as UML standard and formal logic – for the definition of model structures of information within the enterprise. These can ensure a common logical structure for the interoperability of the applications, by referring to the product.

In modelling the various phases of product lifecycle, all the sets of technical information need to be considered, constantly interpreted from the point of view of product; information produced during the idea and design phase need to be also considered. The information model based on the product will constitute a sort of "backbone" for tracing the product evolution and to build the ontological model, making easier the information exchange between different applications linked to the product.

The final expected outcome of the research plan here described will be the formalization of a common information model, almost indifferent to the application type used in manufacturing systems and based on existing standards, such as ISO 10303 and IEC 62264 previously recalled.

Main focus points of the research will be:

i.  study of information reference systems and of applications main models and standard, for the information management of the product;

ii. development of a general reference model, starting from a specific application of PDM (Windchill) and an one for ERP (Sage Adonix), based on a real case of an Italian factory which manufactures bicycles, for the generation of a reference ontology of product information;

iii. formal check of reference model for the ontology of product information, applicatory check on an instanced industrial case for the operational feasibility.

# 6  Conclusions

The interoperability is a concept of growing interest for the enterprise, urged from the competitive pressure imposed by the new market without boundaries. The product is the key concept shared by all applications inside an enterprise: it may serve as a kind of "mediator" to refer all information produced and used by these applications. The thesis here sustained is that an ontological reference model centred on the product takes into account all product points of view.

It is evident how the temporariness of the cooperation is a critical factor for the realization of collaborative networks between manufacturing enterprises, in order to survive in the global market. The scientific studies proposed various answers to this problem: many of these answers can be classified as top-down. The use of a reference system as proposed, in a bottom-up fashion, promises good results in the research of design solution, effective for the temporary cooperation between systems of enterprises, which today has not been reached yet.

**Acknowledgments.** This work is partially supported by the Commission of the European Communities under the sixth framework programme (INTEROP Network of Excellence, Contract N° 508011, <http://www.interop-noe.org>).

# References

1. Morel G., Panetto H., Zaremba M.B., Mayer F.: Manufacturing Enterprise Control and Management System Engineering: paradigms and open issues. *IFAC Annual Reviews in Control*. 27/2, 199-209, Elsevier, December 2003, ISSN: 1367-5788
2. Terzi S., Cassina J., and Panetto H.: Development of a metamodel to foster interoperability along the product lifecycle traceability. Proceedings of the IFIP/ACM SIGAPP INTEROP-ESA conference, Interoperability of Enterprise Software and Applications, February 23-25, Geneva, Switzerland, Springer Science publisher, pp. 1-11, (2005) ISBN: 1-84628-151-2
3. IEC 62264: Enterprise-control system integration, Part 1. Models and terminology, Part 2: Model object attributes. ISO/IEC, (2002) Geneva

4. ISO/TS 10303: STEP modules related to Product Data Management. Industrial automation systems and integration — Product data representation and exchange (2004) Geneva
5. International Organization for Standardization (ISO). Geneva (2005) www.iso.org
6. http://www.zifa.com
7. Bernus P. and Nemes L.: Requirements of the Generic Enterprise Reference Architecture and Methodology. Annual Reviews in Control, 21 (1997) 125-136
8. Bernus P. and Nemes L.: A framework to define a generic enterprise reference architecture and methodology. Computer Integrated Manufacturing Systems, 9 (1996) 179-191
9. Chen, D., Vallespir, B. and Doumeingts, G. : GRAI integrated methodology and its mapping onto generic enterprise reference architecture and methodology. Computers in Industry, 33 (1997) 387- 394
10. McCarthy, I. and Menicou M.: A classification schema of manufacturing decisions for the GRAI enterprise modelling technique. Computers in Industry, 47 (2002) 339-355
11. Scheer A.-W. et al.: ARIS, Business Process Framework, 3 rd edition, Berlin (1999)
12. http://www.pera.net/Methodologies/ARIS/ARIS.html
13. http://www.cimosa.de
14. http://www.gcn.com/enterprisearchitecture
15. http://www.akmii.net
16. Mertins K., Rabe M., Jäkel F-W.: Distributed modelling and simulation of supply chains. International Journal of Computer Integrated Manufacturing, 18/5:342-349, 2005
17. Dahmann J., Fujimoto R. and Weatherly R: The DoD High Level Architecture: an update. (1998)
18. Department of Defence: Defence modelling and simulation Office: High Level Architecture Run-time Infrastructure. Programmer's Guide Version 4 (1998)
19. Zhuge H., Chen J., Feng Y., and Shi Y.: A federation-agent-workflow simulation framework for virtual organisation development. Information & Management, 39 (2002) 325-336
20. ISO IS 15704: Industrial automation systems - Requirements for enterprise reference architectures and methodologies (1999) Geneva
21. ISO IS 14258: Industrial automation systems - Concepts and rules for enterprise models (1999) Geneva
22. CEN ENV 40003:1990 - CIM Systems Architecture - Framework for Enterprise Modelling
23. ISO/DIS 15745-1: Industrial automation systems and integration — Open systems application integration frameworks — Part 1: Generic reference description; (2000), Geneva
24. http://www.ueml.org
25. http://www.interop-noe.org
26. http://www.athena-ip.org
27. Batini C., Lenzerini M., and Navathe S.B.: A Comparative Analysis of Methodologies for Database Schema Integration. ACM Computing Surveys, 18(4) (1986) 323-364
28. Kovacs Z., Le Goff J.M. and McClatchey R.: Support for product data from design to production. Computer Integrated Manufacturing Systems, 11(4) (1998) 285-290
29. Karcher A. and Glander M.: Global distributed engineering – integrating different process paradigms. Journal of Materials Processing Technology, 138 (2003) 31-137

# Understanding Interdependence in Enterprise Systems: A Model and Measurement Formalism

Ronald E. Giachetti

Department of Industrial & Systems Engineering, Florida International University,
10555 W. Flagler Street / (EC 3100), Miami, FL 33174, USA
giachetr@fiu.edu

**Abstract.** Interdependence between the subsystems of an enterprise is one of the driving reasons for integrating the enterprise. Integration attempts to manage those interdependencies so all subsystems work harmoniously together to achieve the enterprise goals. Prior to embarking on an enterprise integration project the interdependencies need to be analyzed. Unfortunately, interdependence between subsystems is still poorly conceptualized. This paper develops a modeling and measurement formalism to analyze interdependence in the enterprise. The model defines interdependence and characterizes the strength of the interdependence through relational measurement theory. The model is supported by empirical findings and illustrated through a case study. Limitations of current conceptualizations of interdependence are discussed and remedies are proposed. The primary contribution is a formal model to define and analyze interdependence in an enterprise, an activity that should occur as part of all enterprise integration projects.

**Keywords:** Enterprise Systems, modeling, measurement.

## 1 Introduction

An enterprise system is an organized collection of interdependent subsystems that must coordinate their activities in order to achieve common enterprise goals. The decomposition of the enterprise into subsystems is a natural strategy to deal with the size and complexity of enterprise systems. There are several ways in which to decompose the enterprise [1]; one of the more common decompositions is functional. The benefits of the decomposition are derived from the differentiation of each subsystem to develop unique knowledge, information, and systems to optimally address local problems. However, the decomposition must be countered with appropriate levels of integration so that the decisions and actions of each subsystem contribute effectively and efficiently to the overall enterprise goals. The need for integration arises due to the interconnectedness between the subsystems. The subsystems are interdependent because of the business processes that cross subsystem boundaries [2]. Not only is the enterprise decomposed from an organizational perspective but also from a technical perspective. The information technologies and related systems that support each organizational unit are specified, designed, and

J. Eder, S. Dustdar et al. (Eds.): BPM 2006 Workshops, LNCS 4103, pp. 261–272, 2006.

implemented to meet local requirements. As a result, when viewing from an enterprise-wide perspective, a heterogeneous mix of technologies emerges and creates additional hurdles to integrating the enterprise.

One of the merits of a good decomposition is to obtain loosely coupled subsystems that minimize the interdependence between subsystems [3]; however, in practice interdependence cannot be eliminated. So while decomposition is done to make enterprise design easier, the decomposition also introduces another level of complexity because complexity arises not just from the size of the system but also from the interrelatedness of the system components and the emergent behaviour that cannot be predicted from the individual system components [3], [4]. As interdependence increases, the enterprise must spend more time and effort on coordination work and utilize more elaborate coordination mechanisms are required to integrate the enterprise system. Malone et al. [5] define coordination work as that work that is performed by a group of actors working together on a task that would not have been performed if a single actor did the task alone. An over-riding concern for the designers and managers of enterprise systems is how to manage the interdependencies between the subsystems so that the overall enterprise systems performance is optimized [6], [7].

Managing dependencies [8] is part of the larger problem of enterprise integration. Enterprise integration (EI) is the study of all the system components, how they are related to each other, and structuring them so as to improve the enterprise's performance [2]. There are many approaches to integrate the enterprise. In an attempt to shed light on the multitude of ways to achieve enterprise integration, [8] defined five integration types of connectivity, data sharing, interoperability, coordination, and alignment that categorize the many approaches applied to integrating the enterprise. The lower level and mostly technical integration types are implemented as an indirect means to effect coordination and organizational alignment. For example, work toward greater interoperability of heterogeneous systems is performed so that the workflow supported by those systems is more seamless or better coordinated. Regardless of the integration approach adopted, all integration approaches strive to improve the performance of the enterprise. It has been established and is generally accepted that integration leads to improved enterprise performance [9], [11]. However, results of integration efforts have been haphazard, with many failures reported in the literature [12], [13]. In order to progress, the central research question in designing enterprise systems is to identify variables that will enable researchers to make consistent and valid predictions of what type of enterprise integration will be most effective in different situations.

To improve the success of enterprise integration this paper seeks to understand the relationships between the subsystems within the enterprise. There are many types of relationships between these subsystems, but the one of primary importance to integration is interdependence. Interdependence is the degree to which the actions and outcomes of one unit are controlled by or contingent upon the actions of another unit. If interdependence is high then the time, cost, and effort necessary to coordinate the process will be high [14], [15]. This paper seeks to define, model, and measure interdependence in an enterprise. In the next section a review of the conceptual development of interdependence is presented. Then in section 2 the modelling framework is presented. The modelling framework shows the development of the definitions of interdependence, how to formally model them, and how to define quantitative measures of interdependence. An illustrative example is provided in section 3. In the conclusions the main findings of the research are summarized and suggestions for future research are made.

## 1.1 Conceptual Development of Interdependence

One of the classical management writers, Fayol [16], listed coordination as one of the critical elements of management. He pointed to the necessity of "harmonizing the separate activities and departments into a single whole". Coordination work is necessary to manage the interdependencies in the enterprise. It was Thompson [17] who in his action theory of organizations paid a great deal of attention to the different types of interdependence existing within organizations and to methods for achieving high levels of cooperation and coordination. Interdependence is "when actions taken by one referent system affect the actions or outcomes of another referent system" [18]. Interdependence relationships can be direct when Unit A requires an action by Unit B (e.g. delivery of materials) or indirect when Unit A requires an action of Unit B contingent on A's own action (e.g. delivery of materials according to a production schedule generated by A) [19]. Interdependence occurs based on the flow of work between organizational units, based on the organizational hierarchy and procedures for decision making, as well as on the social needs and goals of the employees [20].

There are three distinct approaches toward conceptualizing and measuring interdependence. The first approach to measure interdependence is to use the flows (material, information, control) and characterize the difficulty of managing the flows [7], [14], [20], [22]. Thompson proposed a simple ordinal measure scale. In his conceptualization the lowest level of interdependence is pooled resources, then sequential relationships, followed by reciprocal relationships that are the most difficult to coordinate. This basic hierarchy of interdependence types continues to be utilized by researchers today. The approach of modelling and measuring interdependence through studying the work flow patterns assumes the interdependencies arise between tasks – in fact Malone and [7] succinctly define coordination as the management of dependencies. Their work is atypical of much of the other work. They define a taxonomy of dependency types and provide guidelines on how to coordinate each dependency types. The second approach is to conceptualize different types of exchanges between the organization units [18], [19]. In this work, the emphasis is on interdependence in the organizational structure and not the process. The third approach is to develop action theory of organizations, paid a great deal of attention to the different types of interdependence existing within organizations and to methods for achieving high levels of cooperation and coordination. Interdependence is "when actions taken by one referent system affect the actions or outcomes of another referent system" [18]. Interdependence relationships can be direct when Unit A requires an action by Unit B (e.g. delivery of materials) or indirect when Unit A requires an action of Unit B contingent on perceptual constructs of interdependence constructs that can be measure them via survey methods. [23] use a perceptual measure of interdependence because they argue that measuring it by understanding workflows is too difficult. Other researchers have also used perceptual measures of interdependence, usually when interdependence was one of several variables that they were studying [24]. The strength of the survey method is to capture the participants' perspective and provide a richer characterization of all facets of interdependency.

The ordinal scale provided by Thompson was developed to describe the influence of interdependence on organizational structure – it is too crude to guide business process redesign efforts. The extension of the interdependence types through taxonomies is a qualitative analysis. They do not order the dependencies in any way according to strength, they do not rank the coordination mechanisms in terms of usefulness or appropriateness, and they do not discuss the interdependencies of an entire process or system except in an isolated form. Survey methods provide a means to measure interdependence beyond workflow patterns – but they are ill-suited to business process redesign. The reason is surveys provide no model of the enterprise systems nor is it clear how to convert the characterization of interdependence strength into prescriptive actions that can be taken. So, survey data can describe the current as-is interdependence but it cannot be used to understand and predict what interdependence will arise in a to-be enterprise design.

In this work we concur with [7] that interdependence arises from the tasks. However, we view the instance of the interdependence creates a coordination load on the organizational unit or actor responsible for coordinating that (those) tasks involved in the interdependence. So, we relate the interdependence between tasks and organizational structure through the responsibilities of each organization unit for executing a task. Moreover, we combine the merits of survey collection with the merits of process modelling in order to develop an engineering tool to analyze interdependence in enterprise systems as part of the analysis necessary for any enterprise integration project.

## 2 Model Development

Interdependence is the degree to which the actions or outcome of one task affects the actions or outcome of a second task. In this definition, interdependence is viewed as occurring between tasks, which then creates interdependence between the organizational units that are responsible for the tasks. It is important to view interdependence as arising between tasks and not organizational units because the tasks can be decoupled from the organizational unit responsible for its completion. For example, a task requires a certain set of capabilities in order to execute the task. Any actor or organization unit that possesses those capabilities may execute the task. Consequently, management has the flexibility to reassign roles and responsibilities as long as it adheres to the task capability constraints. Any reassignment would change interdependence between organizational units; however the interdependence between tasks would remain unaltered. So, any model must represent both process constructs and organization constructs.

The empirical relationships between the objects are derived from the literature. First, Thompson [17] and many succeeding research state that pooled resources, sequential tasks, and reciprocal tasks are ordered from lowest to highest in terms of interdependence. We add a refinement to the interdependence types to distinguish between two types of sequential interdependence. There is sequential interdependence due to the control flow of activities and a sequential interdependence due to the information flow. In an enterprise, the control flow or sequence of work tasks is not necessarily the same as the information flow. We call the later type an information sequential interdependence.

The introduction of a fourth type disrupts the ordering of interdependence types because it is not clear the ordering of control sequential versus information sequential. We argue that a control sequential interdependence is stronger or at least the same strength interdependence relationship as an information sequential interdependence. The reason is that control flow is like a rely race in which the runner cannot run until he receives the baton. Likewise, in a control flow the succeeding task cannot start until the previous task completes. In an information sequential interdependence the succeeding task frequently has alternative courses of action if the information is delayed or otherwise interfered with. The introduction of this logic leads to a complete ordering of the interdependence types. However, the comparison between control versus information sequential interdependence must be tested and empirically validated.

The current understanding of interdependence is an ordinal scale of the above-mentioned interdependence types. There is insufficient empirical justification to make any stronger claims concerning the relative strength of one interdependence type compared to another type. For example, does a strong sequential relationship equal a weak reciprocal relationship? For this reason we consider the interdependence types separately until more empirical evidence can provide guidance on other courses of action.

A second empirical relationship is reported in [23]. They show that interdependence attributes of frequency, importance, and delay have significant impact on process participants' perception of interdependence. These interdependence characteristics can provide an ordering within each of the four types defined above.

A final observation is interdependence is an asymmetric relationship. For example, task B can be strongly dependent on task A but the reverse may not be true; i.e. task A is only weakly dependent on task B. When discussing relationships in general the term interdependence is preferred since any notion of direction is ambiguous. However, when discussing specific task relationships the term dependent is preferred because it conveys the direction.

## 2.2 Enterprise System Model for Interdependence Measurement

There is a significant body of literature on enterprise modelling (See [2] for a review). A prevalent research approach is the development of enterprise reference architectures that describe the enterprise from many different viewpoints in order to deal with the complexity of the enterprise system. In this work we choose Event Driven Process

Chains (EPC), which are one of the central components of ARIS [25]. EPCs unite the organization, information, and function views defined by ARIS into a single diagram showing the process flow. We choose EPCs because in a single diagram we can represent the primary objects of interest for studying interdependence: control flows, information flows, organizational responsibility, and attributes of these flows. EPC come the closest to representing all of these elements – although in a later section we annotate the EPC to represent the attributes of frequency, importance, and delay of the information flows.

### 2.2.1  Event Driven Process Chain Model

Since, interdependence arises largely due to the business processes in the organization we take a process-centric perspective of the enterprise.

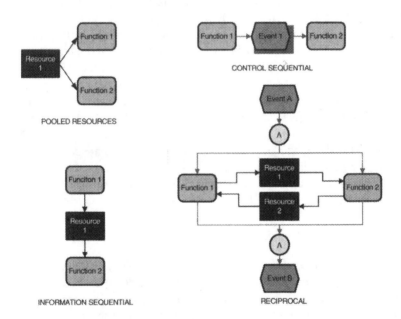

**Fig 1.** Four interdependency types

### 2.3  Measurement of Interdependence

The pattern of work flows alone is insufficient to understand interdependence between tasks. For example, a report can be generated daily and flow to a function but maybe the report is of little use. For this and similar reasons it is necessary to move beyond capturing the patterns of workflow. Attributes of the work flows need to be defined and measured in order to more fully characterize the interdependence. We create an extended event process control diagram that is extended by annotating a standard EPC with the attributes frequency, importance, and timing onto the existing diagram notation.  Let the attributes be defined by the triple $<f, s, d>$ as shown in

**Table 1.** Information Flow Attributes

| Attribute | Scale | Interpretation |
|-----------|-------|----------------|
| Frequency | $f_I : A' \rightarrow \{1,$ $2, 3, 4, 5, 6, 7\}$ | How frequently does this information flow occur? Once a ... {quarter, month, two weeks, week, day, hour, minute} |
| Importance | $s_I : A' \rightarrow \{1,$ $2, 3, 4, 5\}$ | How important is the information flow to the function? { a minor inconvenience to do without it, difficult but possible to function effectively without it, impossible to function effectively without it}[1] |
| Delay | $d_I : A' \rightarrow \{1,$ $2, 3, 4, 5, 6, 7\}$ | How long can this information flow be delayed before the function is negatively affected? {quarter or longer, month, two weeks, week, day, hour, minute} |

Table1. These mappings have been empirically validated [23]. The information flow attributes are used to characterize the strength of pooled resource, information sequential and reciprocal interdependencies.

As previously stated each interdependence type is handled separately. Interdependence between the functions is collected in an $n \times n$ matrix $M$ where each element $m_{ij}$ is the interdependency measure. Each function in a row is dependent on the function in the column to the degree $m_{ij}$. A separate matrix is made for each interdependence type. In the information sequence interdependence matrix the values of $<f_I, s_I, d_I>$ are used to derive $m_{ij}$, which is normalized to be between 0 and 1. In the control sequential matrix the values of $<s_C, d_C>$ are used to derive $m_{ij}$ and are also normalized between 0 and 1.

# 3 Illustrative Application

The interdependence modelling and measurement framework is applied to a telecommunications company that competes in the long-distance domestic and international market. The telecommunications company generated almost $300 million in revenue and employees approximately 180 employees. In this case study we focus on one product, the prepaid calling card. A prepaid calling card is a card in set denominations (e.g. $10, $15, or $20) that customers purchase to make telephone calls. Grocery stores, bodegas, restaurants, and so forth distribute the calling cards. The prepaid cards can be used from any telephone and for any type of call.

The prepaid calling card delivery process was modelled using the annotated EPC described above. To create the model two analysts reviewed the company's existing documentation including procedure manuals and the like. The head of the management systems group that created the procedure manuals was interviewed and consulted with over a six month period. Additionally, the process was observed by the analysts during this same period. Semi-structured interviews of approximately twenty minutes were conducted with the cognizant staff in each department involved in the

---

[1] Scores 2 and 4 are intermediate between described values.

prepaid process. The data collected was incorporated into the model. The model was presented to the company's managers for validation.

Some notable aspects of the process are the telecommunications company acts as a "coordinator" for the entire process. The cards are printed by an outside vendor, they are distributed by an outside distributor who also collects the payments, capacity on the network to carry the calls is negotiated with a network provider, and customer service is partially outsourced. The only actual task, aside from coordination, conducted by the company is marketing of the prepaid calling cards. Otherwise, the company operates as a virtual enterprise that coordinates the activities of specialized providers so as to deliver the service to the customer.

Fig. 2 shows part of the overall EPC diagram for the entire prepaid card process. In order to abridge the diagram the organization units are not shown. Instead, in each task the organization responsible is designated with the abbreviations: D = distributor, S = sales, M = marketing, PM = prepaid manager, and P = printer.

In Fig. 2 the triple characterizing frequency, importance, and delay is depicted on each information flow arc leaving an information resource. For example, the arc from resource PO entering the function Generate Prototype Card is (1, 3, 5). The interpretation is the PO is received quarterly or less, it is difficult but possible to generate the prototype card without the PO, and the PO can be delayed by a day before the function is negatively affected.

The information sequential interdependencies between functions are shown in Table 2. The measures can be used to understand which functions are critical to the overall workflow. For example, the table shows that function 6, Generate order details is a critical function in the overall workflow since other functions have a high dependence on it. This suggests the information output of this function, the Order Details, is important and appropriate use of IT to ensure its accuracy and timely delivery can add to a well coordinated process. Also, function 11, Print Cards has a high interdependence on other functions, specifically functions 7 and 10. These two functions provide the CD-ROM with PINs and the Printing Order. The reason for the high interdependence is the importance of these information resources and the low tolerance for delay. Taking this into consideration managers can examine how the information flows to improve overall efficiency of the process.

The information sequential interdependence can be transferred to the organizational units responsible for each task. These measures can be used to reduce interdependence by modifying each organization unit's task assignments assuming task capability constraints are met, by tracing the sources of the interdependence and enacting means to reduce the interdependence, or by enacting coordination mechanisms to manage the interdependence.

In a business process it is expected that the predominant interdependency type would be sequential. Process designers would try to minimize reciprocal interdependencies – understanding they take more coordination effort. In this extract of the entire prepaid calling card process there are no pooled resource or reciprocal interdependence types – however in the entire process there were several reciprocal interdependence types found.

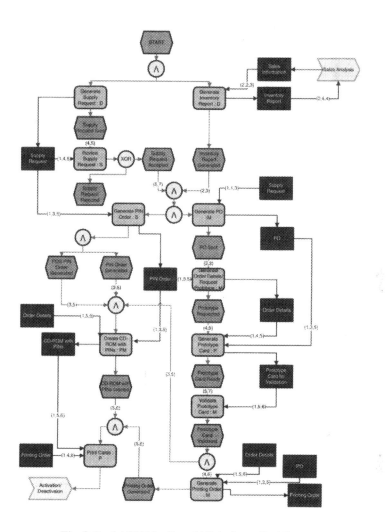

**Fig. 2.** Partial EPC for Prepaid Telephone Card Process

**Table 2.** Information Sequential Interdependence for illustrated example

| FUNCTION | | 1 | 2 | 3 | 4 | 5 | 6 | 7 | 8 | 9 | 10 | 11 | |
|---|---|---|---|---|---|---|---|---|---|---|---|---|---|
| Generate supply request | 1 | | | | | | | | | | | | 0.00 |
| generate inventory report | 2 | | | | | | | | | | | | 0.00 |
| review supply request | 3 | 0.75 | | | | | | | | | | | 0.75 |
| generate PIN order | 4 | 0.67 | | | | | | | | | | | 0.67 |
| generate PO | 5 | 0.33 | | | | | | | | | | | 0.33 |
| Generate order details / prototype | 6 | | | | | 0.67 | | | | | | | 0.67 |
| create CD-ROM with PINs | 7 | | | | | 0.67 | 0.92 | | | | | | 1.58 |
| Generate prototype card | 8 | | | | | | 0.67 | 0.83 | | | | | 1.50 |
| validate prototype card | 9 | | | | | | | | 0.92 | | | | 0.92 |
| generate printing order | 10 | | | | | | 0.67 | 0.92 | | | | | 1.58 |
| print cards | 11 | | | | | | | 0.92 | | | 0.83 | | 1.75 |
| | | 1.75 | 0.00 | 0.00 | 1.33 | 1.33 | 2.67 | 0.92 | 0.92 | 0.00 | 0.83 | 0.00 | |

**Table 3.** Control Sequential Interdependence

| FUNCTION | | 1 | 2 | 3 | 4 | 5 | 6 | 7 | 8 | 9 | 10 | 11 | |
|---|---|---|---|---|---|---|---|---|---|---|---|---|---|
| Generate supply request | 1 | | | | | | | | | | | | 0.00 |
| generate inventory report | 2 | | | | | | | | | | | | 0.00 |
| review supply request | 3 | 0.75 | | | | | | | | | | | 0.75 |
| generate PIN order | 4 | | 0.42 | 1 | | | | | | | | | 1.42 |
| generate PO | 5 | | 0.42 | 1 | | | | | | | | | 1.42 |
| Generate order details / prototype | 6 | | | | | 0.42 | | | | | | | 0.42 |
| create CD-ROM with PINs | 7 | | | | 0.67 | | | | | 0.67 | | | 1.33 |
| Generate prototype card | 8 | | | | | | 0.75 | | | | | | 0.75 |
| validate prototype card | 9 | | | | | | | | 1 | | | | 1.00 |
| generate printing order | 10 | | | | | | | | | 0.83 | | | 0.83 |
| print cards | 11 | | | | | | | 0.92 | | | 0.92 | | 1.83 |
| | | 0.75 | 0.83 | 2.00 | 0.67 | 0.42 | 0.75 | 0.92 | 1.00 | 1.50 | 0.92 | 0.00 | |

An examination of some of the control sequential interdependencies (in Table 3) reveals that some of them are rather weak. For example, function 6 to generate order details is only weakly dependent on function 5 to generate the PO. This indicates there is some parallelism occurring. The Marketing department is generating the order details while they are also generating the PO.

Table 4 shows the control sequential interdependence between organization units. There is a strong interdependency between Marketing and the Printer. Their relationship becomes a possible bottleneck if the workflow is not coordinated well. At the other extreme, the Distributor is not dependent on any other organization unit. However, it should be remembered that this analysis is for illustrative purposes and only a segment of the entire prepaid process is shown. In the full model the Distributor has dependencies on the other units.

**Table 4.** Control sequential interdependence transferred to organization units

| | | D | S | M | PM | P |
|---|---|---|---|---|---|---|
| Distributor | D | | | | | |
| Sales | S | 1.17 | | | | |
| Marketing | M | 0.42 | 1.00 | | | 1.00 |
| Prepaid Manager | PM | | 0.67 | 0.67 | | |
| Printer | P | | | 1.67 | 0.92 | |

## 4 Conclusion

This paper developed a formal model and measurement framework to define and understand the interdependence in an enterprise system. The three interdependence types of pooled resources, sequential, and reciprocal were extended by distinguishing between information sequential and control sequential interdependence. Moreover, in order to measure differences within an interdependence type we introduced attribute measures of frequency, importance, and delay. The inclusion of the interdependence attributes adds a significant refinement to the comparisons that can be made between interdependence types.

The paper formalized and augmented event process chains in order to model the interdependence types. The model enables the analysis of both 'as-is' systems as well as 'to-be' systems. Moreover, the formalization in the model allows the making of a clear distinction between the interdependence types. An advantage of the model we present is it provides for the overlapping of tasks to different degrees. In most process models if tasks are shown sequentially – the assumption is the second task cannot start until the first task completes. Through the use of the control flow attributes, the model presented here allows for tasks that might overlap slightly so that the strict precedence is not mandated. One potential omission that remains in the model (and in most formal modelling efforts) is that there may be many informal communications that take place and would not be immediately apparent to the modeller. To mitigate this possibility the modeller needs to interview process actors and observe the actual process tasks. This suggests that maybe the model should include an additional set of arcs for informal communications. This is a possible future research that needs to be examined.

The study limited itself to interdependence types and characteristics that have been proven through long use and validation in empirical research studies. The exception is we argued that control sequential interdependence is at least equal to or stronger than an information sequential interdependence. This assumption was done in order to maintain the representation condition of measurement theory that requires a weak ordering that is transitive and complete. The relationship between these two types of interdependencies needs to be empirically examined to confirm or reject our hypothesis, and is reserved for future work.

# References

1. M. Harris and A. Raviv, "Organization design," Management Science, vol. 48, pp. 852-866, 2002.
2. F. D. Vernadat, Enterprise modeling and integration. London, UK: Chapman and Hall, 1996.
3. H. A. Simon, "Complex systems: The interplay of organizations and markets in contemporary society," Computational & Mathematical Organization Theory, vol. 7, pp. 79-85, 2001.
4. J. Sutherland and W. J. van den Heuval, "Enterprise application integration and complex adaptive systems," Communications of the ACM, vol. 45, pp. 59-64, 2000.
5. T. W. Malone, J. Yates, and R. I. Benjamin, "Electronic markets and electronic hierarchies," Communications of the ACM, vol. 30, pp. 484-497, 1987.
6. J. F. Rockart and J. E. Short, "IT in the 1990s: Managing Organizational Interdependence," Sloan Management Review, vol. 30, pp. 7-18, 1989.
7. T. W. Malone and K. Crowston, "The interdisciplinary study of coordination," ACM Computing Surveys, vol. 26, pp. 87-119, 1994.
8. R. Giachetti, "Enterprise Integration: An information integration perspective," International Journal of Production Research, vol. 42, pp. 1147-1166, 2004.
9. S. B. Brunnermeier and S. A. Martin, "Interoperability costs in the US automotive supply chain," Supply Chain Management: An International Journal, vol. 7, pp. 71-82, 2002.
10. M. T. Frohlich and R. Westbrook, "Arcs of integration: an international study of supply chain strategies," Journal of Operations Management, vol. 19, pp. 185-200, 2001.

11. K. Kumar and J. Van Hillesgersberg, "ERP: Experiences and evolution," Communications of the ACM, vol. 43, pp. 23-26, 2000.
12. B. Sulon, "Pennsylvania-based Hersey Foods' distribution problems to continue," in Knight-Ridder/Tribune Business News, 1999.
13. A. Osterland, "Blaming ERP," CFO Magazine, vol. January, 2000.
14. V. Albino, P. Pontrandolfo, and B. Scozzi, "Analysis of information flows to enhance the coordination of production processes," International Journal of Production Economics, vol. 75, pp. 7-19, 2002.
15. A. Van de Ven, A. L. Delbecq, and R. Koenig, "Determinants of coordination modes within organizations," American Sociological Review, vol. 41, pp. 32-338, 1976.
16. H. Fayol, General and Industrial Management. London: Pitman, 1949.
17. J. D. Thompson, Organizations in Action. New York: McGraw-Hill, 1967.
18. J. E. McCann and D. L. Ferry, "An approach to assessing and managing inter-unit interdependence," Academy of Management Review, vol. 4, pp. 113-119, 1979.
19. B. Victor and R. S. Blackburn, "Interdependence: An alternative conceptualization," Academy of Management Review, vol. 12, pp. 486-498, 1987.
20. F. Sahin and E. P. Robinson, "Flow coordination and information sharing in supply chains: Review, implications, and directions for further research," Decision Sciences, vol. 33, pp. 505-536, 2002.
21. K. Crowston, "A coordination theory approach to organizational process design," Organizational Science, vol. 8, pp. 157-175, 1997.
22. L. Kunz, Jin, "The Virtual Design Team: A Computational Simulation Model of Project Organizations," Simulation, vol. 64, pp. 160-174, 1995.
23. M. Wybo and D. Goodhue, "Using interdependence as a predictor of data standards: theoretical and measurement issues," Information & Management, vol. 29, pp. 317-329, 1995.
24. J. W. Dean and S. A. Snell, "Integrated manufacturing and job design: moderating effects of organizational inertia," Academy of Management Journal, vol. 34, pp. 776-804, 1991.
25. A. W. Scheer, Business process engineering. Reference models for industrial enterprises. Berlin: Springer-Verlag, 1995.

# Session 2: Model-Based Approach for Enterprise Interoperability

# Semaphore – A Model-Based Semantic Mapping Framework

Andreas Limyr, Tor Neple, Arne-Jørgen Berre, and Brian Elvesæter

SINTEF ICT, Forskningsveien 1, 0373 Oslo, Norway
{Andreas.Limyr, Tor.Neple, Arne.J.Berre,
Brian.Elvesater}@sintef.no

**Abstract.** This paper presents a framework and a tool devised to aid in obtaining information interoperability between enterprise applications. The approach has its foundations in the principles of model-driven architecture (MDA) and architecture-driven modernisation (ADM). The key idea is that mappings between different information formats are defined at a platform-independent level, and that the mechanisms that actually perform the needed data conversion are generated based on the mappings according to the relevant platforms of the systems at hand.

**Keywords:** Interoperability, Mapping, Transformation, UML, MDA.

## 1 Introduction

In the area of interoperability the challenge is to get systems to "speak with each other" in such a manner that the dialog is meaningful for the systems. Work has been going on for a long time to find better ways to enable system interoperability.

When it comes to communication between different software systems it is important that the shared information is understood both syntactically and semantically, because misinterpreted information can cause unexpected, unwanted or even fatal errors. It is therefore important to have a clearly expressed way of making one system understand the information from another system.

In the previous years model-driven development (MDD), where models are seen as the prime artefact in software engineering, has become very wide-spread. This paper describes ongoing work within the area of applying the MDD paradigm to the interoperability problem. The focus of this work has been on the MDD aspects to a larger degree than to more formally based approaches.

This paper is structured as follows; chapter 2 gives an overview of the challenges at hand, chapter 3 presents the Semaphore tool [1], an answer to the challenges, chapter 4 provides an example of using Semaphore, chapter 5 presents a discussion on some topical issues, while chapter 6 provides conclusions and outlines possible further work.

## 2 The Challenges

There are several challenges when it comes to making one system understand another. The first challenge is often the fact that the two systems do not speak the same "language", that is they do not share the same syntax.

J. Eder, S. Dustdar et al. (Eds.): BPM 2006 Workshops, LNCS 4103, pp. 275 – 284, 2006.

Even if the systems use the same syntax it is not certain the semantics are shared. This means the information passed from one system to another can be misinterpreted and close to meaningless.

To address these problems there are some requirements. First of all the syntactical difference should be dealt with. This means the solution should handle systems with different information representation formats, or syntax.

The second requirement is the ability to clearly express a semantic unity between systems. By semantic unity we mean that the shared information is interpreted in the right way by all parties. To support this there is a need for various operations on the source information. Operations such as split, merge and convert should be available. The report [2] describes some challenges related to model mappings and model transformations.

## 3 Semaphore

Semaphore is an attempt at meeting these challenges. It is a syntactic and semantic mapping tool. The specification and implementation of the tool is described in [3], [4]. The idea behind this tool is to define mappings between the information formats at hand through defining the mappings on platform-independent models of the information formats. After defining mappings between a source model and target model transformation code is generated to be used on the instances of the source model. The transformation code will transform an instance of the source model into an instance of the target model according to the mappings performed on the models. This is based on the ideas from the OMG Model Driven Architecture (MDA) paradigm [5].

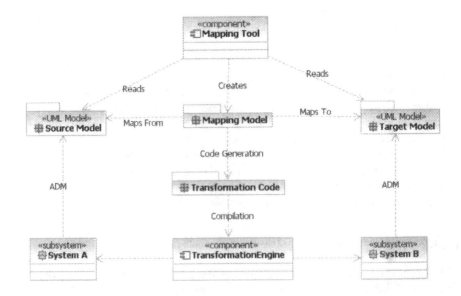

**Fig. 1.** Overview of models and tools

Fig. 1 shows an overview of how the tool relates to the different models and their originating systems. It is important to note that the Semaphore tool is used at design time and that the runtime elements are to be handled by some transformation technology, denoted as *TransformationEngine* in the figure. The transformation engine is viewed as "yet another platform", meaning that the mapping model (the definition of the mapping) is viewed as a platform-independent model, while the *Transformation Code* is viewed as a platform-specific model for the chosen transformation technology.

### 3.1 Input Formats

Information can be exchanged between systems using different formats. Semaphore needs a formal representation of the information structures, i.e. information format definitions. The information format definitions can be in form of XML schemas, SQL table definitions or some other format. Semaphore can be extended with any number of different formats.

To cover up the (possible) syntactical differences we use MDA mentality in abstracting the information format definitions to platform-independent models. Both the source model and the target model are abstracted to platform-independent models and represented as standard Unified Modeling Language (UML) [6] class diagrams. This process can also be seen in relation to architecture-driven modernisation (ADM) principles.

The fact that the mapping tool only takes UML models as input means that the mapping environment is identical, independent of the formats of the source and the target. The magic is in the abstraction of the models and the generation of the (platform specific) transformation code.

### 3.2 Mapping

When the user has imported the right models into the tool, he is presented with three panes; the left pane contains the model of the input and the right the model of the output. The user can then create the mappings by adding mapping elements (called mapping operators) to the centre pane of the tool. The mapping operators are attached to elements, classes or attributes, in the source and target model. This gives a graphical representation of the mapping.

In mapping between the different elements the tool supports different types of mapping operators. Semaphore currently supports the following mapping operators:

- *Root mapping*: One-to-one mapping. This mapping is used to connect the root of the two models.
- *Simple mapping*: One-to-one mapping without any modification. This mapping is also used to create a structure.
- *Concatenate mapping*: Many-to-one mapping. The mapping will simply concatenate the selected input elements to one output element.
- *Split mapping*: One-to-many mapping. The mapping will split the input element into different output elements with regards to a string or character.
- *Substring mapping*: One-to-one mapping. Substring mapping has an index from field and an index to field to specify which part of the input element the output element will consist of.

In order to aid the user in the process of defining the mappings the tool provides a pluggable architecture for mapping helpers. A mapping helper has the task of analysing the models and providing suggestions of possible mappings. The suggested mappings are presented to the user who then can choose to accept or reject them.

A simple helper that checks for similarities in the names of the model elements is provided with the tool as an example. One can also envision that such helpers can be created using more complex strategies, such as strategies based on ontology technologies as seen in [7].

## 3.3  Output

After the mapping is performed it is possible to generate transformation code. The generation of this code can be seen as the goal of the whole exercise. This is done by viewing the mapping definition it self as a model. In fact the mapping definition is a model in it own right adhering to a metamodel defined for this purpose.

The mapping definition model is used as input to a transformation. The transformation can be model to model, where the generated model is used by a transformation engine, but the most common strategy would be to perform a model to text transformation. The transformation code can be in any format, but the purpose of the code is to transform one instance of the source model to one instance of the target model based on the defined mapping.

The transformation code can be from one technology to another, for instance reading from an SQL database and creating XML documents. The tool provides a pluggable architecture for transformation code generation. This means it is possible to create customized transformation code from and to any number of technologies. Semaphore allows for transformation generator code to be written using the model to text technology MOFScript[1], or through the use of Java.

A generator for creating transformation code from XML to XML is provided with the tool. Output of this generator is an XSLT script that can be executed with an XSLT processor.

## 3.4  Tool Implementation

The Semaphore tool is implemented as an Eclipse [8] plug-in. As the Eclipse environment has gained momentum as a developer IDE, the Semaphore tool can easily be integrated into the IDE of developers. This also includes modelling tools both for UML and metamodels such as Rational Software Architect and Borland Together Architect.

In developing Semaphore a number of technologies from the Eclipse projects have been utilised. The Eclipse Modeling Framework (EMF) [9] has been used for handling of the mapping metamodel, the Eclipse UML2.0 project [10] is used to handle the UML models that are used for the mapping. The Eclipse Graphical Editing Framework (GEF) [11] is used to visualise the models and mappings.

The plug-in based Eclipse architecture also allows for the extendible nature of the Semaphore tool, as new mapping helpers, input format transformations and transformation generators are created as plug-ins. This is done through the use of a set of defined extension points provided by the Semaphore tool. Developers can then provide their own plug-ins that implement extensions to the defined extension points.

---

[1] http://www.modelbased.net/mofscript

## 4   Example of Use

In order to give a better understanding of how the Semaphore tool works this section provides an example of applying Semaphore. For this example we will use two simple XML schemas as source and target models. The schemas can be seen in Table 1. The source describes a schema with organisation information with telephone information and address information. The target describes a schema with party information consisting of the same information as the source. These two schemas describe the same information, but have some different naming conventions.

**Table 1.** Example XML Schemas

| Source.xsd | Target.xsd |
|---|---|
| `<xs:element name="street" type="xs:string"/>`<br><br>`<xs:element name="country" type="xs:string"/>`<br><br>`<xs:element name="postalCode" type="xs:string"/>`<br><br>`<xs:element name="telephone" type="xs:string"/>`<br><br>`<xs:element name="OrganisationInfo">`<br>`  <xs:complexType>`<br>`    <xs:sequence>`<br>`      <xs:element ref="Address"/>`<br>`      <xs:element ref="telephone"/>`<br>`    </xs:sequence>`<br>`  </xs:complexType>`<br>`</xs:element>`<br><br>`<xs:element name="Address">`<br>`  <xs:complexType>`<br>`    <xs:sequence>`<br>`      <xs:element ref="street"/>`<br>`      <xs:element ref="country"/>`<br>`      <xs:element ref="postalCode"/>`<br>`    </xs:sequence>`<br>`  </xs:complexType>`<br>`</xs:element>` | `<xs:element name="Address">`<br>`  <xs:complexType>`<br>`    <xs:sequence>`<br>`      <xs:element ref="Country"/>`<br>`      <xs:element ref="PostalZone"/>`<br>`      <xs:element ref="StreetName"/>`<br>`    </xs:sequence>`<br>`  </xs:complexType>`<br>`</xs:element>`<br><br>`<xs:element name="Party">`<br>`  <xs:complexType>`<br>`    <xs:sequence>`<br>`      <xs:element ref="Address"/>`<br>`      <xs:element ref="Telephone"/>`<br>`    </xs:sequence>`<br>`  </xs:complexType>`<br>`</xs:element>`<br><br>`<xs:elementname="PostalZone" type="xs:string"/>`<br><br>`<xs:element name="StreetName" type="xs:string"/>`<br><br>`<xs:element name="Telephone" type="xs:string"/>`<br><br>`<xs:element name="Country" type="xs:string"/>` |

When presented with XSD as input Semaphore will create UML representations of the XSD for use in the mapping process. The conversion is based on some simple rules like an XSD element with a complex type converts to a UML class and an XSD element with a simple type declared inside a complex type is converted to a UML attribute.

After performing a conversion of the source schema and the target schema into UML models, these models are loaded by Semaphore. The first step of mapping these two models is to define a root mapping. The root mapping connects the top levels of the two models. The result of the conversion and the initial root mapping can be seen in Fig. 2.

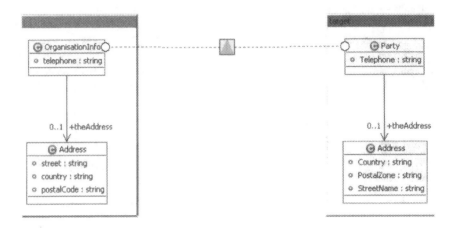

**Fig. 2.** Semaphore with Source.xsd and Target.xsd. There is also a root mapping between OrganisationInfo and Party.

As described earlier, one can perform mappings manually or use mapping helpers to get hints of possible mappings. For this example we will use the "Match by Name" mapping helper to perform a mapping. Right-clicking on the attribute "country" in the source model and selecting "Match by Name" gives one match in the target model. This can be seen in Fig. 3.

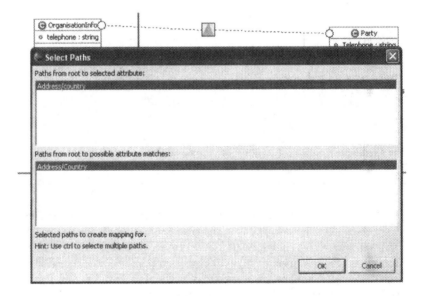

**Fig. 3.** Mapping helper dialog

The state of the mapping diagram after the automatic mapping is performed can be seen in Fig. 4.

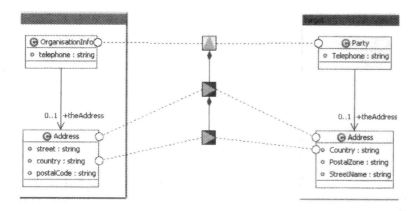

**Fig. 4.** Status after a match by name on Country is performed

The simple mapping is now complete, and one can generate transformation code based on this mapping. This is done by right-clicking anywhere in the diagram and choosing the "Transform from XML to XML" action. This will generate an xslt script capable of taking an XML file adhering to *Source.xsd* and create an XML file adhering to *Target.xsd* according to the mapping. An excerpt of the generated xslt is shown in Table 2.

**Table 2.** Excerpt of the resulting xslt script

```
.....
<xsl:template match="/">
  <Party>
    <Address>
<Country><xsl:value-of
select="/OrganisationInfo/Address/country"/></Country>
    </Address>
  </Party>
</xsl:template>
.....
```

The defined mappings will be valid at a syntactic level, meaning that the elements to be copied to and from are valid, resulting in a syntactically valid schemata for the output format. The semantic validity of the mapping needs to be verified by a human, and is actually done so through the manual mapping steps and by accepting or rejecting the mappings proposed by the mapping helper.

# 5   Discussion

## 5.1   Abstractions to UML

As mentioned in previous chapters Semaphore is based on creating abstractions of the input and output information formats in form of UML models. Semaphore provides a pluggable architecture where one can add new importers that are developed as Eclipse plug-ins. The importers are typically written in Java.

The cost (in form of time) of writing an importer for a new format depends on the nature of the format. The assumption is that formats that describe information elements with properties and associations can be mapped to UML Class models. In this abstraction choices of mapping have to be made, for some formats the mappings are more straight-forward than for others. The complexity of the input format definition scheme and the degree of conceptual similarity with the UML metamodel will be the factors that have the most influence on the cost of developing a new importer.

## 5.2   N2 Versus $N^2$

The Semaphore tool allows for mappings between two models. Potentially one may have multiple input formats for multiple output formats, resulting in mappings between these input and output formats. Mapping between all model pairs will result in N-squared mappings. Mapping between each model and a reference model will result in a linear growth of number of mappings. Given this it is an advantage to map to a reference model. This is shown in Fig. 5, where the mappings between six different models are illustrated.

The reference model may be an ontology, or it may be a commonly agreed UML model. The benefit of the better scalability of this approach is only sustainable as long

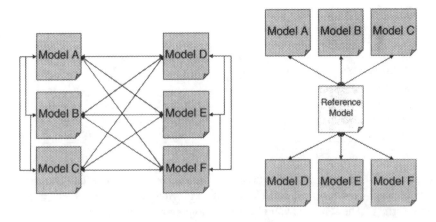

**Fig. 5.** 2N and N-squared

as the reference model is stable. When the reference model is altered there may be a large number of mapping definitions that need to be changed.

Semaphore can be used with the reference model approach. The tool is simply applied between the different models and the reference model as apposed to applying it directly between the input and output model formats.

It should be noted that the number of mapping helpers will not grow in relation to the input and output formats. This is an independent issue as this is based on what strategies one chooses for the helpers. Technically the helpers will work on the PIM level UML models.

## 6   Conclusion and Future Work

The previous chapters have presented Semaphore and shown how it can be applied to a problem. Through this it has been shown that the approach of defining mappings between platform-independent model representations of information formats is viable. One issue that has arose is that when dealing with large models, the graphical view of the mappings may become complex thus limiting the value of using a model diagram approach. This has partly been handled by allowing for mapping sub-trees to be collapsed in the mapping pane.

The pluggable infrastructure of Eclipse has allowed for Semaphore to have a flexible architecture with regards to different input formats, mapping helpers and transformation formats. This will allow for targeting other formats in the future, natural candidates include SQL table definitions among others.

In order to add more weight to the "semantic" part of the concept the idea of using ontology based technologies in mapping helpers has been researched at the conceptual level. Hopefully parts of these ideas can be implemented in the future. The idea would then be to use annotated models in the mapping tool and use technologies such as reasoners to provide mapping suggestions.    The Mapping Helper concept of Semaphore is a natural place to plug such functionality into the system. Related work and tools such as COMA++ [7] has a greater emphasis on the semantic aspects and should be investigated further.    Results related to use of ontology technologies for interoperability from the ATHENA project are natural candidates for integration with Semaphore both for annotation of models (design-time) and reconciliation (run-time). For the latter the reconciliation engine would be viewed as the *TransformationEngine* at hand.

**Acknowledgments.** The work published in this paper is partly funded by the European Commission through the ATHENA IP (Advanced Technologies for interoperability of Heterogeneous Enterprise Networks and their Applications Integrated Project) (IST- 507849) [12] and the INTEROP NoE (Interoperability Research for Networked Enterprise Applications and Software Network of Excellence) (IST-508011) [13]. The work does not represent the view of the European Commission, the ATHENA consortium, or the INTEROP consortium, and the authors are solely responsible for the paper's content.

# References

1. SINTEF, Semaphore website. 2006. http://www.modelbased.net/semaphore/.
2. INTEROP TG3, TG MoMo Roadmap. 2005, INTEROP NoE. http://interop-noe.org/backoffice/workspaces/tg3/documents/task2/roadmap/attachment_download/file.
3. ATHENA A6, Model-driven and Adaptable Interoperability Framework. 2006, ATHENA IP.
4. ATHENA A6, Model-driven and Adaptable Interoperability Infrastructure. 2006, ATHENA IP.
5. Object Management Group, MDA Guide Version 1.0.1, J. Miller and J. Mukerji, Editors. 2003, Object Management Group.
6. Object Management Group, UML 2.0 Superstructure Specification. 2003, Object Management Group.
7. Aumueller, D., et al. Schema and Ontology Matching with COMA++. in SIGMOD. 2005. Baltimore, Maryland, USA.
8. Eclipse Foundation, Eclipse platform. 2005. http://www.eclipse.org.
9. Eclipse Foundation, Eclipse Modeling Framework. 2005. http://www.eclipse.org/emf.
10. Eclipse Foundation, UML2 project. 2006. http://www.eclipse.org/uml2/.
11. Eclipse Foundation, Graphical Editing Framework. 2006. http://www.eclipse.org/gef/.
12. ATHENA, ATHENA Public Web Site. 2005, ATHENA IP. http://www.athena-ip.org.
13. INTEROP, INTEROP Portal. 2005, INTEROP NoE. http://www.interop-noe.org/.

# B2B Protocol Construction as a Basis for Integration Architecture Configuration

Bettina Bazijanec and Klaus Turowski

Business Informatics and Systems Engineering
University of Augsburg,
Universitätsstraße 16, 86135 Augsburg, Germany
{bettina.bazijanec, klaus.turowski}@wiwi.uni-augsburg.de

**Abstract.** Efficient business-to-business collaboration needs an IT-architecture that allows for a preferably automatic configuration of integration services and flexibly supports different collaboration scenarios. This paper presents an approach to construct a B2B protocol from single protocol fragments that address specific collaboration aspects and that are implemented by single components of an B2B integration architecture. Therefore, the resulting B2B protocol description will be mapped to an architecture composition specification in a second step. For the purpose of protocol construction, different types of dependencies between protocols will be described as well as an abstract business transaction pattern that will be extended and refined during the B2B protocol construction process.

**Keywords:** B2B, architecture, collaboration.

## 1 Introduction

In business-to-business collaboration scenarios two coordination problems have to be solved simultaneously: the external coordination problem caused by interaction with one or more independent business partners with potentially different technical capabilities, and the internal coordination problem caused by the usage of existing application systems for implementing inter-organizational business processes. External coordination is achieved by agreeing on a B2B protocol. It defines message exchanges between business partners that are necessary to coordinate collaboration tasks. The order of sending and receiving messages defines a so-called public process for each collaboration partner [3]. The internal coordination problem is solved by defining an internal business process that orchestrates application systems. This is done with the help of some dedicated software that can either be a scripting engine or a more advanced Enterprise Application Integration (EAI) server. It is crucial that business information contained in incoming messages can be handed over to internal application systems and vice versa. Therefore, public and private processes have to be synchronized. For this purpose a so-called binding has to be performed [2]. Binding typically includes integration tasks due to message and sequence mismatches. This may require, for example, transformation, aggregation, or splitting of external

J. Eder, S. Dustdar et al. (Eds.): BPM 2006 Workshops, LNCS 4103, pp. 285 – 296, 2006.

messages before they can be forwarded to the internal business process for further processing [26, 10].

Public processes not only deal with business related messages but also with more technical aspects, e.g. security, reliability, and message transport. Therefore, information is additionally exchanged due to the distributed nature of B2B collaboration (e.g. signatures, passwords, acknowledgement messages). These aspects represent the context of business information exchange and are linked to business protocols but also introduce own message types and exchange sequences (e.g. an authorization protocol that has to be carried out before the business protocol). Consequently, B2B integration systems have to be configured in a way that the external message exchange behavior conforms to the agreed B2B protocol. However, configuration of such systems is tedious and costly as, for example, document mappings have to be defined and processes have to be aligned [8]. The definition of the execution context and the integration of its different aspects into one comprehensive B2B protocol may also be a time-consuming task. There are B2B frameworks like RosettaNet or ebXML that already define many technical and business-related aspects of inter-organizational message exchange but they are not supported by all collaboration partners because there are also many other standards available that only address certain aspects but that may be also be combined to a comprehensive B2B protocol (e.g. MIME, SOAP, cXML, BTP). Hence, there is the need to flexibly adapt to different B2B protocols depending on frequently changing partners and business processes [15, 27].

This paper shows how the definition and implementation of B2B protocols can be simplified by constructing them from predefined protocol artefacts that may be implemented by different architectural components. The remainder is organized as follows: section 2 gives an introduction to our approach and a brief overview of related work. In section 3, different types of dependencies between protocols are described as well as a standard pattern of business transaction that will be used as a basis for the B2B protocol construction process. Section 4 describes how this transaction pattern can be stepwise extended in order to construct the B2B protocol considering a simple purchasing protocol as example. For this purpose three more protocol fragments providing transport, decryption, and validation behaviour are added to the underlying transaction pattern. In section 5, conclusions are drawn and an outlook on future work is given.

## 2 Approach and Related Work

The goal of our approach is to accomplish a mapping between protocol descriptions and suitable configurations of a component-based integration architecture to implement the particular B2B protocol of a given collaboration scenario. Architectural components are used to implement specific protocol fragments that can be composed to a customized integration system. For this purpose two concepts have to be developed: first, a method for construction of a consistent B2B protocol out of single coordination protocols addressing specific aspects relevant for coordination and second, a configuration concept for integration architectures containing mapping rules between B2B protocol description and architectural components. This approach promises a higher degree of flexibility due to the reuse of previously implemented protocols and the automated configuration of the respective architectural components.

In this paper we will focus on the B2B protocol construction, i.e. the definition of public processes for collaboration partners. We will not further discuss binding specific questions and techniques like message transformation. For a detailed description we refer to [2], [10]. Internal business applications are expected to understand exactly the document types sent by the collaboration partner, so that solving message and sequence mismatches between public and private processes is not necessary. We will focus on external coordination and the interplay of different coordination protocols concerning business information exchange, reliability of asynchronous communication, and confidentiality of message content. But unlike other approaches we do not compare two or more public processes in order to test their compatibility or bisimilarity. We start with a common semantic basis in form of abstract business transaction patterns and then built up the overall B2B protocol by consecutively adding protocol fragments to the basis. In each extension step however only such protocol fragments may be used that are supported by each partner. Therefore, some kind of negotiation has to take place but this is also outside the scope of this paper. It rather will be shown which relationships between different coordination aspects are typically present in B2B protocols and how they can be formally described. This description may be either used to analyze given protocols or – as we intend to do – to agree upon a specific B2B protocol. In both cases, the description helps to identify necessary implementation and/or configuration steps. Construction steps may for example add new message exchanges to the basic transaction pattern or replace abstract message descriptions by more specific ones. Also, if concurrent execution of single protocols is needed, separate messages may be composed to one protocol message to send all information at the same time (e.g. authentication header together with a purchase order). After having completed all construction steps the B2B protocol represents a contract between collaboration partners as it contains the definition of all sequences of incoming and outgoing messages (mirrored for each communication partner) including the message definitions, and all necessary parameters (e.g. time-out values).

A related approach of customizing B2B integration systems out of predefined components has been proposed by [12]. They argue that B2B integration systems can be constructed from interaction components that implement B2B protocols and service components that support business activities execution. They subdivide service components into business process oriented components that implement private processes, and business interaction oriented components that are composed from process oriented and interaction components. However, it is not shown how this composition is facilitated and which dependencies components may have. Also, interaction components implement complete B2B protocols, so that these components may be very coarse-grained what may restrict their frequent reuse.

A more fine-grained approach for component reuse based on protocols can be found in the work of [22]. He investigates how components supporting certain protocols can be used to implement a particular business process. Therefore he compares business process and component process descriptions with each other based on methods located in the field of distributed processes and behavioural subtyping where authors investigate compatibility and substitutability of protocols [16], [23], [25]. As already mentioned, this work may be integrated into our approach when determining suitable protocol fragments but not for comparison of complete B2B protocols since they will be constructed. However, some of these approaches already incorporate some concepts (e.g. abstract vs. specific specification in vertical action refinement [19]) that can be used for determining valid construction steps.

Mechanisms for constructing an overall consistent B2B protocol addressing different aspects can be found within the B2B framework ebXML [9]. There, capabilities of the partner's application systems with respect to inter-organizational communication are documented in form of collaboration partner profiles (CPP). The framework also includes a so-called collaboration partner agreement that can be formed out of two CPPs through negotiation. CPPs primarily address security related aspects and only consider ebXML specific description standards. Accordingly, the negotiation process is specific for CPPs.

The idea that B2B protocols can be related to speech acts and therefore have a semantic basis that is useful to build flexible messaging systems has already been described by Moore [18]. He developed a formal language for business communication and a messaging system that can reason about the intended meaning and therefore give suitable responses in a conversation. He evaluated the system in several inter-organizational scenarios but his focus was not on implementation and reuse of existing protocols or protocol standards.

## 3   Protocol Dependencies and Business Transaction Patterns

In order to explain the interrelation of different protocols a formal definition of a protocol is provided first. A *protocol* can formally be defined following the definition of transition systems [11] as a 5-tuple $p=(Q, \Sigma, \delta, s, F)$ where $Q$ is a finite set of states and $\Sigma$ is a finite set of valid labels that represent protocol messages which are exchanged during an interaction. Messages are marked *out* if they represent outgoing messages and *in* if they represent incoming messages. $\delta \subseteq Q \times \Sigma \times Q$ is the transition relation, $s \in Q$ is the initial state, and $F$ is a set of final states. The resulting transition system is specific for a particular role in an interaction. Each outgoing message in the protocol description corresponds to an incoming message of another role's protocol description. As an example, a simple purchase protocol representing a seller's public process can be defined as follows:

$Q = \{q0, q1, q2, q3, q4\}, \Sigma = \{PO, POA, INV, PAY\}, F = \{q4\}, s = q0,$
$\delta = \{(q0, in:PO, q1), (q1, out:POA, q2), (q2, out:INV, q3), (q3, in:PAY, q4)\}$

First, a purchase order (PO) is received which leads to a protocol state change from $q0$ to $q1$. In this state the seller is able to send out a POA message that contains an acceptance of order. After sending out the message, the state changes to $q2$ where it is possible to send an invoice (INV) after having shipped the goods. After that the seller is able to receive an advice of payment (PAY). Fig. 1 shows a graphical representation of the given finite state machine.

The first protocol dependency we want to introduce is the message sequencing dependency. This is the case when a message exchange in one protocol can only happen

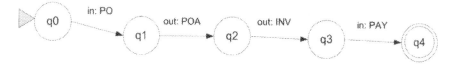

**Fig. 1.** Simple purchasing protocol (seller side)

after an specific message exchange in another protocol, e.g. if the reception of a purchase order has to be acknowledged by a particular message (e.g. ACK) that is not originally part of the business protocol. The definition in Fig. 1 would have to be extended by a further state q1' that is placed between state q0 and q1. The transition relation now would be $\delta = \{(q0, \text{in:PO}, q1'), (q1', \text{out:ACK}, q1), (q1, \text{out:POA}, q2), (q2, \text{out:INV}, q3), (q3, \text{out:PAY}, q4)\}$.

In the protocol definition in Fig. 1 only message types are used (e.g. PO). However, one specific message type can have different syntactic representations and contain multiple message parts that may include document or processing information (e.g. business document and sender's signature). In above definition, a message type corresponds to the type of the included business document. This document is typically put in the message body whereas the message header contains processing (i.e. context related) information. However, the message body may also contain context related information such as a signature. This is particularly true in cases where no business document but only context information will be sent (e.g. an authorization message containing only username and password). When a message body contains more than one message part so-called packaging standards like MIME [13] specify how single parts can be put together and later be identified. Independently from any packaging standard, we propose to specify relationships between different message parts concerning different coordination aspects within a message type definition. Up to date, this information is only implicitly defined in additional trading partner agreements or implementation guidelines [9]. Relationships that can be identified in protocol standards are *enclose*, *encoding*, and *reference*. An enclose relationship (denoted C[DOC]) means that a business document DOC in a message body is sent together with related context information C placed into the header of the message. The brackets ([...]) then represent some packaging syntax. DOC is a document type that represents business information. Encoding (denoted K(DOC)) describes that a business document has been encoded and therefore changed its representation. K may be the name of a compression algorithm or an name that indicates the encryption method. Finally, the reference relationship (denoted S{DOC}) means that some information is included in the message that is related to the document content (e.g. a signature that has been derived from the document and is added to the message). If a message contains independent parts (e.g. documents that both have to be transmitted but do not interrelate) then those are simply separated by comma to denote their ordering (e.g. DOC1,DOC2). It is possible to combine relationships: T[C[DOC1, K(DOC2)]] describes two nested headers T and C that are attached to the message which also contains two documents DOC1 and DOC2, and DOC2 is encoded, i.e. encrypted with K. For example T may be a HTTP header, C a WS-Coordination context, and K the receiver's public key. This would also mean that the square brackets of the C[...]

relationship denote the SOAP packaging standard as required by the WS-Coordination standard. Note that these relationships are already indicators for subsequent architectural mapping: K1(doc) means that the whole message has to be encrypted by one component before the contents of doc can be evaluated by another component. The presented intra-message relationships can now be expressed within a protocol description by using the introduced message composition operators in the message labels.

When describing protocol dependencies, especially intra-message relationships, it is necessary to introduce placeholders for message types because composition and packaging is independent from specific message types. For example, a simple encryption protocol can be defined from the receiver's point of view as:

$$Q = \{q0,q1,q2\}, \Sigma = \{K1(<request>), K2(<reply>)\}, F = \{q2\}, s0 = q0,$$

$$\delta = \{(q0, in:K1(<request>), q1), (q1, out:K2(<reply>), q2)\}$$

Every incoming request is expected to be encrypted with key K1. The fact that <request> is written in lower case and put in angle brackets means that it represents a request with variable type. Every time the receiver gets an encrypted request, a reply message <reply> encrypted with key K2 is sent back. In order to use this abstraction concept a hierarchy of message types has to be developed. A possible abstraction path in such a hierarchy could be: <msg> → <request> → PO. This means that a specific type PO can be used instead of the abstract type <request>, and request can be used instead of the abstract type <msg>. Also, an abstract type <msg> may be replaced by a composed message type as introduced above. To derive a hierarchy of abstract message types their communicative dimension has to be taken into account. Messages can be regarded as communicative acts which express a sender's attitude [21]. This includes the sender's intention what effect it wants to achieve (cf. [4], [20], [14]). Verbs describing these intentions (e.g. inform, request) can be used as abstract message types in protocol definitions since they are already present in many B2B protocol standards. For example, Moore [17] has evaluated several B2B standards and identified many verbs that express intentions. We will not further discuss the definition of an abstract message type hierarchy but introduce some simple abstraction relations within our examples. We rather focus on the use of abstract message types within recurrent patterns of business transaction.

Business protocols are composed of *business transactions* that are basic units of coordination specifying the exchange of business information often using a *send-reply* communication pattern (e.g. *request for quote – quote, purchase order – purchase order acknowledgement*). Unfortunately, there is no common definition of a business transaction in literature so that some authors use this concept only for single pairs of message exchange (e.g. [9]) and others for more complex exchange structures (e.g. [4]). Basically, a business transaction can be seen as an exchange of related messages that leads to a transfer of economic resources (e.g. exchange of goods, money, or information). Although different business protocols may be used for completely different purposes they show recurrent patterns of business transaction when looking at a higher level of abstraction. Definitions of transaction pattern types (also called interaction patterns) can be found in agent and language action literature (cf. [5], [24], [1], [7], [4]). Fig. 2 shows a basic transaction pattern that was built on the basic conversation for action schema [24] and abstractly defines a customer's request for action and a supplier's declaration of the execution result. It is also very similar to the standard pattern of transaction proposed in [4].

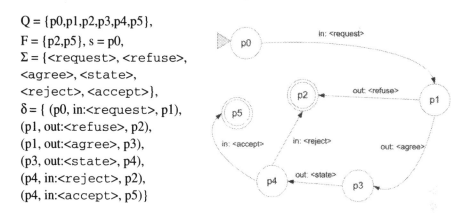

Q = {p0,p1,p2,p3,p4,p5},
F = {p2,p5}, s = p0,
Σ = {<request>, <refuse>, <agree>, <state>, <reject>, <accept>},
δ = { (p0, in:<request>, p1),
(p1, out:<refuse>, p2),
(p1, out:<agree>, p3),
(p3, out:<state>, p4),
(p4, in:<reject>, p2),
(p4, in:<accept>, p5)}

**Fig. 2.** Standard transaction pattern (supplier view)

The transaction starts with an incoming request that is evaluated. The supplier may agree or refuse to perform the requested action. This is done by sending the respective message out to the customer. In case of a refusal the transaction is aborted and no further message will be exchanged (depicted as final state *p2*). After having sent an <agree> message, the requested action will be performed. A <state> message will be sent to the customer by the supplier who indicates that the action has been performed. The customer may accept the outcome or reject it. In both cases the transaction should be aborted (note: in an alternative pattern a reject may also lead back to state *p3* until the outcome is accepted). In the following, we will use this pattern as basis for our protocol construction approach.

## 4  Protocol Construction

So far we have introduced three kinds of protocol dependencies (sequencing, intra-message relationships, and refinement of abstract message types) and also selected the standard pattern of business transaction as a semantic basis for B2B protocol construction. Now, we will show how these concepts can be used to construct a consistent B2B protocol. We assume that collaboration partners have agreed upon following protocol fragments:

**Transport Protocol**

Q = {r0, r1, r2}, F = {r1, r2}, s = r0,
Σ  =  {HTTP[<msg>]},
δ = {(r0, in:HTTP[<msg>], r1),
(r0, out:HTTP[<msg>], r2)}

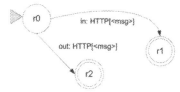

The transport protocol that defines, that all incoming and all outgoing messages will use HTTP for message transport.

**Decryption Protocol**

$Q = \{s0, s1\}$
$\Sigma = \{DES(\texttt{<zrequest>})\}$,
$F = \{t1\}$, $s = s0$,
$\delta = \{(s0, in:DES(\texttt{<request>}), s1)\}$

The decryption protocol defines that all incoming requests should be DES-encrypted. Note, that this also means that all outgoing requests on the communication partner's side have to be encrypted.

**Validation Protocol**

$Q = \{t0, t1, t2, t3\}$, $F = \{t2, t3\}$, $s = t0$,
$\Sigma = \{\texttt{<request>}, \texttt{SCHEMA-}$
$\texttt{ERROR}, \texttt{CONTENT-ERROR}, \texttt{ACK}\}$,
$\delta = \{(t0, in:\texttt{<request>}, t1),$
$(t1, out:\texttt{SCHEMA-ERROR}, t2),$
$(t1, out:\texttt{CONTENT-ERROR}, t2),$
$(t1, out:\texttt{ACK}, t3)\}$

The validation protocol defines that all incoming requests first have to be checked if they conform to the expected message schema and if the message content is readable. If one of these checks fails then an error message is sent out. Otherwise an acknowledgement message is sent back to the requester.

Fig. 3 shows the first construction step. It is based on two dependency types: intra-message relationship and abstract message refinement.

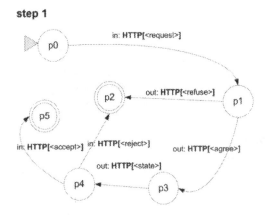

**Fig. 3.** Construction step 1 (transport)

The transport specific message in:HTTP[<msg>] fits to the original message in:<request> because the HTTP-Format is defined upon a more abstract message type (<msg> → <request>). This is also true for all other messages defined by the transaction pattern. Therefore, all message types in the transition system have to be changed.

In Fig. 4 the relevant part of the resulting transition system in step 2 is shown. The decryption protocol maps only to the first transition where incoming requests in:DES(<request>) are considered. So only the message type of the first transition is replaced. There is also an implicit ordering of the intra-message relationship shown in step 2. It is assumed that the encryption relationship is stronger than the transport relationship. This is typically true in B2B protocols but should be explicitly specified.

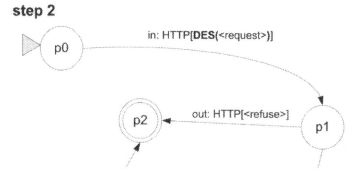

**Fig. 4.** Construction step 2 (decryption)

Fig. 5 shows the result of construction step 3. The first transition of the validation protocol can be integrated into the pattern since the first transition still represents an incoming request. The outgoing error messages of the validation protocol can be mapped to the outgoing refuse message in the pattern.

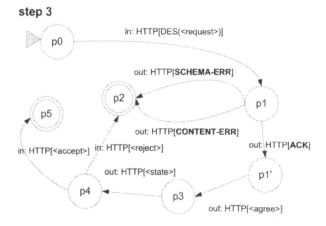

**Fig. 5.** Construction step 3 (validation)

This is possible because protocol errors always lead to the termination of the current transaction unless a retry protocol is in place. There is no retry protocol in this case and therefore the replacement is correct. As there are two possible error messages as answers to the request the refuse transition between state *p1* and *p2* is replaced by two new transitions. By performing this replacement, one of the two possible transaction end states is reached. Reaching all possible transaction end states is an important condition of the protocol construction process. The integration of the validation protocol also shows how sequence relationships are treated. The ACK-message that indicates successful validation of a request does not necessarily replace the <agree> message since it only indicates that the request is valid in the sense of the given validation protocol. In this case a sequencing relationship can be assumed (unless otherwise specified). This means that an additional message exchange transition (out: ACK) and also a new state (*p1'*) are inserted at a given state (here: *p1*).

Finally, Fig. 6 shows step 4 of the B2B protocol construction example where the business protocol from Fig. 1 is used. The integration of this protocol has to be based either on a general mapping of message types to intentions (see for example [17]) or on a specification that comes with the business protocol (here: <request> → PO; <agree> → POA; <state> → INV; <accept> → PAY).

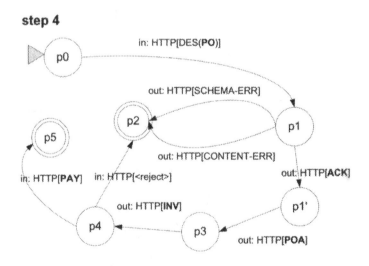

**Fig. 6.** Construction step 4 (business protocol)

The resulting finite state machine for the constructed B2B protocol has still one transition with an abstract message left. This outgoing <reject> message may be replaced by a specific message of another protocol fragment, e.g. a protocol based on the cancellation pattern provided in [4], or a timeout protocol.

# 5  Summary and Outlook

In this paper an approach for the construction of a complete B2B protocol out of several protocol fragments has been showed. This approach is useful when collaboration partner are able to agree upon single protocol standards or parts of B2B frameworks but not on complete B2B protocols. It may also be useful in situations when existing B2B protocols have to be extended an extension points in the external behavior have to be identified. First, three kinds of protocol dependencies have been introduced that enable modelling of sequencing and simultaneity in the message exchange of public processes. Then, a business transaction pattern was described that formed the basis for B2B protocol construction. Several construction steps were explained by means of a comprehensive example. Some basic requirements for protocol construction have been addressed like coverage of all business transaction end states, matching of message exchange direction, matching of transaction continuation/termination, transaction state extension, and the possibility of explicit mappings. Message type definitions and mismatches that cause message transformation have not been considered. Also, negotiation steps for protocol fragments were not part of this paper.

Although checking similarity between public processes of collaboration partners is not necessary in this protocol construction approach, checking similarity of the intermediary B2B protocols between consecutive steps has to be performed. Behavioural subtyping relations like (weak) simulation and optimistic subtyping [16], [6], [22], as well as vertical implementation relations [19] seem to be suitable for protocol construction and will be further examined. Future work will also include the actual mapping of the resulting protocol description to architectural components in order to allow a flexible configuration of the B2B integration system.

# References

1. Bergholtz, M., Jayaweera, P., Johannesson, P., Wohed, P., *Bringing Speech Acts Into UMM*, 1st. Int. REA Technology Workshop 2004.
2. Bussler, C., *B2B Integration*, Springer, Berlin, 2003.
3. Bussler, C., *Public Process Inheritance for Business-to-Business Integration*, Technologies for E-Services, Third International Workshop, TES 2002, pp., pp. 19-28.
4. Dietz, J. L. G., *Generic Recurrent Patterns in Business Processes*, Business Process Management 2003, pp. 200-215.
5. FIPA, *Communicative Act Library Specification*, http://www.fipa.org/specs/fipa00037/.
6. Fischer, C., Wehrheim, H., *Behavioural Subtyping Relations for Object-Oriented Formalisms*, 8th International Conference on Algebraic Methodology And Software Technology 2000, pp. 469-483.
7. Fornara, N., Colombetti, M., *Defining Interaction Protocols using a Commitment-based Agent Communication Language*, Int. Conference on Autonomous Agents and Multiagent Systems 2003.
8. Haller, A., Cimpian, E., Mocan, A., Oren, E., Bussler, C., *WSMX - A Semantic Service-Oriented Architecture*, International Conference on Web Services (ICWS 2005) 2005.
9. Hofreiter, B., Huemer, C., Klas, W., *ebXML: Status, Research Issues, and Obstacles*, 12th Int.l Wrkshp on Research Issues in Data Engineering: Engineering e-Commerce/ e-Business Systems (RIDE.02) 2002, pp., pp. 7-16.

10. Hohpe, G., Woolf, B., *Enterprise integration patterns*, Addison-Wesley, Boston, 2004.
11. Hopcroft, J. E., Motwani, R., Ullman, J. D., *Introduction to Automata Theory, Languages, and Computation*, Addison Wesley, 2001.
12. Hu, J., Grefen, P., *Component Based System Framework for Dynamic B2B Interaction*, 26 th Annual International Computer Software and Applications Conference 2002.
13. IETF, *RFC 2045: Multipurpose Internet Mail Extensions*, http://www.ietf.org/rfc/rfc2045.txt.
14. Kimbrough, S., Moore, S., *On automated message processing in electronic commerce and work support systems: speech act theory and expressive felicity*, ACM Transactions on Information Systems, 15 (1997), pp. 321-367.
15. Medjahed, B., Benatallah, B., Bouguettaya, A., Ngu, A. H. H., Elmagarmid, A. K., *Business-to-business interactions: issues and enabling technologies*, The VLDB Journal, 12 (2003), pp. 59-85.
16. Milner, R., *Communication and Concurrency*, Prentice Hall, Ney York, 1995.
17. Moore, S., *Categorizing automated messages*, Decision Support Systems, 22 (1998), pp. 213-241.
18. Moore, S., *A Foundation for Flexible Automated Electronic Communication*, Information Systems Research, 12 (2001), pp. 34-62.
19. Rensink, A., Gorrieri, R., *Action refinement as an implementation relation*, TAPSOFT 1997, pp. 772–786.
20. Searle, J. R., Vanderveken, D., *Foundations of Illocutionary Logic*, Cambridge University Press, Cambridge, England, 1985.
21. Singh, M., Huhns, M. N., *Service-Oriented Computing: Semantics, Processes, Agents*, John Wiley and Sons Ltd, Chichester, 2004.
22. Teschke, T., *Semantische Komponentensuche auf Basis von Geschäftsmodellen*, Department für Informatik, Universität Oldenburg, Oldenburg, 2003.
23. van der Aalst, W. M. P., Weske, M., *The P2P Approach to Interorganizational Workflows*, Proceedings of the 13th International Conference on Advanced Information Systems Engineering 2001, pp., pp. 140-156.
24. Winograd, T., Flores, F., *Understanding computers and cognition.*, Ablex, Norwood/NJ, 1986.
25. Wombacher, A., Fankhauser, P., Mahleko, B., Neuhold, E., *Matchmaking for Business Processes Based on Choreographies*, IEEE International Conference on e-Technology, e-Commerce and e-Service (EEE'04) 2004, pp., pp. 359-368.
26. Yellin, D. M., Strom, R. E., *Protocol Specifications and Component Adaptors*, ACM Transactions on Programming Languages and Systems, 19 (1997), pp. 292-333.
27. Zirpins, C., Baier, T., Lamersdorf, W., *A Blueprint of Service Engineering*, First European Workshop on Object Orientation and Web Service (EOOWS) 2003.

# A P2P Approach for Business Process Modelling and Reuse

José A. Rodrigues Nt., Jano Moreira de Souza, Geraldo Zimbrão, Geraldo Xexéo, Eduardo Neves, and Wallace A. Pinheiro

COPPE – Universidade Federal do Rio de Janeiro
{rneto, jano, zimbrao, xexeo, eneves, awallace}@cos.ufrj.br

**Abstract.** Business Process Management Systems are largely used nowadays. However, most process models are started from scratch, not having reuse promoted. Large enterprises not using a unique integrated system, and also some of them that do, have the same business process implemented in a variety of ways, due to differences in their units' cultures or environments. A P2P tool is proposed as a way of cooperatively developing business processes models, minimizing the time needed to develop new models, reducing the differences among similar processes conducted in distinct organization units, enhancing the quality of models and promoting reuse.

**Keywords:** Distributed Systems, P2P, Business Process Modelling, BPM, Reuse, Reputation.

## 1 Introduction

Business Process Management (BPM) has gained popularity and strength in the last few years. The failure of traditional approaches for systems modelling in fully addressing the needs of most organizations, especially on aligning the development's final product with business objectives [1], has contributed to this picture. Particularly, modelling the business process can greatly facilitate requirements gathering, still viewed as the source for most failures on projects [2]. Yet, the work on MDA [3], enhancing the value of Platform Independent Models (PIM), also contributes to leveraging the importance of process modelling.

There exist several common, or similar, processes in organizations. For instance, most organizations[1], whether in the same company or not, have a procurement and acquisition process. We believe a cooperative approach can drastically reduce models' development time.

Addressing these issues, we propose the use of a peer-to-peer (P2P) tool to exchange processes models, promoting a "natural" standardization. The proposed tool also allows for the enhancement of existing models, through an evfolutionary ap-

---

[1] The term organization is used in this article with a generic sense, i.e., it can be a company or a company unit.

J. Eder, S. Dustdar et al. (Eds.): BPM 2006 Workshops, LNCS 4103, pp. 297–307, 2006.

proach that helps in organizational learning [4]. Additionally, since modellers can work
independently of any organization, the tool may also be used on an individual basis, as an open repository and reuse promotion mechanism.

## 2   The Problem

A large amount of common business processes do exist among organizations. Due to the increase of attention to business process management [5], organizations tend to fully model their processes. Many times though, models are developed from scratch, with little attention to reuse or process standardization.

In large enterprises, where several non-integrated systems can be found [6], differences among their units or departments could be greatly reduced if there was some way of standardizing their common processes. A cooperative approach can also ease the modelling task among different enterprises, where processes integration may be needed.

The adoption of standardized processes is expected to enhance efficiency and performance, e.g., streamlining the supply-chain process [6], while facilitating reuse and reducing modelling costs. In the networked economy, flexibility and reuse deserve special attention [7].

### 2.1   The Modelling Scenario

Making organizations adopt a standard process is not an easy task. This gets even harder if they are part of different companies. Cross-organizational BP modelling besides justifying special care, especially due to privacy and competitive constraints, can be a complex job [8].

The Business Process Cooperative Editor (BPCE) focuses on the improvement of models, the optimization of modelling activities, and the reuse of models among organizations.

### 2.2   UML for BP Modelling

Business process models are modelled using UML Activity Diagrams. Activity Diagrams were chosen for BP modelling due to the following reasons:

- Being a standard
- Wide use of XMI for model interchange in CASE tools
- IT background of users

For the purpose of BPCE, whole diagrams or fragments are handled as models. This way, a user wanting to develop a new model can do it by assembling existing diagrams, or parts of existing diagrams, to compose a model that suit the established requirements.

## 2.3  Model Exchange

Model exchange can be accomplished in a variety of ways. Actually, the lack of one standard format, widely adopted and used, is still recognized as a problem for the advancement of BPM. It is desirable that an interchange format presents the following characteristics: readability, ease of implementation, platform independence, efficiency, free availability, and support of standards [9].

The XML Process Description Language (XPDL) [10] could be a good choice. Besides being supported by a number of tools, it is capable of handling both UML models (based on the Meta Object Facility – MOF) and Business Process Modeling Notation (BPMN) models.

However, the XML Metadata Interchange Format (XMI), proposed by the OMG [11] appears as a natural choice. The use of XMI is recommended for two reasons:

- The chosen modelling media was the activity diagram, from UML.
- Extensions of the work to deal with software models or other XMI based tasks would be facilitated [12].

Although restricted to interchanging diagrams based on MOF, also from OMG, it is absolutely platform independent [11]. It shall be noted that BPMN has not yet defined a language for diagram interchange [13].

## 2.4  The P2P Approach

To evaluate the adequacy of a P2P approach, an analysis of the proposed system was conducted, based on the work of [14]. An evaluation considering their proposed decision-tree led us to the conclusion that a P2P approach was suitable to our problem.

Summarizing, the use of a P2P approach is justified, in this case, by the following:

- Budget constraints – the low cost entry of P2P systems allows for its use in any organization and also by independent modellers, starting their own cooperation network;
- High relevance, to the participants, of the resources being shared;
- Non-critical nature – the shared models are used as basis for the development of new models and, consequently, are not considered critical, since the modelled business is not actually running on them; and
- Abundance of process models on different and, sometimes, unrelated sources, which could jeopardize a centralized approach. Yet, the possibility of the independent, sometimes "unknown" modeller, to autonomously participate in such a cooperation network, posting its contributions.

Considering that, a P2P system depends on the actual participation of peers and since reuse of one's models builds up a reputation, we believe that such a mechanism motivates the cooperation of peers. However, free-riders might well exist in this scenario [15].

## 3 Implementing the Solution

BPCE is a P2P tool that allows modellers to freely share their models. It is implemented as a four-layer architecture, as described below:

1. Infrastructure layer – implemented by COPPEER [16], it is responsible for the P2P primitives.
2. Repository layer – responsible for storing local models.
3. Searcher layer – has the mechanisms for finding models – the Searcher –, which can be aggregated to build a new model, using COPPEER resources. It also includes a simple tool for visualizing model elements – the Viewer –, prior to being selected for use in the Editor.
4. Editor layer – holds the graphical environment with resources to modelling – the Editor –, including assembling obtained model elements collected from the network of agents.

Fig. 1 shows the conceived architecture.

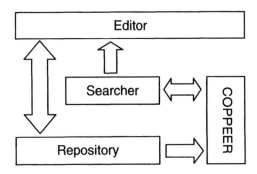

**Fig. 1.** BPCE Architecture

Published models are stored in local repositories – the search space for COPPEER. Whenever a user wants to build a new model, a search can be performed on the Searcher, which uses COPPEER for it. The search returns pointers to model elements[2]. Basic information about found elements is based on their XMI and additional attached data. That basic information is displayed to the user in the Searcher window, where model visualization can be requested. As soon as the local repository receives enough data to graphically display any information about the selected model element, a Viewer, which is part of the Searcher, may be started.

The user can briefly check the found model, using the Viewer. If the user decides to use a model, it can be transferred to the Editor, either to a new Editor window or to an already open one.

---

[2] Model and model elements are sometimes used interchangeably in the article. In the case of activity diagram, model element means a fragment of a model, eventually just an atomic action.

On the Editor, the user can modify the received element, by editing it or by aggregating it to other existing elements. A new version of the same element, or a new one, can then be directly added to the repository, through a publishing mechanism.

An overview of a basic modelling cycle is shown in Fig. 2.

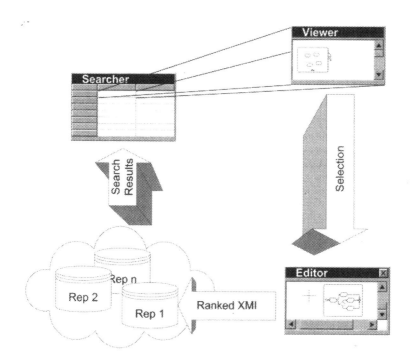

**Fig. 2.** Modelling Cycle

### 3.1 COPPEER – A P2P Framework

The bottom layer, provided by COPPEER [16], takes care of model exchange and allows for the search of models or models' elements related to desired subjects.

The COPPEER framework is an environment for developing and running P2P applications. It is a research project developed at the Database Lab of the Federal University of Rio de Janeiro Graduate School and Research in Engineering (UFRJ/COPPE). It implements a P2P environment under the Complex Adaptive Systems (CAS) paradigm [17].

### 3.2 The Model Editor

The Editor provides resources to assemble and edit model elements. Models prepared on the Editor are published as XMI archives.

Since the appraisals of imported models are done after building a new model, the Editor has a function to publish a model. The published model becomes available on the model repository for use by other peers. Publishing includes the creation of a

Model Object (MO), by the Editor, which aggregates a small image of the published model, its score and its information vector. Such a vector is produced from the XMI representation of the model, discarding the header, common to all published files.

Additionally, when a model is published, the evaluation of the models used to compose it is done. Later on, if the user wants to evolve a published model, the Editor asks for a new evaluation, only if new models are imported and added to the model.

### 3.3  Retrieving Models

Searching the Models' Space is performed using a simple search mechanism, based on the vector model [18]. Each new model has its vector calculated, and preserved, in MO's, created to later use by the Searchers and Viewers.

Since XML tags are also used when calculating vectors, the search can further be directed to specific types of elements, according to activity diagram schema. For example, it can be constrained to *ActivityGroup* [19], by simply adding the term to the query.

Considering the search space can be populated by a large amount of models, user can specify the maximum distance allowed from the query vector, for retrieved models. Retrieved models are presented, ordered by similarity to the query, with their scores.

### 3.4  Ranking Models

In an environment with a large number of choices, ranking turns out to be helpful in optimizing user's work. When there are several models dealing with the same subject, it is to the benefit of the users that some kind of ranking exists, to facilitate the choice of any particular option. The idea of cooperatively filtering the available models can be applied to such a context [20], [21].

A model's score is an indicator of usage of the model. To calculate the score, and assessment of its author's reputation is required. The reputation indicator used in BPCE tries, through tracking models usage, to indicate the quality of the models produce by each user.

While maintaining scores or reputations on a traditional distributed system could be done using a central server, this is not the case in a P2P environment. Some approaches have been already explored [22] and show that in P2P environments, the maintenance of evaluations is not trivial. We assumed, for the sake of reducing complexity, that minor differences among peers' local values are acceptable.

Most P2P reputation systems have two kinds of problems:

- Reputation is based on just a few peers evaluation, losing the big picture; or
- Reputation is based on all peers' evaluations, unnecessarily raising the traffic on the network [23].

The proposed algorithm is not susceptible to the above problems, since the reputation is build up considering all uses of a modeller's model and just this, i.e., it does not require the participation of all peers on the network.

Models are ranked according to their utilization by other modellers. When a retrieved model is used, i.e., the user decides, when using the Viewer, to export it to the Editor, it receives points. Those few points granted, mean that the model has, at least, gotten the attention of the user – however, this is not actually a way to reward the model, but to discard the ones that are not even looked at by users. Later, when a new model is created on the Editor, the user is presented with a list of imported models, where he marks the models actually used to derive the new one. Those selected models receive some additional points, to leverage their ranking, according to their utilization on the new model, i.e., the user can state that an imported model had low, medium or high influence on the new developed model. The received points are weighted by the appraising modeller's reputation.

Synthesizing, a new model has its initial points, based on the score of the models used in its composition and the reputation of its modeller. It keeps receiving points according to its utilization on the development of new models.

A modeler's reputation is calculated based on the reutilization of his models and on his collaboration to the overall ranking process. The modeller receives points each time one of his models is selected and additional points when it is actually used. Points are also granted when he decides to collaborate on the appraisals of the imported models. This can motivate the participation of users in the ranking system. It applies a simplified version of the HYRIWYG reputation system [24].

So, let:

- $I$ be the set of modellers.
- $M$ be the set of models, $J \subset M$ be the set of models from modeller $I$, and $K \subset M$ be the set of imported models in model m.
- $ps_{ijm}$ be the points for selection ( 0 if not selected, 1 otherwise), by modeller $i$, in model $j$, of model $m$.
- $pu_{ijm}$ be the points for use, where not used = 0, low = 1, medium = 2 and high = 3, by modeller $i$, in model $j$, of model $m$.
- $pe_j$ be the points for evaluation, where $pe_j=0$ if the modeller does not evaluate used models, and $pe_j=1$ if he does evaluate, when building his model $j$.
- $R_i$ be the reputation of modeller $i$.
- $wi$ be the weight of memory, $ws$ be the weight of selection, and $wu$ be the weight of use

The evaluation system can then be expressed by:

**Model's Initial Points**

$$PI_m = \frac{\sum_K \left( PM_k * \frac{pu_{ikm}}{3} \right)}{|K|} \tag{1}$$

The initial points' factor evaluates a model, based on the reputation of the models used in its composition. This is done by considering that, if a model is an evolution of other models, it must carry some of their reputation. It can be seen as the model's DNA.

**Model's Selection Points**

$$PS_m = \sum_I \sum_J \left( R_i * PR_i * ps_{ijm} \right) \qquad (2)$$

The selection points factor accounts for the points accrued by the model due to its selection by other modellers, when building new models. A model receives a reward for being, at least, interesting.

**Model's Use Points**

$$PU_m = \sum_I \sum_J \left( R_i * PR_i * pu_{ijm} \right) \qquad (3)$$

The use points factor accounts for the points the models receives on other modellers' appraisals, when also building new models. It is the reward for the actual utilization of the model.

**Model's Total Points**

$$PM_m = wi * PI_m + ws * PS_m + wu * PU_m \qquad (4)$$

Total points are calculated by the formula above. The weights are used to balance the factors. Different organizations or scenarios can require different customizations of the system, manipulating how ranking shall be affected by each of these factors. It is important though, to understand that these weights must be set for once and for all, since the initial evaluation is static, i.e., it is computed at the time the model is built and never more. Also, the other evaluations, although being computed during system's life, are, each of them, computed at the time the model is used, and added to the existing model points.

**Modeller's Reputation (R)**

$$R_i = \frac{PR_i}{\sum_I PR_i} \qquad (5)$$

The modeller's reputation introduces the reputation of the modeller into the scenario. It is defined as above, based on the modeller's points.

**Modeller's Points**

$$PR_i = \left[ \frac{\sum_J PM_j}{|J|} \right] + \left[ \sum_J pe_j \right] \qquad (6)$$

The first factor is the average points the modeller has received on his models. It is the actual score of the modeller.

The second factor is a motivating factor – a reward, given to the modeller, each time he builds a new model, and evaluates the models used to compose it. This feature enhances the cooperation among modellers.

## 4   Conclusion and Expected Benefits

BPCE facilitates the development of new business process models, through reuse. This is done using the P2P paradigm, hiding model exchange complexities from users, and providing users with an easy to use and simple interface.

However, there exist some negative aspects of the approach. Some of them are expected to be mitigated, but some may require some extra effort. The list below is a basic assessment of the cons:

- Trust – while in a controlled membership scenario the problems associated with trustiness may be minimized, this turns out to be much harder in an open environment;
- Participation – heavy dependence on peer's availability, since models are stored on authors' peers, may develop as a problem. Although reputation build up may work as a motivating factor, the unavailability of a node, while not critically compromising the modeller's work, may act as a demotivating factor. Replication can address this problem, reducing its impact;
- Diversity of modelling languages – the system's effectiveness is based on the use of a common standard or, at least, compatibility among shared models. Translators, although feasible, may not be practical; and
- Diversity of tools – even assuming the existence of a unique exchange mechanism, as XMI, our assessment has shown that each tool has some particularities when preparing their XMI files. While BPCE can be adapted to work with several existing tools, the wide use of non-standard resources in XMI files can affect system's effectiveness.

Despite the downside of the coin, we understand that through BPCE, the organization can have its processes shared and adapted. As a result, on the long run, it is expected that the best-fitted processes survive, contributing to evolution and standardization of the organizations' processes. In this sense, it may be seen as a distributed knowledge management tool, supporting organizational learning in the enterprise. Additionally, when used by different enterprises, it can help organizations tune-up their processes and better understand each other.

## 5   Summary and Future Work

BPCE, as presented in the preceding sections, is currently under implementation for deployment in a large company, where the problems stated do exist. Enhancements, as described below, will be implemented on next versions.

Several issues have appeared during the development. Due to the time constraints of the project, we intend to consider them on the next versions of the tool. A small list of issues is provided:

- Ontology based search – besides enhancing search, it allows for customization, including partitioning the search space onto business areas, with their proper ontologies.
- XPDL – support of XPDL and related technologies.
- Security mechanisms – avoiding fraud and selecting what information can be viewed by other users. This deserves special care when conducting cross-organizational modelling. Additionally, the need for anonymity must be studied, since social barriers may difficult sharing.
- Ranking – the present implementation just considers the modeller participation on the ranking process as a binary function, on each new developed model. This can be changed into a system where the points received are also based on the quality of the judgment made by the modeller [24]. In addition, proper experiments shall be conducted to allow for the assessment of the advantages and disadvantages of the algorithm when compared to the other existing ones.

# References

[1] Chan, Y. Why Haven't We Mastered Alignment? The Importance of the Informal Organization Structure. MIS Quarterly Executive, Vol. 1, No. 2, June/2002.
[2] Hofmann, H. Lehner, F. Requirements Engineering as a Success Factor on Software Projects. IEEE Software, v. 18, issue 4, IEEE Press, 2001.
[3] Miller, J. Mukerji, J. editors, MDA Guide Version 1.0.1. OMG 2003.
[4] Liebowitz, J. Building Organizational Intelligence: A Knowledge Management Primer. CRC Press. 1999.
[5] Smith, H. Fingar, P. Business Process Management – The Third Wave. Meghan-Kiffer Press, 2003.
[6] May, M. Business Process Management – Integration in a Web-enabled Environment. Pearson Education Ltd. 2003.
[7] Smith, H. Fingar, P. IT Doesn't Matter – Business Process Do. Meghan-Kiffer Press, 2003.
[8] Lippe, S. Greiner, U. Barros, A. A Survey on State of the Art to Facilitate Modelling of Cross-Organisational Business Processes. 2nd Workshop of German Informatics Society (GI), 11th GI Conference "BTW 2005", 2005.
[9] Mendling, J. Neumann, G. and Nuttgens, M. A Comparison of XML Interchange Formats for Business Process Modelling, in Workflow Handbook 2005. Future Strategies Inc., 2005.
[10] The Workflow Management Coalition, Process Definition Interface – XML Process Definiton Language. WFMC, 2005.
[11] Object Management Group, MOF 2.0/XMI Mapping Specification, v2.1. OMG, 2005.
[12] Rodrigues, E. Rodrigues, J. Mello, R. Porto, F. Mapping OO Applications to Relational Databases using the MOF and XMI. Workshop on Integration and Transformation of UML models – ECOOP 2002, LNCS, v. 2548. Springer-Verlag Heidelfeld, 2002.

[13] Object Management Group, Business Process Modeling Notation Specification, v1.0. OMG, 2006.

[14] Roussopoulos, M. Baker, M. Rosenthal, D. Giuli, T. Maniatis, P. Mogul, J. 2 P2P or not 2 P2P?. Proceedings of the 3rd International Workshop on Peer-to-Peer Systems. LNCS, v. 3279. Springer-Verlag Heidelfeld, 2005.

[15] Parameswaran, M. Susarla, A. Whinston, A. P2P Networking: An Information-Sharing Alternative. IEEE Computer, v. 34, issue 7, IEEE Press, 2001.

[16] Miranda, M. Xexeo, G. Souza, J. Building Tools for Emergent Design with COPPEER. Proceeedings of the 10th International Conference of CSCW in Design – CSCWD 2006. 2006.

[17] Tan, J. Wen, H. Awad, N. Health Care and Services Delivery Systems as Complex Adaptive Systems. Communications of the ACM, vol. 48, issue 5. ACM Press, 2005.

[18] Baeza-Yates, R. Ribeiro-Neto, B. Modern Information Retrieval. ACM Press. 1999.

[19] Object Management Group, UML 2.0 Superstructure, v2.0 formal 05/07/04. OMG, 2005.

[20] Goldberg, D., Nichols, D., Oki, B. M., and Terry, D. Using Collaborative Filtering To Weave An Information Tapestry. Commun. ACM 35, 12 (Dec. 1992), 61-70. ACM, 1992.

[21] Resnick, P. Iacovou, N. Suchak, M. Bergstrom, P. Riedl, J. GroupLens: An Open Architecture for Collaborative Filtering of Netnews. Proceedings of the 1994 ACM Conference on Computer Supported Cooperative Work – CSCW 94. ACM, 1994.

[22] Aberer, K. Despotovic, Z. Managing Trust in a Peer-2-Peer Information System. Proceedings of the 10th International Conference on Information and Knowledge Management (ACM CIKM), New York, USA, 2001.

[23] Kamvar, S. Schlosser, M. Garcia-Molina, H. The Eigentrust Algorithm for Reputation Management in P2P Networks. Proceedings of the 12th International Conference on World Wide Web, Budapest, Hungary - WWW '03. ACM Press, New York, NY, 640-651.

[24] Garcia, A. C., Ekstrom, M., and Björnsson, H. 2004. HYRIWYG: Leveraging Personalization to Elicit Honest Recommendations. In Proceedings of the 5th ACM Conference on Electronic Commerce - EC '04. ACM Press, 2004.

# Session 3: Ontology-Based Approach for Enterprise Interoperability

# Interoperable and Multi-flow Software Environment: Application to Health Care Supply Chain

Pierre Féniès, Michel Gourgand, and Sophie Rodier

LIMOS CNRS UMR 6158
Campus des Cézeaux, 63173 Aubière, France
{fenies, gourgand, rodier}@isima.fr

**Abstract.** In this paper, we propose a generic decisional model allowing to evaluate in a total way (physical flows, financial flows) plannings for any system contained in supply chain. We present a methodology for decision-making aid software conception. This methodology use modelling and simulation concept and show the interest of going towards Advanced Budgeting and Scheduling software for complexes supply chains performance evaluation. To show the generic character of the decisional approach, we apply the chaining of models suggested to the logistic process of Health Care Supply Chain. We give the metrics resulting from the modelling and the simulation of the patient treatment in the Hospital system.

**Keywords:** APS, ABS, Multi flow software environment, interoperability.

## 1 Introduction

Hospital system is an opened system which interacts with external logistic entities or medical service providers. The comparison with industrial supply chain is obvious: the current hospital, taking into account its growing complexity, is closer to an immense logistic chain whose agents aim at satisfying patients. So, Health Care Systems can be seen as a Health Care Supply Chain (HSC) [1].

As medical organizations grow, information flow managing between various components becomes more complex. Health management is a knowledge intensive activity and most organizations have specialist sub-domains, each with its own vocabulary, knowledge base and software applications. The fact that these sub-domains contain multi-platform, multi-vendor application wrappers built around multi-variate data sources further adds to the complexity [2].

So HSC information system needs can be compared with industrial Supply Chain information system needs with regard to data integration and interconnection.

Then, as [3] show it, interoperability appears to be a major approach for the design of applications dedicated to access information. The Supply Chain manager has to possess a set of tools and methods capable of helping him in design problems as in piloting problems but also capable of furthering interoperability of information sources. In fact, decision-making aid software depend increasingly on various

J. Eder, S. Dustdar et al. (Eds.): BPM 2006 Workshops, LNCS 4103, pp. 311–322, 2006.

heterogeneous resources, such as databases, knowledge bases, files, Web-based information, and so on. Moreover, the complexity of a HSC, as of industrial Supply Chain, is due to the structure of the logistic process [4] and to the number of entities which interact simultaneously.

The purpose of this article is to propose an interoperable and multi-flow software environment for HSC which combines simulation and performance evaluation and to connect this decision-making aid software with HSC information system. One of the objectives of this work will be the integration of a decisional and financial applicative brick in the APS (Advanced Planning Scheduling). In fact, thanks to the analysis of existing tools and methods [5] we will show that the latter don't integrate in their decisional approach, in intra-organisational context as in inter-organisational context, the constraints evaluation resulting from financial flow. If decision-making aid tools try to improve the organization profitability by improving a number of physical flow performance criteria, they don't interpret, or inadequately, the physical flow elements in financial flow elements translation.

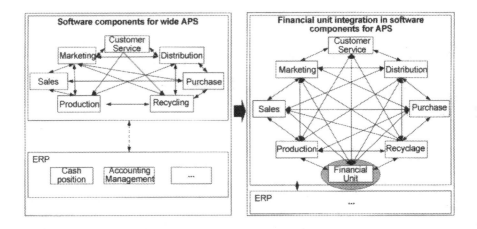

**Fig. 1.** Financial unit integration in software suite of APS type for the Supply Chain

This paper is organized as follows: in next section, a state of the art about integrated decision-making aid software concept and a brief state of decision-making aid software market are given. An interoperable and multi-flow decision-making aid software suite is proposed in section 3. Section 4 is dedicated to the presentation of a study case. Finally, conclusion and future research work are presented.

## 2  State of the Art

In this section, we present a brief state of the art on the necessity of an integrated information system for Supply Chain and Health Care Supply Chain, and in a second part, we briefly compare some decisional tools applicable to Health Care system.

## 2.1 Necessity of Integrated Decision-Making Aid Software

In a literature review [5] show that enterprises have to implement inter-organizational integration due to increasing competition and globalization. This integration is then used as basis for a transparent inter-organizational integration of all members of the whole supply network allowing a continuous exchange of information between the members. Company-internal integration seems to be a precondition for an inter-organizational integration. [6] show that it is possible to integrate and access various heterogeneous information sources within a hospital Intranet based on the ARIANE architecture and the Unified Medical Language System (UMLS) ontology. Their prototype demonstrates the interest of this common ontology when associated with the Information Source MAP (ISM) [7] which provides with a catalogue of existing servers. The use of ontologies to provide interoperability among heterogeneous data sources has been applied in many domains including manufacturing [8] and medical information systems [9,10]. In a literature review about cost models, [11] shows that Activity Based Costing (ABC) system is the best type of cost model for complex system because of its connections with Supply Chain management. As shown by [12], integrating financial flow and physical flow in Supply Chain management is essential to optimize financial flow and we think that there is a need for a general approach for both Supply Chain modelling and its evaluation which combines physical and financial flows thanks to ABC. [13] show that there is not in literature approaches which propose to combine physical flow simulation, financial flow evaluation and data integration.

## 2.2 Existing Software for Decision-Making About Flow

Nowadays the effective decision-making importance grows and many tools were set up on the market in order to answer this request. Information to be presented at the user is the central problems of any decisional project. The decisional tools aim to allow consolidations establishment and to bring closer data, primarily at ends of reporting or decision-making. They are data consultation tools, on variables aggregation or detail levels, and also observed according to variable axes (for example: to measure the costs, the sales or profitability, by geographical area, temporal period or product range). The decisional tools market counts a certain number of solutions as regards Cost Accounting and Budgetary Development. Table 1 retains some software packages, some specialized enough, others generic, which are compared on various criteria. Our study is not exhaustive, and we have only studied the most important editors which propose integrated solutions. For each APS, we study if financial flow is integrated, for example with credit management functions, if costing management models are implemented, and if scorecards with financials metrics are used. This analysis shows that in network configuration, the optimization is done with very simple costs constraints. But in tactical or operational activities, financials constraints are not integrated and are not evaluated. Note that some of the tested APS have links with ERP (for example APO and R3 which are edited by SAP), but these links don't integrate financial evaluation with planning. Moreover, note that discrete event simulations are not used by APS, which only use optimization.

**Table 1.** Encompassing view of various tools functionalities

|  | Dataware House | Process Modelling | Physical flow Opti-mization | Budgetary Develop-ment | Discrete event Simulation |
|---|---|---|---|---|---|
| **Not specialized tools** ADEXA iCollaboration Suite ; ASPEN eSupply Chain Suite ; FUTURMASTER Futurmaster; ORACLE aps; PEOPLE SOFT SupplyChain Planning; SAP Advanced Planer and Optimization (APO); SYNQUEST One2One Solutions. | Not Specified | Yes | Yes | No | No |
| **"Health" specialized tools** SIB Sextant; KEYRUS K@-prim; MC KESSON Evoluance SIAD | Not Specified | Yes | Not specified | Yes | No |

Moreover, to avoid high maintenance costs or to deploy a standard corporate model in an international group, some corporations are implementing ERP systems without or with minimal customization or interoperability [14].

We conclude that if HSC manager want to plan and budget the hospital activities as a whole they must use software which permit a real integration of Supply Chain informational, physical and financial flows in decision making process. This type of software does not actually exist. We propose in next section a type of software which takes into account physical and financial flows thanks to decision making tools and information flow thanks to data warehouse in planning and budgeting activities.

## 3   Proposal of an Interoperable and Multi-flow Decision-Making Aid Software Suite

It is worth noting that there is a need for a general approach for both HCS modelling and its evaluation which combines data from physical, informational and financial flows in one type of software which is a global Advanced Planning and Scheduling (APS) [15]. This one allows solving HCS problem with an integration of all the system flow. We call Advanced Budgeting and Scheduling (ABS) this type of APS which combines all the flows and integrates data from the information system.

First, we propose in this section the ASDI-HSC environment, which means Analysis, Specification, Design, and Implementation for the systems of the Health Care Supply Chain class. In a second time, we present the concept of ABS which is made thanks to ASDI-HSC environment.

### 3.1   Environment for a Multi-flow Tool Design

We use a methodology called ASDI (Analysis, Specification, Design, and Implementation) [16] dedicated to the design and the implementation of modelling, simulation and piloting software environments for a domain.

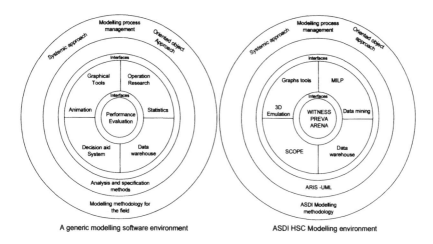

**Fig. 2.** ASDI-HSC environment

Figure 2 only presents the visible elements for the manager. These elements communicate using the interfaces layer. The environment corresponds to the concept of software engineering workshop for the Supply Chain modelling and performance evaluation, whether this one is centred production of goods or services. The ASDI-HSC environment makes it possible to design and establish software suite of ABS type (Advanced Budgeting and Scheduling) which constitutes an evolution in the decision-making aid tools for Supply Chain. ASDI-HSC includes:

- a performance evaluation system, core of the environment; the performance evaluation layer allows the one or more action models development according to the modelling objectives. SIMAN V and WITNESS are indifferently used as core of this software environment. PREVA (PRocess EVAluation) approach [20] thus allows to the action models constitution whose objectives are centred on the value creation, but also on "patient" satisfaction;

- a metric selection part, consisted by SCOPE approach (Supply Chain Operational Performance Evaluation)[1] which allows the balanced scorecards construction and establishment for the behaviours orientation in HSC.

- a data warehouse which allows the access to data necessary to the tools belonging to the various part of the environment ;

- an operational research part which uses Mixed Integer linear Programs (MILP) (For operating theatre…).

- a statistical part, which allows the analysis and the processing the existing data (forecasts of load, learning curves) as well as the study of the results obtained by the core of the environment.

- Graphics tools and 3D emulation which makes possible to animate in 3D with MANTRA 4D the simulation models. This three-dimensional chart tool is very significant to imply the actors in the organizational change.

- a part which contains methods of analysis and specification. ARIS and UML tools are here used as formalisms and methods for specification.

- a modelling methodology of the field which was presented in [13], [16].

## 3.2 ASDI-HSC Environment Use for an Advanced Budgeting and Scheduling Software Design

Figure 3 shows the characteristics of an ABS and the existing connections between the various activities of Supply Chain physical and financial flows, the modelling approaches and the decisional horizons interacting with the various data-processing and mathematical models included in ABS.

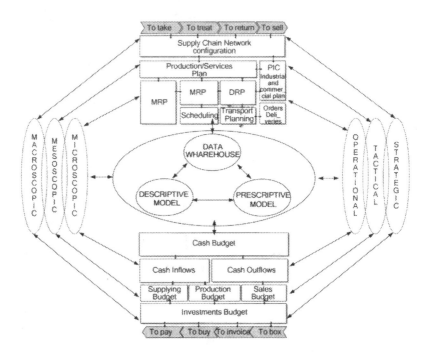

**Fig. 3.** An Advanced Budgeting and Scheduling software

Supposing that the activity "to budget for" for financial flow is the equivalent of the activity "to plan it" for physical flow, we define Advanced Budgeting and Scheduling as a coherent succession of software applications allowing the optimization and the performance evaluation of supply chain physical and financial flows and combining overall (for the whole of the chain) like locally (for an entity) the strategic, tactical, operational decisional horizons [17] with macroscopic, mesoscopic and microscopic modelling approaches. These various applications are connected to the information system of supply chain entities by a data warehouse which reprocesses heterogeneous data resulting from different software applications to feed in information the prescriptive models like descriptive contained in ABS. Usually, prescriptive models [18] are used for decision-making: they are used to make a choice on the design, control and the functioning of supply chain [19], while the descriptive models [19] make it possible to evaluate the decisions made by the prescriptive model or directly by the actors.

Technical and conceptual features of an ABS are given in table 3 which shows the passage from an APS software suite to an ABS software suite. If the context of use of an ABS is the same one (internal Supply Chain as well as external) as an APS, the software functionalities integrate planning and budgeting of the activities (for example, choice of the planning which generates the maximum of cash-flow) and the measuring tools of the performance use concepts more advanced than the few indicators of physical flow. This type of software suite can be used for a complex system of the Supply Chain as for the whole Supply Chain. We integrate in ABS a decisional module which organizes information for Supply Chain managers in the form of prospective scorecard for the ex ante activities evaluation.

**Table 3.** Transition from an APS to an ABS

| | Advanced Planning and Scheduling [15] | Advanced Budgeting and Scheduling |
|---|---|---|
| **Context** | Internal and external Supply Chain | Internal and external Supply Chain |
| **Functionalities** | | |
| Network Design | For physical flow | For physical and financial flows |
| Distribution (DRP) | For physical flow | For physical and financial flows |
| Production (PDP) | For physical flow | For physical and financial flows |
| Supplying (MRP) | For physical flow | For physical and financial flows |
| Scheduling and transport | For physical flow | For physical and financial flows |
| **Decisional Tools** Performance Measurement | Some physical flow metrics | Balanced Scorecard+ PREVA model [16] |
| **Connection with the chain entities information system** | Not detailed | Data warehouses allowing collection of data and information from heterogeneous applications |
| **Software components for decision making tools** | Optimisation (Cplex) and heuristics | Coupling of optimisation/ simulation (prescriptive and descriptive models) |
| **Collaborative Planning** | Collaborative planning gives to the chain entities the quantity of products and services to be produced and delivered on short, medium and long term for a given customer satisfaction rate. | Collaborative planning gives to the chain entities the quantity of products and services to be produced and delivered on short, medium and long term which gives the highest level of value for Supply Chain entities. |

The supply of the centred part on the costs and the financial part of the prospective scorecard is carried out by the model PREVA [20] which makes it possible to translate in a prospective and causal way the impact of physical flow into element of financial flow by a succession of Activity Based Costing models. PREVA evaluate in the medium and long term cash flows generated by Supply Chain and the entities which make it up, but also in the short time the position of treasury of the Chain entities generated by a collaborative planning.

In the APS, the interfacing with each entity information system which makes it up is not carried out. We propose to carry it out in ABS by a data warehouse which allows the collection and the data securisation resulting from heterogeneous applications. Lastly, collaborative plannings of the APS are oriented Patient or Customer Satisfaction (with the logistic meaning of the term) and do not integrate the value creation concept for the actors who take part in the network Supply Chain. Collaborative plannings resulting from an ABS allow, for a level of customer satisfaction given to choose the solution which generates the most value for the whole of the chain actors and to design the division of the latter.

# 4  Application

The generic evaluation model presented previously was applied to a real HSC application. This application is done in collaboration with AXEGE society. In this HSC several cares are done far away the Hospital, for example in the laboratory or in imagery. In hospitals, there is a lot of units which are very often saturated and can't treat all the patients which are addressed to them. The objective of this study is to evaluate, according to physical and financial criteria, various rules of patients priority in the context of systems of health regulation mechanism. For that, the environment previously presented is implemented. In a first paragraph, we present briefly the study case, giving the details of the modelling process, while the second paragraph presents the simulation results which come from the HSC modelling and simulation. Note that many processes are evaluated in the case study and different granularity levels are modelled and evaluated.

## 4.1.  Action Model Modelling and Development

HSC modelling is given on figure 4. Figure 5 shows the links between software applications, information flows, financial flows and physical flows in order to make a decision making aid tool.

We present here an example of application of the decision making aid tool proposed. For the work of modelling and data collection was carried out in collaboration with the Hospital. In the study case, a priority is associated to each treatment. Indeed, the management of the priorities is as follows: an agenda for patient appointment date is made for each day. This last one is elaborated by supposing a processing time of the average patient without taking into account his pathology and its severity. In addition, any patients coming from other departments must be also treated. It is then possible that some schedules patients are not treated the right day. Pathologies differ according to their severity, their medical resources consumption and their remuneration. The objectives of the HSC being multiple (profitability, treatment rate...), the choice of a patients treatments priority rule is complex. We suppose that physical flow is composed of patients flow. Figure 5 presents a chain of patient treatment process in a hospital. It is important to specify that the various interventions are not inevitably carried out within the hospital, indeed the laboratory is for example located on another site. A simulation model under SIMAN V Arena of this system was developed in order to evaluate in a stochastic context the best rule of patients priority management.

Five priority rules (heuristic) are evaluated as follows:

- H1: First patient check-in, first patient treated (current rule).
- H2: The largest criterion of severity (for equivalent criterion of severity, FIFO).
- H3: The largest financial criterion (for equivalent criterion of severity, the financial criterion the most interesting financial criterion).
- H4: Processing time considered on average shortest (with criterion of equivalent time, first in, first out).
- H5: The longest processing time (with criterion of equivalent time, first in, first out).

In the case of identical criterion, rule FIFO is applied.

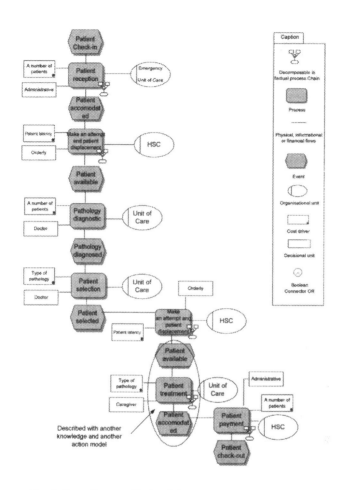

**Fig. 4.** Event Process Chain of the patient way in the Hospital

| | Entity (*) | HSC | Entity (*) | HSC | Entity (*) | HSC |
|---|---|---|---|---|---|---|
| | Real Data | | Previsional Data | | Previsional Information | |
| Physical flows (Patient and logistic flows, 10 different flows) | For each entity and each flow, a data base - 50 data base | Data from different flows and application is collected in a Data warehouse | Previsionnal data are given by Simulation, Arena | Previsionnal data are given by Simulation, Arena | Scorecards with specific entities results, data warehouse | Scorecards and global results, data warehouse |
| Financial flows (one flow, 5 Business unit, and 2 ) | For each Business Unit, a database | Data from different flows and application is collected in a Data warehouse | Previsionnal data are given by PREVA | Previsionnal data are given by PREVA | Scorecards with specific entities results, data warehouse | Scorecards and global results, data warehouse |

*(\*) Internal or external Service Unit, Internal /external Hospital*

**Fig. 5.** Links between software applications and flows in real case study

This simulation is not determinist and finishing. Six families of pathologies: P1 to P6 are considered. The patients check-in follows an exponential law of average 15 mm. The pathologies distribution and the processing time of pathologies by the medical resources are given by table 4. The criterion of pathology severity does not correspond to an emergency criterion. The financial data are "pro format" and are built starting from a regulation system for public health care system. Figure 6 represents the translation of specification model previously defined into simulation model with Arena tool. To realize the simulation of the HSC on 365 days, a time of 15 minutes is necessary.

**Table 4.** Initial data

|  | P1 | P2 | P3 | P4 | P5 | P6 |
|---|---|---|---|---|---|---|
| Distribution law | Seasonality of pathologies | | | | | |
| Processing following a normal distribution | N(14,2) | N(15,5) | N(21,5) | N(25,5) | N(15,5) | N(20,2) |
| Severity (of the least serious to the most serious) | 1 | 2 | 3 | 3 | 2 | 2 |
| Pathology price (€) | 20 | 17 | 22 | 30 | 15 | 25 |
| Pathology margin (€) | 10.62 | 8.75 | 6.5 | 7.98 | 8.8 | 8.37 |

Output variables to observe are: the annual average number of patients treated by pathology, the annual rate of patients satisfaction, the annual rate of medical resources occupation. Input Variables are: Priority rules. Initial state of the system: the Hospital Supply Chain resources are free and the waiting rooms are empty at the beginning of each simulated day. Finishing conditions of the simulation: one day which is simulated begins at 8 AM and finishes at 6 PM. Collect results are: a replication consists of 365 days consecutive without restoring of the "laws". We made 30 replicas of 365 days and determine the average value of each observable variable. The observed variables of the patients treatment of the HSC are then used by the decisional module resulting from PREVA.

### 4.2 Results

The analysis of the physical flow results is carried out using the approach for financial performance evaluation (PREVA). This tool treats the data, which it receives from the simulation model. This data are exported from SIMAN V Arena tool to Scorecards, using the Visual Basic language. Thus starting from the physical flows represented in the simulation model we have the translation of corresponding financial flows. The input data of decisional model detailed previously and which are provided at the end of the simulation are the annual number of patients treated by pathology, the number of patients untreated by pathology, as well as the use ratio of medical resources. Finally, the tool for performance evaluation enabled us to obtain results for each evaluated management rule, these results are represented on figure 6. The analysis of the results (table 5) makes it possible to initially show the sensitivity of the performances indicators compared to various management rules of treatment priority but also to select the best rules for the analyzed system.

**Table 5.** Selection of management rules

| Management Rule | H2 | H3 | H4 | H5 |
|---|---|---|---|---|
| A number of patients | sol < H1 | sol >H1 | Best rule | sol < H1 |
| Satisfaction Patients | sol < H1 | sol >H1 | Best rule | sol < H1 |
| Resources use | id H1 | id H1 | id H1 | id H1 |
| Value Creation | sol < H1 | Best rule | sol >H1 | sol < H1 |
| Generated Cash lows | sol < H1 | Best rule | sol >H1 | sol < H1 |
| Selection | **eliminated** | **H3 & H4 better than H1** | | **eliminated** |

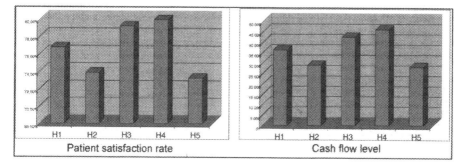

**Fig. 6.** Results

The decisional approach gives criteria of selection which allow, for an equivalent or higher quality of "patient satisfaction", to select the most advantageous rules of management on the financial. If the results presented validate the decisional approach, the various rules of management and their order are relevant only compared to the case study.

# 5 Conclusion

In this paper, a modelling environment for Supply Chains class systems was proposed. This software environment, based on ASDI modelling process has for objective to help the experts in modelling and the managers to model a complex system such as a HSC. The evaluation constraints resulting from financial flows are integrated and give the possibility to propose new decisional software called ABS, which permits the taking into account of performance evaluation methods in interdisciplinary and interoperable context of Supply Chain management. Thanks to this approach, decision making tools using simulations for all the flows (physical, financial and informational flows) are connected together and with information system. This approach is validated in a health care supply chain (with different entities such as laboratories, internal and external unit of care). This generic approach enables us to consider, in a next study, the integration of ABC model and financial flows in optimization models in order to improve running of HSC. An extension of this approach in large external Supply Chain in order to improve their functioning and to allow the managers to share the value creation realized by collaborative planning and to develop interoperability in intra-organizational as in inter-organizational context for other types of supply chain (industrial ...) will be proposed in next works.

# References

1. Féniès, P., Gourgand, M., Tchernev N.: Une contribution à la mesure de la performance dans la supply chain hospitalière : L'exemple du processus opératoire. In 2<sup>ème</sup> conférence francophone en Gestion et Ingénierie de Systèmes Hospitaliers (GISEH). Mons (2004)
2. Orgun B., Vu J.: HL7ontology and mobile agents for interoperability in heterogeneous medical information systems. Computers in Biology and Medicine, (2005)
3. Degoulet P, Fieschi M. Interopérabilité des Systèmes d'Information de Santé - Aspects Syntactiques et Sémantiques. Paris: CIHS, (1997)
4. Tchernev N.: Modélisation du processus logistique dans les systèmes flexibles de production, Thèse de doctorat, Université Blaise Pascal, Clermont Ferrand II, France, (1997)
5. Selk B., Kloeckner S., Albani A.: Enabling interoperability of networked enterprises through an integrative information system architecture for CRM and SCM. First International Workshop on Enterprise and Networked Enterprises Interoperability (ENEI). Nancy (2005)
6. Aymarda S., Fieschia D., Jouberta M., Fieschia M.: Towards Interoperability of Information Sources within a Hospital Intranet. Annual Symposium Library (1998)
7. Masys D., Humphreys B.: Structure and function of the UMLS Information Sources Map. In: Lun K, Degoulet P,Piemme T, Rienhoff O, eds. MEDINFO 92: North-Holland Publ. Comp., (1992)
8. Obitko M., Marik V.: Ontologies for multi-agent systems in manufacturing domain, in: 13th International Workshop on Database and Expert Systems Applications, Aix-en-Provence, France, (2002) 597–602
9. Lanzola G., Falasconi S., Stefanelli M.: Cooperative software agents for patient management, in: Fifth Conference on Artificial Intelligence in Medicine Europe (AIME95) (1995) 173–184
10. Lanzola G., Falasconi S., Stefanelli M.: Cooperating agents implementing distributed patient management, in: Seventh European Workshop on Modelling Autonomous Agents in a Multi-Agent World, (1996) 218–232
11. Shapiro J.: On the connections among activity-based costing and operational research. European Journal of Operational Research, Vol. 118, p 295-314 (1999).
12. Vidal, C.J., Goetschlackx, M.: A global Supply Chain model with transfer pricing and transportation cost allocation, European Journal of Operational Research, Vol. 129. (2001).
13. Chabrol M., Féniès P., Gourgand M., Tchernev N.: Un environnement de modélisation pour le système d'information de la Supply Chain : application au Nouvel Hôpital d'Estaing. Ingénierie des Systèmes d'Information - VOL 11/1, (2006) 137-162
14. Botta-Genoulaz V., Millet P.-A., Grabot B.: A survey on the recent research literature on ERP systems. Computers in Industry, Volume 56, Issue 6, (2005) 510-522
15. Stadtler H., Kilger C.: Supply chain Management and Advanced Planning. Springer (2001).
16. Chabrol M., Chauvet J., Féniès P., and Gourgand M.: A methodology for process evaluation and activity based costing in health care Supply Chain, LNCS as a special issue on Interoperability, Volume 3812, p. 375 – 384, (2006).
17. Ballou R.: Business Logistics Management, Prenctice-Hall Inc Englewood Cliffs,New Jersey (1997).
18. Dietrich B.L.: Taxonomy of discrete manufacturing systems. Journal of Operation Research, (nov-dec 1991).
19. Cooper R, Zmud R.: Information technology implementation research: a technological diffusion approach. Management Science 36 - (2) (1990) 123-39
20. Comelli M., Féniès P., Tchernev N.: Un modèle décisionnel pour l'évaluation de la performance du processus logistique : application sur une unité de consultation ambulatoire d'une Supply Chain hospitalière. 6<sup>ème</sup> Conférence Francophone de MOdélisation et SIMulation (MOSIM). Rabat (2006).

# An Architecture for Proactive Timed Web Service Compositions

Johann Eder[1], Horst Pichler[2], and Stefan Vielgut[2]

[1] Department of Knowledge and Business Engineering
University of Vienna, Austria
[2] Department of Informatics-Systems
University of Klagenfurt, Austria

**Abstract.** Web Services-based business processes spread over the boundaries of companies, requiring the integration of customers, suppliers and partners to achieve inter-organizational business goals. According to organizational rules temporal constraints, like deadlines, must be defined for processes. Violation of these constraints usually results in increased cost and reduced quality of service. Advanced workflow time management approaches allow the prediction of eventually arising time constraint violations and enables proactive initiation of evasive "self healing" actions. This saves time, avoids unnecessary task-compensations and therefor decreases costs. In this paper we present an architecture for Web Service Composition environments which enables the usage of advanced predictive and proactive time management features.

## 1 Introduction

The next step in the evolution of web services are composite web services to support business processes within organizations as well as business processes spanning several organizations like supply chains. Thus the most critical need in companies will be to provide services with a better quality than their competitors. To assess the quality of service (QoS) it is necessary to define measures which are significant indicators for certain quality aspects, where expected or guaranteed process duration ranks among the most important characteristics [15]. Slow web services, invoked by a composite web service, can have an disastrous impact on the overall process response time and even worse result in the violation of time constraints, like a process deadlines. Thus techniques are needed to predict these durations and possible constraint violations based on the anticipated response time of participating web services, enabling us too exchange certain services or to optimize them for faster execution.

These are established problems in workflow management, a closely related application area. Workflow management systems, are used to improve processes by automating tasks and getting the right information to the right place for a specific job function. Additionally it is a necessity to control the flow of information and work in a timely manner by using time-related restrictions, such as bounded execution durations and absolute deadlines, which are often associated

J. Eder, S. Dustdar et al. (Eds.): BPM 2006 Workshops, LNCS 4103, pp. 323–335, 2006.

with process activities and sub-processes [10]. However, arbitrary time restrictions and unexpected delays can lead to time violations, which typically increase the execution time and cost of business processes because they require some type of exception handling [21]. Although currently available commercial products offer sophisticated modelling tools for specifying and analyzing workflow processes, their time-related functionality is still rudimentary and mostly restricted to monitoring of constraint violations and simulation for process re-engineering purposes [6]. Workflow time management deals with these problems and allows for instance the prediction of response times or proactive avoidance of constraint violations. In research several attempts have been made to provide solutions to time management problems (e.g. [5,6,8,11,14,19]).

Nowadays inter-organizational workflows are likely to be assembled from several external processes and services. This can be accomplished by aggregating distributed web services into a web service composition. More than ever slow external services will have a disastrous impact on the overall process response time, cause deadline violations and increase the cost of the process. It seems to be an obvious idea to apply time management approaches to avoid these problems, which requires some adaptations to the original algorithms.

In this paper we present a novel time manager architecture for web service composition environments, where we focus on BPEL executable processes [4,1]. We list and explain required build time and run time components, along with a brief introduction into the necessary parts of time management theory.

The paper is organized as follows. In Section 2 we describe basic workflow time management concepts. Section 3 gives an overview of the architecture. Sections 4 explains already implemented build time components in detail, whereas 5 outlines run time components along with some ideas for still unsolved problems. The paper finishes with some conclusions and a brief outlook in Section 6.

## 2     Workflow Time Management in a Nutshell

The basic concepts of workflow time management are rooted in project planning methods like the Critical Path Method (CPM) or the Program Evaluation Review Technique (PERT) [10]. They determine, among other things, a valid execution interval for each activity in the process. This interval is delimited by the earliest point in time an activity can start, which is determined by preceding activities, and the latest point in time it must end, in order to meet the process deadline. The intervals are calculated based on the knowledge about process control flow structure, the average or estimated durations of activities and time constraints. The phases of time management, its concepts and main ideas are best explained with an example.

### 2.1     Process Build Time

**Process Modelling.** An expert or process designer models the process and augments it with necessary temporal information. Figure 1 visualizes a workflow

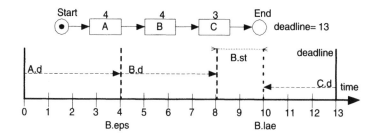

**Fig. 1.** Valid Execution Interval of Activity B

consisting of three activities executed in sequence. Explicit time properties are the estimated duration of activities in basic time units, which are $A.d = 4$, $B.d = 4$ and $C.d = 3$ and a deadline of $\delta = 13$, stating that the overall workflow execution must not exceed 13 time units.[1]

**Calculation of the Timed Graph.** The output of this phase is called *Timed Graph* which augments the process model with valid execution intervals for each node or activity. The time line in Figure 1 shows these execution intervals for activity $B$. A relative time model is used, where 0 denotes the start time of the process. All other points in time are declared or calculated relative to this start time [16]. Based on this information the valid execution interval for activity $B$ is calculated as follows: an activity must not start until all predecessors are finished (since we assume that there is no delay between activities), therefore the earliest possible time $B$ may start is determined by the sum of predecessor durations: $B.eps = 4$. To take the deadline of 13, into account, the point of view has to be reversed, now starting from the end of the workflow. By subtracting the durations of succeeding activities from the deadline, the *latest allowed end B.lae* of activity $B$ is determined: $B.lae = 13 - 3 = 10$. In the figure one can also spot the time span $B.st$, which depicts the *slack* or *buffer* time; this time may be consumed by $B$ without endangering the deadline.[2] The EPS-values for all activities are calculated in a forward pass and the LAE-values in a backward pass, as described in e.g. [14], where along with simple sequences also conditional, alternative and parallel execution structures are considered, as well as upper and lower bound constraints. In order to cope with run time uncertainties like varying execution durations and branching and looping behavior (treatment of blocked loops) a stochastic model was introduced in [11,12], where each time value is represented as histogram, which allows statements for certain confidence thresholds.

---

[1] Although it can not be recommended to represent durations with simple scalar time values, we will still use this representation to reduce the complexity of explanations. In the prototypical implementation we used the probabilistic model presented in e.g. [11,12], where time values are represented as histograms, which allow more differentiated statements about the temporal status of a process.

[2] Slack time is produced by relaxed deadlines or on shorter branches of parallel structures.

## 2.2    Process Instantiation

The workflow engine starts, controls and terminates the control flow of process instances. When starting a new process instance the time manager has to load the according timed graph and adjust it to the current date and time. This step is called *Calendar Mapping*, which in its simplest form just adds the current date and time to each EPS and LAE-value in the timed graph.

## 2.3    Process Run Time

**Monitor State of Execution.** During process execution a time management component must map each currently executed activity with its counterpart-node in the timed graph.

**Predictive Time Management.** The prediction component has several functions: it may be used to predict the rest execution time of the process [11] or to forecast the arrival time of future tasks for certain workflow participants (based on EPS-values) [9]. For this paper the most important feature is the prediction of eventually arising future deadline violations based on LAE-values. E.g. if $B$ ends later than 13 (time units after the start of the process) one can state that it is likely that the deadline will be violated after finishing $C$. In contrast to reactive time management, which solely reacts on constraint violations that already occurred, predictive time management forecasts violations and enables the system to initiate evasive actions [14].

**Proactive Time Management.** Proactive time management will be started after the prediction of violations. Its purpose is to trigger appropriate evasive actions. Consider our running example: before $C$ is even started according evasive actions can be invoked in order to hold the deadline, for instance exchanging activity $C$ with an alternative shorter activity $C'$. We claim that early prediction of time constraint violations and their pro-active treatment saves costs and therefor increases the quality of service [12].

# 3    Architecture for Timed Web Service Compositions

Figure 2 proposes an architecture for a BEPL-based web service environment which enables proactive time management. The architecture consists of the *Process Engine* and the *Time Managers Build Time* and *Run Time* components.

### Time Manager Build Time Components

1. The *Parser* loads the BPEL-definition, parses it and generates an according *Process Graph*.
2. The *Data Collector* augments the graph with additional temporal process information, like expected activity durations and time constraints.

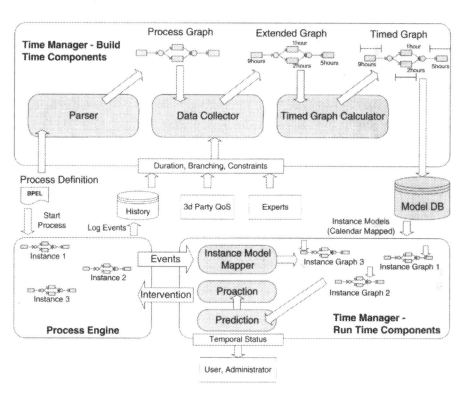

**Fig. 2.** Time Manager Architecture

3. The resulting *Extended Graph* is fed into the *Timed Graph Calculator*, which generates the *Timed Graph*.
4. And finally the *Timed Graph* is stored in the *Model Database*.

## Process Engine

1. The *BPEL-Process Engine* starts new process instances and controls their execution (communication with web services).
2. During the execution of process instances certain events, like start or termination of process activities, are signaled to the run time component of the time manager.
3. In order to avoid possible future violations of time constraints the process engine reacts to intervention signals from the time manager.

## Time Manager Run Time Components

1. When a process is started by the process engine an according signal will be sent to the time manager.
2. The *Instance-Model Mapper* loads the according timed graph from the model database and generates a calendar-mapped copy, called *Timed Instance Graph*, for the process instance.

3. Each time an activity of the process instance starts or ends an according signal will be sent to the instance-model mapper.
4. The *Prediction Component* periodically checks the temporal status of the instance and raises an exception if time constraints are likely to be violated. Additionally it provides an interface to monitor the temporal status of each process instance (e.g. likelihood of deadline violations, expected remaining execution time) which may be accessed by users, service requestors or process administrators.
5. In this case the *Proactive Component* jumps into action, tries to find an alternative (shorter) execution plans in order to prevent a future deadline violation, and sends according intervention instructions to the process engine.

The current status of the prototypical implementation and research tasks is as follows: the build time components are completed and now we focus on the proactive part, namely service exchange algorithms. For the Java-based implementation of the prototype the following tools and technologies were used: Oracle BPEL Server, Eclipse + Oracle BPEL Designer Plugin, Apache Tomcat, Axis Soap Engine and the Xerces2 XML-Parser [22].

# 4   Build Time Components

## 4.1   Parser: Generating the Process Graph

The first step is to parse the web services-based process definition in order to generate a graph-based process representation, which is necessary for the time management calculations performed later. In a service oriented architecture enterprizes or their applications respectively communicate via loosely coupled web services, which are described by standards like the Web Service Description Language (WSDL) [24,1]. As these services do very often not operate in isolation, but in the context of a business process, a description language must be used to define e.g. the data flow between and the execution order of web services. The Process Execution Language for Web Services (BPEL, BPELWS) is such a language [4,1]. Note that we concentrate on executable business processes, which require, similar to processes in workflow systems, a central process execution engine that enacts and controls process instances. In a services-based scenario the engine communicates either synchronously or asynchronously with external web services, which form the steps in a business process. BPEL provides several base activities to communicate with web services, like *invoke, receive* or *reply*. Additionally it provides so called structural activities to define the control flow between base activities, like sequence, switch, flow or while. As BPEL originates from block-structured (XLANG) and activity diagram-based (WSFL) languages the control flow of a BPEL process definition can be represented a directed graph with control nodes [3]. Therefore the transformation of a BPEL-definition into a process graph poses no further problems for the *Parser*.

## 4.2   Data Collector: Generating the Extended Graph

In many workflow systems activities have additional attributes holding expected execution durations, which are mainly used for simulation and process re-engineering purposes [23,18]. Additionally time constraints can be defined to e.g. enable the enforcement of organizational rules.

**Extended Information.** In addition to the control flow structure defined in the process definition, time management algorithms need the following information to calculate their temporal models:

- *Response Time:* Each activity must be augmented with the expected duration, or since we talk about services, call it *response time.*
- *Time Constraints:* Several types of time constraints exist. An overall process *deadline* is a time constraint which restricts the execution duration of the whole process. A *lower bound constraint* is defined between a source and a target activity which are not necessarily adjacent in the graph. It defines a minimum time that must pass after finishing the source activity, before the target activity is allowed to start. An an *Upper Bound Constraint* defines a maximum time that is allowed to pass between the source and the target activity.

**Data Sources.** The function of the *Data Collector* is to gather this additional information and extend the process graph with it, where the following data sources may be accessed:

- *Experts:* Information stemming from organizational rules, like time constraints, must be introduced by expert process modelers. If no other sources are available experts may additionally make estimations about service response times.
- *Process History:* If knowledge about past process execution exists, response times can also be extracted from the process history. The process history (or process log) stores events which occur during process execution, for instance the start or end of activities, along with according time stamps.
- *Third Party:* Sometimes the extraction of response times tends to be a problem, especially in flexible environments where autonomous web services, accessed by the composition, are frequently changing. For these cases response times could also be stored and administered by trusted third parties, which offer an interface to access statistics, similar to or as an extension of a (Web) Service Level Agreement-architecture [7,15].

In order to automate data collection we extended the original WSDL of each service contained in the composition with a time management interface which provides methods (e.g. *getResponseTime*) to access extended data. The (hidden) implementation of these methods provides access to one of the above mentioned types of the data sources and can be uniformly accessed via the web service interface. The implementation may for instance be a query to an experts database or forwarding the request to a third party interface.

## 4.3   Timed Graph Calculator

As BPEL-definitions can be represented as graphs and all possible structural
activities are supported by according control flow structures, as addressed in
e.g. [14,11,12], it already seems that time management algorithms as explained
in Section 2 can be applied without further adaptations. Unfortunately existing
workflow time management approaches are based on one assumption: activities
are interpreted as basic execution units which must be finished in order to proceed with workflow execution. But in Web Service scenarios external services,
applications or sub-processes are started, using a blocking (synchronous) or non-
blocking (asynchronous) communication model. To enable our time management
algorithms to cope with these models it was necessary to examine the structure
of communication scenarios and how they affect EPS- and LAE-values. Recent
publications on web service communication and web service composition, e.g.
[1,20,3], already identified several basic synchronous and asynchronous communication patterns, which we had to consider in our time management calculation
algorithms. A detailed description of how to handle each pattern can be found
in [13].

**Synchronous Patterns.** In a synchronous or blocking model the requester waits
for the response of the provider before it continues execution. The advantage of
this model is its simplicity, as the process state does not change until the response
has been received. The obvious disadvantage is that blocking the execution of
the main process, especially when long running external processes are involved,
increases its execution duration tremendously. For synchronous communication
patterns no special mapping is necessary since after the invocation of an external
service process execution will be blocked until the response is received, which is
exactly the behavior of so called atomic activities in workflow systems.

**Asynchronous Patterns.** Although synchronous communication is appropriate in many situations it may be suboptimal when long-running external services
or sub-processes are called. In an asynchronous or non-blocking model the main
process sends a request to the provider and continues execution without delay. At
a later point in time it receives a response (callback) from the provider, which of
course implies that the main process contains an activity which waits to receive
this response. Asynchronous communication loosely couples sender and receiver.
This accelerates process execution and compensates communication problems
(e.g. network problems). But for time management it poses a problem as visualized on the left-hand side in Figure 3: a web service composition consists
of a sequence of activities, where the first one *invokes* an external web service,
which itself hides a process. As the communication is non-blocking, the process
engine continues execution with succeeding activities (which may for instance
be blocking calls to other services). The last activity *receive* synchronizes the
external web service, as it waits for the response message.[3]

---

[3] For details on callbacks and how response messages are correlated to their appropriate process instances, e.g. using correlation-ids, we refer to [1].

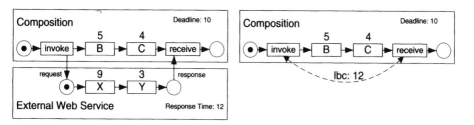

**Fig. 3.** Invocation of an External Web Service

Assuming that the duration of *invoke* and *receive* is 0, one could be tempted to state that the overall execution duration of the composition is 9, which is less than the deadline of 10. But of course it is necessary to consider the response time of the invoked service which is 12, therefore the deadline will be violated. One can see that the time span between invoke and receive is determined by the maximum of the duration of the regular path and the duration of the external service. Please note that in this scenario an external web service with a response time less than 9 hours (which is the sum of durations of $B$ and $D$) would have had no effect on the execution duration of the workflow and the execution intervals of its activities, as in this case the longer regular path via $B$ and $D$ would determine these values.

In order to calculate the timed graph we have to introduce a temporal relationship between the invoking and the receiving activity, where asynchronous communication with a web service can be easily mapped to a lower bound constraint (see right-hand side in Figure 3). The forward and backward calculations may then be performed as explained in [14], which states that for activities which are connected by a lower bound constraint the longest path determines the according time intervals. A required prerequisite is to connect the *invoke* and the adhering *receive* activity with a lower bound. This can be automated during parsing if the BPEL-definition contains according partner links and bindings [1,22]. Note also that since the invoked service may reside anywhere its structure will be unknown and it must therefore be treated as a black box. The only knowledge required is its expected response time which can for instance be determined by retrieving the QoS-information on this service from a trusted third party.

### 4.4   Model Database

At the last step of the build time phase the timed graph must be stored in the *Model Database*. The model database holds a timed graph for each time-managed process. The model is stored as an XML-representation of the timed graph model, which consists of nodes, edges and temporal relations. Nodes hold temporal information (EP- and LA-values) and a mapping to the WSDL-specification and according partner links. Edges connect nodes and temporal relations represent time constraints like lower bounds.

# 5   Run Time Components

## 5.1   Instance-Model Mapper

To monitor the progress of a process instance and its temporal status the time manager needs to be notified of certain events, which are: start of a process or activity, end of a process or activity and the abnormal termination of a process. Each of these events must be signaled to the *Instance-Model Mapper* which reacts as follows:

**Start Process.** The mapper generates a copy, called *Timed Instance Graph*, of the according timed graph which it loads from the model database. Afterwards each EPS and LAE-value in this graph is mapped to the real calendar, which means that the current date and time is added. Consider the example from Section 2: in the original model the valid execution interval is defined as relative distance to the start time 0 of the process, e.g. $B.eps = 4$ and $B.lae = 10$. Assuming that the time unit used is *hours* and the (current) time at the start of the process is $Monday\ 1st, 8am$ the interval in the instance graph will be calendar-mapped as follows: $B.eps = Monday\ 1st, 12am$ and $B.lae = Monday\ 1st, 6pm$. Of course this applies for the intervals of all activities the timed instance graph, as well as for the overall deadline which is mapped to $Monday\ 1st, 9pm$. Additionally the *execution pointer* is initialized with a reference to the start activity (in the timed instance graph).

**Start Activity, End Activity.** The mapper updates the execution pointer such that it references the currently executed activity (in the timed instance graph).

**End Process, Cancel Process, Termination Due to Failure.** The mapper discards the timed instance graph.

## 5.2   Predictive Time Manager

This component checks periodically and on arrival of certain events if the current execution status is likely to cause time constraint violations in the future. E.g. activity $B$ finishes at time $Monday\ 1st, 7pm$ and the process enginge signals *end of activity* $B$ to the time manager. By comparing the actual end time of $B$ with its latest allowed end time $B.lae = 6pm$ the time manager finds out that a deadline violation is likely to occur. Actually it predicts that after the execution of $C$ the process will most likely finish at $10pm$, which is 1 hour after the calendar-mapped deadline, and therefore 1 hour to late. It raises an according exception which must be handled by the *Proactive Time Manager*.

   As an additional feature the prediction componente provides an interface to monitor the temporal information and status of each process instance which may be accessed by users, service requestors or process administrators. Service requestors might for instance be interested in the expected completion date/time of a certain process instance. Process administrators might want to know the temporal status of an instance. In [14] the *traffic light model* was introduced, which proposes different temporal states that are set according to the likelihood of a deadline violation: green (everything ok), yellow (problems possible) and red (violation most likely to occur).

## 5.3  Proactive Time Manager

When this component catches an exception the process is already late, which means that the rest of the process must be sped-up in order to reach the given deadline. We just started to research methods to exchange services with faster alternatives. Of course it is possible that these alternative services have some drawbacks (which is the reason that they were not chosen in the first place), e.g. they might be more expensive. The first input parameter for such an algorithm is the amount of time that must be saved; consider the running example: activity $B$ is late by one hour, therefore the succeeding activities must be accelerated by at least one hour, in order to meet the deadline. Additionally such an algorithm will need to know which services are exchangeable, along with a set of alternative services for each of them (we plan to realize a static approach in the prototypical implementation). The next step is the generation of an alternative constraint-violation free process execution plan. This is not so straightforward as it seems at first glance. E.g. exchanging a service with a shorter alternative might not affect the execution duration of the process at all, if it for example resides on a path where still slack time is available. Additionally it might be necessary to exchange more than one service. However, in every case a partial recalculation of the timed instance graph will be necessary. Finally the process engine must be informed about the changes it has to apply on the (still running) process instance.

# 6  Current Work, Future Work and Conclusions

The prediction and proactive avoidance of deadline violations decreases costs of processes and increases their quality of service. In this paper we proposed a time manager architecture for web service composition environments, showed how to apply workflow time management algorithms, explained in detail how build time and some run time components work and provided some ideas of how to solve still open run time problems. To prove the feasibility of our concepts we implement a web services-based time management framework, where we currently concentrate on the run time aspects, especially on repair and service exchange algorithms. Additionally we examine the applicability of proactive time management features on other quantifiable quality dimensions, like cost or reliability. The integration of proactive repair mechanisms into process automation environments is subject of ongoing research.

# References

1. G. Alonso, F. Casati, H. Kuno, V. Machiraju. Web Services: Concepts, Architectures and Applications. Springer Verlag, ISBN 3-540-44008-9, 2005.
2. W. M. P. van der Aalst and H. A. Reijers. Analysis of discrete-time stochastic petrinets. In *Statistica Neerlandica, Journal of the Netherlands Society for Statistics and Operations Research,* Volume 58 Issue 2, 2003.
3. Petia Wohed and Wil M.P. van der Aalst and Marlon Dumas and Arthur H.M. ter Hofstede. Pattern Based Analysis of BPEL4WS. QUT Technical report, FIT-TR-2002-04, Queensland University of Technology, Brisbane, 2002.
4. Business Process Execution Language for Web Services Version 1.1 - BPEL4WS Specification. BEA, IBM, Microsoft, SAP and Siebel, 2004.
5. G. Baggio and J. Wainer and C. A. Ellis. Applying Scheduling Techniques to Minimize the Number of Late Jobs in Workflow Systems. In *Proc. of the 2004 ACM Symposium on Applied Computing (SAC)*. ACM Press, 2004.
6. C. Combi and G. Pozzi. Temporal conceptual modelling of workflows. LNCS 2813. Springer, 2003.
7. J. Cardoso and A. Sheth and J. Miller. *Workflow Quality of Service.* Proceedings of the International Conference on Integration and Modeling Technology and International Enterprise Modeling Conference (IEIMT/IEMC'02), Kluwer Publishers, 2002.
8. P. Dadam and M. Reichert. The ADEPT WfMS Project at the University of Ulm. In Proc. of the 1st European Workshop on Workflow and Process Management (WPM'98). Swiss Federal Institute of Technology (ETH), 1998.
9. J. Eder, W. Gruber, M. Ninaus, and H. Pichler. Personal Scheduling for Workflow Systems. LNCS 2678, Springer Verlag, 2003.
10. J. Eder and E. Panagos. Managing Time in Workflow Systems. Workflow Handbook 2001. Future Strategies Inc. Publ. in association with Workflow Management Coalition (WfMC), 2001.
11. J. Eder and H. Pichler. Duration Histograms for Workflow Systems. In Proc. of the Conf. on Engineering Information Systems in the Internet Context 2002, Kluwer Academic Publishers, 2002.
12. J. Eder and H. Pichler. Probabilistic Workflow Management. Technical report, Universitt Klagenfurt, Institut fr Informatik Systeme, 2005.
13. J. Eder and H. Pichler. Avoidance of Deadline Violations for Interorganizational Business Processes. Seventh International Baltic Conference on Databases and Information Systems DB&IS, Technika, 2006.
14. J. Eder, E. Panagos, and M. Rabinovich. Time constraints in workflow systems. LNCS 1626. Springer, 1999.
15. M. Gillmann, G. Weikum, and W. Wonner. Workflow management with service quality guarantees. In *Proceedings of the 2002 ACM SIGMOD International Conference on Management of Data.* ACM Press, 2002.
16. H. Jasper and O. Zukunft. Time Issues in Advanced Workflow Management Applications of Active Databases. In *Proc. of the 1st International Workshop on Active and Real-Time Database Systems.* Workshops in Computing, 1995.
17. B. Kiepuszewski, A. ter Hofstede, C. Bussler. On Structured Workflow Modeling. In: Proceedings of the 12th Conference on Advanced Information Systems Engineering (CAISE). Stockholm, Sweden, June 2000.
18. M. Laguna and J. Marklund. Business Process Modeling, Simulation and Design. *ISBN 0-13-091519-X.* Pearson Prentice Hall, 2005.

19. O. Marjanovic and M. Orlowska. On modeling and verification of temporal constraints in production workflows. Knowledge and Information Systems, 1(2), 1999.
20. E. Newcomer. Understanding Web Services. Verlag: Addison-Wesley, ISBN 0-201-75081-3, 2002.
21. E. Panagos and M. Rabinovich. Predictive workflow management. In Proc. of the 3rd Int. Workshop on Next Generation Information Technologies and Systems, Neve Ilan, ISRAEL, 1997.
22. S. Vielgut. Time Management in Web Service Orchestrations. Master Thesis, University of Klagenfurt, 2005.
23. Workflow Process Definition Interface. A Workflow Management Coalition Specification. Document number WFMC-TC-1025, 2002.
24. E. Christensen and F. Curbera and G. Mereditih and S. Weerawarana Web Service Definition Language 1.1 - WSDL Specification IBM, Microsoft, 2001.

# Ontology Knowledge Spaces for Semantic Collaboration in Networked Enterprises*

Silvana Castano, Alfio Ferrara, and Stefano Montanelli

Università degli Studi di Milano
DICo - Via Comelico, 39, 20135 Milano - Italy
{castano, ferrara, montanelli}@dico.unimi.it

**Abstract.** In this paper, we define a reference conceptual framework to organize *ontology knowledge spaces* and related *semantic collaboration schemes* for coordinated and virtual access to heterogeneous and distributed information resources inside and outside the enterprise, at both intra- and inter-enterprise level under different collaboration requirements and goals. The framework exploits ontology knowledge spaces and enabling services for searching and retrieving the relevant information resources, namely those semantically related to a target request, both in a stable and emergent collaboration scenarios.

## 1 Introduction

Large enterprises, e-government organizations, business organizations, and internetworking communities in general, need today a coordinated and virtualized access to distributed information resources to realize novel forms of networked enterprises (e.g., virtual organizations, networks of cooperating organizations), often to rapidly respond to opportunities or challenges that cannot be anticipated in advance. Accessing heterogeneous and distributed information resources in a coordinated and virtual way through complex, possibly cross-organizational, business processes requires appropriate semantic interoperability techniques to enable a seamless access and retrieval of the right information resources, in the time frame that the users require, while preserving the information representation and management requirements of each single party involved in the collaboration [1,12]. In addition, a further requirement for effective semantic interoperability techniques regards the availability of ontology-based descriptions of information of interest in use by an organization. Ontologies are generally recognized as an essential tool for allowing communication and knowledge sharing among distributed users and applications, by providing a semantically rich description and a common understanding of a domain of interest.

In this paper, we define a reference conceptual framework to organize *ontology knowledge spaces* and related *semantic collaboration schemes* for coordinated

---

* This paper has been partially funded by NoE INTEROP, IST Project n. 508011 - 6th EU Framework Programme.

J. Eder, S. Dustdar et al. (Eds.): BPM 2006 Workshops, LNCS 4103, pp. 336–347, 2006.

and virtual access to heterogeneous and distributed information resources inside and outside the enterprise, at both intra- and inter-enterprise level under different collaboration requirements and goals. The framework exploits ontology knowledge spaces and enabling services for searching and retrieving the relevant information resources, namely those semantically related to a target request, both in a stable and emergent collaboration scenarios. To this end, we combine both a mediation approach for integrated access to heterogeneous information sources, typical of data integration systems [3,8,9], and a discovery approach typical of open networked systems [2,7], to provide a comprehensive framework for semantic collaboration in networked enterprise contexts. With respect to networked collaboration, recent research in P2P systems focuses on providing techniques for evolving from basic P2P networks supporting only file exchanges using simple filenames as metadata, to more complex systems like schema-based P2P networks, capable of supporting the exchange of structured contents (e.g., documents, relational data) by exploiting explicit schemas to describe knowledge, usually using RDF and thematic ontologies as metadata [10,11]. With respect to these latter approaches, the paper presents collaboration techniques for semantic collaboration that work without super-peer nodes and integrated schemas, but rather on the presence of autonomous information ontologies and on dynamic query through a knowledge discovery service at each enterprise party. Main contributions of our work regards the organization of the ontology knowledge into multiple spaces capable of providing different semantic views targeted to different semantic collaboration purposes. Moreover, we discuss how such knowledge spaces can be used by enabling services for enforcing semantic collaborations both at intra- and inter-enterprise level.

The paper is organized as follows. In Section 2, we describe the reference conceptual framework for organizing the enterprise ontology knowledge spaces. The stable semantic collaboration scheme and the emergent semantic collaboration scheme are presented in Section 3 and 4, respectively. In Section 5, an application example regarding the stable/emergent collaboration schemes is discussed. Finally, concluding remarks are provided in Section 6.

# 2   Enterprise Knowledge for Semantic Collaboration

An important requirement to consider when addressing the problem of semantic collaboration and knowledge sharing in intra/inter enterprise contexts, is related to the fact that each enterprise needs to share a large number of heterogeneous information resources (e.g., databases, XML documents). In this respect, ontology specification is generally employed for providing a semantic description of the resources to be shared for semantic collaboration. In this paper, we propose an *enterprise-level* ontology knowledge organization in multiple spaces with the aim to provide multiple semantic views targeted to different semantic collaboration purposes.

## 2.1  Ontology Knowledge Spaces

As shown in Figure 1, three different ontology knowledge spaces are defined in
the enterprise-level ontology, namely the *resource knowledge* space, the *mapping
knowledge* space, and the *network knowledge* space. They are defined to be used
for supporting different semantic collaboration schemes.

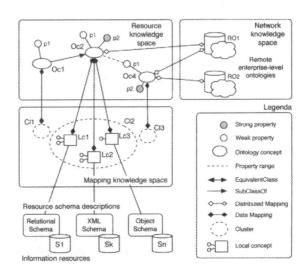

**Fig. 1.** The enterprise-level ontology spaces

**Resource knowledge space.** This knowledge space provides a reference description of the enterprise information resources in terms of ontology concepts
and semantic relations, possibly according to a Semantic Web-compatible specification language (e.g., OWL). Ontology concepts are characterized by a name,
and a set of properties that represents their features. Each property is associated with a name and a value, which can be a datatype or a reference to another
ontology concept. Properties can be *strong* is they are mandatory (i.e., they
have minimal cardinality $\geq 1$), or they can be *weak* if they are optional (i.e.,
they have minimal cardinality $= 0$). Semantic relations are defined between
ontology concepts in the resource knowledge, to express the most appropriate
relationship existing between them. In particular, semantic relations that can be
specified include the typical relations provided by the Semantic Web languages
(e.g., equivalentClass, subClassOf in the OWL language). Ontology concepts in the
resource knowledge space are connected with the mapping knowledge by means
of data mappings and with the network knowledge by means of distributed
mappings.

**Mapping knowledge space.** This knowledge space describes how to map ontology concepts onto the underlying information resources described through

local concepts. A local concept provides metadata information about the name and the structure of a specific information resource. To overcome (semantic) heterogeneity, local concepts that have semantic affinity, namely, that describe the same information resources using the same or similar terminology (e.g., synonyms) and the same or compatible structure in different enterprise sources are grouped into clusters. The local concepts in each cluster are connected with the corresponding ontology concept in the resource knowledge space through data mappings. A *data mapping* is a correspondence between an ontology concept *oc* and a local concept *lc*. A data mapping defines how to map the structure of *oc* (i.e., its name and its properties) on the specific structure of *lc*. Given *oc* and its associated cluster of local concepts, all the data mapping for *oc* are conceptually organized into a *data mapping table*, where columns represent the properties of *oc* and the rows represent the corresponding element in the structure of the local concepts. We note that the data mapping tables provide information regarding the semantic similarity of the information resources within the enterprise (intra-enterprise knowledge) and are exploited to enforce an intra-enterprise collaboration scheme (see Section 3). In general, data mapping and data mapping tables can be semi-automatically defined by relying on an integration/unification process like in the GAV-based data integration systems [3,8].

**Network knowledge space.** This knowledge space describes the knowledge that the enterprise has acquired about the other parties in the networked enterprise. In particular, the network knowledge keeps track of the semantic similarity between the ontology concepts in the resource knowledge and the knowledge in the remote enterprise-level ontologies through distributed mappings. A *distributed mapping* is a correspondence between an ontology concept *oc* and a remote enterprise-level ontology *eo* of the networked enterprise. In particular, a distributed mapping links an ontology concept *oc* to the ontology of an external party of the networked enterprise that contains ontology descriptions of resources semantically related to *oc*. Currently, we are enforcing also a more advanced distributed mapping approach in order to associate each ontology concept *oc* also with the specific remote concepts that have a high level of similarity with *oc*. This last approach allows us to maintain more specific mapping information and a policy for updating the network knowledge with respect to the changes in the remote ontologies. For a detailed description of these latter mapping approach the reader can refer to [4]. Given *oc*, the set of its distributed mapping is conceptually organized into a *distributed mapping table*, where rows specify the location metadata of the involved remote enterprise-level ontologies (e.g., name, uri, version). In other words, the network mapping table provides information regarding the semantic neighbors of the enterprise within the networked enterprise (inter-enterprise knowledge) and can be exploited to enforce an inter-enterprise collaboration scheme (see Section 4).

## 2.2    Semantic Collaboration Schemes

Semantic collaboration is concerned with cooperative interaction of autonomous parties, possibly within a networked enterprise, with the aim to achieve a common goal. Using available ontology knowledge spaces, appropriate collaboration schemes and related enabling services are defined to reflect the nature of collaboration, and to comply with several technical requirements with respect to automated and semantically enabled collaboration support. We distinguish two main different semantic collaboration schemes, namely the *stable collaboration* and the *emergent collaboration*. The stable collaboration is suited for intra-enterprise contexts where information resources are assumed to change quite rarely and the enterprise-level ontology is built and maintained by a team of enterprise experts to reflect the internal enterprise requirements for integrated information resource access. The stable collaboration scheme allows the enterprise users to specify single target queries on the resource knowledge space of the enterprise-level ontology with the aim to exploit the mapping knowledge space and to retrieve all the relevant data contained in the underlying, possibly heterogeneous, information sources.

The emergent collaboration is suited for inter-enterprise contexts (i.e., networked enterprises) where the collaboration constraints may change and a rapid response by the participants is needed to reorganize the collaboration according to the new emergent requirements. The emergent collaboration scheme allows the enterprise users to specify target queries on the resource knowledge space of the enterprise-level ontology with the aim to exploit the network knowledge space and to dynamically identify the enterprise parties within the networked enterprise that can provide relevant knowledge with respect to a given target request.

## 3    Stable Semantic Collaboration

The goal of the stable semantic collaboration is to allow a uniform and integrated access to a multitude of heterogeneous information resources at intra-enterprise level.

### 3.1    Collaboration Scheme

In the stable collaboration, a mediation/acquisition service provides centralized query processing as shown in Figure 2. In particular, starting from a search query formulated over the resource knowledge space, the mediation/acquistition service reformulates this query in terms of each local information resource by exploiting the mapping knowledge and by generating a number of sub-queries against the involved local sources. The local queries are then executed by means of the wrappers associated with each source, and the results (i.e., specific resource instances) are collected by the mediator and sent back to the requesting client submitting the query. Based on the data provided by each source, the mediation/acquisition service provides an integrated result to the original search query.

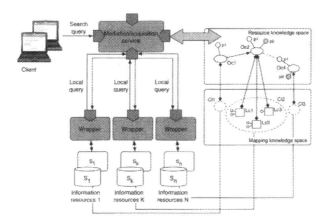

**Fig. 2.** Service architecture of the stable semantic collaboration

## 3.2   Enabling Services

The main service enabling the stable semantic collaboration is the mediation/-acquisition service. Given a search query formulated over the concepts of the resource knowledge space, the mediator locates the involved local concepts by exploiting the mapping knowledge space and reformulates the query in terms of such local concepts. In particular, query processing is composed by three steps: i) *cluster selection*, ii) *query reformulation* and iii) *answer composition*.

**Cluster selection.** The aim of the cluster selection step is to select clusters of the mapping knowledge that contain local concepts which can satisfy a given search query. Moreover, within a cluster, only local concepts that are relevant for the target query are identified, in order to minimize the query reformulation step. Given a SQL-like search query $\mathcal{SQ}$ of the form: ⟨SELECT * | property name [,...] FROM ontology concept name [,...] [WHERE property condition [,...]]⟩ we consider the data mappings associated with the ontology concept(s) listed in the FROM clause of $\mathcal{SQ}$. For each ontology concept, the data mapping table is exploited in order to select the local concepts in CI that can satisfy $\mathcal{SQ}$. In order to perform such an activity, the mediator considers the search query condition in the WHERE clause and it selects only those local concepts which can satisfy at least one factor in the query condition.

**Query reformulation.** In the query reformulation step the mediator composes a local query $\mathcal{LQ}_i$ for each selected local concept $Lc_i$. By exploiting the appropriate data mappings, the SELECT and WHERE clauses of $\mathcal{SQ}$ are rewritten appropriately in terms of the corresponding local concept structure.

**Answer composition.** Local queries $\mathcal{LQ}_i$ formulated in the query reformulation step are executed against the corresponding information sources, by means of their query wrappers. The local query replies are then collected and properly composed by the mediator and sent back to the requesting client.

## 4    Emergent Semantic Collaboration

The goal of the emergent collaboration is to support dynamic knowledge sharing and resource discovery at inter-enterprise level in dynamic networked enterprises/communities, where the all cooperating parties have equal roles and capabilities and can decide to join and leave the community at any moment (e.g., Peer-to-Peer (P2P) networks, Grids). Networked enterprises can dynamically cooperate and share resources often in response to opportunities or challenges that cannot be anticipated in advance and require a rapid response. In this contexts, enterprise parties dynamically take part to the collaboration by exposing their resource knowledge space and interact each other directly by submitting queries for knowledge sharing and resource discovery purposes.

### 4.1    Collaboration Scheme

Differently from the stable collaboration, in the emergent collaboration the client cannot refer to a unique enterprise-level ontology to formulate his requests. Instead, each enterprise party in the system provides part of the overall information available from a distributed environment, and acts both as a client and as a server in the system. The architecture of the emergent collaboration is shown in Figure 3. In the emergent collaboration, two different query types are sup-

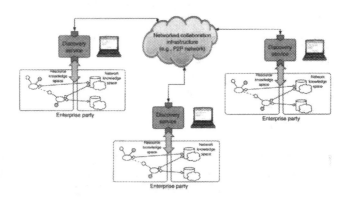

**Fig. 3.** Service architecture of the emergent collaboration

ported, namely the *probe query* and the *search query*. A probe query is used for discovering potential collaborating enterprise parties, and contains specifications of target concepts describing the resources of interest. A search query is used in order to acquire resource data related to one or more target resources, once a collaborating enterprise has been identified. The emergent collaboration is realized by means of a discovery service, which is responsible for performing i) probe query composition and propagation, and ii) probe query processing invocation. The discovery service is invoked by an enterprise party in order to identify the collaborating parties within the networked organization that can provide relevant information resources with respect to a target request, based on the ontology descriptions of its resource knowledge space. Once an enterprise party providing relevant information resource with respect to the target request is discovered, specific search queries can be directly submitted to the mediation/acquisition service provided by the remote party. Each enterprise party can provide a standard access to its mediation/acquisition service by means of a Web Service. Standard protocols (e.g., SOAP,WSDL) can be adopted to interact with the Web Service. The SOAP protocol provides well-defined XML-based message communications to send and receive search queries, while the WSDL document provides the specification of the set of methods supported by the remote mediation/acquisition service as well as the structure of the returned data extracted from the information resources.

## 4.2   Enabling Services

The discovery service is based on three main steps: i) the *query formulation and propagation*; ii) the *query resolution*; iii) the *answer management*.

**Query formulation and propagation.** A requesting enterprise party (querier) interested in enriching its knowledge with respect to one or more concepts of interests (target concept(s)), submits a probe query containing the target concept(s) with the intention to find those parties of the networked enterprise which store semantically related concepts in its enterprise-level ontology. An expressive probe query representation capable to support the description of ontology concepts, properties, and semantic relations is adopted. To this end, a reference query template is defined as follows:

```
FIND          Target concept name [, . . . ]
[WITH         Property name [, . . . ]]
[WHERE        Property conditions,
              ⟨Related concept, semantic relation name⟩[, . . . ]]
```

where the FIND clause contains a list of target concept(s) names; the WITH clause an optional list of properties related to the target concept(s); and the WHERE clause an optional list of conditions to be verified by the property values, and/or an optional list of concepts related to the target by a semantic relation. The probe query is then sent to the other enterprise parties according to the routing protocols of the underlying collaboration infrastructure.

**Query resolution.** Receiving a probe query, each enterprise party is interested in comparing the incoming request against its enterprise- level ontology, in order to discover whether it can provide concepts matching the target. Appropriate ontology matchmaking techniques are required to cope with different levels of detail in concept descriptions. In such a dynamic context, the aim of matching techniques is to allow a dynamic choice of the kind of features to be considered in the matching process, with the goal of providing a wide spectrum of metrics suited for dealing with many different matching scenarios [5]. In particular, the meaning of ontology elements in the enterprise-level ontology and in the query depends basically on the names chosen for their definition and on the relations they have with other elements. Based on these considerations, the matching process compares the target concept descriptions contained in the probe query with the ontology definitions in order to evaluate the semantic affinity between them. Finally, the matching process returns a (possibly empty) list of concepts semantically related to the target, which is replied to the querier by means of a query answer.

**Answer management.** Collecting query replies from the answering parties, the querier has to manage the received additional knowledge. Such an additional knowledge can serve the querier with two main purposes. The first purpose is to enrich the network knowledge of the querier by introducing the description of new enterprise parties that provide resources semantically related to one or more ontology concepts of the querier. The second purpose is to exploit the new ontology concepts in order to compose specific search queries to be submitted to the remote enterprise party. In this case, the querier can send the search query, by exploiting directly the mediation/acquisition service of the remote enterprise party.

## 5    Application Example

In Figure 4, we show a portion of an enterprise ontology in the Travel domain where we consider three information resources of a travel agency enterprise. The Accommodation local concept is extracted by the relational database Reservation_DB (S1) and describes accommodations that are characterized by the name, price, location, and affiliation. The Hotel local concept is extracted by the XML source Travel (S2) and describes hotels featured by an hotel name, a category, a cost, a region, and a country. Finally, from the object-relational database German_hostels (S3), we extract the local concept Hostel, featured by the name and the cost. As an example of ontology concept, we consider the Accommodation

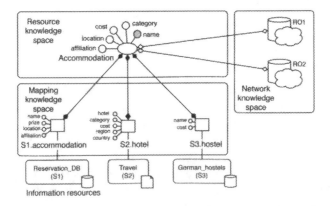

**Fig. 4.** Example of an enterprise-level ontology in the Travel domain

concept in the resource knowledge space. The Accommodation concept has been derived from the local concepts presented above. The correspondences between the ontology concept and the local concepts are represented by appropriate data mappings, that are represented in the data mapping Table 1. The data mapping

**Table 1.** Data mapping table for the Accommodation ontology concept

| Accommodation | name | category | cost | location | affiliation |
|---|---|---|---|---|---|
| $S_1$.Accommodation | name | NULL | price | location | affiliation |
| $S_2$.Hotel | hotel | category | cost | region OR country | NULL |
| $S_3$.Hostel | name | NULL | cost | 'Germany' | NULL |

table provides information on the local concept properties that correspond to each global property. In particular, the NULL value denotes that the global property does not have a corresponding local property in a given local concept (e.g., category). The OR clause is used to represent property patterns that correspond to a given ontology property. For example, the location property of the Accommodation concept has been mapped on the region and country properties of the Hotel local concept. Moreover, data mappings allow to map a global property on a constant value denoting a value for properties that does not have a corresponding local property in a given local concept. For example, the location property of the Accommodation concept has been mapped on the 'Germany' constant value for the Hostel local concept, denoting that the Hostel concept provides information only about hostels in Germany.

The Accommodation ontology concept is also associated with two remote enterprise-level ontologies of two other enterprise parties in the networked enterprise, namely RO1 and RO2. The correspondence between the Accommodation concept and the remote ontologies is represented by the distributed mapping shown in the distributed mapping Table 2.

**Table 2.** Distributed mapping table for the Accommodation ontology concept

| ontology concept: Accommodation | | |
|---|---|---|
| Name | URI | Version |
| RO1 | http://www.enterprise1.com/ontology | 1.0 |
| RO2 | http://www.enterprise2.com/ontology | 2.0 |

In the following, we show an example of retrieval of resources about accommodations. The querier first search accommodation data within his enterprise, then, in order to extend the result set, he exploits the emerging collaboration scheme by sending the query over the network.

**Stable collaboration.** As an example of stable collaboration, we consider the search query SELECT name FROM accommodation WHERE location = 'Italy' AND cost ≤ 100, performed against the Accommodation concept shown in Figure 4. The query aims to identify low-priced accommodations in Italy. By exploiting the data mappings, the global query condition is reformulated as: location = 'Italy' AND cost ≤ 100. For each local concept in $Cl_1$, the mediation/acquisition service verifies if it can satisfy the condition. In our example, the Accommodation and the Hotel local concepts are selected, but not the Hostel concept, as its location is 'Germany', and thus the condition factor location = 'Italy' can not be satisfied. As a consequence, in the query transformation step, the search query above is reformulated into two local queries, one for each selected local concept. The obtained local queries are shown in Figure 5.

| $\mathcal{LQ}_1$ | | $\mathcal{LQ}_2$ | |
| --- | --- | --- | --- |
| SELECT | name | SELECT | hotel |
| FROM | accommodation | FROM | hotel |
| WHERE | location = 'Italy' AND price ≤ 100 | WHERE | (region = 'Italy' OR country = 'Italy') |
| | | AND | cost ≤ 100 |

Fig. 5. Example of query reformulation

**Emergent collaboration.** As an example of emergent collaboration, we suppose that the querier intends to enlarge its knowledge with respect to the Accommodation concept. To this end, he submits to the network the following query, searching for parties storing similar concepts: FIND accommodation WITH name, category, location, affiliation. The query is received by two remote enterprise parties $EP_3$ and $EP_4$ which apply ontology matching techniques to evaluate the semantic affinity between the query and the concepts contained in their enterprise-level ontologies. According to the ontology matching results, the two parties reply with their concepts Hotel and Hostel, respectively. On the basis of these two results, the querier updates its network knowledge by defining two new distributed mappings. The first mapping links the Accommodation concept in the querier ontology to the enterprise-level ontology of $EP_3$, while the second mapping links the Accommodation concept to the enterprise-level ontology of $EP_4$. Moreover, the querier can formulate hotel or hostel specific search queries for the mediation/acquisition services of $EP_3$ and $EP_4$, respectively.

## 6 Concluding Remarks

In this paper, we have presented a conceptual framework to organize ontology knowledge spaces and enabling services for supporting different levels of semantic collaboration at both intra- and inter-organization level. We have also described stable and emergent semantic collaboration schemes targeted to different networked collaboration scenarios. Stable and emergent collaborations can be enforced through specific software tools. For instance, the stable collaboration can be enforced by relying on the ARTEMIS tool environment and related mediation functionalities. In particular, ARTEMIS implements the mediation service, by providing a query processing environment over an integrated schema of heterogeneous datasources [3]. Furthermore, the emergent collaboration can be enforced by relying on the HELIOS tool environment for knowledge discovery and sharing in peer-based systems. In particular, HELIOS is implemented as a toolkit that can be used by each enterprise to realize the discovery service [6].

# References

1. H. Afsarmanesh, C. Garita, and L.O. Hertzberger. Virtual Enterprises and Federated Information Sharing. In *Proc of the 9th Int. Conference on Database and Expert Systems Applications (DEXA 1998)*, pages 374–383, Vienna, Austria, 1998.
2. J. Broekstra and et al. A Metadata Model for Semantics-Based Peer-to-Peer Systems. In *Proc. of the 1st Int. WWW Workshop on Semantics in Peer-to-Peer and Grid Computing (SemPGRID)*, Budapest, Hungary, May 2003.
3. S. Castano, V. De Antonellis, and S. De Capitani Di Vimercati. Global Viewing of Heterogeneous Data Sources. *IEEE Transactions on Knowledge and Data Engineering*, 13(2):277–297, March/April 2001.
4. S. Castano, A. Ferrara, and S. Montanelli. Evolving open and independent ontologies. *International Journal of Metadata, Semantics and Ontologies*, 2006. To appear.
5. S. Castano, A. Ferrara, and S. Montanelli. Matching Ontologies in Open Networked Systems: Techniques and Applications. *Journal on Data Semantics*, V, 2006.
6. S. Castano, A. Ferrara, and S. Montanelli. *Web Semantics and Ontology*, chapter Dynamic Knowledge Discovery in Open, Distributed and Multi-Ontology Systems: Techniques and Applications. Idea Group, 2006.
7. A. Halevy, Z. Ives, D. Suciu, and I. Tatarinov. Schema Mediation in Peer Data Management Systems. In *Proc. of the 19th Int. Conference on Data Engineering (ICDE 2003)*, Bangalore, India, 2003.
8. M. Lenzerini. Data Integration: A Theoretical Perspective. In *Proc. of the 21st ACM SIGACT-SIGMOD-SIGART Symposium on Principles of Database Systems (PODS 2002)*, Madison, Wisconsin, USA, 2001.
9. J. Madhavan, P. A. Bernstein, and E. Rahm. Generic Schema Matching with Cupid. In *Proc. of the 27th Int. Conference on Very Large Data Bases (VLDB 2001)*, Rome, Italy, 2001.
10. W. Nejdl and et al. EDUTELLA: a P2P Networking Infrastructure Based on RDF. In *Proc. of the 11th Int. World Wide Web Conference (WWW 2002)*, Honolulu, Hawaii, USA, May 2002.
11. S. Gribble and A. Halevy and Z. Ives and M. Rodrig and D. Suciu. What Can Databases Do for Peer-to-Peer? In *Proc. of the 4th Int. Workshop on the Web and Databases (WebDB 2001), in conjunction with ACM PODS/SIGMOD 2001*, Santa Barbara, California, USA, May 2001.
12. N. Silva, J. Rocha, and J. Cardoso. E-Business Interoperability Through Ontology Semantic Mapping. In *Proc. of the PRO-VE Working Conference*, Lugano, Switzerland, 2003.

# About Semantic Enrichment of Strategic Data Models as Part of Enterprise Models[*]

Claudia Diamantini[1] and Nacer Boudjlida[2]

[1] DIIGA, UNIVPM, Ancona, Italy
diamantini@diiga.univpm.it
[2] UHP Nancy 1, LORIA, France
Nacer.Boudjlida@loria.fr

**Abstract.** The paper presents the outcomes of a practical experiment aimed at the identification of the various types of annotations that can be attached to enterprise strategic data models. The work is part of a more extensive experimentation on different enterprise models perspectives developed inside the "Semantic Enrichment of Models and Architecture & Platforms" task group of the FP6 IST-508-011 NoE INTEROP, whose goal is to evaluate the appropriateness (and the possible incompleteness) of existing semantic enrichment concepts, techniques, services and tools. Besides the need for multiple ontologies, the experiment enlighten a rather new perspective with respect to the literature on semantic annotation, related to the fact that mathematical objects have to be taken into consideration.

## 1 Introduction

Semantic enrichment is the process of associating to data a description of their meaning, in order to improve human understanding, machine interoperability, and advanced automatic information management (retrieval, mining, presentation). Nowadays, semantic enrichment is almost a synonym of annotating source data with formal descriptions of concepts in a domain ontology. It is mainly considered in the semantic web scenario, where it is applied to semi-structured and unstructured documents [19,8,15,20]. However, semantic enrichment has been applied also to structured data, like database schema, to enhance database interoperability and to enable intelligent access to heterogeneous sources [12,10,6]. Some approach to ontology mapping exploits semantic enrichment of ontologies as well [21]. To the best of our knowledge, few works in the literature takes the semantic enrichment problem from the perspective of a model-based view of enterprise systems (see e.g. [14] for semantic annotation of process models). Therefore, in the framework of the FP6 IST-508-011 INTEROP Network of Excellence (http://www.interop-noe.org), the research group entitled "Semantic Enrichment of Models and Architecture & Platforms" adopted a pragmatic approach to experience semantic enrichment

---

[*] Part of this work is supported by the FP6 IST-508-011 NoE INTEROP.

J. Eder, S. Dustdar et al. (Eds.): BPM 2006 Workshops, LNCS 4103, pp. 348–359, 2006.

of enterprise models. The aim of the intended experimentation is to pragmatically locate, by means of the analysis of case studies, the various types of annotations that can be attached to a model to make it more readable and exchangeable, in order to evaluate the appropriateness (and the possible incompleteness) of concepts, techniques, services and tools developed in the semantic web scenario [3]. This paper presents the outcomes of the study performed at the strategic enterprise level. At this level, enterprises develops a strategy through a complex planning and control cycle. In this cycle, a model of the enterprise is considered, that is compared against a "to-be" state, being it either the realization of a given vision and mission or a reference best practice. A gap analysis may then leads to the definition of the necessary steps to fill that gap. The models considered at this level by strategy experts and top management are defined by a set of measurable performance indicators coming from inside and outside the organization. In the information system view, the reference architecture for strategic support is based on the data warehouse (DW), that enables multidimensional analysis of performance indicators by means of OLAP tools and reports. Hence, we consider the DW model as part of an enterprise model at the strategic level. Also, an OLAP report can be considered as a view over the DW (and hence a view of the enterprise model), realized by slice-and-dice, roll-up and drill-down operations. However, a report may contain further information, derived from the DW and calculated at report generation time. Furthermore, reports are the main tool used by managers for their activity. For these reasons, in this paper we focus on OLAP reports, instead of the DW to study the kind of semantic information which can be found at the strategic enterprise level. The results of this study point out that annotations based on links to an ontology (that is the main kind of semantic annotation considered in the semantic web scenario) can be useful at this level, provided that different kinds of ontologies are provided. However they cannot by themselves express the whole body of semantic information appearing at the strategic level. In order to fully describe the meaning of strategic data, also a description of the way they have been generated has to be given. Hence, annotation languages should be defined that are expressive enough to describe the semantics of mathematical formulas, forecasting processes and models.

The rest of the paper is organized as follows: section 2 shortly introduces considerations about semantic annotation and annotation of models, section 3 briefly reviews the theory underpinning the definition of a strategy, section 4 describes the organization of strategic data and gives a reference example, derived from the analysis of the case study. This example is exploited in section 5 to review the different kinds of semantic information that are worth of being associated with strategic data. Section 6 ends the paper.

# 2 Semantic Annotations of Models

*Annotate*: to add a brief explanation or opinion to a text or drawing (Cambridge advanced learner's dictionary, *http://dictionary.cambridge.org/*)

*Annotation*: A comment attached to a particular section of a document. Many computer applications enable you to enter annotations on text documents, spreadsheets, presentations, and other objects. This is a particularly effective way to use computers in a workgroup environment to edit and review work. . . (Webopedia, *http://www.webopedia.com*).

The purpose of annotations is to describe the content of "something" (we will call it the *annotated object*) and therefore annotations may be considered as meta-data. They have been used for a while for texts and hypertext documents as well as in some communities like biologists [2,8]. They may be provided under different forms, like links, paths, notes, comments, highlights of selected words, numbered steps in a process, etc.

Hereafter, we present a review of the annotation concept, describing the typology of annotations together with the link between annotations and ontologies (section 2.1), the requirements for annotations to be consistently first provided and second interpreted (section 2.2), and the possible services for annotations (section 2.3). Finally, we illustrate the annotation of models (section 2.4).

### 2.1   Typology of Annotations

Different types of annotations may be distinguished; these include:

1. *Textual annotations* that consist in added notes and comments to the *annotated object*.
2. *Link annotations* that extend the textual annotation notion: the annotation content is reachable through a provided link.
3. *Semantic annotations*: while textual annotations and link annotations are primarily intended toward humans, semantic annotation content is some semantic information intended to be readable by humans as well as machines. For instance, the current work on semantic annotations of Web resources and services is intended to serve for sophisticated Web resources retrieval, discovery and composition as well as for reasoning [20].

Further, annotations may appear as informal (like a margin note) or formal: That means that the annotation expressions may range from annotation expressed according to a given structured language (like RDF and RDF Schema) with a formal syntax, to annotations expressed in some sound and well-founded language (like First Order Logic, Description Logic, etc.), which have also a formal semantics. It is obvious that the more formal the semantics of the language is, the more the machine-readability of the annotation increases. This assumes that no implicit assumptions are made and no ambiguity persists to enable a common interpretation and understanding of the annotations.

Therefore, in addition to the annotation definition language used, a common understanding of the provided annotations is required. Part of this common understanding may rely on the use of one or several ontologies that provide "a representation of a shared conceptualization of a particular domain"[23]. It means that *(i)* the conceptualization has to be agreed by the authors of the annotation (let us call them the *annotation providers*) and by the ones who exploit the annotations (let's call them the *annotation consumers*) and that, *(ii)* for some types of annotations, the annotation contents are linked to concepts in the ontology.

## 2.2   Semantics of Semantic Annotations[1]

Additionally, in order for the annotation to be interpreted and processed consistently, *annotation consumers* need to understand the meaning of the annotations that are provided to them [1]. Consider a very simple example: a theorem being stated in a document. What types of annotations may be associated with it? One can annotate that theorem providing a link to its demonstration or providing the demonstration itself, someone else may annotate the document with a list of possible applications of the theorem, etc. The interpretation and the processing of the annotations are then obviously different.

As an illustration of types of annotation contents, [1] introduces a classification considering a resource U#X annotated with a concept expression C, U being the URL of a web page and X being an XPointer expression leading to a region of the document. That classification includes the following types of annotations.

- *Decoration* and *Linking*, very similar to the textual and to the link annotations mentioned before;
- *Instance Identification*: the annotated object (U#X) is an instance of a given class and the annotation content may be a link to that class;
- *Aboutness*: no assertion is made about the existence of an instance of the concept C, but there is a loose association with the concept;
- *Pertinence*: the target of the annotation may be of interest for the *annotated object*.

## 2.3   Services for Annotations

Another matter concerns the way the annotations are actually provided and associated with the *annotated object*. There is a progressive move from manual to automatic or semi-automatic annotation provision (for some example of annotation tools, see for instance *http://annotation.semanticweb.org/tools/* and [16]). An *annotation provider* uses at the same time ontology management services and annotation management services while modelling the various enterprise perspectives that may constitute a model of an enterprise: annotations that are incorporated into a model or into parts of a model refer to given ontologies. Since the content of some types of annotations relies on given ontologies, it seems clear that ontology services (like querying or browsing an ontology) have to be coupled with annotation services.

From a software architecture perspective, [13] distinguishes between a proxy based approach and a browser based approach for annotating web resources. In the proxy based approach, annotations and annotated documents are merged by the proxy; the browser only services the merged documents. In a browser

---

[1] Title borrowed from[1].

based approach, an application of the browser merges the annotations with the documents while browsing. In addition, annotations can be stored separately and provided thanks to an annotation service offered by an annotation server.

## 2.4    Annotation of Enterprise Models in a Model Based Approach

In a model-based approach, various levels of models and instances are considered, every level having its proper concepts, rules and constraints, and it may be linked to other levels using various types of relationships (is_instance_of, derives_from, etc.). Figure 1 illustrates such types of levels and instances [5,7], where:

- the meta-model level concerns the ways models are designed, specified, validated, instantiated, etc. This level itself may be specified as a (meta)model;
- the generic/specific model level comprises the specification of models. When these are generic, they may serve for deriving specific models. Models at these levels are instances of the meta-model level.
- the model instance level: while the two preceding levels are abstract ones, this level comprises concrete objects like resources allocated to some tasks, task assignments to actors, software systems assigned for realizing activities.
- the instance level is the level of the actual objects and activities.

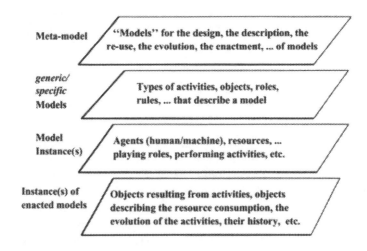

**Fig. 1.** Model and instance levels

Every level may be fitted with appropriate software support, which means that the set of enterprise applications and software systems may cover the levels horizontally (i.e. a software support is provided for the activities that are performed at a given level) as well as vertically (i.e. a support is provided for "going down" from one level to another).

The consequence is that interoperability is required within a level and between levels. For example, at the generic/specific model level, one can imagine that various enterprise modelling tools or environments are cooperatively used to specify an enterprise model according to their respective meta-models as described at the meta-model level.

This figure becomes more complex when we consider networked enterprises interoperability where every "node" of the networked enterprises may have its proper meta-models, generic/specific models, software systems and platforms, and so on. This means that interoperability ranges from very fine granule objects and software (for example, a function that concatenates strings) to the interoperability of two or more networked organizations.

Therefore, for interoperability purposes, intra-levels and inter-levels semantic annotations are conceivable to enable consistent model exchange and model sharing between actors in an enterprise as well as in a networked enterprise. However, at this stage of our work, we are not able to provide a complete list of the types of annotations that may be suited for each level and for moving between levels. To the best of our knowledge, few work is reported in the literature about semantic enrichment of models since most of the on-going work mainly deals with Web resources and services. Therefore, we adopted a pragmatic approach to experience semantic enrichment of enterprise models.

The role of the intended experimentations is to help in the identification of the various types of annotations that can be attached to a model to make it more readable and exchangeable. The next section reports on the current state of that identification with respect to enterprise strategic models. Further details about additional enterprise models perspectives can be found in [3].

# 3  Strategic Planning

One of the most comprehensive definitions of strategy is given by [11, p. 14]: "Strategy determines and reveals the organizational purpose in terms of long-term objectives, action programs, and resource allocation priorities; ...; attempts to achieve a long-term sustainable advantage in each of its businesses by responding appropriately to the opportunities and threats in the firm's environment, and the strengths and weaknesses of the organization...".

Strategic planning is a complex process of "dynamic, continuous activities of self-analysis" [17, p.37] oriented to the definition of a strategy. Strategic planning strongly recommends to base the analysis on a set of measurable, objective indicators characterizing internal and external facts that are relevant to the enterprise vision and mission. In the literature different complementary methodologies have been devised to perform this strategic information needs analysis, like Critical Success Factors, Key Performance Indicators, Management Accounting and Balanced Score Card methods [4,18]. These methodologies have been adopted to define a set of indices for our case study. We do not go deeper into the process of information needs analysis due to lack of space and since it is out of the scope of the present paper.

# 4    The Information System View of Strategic Planning

The reference architecture of information systems for strategic support is based on the data warehouse architecture. The logical data model in a data warehouse is the multidimensional model. In the multidimensional model, measured indices (the facts) are analyzed (i.e. aggregated/disaggrgated) w.r.t. different dimensions, like time, organization and product hierarchies.

Figure 2 gives a simplified example of data warehouse schema, showing part of the set of indices defined for the considered case study.

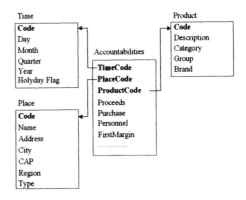

**Fig. 2.** A Simplified Data Warehouse Schema

The data warehouse feeds OLAP analysis and presentation tools, like report generators. Figure 3 shows an example of the typical content and structure of an OLAP report, which is suited for the next discussion on semantic annotation.

| | | | | proceeds | purchase | personnel | first margin | amortization | other costs | various | income | sold products | unit cost |
|---|---|---|---|---|---|---|---|---|---|---|---|---|---|
| Products | Total | Quart.I | Actual | 2,100 | 720 | 850 | 530 | 200 | 200 | 20 | 110 | 1,200 | 1,100 |
| | | | BDGT | 2,000 | 720 | 800 | 480 | 200 | 225 | 20 | 35 | 1,100 | 1,100 |
| | | Quart.II | Actual | 2,000 | 750 | 800 | 450 | 200 | 300 | 15 | -65 | 1,100 | 1,100 |
| | | | BDGT | 2,000 | 720 | 800 | 480 | 200 | 225 | 20 | 35 | 1,100 | 1,100 |
| | | Proj. To Year | Actual | 5,600 | 2,210 | 2,400 | 990 | 600 | 800 | 60 | -470 | 3,400 | 3,300 |
| | | | BDGT | 6,000 | 2,160 | 2,400 | 1,440 | 600 | 675 | 60 | 105 | 3,300 | 3,300 |
| | | | Diff. | -400 | 50 | 0 | -450 | 0 | 125 | 0 | -575 | 100 | 0 |
| | Batteries | Quart.I | Actual | 1,400 | 480 | 567 | 353 | 133 | 133 | 13 | 73 | 800 | 733 |
| | | | BDGT | 1,333 | 480 | 533 | 320 | 133 | 150 | 13 | 23 | 733 | 733 |
| | | Quart.II | Actual | 1,333 | 500 | 533 | 300 | 133 | 200 | 10 | -43 | 733 | 733 |
| | | | BDGT | 1,333 | 480 | 533 | 320 | 133 | 150 | 13 | 23 | 733 | 733 |
| | | Proj. To Year | Actual | 3,733 | 1,473 | 1,600 | 660 | 400 | 533 | 40 | -313 | 2,267 | 2,200 |
| | | | BDGT | 4,000 | 1,440 | 1,600 | 960 | 400 | 450 | 40 | 70 | 2,200 | 2,200 |
| | Mob. Phones | Quart.I | Actual | 700 | 240 | 283 | 177 | 67 | 67 | 7 | 37 | 400 | 367 |
| | | | BDGT | 667 | 240 | 267 | 160 | 67 | 75 | 7 | 12 | 367 | 367 |
| | | Quart.II | Actual | 667 | 250 | 267 | 150 | 67 | 100 | 5 | -22 | 367 | 367 |
| | | | BDGT | 667 | 240 | 267 | 160 | 67 | 75 | 7 | 12 | 367 | 367 |
| | | Proj. To Year | Actual | 1,867 | 737 | 800 | 330 | 200 | 267 | 20 | -157 | 1,133 | 1,100 |
| | | | BDGT | 2,000 | 720 | 800 | 480 | 200 | 225 | 20 | 35 | 1,100 | 1,100 |

**Fig. 3.** An example of typical report

# 5    Semantic Enrichment of Strategic Data

As already said, reports can be considered as views over the data warehouse, realized by slice-and-dice, drill-down and roll-up operations. Hence, if we accept that a data warehouse is the reference model at strategic level, the model of a report is part of an enterprise model; a specific report being an instance of its model. Models and instances can be both subject to annotations. An OLAP report may contains indices not explicitly stored in the data warehouse, calculated from the basic facts at report generation time. In our example, unit cost and all the rows labeled *Proj. to year* (which are estimates of the indices for the coming months) are elements of this type. Furthermore, reports are the main tool used by managers for their activity. For this reason, we focus our analysis on reports instead of the data warehouse.

By inspecting the report example we identified the following types of semantic information (see figure 4): (a) Meaning of a term (b) Temporal and metric unit information (c) Forecasting models (d) Derivation and aggregation rules.

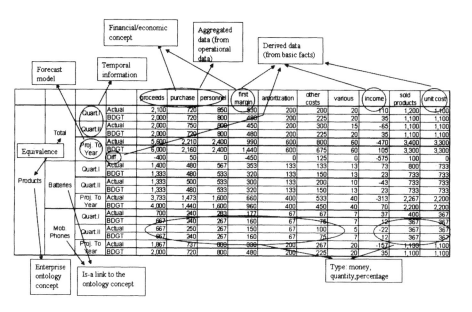

**Fig. 4.** Kind of relevant semantic information

## 5.1    Meaning of Terms

Meaning of terms can be expressed by linking the terms to concepts of a common domain ontology.

The Edinburgh Enterprise Ontology (EO) [24] has been taken into consideration. Report terms can be related to ontology concepts in different ways: for instance, terms like *Batteries* (*Mob. Phones*) can be considered an *instance of* the *Product* concept in EO, explaining that in our context, batteries (mobile phones) are particular kinds of products. Similarly, the term *Products* has an *equivalence* relation with the same ontology concept.

Other kinds of relations could be envisaged as well: for instance intra-model relations like a *part-of* relation between *Batteries* and *Mob. Phones*, or an *equivalence* relation between *Products* and *Total*.

At the strategic level, the enterprise ontology is no more sufficient, since indices express concepts that are better referred to the financial and economic domain, like purchase, cost, proceeds, margin, amortization and so on.

To express the meaning of such indices, we may refer to a specific ontology like the Financial Ontology by Teknowledge (http://ontology.teknowledge.com). For instance, we might define an instance-of relation between the term *proceeds* and the ontology concept *Income*.

### 5.2    Temporal and Metric Information

Metric information is perhaps the most standardized and well-known kind of information. Probably it is not necessary to define specific ontologies. Simple annotations reporting the symbol of the unit measure ($, %,... ) might suffice. In some situation, information about unit conversion (e.g. from $ to euro) might be useful. In this case, rather than a fixed conversion, it is preferable to establish a link to an external, official exchange organization. Let us note that, despite its simplicity, information about unit measure gives important insights to understand the meaning of numbers in the report.

Temporal information appears in the report (e.g. the term *Quart.I*). It can be annotated in the simplest way by resorting to the Edinburgh Enterprise Ontology, which contains temporal concepts like Time_Interval, Time_Line and Time_Point. In order to enable temporal reasoning, more specific ontologies should be exploited.

### 5.3    Forecasting Models

Intermediate reports usually contain estimates of quantities which are not already known. In the example, it is assumed that the report is generated at the end of the second quarter of the year, hence it contains performance indices which are calculated from transactional data for the first and second quarter, while it gives an estimate for the remaining part of the year. A fundamental information to understand the meaning of terms like *Proj. to year* is the actual method (for instance, linear or non linear regression) used to estimate the unknown quantity, on the basis of known data. This information can be given in different ways:

- by a link to a suited mathematical ontology
- by a link to a formal description of the method
- by a link to a formal description of the model

At the best of our knowledge, mathematical ontologies suited to our end does not exist. Formal description of the method means the description of the process which leads to the estimate, given in some process description language. It can either refers to an abstract description of the method or to the actual program which performs calculation. Finally, formal description of the model means for instance to give the parameters of the linear/non linear equation interpolating known data. Model description languages like the Predictive Model Markup Language (PMML) can be used to this end [9].

### 5.4 Derivation and Aggregation Rules

Index values are calculated by elaborating upon transactional data. Basically, we can distinguish two kinds of elaboration:

- *Aggregation*: used to generate synthetic data at different levels of granularity. Aggregation is performed by functions like average, sum, etc.;
- *Derivation*: used to calculate derived indices (e.g., in the example the first margin concept is defined as the difference between proceeds and the costs for purchase and personnel)

We point out that the actual definition of the function used to calculate a derived index is the most important semantic information to give about the index: as a matter of fact, an important limitation to interoperability at strategic level, even in homogenous environments like a single enterprise, is the semantic heterogeneity of derived indices. Although theoretically enterprises could/should define a standardized set of indicators, this is not actually the case for many true enterprises. The reason is related to the existence of some form of autonomy for organization units: this is the case for example of public administrations, multiple division structures, franchising etc. This autonomy can lead organization units to define their own indicators and hence to heterogenous indices definition. For instance, the *unit cost* can be simply defined as the total cost divided by the total number of goods produced, but the calculus of total cost is not a standardized procedure, which may or may not include some type of cost, relate the cost to the production volume by either a linear or non linear function etc. Similarly, a *productivity* index might be defined either by the ratio between proceeds and the number of employees, or between the net income and the number of employees. Employees can be counted by "heads", or by "hours-equivalent", taking into consideration part-time and full-time contracts. As another source of heterogeneity, indicators can change in time, due to different analysis needs, or modified external and internal conditions like changes in enterprise rules or national/international laws. In this scenario, the usage of annotation can be envisioned to enhance communication and comprehension among managers, simplify the process of budget formation by comparison and reconciliation of local performance indicators, or to compare and reason on reports generated at different times.

## 6   Conclusions

The simulation of a strategic information needs analysis for the case study we used, allows to enlighten novel kinds of information which is typical of strategic planning and control activities. This information comes in the form of financial and economic concepts, aggregated and derived data, and forecasting models.

Hence it is argued that a single enterprise ontology is not sufficient to describe the concepts in OLAP reports, and that specific financial/economic and mathematical ontologies are needed. Also, it is argued that the traditional mapping of terms to ontology concepts cannot by itself express the whole body of semantic information appearing at the strategic level. Rather, annotation languages should be defined which are expressive enough to describe the semantics of mathematical formulas, forecasting processes and models. The problem of semantic description of mathematical objects has been addressed only recently, by the MathML [25] and the OpenMath [22] standards. The best known language for the description of forecasting (or predictive) models is the Predictive Model Markup Language (PMML) [9]. Further work will be devoted to evaluate the appropriateness of these languages for our purpose, and to device specific annotation services and tools.

From a more general standpoint, considering the variety of enterprise models perspectives, we feel that a single ontology may not cover all the reequired types of annotations. Will we then fall in the problem of heterogeneous ontologies?

**Acknowledgement.** The authors are indebted to Stefano Tinella (Troux, Norway) for fruitful discussions about Strategic and Business enterprise models.

# References

1. S. Bechhofer, L. Carrand C.A. Goble, S. Kampa, and T. Miles-Board. The Semantics of Semantic Annotation. In *Proceedings of CoopIS/DOA/ODBASE*, pages 1152–1167, Irvine, California, USA, October 30-November 1 2002. LNCS# 2519.

2. N. Boudjlida, M-D. Devignes, and M. Smal-Tabonne. Services for a Genomics Open Distributed Environment, a position paper. In *XEWA-00, The XML Enabled Wide-Area Searches for Bioinformatics Workshop*, League City, Texas, December 2000. http://www.casc.llnl.gov/xewa/.

3. Boudjlida, N. et alii. A practical experiment on semantic enrichment in a homogeneous environment. Deliverable DTG4.1, IST-508 011 NoE INTEROP, 2006.

4. Bracchi,G.,Francalanci,C. and Motta,G. *Sistemi Informativi e Aziende in Rete.* McGraw-Hill Italia, 2001.

5. G. Canals, N. Boudjlida, J.C. Derniame, C. Godart, and J. Lonchamp. *ALF: A Framework for Building Process-Centered Software Engineering Environments*, chapter 7, pages 153–187. Research Studies Press, Taunton, Somerset England, 1994. In "Software Process Modeling and Technology", A. Finkelstein, J. Kramer and B.A. Nuseibeh, editors.

6. Castellanos, M. Semantic Enrichment of Interoperable Databases. In *IEEE Workshop on Research Directions in Interoperability*, April 1993.

7. J-C. Derniame, B-A. Kaba, and D. Wastell, editors. *Software Process: Principles, Methodology and Technology.* Springer-Verlag, LNCS# 1500, 1999.

8. European Bioinformatics Institute. *Symposium on Semantic Enrichment of Scientific Literature*, Hinxton, Cambridgeshire, UK, February 2006.

9. Grossman, R., Hornik, M. and Meyer, G. Evolving Data Mining into Solutions for Insights: Data Mining Standards Initiatives. *Communications of the ACM*, 45(8):59–61, August 2002.

10. Hakkarainen, S. *Dynamic Aspects and Semantic Enrichment in Schema Comparison*. PhD thesis, Stockholm University, 1999.

11. Hax, A. C. and Majluf, N. S. *The Strategy Concept and Process, A Pragmatic Approach*. Prentice Hall, Upper Saddle River, NJ, 1996.

12. Hohenstein, U. Using Semantic Enrichment to Provide Interoperability between Relational and ODMG Databases. In *International Hong Kong Computer Society Database Workshop*, pages 210–232, 1996.

13. M-R. Koivunen and R. Swick. Metadata Based Annotation Infrastructure offers Flexibility and Extensibility for Collaborative Applications and Beyond. In *Proc. of the KCAP 2001 Workshop on Knowledge Markup & Semantic Annotation*, 2001.

14. Lin, Y., Strasunskas, D., Hakkarainen, S., Krogstie, J., and Solvberg, A. Semantic Annotation Framework to Manage Semantic Heterogeneity of Process Models. In *Proc. of the 18th Conference on Advanced Information Systems Engineering*, Luxemburg, Springer-Verlag, LNCS# 4001, pages 433-446, 2006.

15. Missikoff, M. et alii. Ontology-Based Integration and Interoperability of Enterprise Modelling, Architectures and Platforms: State of the Art and State of the Practice. Deliverable no. DWP8.1, FP6 IST-508 011 NoE INTEROP, November 2004.

16. Reeve, L., Han, H. Survey of semantic annotation platforms. In *Proc. of the 2005 ACM symposium on Applied Computing*, pp.1634–1638, Santa Fe, New Mexico, 2005

17. Rowley, D. J., Lujan, H. D., and Dolence, M.G. *Strategic Change in Colleges and Universities*. Jossey-Bass Publishers, San Francisco, CA, 1997.

18. Seung Ki Min, Eui-Ho Suh and Su-Yeon Kim. An Integrated Approach Toward Strategic Information Systems Planning. *The Journal of Strategic Information Systems*, 8(4):373–394, 2000.

19. SEWASIE: SEmantic Webs and AgentS in Integrated Economies. IST-2001-34825 EU Project. http://www.sewasie.org/.

20. S. Sivashanmugam, K. Verma, A. Sheth, and J. Miller. Adding Semantic to Web services Standards. In *Proceedings of the 1st Intern'l Conference on Web Services (ICWS'03)*, pages 395–401, Las Vegas, Nevada, June 2003.

21. Su, X., Hakkarainen, S. and Brasethvik, T. Semantic enrichment for improving systems interoperability. In *ACM Symposium on Applied Computing*, pages 1634–1641, 2004.

22. The OpenMath Society. *The OpenMath Standard Version 2.0*. http://www.openmath.org/cocoon/openmath/standard/om20-2004-06-30/omstd20.pdf, 2004.

23. M. Uschold and M. Gruninger. Ontologies: Principles, Methods and Applications. *Knowledge Engineering Review*, 11(2), 1996.

24. Uschold, M., King, M., Moralee, S. and Zorgios, Y. v The Enterprise Ontology. *The Knowledge Engineering Review*, 13, 1998.

25. W3C Math Working Group. *Mathematical Markup Language (MathML) Version 2.0 (Second Edition)*. http://www.w3.org/Math, Oct. 2003.

# Workshop on Grid and Peer-to-Peer Based Workflows GPWW 2006

# Workshop on Grid and Peer-to-Peer Based Workflows (GPWW 2006) Preface

Nowadays, many data- and/or computation-intensive applications in the area of e-science and e-business involve coordinated sharing of highly distributed resources in a grid environment. In this context, a collaborative workflow management system is always required as part of the sophisticated problem solving process. Efficient management of workflow in grid environments has become increasingly important. Issues such as grid workflow infrastructure based on the Grid toolkits, grid workflow modeling and specification, grid workflow verification and validation, and decentralized grid workflow execution based on peer-to-peer technology have already evoked a high degree of interest.

With the success of the 1st workshop, which was held in Melbourne, Australia in 2005, the 2nd International Workshop on Grid and Peer-to-Peer based Workflows (GPWW) was held in conjunction with the 4th International Conference on Business Process Management (BPM 2006), in Vienna, Austria. The aim of this workshop was to bring together researchers and practitioners from academia, industry and governments to report advances in grid and peer-to-peer based workflow research.

Overall, we received 11 submissions from Australia, Belgium, China, Germany, Hungary, Italy, Korea, Netherlands, Poland and USA. Each paper was carefully reviewed by 3 members from the International Program Committee. Based on the quality of the submissions and their relevance to the workshop themes, the Program Committee accepted 5 papers to be included in the workshop proceedings.

We would like to thank all the members of the Program Committee for reviewing the papers in a very short time period. We are grateful to all the colleagues who submitted papers to GPWW. We would also like to thank the organizers of BPM 2006 for their cooperation and partnership. Finally, we acknowledge the professional support from Springer, who published the proceedings in its LNCS series.

June 2006

Yun Yang
Jun Shen
Jun Yan
Jinjun Chen
(Editors)

# Workshop Organization

## Organizers

Yun Yang, Swinburne University of Technology, Australia
Jun Shen, University of Wollongong, Australia
Jun Yan, University of Wollongong, Australia
Jinjun Chen, Swinburne University of Technology, Australia

## International Program Committee

Ilkay Altintas, San Diego Supercomputing Center, UCSD, USA
Boualem Benatallah, University of New South Wales, Australia
Rajkumar Buyya, The University of Melbourne, Australia
Ewa Deelman, University of Southern California, USA
Schahram Dustdar, Vienna University of Technology, Austria
Geoffrey Fox, Indiana University, USA
Volker Gruhn, Leipzig University, Germany
John Grundy, Auckland University, New Zealand
Vassilios Karakostas, City University London, UK
Kwei-Jay Lin, University of California at Irvine, USA
Chengfei Liu, Swinburne University of Technology, Australia
Michael Schrefl, University of Linz, Austria
Markus Stumpter, University of South Australia, Australia
Kunal Vemar, University of Georgia, USA
Jian Yang, Macquarie University, Australia
Hai Zhuge, Institute of Computing Technology, CAS, China

## External Reviewers

Georg Grossmann, Australia
Aneesh Krishna, Australia
Jia Yu, Australia
Xiaohui Zhao, Australia

# Requirements for a Workflow System for Grid Service Composition

Niels Joncheere, Wim Vanderperren, and Ragnhild Van Der Straeten

System and Software Engineering Lab (SSEL)
Vrije Universiteit Brussel
Pleinlaan 2, 1050 Brussels, Belgium
{njonchee, wvdperre, rvdstrae}@vub.ac.be

**Abstract.** In this position paper, we propose a new generation workflow system for grid services. We observe that grid computing has become an increasingly important application domain in computer science. Grid services — a new technology based on web services — are expected to become the de facto standard for grid computing. Similar to web services, an effective mechanism is needed for the composition of grid services. Existing technologies, however, have a number of important drawbacks: they have limited or no support for modularization of crosscutting concerns, for dynamic workflow adaptation, and for high-performance computing. We propose a new generation workflow system that is tailored specifically for grid services, and that tackles these problems, among others.

**Keywords:** Aspect-oriented software development, grid services, workflow languages.

## 1 Introduction

Over the last years, *grid computing* has become an increasingly important research domain within computer science. "The Grid" can be described as *a service for sharing computing power and data storage capacity over the Internet.*[1] The specific problem that lies at the heart of this technology is *coordinated resource sharing and problem solving in dynamic, multi-institutional virtual organizations* [1]: the large scope of many current scientific problems makes it increasingly difficult to solve them using only one computer system, and forces the use of a distributed solution. By creating a virtual organization of different resources, which typically don't belong to the same owner but are connected through the Internet, it is possible to address these problems. A recent challenge is the use of grid technology beyond scientific applications, more specifically in the production and design of products in industrial environments. Such design tasks typically require the use of multiple complex simulation- and optimization tools, which are used as part of a design process workflow.

---

[1] http://gridcafe.web.cern.ch/gridcafe/

J. Eder, S. Dustdar et al. (Eds.): BPM 2006 Workshops, LNCS 4103, pp. 365–374, 2006.

Since 2002, a standardization effort for grid computing has been active under the form of the Open Grid Services Architecture (OGSA).[2] This initiative aims to promote the acceptance and application of grid technologies through standardization. Its main task is the harmonization of academic activities concerning the Grid, with *web services* [2], a technology which also has a lot of industry support. Web services are applications that are accessible through the Internet and which use SOAP/XML for the transmission of information and WSDL/UDDI for the description and discovery of other web services. The OGSA standardization work has led to the development of *grid services* [3], which are actually a subclass of web services, with additional properties relevant for grid computing. It is expected that grid services will soon become the de facto standard for grid computing.

Although the services themselves have been standardized, composing grid services is still an open issue. Grid services are currently typically composed by manually writing the necessary glue-code in programming languages such as C and Java. In the web services world, however, it has been identified that a composition of web services is more naturally captured by dedicated workflow languages than by general-purpose programming languages. Languages such as BPEL4WS [4] and WS-CDL [5] have already been well accepted in the web services community. Because grid services are a kind of web services, it is in principle possible to recuperate these workflow languages for grid services. However, we identify several problems with current practice web service workflow languages:

- Most workflow languages do not have a clearly defined semantics [6].
- Most languages are not suitable for high-performance computing.
- There is insufficient support for the modularization of *crosscutting concerns* [7].
- There is insufficient or no support for dynamic adaptation of workflows.

The goal of this position paper is to identify the main limitations of current approaches for grid service composition, and to specify the requirements of a workflow system that is specifically tailored for grid service composition, and which therefore addresses these limitations, among others.

The outline of the paper is as follows. In Section 2, we analyze current approaches for grid service composition and identify their main limitations. In Section 3, we specify the requirements for a workflow system for grid services based on these limitations. In Section 4, we illustrate the applicability of our approach by describing the context in which it would typically be used. In Section 5, we present related work, and in Section 6, we state our conclusions.

## 2   Limitations of Current Approaches

Several workflow approaches for grid computing currently exist [8,9,10,11,12,13]. These approaches, however, use their own service and communication standards,

---

[2] http://www.globus.org/ogsa/

which makes them incompatible with each other. Furthermore, most of them are not suited for the new grid services standard. Therefore, composing grid services is currently typically handled by manually programming glue-code. Existing workflow systems for web services can technically be used for composing grid services, as grid services are a special kind of web services. There are, however, several problems with current workflow systems for web services which make them less suited for the grid services context.

Currently, BPEL4WS is well supported and widely accepted as the de facto standard for web service composition. We therefore limit our discussion of limitations to BPEL4WS; most of the limitations are also applicable to the other, less frequently used approaches. Note that our approach itself is not based on BPEL4WS; we merely discuss it here because it is representative of the state of the art in workflow languages.

## 2.1   Semantics

van der Aalst [6] observes that most workflow languages for web services do not have a clearly defined semantics. BPEL4WS is a combination of WSFL [14] and XLANG [15], which are in their turn based on other, earlier languages. A large amount of the functionality of the original languages has ended up in the new language. This makes BPEL4WS expressive at the price of being complex.

## 2.2   High-Performance Computing

Another important topic regarding workflow languages for grid services is the support for the specific requirements that are typically of importance with high-performance computing. In such an environment, it is common that large amounts of data need to be transferred from one step in a workflow to another. Special attention should be directed to how this happens: it would, for example, be unacceptable if all these data were transferred to a central workflow coordinator before being transferred to a next step. This is, however, current practice in BPEL4WS workflow systems.

## 2.3   Separation of Concerns

BPEL4WS does not have sufficient support for separation of concerns [16]. It is very difficult to modularize BPEL4WS processes in an effective way, because each process must be specified in a single XML file. Furthermore, it is not possible to specify sub-processes separately. Complex processes thus give rise to large XML files, which can become difficult to understand and maintain. A workaround for this problem is to expose sub-processes as separate services, but this is not always desirable, as it introduces additional overhead and scoping problems.

Even if BPEL4WS would support sub-processes, one would still not be able to modularize every concern successfully. Kiczales *et al.* [7] recognize that some concerns of an application cannot be modularized using existing software development methods: the implementation of these concerns is completely spread out over the different modules of the system. The same logic is repeated among different modules, resulting in code duplication. This code duplication makes it very difficult to add, modify or remove these concerns [17]. Examples of such *crosscutting concerns* are security concerns such as access control and confidentiality [18], debugging concerns such as logging [19] and timing contract validation [20], and business rules such as billing [21].

The goal of *aspect-oriented software development* (AOSD) is to achieve a better separation of concerns, by allowing crosscutting concerns to be specified in separate modules called *aspects*, so that adding, modifying or removing these concerns does not require changes to the rest of the system. As the crosscutting concerns we mentioned above are encountered frequently in BPEL4WS workflows [22,23,24,25], a solution for better modularization based on aspect-oriented techniques is necessary.

### 2.4   Dynamism

BPEL4WS does not support altering the workflow specification while it is running. The only exception is altering the concrete partner bindings (web services) when the additional standard WS-Addressing [26] is employed. In a grid services context, where long-running computations are the norm, dynamic workflow adaptation is essential in order to manage changing requirements.

## 3   A New Generation Workflow System

The goal of our approach is to offer a new generation workflow system, which is specifically tailored for grid service composition, and which therefore addresses the problems that were identified above, among others. This section specifies the requirements for this workflow system. These requirements can be divided into six properties, namely workflow, AOSD, dynamism, modularity, high-performance computing, and semantics. Each of these properties is discussed in further detail below.

### 3.1   Workflow

Every workflow language needs to define the basic activities that it supports, and how these activities can be ordered. Concerning the basic activities, we support invoking grid services (both synchronously and asynchronously), and assigning and retrieving variables.

Concerning the ordering of activities, existing literature is useful when deciding which kinds of orderings must be supported. For example, van der Aalst *et al.* [27] have identified a number of recurring workflow patterns, from elementary to complex, based on an extensive study of existing workflow languages. These patterns can be divided into six categories: basic control patterns, advanced branching- and synchronization patterns, structural patterns, patterns involving multiple instances, state-based patterns, and cancellation patterns. Our workflow language naturally supports the basic control patterns (such as sequence and exclusive choice), but regarding the more complex patterns, we need to weigh expressivity against clarity.

## 3.2   AOSD

Just like with regular software, some concerns of a grid service composition (such as billing and logging) cannot be modularized using current technologies: they end up scattered across the composition, and tangled with one another. This makes it difficult to add, modify or remove these concerns. In order to avoid such problems, one of the main properties of our workflow system is that it supports AOSD in order to allow the modularization of crosscutting concerns.

We propose a joinpoint model that allows advices to be executed before, around and after each basic workflow activity (e.g. service invocations and variable assignments). Pointcuts are expressed in a language based on logic programming, which allows selecting joinpoints based on the names and types of the corresponding workflow activities. Advices are expressed in the basic workflow language.

Because workflows involving grid services typically run for a long time, and on expensive infrastructure, it is important that the chance of encountering unexpected behavior is minimized. Therefore, we require that all properties of aspect-oriented interactions (such as the order in which multiple advices, which are applicable on the same joinpoint, are applied) are specified in advance.

## 3.3   Dynamism

Grid workflows often take a lot of time to complete, because of the complicated calculations and the large amounts of data that are involved. Additionally, they run on complicated, expensive infrastructure, which may be used on a pay-per-use basis. This makes it prohibitively expensive if workflows do not behave as expected, and have to be restarted.

This problem is our motivation for requiring that all properties of aspect-oriented interactions are specified in advance. However, this does not solve the problem completely: suppose that a certain business unit of a company is awaiting the results of a grid workflow that is taking more time to complete than expected. In such a case, it could be useful if the workflow could be modified while it is running in order to get it to finish faster (e.g. by removing certain parts of the workflow that are not considered essential to obtain the results needed by the business unit).

As another example, consider the case where an error is discovered near the end of a workflow that has already performed a lot of useful computations. In this case, correcting part of the workflow while it is running would certainly be preferable to terminating it and restarting it after the workflow is corrected.

Therefore, our workflow system supports dynamic workflow adaptation, i.e. it is possible to modify workflows while they are being executed. We allow pieces of workflow to be added, replaced or removed in any place where the control flow has not yet passed at the time of the modification. We aim to prevent introducing specific language constructs for this purpose: a piece of workflow should not need to know that part of it might be adapted during its execution, or that it might be used to replace another piece of workflow.

The dynamism we discussed above concerns the basic workflow description. However, dynamism can be useful with respect to AOSD, too: several aspect-oriented programming (AOP) languages [28,29] already support dynamic enabling and disabling of aspects in order to facilitate adapting to concrete situations. Therefore, our workflow system supports such *dynamic AOP*, too. Although dynamic AOP once had a reputation of introducing high performance overhead, recent work [30] has shown that it is possible to implement dynamic AOP efficiently using techniques such as just-in-time compilation and caching.

### 3.4 Modularity

Because of our system's support for AOSD, it facilitates modularizing crosscutting concerns. Using current workflow languages, however, it is not always possible to effectively modularize even the basic workflow. For example, a BPEL4WS process is always a single monolithic specification, which makes it impossible to reuse parts of a process elsewhere (unless these parts are modeled as separate web services, which introduces a large amount of overhead).

Therefore, we support sub-processes by allowing parts of a workflow to be specified in separate modules. These modules can then evolve independently from the main workflow, and can be reused in other workflows. It is clear that such an approach is an improvement on a number of current approaches.

### 3.5 High-Performance Computing

In traditional web services applications, the messages that are exchanged between services are typically very small. In grid computing, on the other hand, it is common that large streams of data need to be transferred. Therefore, requiring that all data pass through a central workflow coordinator — as is the case with conventional workflow languages such as BPEL4WS — is unacceptable, as it would require much more network capacity than is actually necessary. We therefore aim to remedy this problem by providing a distributed workflow coordinator that makes sure large data streams are routed directly to the next step in the workflow.

In order to provide this functionality, we introduce a language construct that allows specifying which data streams may be large and may thus require more efficient modes of network transport. On the other hand, the workflow engine may decide which streams of data are large, and handle them accordingly, if such information is not specified.

### 3.6 Semantics

It has been argued that most current workflow languages do not have a clearly defined semantics [6]. Among others, this hampers compatibility between different engines for a same workflow language. Therefore, we aim to define a formal operational semantics for our workflow language.

# 4   Applicability

Existing work on grid computing mostly focuses on scientific applications, such as bio-informatics or high-energy physics. Our approach, however, is aimed at design and production in industrial settings — an increasingly important application domain for grid services.

A lot of design activities in such industrial setting traditionally require prototypes to be built and tested in order to obtain important information on the design (e.g. crashing an automobile into a wall in order to discover safety information, placing a model of a plane in a wind tunnel in order to discover aerodynamics information, etc.). Innovation in computer science has made it possible to simulate this kind of tests. Because this kind of virtual prototyping requires a lot of computing power and involves a lot of data, such problems cannot be solved easily using only one computer system. Using grid computing, however, these problems can be solved effectively.

The industrial partner for our research currently sells such virtual prototyping grid software to clients that wish to test their products. These clients then use their own grid infrastructure to run the simulations. This limits the applicability of the industrial partner's products, as the required infrastructure's cost may be prohibitively high.

Our workflow system would, however, enable a completely new business model, in which clients use the infrastructure of the industrial partner on a customizable basis. In such a scheme, clients would not be forced to invest in specific infrastructure any more, and the industrial partner would not be forced to spend time on offering support for clients' local software.

The contracts of the industrial partner with its clients may vary a lot: one client may require other grid services than another, the service level agreements may differ, or different billing schemes (pay-per-use, flat-fee, etc.) may be used. Our workflow system would facilitate enforcing such different contracts, as these could be modularized as aspects.

Of course, the applicability of our approach is not limited to the virtual prototyping case presented above: the properties of our system, such as support for AOSD and dynamic workflow adaptation, are also useful in the traditional scientific application domain of grid computing, and even in the application domain for web services.

# 5   Related Work

An aspect-oriented extension to BPEL4WS — AO4BPEL [23] — has been proposed. This extension supports dynamic adaptation of aspects. However, because it is an extension to BPEL4WS, it inherits the deficiencies identified in this paper, such as limited support for modularization (of non-crosscutting concerns) and high-performance computing. Another approach that recuperates aspect-oriented ideas in the domain of web services is the Web Services Management Layer [25]. The WSML modularizes redirection, advanced selection policies, and management concerns such as caching and billing using aspects. The WSML does, however, not directly support web service composition and relies on BPEL4WS for that end. As such, it also inherits the disadvantages discussed in this paper.

Currently, grid services are mostly composed manually, by writing programs in traditional programming languages (such as C and Java), which use libraries such as the ones provided by the Globus Toolkit[3] to interact with concrete grid services. This situation obviously has a lot of drawbacks, as these languages do not support dynamic adaptation of the composition, or modularization of crosscutting concerns. Recently, however, a number of approaches have been proposed that aim to remedy these problems.

GridNexus [31] is a graphical system for creating and executing scientific workflows in a grid environment. A GUI allows developers to specify processes by creating directed acyclic graphs whose nodes perform simple computing tasks, or invoke grid services. Processes can be saved as composites, which can then be reused in other processes. Visual process specifications are represented by scripts written in a language called JXPL, which can be executed by an appropriate engine. By using such scripts, the user interface is separated from workflow execution. Although this approach is a serious improvement on manual grid service composition, it is targeted mainly at scientific grid applications, and not at industrial applications. It does not support dynamic workflow adaptation nor advanced separation of concerns.

Kepler [32] is a graphical workflow system similar to GridNexus (both approaches even use the same GUI technology). Like GridNexus, processes are directed acyclic graphs. The most important difference is that Kepler does not translate diagrams to scripts in order to execute workflows: workflows are executed by the GUI, thus increasing coupling between process definition and execution. Kepler is also aimed at scientific applications, and does not support dynamic workflow adaptation nor advanced separation of concerns.

## 6    Conclusions

In this position paper, we observe that, although the application domain for grid services is rapidly expanding, current approaches for grid service composition have a number of disadvantages that limit their applicability, and thus hamper the acceptance of grid services in industrial settings. The most important disadvantages are insufficient support for AOSD, for dynamic workflow adaptation, and for high-performance computing.

Therefore, we propose a new generation workflow system, which is specifically tailored for grid service composition, and thus tackles these problems, among others. We present the requirements for our workflow system, and illustrate its applicability. Our future work will be directed at performing a first iteration on the design and implementation of our system.

---

[3] http://www.globus.org/toolkit/

# References

1. Foster, I., Kesselman, C., Tuecke, S.: The anatomy of the grid: Enabling scalable virtual organizations. International Journal of High Performance Computing Applications **15**(3) (2001) 200–222
2. Alonso, G., Casati, F., Kuno, H., Machiraju, V., eds.: Web Services: Concepts, Architectures and Applications. Springer-Verlag, Heidelberg, Germany (2004)
3. Foster, I., Kesselman, C., Nick, J.M., Tuecke, S.: The physiology of the grid: An open grid services architecture for distributed systems integration (2002) http://www.globus.org/alliance/publications/papers/ogsa.pdf.
4. Andrews, T., Curbera, F., Dholakia, H., Goland, Y., Klein, J., Leymann, F., Liu, K., Roller, D., Smith, D., Thatte, S., Trickovic, I., Weerawarana, S.: Business Process Execution Language for Web Services version 1.1 (2003) http://www.ibm.com/developerworks/library/ws-bpel/.
5. Kavantzas, N., Burdett, D., Ritzinger, G.: Web Services Choreography Description Language version 1.0. W3C Working Draft 27 April 2004, World Wide Web Consortium (2004) http://www.w3.org/TR/2004/WD-ws-cdl-10-20040427/.
6. van der Aalst, W.M.P.: Don't go with the flow: Web services composition standards exposed. IEEE Intelligent Systems **18**(1) (2003) 72–76
7. Kiczales, G., Lamping, J., Mendhekar, A., Maeda, C., Lopes, C., Loingtier, J.M., Irwin, J.: Aspect-oriented programming. Technical Report SPL97-008 P9710042, Xerox PARC (1997)
8. Bhatia, D., Burzevski, V., Camuseva, M., Fox, G., Furmanski, W., Premchandran, G.: WebFlow — a visual programming paradigm for web/Java based coarse grain distributed computing. Concurrency — Practice and Experience **9**(6) (1997) 555–577
9. Basney, J., Livny, M.: Deploying a high throughput computing cluster. In Buyya, R., ed.: High Performance Cluster Computing: Architectures and Systems, Volume 1. Prentice Hall (1999)
10. Furmento, N., Mayer, A., McGough, S., Newhouse, S., Field, T., Darlington, J.: Optimisation of component-based applications within a grid environment. In: Proceedings of the 14th International Conference on High Performance Computing and Communications (SC 2001), Denver, CO, USA (2001)
11. Romberg, M.: The UNICORE grid infrastructure. Scientific Programming, Special Issue on Grid Computing **10**(2) (2002) 149–157
12. Lorch, M., Kafura, D.: Symphony — a Java-based composition and manipulation framework for computational grids. In: Proceedings of the 2nd International Symposium on Cluster Computing and the Grid (CCGrid 2002), Berlin, Germany (2002) 136–143
13. Gannon, D., Bramley, R., Fox, G., Smallen, S., Rossi, A., Ananthakrishnan, R., Bertrand, F., Chiu, K., Farrellee, M., Govindaraju, M., Krishnan, S., Ramakrishnan, L., Simmhan, Y., Slominski, A., Ma, Y., Olariu, C., Rey-Cenvaz, N.: Programming the grid: Distributed software components, P2P and grid web services for scientific applications. Cluster Computing **5**(3) (2002) 325–336
14. Leymann, F.: Web Services Flow Language (WSFL 1.0). IBM (2001)
15. Thatte, S.: XLANG — web services for business process design. Microsoft (2001) http://www.gotdotnet.com/team/xml_wsspecs/xlang-c/default.htm.
16. Parnas, D.L.: On the criteria to be used in decomposing systems into modules. Comm. ACM **15**(12) (1972) 1053–1058

17. Elrad, T., Filman, R.E., Bader, A.: Aspect-oriented programming. Comm. ACM **44**(10) (2001) 29–32
18. De Win, B., Joosen, W., Piessens, F.: Developing secure applications through aspect-oriented programming. In Filman, R.E., Elrad, T., Clarke, S., Akşit, M., eds.: Aspect-Oriented Software Development. Addison-Wesley, Boston (2005) 633–650
19. Kiczales, G., Hilsdale, E., Hugunin, J., Kersten, M., Palm, J., Griswold, W.G.: An overview of AspectJ. In Knudsen, J.L., ed.: Proc. ECOOP 2001, LNCS 2072, Berlin, Springer-Verlag (2001) 327–353
20. Vanderperren, W., Suvée, D., Jonckers, V.: Combining AOSD and CBSD in PacoSuite through invasive composition adapters and JAsCo. In: Proceedings of Net.ObjectDays 2003, Erfurt, Germany (2003) 36–50
21. D'Hondt, M., Jonckers, V.: Hybrid aspects for weaving object-oriented functionality and rule-based knowledge. In Lieberherr, K., ed.: Proc. 3rd Int' Conf. on Aspect-Oriented Software Development (AOSD-2004), ACM Press (2004) 132–140
22. Arsanjani, A., Hailpern, B., Martin, J., Tarr, P.: Web services: Promises and compromises. Queue **1**(1) (2003) 48–58
23. Charfi, A., Mezini, M.: Aspect-oriented web service composition with AO4BPEL. In Zhang, L.J., ed.: Proceedings of the 2nd European Conference on Web Services (ECOWS 2004), Erfurt, Germany, Springer-Verlag (2004) 168–182
24. Cottenier, T., Elrad, T.: Dynamic and decentralized service composition with Contextual Aspect-Sensitive Services. In: Proceedings of the 1st International Conference on Web Information Systems and Technologies (WEBIST 2005), Miami, FL, USA (2005)
25. Verheecke, B., Vanderperren, W., Jonckers, V.: Unraveling crosscutting concerns in web services middleware. IEEE Software **23**(1) (2006) 42–50
26. Box, D., Christensen, E., Curbera, F., Ferguson, D., Frey, J., Hadley, M., Kaler, C., Langworthy, D., Leymann, F., Lovering, B., Lucco, S., Millet, S., Mukhi, N., Nottingham, M., Orchard, D., Shewchuk, J., Sindambiwe, E., Storey, T., Weerawarana, S., Winkler, S.: Web Services Addressing (WS-Addressing). W3C Member Submission 10 August 2004, World Wide Web Consortium (2004) http://www.w3.org/Submission/2004/SUBM-ws-addressing-20040810/.
27. van der Aalst, W.M.P., ter Hofstede, A.H.M., Kiepuszewski, B., Barros, A.P.: Workflow patterns. Distributed and Parallel Databases **14**(3) (2003) 5–51
28. Popovici, A., Gross, T., Alonso, G.: Dynamic weaving for aspect-oriented programming. In Kiczales, G., ed.: Proc. 1st Int' Conf. on Aspect-Oriented Software Development (AOSD-2002), ACM Press (2002) 141–147
29. Suvée, D., Vanderperren, W.: JAsCo: An aspect-oriented approach tailored for component based software development. In Akşit, M., ed.: Proc. 2nd Int' Conf. on Aspect-Oriented Software Development (AOSD-2003), ACM Press (2003) 21–29
30. Vanderperren, W., Suvée, D.: Optimizing JAsCo dynamic AOP through HotSwap and Jutta. In Filman, R., Haupt, M., Mehner, K., Mezini, M., eds.: DAW: Dynamic Aspects Workshop. (2004) 120–134
31. Brown, J.L., Ferner, C.S., Hudson, T.C., Stapleton, A.E., Vetter, R.J., Carland, T., Martin, A., Martin, J., Rawls, A., Shipman, W.J., Wood, M.: GridNexus: A grid services scientific workflow system. International Journal of Computer & Information Science **6**(2) (2005) 72–82
32. Altintas, I., Berkley, C., Jaeger, E., Jones, M., Ludäscher, B., Mock, S.: Kepler: An extensible system for design and execution of scientific workflows. In: Proceedings of the 16th International Conference on Scientific and Statistical Database Management (SSDBM 2004), Santorini, Greece (2004)

# Web Services Composition in Autonomic Grid Environments

Danilo Ardagna, Silvia Lucchini, Raffaela Mirandola, and Barbara Pernici

Politecnico di Milano

**Abstract.** To cope with the competitiveness of the market place, e-business applications should be developed exploiting the flexibility of service oriented paradigm and the challenges of the grid computing technologies and should guarantee the fulfillment of quality requirements. In this paper we present a reference framework to support the execution of Web services based e-business applications in autonomic grid environments. Specifically, we tackle the problem of selection of Web services that assure the optimum mapping between each abstract Web service of a business process and a Web service which implements the abstract description, such that the overall quality of service perceived by the user is maximized. The proposed solution guarantees the fulfillment of global constraints, considers variable quality of service profile of component Web services and the long term process execution.

## 1 Introduction

The competitiveness of the market place and the advent of on demand service computing pave the way for the development of e-business applications that exploit both the flexibility of service oriented paradigm of development and the challenges of the grid computing technologies. At the same time, QoS in the context of software engineering and Web services has seen a flurry of recent research activity. Different approaches have been followed so far, spanning the use of QoS ontologies [15], the definition of ad-hoc methods in QoS-aware framework [19,22], and the application of optimization algorithms [23,4,11,7].

Our work aims at merging these trends as it intend to pursue the QoS-driven selection and composition of Web services for e-business applications in (autonomic) grid environment.

QoS requirements are difficult to satisfy especially due to the high variability of Internet application workloads. Internet workloads can vary by orders of magnitude within the same business day [9]. Such variations cannot be accommodated with traditional allocation practices, but require autonomic computing self-managing techniques [13], which dynamically allocate resources among different services on the basis of short-term demand estimates.

This dynamic fulfillment of varying QoS requirements can be enhanced by grid computing, which is proposed as an infrastructure providing transparent resource sharing between collaborating organizations [12]. Grid middlewareprovides basic

J. Eder, S. Dustdar et al. (Eds.): BPM 2006 Workshops, LNCS 4103, pp. 375–386, 2006.

mechanisms to manage the overall infrastructure of a service center, implementing service differentiation and performance isolation for multiple Web services sharing the same physical resources, and simplifying the re-configuration of the physical infrastructure.

Recently, Grid middleware is evolving to implement Web service standards. Grid and Web services framework mutual convergence can favor the integration of business process across extended enterprises in order to maximize the QoS requirements for the end user and optimize the use of physical resources.

In the literature resource allocation and scheduling in scientific grid workflows has been analyzed in depth [21,26]. Resource management spans task-based algorithms that greedily allocate tasks to resources and workflow-based algorithms that search for an efficient allocation for the entire workflow [8]. Another aspect/dimension that distinguishes the various approaches concerns the type of resource manager considered: centralized or distributed [21]. A comprehensive survey of different workflow management systems and grid ongoing research projects is presented in [5].

However scientific workflows and composed e-business processes have different computing requirements, which pose diverse constraints on the re-configuration of the infrastructure. In this paper we present a reference framework to support the execution of Web services based e-business applications in autonomic grid environments. The problem of selection of Web services in composed services will be analyzed in depth. The goal is to discover the optimum mapping between each abstract Web service of a business process and a Web service which implements the abstract description, such that the overall QoS perceived by the user is maximized and some global constraints (i.e. constraints over the whole business process) are guaranteed. Furthermore, we assume that Web services are characterized by a variable quality of service profile and the long term execution of the composed service will be considered.

The paper is organized as follows. In Section 2 we describe the composed Web service specification and the quality model adopted. Section 3 is devoted to the description of the problem of resource allocation in grid environments. Finally, conclusions are drawn in Section 4.

## 2    Business Process Specification and Quality Model

A Web service is modeled as a software component which implements a set of operations. Web services are registered with associated keywords and their WSDL specification in a service registry [6]. We assume that the registry stores also for each operation $o$ of a Web service $j$, the values of QoS $q_{j,o}(t)$ and the number of instances that can be executed during a specific time interval.

A composite service is specified as a high-level business process in BPEL language in which the composed Web service is specified at an abstract level. In the following we refer to an *abstract Web service* as a *task* $t_i$, while Web services selected to be executed are called concrete Web services. Some annotations are added to the BPEL specification in order to identify:

- global and local constraints on quality dimensions;
- the maximum number of iterations for cycles;
- the expected frequency of execution of conditional branches;
- user preferences, a set of normalized weights $\{\omega_1, \omega_2, \ldots, \omega_N\}$, $\sum_{n=1}^{N} \omega_n = 1$, indicating the user preferences with respect to the set of quality dimensions;
- Web service dependency constraints.

Global constraints specify requirements at process level, while local constraints define quality of Web services to be invoked for a given task in the process. The optimization problem will consider statistically all of the possible execution scenarios of the composite service, according to their probability of execution.

The maximum number of iterations and frequency of execution of conditional branches can be evaluated from past executions by inspecting system logs or can be specified by the composite service designer. If an upper bound for cycles execution cannot be determined, then the optimization could not guarantee that global constraints are satisfied [23]. At compile time, cycles are unfolded according to the maximum number of iterations.

Finally, Web service dependency constraints impose that a given set of tasks in the process is executed by the same Web service. This type of constraints allows considering both stateless and stateful Web services in composed services. Constraints and BPEL annotations are specified by WS-Policy (see [3]).

QoS profiles follow a discrete stepwise function, that is periodic with period $T$ (see Figure 1). QoS profiles are obtained as result of the local grid resource allocation as it will be discussed in Section 3.1. In the following the continuous time will be denoted by $t$, while the discrete time interval will be denoted by $u$. The discretization interval will be denoted by $\triangle$ and we assume that the QoS profile is constant in every interval of length $\triangle$. In autonomic systems $\triangle$ is about half an hour [2], while, if we assume that the incoming workload has a daily seasonal component, $T$ is 24 hours.

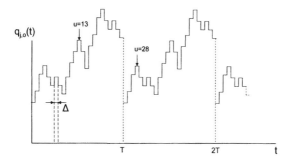

**Fig. 1.** Example of Periodic QoS Profile

In Figure 1, the time interval $u = 13$ and $u = 28$ are highligted, where $T = 24 \cdot \triangle$ and $\triangle = 1$ hour. The index $u$ can range in $[1, \lceil E/\triangle \rceil]$.

For the periodicity we have:

$$q_{j,o}(t) = q_{j,o}(t + uT) \quad u \in [1, \lceil E/\triangle \rceil] \tag{1}$$

and

$$q_{j,o,u} = q_{j,o,u \bmod (T/\triangle)} \quad u \in [1, \lceil E/\triangle \rceil] \tag{2}$$

The problem of maximization of QoS is multi-objective since several quality criteria can be associated with each operation $o$ of a Web service $j$ in the time interval $u$. In this paper we focus on Web services *execution time* ($e_{j,o,u}$), *availability* ($a_{j,o,u}$), *price* ($p_{j,o,u}$), and *reputation* ($r_{j,o,u}$). In the following we will indicate with $E$, $A$, $B$, and $R$ the execution time, availability, budget, and reputation global constraints for the composed service execution. This set of quality dimensions have been the basis for QoS consideration also in other approaches both in the Web service and grid community [23,18,17].

Note that, if the same service is accessible from the same provider, but with different quality characteristics (e.g. quality level), then multiple copies of the same service will be stored in the registry, each copy being characterized by its quality profile.

Finally we denote with $N_{j,o,u}$ the number of instances of operation $o$ of Web service $j$ which can be executed in the time interval $u$; we assume that the Web services execution is supported by limited resources.

# 3    Resource Allocation in Grid Environments

The grid domain is characterized by the Virtual Organization (VO) concept, that is a set of individuals and/or institutions which share computing resources. Resource sharing is regulated and controlled by defining the set of shared computing and storage elements [1,12], who is allowed to access them and which are the conditions under which resource sharing occurs. A VO lets different individuals and/or institutions to share resources in a controlled way, so that VO members can collaborate to obtain a common objective. In the scenario considered in this paper, resources are represented by concrete Web services which are physically deployed in multiple VOs, and are executed by *Local Grids*. A VO can use concrete Web services, that are located in different VO sites, to execute a particular abstract composed service. Local Grid includes also: a *Service Registry*, a *Local Resource Allocation* module and a *Broker* (see Figure 2). The registry stores the WSDL specification, the QoS profile and the number of instances which can be executed in the time interval $u$ for every operation. The broker receives composed Web service execution requests from VO members and external users, consults the local and remote registries and determines the execution plan (i.e. abstract to concrete Web service assignment) for the composed service execution. Local grid resources are reserved according to the execution plan identified by the broker. VOs and the end user establish Service Level Agreement (SLA) contracts for the service provisioning and $N_{j,o,u}$ is updated accordingly.

Resource management introduces two different optimization problems which corresponds to the VOs (providers) and users perspectives: (i) each VO would like to maximize the SLA revenues and the use of physical resources, (ii) the end user is interested in the maximization of the QoS of the composed service execution.

SLA revenues maximization is performed locally by the local resource allocation module, while QoS maximization is evaluated by brokers. Note that brokers of different local grids can collaborate to identify the optimum abstract to concrete Web service mapping and a composed service can be executed by concrete Web services located in different local grids.

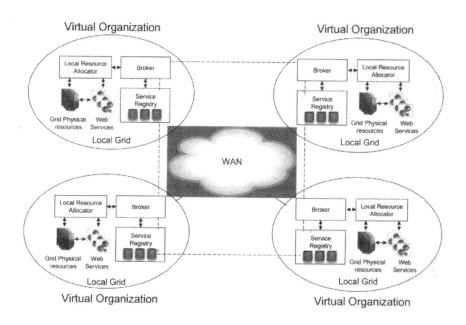

**Fig. 2.** Grid Reference Framework

This paper focuses on the maximization of the QoS for the end user which will be discussed in depth in Section 3.2. Local grid resource management has been presented in previous work [24,2] and will be briefly summarized in Section 3.1.

## 3.1   Local Resource Allocation

Each VO needs to allocate local grid physical resources to different Web service operation invocations $ws_{j,o}$ in order to maximize the revenues from SLA, while minimizing resource management costs. One of the main issues is the high variability of the incoming request workload which can vary by orders of magnitude within the same business day [9]. It is difficult to estimate workload requirements in advance, and planning the capacity for the worst-case scenario is either infeasible or extremely inefficient. In order to handle workload variations, many service centers have started employing autonomic techniques [14], that allow the dynamic allocation of physical resources among different Web services invocations on the basis of short-term demand estimates. The goal is to meet the application requirements while adapting the physical infrastructure. The adoption of grid computing is very promising in this application area, since basic mechanisms to provide resource virtualization, service differentiation, performance isolation, and dynamic re-configuration of the physical infrastructure are implemented by the grid middleware layer [12,1].

The local resource allocation is performed periodically with period $\Delta'$ (e.g., 10-30 minutes [25,2]) on the basis of a short-term workload prediction (see Figure 3a). Note that $\Delta'$ is lower than $\Delta$, the discretization time interval adopted to model the QoS in the service registry. The short term predictor forecasts the number of Web services invocations for the next control interval denoted as $\hat{N}_{j,o}(t)$. The local resource allocator uses also some low level information provided by the grid monitoring infrastructure in order to identify requests of different Web services operations and to estimate requests service times (i.e., the CPU and disk time required by the physical infrastructure to execute each operation).

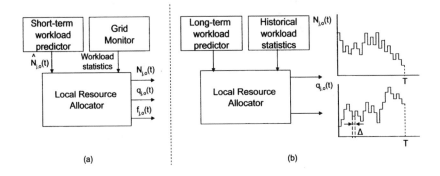

**Fig. 3.** Local Resource Allocation

In order to maximize revenues from SLA, the local resource allocator determines the fraction of capacity assigned to each Web service invocation $f_{j,o}(t)$, relying on the virtualization mechanism and performance isolation provided by the grid infrastructure. The local resource allocator employs also an admission control scheme [20] that may reject requests in order to guarantee that the QoS requirements are met, or to avoid service instability caused by capacity restrictions. Overall, the local resource allocator determines the number of Web service operation invocations $N_{j,o}(t) \leq \hat{N}_{j,o}(t)$ allowed for the next control interval, its corresponding QoS level $q_{j,o}(t)$, and the fraction of capacity of the physical grid infrastructure $f_{j,o}(t)$ devoted to its execution.

As we discussed in [2], the local resource allocator algorithm can be used with a long-term workload predictor and historical workload statistics from systems log (see Figure 3b) in a simulation environment in order to determine $N_{j,o}(t)$ and the quality profile on the long term. If we assume that the incoming workload has a daily periodic component, as frequently happens in practice [16], $N_{j,o}(t)$ and $q_{j,o}(t)$ are also periodic and can be described with granularity $\triangle > \triangle'$ in a service registry.

Note that, resource allocation is performed at local grid level since a global resource allocation scheme which determines $N_{j,o}(t)$ and $q_{j,o}(t)$ for the whole grid infrastructure introduces a high overhead [10]. Furthermore, by implementing a local resource allocation policy VOs have a greater control of their own physical infrastructure.

## 3.2   Maximizing QoS for the End-User

Requests of execution of composed Web service from VOs or external users are submitted to grid brokers specifying the preferences (weights) and the set of local and global constraints. A broker solves the Web Service Selection problem (WSC) which consists in finding the optimal mapping between process tasks and Web service operations.

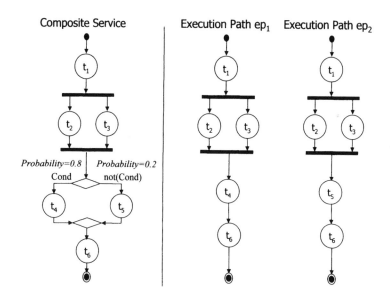

**Fig. 4.** Execution Paths

In the following, Web services will be indexed by $j$ while operations will be indexed by $o$. We will indicate with $WS_i$ the set of indexes of Web services $ws_j$ candidate for the execution of task $t_i$, with $OP_j$ the set of indexes of operations implemented by Web service $ws_j$, and with $ws_{j,o}$ the invocation of operation $o \in OP_j$ of Web service $ws_j$. Let be $I$ the number of tasks of the composed service specification and $J$ the number of candidate Web services. We assume that cycles are unfolded according to the maximum number of iterations. For the sake of simplicity in the following definitions we assume that a composite service is characterized by a single initial task $t_1$ and a single end task $t_I$:

- *Execution Path.* A set of tasks $\{t_1, \ldots, t_i, \ldots, t_I\}$ such that $t_1$ is the initial task, $t_I$ is the final task and no $t_{i_1}$, $t_{i_2}$ belong to alternative branches. Execution paths will be indexed by $k$ and denoted by $ep_k$. We will indicate with $\mathcal{A}_k$ the set of indexes of tasks included in the execution path and with $K$ the number of different execution paths arising from the composed service specification. Note that an execution path can include parallel sequences (see Figure 4).
- *Execution Plan.* An execution plan of an execution path $ep_k$ is a set of ordered triples $\{(t_i, ws_{j,o}, x_i)\}$, indicating that every task $t_i$ included in $ep_k$ is executed at time instant $x_i$ by invoking $ws_{j,o}$. Execution plans will be indexed by $l$ and denoted as $epl_l^k$.
- *Global Plan.* The global plan is a set of ordered triples $\{(t_i, ws_{i,o}, x_i)\}$, which associates every task $t_i$ to a given Web service operation invocation $ws_{j,o}$ at time instant $x_i$ and satisfies local and global constraints for all execution paths.

Note that, the set of execution paths of an activity diagram identifies all the possible execution scenarios of the composite service. The optimization problem will consider all of the possible execution scenarios according to their probability of execution, which can be evaluated by the product of the frequency of execution of branch conditions included in execution paths and annotated in the BPEL specification. Under these definitions, a local constraint can predicate only on properties of a single task. Vice versa, global constraints can predicate on quality attributes of an execution path or on a subset of tasks of the activity diagram, for example a set of subsequent tasks or a sub path. In the current implementation, exceptions are not considered in the optimization problem, global constraints will be guaranteed only for the nominal execution of the composite service.

The WSC problem is formulated as a mixed integer linear programming problem. The decision variables of our model are the followings:

- $y_{i,j,o,u} \in \{0,1\}$ is equal to 1 if the task $t_i$ is executed by Web service $j \in WS_i$ with the operation $o \in OP_j$ during the time interval $u$, 0 otherwise;
- $w_{i,u} \in \{0,1\}$ is equal to 1 if the task $t_i$ is executed during time interval $u$, 0 otherwise;
- $x_i \in \mathbb{R}^+$ indicates the time instant in which task $t_i$ is executed.

Let us denote with the variable $\mathcal{Y} = [y_{i,j,o,u}]$ the characteristic vector of a generic execution plan $EPL$; in the following, execution plans will be represented by their characteristic vector.

The goal of the WSC problem is to maximize the average aggregated value of QoS. The average is obtained by considering all of the possible execution scenarios, i.e., all of the execution paths arising from the composed service specification, and their probability of execution $freq_k$. As we have discussed in [4] the aggregated value of QoS can be obtained by applying the Simple Additive Weighting (SAW) technique, one of the most widely used techniques to obtain a *score* from a list of dimensions.

Let us denote with $score_k(\mathcal{Y})$ the aggregated value of QoS of the execution plan $\mathcal{Y}$ along the execution path $ep_k$. If we number the quality dimensions as $exeTime = 1$, $avail = 2$, $price = 3$, $rep = 4$ the overall score along the execution path $ep_k$ associated with an execution plan $\mathcal{Y}$ is evaluated as (for deeper details see [4]):

$$score_k(\mathcal{Y}) = \omega_1 \frac{\max exeTime_k - exeTime_k(\mathcal{Y})}{\max exeTime_k - \min exeTime_k} + \omega_2 \frac{avail_k(\mathcal{Y}) - \min avail_k}{\max avail_k - \min avail_k} +$$
$$+\omega_3 \frac{\max price_k - price_k(\mathcal{Y})}{\max price_k - \min price_k} + \omega_4 \frac{rep_k(\mathcal{Y}) - \min rep_k}{\max rep_k - \min rep_k} \tag{3}$$

Our goal is to maximize the weighted average of the score of execution paths where weights are given by execution path frequency of execution $freq_k$. The WSC problem can be formulated as:

P1)
$$\max \sum_{k=1}^{K} freq_k \cdot score_k(\mathcal{Y})$$

$$\sum_{j \in WS_i} \sum_{o \in OP_j} \sum_{u=1}^{\lceil E/\Delta \rceil} y_{i,j,o,u} = 1 \quad i = 1, \ldots, I \tag{4}$$

$$w_{i,u}(u-1)\Delta \leq x_i \quad i = 1, \ldots, I; u = 1, \ldots, \lceil E/\Delta \rceil \tag{5}$$

$$u\Delta w_{i,u} + E(1 - w_{i,u}) \geq x_i \quad i = 1, \ldots, I; u = 1, \ldots, \lceil E/\Delta \rceil \tag{6}$$

$$w_{i,u} = \sum_{j \in WS_i} \sum_{o \in OP_j} y_{i,j,o,u} \quad i = 1, \ldots, I; u = 1, \ldots, \lceil E/\Delta \rceil \tag{7}$$

$$y_{i,j,o,u} \leq N_{j,o,u} \quad i = 1, \ldots, I; \forall j \in WS_i; \forall o \in OP_j; u = 1, \ldots, \lceil E/\Delta \rceil \tag{8}$$

$$\sum_{j \in WS_i} \sum_{o \in OP_j} \sum_{u=1}^{\lceil E/\Delta \rceil} e_{j,o,u \bmod(T/\Delta)} y_{i,j,o,u} = exeT_i \quad i = 1, \ldots, I \tag{9}$$

$$x_{i_2} - (exeT_{i_1} + x_{i_1}) \geq 0 \quad \forall t_{i_1} \rightarrow t_{i_2} \tag{10}$$

$$exeTime_k = x_I + exeT_I; \quad k = 1, \ldots, K \tag{11}$$

$$avail_k = \prod_{i \in A_k} \prod_{j \in WS_i} \prod_{o \in OP_j} \prod_{u=1}^{\lceil E/\Delta \rceil} a_{j,o,u \bmod(T/\Delta)}^{y_{i,j,o,u}} \quad k = 1, \ldots, K \tag{12}$$

$$price_k = \sum_{i \in A_k} \sum_{j \in WS_i} \sum_{o \in OP_j} \sum_{u=1}^{\lceil E/\Delta \rceil} p_{j,o,u \bmod(T/\Delta)} y_{i,j,o,u} \quad k = 1, \ldots, K \tag{13}$$

$$rep_k = \frac{1}{|A_k|} \sum_{i \in A_k} \sum_{j \in WS_i} \sum_{o \in OP_j} \sum_{u=1}^{\lceil E/\Delta \rceil} r_{j,o,u \bmod(T/\Delta)} y_{i,j,o,u} \quad k = 1, \ldots, K \tag{14}$$

$$exeTime_k \leq E \quad k = 1, \ldots, K \tag{15}$$

$$avail_k \geq A \quad k = 1, \ldots, K \tag{16}$$

$$price_k \leq B \quad k = 1, \ldots, K \tag{17}$$

$$rep_k \geq R \quad k = 1, \ldots, K \tag{18}$$

$$x_i \in \mathbb{R}^+ \quad i = 1, \ldots, I; \quad exeTime_k, avail_k, price_k, rep_k \in \mathbb{R}^+ \quad k = 1, \ldots, K;$$
$$y_{i,j,o,u}, w_{i,u} \in [0,1] \quad \forall i, j, o, u$$

Constraint family (4) garantees that each task $t_i$ is assigned to only one concrete $ws_{j,o}$ and its execution can start in a specific time interval $u$. Constraint families (5) and (6) relate variable $x_i$ and variable $w_{i,u}$. If $w_{i,u}$ is set to 1 then $x_i$ value belongs to $u$ interval, otherwise $x_i$ can assume any value between [0,E]. For example if $w_{i,5} = 1$ then we can obtain from constraint (5) $x_i \geq 4\triangle$ and from constraint (6) $x_i \leq 5\triangle$; on the other hand if $w_{i,5} = 0$ we obtain $x_i \geq 0$ and $x_i \leq E$. Constraint family (7) relates variables $w_{i,u}$ and $y_{i,j,o,u}$, indeed if the task $t_i$ is executed by invoking in interval $u$ the operation $o$ of Web service $j$, i.e. $y_{i,j,o,u} = 1$, then $w_{i,u}$ is raised to 1. Family constraint (8) guarantees that the number of parallel Web service operation invocations that can be executed in the same interval $u$ must be lower or equal to the number of available invocation instances. Constraint (9) expresses the duration of every task in term of the duration of selected service. Note that for constraints (4) and (7) there is only one operation invocation in a specific interval and hence a task duration is given by the selected Web service operation execution time. Constraint family (10) represents precedence constraints for subsequent tasks in the activity diagram. If a task $t_{i_2}$ is a direct successor of task $t_{i_1}$ (indicated as $t_{i_1} \rightarrow t_{i_2}$), then execution of task $t_{i_2}$ starts after task $t_{i_1}$ termination. Constraint family (11) evaluates the execution time of an execution path (and hence the execution time of the composed process, from Section 2 we assume that the composed process has a single start and a single end task) as the sum of the starting time of the last task $t_I$ and its corresponding execution time. Constraints families (12)-(14) express execution path $ep_k$ availability, price and reputation (see [4]). Finally, constraint families (15)-(18) are the global constraints to be fulfilled.

Problem P1) can include Web service dependency constraints which can be formulated as follows. If two task $t_{i_1}$, $t_{i_2}$ must be executed by the same Web service, then the following constraint families are introduced:

$$\sum_{o \in OP_j} \sum_{u=1}^{\lceil E/\triangle \rceil} y_{i_1,j,o,u} = \sum_{o \in OP_j} \sum_{u=1}^{\lceil E/\triangle \rceil} y_{i_2,j,o,u} \quad \forall j \in WS_{i_1} \cap WS_{i_2};$$

$$\sum_{o \in OP_j} \sum_{u=1}^{\lceil E/\triangle \rceil} y_{i_1,j,o,u} = 0, \forall j \in WS_{i_1} \setminus WS_{i_2};$$

$$\sum_{o \in OP_j} \sum_{u=1}^{\lceil E/\triangle \rceil} y_{i_2,j,o,u} = 0, \forall j \in WS_{i_2} \setminus WS_{i_1}.$$

Local constraints can predicate on properties of a single task and can be included in the model as follows. For example if the designer requires that the price for task $t_{i_1}$ has to be less or equal than a given value $\overline{p}$, then the following constraint is introduced:

$$\sum_{j \in WS_{i_1}} \sum_{o \in OP_j} \sum_{u=1}^{\lceil E/\triangle \rceil} p_{j,o,u} y_{i_1,j,o,u} \leq \overline{p} \tag{19}$$

The Problem P1) has integer variables and a non-linear constraint family (the availability bounds expressed by equations (12) and (16)). Availability bounds can be linearized by applying the logarithm function (see [23]). In [4], by assuming a constant quality profile, we have shown that the problem of selection of Web services with QoS constraints is equivalent to a Multiple choice Multiple dimension Knapsack Problem which is NP-hard, hence P1) is NP-hard.

An optimization tool based on *CPLEX*, a state of the art integer linear programming solver, is under development. The performance of the approach will be evaluated by varying the size of the WSC instances, i.e., by varying the number of tasks and candidate Web services.

## 4  Conclusions

This paper presents a framework for the development of e-business applications built on autonomic grid computing infrastructure, where the service selection and composition is performed to guarantee that the overall quality perceived by the user is maximized. Our short/medium term goal includes the realization/implementation of the proposed approach and its validation on an industrial case study. In particular, the execution of a distributed ERP software to support small and medium enterprises which share computing resources in a grid environment will be considered. The long term goal is the realization of a framework where different kind of selection and composition methods are provided; in such a way the user can choose the methods best suited for his application and quality requirements.

**Acknowledgements.** The work reported in this paper has been partially supported by the DISCORSO FAR Italian Project. Thanks are expressed to Giuliana Carello and Marco Trubian for many fruitfull discussions on optimization issues. We are grateful to Engineering Ingegneria Informatica and especially to Gabriele Giunta for technical support.

## References

1. The egee Project (Enabling Grid for E-Science). http://public.eu-egee.org/test/.
2. J. Almeida, V. Almeida, D. Ardagna, C. Francalanci, and M. Trubian. Resource management in the autonomic service-oriented architecture. In *ICAC 2006 Proc.*, 2006. In Press.
3. D. Ardagna, C. Cappiello, P. Plebani, and B. Pernici. A Framework for Describing and Supporting Adaptive Context-aware Web Services. Politecnico di Milano Technical Report 2006.48 http://www.elet.polimi.it/upload/ardagna/Tech2006-48.pdf, June 2006.
4. D. Ardagna and B. Pernici. Global and Local QoS Guarantee in Web Service Selection. In *BPM 2005 Workshops Proc.*, pages 32–46, 2005. Nancy.
5. D. Berlich, M. Kunze, and K. Schwarz. Grid computing in Europe: from research to deployment. In *CRPIT '44: Proc. of the 2005 Australian workshop on Grid computing and e-research*, pages 21–27, Darlinghurst, Australia, Australia, 2005. Australian Computer Society, Inc.

6. D. Bianchini, V. D. Antonellis, B. Pernici, and P. Plebani. Ontology-based methodology for e-Service discovery. *Information Systems*, 31:361–380, 2006.

7. G. Canfora, M. Penta, R. Esposito, and M. L. Villani. QoS-Aware Replanning of Composite Web Services. In *ICWS 2005 Proc.*, 2005.

8. J. Cao, S. A. Jarvis, S. Saini, and G. R. Nudd. GridFlow: Workflow Management for Grid Computing. In *CCGRID 2003 Proc.*, Jul. 2003.

9. J. S. Chase, D. C. Anderson, P. N. Thakar, A. M. Vahdat, and R. P. Doyle. Managing energy and server resources in hosting centers. In *SOSP 2001 Proc.*, pages 103–116, 2001. Banff.

10. L. Chunlin and L. Layuan. A distributed utility-based two level market solution for optimal resource scheduling in computational grid. *Parallel Comput.*, 31(3+4):332–351, 2005.

11. D. B. Claro, P. Albers, and J. K. Hao. Selecting Web Services for Optimal Composition. In *ICWS 2005 Workshop Proc.*, 2005. Orlando.

12. I. Foster, C. Kesselman, and S. Tuecke. The Anatomy of the Grid: Enabling Scalable Virtual Organizations. *Intl. J. of Supercomputer Applications*, 2001.

13. J. O. Kephart and D. M. Chess. The vision of autonomic computing. *IEEE Computer*, 1(31):41–50, 2003.

14. Z. Liu, M. Squillante, and J. L. Wolf. On Maximizing Service-Level-Agreement Profits. In *Proc. of ACM Eletronic Commerce Conference*, October 2001.

15. E. M. Maximilien and M. P. Singh. A Framework and Ontology for Dynamic Web Services Selection. *IC*, 8(5):84–93, Sept./Oct. 2004.

16. D. Menascé, V. Almeida, and L. Dowdy. *Performance by Design*. Prentice Hall, 2003.

17. D. Menasce and E. Casalicchio. QoS in Grid Computing. *IEEE Internet Computing*, July–Aug 2004.

18. M. Ouzzani and A. Bouguettaya. Efficient Access to Web Services. *IEEE Internet Comp.*, 37(3):34–44, 2004.

19. C. Patel, K. Supekar, and Y. Lee. A QoS Oriented Framework for Adaptive Management of Web Service Based Workflows. In *Proc. of DEXA 2003*, volume 2376 of *LCNS*, pages 826–835. Springer-Verlag, 2003.

20. H. G. Perros and K. H. Elsayed. Call Admission Control Schemes : A Review. *IEEE Magazine on Communications*, 1996.

21. J. Yu and R. Buyya. A taxonomy of scientific workflow systems for grid computing. *SIGMOD Rec.*, 34(3):44–49, 2005.

22. T. Yu and K. J. Lin. A Broker-Based Framework for QoS-Aware Web Service Composition. In *Proc. of 2005 IEEE Int'l Conf. on e-Technology, e-Commerce and e-Service*, Mar. 2005.

23. L. Zeng, B. Benatallah, M. Dumas, J. Kalagnamam, and H. Chang. QoS-Aware Middleware for Web Services Composition. *IEEE Trans. on Soft. Eng.*, May 2004.

24. L. Zhang and D. Ardagna. SLA based profit optimization in autonomic computing systems. In *ICSOC 2004 Proc.*, pages 173–182, 2004. New York.

25. L. Zhang and D. Ardagna. SLA Based Profit Optimization in Autonomic Computing Systems. In *ICSOC 2004 Proc.*, pages 173–182, 2004.

26. L. J. Zhang and L. Bing. Requirements driven dynamic services composition for web services and grid solutions. *Journal of Grid Computing*, 2(2):121–140, 2004.

# Event-Based Peer-to-Peer Process Enactment for Ubiquitous Web Service Devices

Jae-Yoon Jung[1,2], Jonghun Park[2], Seung-Kyun Han[2], and Kangchan Lee[3]

[1] Eindhoven University of Technology, The Netherlands
jjyjung@gmail.com
[2] Seoul National University, Republic of Korea
jonghun@snu.ac.kr, jackleg83@gmail.com
[3] Electronics & Telecommunication Research Institute, Republic of Korea
chan@etri.re.kr

**Abstract.** Web service technology is a representative means of heterogeneous system integration and communication. Process language standards, such as WS-BPEL and WS-CDL, have accelerated the usability of web services in business area. However, recently emerging web service devices in ubiquitous environments still have a difficulty in coordinating their processes because of the limited computing power and storage. This research proposes a framework of event-based process enactment for ubiquitous web service devices. The framework adopts P2P architecture where devices communicate with one another via web services eventing. The schema of ECA rules and messaging protocol are presented for P2P process enactment so that service devices can interact each other and accomplish their process execution based on the ECA rules. Our proposed framework is expected to be useful in ubiquitous service environments since it enables a scalable and light-weighted process enactment through event-based web service technology.

**Keywords:** Peer-to-peer process, web services eventing, ubiquitous computing, Event-Condition-Action rules.

## 1 Introduction

Ubiquitous computing environments are increasingly becoming heterogeneous and service rich domains [7]. In such environments, distributed devices with particular services are interconnected each other via various types of networks. While web service technology is becoming a de facto standard for integration of business applications [14], it is also rapidly emerging as an effective means for achieving interoperability among the devices in ubiquitous computing networks [11]. There are several ongoing efforts that attempt to embed the web services into various forms of computing devices in order to establish pervasive networks. These include Microsoft's invisible computing project [10] and UPnP 2.0 [12]. In particular, recently proposed web service standards, such as WS-Eventing [2] and WS-Addressing [3], are accelerating the deployment of web service technology into the ubiquitous environments.

J. Eder, S. Dustdar et al. (Eds.): BPM 2006 Workshops, LNCS 4103, pp. 387–399, 2006.

In the meantime, workflow technology has changed the paradigm of information system. Process-centric system architecture has facilitated heterogeneous systems to collaborate with one another on the control of process enactment engines [5]. The centralized coordination mechanism based on the client/server structure has supported managerial control to administrators and efficient job assignment to participants. Web service technologies have been also enhanced through development of process standards, such as WS-BPEL [1] and WS-CDL [9]. Moreover, research results on web service discovery and semantic web service are accelerating the wide spread of web service technologies by discovering service providers based on ontology and comparing their quality of services [13].

Yet, ubiquitous computing environments have difficulty in adopting the recent advancements from process technology mainly due to the nature of centralized service coordination. Ubiquitous computing assumes that various service devices, such as sensors, service appliances, and controllers, are interacting for the purpose of user convenience in any time and any place. Although process execution is requisite to effective user supporting, the centralized mechanism can hinder scalable network and efficient interaction among service devices, requiring a new framework for ubiquitous process enactments.

This paper introduces an event-based peer-to-peer (P2P) process enactment framework for ubiquitous service devices. In the framework, service devices interact with one another via web service eventing messages, and each device executes independently sub-processes expressed in Event-Condition-Action (ECA) rules. The event-based mechanism enhances network efficiency and scalability since service devices in P2P network can communicate each other directly without centralized coordination and also execute their sub-processes independently.

Specifically, we present an ECA rule description language for Web Services (named WS-ECA) that employs WS-Eventing specification as an eventing format in P2P network. WS-ECA can support primitive events, such as time, service, internal and external events, as well as composite events with logical operators. WS-Eventing, proposed by Microsoft, et al., provides a messaging protocol for delivering subscription, notification, and fault messages to implement event-driven interactions based on web services [2]. The content of notification events can be described without restrictions for specific applications. Furthermore, we also propose a schema of the message protocol for process enactment by extending the notification events in WS-Eventing. The protocol is composed of the messages for process deployment, initiation, enactment, and audit reporting.

In the following, Section 2 introduces the framework of event-based P2P process enactment for ubiquitous service computing, and Section 3 and 4 present the WS-ECA language and messaging protocol for the framework, respectively. An example of P2P process enactment in a home networking scenario is described in Section 5. Finally, Section 6 concludes the paper.

## 2   P2P Process Enactment in Ubiquitous Service Computing

This section describes an event-based P2P process enactment framework for ubiquitous service devices. In the proposed framework, service devices interact with one another via web services eventing, and each device executes sub-processes expressed in terms of ECA rules. The eventing-based mechanism facilitates scalability and efficiency since the devices participate in service network as a peer and interact with each other directly without centralized coordination. The considered P2P network adopts WS-Eventing specification as an event message format, and employs a WS-ECA proposed in this paper.

The framework has three main characteristics: (1) event-based communication via web service technology (2) process enactment in a scalable P2P network, and (3) lightweight process execution based on ECA rules. These characteristics of proposed framework offer several advantages compared to centralized process coordination as follows:

- *Scalable collaboration network*: Process enactment is accomplished by event-driven communication in a P2P network. In ubiquitous environments there are frequent joining and leaving of a number of devices. Web services eventing enables heterogeneous service devices to seamlessly communicate each other.
- *Decentralized coordination*: P2P processes are executed according to ECA rules of service devices that are interacting via web services eventing. The ECA rules governing the behavior of devices are distributed across the network and executed independently by individual devices.
- *Light-weight implementation*: Contrary to the full-blown process modeling languages such as WS-BPEL and WS-CDL that require heavy process engines, the proposed framework adopts active rules that can be executed via web services eventing. This enables light-weight implementation of process execution and message communication for web service-enabled devices.

## 2.1 P2P Process Enactment Framework

The framework for P2P process enactment defines three types of peers, and the peers perform five steps throughout their life cycle similar to conventional workflow systems: process design, deployment, initiation, enactment, and audit reporting. Figure 1 illustrates the P2P process enactment framework with the five steps.

First, designer peers can create new P2P processes and deploy them to service peers. The peers should know what service peers are included in the network and what services are provided by the peers. The discovery procedure can be adopted from previous research results on service discovery and semantic web services [7, 13], and it is beyond the scope of this paper. In the step of process deployment, a global process is composed of several sub-processes based on their roles, and the sub-processes are described according to ECA rules so that they can interact with one another through triggering events. The ECA rules are explained in detail with the proposed WS-ECA schema in Section 3. An ECA rule may be registered to multiple peers in the same role group since duplicated registration can address the problem of dynamic participation of service peers in the network.

Subsequently, administrator peers can initiate a process from the list of deployed processes. The peer can make a selection of some peers in each service role or assign a priority among them in consideration of their connectivity and the user's preference. Finally, service peers execute the rules and services of initiated processes while they inform one another of the status of sub-process execution. The detailed procedure of process enactment is explained in Section 4.

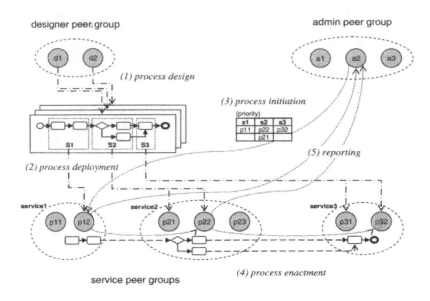

**Fig. 1.** P2P process enactment framework

## 3  ECA Rule Description Language for Web Service Devices

This section describes the schema of WS-ECA, the proposed rule description language for ubiquitous web service devices. The rules can be triggered by either the external events in the form of WS-Eventing or the internal events generated from the timer or internal systems. While external events can be used for initiation of sub-processes and message flow between two sub-processes, internal events are used for modeling state transitions and gateways in sub-processes. The basic structure of the proposed WS-ECA is defined as follows.

```
<ECARule name="xs:NCName" targetNampespace="xs:anyURI"
      xmlns="http://di.snu.ac.kr/2005/eca/"
      xmlns:xs="http://www.w3.org/2001/XMLSchema" >
   <variables>? <variable ... />+ </variables>
   <events> event+ </events>
   <actions> action+ </actions>
   <rules>
        <rule name="xs:NCName">+
           <event name="xs:QName"/>
           <condition expression="XPath Expression"/>
           <action name="xs:QName"/>
        </rule>
   </rules>
<ECARule>
```

**Fig. 2.** The overall WS-ECA schema

The schema supports the primitive events and actions as well as the composite ones for ECA rule processing in ubiquitous service devices. Event is an incident that triggers a rule, and it can be internal or external to a service device. Specifically, the schema supports four types of primitive events. First, time event is generated by a timer at the point that a user has specified. The time event has three subtypes: *absolute*, *periodic*, and *relative*. The *absolute* type event is generated once, the *periodic* type event occurs periodically, and the *relative* type event occurs at specific time before or after another event. Second, internal event is generated by the internal system including the rule engine and the device itself. It can be used to recognize the state change of the device or to trigger other rules (i.e. rule chaining). A sub-process is implemented by chaining several rules. Third, external event is delivered from an external device in order to initiate a sub-process or exchange the state of a sub-process. External events are conformant to the schema extended from WS-Eventing specification, which is described in detail in Section 4. Finally, service event can be one of two types: *before* and *after*. The *before* (*after*, respectively) type is generated before (after, respectively) a specific service of a device begins (finishes, respectively).

```
<events>
   <timeEvent type="once" name="xs:NCName"> xs:dateTime </timeEvent>
   <timeEvent type="periodic" name="xs:NCName" unit="xs:duration">
       xs:dateTime </timeEvent>
   <timeEvent type="relative" name="xs:NCName" baseEvent="xs:NCName"
       interval="xs:duration"/>
   <intEvent name="xs:NCName"/>
   <extEvent name="xs:NCName" eventID="xs:anyURI"/>
   <svcEvent type="before" name="xs:NCName" service="xs:QName"/>
   <svcEvent type="after" name="xs:NCName" service="xs:QName"/>

   <compositeEvent type="OR" name="xs:NCName" TTL="xs:duration">
       event+ </compositeEvent>
   <compositeEvent type="AND" name="xs:NCName" TTL="xs:duration">
       event+ </compositeEvent>
   <compositeEvent type="SEQ" name="xs:NCName" TTL="xs:duration">
       event+ </compositeEvent>
   <compositeEvent type="NOT" name="xs:NCName" TTL="xs:duration">
       event+ </compositeEvent>
</events>
```

**Fig. 3.** Event schema of WS-ECA

More than one of the above four primitive events may be composed into a composite event by use of the following logical operators. First, disjunction event of type *"OR"* has more than one sub-event. One or more of the sub-events must occur within a specific time interval. Second, conjunction event of type *"AND"* has more than one sub-event. All of the sub-events must occur one or more times within a specific time interval. Third, sequence event of type *"SEQ"* has more than one sub-event. All of the sub-events must ever occur sequentially within a specific time interval. Finally, negation event of type *"NOT"* has only one sub-event. The sub-event must not occur within a specified time interval. A composite event can be defined recursively by using the above logical operators. The XML schema for the proposed event structure is shown in Figure 3.

The condition part of WS-ECA rules is a boolean statement that must be satisfied in order to activate a rule. It is described in terms of an XPath expression [4], and the expression in a condition may refer to values from the event definition and use the variables defined in a WS-ECA document. The syntax for the variables is presented in Figure 4. Variables may refer to specific elements of an event defined in WS-ECA rules (called *event variables*) or they may be used to represent a state of a device (called *device variables*). They can be also used to express the conditions or to assign necessary input data for actions such as service invocations and event generation. We define two extension functions to assign the value to a variable as shown in Table 1. The first function extracts a specific value from an event variable, and the second returns the date and time information.

```
<variables>?
   <variable name="xs:NCName" deviceVar="xs:QName"?
      eventVar="eca:getVariable(event QName, path PathExpr)"? />+
</variables>
```

**Fig. 4.** Variable schema of WS-ECA

**Table 1.** Extension functions to XPath's built-in functions

| Functions | Return type | Return value |
|---|---|---|
| eca:getVariable(event QName, path PathExpr) | xs:any | Specific value from an event variable |
| eca:getDateTime(event QName) | xs:dateTime | Date and time information |

The action part of the WS-ECA contains the instructions that are executed when a triggered rule is activated. A primitive action can be (i) invokeService(svc) that invokes internal or external service svc, (ii) createExtEvent(evt) that generates an external event evt and publishes it to subscribing devices, and (iii) createIntEvent (evt) that generates an internal event evt and triggers corresponding rules of a device. invokeService action can be used for invocation of internal services during executing sub-processes, in addition to the invocation of external services if it does not influence the control flow of sub-processes. And, createExtEvent and createIntEvent actions are used for representing control flow and message flow of P2P processes, respectively.

As in the case of events, the actions also may consist of above primitive actions or their compositions. A composite action is defined by use of more than one primitive or composite action with two operators: conjunction and disjunction operators. The syntax of actions is omitted due to the space limitation.

## 4   Eventing Protocol for P2P Process Enactment

P2P process network includes three kinds of peers, namely designer, service, and administrator peers. Service peers subscribe their roles to designer peers. The role is used as a criterion of service assignment for deploying processes. Next, designer peers create new processes based on WS-ECA schema, and then deploy the processes to service peers according to their roles. Finally, administrator peers can initiate deployed processes and require the audit reporting. The life cycle of P2P processes and their message protocols are defined as follows:

**Process design.** Designer peers create P2P processes by using WS-ECA rules and the WS-Eventing messages. In designing the process, four types of primitive events - time, service, internal, and external events - can be used for composing or choreographing services. In particular, external events can be employed to express message flows among sub-processes while internal events can be used to express control flows in sub-processes. In addition, AND, XOR, OR splits and joins can be also expressed by using composite events and conditions in the rules. The proposed concept of process design will be described with an example in the next section.

**Process deployment.** Process deployment is a procedure of registering all sub-processes to participating devices according to their roles. There are two kinds of sub-processes: one is embedded sub-processes, which can be initiated by the global process, and the other is independent sub-processes, which can be reused by another process by using its triggering event. To deploy a sub-process, a designer peer sends DeployProcess messages to service peers with the corresponding role, and the message contains descriptions of a new process, ECA rules, and deployment information. Figure 5 shows the schema of DeployProcess message.

**Process initiation.** Two kinds of initiation methods are supported in our framework. One is manual initiation by administrator peers sending InitiateProcess messages, and the other is automatic initiation via triggering events, which can be periodic time events, internal events occurred by device state changes, and external events through WS-Eventing. InitiateProcess message contains information of administrator, priorities of service providers, policy of audit reporting, etc.

**Process enactment.** An initiated process is executed according to the ECA rules that comprise the sub-process. After finishing a sub-process, the service peer sends TransitProcess messages to a set of descendant service peers for triggering the next sub-processes. The TransitProcess messages contain the history of the executed sub-processes and instances as UUID, which enables service peers to discriminate returned processes from new ones.

**Audit reporting.** This step is not mandatory. In case audit reporting was set when the process has been designed or initiated, the service peers should send ReportAudit messages to the administrator peer. The messages are sent as soon as service peers finish each service in the sub-process. If connection is lost or a response message is not received, the service peer sends again to the peer performing the next sub-process and then the message will be sent again to the administrator peer with the next audit reporting message. Figure 6 shows the schema of ReportAudit message.

Table 2 shows the list of protocol messages defined for the five steps of P2P process life cycle. The schema of all messages is specified through extending and conforming to WS-Eventing specification. In each step, a pair of messages is

**Table 2.** Process enactment life cycle and message protocol

| Life cycle | Peers | Messages |
|---|---|---|
| Process design | designer peer | N/A |
| Process deployment | designer peer → service peers | DeployProcess(Response) |
| Process initiation | admin/service peer → service peer | InitiateProcess(Response) |
| Process enactment | service peer → service peers | TransitProcess(Response) |
| Audit reporting | service peer → admin peer | ReportAudit(Response) |

exchanged between two peers. For instance, after DeployProcess message is sent from designer peer to service peers, DeployProcessResponse messages should be replied from service peers to design peer.

```
<s:Envelope xmlns:s="http://www.w3.org/2003/05/soap-envelope"
   xmlns:wsa="http://schemas.xmlsoap.org/ws/2004/08/addressing"
   xmlns:wse="http://schemas.xmlsoap.org/ws/2004/08/eventing"
   xmlns:p2p=" http://di.snu.ac.kr/2006/p2p">
 <s:Header>
   <wsa:Action>http://di.snu.ac.kr/2006/p2p/DeployProcess</wsa:Action>
   ...
 </s:Header>
 <s:Body>
   <p2p:DeployProcess>
     <p2p:ProcessDescriptionURI>xs:anyURI</p2p:ProcessDescriptionURI>
     <p2p:ECARuleDescriptionURI>xs:anyURI</p2p:ECARuleDescriptionURI>
     <p2p:DeploymentDescription>
       <p2p:Deployer> xs:any </p2p:Deployer>?
       <p2p:Time> xs:dateTime </p2p:Time>?
       <p2p:Expires> [xs:dateTime | xs:duration] </p2p:Expires>?
       <p2p:Version> xs:any </p2p:Version>?
     </p2p:DeploymentDescription>?
   </p2p:DeployProcess>
 </s:Body>
</s:Envelope>
```

**Fig. 5.** The schema of DeployProcess messages

```
<s:Envelope ...>
 <s:Header>
  <wsa:Action>http://di.snu.ac.kr/2005/p2p/ReportAudit</wsa:Action>...
 </s:Header>
 <s:Body>
   <p2p:ReportAudit>
     <p2p:ProcessDescriptionURI>xs:anyURI</p2p:ProcessDescriptionURI>
     <p2p:ServiceDescriptionURI>xs:anyURI</p2p:ServiceDescriptionURI>
     <p2p:AuditDescription>
       <p2p:ServiceName> xs:NCName </p2p:ServiceName>
       <p2p:Time> xs:dateTime </p2p:Time>
       <p2p:Status> xs:any </p2p:Status>
     </p2p:AuditDescription>
   </p2p:ReportAudit>+
 </s:Body>
</s:Envelope>
```

**Fig. 6.** The schema of ReportAudit messages

# 5  Example

In this section, P2P process enactment is illustrated with an example of "morning cook process" in a home networking environment, as shown in Figure 7. Suppose that Jack set a get-up time of the alarm clock to 7:00 AM before sleeping. In the morning, the alarm clock informs the rice cooker of '20 minutes before get-up' (represented as extEvent(alarm(msg))). The cooker starts to cook the rice (represented as invoke Service(cook())), and in case that the amount of rice is not enough, it will alert that to the alarm clock (represented as extEvent(out-of-rice)) at get-up time. When the rice cooking is completed, the cooker informs a coffee maker. And after 10 minutes (represented as timeEvent(10min before extEvent(cooking-completion))), the coffee maker will start to prepare coffee (represented as invokeService (makeCoffee())).

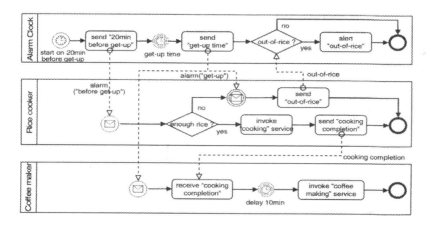

**Fig. 7.** Example of morning cooking service

Based on the structure and syntax of the WS-ECA presented in Section 3, we can define WS-ECA rules for the morning cooking. For example, the process of the rice cooker is described by use of the ECA rules, and it is shown in Figure 8. In addition,

| |
|---|
| *on* **extEvent**(alarm(msg))<br>*if* alarm.msg='20min before get-up'<br>*do* **invokeService**(cook()) |
| *on* **beforeServiceEvent**(cook())<br>*if* rice is not enough<br>*do* **createIntEvent**(out_of_rice) |
| *on* **extEvent**(alarm) after **intEvent**(out_of_rice) within 1hr<br>*if* alarm.msg='get-up'<br>*do* **createExtEvent**(out-of-rice) |
| *on* **afterServiceEvent**(cook())<br>*if* cooking is succeeded.<br>*do* **createExtEvent**(cooking-completion) |

**Fig. 8.** ECA rules of the rice cooker

```
<ECARule name="rice-cooker-rules"
    targetNampespace="http://di.snu.ac.kr/ rice-cooker/rules/"
    xmlns:xsd="http://www.w3.org/2001/XMLSchema"
    xmlns:rc="http://di.snu.ac.kr/ rice-cooker/WSDL/"
    xmlns="http://di.snu.ac.kr/2005/eca/">
  <variables>
    <variable name="hasEnoughRice" type="xsd:boolean"/>
  </variables>
  <events>
   <intEvent name="cookingEvt"/>
   <extEvent name="alarm"
       eventID="http://di.snu.ac.kr/event/alarm-clock/alarm"/>
   <svcEvent type="before" name="before-cooking" service="rc:cook"/>
   <svcEvent type="after" name="after-cooking" service="rc:cook"/>
   <compositeEvent type="SEQ" name="getting-up-after-out-of-rice"
TTL="PT1H">
       <event name="cooking"/><event name="alarm"/>
   </compositeEvent>
  </events>

  <actions>
      <createIntEvent name="cooking" intEvent="cookingEvt"/>
      <createIntEvent name="out-of-rice" intEvent="outofriceEvt"/>
      <createExtEvent name="cooking-completion" extEvent=
    "http://di.snu.ac.kr/event/rice-cooker/cooking-completion"/>
      <invoke name="invokeCooking" service="rc:cook"/>
      <invoke name="alert-out-of-rice" service="rc:alert">
       <rc:contents>out of rice</rc:contents>
      </invoke>
  </actions>
  <rules>
    <rule name="cooking-rule">
       <event name="alarm"/>
       <condition expression="/alarm/msg='20min before get-up'"/>
       <action name="cooking"/>
    </rule>
    <rule name="enough-rice-rule">
       <event name="cookingEvt"/>
       <condition expression="hasEnoughRice=true"/>
       <action name="invokeCooking"/>
    </rule>
    <rule name="not-enough-rice-rule">
       <event name="cookingEvt"/>
       <condition expression="hasEnoughRice=false"/>
       <action name="out-of-rice"/>
    </rule>
    <rule name="out-of-rice-alarm-rule">
       <event name="getting-up-after-out-of-rice"/>
       <condition expression="/alarm/msg='get-up'"/>
       <action name="alert-out-of-rice"/>
    </rule>
    <rule name="cooking-completion-rule">
       <event name="cooking-completion"/>
       <condition expression="true"/>
       <action name="cooking-completion"/>
    </rule>
  </rules>
</ECARule>
```

**Fig. 9.** WS-ECA rules of the rice cooker

```
<s:Envelope xmlns:ac="http://di.snu.ac.kr/event/alarm-clock/" ... >
<s:Header>
<wsa:Action>http://di.snu.ac.kr/2006/p2p/InitiateProcess</wsa:Action>
 <wsa:MessageID>uuid:7dd22961-78ee-4b66-8766-f6b388f6b9dd </wsa:MessageID>
 <wsa:To> http://home.example.com/rice-cooker</wsa:To>
</s:Header>
<s:Body>
  <p2p:InitiateProcess>
    <p2p:ProcessDescriptionURI> ... </p2p:ProcessDescriptionURI>
    <p2p:ECARuleDescriptionURI> ... </p2p:ECARuleDescriptionURI>
    <p2p:InitiationDescription>
      <p2p:Initiator> Jack </p2p:Initiator>
      <p2p:Time> 2006-03-01T07:00:00Z </p2p:Time>
      <p2p:ProcessType> embedded sub-process </p2p:ProcessType>
    </p2p:InitiationDescription>
  </p2p:InitiateProcess>
  <ac:alarm> <ac:msg> 20min before get-up </ac:msg></ac:alarm>
</s:Body>
</s:Envelope>
```

**Fig. 10.** InitiateProcess messages for the rice cooker

Figure 9 shows the WS-ECA document for the rice cooker, rice-cooker.xml, which is initiated by the InitiateProcess message presented in the Figure 10.

# 6  Conclusions and Discussion

Process management is one of the widely deployed technologies in area of modern business information systems. Nevertheless, centralized process enactment and control have resulted in several shortcomings such as workload of servers, single point of failure, and network inefficiency. To address these limitations, grid and P2P approaches have been recently proposed in many areas. In particular, grid approach is taken in many scientific workflow projects, such as bioinformatics, GIS, and physics computing [8]. Since scientific problem-solving usually requires high performance computing as well as huge data set, the centralized coordination approach may result in serious inefficiency of process enactments. On the other hand, P2P workflow does not have a long history. It concentrates on the scalability and connectivity in ad hoc networks rather than the load balancing of computing resources. Fakas and Karacostas [6] proposed P2P workflow architecture based on web directory, which enables peers to search one another and offer their services via web service technology. Nevertheless, since the approach requires a heavy process engine and centralized directory service, it is rather similar to the distributed workflow research. Recently, Yan, et al. [15] presented P2P infrastructure for workflow management. The work focused on distributed data storage in consideration of P2P network construction. In contrast to their work, this paper addressed the problem of efficient process enactment in ubiquitous computing environment.

Specifically, ubiquitous computing systems have difficulty in adopting centralized process enactment approaches. In such systems, the process-centric coordination is required when a number of devices are interacting with each other and with surrounding service users. The decentralized process enactment is therefore required to effectively address the characteristics, such as unstable network connection and dynamic device participation, as well as limited device capabilities.

This paper introduced an event-based P2P process enactment framework for ubiquitous service devices. The framework aimed at light-weight process enactment without requiring centralized coordination for the purpose of scalability, efficiency, and fault tolerance. As a result, we took an event-based coordination approach, and presented an event-based rule description language, named WS-ECA, as well as a messaging protocol for P2P process enactment by extending WS-Eventing specification. WS-ECA enables service devices to interact with each other while they exchange web service-based event messages. Contrary to the existing web service based process execution languages such as WS-BPEL and WS-CDL that are specifically defined for supporting long-running, transactional business processes, the proposed WS-ECA attempts to support instantaneous, reactive interactions of web service enabled devices in P2P process environments.

The presented framework on event-driven process enactment is expected to contribute to efficient implementation of emerging ubiquitous service-based systems.

## Acknowledgement

This work was supported by the Korea Research Foundation Grant funded by the Korean Government (MOEHRD). (KRF- 2005-214-D00397).

## References

1. Andrews, T. *et al.*: Business Process Execution Language for Web Services: Version 1.1. OASIS (2003) http://www-128.ibm.com/developerworks/library/specification/ws-bpel/
2. Bank, D. *et al.*: Web Services Eventing. 2004. http://ftpna2.bea.com/pub/downloads/WS-Eventing.pdf
3. Box, D. *et al.*: Web Services Addressing. W3C Member Submission (2004). http://www.w3.org/Submission/ws-addressing/
4. Clark, J., DeRose, S.: XML Path Language (XPath) Version 1.0, W3C Recommendation, 1999, http://www.w3.org/TR/xpath
5. Dumas, M. van der Aalst, W.M.P., Hofstede, A.H.: Process-Aware Information Systems: Bridging People and Software Through Process Technology. John Wiley & Sons Inc. (2005)
6. Fakas, G.J., Karakostas, B.: A peer to peer (P2P) architecture for dynamic workflow management, Info. Soft. Tech. 46 (2004) 423-431
7. Friday, A., Davies, N., Wallbank, N., Catterall, E., Pink, S.: Supporting Service Discovery, Querying and Interaction. In Ubiquitous Computing Environments. Wireless Networks 10 (2004) 631–641
8. Jung, J.-Y., Lee, W., Kang, S.-H.: Process Decomposition and Choreography for Distributed Scientific Workflow Enactment. In Proc. of Int'l Conf. Comp. Sci. and its App. (ICCSA'06), LNCS 3984, Springer-Verlag, Berlin (2006) 942-951
9. Kavantzas, N. *et al.*, Web Services Choreography Description Language Version 1.0, W3C Candidate Recommendation (2005) http://www.w3.org/TR/ws-cdl-10/
10. Microsoft, The Microsoft invisible computing project web site, http://research.microsoft.com/invisible/

11. Sashima, A., Izumi, N., Kurumatani, K.: Location-Mediated Coordination of Web Services in Ubiquitous Computing. In Proc. of IEEE Int'l Conf. Web Services (ICWS'04) (2004) 109-114.
12. UPnP, The UPnP forum web site, http://www.upnp.org
13. Verma, K., *et al.*: METEOR-S WSDI: A Scalable P2P Infrastructure of Registries for Semantic Publication and Discovery of Web Services, Info. Tech. and Mgt. 6 (2005) 17-39
14. Vinoski, S.: Integration with Web Services. IEEE Internet Comp., 7(6) (2003) 75-77.
15. Yan, J., Yang, Y., Raikundalia, G.K.: SwinDeW- p2p-Based Decentralized Workflow Management System. IEEE Trans. Sys., Man, and Cyber. – Part A. In Press.

# Expressing Business Process Models
# as OWL-S Ontologies

Muhammad Ahtisham Aslam[1], Sören Auer[1,2], Jun Shen[3], and Michael Herrmann[4]

[1] Betriebliche Informationsysteme, Universität Leipzig, Germany
{aslam, auer}@informatik.uni-leipzig.de
[2] Computer and Information Science Department, University of Pennsylvania, USA
auer@seas.upenn.edu
[3] School of IT and CS, University of Wollongong, Australia
jshen@uow.edu.au
[4] DaimlerChrysler AG, Sindelfingen Germany
michael.hm.herrmann@daimlerchrysler.com

**Abstract.** BPEL4WS is a well-established business process standard that can be used to orchestrate service-based workflows. However, the rapid growth and automation demands of e-business and grid applications require BPEL4WS to provide enhanced semantic annotations to achieve the goal of business processes automation. Here, OWL-S (OWL for Web Services) is designed to represent such kind of semantic information. Furthermore, there exists a similarity in the conceptual model of OWL-S and BPEL4WS that can be employed to overcome the lack of semantics in BPEL4WS by mapping the BPEL4WS process model to the OWL-S suite of ontologies. The mapped OWL-S service can be used to increase flexibility and to automate BPEL based grid scenarios even further. This is achieved by dynamic discovery, composition and invocation of OWL-S services, for example within e-business and grid environments. Hence, the aim of this paper is to establish a mapping from the BPEL process model to the complete OWL-S suite of ontologies. We present a mapping strategy and a tool supporting this strategy. This allows the semantic annotation of workflows defined as BPEL4WS processes to enable the automation of a variety of e-business tasks.

## 1 Introduction

Combining Web Services and Grids is a promising way to leverage existing work in both business and scientific environments. BPEL4WS is a standard language to define workflows as a combination of Web Services interactions. BPEL4WS combines the power of graph oriented (WSFL) language and procedural workflow language (XLANG). Strong support for Web Services in BPEL makes it very attractive workflow language for the use in Grid environments. A BPEL workflow is a Web Services orchestration and can act itself as a Web Service. A BPEL process seen as a Web Service can be combined with other Web Services to create new ones. But such an interaction and combination of a BPEL process with other Web Services has the same syntactical limitations as the syntax of the base Web Services. With such syntactical limitations, processes defined by using a workflow language (e.g. BPEL4WS) cannot be automated to meet the demands of rapidly growing e-business world.

J. Eder, S. Dustdar et al. (Eds.): BPM 2006 Workshops, LNCS 4103, pp. 400–415, 2006.
© Springer-Verlag Berlin Heidelberg 2006

We consider a B2B interaction in which two business partners have defined their business processes as BPEL processes. Integrating these processes to perform some complex business task requires prior agreements between both business partners. But such kind of manual discovery of compeers and making prior agreements between them is not an efficient and flexible approach for the automation and integration of BPEL processes. Even exporting such a workflow, as a Web Service is not enough for the purpose of automation of BPEL based Grid service scenarios. Mapping a business process (BPEL process) to an OWL-S service description will support business process automation by enabling semantic base discovery, invocation and composition by semantic enabled systems.

In this paper we present a mapping strategy to map BPEL processes to the OWL-S ontology and its prototypical implementation as a tool[1] (BPEL4WS2OWL-S Mapping Tool) that can be used to map BEPL4WS processes to the complete OWL-S suite of ontologies. Our work is an extension and improvement to work by CICEC Lab [8] that has the following drawbacks:

- Atomic processes are not supported according to OWL-S specifications.
- Atomic processes cannot be invoked and executed in resulting OWL-S service.
- Complex message types are not supported.
- No data binding is supported between atomic processes.
- Data flow between atomic processes is defined in separate OWL file, which is not according to OWL-S specifications.
- Mapping does not support the OWL-S specification.
- *Profile* and *Grounding* ontologies are not supported.

Since, *Profile* ontology is not supported by [8], therefore, mapped OWL-S *Process Model* ontology cannot describe its capabilities so that it can be discovered on the basis of matching semantics. Also, unavailability of *Grounding* ontology results in communication restrictions with other semantic enabled services. [8] Supports only mapping from BPEL process model to OWL-S *Process Model* ontology and this mapping also have many drawbacks and limitations as discussed above. Therefore, work by CICEC Lab (Jun Shen and Yun Yang) needs to be enhanced and improved to support more consistent mapping to *Process Model* ontology. Also, such a mapping will have real world effects if mapping from BPEL process model to complete OWL-S suite of ontologies (*Profile, Process Model* and *Grounding*) will be supported.

Our work is an effort to achieve more consistent mapping, resulting in full OWL-S suite of ontologies (*Profile, Process Model* and *Grounding* ontologies). Our work supports complex message types to create more consistent data flow. WSDL operations are mapped to OWL-S *atomic processes* (with *Profile, Process Model* and *Grounding*). Data flow between *atomic processes* is supported and the mapped OWL file has the complete OWL-S suite of ontologies (*Profile, Process Model* and *Grounding*). Also, atomic processes are grounded with real WSDL services so that they can be invoked and executed on network.

The remaining paper is organized as follows: In section 2 we discuss some important concepts, concerning the relevant technologies (i.e. BPEL, OWL-S) and

---

[1]  http://bpel4ws2owls.sourceforge.net/

some introductory sentences about the OWL-S API being an important part of mapping implementation. In section 3 we discuss the mapping specifications (for mapping BPEL4WS process model to OWL-S suite of ontologies) and mapping of BPEL process model to OWL-S *Process Model* ontology. Section 4 describes how *Profile* and *Grounding* ontologies are created during mapping process. Section 5 descries the architecture and user interface of our mapping tool. In section 6 we discuss the limitations of our work. Section 7 discusses the related work and sections 8 draw the conclusion of our work and discuss the future plans.

## 2 Background

### 2.1 BPEL4WS

Different workflow languages (e.g. WSFL [9], MS XLANG [10] and BPEL4WS [2]) were developed to bring the use of Web Services to a higher level by composing them together to perform complex business tasks that a single Web Service cannot perform. Among these languages BPEL got more attraction of the community for modeling business processes as a composition of Web Services. A BPEL process is modeled by using BPEL *primitive and structured activities*. Figure 1 gives an overview of BPEL activities. Figure 1 shows that BPEL has two kinds of activities *basic* or *primitive activities* and *structured activities*. *Primitive activities* (e.g. *invoke, receive* and *reply*) are used to model interaction between business partners, where as workflow in a BPEL process model is modeled by using the *structured activities* (e.g. *sequence, flow* etc.) BPEL *primitive activities* can be nested in *structured activities* according to requirements (e.g. *sequence* activity can be used to perform sub activities in a sequence). *Flow* activity can be used to perform sub-activities concurrently and to synchronize sub-activities. Key components of a BPEL process model are partners, which associate a Web Service defined in an accompanying WSDL document with a particular role and variables. Variables contain the messages passed between partners and correspond to message in accompanying WSDL documents [11]. But effective dynamic service binding cannot be performed by solely matching WSDL messaging interfaces.

| BPEL4WS Activities | |
|---|---|
| Primitive Activities | Structured Activities |
| • Receive<br>• Send<br>• Invoke | • Sequence<br>• Flow<br>• Switch<br>• While<br>• etc. |

**Fig. 1.** BPEL4WS activities table

Since, expressiveness of WSDL service behavior is restricted to interaction specifications and BPEL uses WSDL portType as service information, therefore, BPEL inherits the limitations of WSDL. Furthermore, BPEL cannot express the inheritance and relationships among the Web Services. It cannot provide well-defined semantics for automated composition and execution. Moreover, these languages are based on XML in essence; they are limited in semantic descriptions without enough ontology support [12].

## 2.2 OWL-S

Towards ultimate goal of seamless interaction among networked programs and devices, industry has developed orchestration and process modeling languages such as WSFL [9], MS XLANG [10] and recently BPEL4WS [2]. Unfortunately, lack of support for semantically enriched information in these modeling languages leaves us a long way from seamless interoperation. Researchers in the Semantic Web community have taken up this challenge proposing top-down approaches to achieve aspects of Web Service interoperation [11]. OWL-S, OWL ontology for Web Services, is developed to provide Web Services semantics and consists of three types of knowledge: *Profile, Process Model* and *Grounding*.

*Profile* provides semantically enriched information about capabilities of a service and what a service is doing. *Profile* specifies *inputs* required by a service and *outputs* generated by a service, pre-conditions that need to be true for using the service and effects that service produce in surrounding world after its execution.

Rather than a program that can be executed, a *Process Model* is specification of ways a client may interact with a service. A *Process Model* can have one or more *simple, atomic* and *composite processes*. An *atomic process* is a description of a service that can be executed in single step and expects a message as an input and may return a message in response as an output. A *composite process* maintains the state of the process. A *composite process* may consist of sub *composite* or *atomic processes*. *Simple processes* are non-invoke able processes and have no grounding, but like *atomic processes* they can be executed in single step.

*Grounding* specifies how to access a service. Technical details, for example, communication protocols, message formats, port numbers used to contact the service, are specified in *Grounding*. Normally, the *Grounding* suffices to express how the components of a message are bundled (i.e. how inputs are put together to make a message to a service, and how replies are disassembled into the intended outputs) [3].

## 2.3 OWL-S API

OWL-S API provides a Java API for programmatic access to read, execute and write OWL-S service descriptions. The API provides an Execution Engine that can invoke *atomic processes* that have WSDL [4] or Universal Plug and Play Language (UPnP) [13] groundings, and *composite processes* that uses OWL-S control constructs (e.g. *Sequence, Split* etc.) [14]. OWL-S's exchange syntax is RDF/XML and many processors work with an RDF based model, in part, to facilitate the smooth integration of OWL-S service descriptions with other Semantic Web knowledge bases. However working with the RDF triples directly can be quite cumbersome and confusing and the OWL-S API was designed to help programmers to access and manipulate OWL-S service descriptions programmatically [14]. We have also implemented the use of OWL- S API in our tool to write the OWL-S services, for the BPEL process model, according to mapping specifications discussed in the next section.

## 3  Mapping Specifications

In this section we discuss the mapping from BPEL process to the OWL-S ontology. We also discuss the criteria used for mapping in areas where specifications of the BPEL and the OWL-S do not support direct mapping. For example *Assignment* activity in BPEL has no equivalent control construct in OWL-S so that it can be directly translated to OWL-S control construct.

### 3.1  Overview

Figure 2 gives an overview of mapping specifications. Figure 2 shows that BPEL *primitive activities* are mapped to OWL-S *Perform* control constructs. If a *primitive activity* is an I/O activity (used to create the interface of the BPEL process) then this activity is used to create the *Profile* of the resulting OWL-S service. Also, figure 2 shows that BPEL *structured activities* are mapped to relevant OWL-S control constructs. On the basis of this mapping overview the next section describes the mapping of BPEL process model to OWL-S *Process Model* ontology in more detail.

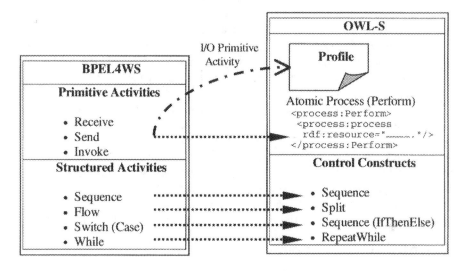

**Fig. 2.** Overview of mapping specifications

### 3.2  Mapping to OWL-S Process Model

OWL-S has three kinds of processes, *simple processes, atomic process* and *composite process.* Where as the BPEL have two kinds of processes, *abstract processes* and *executable processes. Abstract processes* provide means of synchronization with other processes at various level of granularity for the purpose of planning and reasoning [12]. *Simple processes* in OWL-S also play the same role as BPEL *abstract processes* by providing a level of abstraction. To keep the complexity of work within limitations, in the current version, synchronization between processes is not supported therefore, we restrict our self on the mapping of *executable processes* to *atomic* and *composite processes*.

### 3.2.1 Atomic Processes.

*Atomic process* corresponds to an action a service can perform in a single interaction and which can be executed in a single step by sending and receiving appropriate messages. Also, an atomic process has no sub-process.

BPEL process gives flow information of different activities in a business process. Where as, messages exchanged between partners, port types and partner links, expressing business partners and relation between partners are expressed in BPEL's corresponding WSDL file. A business process interacts with partner services through interfaces supported by corresponding Web Services. Operations supported by partner services (WSDL services) can be used to perform some specific task (supported by that Web Service operations) by sending them an input message and probably receiving some output message. Like an operation supported by a Web Service, an *atomic process* in OWL-S is a process that can perform some action in a single step. Therefore, partner Web Services (WSDL Services) are parsed and corresponding *atomic processes* (with *Profile, Process Model* and *Grounding*) are created for each supported operation. Each *atomic process* is grounded with real Web Service (WSDL service), so that it can be invoked in resulting OWL-S composite service to perform some specific task.

For more clarification consider the "Translation And Dictionary" process example (available with our tool). The example contains a BPEL file and relevant WSDL file and two WSDL services ("DictionaryService.wsdl" and "TranslatorService.wsdl", having operations "getMeaning" and "getTranslation" respectively). The figure 3 shows the partner link for the interacting Web Service in the BPEL's corresponding WSDL file.

```
<plnk:partnerLinkType name="Dictionary_Ser_PortType">
 <plnk:role name="portRole">
  <plnk:portType name="q1:DictionaryPortType" />
 </plnk:role>
</plnk:partnerLinkType>
```

**Fig. 3.** "Partner Link" in BPEL's corresponding WSDL file showing interaction with "Dictionary Service".

Figure below (fig. 4) shows supported operation "getMeaning" in the "DictionaryService.wsdl" file.

```
<wsdl:portType name="DictionaryPortType">
 <wsdl:operation name="getMeaning">
  <wsdl:input message="tns:DictionaryRequest" />
  <wsdl:output message="tns:DictionaryResponse" />
 </wsdl:operation>
</wsdl:portType>
```

**Fig. 4.** WSDL operation "getMeaning" will be mapped to OWL-S atomic process "getMeaningProcess".

So according to specifications, the tool creates *atomic process* "getMeaningProcess" for Web Service operation "getMeaning". Similarly all partner services (WSDL services) are parsed and *atomic processes* "OWL files" are created for each supported operation. Also, tool will not be able to create the *atomic process* for a Web Service operation, if the WSDL service would not be accessible on network.

**3.2.2    Primitive Activities and Atomic Processes.** OWL-S *Perform* control construct can be used to perform an *atomic process*. BPEL *primitive activities* (e.g. *receive, reply* and *invoke*) can be used to perform a Web Service operation by sending and receiving appropriate messages. Due to their logical matching behavior we map BPEL *primitive activities* to OWL-S *Perform* control constructs to perform relevant atomic processes. *Receive* activity is used to receive some message from some resource (e.g. from some Web Service). *Reply* activity is used to send a message in response to some *receive* activity. Where as the *invoke* activity represents combine behaviour of both *receive* and *reply* activities (i.e. it invoke a service by sending it an input message and then receive a message as an output of Web Service operation). Figure 5 shows *invoke* activity statement in a BPEL process.

```
<invoke partnerLink="Dictionary_Ser_Port"
        portType="q3:DictionaryPortType"
        operation="getMeaning"
        inputVariable= "Message_1_To_Dic_Service"
        outputVariable= "Message_1_From_Dic_Service"/>
```

**Fig. 5.** Invoke activity sending and receiving message from"Dictionary Service"

Figure 5 shows an *invoke* activity statement which sends an input message "Message_1_To_Dic_Service" to perform "getMeaning" operation and receives a message "Message_1_From_Dic_Service" as a response of "getMeaning" operation. Like OWL-S *atomic processes*, the BPEL *primitive activities* can be used to perform some specific operation in a single step and they have no sub activity to be performed. We map these BPEL *primitive activities* to OWL-S *Perform* control constructs (as shown in figure 6).

```
<process:Perform>
<process:process df:resource="http://examples.org/DummyURI.owl
    #getMeaningProcess"/>
</process:Perform>
```

**Fig. 6.** OWL-S Perform control construct to perform atomic process "getMeaningProcess"

Where as, the "getMeaningProcess" is *atomic process* that can be performed in single step and is supported by the "getMeaning.owl" file created in section 3.2.1.

**3.2.3    Structured Activities and Composite Processes.** *Structured Activities* in a BPEL process model describe the order in which set of the child *primitive* or *structured activities* is performed. For example *structured activity* (*sequence*) describes that the child *primitive* or *structured activities* within a *sequence* activity are performed in a sequence. Similar to BPEL *structured activity (sequence)*, the OWL-S has *Sequence* control construct, which is used to perform the child *atomic* or *composite processes* in a sequence. Due to their logical matching behavior, BPEL *structured activities* are mapped to OWL-S control constructs with in an OWL-S *composite process*.

A *composite process* is not a behavior a service will do, but a behavior (or set of behaviors) the client can perform by sending and receiving a series of messages [3]. A *composite process* may consist of sub *atomic* or *composite processes*. Like BPEL *structured activities*, the OWL-S uses its control constructs to define control flow between sub *atomic* and *composite processes*.

Let us consider the example below (taken from "Translation And Dictionary" example available with our tool), describing that *structured* activity *(sequence)* has two sub *primitive activities* that can be performed in a sequence with in a BPEL process model.

```
<sequence>
..........................
    <invoke partnerLink="To_Translation_Service_Port_1"
        portType="q2:TranslatorPortType"
        operation="getTranslation"
        inputVariable="Message1_To_Translation_Service"
        outputVariable="Message1_From_Translation_Service"/>
..........................

..........................
    <invoke partnerLink="Dictionary_Ser_Port"
        portType="q3:DictionaryPortType"
        operation="getMeaning"
        inputVariable="Message_1_To_Dic_Service"
        outputVariable="Message_1_From_Dic_Service" />
..........................
</sequence>
```

**Fig. 7.** Sequence activity having child primitive activities (invoke)

Figure 8 shows the OWL-S control construct *Sequence* as a result of mapping of BPEL *structured activity (sequence)*. Figure 8 shows that *Sequence* control construct has two *atomic processes* (i.e. "getTranslationProcess" and "getMeaningProcess") that can be performed in a sequence. Where two *Perform* control construct statements are result of mapping of two *invoke* activities with in BPEL *sequence* activity (as discussed in section 3.2.2).

*Flow* activity in BPEL is used to create concurrency and synchronization between sub-activities and has an equivalent OWL-S control construct *Split*. In OWL-S, *Split* control construct is used for concurrent execution of process components and *Split-Join* control construct is used to define processes that have partial synchronization. But in current version we have implemented the mapping of *flow* activity to *Split* control construct and synchronization between process components is not yet supported.

*Switch, structured activity* supports conditional behavior. A conditional branch is defined by the *case* element, which can have optional *otherwise* branch. The BPEL *switch* activity is mapped to OWL-S sequence *(Sequence)* of *If-Then-Else* control constructs. Where each *case* element is mapped to an *If-Then-Else* control construct

```
<process:CompositeProcess
        rdf:about="http://www.BPEL2OWLS.org/ChangeTestURI.owl#TestProcess">
<process:composedOf>
 <process:Sequence>
  <process:components>
   <process:ControlConstructList>
    <list:first>
     <process:Perform>
      <process:process
              rdf:resource="http://examples.org/DummyURI.owl#getTranslationProcess"/>
     </process:Perform>
         ............

         ............
      <process:ControlConstructList>
        <list:first>
         <process:Perform>
          <process:process
                  rdf:resource="http://examples.org/DummyURI.owl#getMeaningProcess"/>
         </process:Perform>
        </list:first>
         ............

         ............
      </process:ControlConstructList>
     </list:rest>
    </process:ControlConstructList>
   </process:components>
  </process:Sequence>
 </process:composedOf>
</process:CompositeProcess>
```

**Fig. 8.** OWL-S sequence control construct statement

and *otherwise* part of the *case* statement is mapped to *Else* part of *If-Then-Else* control construct. Figure below (figure 9) shows the BPEL *switch* activity having a *case* element and *case* condition statement.

```
<switch name="Solvency_Switch">
 <case condition="bpws:getVariableData('status', 'status', '//type')=3">
  <sequence name="Solvency_Sequence">
      ........ ..
  </sequence>
 </case>
</switch>
```

**Fig. 9.** BPEL switch activity statement

Figure 10 shows the mapping of the BPEL *switch* activity to the OWL-S sequence of *If-Then-Else* control constructs.

```
<process:Sequence>
 <process:components>
  <process:ControlConstructList>
   <list:first>
    <process:If-Then-Else>
     <process:then>
      <process:Sequence>
          ...........................

          ...........................
      </process:Sequence>
     </process:then>
       ...........................

       ...........................
    </process:If-Then-Else>
   </list:first>
  </process:ControlConstructList>
 </process:components>
</process:Sequence>
```

**Fig. 10.** Mapping of "switch" activity to OWL-S sequence (Sequence) of If-Then-Else control constructs

Also, the *while* activity in BPEL is mapped to the *Repeat-While* control construct in OWL-S, to repeatedly perform a specific process.

**Conditions:** mapping for condition statements is not fully supported in this version. Also, there exist no appropriate way to map the statement part "bpws:getVariableData(... " to OWL-S, that's why in this version automatic mapping of condition is not fully supported. But information about the condition statement can be found in OWL-S process ontology (e.g. in "Demo.owl" file, in case of our Demo example project). This condition statement can be used to manually create the *SWRL* expressions for conditions in OWL-S.

### 3.3   Data Flow

According to the BPEL and the OWL-S specifications there are no logically equivalent activities in BPEL and OWL-S for direct mapping of the *Assignment* activity, which can be used to define data flow between process components in the OWL-S *composite process*. Therefore, here, we discuss the criteria we have implemented for defining data flow between *atomic processes* within a *composite process*.

The BPEL *Assignment* activity can be used to assign an output message or message part of a *primitive activity*, as an input message or message part of other *primitive activity*. According to mapping specifications, *invoke* activities before and after *Assignment* activity are mapped to the OWL-S *Perform* control constructs (as discussed in section 3.2.2) and message and message parts in the *from* and *to* part of *Assignment activity* are used to create the data flow between these *atomic processes*. Figure 11 gives a simplified view of criteria we used to create data flow. Figure 11 shows that *primitive activities* (performing operations "Operation1" and "Operation 2" respectively) before and after *Assignment* activity are mapped to *atomic processes* ("Atomic Process 1" and "Atomic Process 2" respectively) and message and message parts of these activities used in *Assignment* activity are mapped to data flow statements in OWL-S by using *<Process:hasDataFrom>* and *<Process:InputBinding>* constructs.

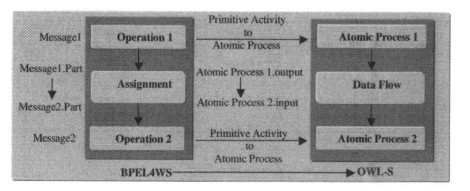

**Fig. 11.** Mapping of Assignment activity to create data flow between process components

## 4 Profile and Grounding Ontologies

In above section we have discussed in detail, how a BPEL process model is mapped to OWL-S *Process Model* ontology. This section describes how *Profile* and *Grounding* ontologies are created during the whole mapping process.

### 4.1 Profile

A BPEL process can have multiple interfaces as *receive, reply* or *invoke* activities. These activities can have input/output messages, which are defined in the BPEL's corresponding WSDL file. Such activities can be used to receive and send a message as an input and output of a BPEL process. Therefore, among these multiple input and output *primitive activity* options, message variable of the first *receive primitive activity* that receives a message from the outer world is selected to define the input of the OWL-S *composite process*. Message parts of this message variable are defined as input parameters of the resulting *Profile* ontology and these input parameters are annotated with dummy ontological concepts to define semantics of resulting OWL-S service. If a *receive* activity has corresponding *reply* activity then message variable of this *reply* activity is used to set the output of the OWL-S *composite process*. If a *receive* activity don't has corresponding *reply* activity then first *primitive activity* (i.e. first *invoke* activity) sending some message to the outer world (working as an interface of BPEL process) is taken as an output activity to define the output of the OWL-S *composite process*. Message variable of this activity is used to define the output parameters in the *Profile* ontology of resulting OWL-S service and theses output parameters are also annotated with dummy ontological concepts to provide semantics of mapped BPEL process as OWL-S service. End user of the mapping tool needs to replace these URIs of dummy ontological concepts with their domain ontologies.

A *primitive activity* is declared as an Input/Output (I/O) activity if its port type and operation is supported by the BPEL's corresponding WSDL file. Even though, OWL-S specifications support multiple instances of *Profile* ontology for one instance of *Process Model* ontology but tool create one instance of *Profile* ontology for one instance of *Process Model* ontology. Therefore, in case, if a BPEL process has more

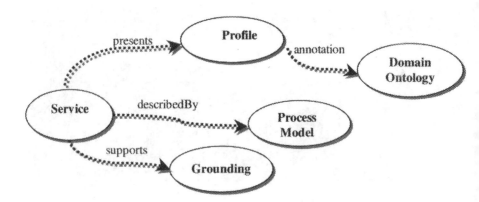

**Fig. 12.** Annotating input/output parameters in Profile ontology with domain ontology

than one I/O *primitive activities* (which create the interface of BPEL process) then only one instance of *Profile* ontology is created according to above discussed specifications.

## 4.2 Grounding

*Grounding* of a service specifies details about how to access a service. In case of our mapped OWL-S service, *Grounding* of OWL-S composite service specifies the address of the grounding of each *atomic process* (as shown in fig. 13). Also, concrete messages are specified explicitly in *Grounding*. Of course, it is not possible to automatically define the XSL Transformation [15] for complex messages. Web Services Description Language (WSDL) service, being XML format for describing network services is referred in *Grounding* of each *atomic process* to have access to the original implementation of WSDL service.

```
<grounding:WsdlGrounding
          rdf:about="http://www.BPEL2OWLS.org/ChangeTestURI.owl#TestGrounding">
  <grounding:hasAtomicProcessGrounding
          rdf:resource="http://examples.org/DummyURI/getMeaning.owl#
          getMeaningAtomicProcessGrounding"/>
  <grounding:hasAtomicProcessGrounding
          rdf:resource="http://examples.org/DummyURI/getTranslation.owl#
          getTranslationAtomicProcessGrounding"/>
</grounding:WsdlGrounding>
```

**Fig. 13.** Service Grounding for "Translation And Dictionary" example

In figure 13 "getMeaningAtomicProcessGrounding" and "getTranslationAtomic-ProcessGrounding" are groundings for "getMeaningProcess" and "getTranslation-Process" defined in "getMeaning.owl" and "getTranslation.owl" created in section 3.2.1.

# 5   BPEL4WS2OWL-S Mapping Tool

In this section we describe the internal architecture of the tool and its user interface. Figure 14 gives a simplified view of the architecture of the tool and shows that tool consists of three major components (i.e. WSDL Parser, BPEL Parser and OWL-S Mapper which uses the OWL-S API).

Function of the WSDL Parser is to parse each of the Web Services (WSDL files) taking part in BPEL process composition and to transfer information about Web Service operations to the OWL-S Mapper. The OWL-S Mapper creates an OWL-S *atomic process* (with *Profile, Process Model* and *Grounding* ontologies) for each Web Service operation. The mapped OWL-S *atomic processes* are stored in a separate OWL file and saved in project atomic processes directory. Then BPEL Parser is activated which parses the BPEL process model file. BPEL *primitive activities* with in a BPEL process model that are used to perform a Web Service operation, are transferred to OWL-S Mapper with information about Web Service operation performed by that *primitive activity*. The OWL-S Mapper maps these *primitive activities* to OWL-S *Perform* control construct statements that are used to perform the relevant *atomic processes*. Where as, OWL-S Mapper has already created and saved the *atomic process* that an OWL-S *Perform* control construct has to perform. Also, BPEL Parser transfers each BPEL *structured activity* to OWL-S Mapper, which maps the BPEL *structured activity* to relevant OWL-S control construct within the OWL-S *composite process*. Notice that the BPEL Parser takes care for *primitive activities,* which are working as an interface of the BPEL process model. The OWL-S Mapper uses message parts of these activities to create the input/output parameters of *Profile* ontology of resulting OWL-S service (as discussed in section 4.1).

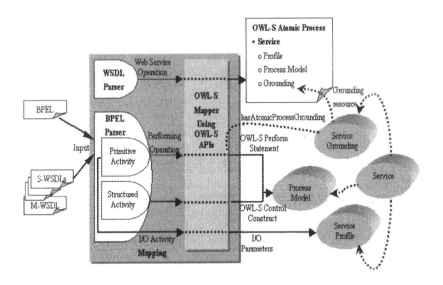

**Fig. 14.** Architecture of BPEL4WS2OWL-S Mapping Tool

The "BPEL4WS2OWL-S mapping tool" provides an easy to use interface (fig.15) employing menus and buttons to perform the mapping process. The mapping process includes creating a new project, adding input BPEL and WSDL files, validating the

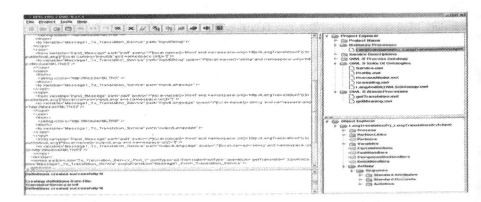

**Fig. 15.** An overview of BPEL4WS2OWL-S mapping tool

input files, building the project (to create object view of input files) and finally mapping the project. The resulting OWL-S ontology files can be viewed in the project explorer (upper right window) and the contents of these files can be seen in upper left window of the tool. The lower left window acts as an output window to see the output of different mapping actions. The lower right window is an object explorer, which gives an object view of the input files.

# 6 Limitations

Here, we describe the limitation of our work in two phrases: one is the OWL-S specifications limitation and other is the mapping implementation. OWL-S is not as mature as BPEL, for example, equivalent of BPEL activities like *Assignment, Fault Handler, Terminate* etc. are not available in OWL-S for direct mapping from BPEL to OWL-S. Information about pre and post-conditions is not described in BPEL so that it can be used in automatic mapping. Input and output parameters in the resulting *Profile* ontology need to be annotated with real world domain ontologies by the end user. Second phrase is about limitations of mapping implementation. For example, synchronization between process components is not supported. Conditions are partially supported. These are the areas where mapping implementation can be improved with further research and development to create more consistent mapping.

Therefore, mapping support in our tool is limited in above discussed areas and needs to further improvements in our tool to produce more consistent mapping. Also, tool needs to be continuously updated with coming versions of related technologies.

# 7 Related Work

In this paper, we have presented an approach to map syntax based Web Services composition (BPEL process model) to Semantic Web Services composition (OWL-S composite service). Our work supports the mapping of the BPEL process model to the complete OWL-S suite of ontologies. The resulting OWL-S service can be used for dynamic discovery, invocation and composition by semantic enabled systems.

As discussed before that [8] presents an initial kind of mapping to map BPEL process to OWL-S *Process* ontology (with above discussed limitations) to facilitate p2p based service flow system. WSDL2DAML-S [17] (updated to WSDL2OWL-S) presents an approach to add semantics to Web Services by translating Web Service operation to OWL-S ontology. WSDL2OWL-S partially supports the translation to *Process Model* and *Profile* ontologies because Web Services technology (WSDL) do not provide all information that is needed for complete WSDL to OWL-S translation. There have also been other efforts to add semantics to different technologies. WSDL-S [16] is an effort by LSDIS Labs to add semantics to WSDL. WSDL-S's approach is to enhance WSDL tags to add semantics (by annotating them with domain ontologies) to Web Services rather than to define a separate ontology to describe Web Services semantically. WSDL-S also adds new tags to WSDL specifications to support pre and post conditions. [11] Presents an approach to enhance dynamic discovery and composition of semantically enriched Web Services with in a BPEL process model. [11] Propose, rather than to bind a service in a BPEL process at design time, user should define semantic requirements of a required service with in a BPEL process. Our work is a more consistent effort to add semantics to BPEL process model by mapping it to OWL-S composite service in which each Web Service operation is an OWL-S *atomic process*.

# 8   Conclusion and Future Work

As discussed above that end user needs to develop the domain ontologies and to change the *Profile* ontology of resulting OWL-S service by annotating input/output parameters with these domain ontologies. Therefore, a tool is needed that can be used to develop domain ontologies and an editor which can be used to edit the resulting OWL-S ontology (*Profile* ontology) with these domain ontologies. Once completed, the resulting OWL-S service can provide richer business process semantics in the form of OWL-S ontology for flexible integration and automation of workflows in peer-2-peer workflow systems and in Data Grid applications. For example the approach discussed in [11] can be used to dynamically discover, invoke and compose theses Semantic Web Services to complete a process. Also resulting OWL-S ontology can be edited to create more complex Semantic Web Services by composing different atomic and composite services together.

"Protégé" with its plug-in "OWL-S Editor" is an ideal framework to develop domain ontologies and to edit resulting OWL-S service with these domain ontologies. "Protégé" is an ontology development tool and "OWL-S Editor" is an editor, which can be used to visually develop and edit OWL-S services. "OWL-S Editor" is available as a plug-in for "Protégé". We are working to produce more consistent mapping from BPEL to OWL-S to overcome the above-discussed limitations of our work. We are also working to improve our tool as a "BPEL4WS2OWL-S import plug-in" for "Protégé" and "OWL-S Editor", so that the mapped OWL-S services can be directly imported in "OWL-S Editor" for editing.

# References

1. WISEINFO: [online] Available http://wiseinfo.info/web-service.htm
2. Business Process Execution Language for Web Services Version 1.1. 5th May 2003. [online] Available ftp://www6.software.ibm.com/software/developer/library/ws-bpel.pdf.
3. OWL-S: Semantic Markup for Web Services. [online] Available http://www.daml.org/services/owl-s/1.1/overview/.
4. Web Services Description Language (WSDL) 1.1. [online] Available http://www.w3.org/TR/wsdl.
5. UDDI Version 3.0.2: UDDI Specifications Technical Committee Draft, Dated 20041019. [online] Available http://www.uddi.org/specification.html
6. A First Overview of BPEL4WS. January 25, 2.005. [online] Available http://jroller.com/page/coreteam /Weblog?catname=%2FWorkflow
7. OWL-S' Relationship to Selected Other Technologies [online] Available http://www.daml.org/services /owl-s/1.1/related.html.
8. J. Shen, Y. Yang, C. Zhu and C. Wan. "From BPEL4WS to OWL-S: Integrating E-Business Process Descriptions", Proc. of 2nd IEEE International Conference on Services Computing (SCC 2005), pp.181-188, Orlando, USA, July 2005.

9. Frank Leymann. Web Services Flow Language (WSFL 1.0) May 2001. [online] Available http://www-306.ibm.com/software/solutions/webservices/pdf/WSFL.pdf.
10. UDDI Version 3.0.2: UDDI Specifications Technical Committee Draft, Dated 20041019. [online] Available http://www.uddi.org/specification.html
11. Daniel J. Mandell and Sheila A. McIlraith: Adapting BPEL4WS for the Semantic Web: The Bottom-Up Approach to Web Service Interoperation. Proceedings of the Second International Semantic Web Conference 2003.
12. Jun Shen, Yun Yang, Jun Yan, A P2P based Service Flow System with Advanced Ontology Profiles, accepted by International Journal of Advanced Engineering Informatics.
13. http://upnp.org/
14. Evren Sirin: OWL-S API. [Project Home Page] Available http://www.mindswap.org/2004/owl-s/api/.
15. XSL Transformations (XSLT) : [online] Available http://www.w3.org/TR/xslt.
16. R. Akkiraju, J. Farell, J.A. Miller, M. Nagarajan, A. Sheth and K. Verma : "Web Service Semantics – WSDL-S" [online] Available http://www.w3.org/2005/04/FSWS/Submissions/17/WSDL-S.htm.
17. M. Paolucci, N. Srinivasan, K. Sycara, and T. Nishimura, "Toward a Semantic Choreography of Web Services: From WSDL to DAML-S" In Proceedings of the First International Conference on Web Services (ICWS'03), Las Vegas, Nevada, USA, June 2003, pp 22-26.

# Combining *i\** and BPMN for
# Business Process Model Lifecycle Management

George Koliadis, Aleksandar Vranesevic, Moshiur Bhuiyan,
Aneesh Krishna, and Aditya Ghose

School of Information Technology and Computer Science (SITACS),
University of Wollongong (UOW), NSW 2522, Australia
{gk56, av85, mmrb95, aneesh, aditya}@uow.edu.au

**Abstract.** The premise behind 'third wave' Business Process Management (BPM[1]) is effective support for change at levels. Business Process Modeling (BPM[2]) notations such as BPMN are used to effectively *conceptualize* and *communicate* process configurations to relevant stakeholders. In this paper we argue that the management of change throughout the business process model lifecycle requires greater conceptual support achieved via a combination of complementary notations. As such the focus in this paper is on the co-evolution of operational (BPMN) and organizational (*i\**) models. Our intent is to provide a way of expressing changes, which arise in one model, effectively in the other model. We present constrained development methodologies capable of guiding an analyst when reflecting changes from an *i\** model to a BPMN model and vice-versa.

## 1 Introduction

Business process models play a key role in both organizational management [1] [2] and enterprise information systems development [3]. Many notations developed for the task of modeling business processes, have their own focus of *application* and appropriate *audience* [4] [5] [6] [7] [8]. High-level conceptual models provide an understanding of an organization from an intentional and social perspective [9] for reasoning support during redesign [9]. In comparison, lower-level technical models are especially suited for applications in the description, execution and simulation of business processes [8].

Business process development should be based on principled high-level models of the enterprise and the business context. Commonly, processes are formulated in an ad-hoc fashion without reference to these high-level models. Some of the most prominent modeling notations enlisted are focused towards technically-oriented data, and process modeling notations such as ER, Data-Flow, Systems Flowcharting and UML and workflow modeling [10]. In this work, we offer constrained development methodologies to guide development of process models from higher-level conceptual models. This supports life-cycle management in the following sense: when changes occur to the high-level model, these can be reflected in the process model, and vice-versa. In this paper, Section 2 provides a background to business process modeling

J. Eder, S. Dustdar et al. (Eds.): BPM 2006 Workshops, LNCS 4103, pp. 416–427, 2006.

with an overview of our chosen notations. Section 3 illustrates concepts/methods provided in our methodologies (with examples). The paper is concluded in Section 4.

## 2   Background

The notations used for modeling business processes have been categorized in many works, based on their conceptual features [4] [5] [6] [7] [8]. The common principle recognized in all analyses is that some notations are more suited towards specific *audiences* (i.e. with either technical/non-technical backgrounds) or *applications* (i.e. possibly for description, re-design or execution) throughout the business process lifecycle. Many notations focus on specific aspects, with limited relation/traceability to other important business process aspects. This has brought about the need for an enterprise view [6] to support the development and maintenance of rich models that provide an enhanced ability to *conceptualize, communicate* and *understand* business processes, and their context of operation.

   In related work, some preliminary ideas in [11] have been proposed for developing a BPMN model given the existence, and agreement to, an *i** model of the process. Six steps are provided for mapping between constructs, with no consideration for reflecting change and consistency made. Also, an approach for deriving a BPMN model from a business model is proposed in [12], achieved through the intermediate translation of the business model into an activity dependency model that can then be translated into a business process model. In this work, we provide a simpler approach aimed at reducing added complexity and/or misinterpretations during modeling. Furthermore, much work has been completed on supporting guided translation and co-evolution of *i** into various other behavioral modeling notations and languages [13] [14] [15]. The primary aim in these approaches is to further develop detailed design artifacts that can lead onto implemented systems, or directly be used in the configuration of agent-based systems. However, our primary focus is on modeling lifecycle support during BPM[1] projects whereby the concern is for the development and/or assessment of detailed business process designs. The work in this paper extends previous work in [16]. In comparison to previous work, we take the following approach to lifecycle management: when changes to a business process model (i.e. BPMN – [17]) occur, these changes must ensure some notion of consistency with a higher-level enterprise model, and vice versa. In this instance, an *i** model [9].

### 2.1   Agent-Oriented Conceptual Modeling (AOCM) with *i**

*i** supports modeling rich organizational contexts by offering high-level social/anthropomorphic abstractions (such as goals, tasks, soft goals and dependencies) as modeling constructs for reasoning support during business process redesign [9] [7]. Figure 1 represents a simple *i** *Meeting Scheduling* model. The central concept in *i** is that of intentional actor. These can be seen in the Meeting Scheduling model as nodes representing the intentional/social relationships between three (3) actors required to schedule a meeting: a *Meeting Initiator* (MI); *Meeting Scheduler* (MS); and, *Meeting Participant* (MP).

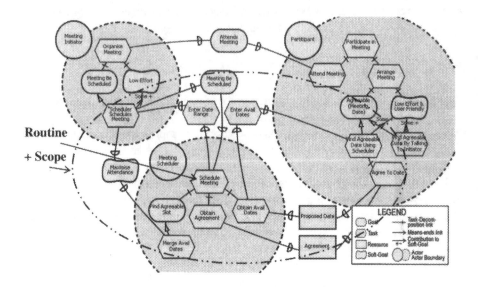

**Fig. 1.** An *i\** Strategic Rationale (SR) Meeting Scheduling Model with a Routine Illustrated

The *i\** framework consists of two modeling components [9] Strategic Dependency (SD), and Strategic Rationale (SR) models. The SD model consists of a set of nodes and links. Each node represents an actor, and each link between the two actors indicates that one actor depends on the other for something in order that the former may attain some goal. The depending actor is known as *depender*, while the actor depended upon is known as the *dependee*. Dependancies may involve *goals* to be achieved (e.g. *MeetingBeScheduled*), *tasks* to be performed (e.g. *EnterAvailDates*), *resources* to be furnished (e.g. Agreement), or *soft-goals* (optimization objectives or preferences) to be satisficed (e.g. *MaximizeAttendance*).

The SR mode further represents internal motivations and capabilities (i.e. processes or routines) accessible to specific actors that provide illustration of how dependencies can be met. In *i\**, a *routine* [9] specifies an intended course of action an actor may pursue given a set of alternatives. These elements and their relationships represent the strategic requirements of a business process when invoked in a specific context. For example, to *ScheduleMeeting* (illustrated in Figure 1 with its Scope) that includes three sub-tasks and six dependencies with two additional actors. Tasks in *i\** may be primitively workable whereby the actor responsible for the element believes that it can achieve its requirements at execution time – i.e. it is sufficiently reduced during decomposition. In comparison to BPMN however, a primitively workable element may still be represented as a sub-process as the term does not imply a 'primitively executable action' (i.e. application of analyst / designer discretion). Furthermore, for a routine to be workable, all involved actors must be committed to satisfying their dependencies [9].

The Tropos project [18] aims to provide methodological support for advancing the *i\** framework further towards architectural and detailed design where dynamic / behavioral aspects are of importance. Specifically, Formal Tropos (FT) – see [19], is a part of the Tropos project that provides a specification language for modeling dynamic aspects of an *i*\* model via formal annotation of *Creation* and *Fulfillment* conditions. These conditions are specified using first-order typed linear temporal logic and prescribe the constraints on an elements lifecycle. In this work, we take the same approach to annotation (with the use of fulfillment conditions annotated to *i*\* models). In comparison, our work is illustrated via informal annotations.

## 2.2 Business Process Modeling with BPMN

The Business Process Modeling Notation (BPMN), developed by the Business Process Management Initiative (BPMI.org) [17] is primarily a technically-oriented business process modeling notation that supports the assignment of activity execution control to entities within an organization via 'swim-lanes'. BPMN has the capability to map directly to executable process languages including XPDL [20] and BPEL [17] [21]. Furthermore, an analysis of BPMN [22] also stated its high maturity in representing concepts required for modeling business process, apart from some limitations in terms of representing state, and the possible ambiguity of the swim-lane concept.

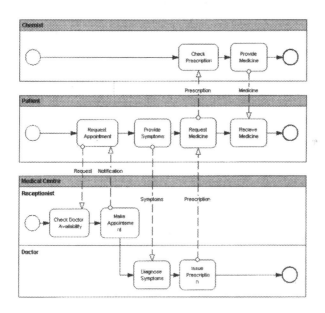

**Fig. 2.** A BPMN Patient Treatment Business Process Model

Figure 2 represents a simple BPMN Patient Treatment process. Processes are represented in BPMN using **flow nodes**: *events* (circles), *activities* (rounded boxes), and *decisions* (diamonds); **connecting objects**: *control flow links* (unbroken directed lines), and *message flow links* (broken directed lines); and **swim-lanes**: *pools* (high-level rectangular container), and *lanes* partitioning pools. These concepts are further discussed in [17].

# 3   Constrained Development Methodologies

We propose constrained development methodologies to guide the derivation or maintenance of one type of model given the availability of the other. The development is supported with the introduction of two concepts: *fulfillment conditions* (i.e. as in [19]) and *effect annotations*.

An *effect* is broadly defined as the result (i.e. product or outcome) of an activity being executed by some cause or agent. An *effect annotation* is a specific statement relating to the outcome of an activity, associated to a *state altering construct* in a given model. During BPM$^2$, effects are annotated to atomic tasks/activities or subprocesses within an actor's lane. The execution of a number of activities in succession results in a *cumulative effect* that includes the specific effects of each activity in the sequence. We also note the fact that certain effects can undo prior effects (i.e. in the case of compensatory activities). Effect annotations may possibly be formalized using the formal layers of some currently well-developed Goal-Oriented Requirements Engineering (GORE) methodologies [23] [19], however, we only state their applicability in this work, and aim towards possible integration in the future.

*Fulfillment conditions* are annotated to *tasks* and *goals* assigned to actors in an SR diagram, and *dependencies* (i.e. not including *soft-goals* as these are used during assessment of alternatives and describe non-functional properties to be addressed) in an *i\** model. A *fulfillment condition* [19] is a statement specifying the required conditions realized upon completion of a given task, goal or dependency. Fulfillment conditions recognize the required effects on a business process model. For example, a fulfillment condition for a task dependency to *EnterADateRange*, may be the *DateRangeCommunicated* effect (subsequently required by the task assigned to a dependee actor).

## 3.1   Annotation and Propagation

Tasks, goals and dependencies are annotated with fulfillment conditions in an *i\** model. Additionally, the tasks assigned to participants in a BPMN model are annotated with effects for assessment against fulfillment conditions.

Tasks associated to dependencies on the *dependee* side may require additional effects when related to a BPMN model. That is, the fulfillment conditions for a dependency may not be explicitly stated against the tasks. For example, the fulfillment condition for *ProposedDateProvided* (i.e. annotated to the *ProposedDate* resource dependency in Figure 1) will be propagated to the *ObtainAvailDate* task. This should occur during annotation, whenever a fulfillment condition is annotated to a *resource*, *goal* or *task* dependency.

Effect annotations in BPMN models are propagated via *trajectories*. A trajectory is a sequential execution of activities terminating at an end state that represents the operational goal of the process. Control flow links between events, activities, and gateways within a BPMN model indicate the flow of trajectories. Effects within a process are accumulated during forward traversal through a trajectory. This accumulation ensures that any compensatory activities, that may undo effects, are also taken into account during traversal.

### 3.1.1 Annotating the Meeting Scheduling Model (Figures 1 and 4)

**Table 1.** Annotation of Fullfillmnent Conditions to Respective Tasks/Dependancies

| Task/Dependency (Figure 1) | Fulfillment Conditions | Task Annotation (Post Development – Figure 4) |
|---|---|---|
| MI: SchedulerSchedules Meeting | DateRangeEnteredIntoScheduler; | 1; |
|  | DateRangeCommunicatedToScheduler | 1; |
| MS: ScheduleMeeting | AgreedDateKnownToInitiator | 4 |
| MS: ObtainAvailableDates | ProposedDateProvided; | 2 (message); |
|  | AvailableDatesObtained; | 2; |
|  | AvailableDatesStored; | 2; |
|  | AvailableDatesValidated | 2 |
| MS: ObtainAgreement | AgreementObtained; | 4; |
|  | AgreementRecorded | 4 |
| MS: MergeAvailableDates | AvailableDatesMerged | 3 |
| P: AgreeToDate | DateAgreedTo; AgreementProvided; | 6; 6 (message) |
| P: FindAgreeableDateUsing Scheduler | AvailDatesEnteredIntoScheduler; | 5; |
|  | AgreeableDateFoundUsingScheduler | 6 |
| MS-Dep->MI: EnterDateRange | DateRangeCommunicatedToScheduler | 1 |
| MI-Dep->MS: MeetingBeScheduled | AgreedDateKnownToInitiator | 4 |
| MS-Dep->P: EnterAvailDates | AvailDatesEnteredIntoScheduler | 5 |
| P-Dep->MS: ProposedDate | ProposedDateProvided | 2 |
| MS-Dep->P: Agreement | AgreementProvided | 6 (message) |

## 3.2 Scope Projection

In order to evaluate consistency between the two notations, we provide some rules for projecting the scope of the *i\** model. In the current case, *i\** models are likely to represent a broader scope in comparison to a specific BPMN model as they are applied to capture the greater organizational context. Scope projection is based on an identification of the business process (represented in BPMN) as a *routine* assigned to an actor in an *i\** model.

- *Rule 1:* The root node of the routine traceable to the process in consideration and all tasks in its first level of decomposition from are to be within scope.
- *Rule 2:* All dependencies that are associated to a task within the scope of the routine, where the actor in control of the routine (initiator) is the depender are within the scope of the process; as well as the tasks assigned to dependee actors.
- *Rule 3:* All dependencies that are associated to a task within the scope of the routine, where the intiator is the dependee are within the scope of the process iff the task assigned to the depender is part of some decomposition of a task in the scope of the process as per Rule 2; as well as the tasks assigned to the depender actors.

## 3.3 Consistency Evaluation

We introduce consistency rules to provide a mechanism for ensuring consistency between *i\** and BPMN models (developed with consideration to [19]).

- *Rule 1:* Every actor in an *i\** model required as a participant in the routine (traceable to the business process) and any of their tasks must be represented in the BPMN model (and vice versa), assessed via application of scope projection rules.
- *Rule 2:* There must exist a trajectory in the process model, whereby the operational objective (as encoded in the accumulated fulfillment conditions of traceable tasks) of the routine is achieved, and the sequence of activities is consistent with the requirements specified in the routine as further outlined below:
    - *Rule 2.1:* The accumulated effect of all tasks and goals traceable to the routine must achieve accumulated routine fulfillment conditions during forward traversal of at least one trajectory in the process model; AND,
    - *Rule 2.2:* The fulfillment of a task on the depender side of a dependency must not be realized before the fulfillment of the dependency upon accumulation of effects during forward traversal of the same trajectory.

### 3.4 Constrained Development of a Business Process Model Given a High-Level Conceptual Model

These steps are based on the aforementioned consistency rules aimed towards providing analyst guidance during initial model development.

- *Step 1: Identify internal and external actors in i\* diagram.*
- *Step 2: Map elements to equivalent constructs within the BPMN model.* See substeps below.
    - *Step 2.1: Map Participants.* The greater organization for which the *i\** model is represented is signified as a pool in BPMN. Any external participants are also represented as pools. Internal organizational actors are represented as lanes within the organizational pool.
    - *Step 2.2: Map Activities.* Tasks within *i\** are represented as either subprocesses or atomic activities within BPMN assigned to actors within pools and lanes.
- *Step 3: Sequence required tasks/sub-processes and introduce control and sequence flow links by analyzing fulfillment conditions.* Tasks placed within each pool or lane are now sequenced to conform to routine requirements by taking Consistency Rule 2 (see: Section 3.3) into consideration. This requires that tasks be sequenced using control flow links in a manner that results in a trajectory satisfying fulfillment conditions on an *i\** model. Control flow links are used to indicate realization of dependencies between actors within the same organization. In order to realize dependencies between organizational boundaries, a message flow link is used to represent the dependency going from the depender lane to the dependee lane. This may require single/multiple messages between tasks derived via analysis of fulfillment conditions.
- *Step 4: Elaborate on sub-processes.* The choice to introduce tasks or subprocesses into the BPMN diagram for specific tasks in the *i\** model is made in *Step 2.2.* The analyst can develop each sub-process guided by the list of required fulfillment conditions annotated to the *i\** task that the sub-process realizes.

Figure 3 illustrates the application of the constrained development methodology in the context of the Meeting Scheduling model represented in Figure 1, with annotations applied in Table 1. Much of the detail has been omitted for brevity. The following section describes a possible change requirement and its reflection within an *i** model for further analysis.

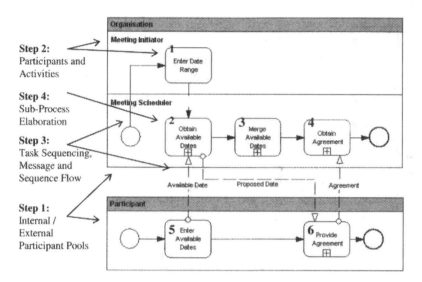

**Fig. 3.** BPMN Process Model derived using the Constrained Development Methodology

### 3.4.1 Reflecting Changes in an *i** Model to an Associated BPMN Model

The scope projection techniques are used to assess whether a change in an *i** model will impact a BPMN model. These guidelines aim to support the reflection of change between *i** and BPMN models for the specific instances of impacting change outlined below.

- *Step 1:* For each classification outlined below apply associated changes.
    - *Addition of an actor.* If a new actor has been added to the *i** model, a swimlane (i.e. for an internal actor) or pool (i.e. for an external actor) will need to be placed on the process model. Additionally, new dependencies must exist between the actor and existing actors (described below). These dependencies will be included for all new actors where the dependency is related to the routine and actor is the dependee. However, where the actor is the depender they will only be included if linked to a task in an existing dependency graph (see Scope Projection rules).
    - *Addition of a goal/task/resource dependency.* If a new dependency has been added to the *i** model, then this may require the addition of new activities/sub-processes and message flow links within the BPMN model (as described below).

- *Addition of a goal or task.* The addition of a goal or task will require the addition of a task within the BPMN model. The addition of these tasks must be scoped to their respective actors, and any dependencies must be realized via message-flow links where one of the actors is external to the organization.
- *Step 2:* Re-apply consistency rules to both models to assess whether consistency has been maintained.

Consider the following example applied to the *Meeting Scheduling* example in Figure 1 (*i\**) and Figure 3 (BPMN). A new requirement within in the form of a task dependency between the *Meeting Initiator* (i.e. the dependee) and the *Meeting Scheduler* (i.e. the depender) to *ProvideParticipantPrioritization*. Participant prioritization means that the *Meeting Initiator* must now prioritize the current list of participants in order for the *Meeting Scheduler* to *MergeAvailableDates* and *FindAnAgreeableSlot* effectively.

Given the application of our approach for guiding an analysts decision, it can be inferred that the effect for *ParticipantPrioritizationProvided* will propagate within the *i\** model as a fulfillment condition on the *SchedulerSchedulesMeetingTask*. Furthermore, given *Consistency Rule 3*, requires that *ParticipantPrioritizationProvided* occurs prior to the fulfillment of the *MergeAvailableDates* fulfillment conditions. This information can then be used to highlight the scope of change within the BPMN model to a point within a trajectory prior to the required effects of *MergeAvailableDates*, where an activity controlled by the initiator is able to realize the required effect.

### 3.5 Constrained Development of a High-Level Conceptual Model Given a Business Process Model

The following steps provide systematic guidance for developing an *i\** model given an already existing process model. Figure 5, illustrates the constrained development of the *Patient Treatment* BPMN model in Figure 2.

- *Step 1: Map elements to equivalent constructs within the i\* model.*
  - *Step 1.1: Map Participants.* Both pools and lanes in a BPMN model represent actors in an *i\** model. These can be directly translated into the model.
  - *Step 1.2: Map Activities.* Represent activities and sub-processes as 'primitively workable' tasks assigned to actors in *i\**.
- *Step 2. Apply intentional reasoning.*
  - *Step 2.1: Query the Intention of Tasks.* Intentional reasoning is applied to identify higher-level intentional elements and dependencies by querying the intention of tasks. This step aims to guide the further understanding and representation of an actors motivations.
  - *Step 2.2: Query the Intention of Flow-Links.* Analyze control and message flow between actor boundaries to identify goal, task and resource dependencies. These types of links can be used as a primary heuristic for identifying possible dependencies between actors.
- *Step 3: Identify soft-goal dependencies in the i\* model.* The representation of soft-goals (including dependencies) are not in the scope of the BPMN notation.

### 3.5.1  Reflecting Changes in a BPMN Model to an Associated *i** Model

These steps indicate how BPMN model change may be reflected in the *i** model:

- *Step 1:* For each classification of change, apply the following changes.
    - *Addition of a swimlane or pool.* If a swimlane or pool is added, then a new ac-
      tor will be required within the *i** model. This will include the addition of new
      dependencies and tasks within the *i** model. A primary heuristic for identifying
      dependencies includes message flow links and control flow links between pools
      and lanes (message flow ndicates a resource dependency for some information).
    - *Addition a task to an existing swimlane or pool.* If a new task is added to a
      swimlane or pool, this will require a task to be decomposed from the root node
      of the routine traceable to the current process.
- *Step 2:* Re-apply consistency rules assess whether maintenance.

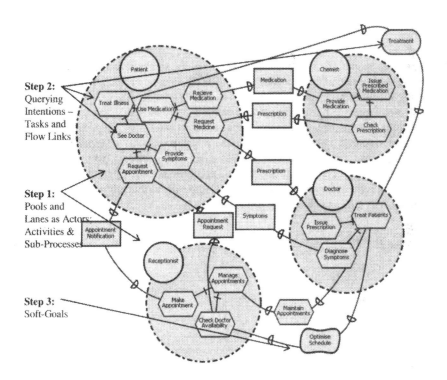

**Fig. 4.** An *i** 'Patient Treatment' Process

Consider now a scenario where the business process model is modified to improve
the performance of the *IssuePrescription* task which has been identified to be a major
operational bottleneck. The task is improved by including a task before hand which
checks the patient's previous medical history to identify previous prescriptions for the
patient for similar illnesses (e.g. common flu). We name the task *CheckPatientMedi-
calHistory*. Furthermore, the client is now encouraged to provide information on his

medical background, which we represent as a task named *ProvideMedicalHistoryInformation*. We now proceed to add an additional task within the bounds of the Doctor agent and an additional task within the bounds of the Patient agent.

As in the previous case we use intentional reasoning to identify that the added task, within the Doctor agent, contributes to the higher level task of *TreatingPatients*. We apply the same technique to justify the placement of the *ProvideMedicalHistoryInformation* task as a decomposition task under the *RequestMedicine* task.

The added message flow in the BPMN diagram is represented as a resource dependency between the Patient and the Doctor, where the Doctor requires the Patient to provide his previous medical history. We also introduce the soft-goal between the Patient and the Doctor, titled *TimelyDrugPrescription*, indicating the fact that the Doctor will try to improve the time required to prescribe medication to the Patient.

# 4   Conclusion

In this work, we have illustrated an initial approach for supporting the lifecycle of business process models with the complementary use of *i\** - a well developed notation for modeling organizational contexts, and BPMN – a newly developed notation for modeling business processes. The approach for reflecting changes in organizational context to changes in the design of business processes provides an effective mechanism for aligning business processes with organizational objectives. Similarly, operational improvements can be mapped back to organizational objectives to facilitate analysis and ensure no conflicts exist with existing objectives. Although these steps are preliminary we believe their systematic nature makes them available for automation in all phases, and are pursuing this task, through the development of a software tool, along with further refinement of the approach.

# References

1. Smith, H. Fingar, P.: Business Process Management – The Third Wave. Meghan-Kiffer Press, Tampa Florida (2003)
2. Hammer, M. Champy, J.: Reengineering the Corporation: A Manifesto for Business Revolution. HarperBusiness, (1993)
3. Dumas, M. Aalst, W. M. P. and Hofstede, A. H.: Process-Aware Information Systems: Bridging People and Software Through Process Technology. Wiley-Interscience (2005)
4. Bider, I. Johannesson, P.: Tutorial on: Modeling Dynamics of Business Processes – Key for Building Next Generation of Business Information Systems. In: The 21st International Conference on Conceptual Modeling (ER2002), Tampere, FL, October 7-11 (2002)
5. Kavakli, V. and Loucopoulos, P.: Goal-Driven Business Process Analysis - Application in Electricity Deregulation. In: Information Systems, 24(3) (1999) 187-207
6. Loucopoulos, P. and Kavakli, E.: Enterprise Modeling and the Teleological Approach to Requirements Engineering. In: International Journal of Intelligent and Cooperative Information Systems 4(1) (1995) 45-79
7. Katzenstein G. Lerch F. J.: Beneath the surface of organizational processes: a social representation framework for business process redesign. In: ACM Transactions on Information Systems (TOIS), 18(4) (2000) 383-422

8. Yu, E.: Models for Supporting the Redesign of Organizational Work. In: Proceedings, Conf. on Organizational Computing Systems (COOCS'95) Milpitas, California, USA, August 13-16 (1995) 225-236

9. Yu, E.: Modelling Strategic Relationships for Process Reengineering. PhD Thesis, Graduate Department of Computer Science, University of Toronto, Toronto, Canada (1995) ~124

10. Davies, I, Green, P. Rosemann, M. Gallo, S.: Conceptual Modelling – What and Why in Current Practice. In: Lecture Notes in Computer Science, Volume 3288 (2004) 30-42

11. Cysneiros, L.M. Yu, E. Addressing Agent Autonomy in Business Process Management - with Case Studies on the Patient Discharge Process. In: Proc. of the 2004 Information Resources Management Association Conference, New Orleans, May, (2004)

12. Andersson, B. Bergholtz, M. Edirisuriya, A. Ilayperuma, T. Johannesson, P.: A Declarative Foundation of Process Models. In: Lecture Notes in Computer Science, Volume 3520 (2005) 233–247

13. Krishna, A., Ghose, A. K., Vranesevic, A.: Agent-Oriented Conceptual Models to UML Sequence Diagrams via Effect Annotations. Special issue on Agent-Oriented Software Development Methodologies-International Journal of Multi-Agent and Grid Systems. In-press. (2006)

14. Dasgupta, A., Salim, F., Krishna, A., Ghose, A. K.: Hybrid Modelling using *i** and AgentSpeak (L) Agents in Agent-Oriented Software Engineering. To appear in: The Proceedings of 8th International Conference on Enterprise Information System (ICEIS-2006), Paphos, Cyprus, May 23-27 (2006)

15. Krishna, A., Guan, Y., Sambattheera, C., Ghose, A. K.: Agent-based Prototyping of Web-based Systems. To appear in: The Proceedings of the 19th International Conference on Industrial and Engineering Applications of Artificial Intelligence and Expert Systems (IEA-AIE-2006), Springer-Verlag Lecture Notes in Computer Science, Annecy, France, 27-30 June (2006)

16. Koliadis, G. Vranesevic, A. Bhuiyan, M. Krishna, A. Ghose, A.: A Combined Approach for Supporting the Business Process Model Lifecycle. To appear in: The Proceedings of the 10th Pacific Asia Conference on Information Systems (PACIS), July 6-9, Kuala Lumpur, Malaysia (2006).

17. White, S. Business Process Modeling Notation (BPMN) Version 1.0. Business Process Management Initiative (BPMI.org), May (2004)

18. Giorgini, P. Kolp, M. Mylopoulos, J. Pistore, M.: The Tropos Methodology: an overview. In: Methodologies And Software Engineering For Agent Systems. Kluwer Academic Publishing (2004)

19. Fuxman, A. Liu, L. Mylopoulos, J. Pistore, M. Roveri, M. Traverso, P.: Specifying and analyzing early requirements in Tropos. In: Requirements Engineering, Springer London, 9(2) (2004) 132–150

20. Fischer, L.: Workflow Handbook 2005. Workflow Management Coalition, (WfMC) (2005)

21. Ouyang, C. W.M.P. van der Aalst, Dumas, M. and ter Hofstede, A.H.M.: Translating BPMN to BPEL. BPM Center Report BPM-06-02, BPMcenter.org, (2006)

22. Becker, J. Indulska, M. and Rosemann, M. Green, P.: Do Process Modelling Techniques Get Better? A Comparative Ontological Analysis of BPMN. In: Campbell, Bruce and Underwood, Jim and Bunker, Deborah, Eds. Proceedings 16th Australasian Conference on Information Systems, Sydney, Australia (2005)

23. Lamsweerde, A. Goal-Oriented Requirements Engineering: A Guided Tour. In: The 5th International Symp. In Requirements Engineering (RE'01), Aug. (2001)

# Advances in Semantics
# for Web Services
# (semantics4ws 2006)

# Advances in Semantics for Web Services (semantics4ws 2006) Preface

These proceedings contain the papers accepted for presentation at the "Advances in Semantics for Web services (semantics4ws 2006)" workshop held in Vienna, Austria, on September 4, 2006, in conjunction with the Fourth International Conference on Business Process Mangement (BPM 2006).

The main topics of this workshop are related to applicability of semantic technologies to Web services. Web services have added a new level of functionality to the current Web by taking a first step towards seamless integration of distributed software components using Web standards. Nevertheless, current Web service technologies around SOAP, WSDL and UDDI operate at a syntactic level and, therefore, although they support interoperability (i.e., interoperability between the many diverse application development platforms that exist today) through common standards, they still require human interaction to a large extent. For example, the human programmer has to manually search for appropriate Web services in order to combine them in a useful manner, which limits scalability and greatly curtails the added economic value envisioned with the advent of Web services.

Recent research (which we refer to as Semantic Web Services – SWS), which draws on a variety of fields such as Semantic Web, knowledge representation, formal methods, software engineering, process modeling, workflow, and software agents, is gaining momentum, in particular in the context of Web services usage. Research in the above mentioned fields can be exploited to automate Web services-related tasks, like discovery, selection, composition, mediation, monitoring, and invocation, thus enabling seamless interoperation between them while keeping human intervention to a minimum. Although several initiatives, like OWL-S, WSMO, WSDL-S, or IRS, have emerged in this area aiming at addressing the problem of semantics in Web services, many major challenges still need to be addressed and solved in this field.

In this context, this workshop aims to provide a forum in which to focus on selected core technical challenges for deployment of Semantic Web Services, and reach a better understanding of the relationships between commercial Web service standards, current SWS research efforts, and the ultimate requirements for full-scale deployment of these technologies. More specifically, this workshop aims to tackle the research problems (as well as recent practical experiences) around methods, concepts, models, languages and technology that enable semantics in the context of Web services, as well as discussing recent advances in semantics for Web services. Of particular interest are the architectural, technical, and developmental foundations of SWS, and showing how they combine synergistically to enable service automation on the scale required by today's Internet-connected enterprises.

This workshop aims to bring together researchers and industry practitioners (e.g., leading modelers, architects, system vendors, open-source projects, developers, and end-users) addressing many of these issues (including recent developments in tools and techniques, and real-world implementations of SWS applications), and promote and foster a greater understanding of how semantics can assist automation in Web services, thus helping people develop and manage services more efficiently and effectively.

The workshop organizers would like to thank the authors for their high-quality submissions and the members of the program committee for their reviewing and review coordination efforts.

June 2006

Steven Battle  
John Domingue  
David Martin  
Dumitru Roman  
Amit Sheth  
(Editors)

# Workshop Organization

## Program Chairs

Steven Battle, Hewlett-Packard Labs, UK
John Domingue, The Open University, UK
David Martin, SRI International, USA
Dumitru Roman, DERI Innsbruck, Austria
Amit Sheth, University of Georgia, USA

## Program Committee

Rama Akkiraju, IBM, USA
Abraham Bernstein, University of Zurich, Switzerland
Carine Bournez, W3C, France
Jorge Cardoso, University of Mediera, Portugal
Sanjay Chaudhary, DA-IICT, India
Emilia Cimpian, DERI Innsbruck, Austria
Marin Dimitrov, Ontotext, Bulgaria
Dieter Fensel, DERI Innsbruck, Austria
Karthik Gomadam, University of Georgia, USA
Michael Gruninger, University of Toronto, Canada
Sung-Kook Han, Won Kwang University, South Korea
Rick Hull, Lucent, USA
Deepali Khushraj, Nokia, Finland
Michael Kifer, State University of New York at Stony Brook, USA
Michael Maximilien, IBM, USA
Sheila McIlraith, University of Toronto, Canada
Brahim Medjahed, University of Michigan, USA
Adrian Mocan, DERI Innsbruck, Austria
Massimo Paolucci, DoCoMo Euro-Labs, Germany
Brahmananda Sapkota, DERI Galway, Ireland
Tony Shan, Wachovia Bank, USA
Monika Solanki, De Montfort University, UK
Ioan Toma, DERI Innsbruck, Austria
Stuart Williams, HP Bristol, UK

## External Reviewers

Alessio Gugliotta
Farshad Hakimpour
Stijn Heymans
Carlos Pedrinaci

James Scicluna
Kunal Verma
Christoph Kiefer

# The Semantics of Business Service Orchestration

Bill Karakostas[1], Yannis Zorgios[2], and Charalampos C. Alevizos[1]

[1] Centre for HCI Design, School of Informatics, City University, London, UK
{billk, C.Alevizos}@soi.city.ac.uk
[2] CLMS (UK) LIMITED, Croydon, UK
yz.clms@gmail.com

**Abstract.** Business services are deliveries of capabilities to consumers. The way such capabilities are selected, combined and delivered makes for the flexibility in services provision compared to, for example, manufacturing of tangible goods. The coordination ('orchestration') of services is an essential requirement for the delivery of more complex services. However, current technologies for web service orchestration assume a procedural 'program-like' approach that as we argue in this paper reduces the flexibility to adapt the composite service in response to changing requirements. This paper proposes that service orchestration should be carried out at the business level, preserving the business semantics and transformed if required to specific orchestration execution models such as BPEL4WS, using MDA techniques.

**Keywords:** Service composition, Service orchestration, Service semantics, IDEF0, MDA, BPEL4WS.

## 1 Introduction

*Web services* make software functions available programmatically over the Internet and may be used as building blocks for applications. A composite web service is one that is built using multiple component web services and is typically specified using a language such as BPEL4WS [1] or WSIPL [2].

In a broader sense, a *service* is a set of capabilities delivered to a consumer. A capability is access to a tangible resource such as a piece of equipment, or to an intangible one such as information. Thus, a flight service offers a passenger the capability to fly to some destination via the airline's resources (i.e. airplanes). Since computers, however, can only deal with intangible (i.e. information) resources, in this paper we will only be concerned with information-based services.

Services are often confused with the mechanisms that are used for their delivery: *processes*. Services are conceptually different from processes in the sense that unlike processes they are not procedural transformations of inputs to outputs. A banking loan service, for example, is not about transforming loan applications to loans- it is about giving customers access to financial resources of the bank.

Research in service orchestration is currently driven by the popularity of web services. Therefore current approaches to service orchestration, such as WFSL,

J. Eder, S. Dustdar et al. (Eds.): BPM 2006 Workshops, LNCS 4103, pp. 435–446, 2006.

XLANG, more recently BPEL4WS and others are XML based and focus on the coordination of executable web services. Languages, such as BPEL4WS, utilise high-level scripting notation to control the sequence and flow of service execution. They define standard programming language constructs for sequences, loops, spawning, conditional execution, and exception handling.

However, we argue that by thinking about services orchestration in execution terms, we loose the ability to separate business services from their implementation and hence the ability to independently change the business service from its delivery mechanisms. In this paper, therefore, we propose an execution language-independent way to represent business services and their orchestrations.

Our service modelling and orchestration language is based on the IDEF0 modelling standard [3]. IDEF0 allows the specification of services and their dependencies (orchestrations) in an execution independent way that allows flexible adaptation of orchestrations by reconfiguring service dependencies. The reconfiguration is accomplished through declarative specifications of controls that constrain the behaviour of individual services or of the orchestration as a whole.

The structure of the paper is as follows: Section 2 defines the notation and semantics of the service description language. Section 3 defines the formal semantics of service execution and service orchestration. Section 4 uses a travel agent example to illustrate our approach to service orchestration. Section 5 discusses the service orchestration engine. Finally, Section 6 positions our research against related approaches and identifies directions for further research.

## 2   A Service Description Language

Our service modelling approach is based on an extended version of the process analysis and modelling method known as IDEF0 [3]. IDEF0 in turn is based on the Structured Analysis and Design Technique (SADT), a graphical approach to system description, introduced by Douglas T. Ross in the early 1970s. An IDEF0 activity diagram contains one or more levels of decomposition of a process. Boxes within a diagram show the sub-processes of the parent process named by the diagram. Arrows between the boxes show the flow of products between processes (Figure 1).

A business service is modelled as consisting of a number of inputs, outputs, controls and mechanisms:

- *Inputs* denote the capabilities that are required for the provision of the service.
- *Outputs* are the capabilities offered by the service to its consumers.
- *Controls* are the methods, procedures, standards etc. controlling the provision of the service.
- Finally, *mechanisms* are the processes and resources used in the provision of the service.

The key advantages of IDEF0 over alternatives, such as UML activity diagrams in service orchestration modelling, are as follows:

1. IDEF0 supports hierarchical service decomposition. A service can be decomposed into its constituting services and this can be repeated for several levels until services are atomic i.e. they cannot be decomposed any further. In contrast, UML activity diagrams are flat.
2. An IDEF0 model does not imply an order of service execution; services in an IDEF0 model are not executed in any particular order, as it might be implied by the layout of the model (e.g. from left to right). Moreover, arrows connecting services do not signify execution control, but dependencies between services, in contrast to control flow representations in models such as Petri nets or UML 2.0 activity diagrams [4].

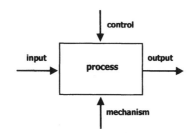

**Fig. 1.** Process model in IDEF0 notation

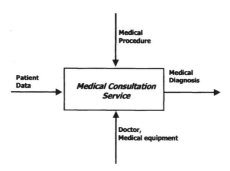

**Fig. 2.** Example of a Medical Consultation Business Service in IDEF0 notation

Figure 2 shows an example of modelling a medical consultation business service as a Level 0 IDEF0 model. Input capabilities to the service are access to patient data such as the patient's medical history etc. The output capability is a medical diagnosis that, for example, will enable a treatment to be prescribed. The practitioner doctor and any equipment he uses constitute the mechanisms of the service. Finally, the provision of this service is controlled by the medical procedures and practices that they may apply to this particular type of medical consultation.

A formal definition of a service is therefore as follows:

A service S is a 4-*tuple (I, C, O, M)* where:

- I is a set of *input capabilities* $I_1, I_2,..., I_n$ [defined as I(S)] that are required for the service to be delivered. A capability is a complex (tangible or intangible) entity and is described by a set of attributes that draw values from some domain. As explained already, capabilities are usually referring to the availability of information or tangible resources such as humans, machinery, money etc.

$$I(S): \forall\, i,\, 1 \le i \le n,\, I_i \in I(S) \tag{1}$$

- C is a set of *control rules* $C_1, C_2,..., C_n$ [defined as C(S)] that constrain the service execution, based on the input capabilities of the service. The concept of control is explained in section 3 of the paper.

$$C(S): \forall\, i,\, 1 \le i \le n,\, C_i \in C(S) \tag{2}$$

- O is a set of *output capabilities* $O_1, O_2,..., O_n$ [defined as O(S)] that are delivered by the service to its consumers.

$$O(S): \forall\, i,\, 1 \le i \le n,\, O_i \in O(S) \tag{3}$$

- M is the *mechanism* used for the delivery of the service [defined as M(S)]. M is the process that will deliver the service.

$$M(S): \forall\, i,\, i = 1,\, M_i \in M(S) \tag{4}$$

## 3  Service Execution Semantics

### 3.1  Service Execution

Because a service is not a process, it is not appropriate to use program execution concepts such as for example execution paths, synchronisation etc. We say that at anytime a service can be only in of the two possible states '*available*' or '*unavailable*'. A service is '*available*' if and only if all the capabilities for its delivery are present and all conditions for its delivery (as defined by the service's control rules) are fulfilled – otherwise it is '*unavailable*'.

A control rule is a logic expression that evaluates to true or false. Control rules are defined in terms of capabilities. A control rule is therefore a function from LP -> {*true, false*}, where LP are all the possible logic expressions constructed using logical operators ($\neg \lor \land$) and the properties and values of the input capabilities in an IDEF0 service model. Essentially, a control rule is a precondition on the availability of a service and is defined in terms of the input capabilities properties. More formally, a service S is '*available*' at time t if input capabilities $I_1, I_2, ... , I_n$ are available at time t and all control rules $C_1, C_2, ... , C_n$ applying to that service evaluate to true.

$$\text{available}(S^t){:}(\forall\, I_i^t \in I(S^t),\, \text{available}(I_i^t){=}\text{true}) \land (\forall\, C_i^t \in C(S^t),\, \text{eval}(C_i^t){=}\text{true}) \tag{5}$$

Below are some example control rules from the problem domain of flight booking. The same problem domain will be used in the more extensive example of Section 5.

As the following control rules are defined in terms of resource capabilities, such resources, their properties and their domains need to be defined first as in Table 1.

**Table 1.** Classes of resources in the flight booking domain

| Class | Properties |
|-------|-----------|
| Flight | FlightNo : Int<br>FlightDeparture : Date<br>DepartureAirportCode : AirportCode |
| Passenger | PassengerDetails : PersonalDetails<br>PassportStatus : {'valid', 'invalid'} |
| Ticket | Type : {'first', 'business', 'economy'}<br>Farevalue : Money |
| FlightBooking | BookingRef : ReferenceNumber<br>FlightRef : Flight<br>PassengerRef : Passenger<br>TicketRef: Ticket |

And the corresponding UML class diagram is:

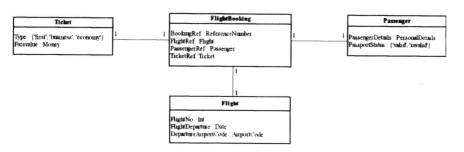

**Fig. 3.** Class diagram for Flight and Hotel booking

The following control rules can then be defined, first in English natural language and then as the equivalent logic expressions:

*Control Rule 1*: The booking of an economy ticket is allowed only if the departure date is a Saturday.

| | |
|---|---|
| available(FlightBooking) $\Leftarrow$ FlightBooking.TicketRef.Type = 'economy' $\Leftarrow$ DayOfTheWeek(FlightBooking.FlightRef.FlightDeparture) = 'Saturday' | (6) |

*Control Rule 2*: Bookings are allowed only if the passenger's passport status is 'valid'.

| | |
|---|---|
| available(FlightBooking) $\Leftarrow$ <br><br>      FlightBooking.PassengerRef.PassportStatus='valid' | (7) |

The above are complex control rules that constrain the allowed combinations of values in the service resources. Other control rules may only constrain the presence of resources to provide input capabilities to a service, i.e. a service cannot be available if the input resources do not exist.

*Control Rule 3*: A flight can only be booked if the passenger's details are known.

| | |
|---|---|
| available (FlightBooking) $\Leftarrow$ FlightBooking.PassengerRef $\neq null$ | (8) |

### 3.2 Service Orchestration

An orchestration is a set $\Sigma$ consisting of services $S_1, S_2, ..., S_n$ where each service is connected to some other service via a capability which is used as input, output or control i.e. the output of a service can be either input to another service, control for another service or both. This can be expressed formally as:

| | |
|---|---|
| $\forall\ S_i \in \Sigma\ \exists\ S_k \in \Sigma : \left( \exists\ j \in S_k(C) \land j \in S_i(I) \right) \lor$ <br> $\left( \exists\ j \in S_k(O) \land j \in S_i(C) \right) \lor$ <br> $\left( \exists\ j \in S_k(I) \land\ j \in S_i(O) \right)$ | (9) |

A service orchestration can be considered as a composite service $S_i$ that can be decomposed into a network of services $S_{i1}, S_{i2}, ..., S_{in}$, where each $S_{ik}$ can be composite or atomic. A service is atomic if it delivers capabilities to a higher order service but itself does not use the capabilities of another service. Services that are not atomic can be further decomposed allowing as a result multiple levels of orchestration.

There are three conditions for an atomic service $S_i$ to be valid and be able to participate in an orchestration:

1. Service must have at least one input capability. Using definition (1) we have:

| | |
|---|---|
| $\exists\ I_k \in I(S_i), 1 \leq k \leq n, S_i \in \Sigma$ | (10) |

2. Service must have at least one output capability. Using definition (2) we have:

| | |
|---|---|
| $\exists\ O_k \in O(S_i), 1 \leq k \leq n, S_i \in \Sigma$ | (11) |

3. Service must have a mechanism. Using definition (4) we have:

| | |
|---|---|
| $\exists\ M_k \in M(S_i), k = 1, S_i \in \Sigma$ | (12) |

## 4  A Service Orchestration Example

We will use a travel agent scenario that is frequently sited in service orchestration papers. A travel agent undertakes to fulfil the requirements of a customer for a trip by arranging both the customer's flight and hotel accommodation. The customer requires that the flight's actual date must be as close as possible to his desired date for travel, and that there must be available hotel accommodation for that date. The task of the travel agent is to orchestrate external services for flight and hotel booking in a way that meets the customer requirements. There are mutual dependencies between the services as hotel reservation can only be made after a suitable flight has been found. However the flight service depends also on the hotel booking service, as if there are no hotels availability for the found date then an alternative flight must be sought.

To describe the above service in a procedural (e.g. BPEL4WS style) we can use the UML activity diagram of Figure 4.

However, this procedural approach makes the evolution of the provided services more difficult. Suppose that the travel agency extends its range of services by providing also a car booking service. The newly added service of car booking, adds a new set of dependencies to the existing services. To introduce them in the previous activity diagram (or the equivalent BPEL4WS program) we would be required to do modifications in several places as now three conditions need to be satisfied simultaneously in order for the composite service to be available (Figure 5).

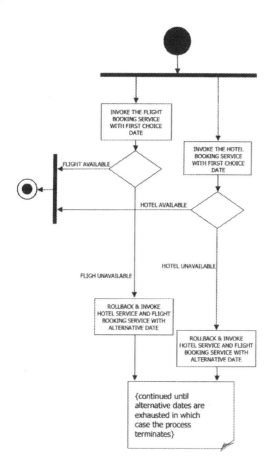

**Fig. 4.** Activity diagram for Flight and Hotel booking

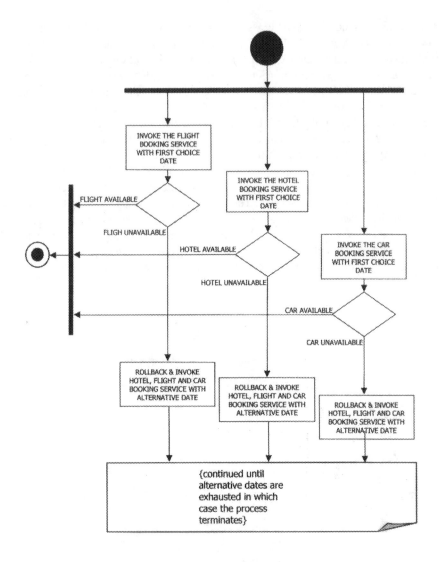

**Fig. 5.** Activity diagram for Flight, Hotel and Car booking

To model the same scenario in our approach, we first define the following three services:

| $S_{BookFlight}$ (*INPUT* : SETOF Date , |
|---|
| *OUTPUT* : FlightBooking, |
| *CONTROL*: FlightBookingControl , |
| *MECHANISM* : FlightBookingWebService) |

(13)

$$S_{BookHotel}(INPUT : \text{SETOF Date},$$
$$\qquad OUTPUT : \text{HotelBooking},$$
$$\qquad CONTROL : \text{HotelBookingControl},$$
$$\qquad MECHANISM : \text{HotelBookingWebService}) \qquad (14)$$

$$S_{BookCar}(INPUT : \text{SETOF Date},$$
$$\qquad OUTPUT : \text{CarBooking},$$
$$\qquad CONTROL : \text{CarBookingControl},$$
$$\qquad MECHANISM : \text{CarBookingWebService}) \qquad (15)$$

We then specify the control rules as follows:

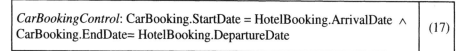

*FlightBookingControl*: FlightBooking.OutDate=HotelBooking.ArrivalDate ∧
FlightBooking.ReturnDate=HotelBooking.DepartureDate                        (16)

*CarBookingControl*: CarBooking.StartDate = HotelBooking.ArrivalDate ∧
CarBooking.EndDate= HotelBooking.DepartureDate                             (17)

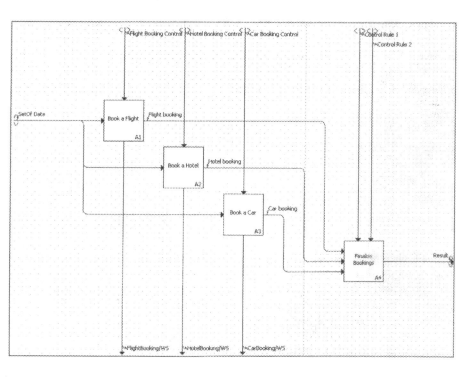

**Fig. 6.** Services of travel agent scenario as encoded in the IDEF0 model

Note that although the control rules can be added at different times (i.e. as the service is modified) the declarative style of definitions allows rules to be processed independently from each other by an inference engine. Thus by using the transitivity property, an inference engine like the Service Orchestration Engine described in the next section, can deduce that there is a dependency between the flight booking service and the car booking service in two different control rules:

| FlightBooking.OutDate= HotelBooking. ArrivalDate = CarBooking.StartDate | (18) |
|---|---|

And

| FlightBooking.ReturnDate=HotelBooking.Departuredate= CarBooking. EndDate | (19) |
|---|---|

The IDEF0-based graphical representation of the travel agent services with all possible dependencies shown as control rules is shown in Figure 6.

## 5   Service Orchestration Engine

Service Orchestration Engine is a service execution engine that is similar to BPEL4WS processors, i.e. applications that execute BPEL4WS programs. However, the main difference between the Service Orchestration Engine and a BPEL4WS engine is that the former does not implement a procedural style of execution. The Service Orchestration Engine allows for flexible rearrangements in the service orchestration, which unlike BPEL4WS does not require modifications to an orchestration program, as it implements a declarative rather than procedural style of orchestration. Effectively, the Service Orchestration Engine is a constraint-checking engine. Given an orchestration, the engine will evaluate for each service all controls that apply to the service either directly, as modelled at the time of the service definition, or because such controls refer to the service's input capabilities. Only if all relevant controls evaluate to true, the service will be considered to be *'available'*.

Formally given an orchestration $\Sigma$:

$$\exists\ S \in \Sigma : available(S)\ \text{iff}\ \forall\ c \in C(S), eval(c) = true \qquad (20)$$

Service orchestration does not exclude the possibility that some of the services making up the orchestration will themselves be composite services, orchestrated in a procedural BPEL4WS style. Additionally, a service orchestration as defined in this paper can be automatically transformed into a BPEL4WS or other language service orchestration equivalent. This approach is described in more detail in [5].

Model-driven architecture is at the core of our approach to provide a seamless transition from business services to web services design and orchestration. IDEF0 models of the services are used as platform independent models (PIM) that capture the semantics of business services and produce flexible orchestrations.

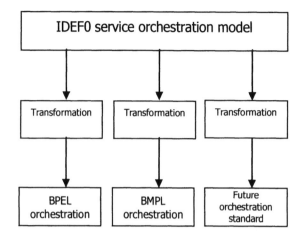

**Fig. 7.** Transforming declarative service orchestrations to procedural ones

Inside the PIMs, business services are systematically decomposed by the business expert into networks of activities. Web services are identified and co-designed with the other business activities. This approach leads to flexible business process orchestrations as it captures business services behaviour semantics as well as the corresponding web services behaviour and the relation between the two. Finally, based on these models, actual processes in BPEL, BPML or other standard can be generated using separate modules [5]. Each module can generate a specific executable process and can be easily replaced and reused in case a standard has been revised. Finally, with IDEF0 generic modules an executable process can be created in more than one standard simultaneously.

## 6  Discussion and Conclusions

The advantages of service orchestration have been analysed from organizational, managerial, strategic, operational and technical perspectives, e.g. in [6]. While clearly all approaches to service orchestration today are concerned with the orchestration of executable web services, e.g. [7], we argue that for flexibility reasons orchestration must be implemented at the business process level. Other approaches have also considered the problem of service composition  as an AI planning problem e.g. [8].

Building generic IDEF0 service models and specifying each service in the model using the semantics defined in this paper, allows for flexible orchestration of business services that are independent of particular service execution environments. This approach improves the reusability of generic services in different situations and it also enables the customization of the services based on the configuration parameters. It also helps in the success of new business models, where services are bought in from external parties. Off-the-shelf IDEF0 service models can be bought and used in orchestrations to implement complex solutions, such as for supply chain models, e-government applications and other business-to-business types of collaboration.

**Acknowledgements.** The service orchestration semantics described in this paper are based on the IDEF0 execution engine of CLMS (UK) which is the core element of the CLMS Platform that is used to deliver distributed system solutions.

# References

1. IBM, et al. *Business Process Execution Language for Web Services version 1.1.* 2002 [cited; Available from: http://www-128.ibm.com/developerworks/library/specification/ws-bpel/.
2. Lo, E., et al., *WSIPL: An XML Scripting Language for Integrating Web Service Data and Applications.* To appear in Web Intelligence and Agent Systems (WIAS), 2005.
3. *Draft Federal Information Processing Standards Publication 183, Standard for integration definition for function Modeling (IDEF0).* 1993, National Institute of Standards and Technology (NIST).
4. Storrle, H., *Semantics and Verification of Data-Flow in UML 2.0 Activities*, in *Proc. Intl. Ws. on Visual Languages and Formal Methods (VLFM'04).* 2004: Rome, Italy.
5. Karakostas, B., Y. Zorgios, and C.C. Alevizos, *Automatic derivation of BPEL4WS from IDEF0 process models.* To appear in Journal of Software & System Modeling, Springer-Verlag, 2006.
6. Gortmaker, J., M. Janssen, and R.W. Wagenaar. *The Advantages of Web Service Orchestration in Perspective.* in *Proceedings of the 6th international conference on Electronic commerce.* 2004. Delft, The Netherlands: ACM International Conference Proceeding Series; Vol. 60.
7. Courbis, C. and A. Finkelstein. *Weaving Aspects into Web Service Orchestrations.* in *3rd IEEE International Conference on Web Services (ICWS'2005).* 2005. Orlando, Florida, USA.
8. Carman, M., L. Serafini, and P. Traverso, *Web Service Composition as Planning*, in *International Conference on Automated Planning & Scheduling (ICAPS).* 2003: Trento, Italy.

# Requirements for Automated Service Composition[*]

Harald Meyer and Dominik Kuropka

Hasso-Plattner-Institute for IT-Systems-Engineering
Prof.-Dr.-Helmert-Strasse 2-3, 14482 Potsdam, Germany
{harald.meyer, dominik.kuropka}@hpi.uni-potsdam.de

**Abstract.** Automated service composition is an important approach to create aggregate services out of existing services. Several different approaches towards automated service composition exist. They differ not only in the used algorithms but also in provided functionality. While some support the creation of compositions with alternative or parallel control flow, others are missing this functionality. This diversity yields from a missing consensus on the required functionality to automatically compose real-world services. Hence, with this paper we aim at providing the foundation for such a consensus. We derived the required functionality from multiple business scenarios set up in the Adaptive Services Grid (ASG) project.

## 1 Introduction

Cooperation between enterprises on global level is essential to conduct successful business. Service composition yields the possibility to aggregate services from inside and outside of enterprises to new composed services which raises the value of the whole service chain. Compositions are currently modeled manually. This leads to inflexible service compositions with in-optimal quality as manual modeling makes adjustments for individual service requests too expensive. Automating the creation of compositions increases flexibility and quality. Furthermore it reduces the probability of enactment failures caused by services used in the model which either disappeared or have been modified over the time. Automated service composition will include newly registered services automatically while de-registered services will no longer be used in compositions.

Several approaches for automated service composition differing in provided functionality exist. While they motivate automated service composition, a consensus on the required functionality to perform automated service composition is missing. Zeng et al. [1] present an automated composition approach based on a rule inference engine. They describe the supported functionality of their system $DY_{flow}$ like the composition of parallel and alternative control flow or the

---

[*] This paper presents results of the Adaptive Services Grid (ASG) project (contract number 004617, call identifier FP6-2003-IST-2) funded by the Sixth Framework Program of the European Commission.

J. Eder, S. Dustdar et al. (Eds.): BPM 2006 Workshops, LNCS 4103, pp. 447–458, 2006.
© Springer-Verlag Berlin Heidelberg 2006

annotation of services with Quality of Service (QOS) properties. Pistore et al. [2] use their model-checking planner *MBP* to do automated service composition. It supports non-deterministic services and partial observability of service effects. They explain that these features are necessary to model real-world services. Sirin et al. [3] implement automated service composition through Hierarchical Task Network (HTN) planning. For them an important feature of service composition is the hierarchical decomposition of complex task to atomic—invokable— services. The approach by Berardi et al. [4] is based on the automatic synthesis of finite state machines. In [5] they extend this approach to non-deterministic finite state machines to support real-world, external services. This small selection underlines that no common understanding on the required features exists. While rationale is provided for the extended features of each approach, the features are mostly rooting from the origins of the used algorithms. As most algorithms come from the area of automated planning, features are aimed at supporting problems in typical planning domains[1]. Features like parallel control flow that are usually not of importance in such domains are rather sparsely supported.

In this paper we aim at creating a consensus on the required features for automated service composition. We will motivate them through a real world business scenario. Following this introduction a scenario is presented that forms the basis for our requirements analysis. In Section 3 we present the functional requirements on a service composition component. Finally, Section 4 contains a summary of the presented requirements and an outlook.

## 2    Use Case Scenario

The *attraction booking* use case scenario presented here serves as the motivating scenario in the Adaptive Services Grid (ASG)[2] project. The goal of the ASG project is to develop a reference architecture for adaptive service matchmaking, composition, binding and enactment. Furthermore a prototypical implementation for testing and evaluation purposes of this reference architecture is provided by the project. The scenario allows customers to retrieve information about attractions in the immediate surrounding of the customer by using a mobile device. Additionally customers may request directions and maps to the attraction or they can directly book tickets with their mobile device.

Based on the customer's current position and the specified query, the system compiles a list of attractions. This list is displayed as it is or as a map showing the position of the customer and the attractions found. The customer can then request additional information for specific attractions. This includes its address, opening hours or price. The customer can also request a route description to lead him to the attraction. If the attraction is bookable, the customer can book

---

[1] Domains at the biannual International Planning Competition (IPC) [http://ipc.icaps-conference.org] include for example controlling ground traffic at an airport or the flow of oil through a pipeline network.

[2] http://asg-project.org

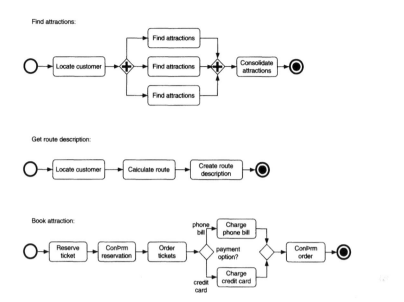

**Fig. 1.** Example compositions for attraction booking use cases

a digital ticket. The route description consists of a map and a textual description. While the map shows streets and buildings, indicating the path as a colored line, the textual description includes street names and directions (e.g.: where to turn left or right). To book a specific attraction or event, the customer selects the number of people to attend the event. The system then offers the customer a number of tickets for a certain price category. If the customer decides to accept the offer, he is charged the specified amount of money. In return he receives the given number of digital tickets for the event. The attraction booking booking scenario encompasses the three use cases find attractions, get route description, book attraction.

All three are fulfilled by enactment of proper service compositions. Figure 1 shows some example compositions for each use case. The activities inside the compositions represent service invocations. The shown compositions are tailored exactly to the specific user request. For example, if the customer's location is already specified in the service request, the invocation of a localization service is not necessary. A similar flexibility applies to the booking of an attraction. No payment option is specified in the shown example. Instead the user selects a payment option just before payment. But the customer may have already specified his preferred payment option in a profile. The client application on the mobile device then transfers the information about the user preference and the customer does not have to select a payment option. If service providers register new attraction information services or remove old services, future queries for attraction information will incorporate these changes of the service landscape. In this scenario automated service composition allows changes in the set of available services and in the client application (new use cases, additional information) without requiring manual adjustment of the service compositions.

# 3  Functional Requirements of Service Composition

In the previous section a use case scenario from the ASG project was introduced. In the ASG project, the industry partners developed and evaluate five different scenarios for their business areas. The attraction booking scenario together with another scenario proved to scenarios with the biggest market potential. Our approach was to derive the requirements from these two scenarios. We will use the attraction booking scenario in this section to motivate the requirements on a service composition component and a composition language. The composition language defines how service compositions look like. The requirements are ordered according to the categories elements of composition, control flow, data flow, data model, and quality of service.

This categorization is based on the process representation perspectives by Curtis, Kellner, and Over [6]. While other approaches [7,8,9] propose additional aspects or categories, our first four categories represent the core of all these approaches. We see quality of service and the optimization for it as one of the main advantages of automated service composition. If we did not introduce an own category for it QOS requirements would be scattered among the elements of composition (QOS properties of services) and the control flow (QOS fulfillment of service compositions).

## 3.1  Requirements on the Elements of Composition

The elements of composition are the building blocks from which service compositions are created.

*Req. 1: Elements of composition are services interactions.* The elements of a composition are activities that perform a task. All these activities must be service interactions. This does not limit generality as we can encapsulate all other activities—even manual—in services. For example: In the above scenario the activity to locate a customer is realized by a service. Each service performs exactly one task and is stateless. It is therefore not necessary to support more than one operation per service. Besides invoking services, a composition can itself be invoked as a service.

*Req. 2: Elements of composition are service compositions.* Service interactions are the atomic elements of compositions. To improve reusability existing service compositions are used as elements of compositions as well. Service compositions can be either manually modeled or they can be results from previous composition requests. Using manually modeled compositions allows to express process parts that cannot be created by the composer automatically (e.g. loops are impossible with most composition approaches). Reusing previous automated service compositions is useful in most scenarios especially if equal functionalities are often requested.

*Req. 3: Services have input and output parameters.* Services perform a specified functionality and this functionality usually depend on data provided in the service request as input parameters. For example the localization of a customer needs the customer's telephone number as input data. Services usually also return a result (e.g.: the customer's location). To allow the input and output of data, parameters are needed. A service has zero or more input and output parameters. In reality, mapping between the input and output parameters of different services is a complicated task [10]. Here we assume that input and output parameters correspond to concepts from one ontology.

*Req. 4: Service functionality is described semantically.* Service functionality is described semantically to allow automated service composition. Besides input and output parameters, specifications of services include preconditions and effects. The precondition of a service specifies the assumptions that must hold in order to invoke the service. The effect defines the changes to the current state that result from invoking the service on the world beyond the output parameter. Preconditions and effects describe the state of the world and the state of available information. To do so, logical relations between input parameters, between output parameters and between input and output parameters can be defined. Additional variables that are not parameters of a service might be necessary to describe functionality for instance by referring to objects of the world which are not directly inputs or outputs of a service. In order to express preconditions and effects a logical language is necessary. In the semantic community well known and often used languages are Description Logics [11] and Frame Logics [12].

*Req. 5: Services can have more than one precondition or effect.* It is common that a service has more than one precondition or effect. This can be implemented by most logical languages though conjunction of several logical expressions.

*Req. 6: Services can be invokable in different situations.* Often a service is not just invokable in more than one situation. Confirming the order in the *book attraction* composition from Figure 1 can be invoked if the tickets have been paid by credit card or through the telephone bill. This can be achieved by having two distinct order confirmation services—one for credit card payment and one for telephone bill payment—or by supporting disjunction in the precondition. All possible situations in which the service is invokable are linked via disjunction and if just one of them is true, the service can be invoked.

*Req. 7: Services can have uncertain effects.* Services can have more than one possible outcome and it might be impossible to determine the concrete output in advance. Uncertain effects can be expressed through disjunction possible effect. Disjunctive effects increase the complexity of automated service composition [13,14] but they are usually unavoidable when real world services have to be modeled.

## 3.2   Control Flow Requirements

The control flow of a process or service compositions defines the order in which the elements of composition are enacted. This includes simple sequential ordering but also complex parallel or alternative control flows. Figure 1 shows sequential, parallel, and alternative control flows.

Requirements regarding control flow can be separated into two types of requirements: Requirements regarding composition language and requirements regarding automated composition functionality. The first one describe what can kind of control flow can be modeled and how it can be expressed. The second one describe which subset of these composition language features can be automatically composed. With workflow patterns [15] a categorization for different control flow constructs exists for the workflow management domain. Requirements analysis regarding control flow will be performed according to these patterns.

*Req. 8: Composition of sequential control flow.* In a *Sequence* of activities the activities are enacted one after another in a well-defined order. Figure 1 shows a sequence in the *get route description* composition: First the customer is located, then a route is calculated, and finally a description for the route is generated.

*Req. 9: Composition of parallel control flow.* Parallel control flow allows the parallel invocation of activities. Figure 1 in the *find attractions* composition shows an example for parallel control flow. The different attraction information services are invoked in parallel. In general every usage of parallel control flows can be sequentialized. But sequentialization can dramatically reduce process performance. For the application to real world scenarios it is therefore mandatory. Parallel control flow is implemented by two different patterns: *Parallel Split* and *Synchronization*. A parallel split splits a single thread of control into multiple threads. A synchronization merges them later.

*Req. 10: Composition of alternative control flow.* Alternative control flows are parts in a process where—depending on some condition—one out of many possible control flows is selected. One example is displayed in Figure 1 in the *book attraction* composition. It shows the realization of an alternative control flow using the workflow patterns *Exclusive Choice* and a *Synchronizing Merge*.

*Req. 11: Composition Language supports workflow patterns.* So far all control flow requirements were requirements regarding the functionality of the composition component. However the composition output, an instance of the composition language, has also to be considered. The basic requirement on the composition language regarding control flow is modeling support for the above-mentioned required workflow pattern. This can be achieved through a graph-structured or a block-structured approach. In a graph-structured approach activities are vertices that are connected through edges symbolizing ordering constraints. In a block-structured approach structured activities exist that contain other activities and determine their enactment order. While a graph-structured approach is more generic, a block-structured approach is easier to visualize and to reason about. In general it is best to support both approaches like WS-BPEL [16] does. The composition language should also support the patterns that cannot be composed automatically.

*Req. 12: Composition is block-structured.* Supporting structured activities in the composition language does not mean that the composer outputs a block-structured result. Actually, service composition generates a partially-ordered set of services that can be represented as a graph. As already mentioned block-structuring has its advantages and should be preferred when possible. To have block-structured compositions, either the composition algorithm could support them directly or post-processing could be performed. The first approach is a new research area, so it is unclear whether it can be successful. Hierarchical-Task-Network planners [17,18,19] generate block-structured plans. But they do not actually generate block structures, but rather reuse them. Post-processing rises the problem of complexity. As shown in [20] reordering compositions subsequently can be as complex as composition itself.

## 3.3   Data Flow Requirements

The data flow of composition defines how data is exchanged between services. Services have input and output parameters. The output of one service can be the input for another service. Data flow requirements include for example the ability to exchange data and the usage of process input data. The following four requirements regarding data flow are all defined over activities instead of services. The process enactment engine stores the outputs of invoked services and sends them to services that require them. Hence, data is exchanged between the activities of the composition.

*Req. 13: Activities exchange data.* The fundamental data flow requirement is the ability to exchange data. Exchanging data between activities and therefore data flow is supported in nearly all process meta-models [6,21]. Activities have formal parameters that are replaced by actual data when invoked. This data can either be process input data or output from other activities.

In workflow management, two different approaches to model data flow are in use. With the first approach all data is stored on the process level. Input parameters of activities are read from this central storage. Output parameters are stored in this central storage or the so called *blackboard*. With the second approach, data actually flows between activities. Explicit data flow connectors connect the outputs of one activity with the input of another one. So the main difference is that in the first approach all data exchange must be done through the central storage. If the output of one activity is used by two other activities, it is still written only once to the storage and read twice. In the second approach two distinct data connectors exist. WS-BPEL uses the blackboard approach through process variables [16]. In contrast, Leymann and Roller [21] propose a meta-model, used in IBM MQSeries Workflow, that facilitates explicit data connectors. The flexibility gained by the blackboard approach, stands in contrast to the fact that it is harder to follow the implicit data flow. This requirement and service composition in general are agnostic to the selected approach of data flow representation.

*Req. 14: Activities use process input data.* Certain data elements in the attraction booking scenario like *PhoneNumber* and *Attraction*, are not produced by any activity. These data elements are part of the process data and are inputs for the process. Processes must have such data, and activities must be able to use them.

*Req. 15: Data exchange implies control flow.* Control flow embeds an ordering constraint between two activities if one activity depends on another one. Dependencies are for example causal links (e.g.: an activities creates the precondition of another one) or the protection of causal links. Causal links do not only exist on the level of semantic service descriptions, but also for input and output parameters. If one activity uses the output of another activity as an input a causal link between the two activities exist. Therefore an ordering constraint between the two activities must be included.

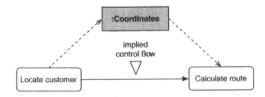

**Fig. 2.** Control flow implied by data flow

Refer to Figure 2 for an example: Even if the customer localization service and the route calculation service are not linked through preconditions and effects, it is necessary to add an ordering constraint between them as the route calculation service uses the coordinates created by the localization service.

*Req. 16: Activities create new variables.* While this requirement sounds trivial and self-evident, it actually is not for automated planning / composition. Activities create new variables, means that activities do not just write data into already defined variables, but they create variables on the fly. With automated planning this is normally not possible. All the variables that are usable during composition must be defined in advance. This includes also intermediate variables that are neither used in the input nor in the output. When retrieving a route description in the Attraction Booking scenario, a coordinates variable must be defined. This coordinates variable is never used in the input or the output of the request. It is also not obvious why such a variable could be necessary. Hence, by adding this variable we are encoding assumptions about automatically created service composition into the service request. This is bad as it hampers flexibility. Other service compositions are possible that do not need this variable.

Defining all necessary variables requires a lot of information about the available services and at least a rough idea on how the composition could look like. Therefore it is required here that activities can create new variables and that the service composer takes them into account.

## 3.4   Data Model Requirements

The data model defines how data elements are described. The data model is of importance for the service composition component, as it has to use data elements to replace the formal parameters with actual parameters. We assume that all services use one data model (ontology). Without this assumption complex problems in structural and semantic heterogeneities [22,10] arise that often cannot be solved automatically.

*Req. 17: Data elements are typed.* Data elements are exchanged between services as parameters. To ensure that only valid data elements are passed as parameters it makes sense to type them. Besides predefined types, user-defined types are necessary as well. Type-safety not only prevents service enactment from invoking services with wrong parameters, it also eases planning. With typed data elements and parameters the search space of the service composer is reduced. So the composer can already eliminate many of the potential compositions.

*Req. 18: Data element types are defined in an ontology.* Service specifications are annotated semantically to allow automated service composition. Service specifications therefore include preconditions and effects. Both are modeled as logical expressions. To use input parameters, output parameters and variables in these logical expressions, the types of data elements are described in an ontology.

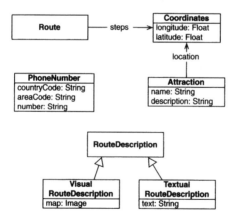

**Fig. 3.** Extract from the Attraction Booking ontology

An ontology is a model of linguistic means of expression on which several actors have agreed on and which are (or can be) used by those actors. [23] In this context a model is a representation of an (not necessary tangible) object system written by the mean of a formal (but not necessary textual) modeling language. So an ontology defines concepts and their relations which are important in a specific domain. Figure 3 shows the ontology of the Attraction Booking scenario modeled using the Unified Modeling Language.

*Req. 19: Composer is aware of data element structure.* Besides having data elements with ontology-based types it is also necessary that the composer is aware of the internal structure of data elements described using an ontology. To do so the composer has to understand a logic language that can represent such structured information. Frame Logic [12] is an enhancement of first-order logic as it adds object-oriented concepts like object identity, inheritance and complex objects.

*Req. 20: Data elements can be used to evaluate control flow conditions.* Requirement 9 stated that the composer can compose alternative control flows. An alternative control flow can be the result of an *Exclusive Choice* or a *Multiple Choice*. Both have one incoming and multiple outgoing control flows. To decide which control flows are actually executed, conditions are assigned to the individual flows. In our example, booked tickets for an attraction can be paid by via telephone bill or credit card. Based on the user provided payment option, the correct service is invoked. Conditions are expressed over data elements. So the composer must be able to create such conditions to enable a proper execution of the composition at run-time.

### 3.5   Quality of Service Requirements

The quality of service (QOS) requirements here are part of the functional requirements. They describe functionality that is needed to ensure quality of service properties for service compositions defined in a service request. The requirements on the representation of quality of service properties for service requests and service specifications is out of scope of this requirements analysis. Together with a solution strategy for calculating QoS of compositions a detailed analysis can be found in [24] and [25].

*Req. 21: Composer uses QOS properties.* In order to fulfill QOS requirements stated in a service request the composer must use the QOS properties specified by services. Based on the values of the properties for different services the composer is able to select the best service.

*Req. 22: Compositions fulfill QOS requirements from service request.* To use the quality of service properties to select the best service compositions, it is important to describe the relevant quality of service properties and their desired values in the service request. A service request in the Attraction Booking scenario could state that finding attractions costs at most 0.10 €. Accordingly, all services invoked can only cost 0.10 €. Then the service composer selects and composes service compositions according to these quality of service parameters.

## 4   Conclusion

In this paper we presented the core requirements towards automated service composition. We identified 22 requirements regarding the elements of composition, the control flow, the data flow, the data model, and the usage of quality of service properties. They described expected functionality of a component for automated service composition and requirements regarding the languages to specify services and service compositions. These requirements can be used as a starting point to develop a new component for the automated service composition, to evaluate existing ones, and to justify their extension.

Our future work in the ASG project is to realize a component for the automated service composition that fulfills all identified requirements. We will also verify these requirements in another use case prototype that is currently implemented.

# References

1. Zeng, L., Benatallah, B., Lei, H., Ngu, A., Flaxer, D., Chang, H.: Flexible Composition of Enterprise Web Services. Electronic Markets – Web Services **13** (2003) 141–152
2. Pistore, M., Barbon, F., Bertoli, P., Shaparau, D., Traverso, P.: Planning and monitoring web service composition. In: Workshop on Planning and Scheduling for Web and Grid Services (held in conjunction with The 14th International Conference on Automated Planning and Scheduling. (2004) 70 – 71
3. Sirin, E., Parsia, B., Wu, D., Hendler, J., Nau, D.: Htn planning for web service composition using shop2. Journal of Web Semantics **1** (2004) 377–396
4. Berardi, D., Calvanese, D., Giacomo, G.D., Lenzerini, M., Mecella, M.: Automatic composition of e-services that export their behavior. In: Proceedings of the First International Conference on Service-Oriented Computing. Volume 2910 of Lecture Notes In Computer Science., Heidelberg (2003) 43–58
5. Berardi, D., Calvanese, D., Giacomo, G.D., Mecella, M.: Composition of services with nondeterministic observable behaviour. In: Proceedings of the Third International Conference on Service-Oriented Computing. Volume 3826 of Lecture Notes In Computer Science., Heidelberg (2005) 520–526
6. Curtis, B., Keller, M.I., Over, J.: Process modeling. Communications of the ACM **35** (1992) 75 – 90
7. Jablonski, S., Böhm, M., Schulze, W., eds.: Workflow Management – Entwicklung von Anwendungen und Systemen. dpunkt Verlag (1997)
8. Weske, M., Vossen, G.: Workflow Languages. International Handbooks on Information Systems. In: Handbook on Architectures of Information Systems. Springer (1998) 359 – 379
9. Alonso, G., Casati, F., Kuno, H., Machiraju, V.: Web Services – Concepts, Architectures and Applications. Data-Centric Systems and Applications. Springer (2004)
10. Nagarajan, M., Verma, K., Sheth, A.P., Miller, J.A., Lathem, J.: Semantic interoperability of web services – challenges abd experiences. In: Proceedings of the 4th IEEE Intl. Conference on Web Services. (2006) (to appear).
11. Baader, F., Calvanese, D., McGuiness, D.L., Nardi, D., Patel-Schneider, P.F.: The Description Logic Handbook: Theory, Implementation, Applications. Cambridge University Press, Cambridge, UK (2003)
12. Kifer, M., Lausen, G., Wu, J.: Logical foundations of object-oriented and frame-based languages. Journal of the Association for Computing Machinery **42** (1995) 741 – 843

13. Erol, K., Nau, D.S., Subrahamnian, V.: Complexity, decidability and undecidability results for domain-independent planning: A detailed analysis. Technical Report CS-TR-2797, UMIACS-TR-91-154, SRC-TR-91-96, University Of Maryland (1991)
14. Ghallab, M., Lau, D., Traverso, P.: Automated Planning - theory and practice. Morgan Kaufmann (2004)
15. van der Aalst, W., ter Hofstede, A., Kiepuszewski, B., Barros, A.: Workflow patterns. Distributed and Parallel Databases **14** (2003) 5 – 51
16. Organization for the Advancement of Structured Information Standards (OASIS): Web Services Business Process Execution Language (WS-BPEL). (2004) http://www.oasis-open.org/committees/tc_home.php?wg_abbrev=wsbpel.
17. Sacerdoti, E.: The nonlinear structure of plans. In: Proceedings of the International Joint Conference on Artificial Intelligence. (1975) 206 – 214
18. Erol, K., Handler, J., Nau, D.S.: Semantics for hierarchical task-network planning. Technical Report CS-TR-3239, UMIACS-TR-94-31, ISR-TR-95-9, University Of Maryland (1994)
19. Nau, D., Au, T.C., Ilghami, O., Kuter, U., Murdock, W., Wu, D., Yaman, F.: Shop2: An htn planning system. Journal on Artificial Intelligence Research **20** (2003) 379 – 404
20. Bäckström, C.: Computational aspects of reordering plans. Journal Of Artificial Intelligence **9** (1998) 99 – 137
21. Leymann, F., Roller, D.: Production Workflow: Concepts and Techniques. Prentice Hall (2000)
22. Sheth, A.P.: Changing focus on interoperability in information systems: From system, syntax, structure to semantics. In: Interoperating Geographic Information Systems, Kluwer Academic Publishers (1998) 5–30
23. Kuropka, D.: Modelle zur Repräsentation natürlichsprachlicher Dokumente – Information-Filtering und -Retrieval mit relationalen Datenbanken. Logos Verlag, Berlin (2004)
24. Cardoso, J., Sheth, A.P., Miller, J.: Workflow quality of service. In: Proceedings of the International Conference on Enterprise Integration and Modeling Technology, Deventer, The Netherlands, The Netherlands, Kluwer, B.V. (2002) 303–311
25. Cardoso, J., Sheth, A.: Semantic e-workflow composition. J. Intell. Inf. Syst. **21** (2003) 191–225

# Semi-automatic Semantic-Based Web Service Classification

Miguel Ángel Corella and Pablo Castells

Universidad Autónoma de Madrid, Escuela Politécnica Superior
Campus de Cantoblanco, 28049 Madrid, Spain
{miguel.corella, pablo.castells}@uam.es

**Abstract.** With the expectable growth of the number of Web services available on the WWW and service repositories, the need for mechanisms that enable the automatic organization and discovery of services becomes increasingly important. Service classification using standard or proprietary taxonomies is a common and simple facility in this context, complementarily to more sophisticated service management retrieval techniques. In this paper we propose a heuristic approach for the semi-automatic classification of Web services, based on a three-level matching procedure between services and classification categories, assuming a corpus of previously classified services is available. An experimental test of the proposed techniques is reported, showing positive results.

## 1 Introduction

Since the emergence of the semantic Web [3], many research efforts have been aiming to use semantics to endow Web services with a higher potential for automation. These efforts have given rise to the semantic Web services vision [18]. The basis of this trend is to add semantic information to current Web service descriptions (in WSDL [6] format) to enable their analysis and manipulation by software programs enacting further automation capabilities for such tasks as service selection, invocation, composition, or discovery [11] and other tasks related to Web services but not often mentioned as being target of semantic-based technologies. In this paper we focus on the classification of Web services, this is, the assignment of a class to a service, at publication time, indicating the domain (i.e. the business focus) to which a service belongs.

Today, UDDI [14] is the most widely accepted and used protocol for publishing and searching Web services on the Web. These actions are usually performed within UDDI registries, which can be defined as service repositories available (and easy accessed through a URL) on the Internet. In these registries, services can be classified using one or several service taxonomies (such as UNSPSC[1] – United Nations Standard Products and Service Code, NAICS[2] – North American Industry Classification System, or even user-defined taxonomies created in UDDI format, since UDDI specification v.2). Nevertheless, this classification has to be performed manually by a

---

[1] http://www.unspsc.org/
[2] http://www.census.gov/naics

J. Eder, S. Dustdar et al. (Eds.): BPM 2006 Workshops, LNCS 4103, pp. 459–470, 2006.

human publisher. Due to the huge quantity of classes in standard service taxonomies like the ones already mentioned, the classification process is usually costly. Furthermore, taxonomies are subject to evolution, change or even replacement by new ones, making even heavier the maintenance effort load on repository administrators.

The purpose of the work presented here is to provide automatic mechanisms to help service publishers in the classification task at publication time. For this aim, we propose a heuristic-based classification system that compares a new service with the ones already classified in order to predict the appropriateness of the available classification categories for the new service, and produce a ranked list of candidate classes. Service classification is not only a must for manually browsing and managing service repositories, but can in fact be used for simple but efficient forms of service annotation and semi-automated discovery, complementary aid for automatic selection, etc.

The paper is organized as follows: Section 2 introduces some related work already presented in the domain of Web service classification and other related knowledge areas. Section 3 defines the problem of Web service classification in a more formal way and motivates why service semantics are needed in order to successfully solve it. The presentation and brief explanation of our classification heuristic is described in Section 4. Section 5 describes a framework where the classification method has been implemented and tested. Section 6 reports the experimental results obtained with our approach. Finally, Section 7 provides conclusions and outlines future work directions.

## 2  Related Work

The problem of the automatic classification of Web services has been addressed in prior work from two main approaches, that we may class as heuristic (e.g. [15]) and non-heuristic (e.g. [5] and [10]). In [10], two different strategies are proposed. The first one is based on using the information contained in non-semantic service descriptions to select a category in which the service fits best, by using Natural Language Processing, machine learning and text classification techniques. The second one consists of using the same information contained in service descriptions to dynamically create the categories in which the service should be classified, using clustering techniques. In both approaches the classification process is based on the extraction of relevant words from service descriptions, the construction of term vectors with those relevant words and the usage of classification mechanisms (e.g. Naïve Bayes) to perform the vector classification. This way, the service classification problem is solved by a text classification approach. From our point of view, this approach has two main drawbacks. First, the hypothesis of finding relevant and meaningful words in service descriptions is a very optimistic starting point. Next, doing clustering implies that the created categories do not have meaningful names, and the classification taxonomy changes over time. These two problems do not matter at publication time, but can be an issue if the classification information is intended to be used for service discovery, since users could neither select services by category (they do not have a name), nor get properly acquainted with the taxonomy, as its structure may change frequently.

The approach to classification proposed in [5] follows similar steps as those described in [10]. The main difference is that the method used to classify term vectors is based on Support Vector Machines. In addition, in this proposal, service publishers are provided with some extra information, more precisely, with a concept lattice extracted using Formal Concept Analysis over service descriptions. This extra information allows service publishers to know how the words used in their service descriptions contribute to the selection of a specific category, helping them to e.g. modify some words of their descriptions which may cause ambiguity in the classification process. As this approach also applies Natural Language Processing techniques on service descriptions, the same drawback as pointed out above can be found here, namely the assumption that meaningful textual information can be found in service descriptions (operation and parameter identifiers, comments, etc.) does often not hold.

In [15], a framework to semi-automate the semantic annotation of Web services (i.e. parameter description based on ontology concepts, semantic service classification, etc.) is presented. For classification, an algorithm to match Web service data types (in XML Schema[3]) and domain ontology concepts is defined based on schema matching. Assuming a 1-1 correspondence between domain ontologies and service categories, the classification is done by selecting the category that corresponds to the domain ontology that yields the highest similarity when compared to the service. The drawback here is that best practices in Web service definition prescribe document-based service descriptions, this is, service messages should consist of a unique part defined by a complex schema containing all the service parameters. With this form of description it is difficult to find similarities with domain ontology concepts as, usually, no single domain concept will contain the complete structure of service messages.

Another relevant area for our work is that of service matchmaking (see e.g. [12] and [16]). This research topic is related to Web service classification in that our approach to service classification computes similarity degrees between services in order to assign them a common category, and service matchmaking aims to find services that match a concrete capability description, e.g. in order to invoke matching services and/or compose them into more complex processes. The main difference between this research area and our addressed problem is that while in our view, service classification admits some degree of fuzziness in service matching, i.e. we consider a continuous similarity measure, work on service matchmaking typically does not, and is based on discrete matching levels (e.g. "no match", "partial match", "complete match").

# 3  The Service Classification Problem

As mentioned earlier, service classification is a common necessity to make service administration and retrieval manageable for human users. Moreover, it can serve as a complementary aid for automatic service discovery and selection techniques. Nevertheless, there are often usability problems involved in service categorization which cause difficulties for the creation, validation, and use of classifications in real-world environments. Such problems include:

---

[3] http://www.w3.org/TR/2001/REC-xmlschema-2-20010502

- Classification taxonomies can be extremely large, comprising thousands of categories (e.g. UNSPSC ~ 20,000 classes, NAICS ~ 2,300 classes).
- The number of services in a repository can grow quite large, making it virtually impossible for repository administrators to validate the information published along with a service.
- The placement of a service under a proper category requires a considerable amount of knowledge of the taxonomy, the application domain, etc., in order to make appropriate classification decisions. Few publishers or administrators have this knowledge with sufficient width and depth.

Our work aims at alleviating the administrator's work, and reducing the publication effort for service providers, by supplying them with a ranked set of likely appropriate categories when a new service has to be published in the repository. Our proposal approaches the classification problem as follows. Given a set of services already classified under a given taxonomy, and a new service description to be published, the unclassified service is compared with the classified ones, whereby a measure of the likelihood that the service should be assigned a certain category is computed.

WSDL descriptions provided by current technologies are not suitable for this purpose, as they only focus on the syntactic view of the services, which is not sufficient to support valid service classification criteria in practice.

## 3.1 The Need for Service Semantics

Consider this example: take two Web services, the first one defining currency conversion capabilities, and the second one describing a trip time calculator. A typical description of such functionalities in WSDL is provided in Appendix A at the end of this paper. Since WSDL service descriptions only include functional information (i.e. syntactic information about the service interface), the only available description elements to compare services are service operations, messages, and data types. As can be seen in the example, the currency converter service has one operation, involving:

- An input message containing an amount of money of type double, and two currency codes, of type string.
- An output message containing the converted amount (a double).

On the other hand, the trip time calculator service has also one operation, involving:

- An input message containing an average speed of type double, and two city names, of type string.
- An output message containing the trip time in minutes (a double).

From a conceptual point of view, these two services should yield a low similarity measure value when compared. However, since the WSDL interfaces are syntactically equivalent, their comparison would produce a very high result value.

- In conclusion, WSDL-based descriptions are not sufficient, and would often lead to inconsistent similarity values, and therefore, to service misclassification. Semantic Web service descriptions can solve this problem by providing means to describe service inputs and outputs from a conceptual point of view. A typical description of the examples as semantic Web services is included in Appendix B. We use WSMO [17] in the example, but our classification approach (as it is based on abstract mathematical similarity formulas) is language agnostic, so it is compatible with other semantic Web service languages such as OWL-S [13], WSDL-S [1], or SWSO [2].

# 4 Classification Heuristic

As introduced in earlier sections, our heuristic approach consists of the comparison of unclassified services with classified ones. The heuristic is divided into three levels, corresponding to the comparison between different service elements involved in the classification procedure, as we explain next. We will omit here all the mathematical formalization details, which can be found in [7].

**Service Category Level.** Since services have to be assigned a category as a result of the classification procedure, the consideration of this level is quite obvious. It is needed in order to find evidence that a service should belong to a specific category. This is the highest level of granularity in the classification method, at which a final service-category matching degree is obtained, which is used to sort the ranked service category list proposed to service publishers. The proposed computation for this measure is defined by:

$$P(s:c) \sim \sum_{A \subset \tau^{-1}(c)} (-1)^{|A|+1} \prod_{x \in A} \text{sim}(s,x)$$

where $P(s:c)$ is the evidence that the service $s$ should belong to the category $c$ formalized in a probabilistic way and estimated by the inclusion-exclusion principle [19] applied to a set of computed similarity values $\text{sim}(s,x)$, between service $s$ and all the services under category $c$. Thus, the predicted appropriateness of a category for a service increases with the similarity between the service and the classified services.

**Service Description Level.** The comparison between services is based on the assumption that services of the same category are likely to deal with similar concepts as inputs/outputs. Therefore, operation structures (i.e. conceptual roles and grouping of the data involved in the operations) are considered relevant for service-level comparisons. In fact, the similarity between two services is measured in terms of the similarity between service operation sets, and it is computed as the average of the best possible pairwise similarities obtained by an optimal pairing of the operations from the two sets. For this purpose, the similarity between two operations is computed as:

$$\text{sim}(op,op') = \text{sim}\left(I_{op}, I_{op'}\right) \cdot \text{sim}\left(O_{op}, O_{op'}\right)$$

where $I_{op}$, $I_{op'}$, $O_{op}$ and $O_{op'}$ are the set of input and output parameters of the operations $op$ and $op'$ respectively. The similarity between two parameter sets is computed in turn as the average of the best possible pairwise similarities obtained by an optimal pairing of the parameters from the two sets.

**Service Parameter Level.** The comparison of service parameters in our approach is based on the similarity between the ontology concepts used to annotate them. A considerable body of research has addressed the problem of matching ontology concepts (e.g. [4], [8], [9]). In our current experiments, we have tested our own concept to concept similarity measure, specifically devised and tuned to our approach. The similarity between two ontology concepts $t$ and $t'$ is measured by:

$$\text{sim}(t,t') = \left(1 - \frac{\alpha}{h(T)} \cdot \frac{|d-d'|}{d+d'}\right) \cdot \frac{1}{\min(d,d')} \cdot \left(1 - \frac{\max(d,d')-1}{h(T)}\right)$$

where $h(T)$ is the total height of the concept hierarchy in the ontology, $d$ and $d'$ are the distances from $t$ and $t'$, respectively, to their lowest common ancestor, and $\alpha \in [0,1]$ is a parameter that ensures a minimum non-zero similarity value to soften the impact of this measure on the overall heuristic. In our tests, $\alpha$ was tuned empirically to 0.8.

# 5 Implementation

We have implemented the techniques described in the previous sections into a service classification framework, serving the double purpose of a) demonstrating a practical environment where users can classify and store their services in a repository, and b) setting up experiments to test and evaluate our approach .

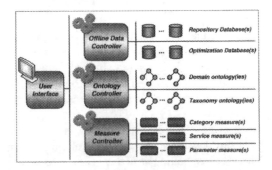

**Fig. 1.** Classification framework architecture showing the three main component types of the implementation: offline data controllers, ontology controllers and measure controllers

Figure 1 shows a high-level view of the main architectural components of this framework. These include:

- Offline Data Controllers: They are responsible for controlling the access to offline information stored in different databases. This offline information storage allows both the persistence of the service repository and the optimization of the execution time. For instance, since our techniques involve a combinatory comparison between services, parameters, etc., many similarity values are computed in advance and stored in the database, The offline data controllers are compatible with any service repository, by implementing a bridge from the repository to our database.

- Ontology Controllers: They interface with the different ontologies that may be involved in the classification process. These include both domain ontologies containing the concepts used in semantic Web service descriptions, and service taxonomies, represented in an ontological format. Again the generality of these components allows plugging any ontology into the framework.

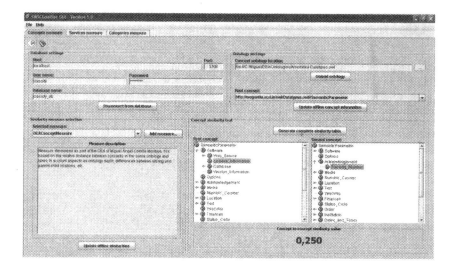

**Fig. 2.** Screenshot of the classification framework to use and test our approach

- Measure Controllers: They interface with the similarity measures involved in the heuristic. Once again, these abstraction components enable using any similarity measure at each level provided that it complies with the controller interface.

The above components are provided to achieve as much generality as possible. This way, our framework can be easily configured for the classification of services described with any domain ontology, into any taxonomy, based on any matching functions (at each comparison level), and using in any repository implementation standard (e.g. UDDI). This flexibility is also a valuable feature to facilitate the tests involved in our research. A screenshot of the framework user interface is shown in Figure 2.

## 6  Experiments and Evaluation

The approach proposed here was tested and evaluated in the implemented framework. The corpus used in the experiments is a repository containing 164 semantic Web service descriptions (in OWL-S), annotated using an ontology containing over 400 atomic concepts (i.e. no complex concept definitions, as e.g. OWL or WSML support, were used yet in our experiments). The services were manually classified using a taxonomy containing 23 different service categories. The service repository was essentially the one used in several other studies [5, 10, 15], and available in A. Heβ's Web page[4]. We have reused the domain ontology and the taxonomy included in this corpus, but have mapped the service descriptions to WSMO in order to reuse some tools available or developed in our research group (e.g. an input/output concept extractor or a translator to Racer[5] logical axioms enabling reasoning in our future work).

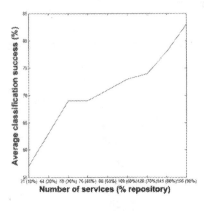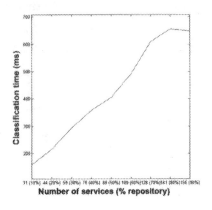

**Fig. 3.** Average classification success rate (i.e. correct class is at top of the ranking) vs. the services used as evidence (left), and average service classification time vs. the number of services in the repository (right). The test was performed with a repository of 164 services.

Using this corpus, we have conducted several effectiveness and performance tests by using a part of the repository as evidence (i.e. classifications taken as a given), and the rest for testing (i.e. services to be classified). The experiments were run for different ratios of evidence vs. test corpus sizes, in order to observe the evolution of the performance measures with respect to the amount of training data. The results obtained in the experiments are shown in Figure 3. The tested features are:

- Classification success rate: In this test we measured the average percentage of correct classifications with respect to the percentage of the repository used as evidence and test. A correct classification is one that ranks first the right (manually assigned) category of a service in the ranking of possible categories. This provides an estimation of the average probability of offering the correct category as first option. It can be seen that the success rate is about 83% when almost all the available corpus of 164 (but eight) services is used as evidence. In the cases where the method failed, the correct class was usually second or third in the ranking.
- Time performance: Although this is not a critical issue for classification, since this process can be performed offline at service publication time, our framework aims to be as efficient as possible. Thus we have measured the average classification time with respect to the size of the repository, which shows linear growth up to less than 7 s., on an Intel® Pentium® M, 1.73 GHz and 1 GB of RAM available.

---

[4] http://www.few.vu.nl/~andreas/projects/annotator/owl-ds.html
[5] http://www.racer-systems.com

# 7 Conclusions and Future Work

We have presented an efficient service classification approach based on conceptual service descriptions, that can be used to assist publishers, consumers and repository administrators in manual service categorization and retrieval tasks. As a continuation of the work presented here, we plan to investigate the potential of the proposed classification capabilities to enhance automatic service retrieval mechanisms. The heuristics have been tested on a corpus use in prior research by different authors, showing positive results. The generality of the implemented framework allows the easy integration and testing of different similarity measures at the three proposed granularity levels.

Besides the combination of our approach with service discovery techniques, as future work we envisage the extension of the algorithms to deal with more complex ontology-based descriptions of concepts, service capabilities (by Boolean expressions), etc. This involves a generalization of our basic matching functions, which could benefit from available ontology-oriented reasoners, and could link to ongoing related research in service matchmaking. Further experimentation and testing of our approach is foreseen as well, such as the comparison with other existing techniques, similarity measures, as well as the combination of several measures into improved ones, tests on larger repositories, performance tests with respect to further corpus features (such as taxonomy and ontology size, service disparity), etc.

## Acknowledgements

This research was supported by the Spanish Ministry of Industry, Tourism and Commerce (CDTI05-0436) and the Ministry of Science and Education (TIN2005-0685). Thanks are due to Rubén Lara for all his feedback and ideas on the research presented.

## References

1. Akkiraju, R., Farrel, J., Miller, J., Nagarajan, M., Schmidt, M., Sheth, A., Verma, K: Web Service Semantics – WSDL-S, Technical Note, Version 1.0, 2005.
2. Battle, S., Bernstein, A., Booley, H., Grosof, B., Gruninger, M., Hull, R., Kifer, M., Martin, D., McIlraith, S., McGuiness, D., Su, J., Tabet, S.: Semantic Web Service Ontology (SWSO), Version 1.0, 2005.
3. Berners-Lee, T., Hendler, J., Lassila, O.: The semantic web. Scientific American, 2001.
4. Bernstein, A., Kaufmann, E., Bürki, C., Klein, M.: How similar is it? Towards personalized similarity measures in ontologies. In the 7th Internationale Tagung Wirtschaftsinformaitk. Bamberg, Germany, 2005, pp. 1347-1366.
5. Bruno, M., Canfora, G., Di Penta, M., Scognamiglio, R.: An approach to support web service classification and annotation. In Proceedings of the IEEE International Conference on e-Technology, e-Commmerce and e-Services (EEE 2005), Hong Kong 2005.
6. Christiensen, E. et al: Web Service Description Language (WSDL), v1.1.

7. Corella, M. A., Castells, P.: A Heuristic Approach to Semantic Web Services Classification. In Proceedings of the 10<sup>th</sup> International Conference on Knowledge-Based & Intelligent Information & Engineering Systems (KES 2006), Bournemouth, UK, 2006.

8. Culmore, R., Rossi, G., Merelli, E.: An ontology similarity algorithm for BioAgent. In NETTAB 02 Agents in Bioinformatics. Bologna, Italy, 2002.

9. Ehrig, M., Haase, P., Stojanovic, N.: Similarity for ontologies – a comprehensive framework. Workshop on Enterprise Modelling and Ontology at PAKM 2004. Austria, 2004.

10. Heβ, A., Kushmerick, N.: Automatically attaching semantic metadata to Web Services. In Workshop on Information Integration on the Web (IIWeb2003), Acapulco, Mexico, 2003.

11. Keller, U., Lara, R., Lausen, H., Polleres, A., Fensel, D.: Automatic Location of Services. In 2<sup>nd</sup> European Semantic Web Conference (ESWC 2005). LNCS Vol. 3532 pp. 1-16.

12. Li, L., Horrocks, I.: A software framework for matchmaking based on semantic web technology. In the International Journal of Electronic Commerce, 8(4):39 – 60. 2004.

13. Maritn, D., Burnstein, M., Hobbs, J., Lassila, O., McDermott, D., McIlraith, S., Narayanan, S., Paolucci, M., Parsia, B. et al: OWL-S: Semantic markup for web services, v1.1, 2004.

14. OASIS: UDDI: The UDDI technical white paper, 2004.

15. Oldham, N., Thomas, C., Sheth, A., Verma, K.: METEOR-S Web Service Annotation Framework with Machine Learning Classification. In Proc. of the 1<sup>st</sup> Int. Workshop on Semantic Web Services and Web Process Composition (SWSWPC'04), California, July 2004.

16. Paolucci, M., Kawamura, T., Payne, T., Sycara, K.: Semantic Matching of Web Service Capabilities. In Proceedings of the First International Semantic Web Conference, 2002.

17. Roman, D., Lausen, H., Keller, U., de Brujin, J., Bussler, C., Domingue, J., Fensel, D., Hepp, M., Kifer, M., König-Ries, B., Kopecky, J., Lara, R., Oren, E., Polleres, A., Scicluna, J., Stollberg, M.: Web Service Modeling Ontology (WSMO), 2005.

18. Terziyan, V. Y., Kononenko, O.: Semantic web enabled web services: State-of-the-art and industrial challenges. In Proc. International Conference on Web Services (ICWS), 2003.

19. Whitworth, W. A.: Choice and Chance, with one thousand exercises. Hafner Pub. Co. New York, 1965.

# Appendix A: WSDL Example Descriptions

## Example Service 1: Currency Converter

```
<wsdl:definitions ... >
 <wsdl:types>
  <schema targetNamespace="http://nets.ii.uam.es/CurrencyConverter"
          xmlns="http://www.w3.org/2001/XMLSchema">
   <complexType name="CurrencyConverterRequest"> <sequence>
     <element name="amount" type="xsd:double"/>
     <element name="currencyCode1" type="xsd:string"/>
     <element name="currencyCode2" type="xsd:string"/>
    </sequence> </complexType>
   <complexType name="CurrencyConverterResponse"> <sequence>
     <element name="convertedAmount" type="xsd:double"/>
    </sequence> </complexType>
  </schema>
 </wsdl:types>
 <wsdl:message name="convertCurrencyRequest">
    <wsdl:part name="request" type="impl:CurrencyConverterRequest"/>
 </wsdl:message>
 <wsdl:message name="convertCurrencyResponse">
    <wsdl:part name="response" type="impl:CurrencyConverterResponse"/>
 </wsdl:message>
 <wsdl:portType name="CurrencyConverterPortType">
    <wsdl:operation name="convertCurrency" parameterOrder="request">
       <wsdl:input message="impl:convertCurrencyRequest"
                   name="convertCurrencyRequest"/>
       <wsdl:output message="impl:convertCurrencyResponse"
                   name="convertCurrencyResponse"/>
    </wsdl:operation>
 </wsdl:portType>
...
</wsdl:definitions>
```

## Example Service 2: Trip Time Calculator

```
<wsdl:definitions ...>
 <wsdl:types>
  <schema targetNamespace="http://nets.ii.uam.es/TripTimeCalculator"
          xmlns="http://www.w3.org/2001/XMLSchema">
   <complexType name="TripTimeCalcualtorRequest"> <sequence>
     <element name="averageSpeed" type="xsd:double"/>
     <element name="departureCity" type="xsd:string"/>
     <element name="destinationCity" type="xsd:string"/>
    </sequence> </complexType>
   <complexType name="TripTimeCalculatorResponse"> <sequence>
     <element name="tripDuration" type="xsd:double"/>
    </sequence> </complexType>
  </schema>
 </wsdl:types>
 <wsdl:message name="tripTimeCalculatorRequest">
    <wsdl:part name="request" type="impl:TripTimeCalculatorRequest"/>
 </wsdl:message>
 <wsdl:message name="tripTimeCalculatorResponse">
    <wsdl:part name="response" type="impl:TripTimeCalculatorResponse"/>
 </wsdl:message>
 <wsdl:portType name="TripTimeCalculatorPortType">
    <wsdl:operation name="calculateTripTime" parameterOrder="request">
       <wsdl:input message="impl:tripTimeCalculatorRequest"
                   name="calculateTripTimeRequest"/>
       <wsdl:output message="impl:tripTimeCalculatorResponse"
                   name="calculateTripTimeResponse"/>
    </wsdl:operation>
 </wsdl:portType>
...
</wsdl:definitions>
```

# Appendix B: WSMO Example Descriptions

## Example Service 1: Currency Converter

```
namespace {
   _"http://nets.ii.uam.es/CurrencyConverter#",
   dc _"http://purl.org/dc/elements/1.1#",
   sample _"http://nets.ii.uam.es/SampleOntology#",
}
webService _"http://nets.ii.uam.es/CurrencyConverter"
   capability ConverterCapability
       sharedVariables {?ccode2}
       precondition
          definedBy
             ?amount memberOf sample#MoneyAmount and
                ?amount[sample#fromCurrency hasValue ?ccode1] and
             ?ccode1 memberOf sample#CurrencyCode and
             ?ccode2 memberOf sample#CurrencyCode.
       postcondition
          definedBy
             ?convertedAmount memberOf sample#MoneyAmount and
                ?convertedAmount[sample#fromCurrency hasValue ?ccode2].
```

## Example Service 2: Trip Time Calculator

```
namespace {
   _"http://nets.ii.uam.es/TripTimeCalculator#",
   dc _"http://purl.org/dc/elements/1.1#",
   sample _"http://nets.ii.uam.es/SampleOntology#",
}
webService _"http://nets.ii.uam.es/TripTimeCalculator"
   capability CalculatorCapability
       precondition
          definedBy
             ?speed memberOf sample#Speed and
                ?speed[sample#inUnits hasValue "km"] and
             ?city1 memberOf sample#City and
             ?city2 memberOf sample#City.
       postcondition
          definedBy
             ?tripTime memberOf sample#Duration and
                ?tripTime[sample#inUnits hasValue "min"].
```

# Modeling, Matching and Ranking Services Based on Constraint Hardness

Claudia d'Amato[1] and Steffen Staab[2]

[1] Department of Computer Science, University of Bari - Italy
`claudia.damato@di.uniba.it`
[2] ISWeb, University of Koblenz-Landau - Germany
`staab@uni-koblenz.de`

**Abstract.** A framework for modeling Semantic Web Service is proposed. It is based on Description Logic (DL), hence it is endowed with a formal semantics and, in addition, it allows for expressing constraints in service descriptions of different strengths, i.e. *Hard* and *Soft Constraints*. *Semantic service discovery* can be performed by matching DL descriptions, expressing both Hard and Soft constraints, and exploiting DL inferences. Additionally, a method for solving the problem of *ranking* services is proposed which is based on the use of a semantic similarity measure for DL. This method can rank (matched) service descriptions on the grounds of their semantic similarity w.r.t. the service request, by preferring those that are able to better satisfy both Hard and Soft Constraints.

## 1 Introduction

In the last few years, the Web had two revolutionary changes, Web Service technology and the Semantic Web technology, that transformed it from a static document collection into an intelligent and dynamically integrated collection of resources. The former has allowed uniform access via Web standards to software components residing on various platforms and written in various programming languages. The latter has enriched existing Web data with their meaning, logically expressed with formal descriptions that are machine processable, thus facilitating access and integration. The major limitation of Web Services is that their retrieval and composition still require manual effort. To solve this problem, researchers have augmented Web Services with a semantic description of their functionality [8, 11]. By reusing a common vocabulary, service modelers can produce semantic service descriptions that can be shared and understood on the Web. Such vocabulary is defined by upper-level ontologies such as OWL-S[1] and WSMO[2] for *Semantic Web Services*.

In this paper we propose a framework for describing services, based on Description Logic (DL) [1]. DL is the theoretical foundation of OWL[3] language and it is endowed by a formal semantics, thus allowing expressive service descriptions. Moreover the service discovery task can be performed by algorithms defined in terms of standard and non-standard DL inferences. The use of DL in service descriptions and discovery task

---

[1] http://www.daml.org/services/owl-s/1.0/
[2] http://wsmo.org
[3] The ontology language for the Semantic Web, http://www.w3.org/2004/OWL/.

J. Eder, S. Dustdar et al. (Eds.): BPM 2006 Workshops, LNCS 4103, pp. 471–482, 2006.

is not new [7, 5, 13, 10, 14, 6, 3]. However in [7] it is showed that primitives, modeled by DL, sometimes produce counterintuitive results. This issue is analyzed in [6], where preliminary guidelines for modeling service descriptions are presented. Moreover, the notion of *variance* is introduced, namely a service description usually represents numerous variants of a concrete service. Exploiting this notion, a service discovery algorithm is proposed. The assumption is that precise control of *variance* in service description is crucial to ensure quality of the discovery process.

The framework that we propose enriches the guidelines of [6]. However, in a real scenario it is important to express another form of variance in service descriptions (and particularly in the service request side), represented by the optional and the mandatory aspects of a service description. Hence we introduce the notion of *Hard* and *Soft Constraints*. Namely, we call *Hard Constraints* (HC) those features of a service description that have to be necessarily satisfied by the target services and we call *Soft Constraints* (SC) those features whose satisfaction is only preferable. To be able to distinguish *HC* and *SC* is important both for *business-to-consumer* interaction and for service discovery task. In fact with respect to business-to-consumer interaction, *HC* and *SC* allow to express the real necessities of the user; with respect to the process discovery task, the distinction between *HC* and *SC* make possible to relax some needs, increasing the possibility of satisfying a request. We propose a way to express these kind of constraints and how to deal with them during the service discovery phase.

Furthermore, we propose a new procedure for ranking the services (discovered in the previous phase), that is able to manage the variance introduced by *HC* and *SC*. The procedure uses a semantic similarity measure for DL concept descriptions that assigns higher ranks to services that are more similar to the requested service and that satisfy both its *HC* and *SC*, while services that are less similar and/or satisfy only *SC* of the request receive a low rank.

The paper is organized as follows. The DL framework for describing services is presented in the next section. In Sect. 3 the discovery and ranking processes are detailed. The conclusions of this work are drawn in Sect. 4.

## 2    Modelling Service Descriptions

The main reason of the attention to service descriptions is the need of automating processes such as service discovery and composition. A *service description* is expressed as a set of constraints that have to be satisfied by the service providers. It can be thought as an abstract class acting as a template for *service instances*; namely, a service description defines a space of possible service instances (as in [12]), thus introducing *variance*.

Variance is the phenomenon of having more than one instance and/or more than one interpretation for a service description. Following [6], we distinguish between *variance due to intended diversity* and *variance due to incomplete knowledge*. To explain these concepts, the notion of *possible worlds* (borrowed from the first-order logic semantics) is used. Under open-world semantics, a modeler must explicitly state which service instances are not covered by the service description. For each aspect of the service description that is not fully specified there are *several possible worlds*, reflecting a way of resolving incompleteness (*variance due to incomplete knowledge*). Besides, given a possible world, the lack of constraints possibly allows for many instances satisfying a service description (*variance due to intended diversity*).

Let us consider the following service description (for a request):
Flight(flight) *and* operatedBy(flight,company)*and* departureTime(flight,time) *and* arrivalTime(flight,time) *and* from(flight,Germany) *and* to(flight,Italy)
and the *Service instances:*

- Flight(0542) *and* operatedBy(0542,ryanair) *and* departureTime(0542,8:00) *and* arrivalTime(0542,9:40) *and* from(0542,Hahn) *and* to(0542,Bari)
- Flight(0721) *and* operatedBy(0721,hlx) *and* departureTime(0721,12:00) *and* arrivalTime(0721,13:10) *and* from(0721,Cologne) *and* to(0721,Milan)

This description represents the request of flights from Germany to Italy, independently from departure and arrival time, company and cities involved. This lack of constraints allows many possible instances (as above), inducing *variance due to intended diversity*.

Now, let us consider the service instance below:
Flight(512) *and* operatedBy(512,airBerlin)*and* departureTime(512,18:00) *and* arrivalTime (512,19:30) *and* from(512,Berlin) *and* to(512,London)

This is also a correct instance of the service request reported above, because the fact that London is not an Italian city is left unspecified in the KB. So there can be a possible world in which London is an Italian city. Here the absence of constraints induces *variance due to incomplete knowledge*.

In order to cope with the effects of the *variance* on the semantics of a service description, it is necessary to adopt a language for service representation characterized by well-defined semantics. This is one of the peculiarities of the DL family. We intend to enrich the framework in [6] for describing services using DL, by showing how to deal with *HC* and *SC* expressed in service descriptions. The framework is reported below.

- A service description is expressed by a set of DL-axioms $D = \{S, \phi_1, \phi_2, ..., \phi_n\}$, where the axioms $\phi_i$ impose restrictions on an atomic concept $S$, which represents the service to be performed.
- Domain-specific background knowledge is represented by a *knowledge base* (KB) that contains all relevant domain-level facts.
- A *possible world*, resolving incomplete knowledge issues, is represented by a single DL model (interpretation) $I$ of $KB \sqcup D$.
- The service instances that are acceptable w.r.t. a service description $D$, are the individuals in the extension $S^I$ of the concept $S$ representing the service.
- Variance due to intended diversity is given by $S^I$ containing different individuals.
- Variance due to incomplete knowledge is reflected by $KB \sqcup D$ having several models $I_1, I_2, .....$.

The axioms in a service description $D$ constrain the set of acceptable service instances in $S^I$. These constraints are generally referred to the properties used in a description. Here, various ways for constraining a property using DL are reported.

**Variety:** a property can either be restricted to a fixed value or it can range over instances of a certain class. This is expressed by $\forall r.i$ (or $\exists r.i$) and $\forall r.C$ (or $\exists r.C$), respectively. For any acceptable service instance, the value of such a property must either be an individual or a member of a class.

**Multiplicity:** a property can either be multi-valued, allowing service instances with several property values, or single-valued, requiring service instances to have at most one value for the property. By the number restriction $\leq 1\ r$, a property is marked as single-valued. Using the restrictions $\leq m\ r$ (with $m \geq 2$) $\geq n\ r$, $\exists r.\top$, $\exists r.C$, and $\forall r.C$ a property is marked as multi-valued.

**Coverage:** a property can be explicitly known to cover a range. If a property is *range-covering*, the service description enforces that in every possible world, there is an acceptable service instance with this property value. This introduces variance due to intended diversity. This kind of constraint is expressed by an axiom of the form $C \sqsubseteq \exists r^-.S$ in $D$, where the concept $C$ is the range of the property $r$ to be covered. A non-range-covering property induces variance due to incomplete knowledge, as in distinct possible worlds different subsets of the range will be covered.

*Example 2.1.* Let us consider the following requested service description
$D_r = \{\ S_r \equiv$ Company $\sqcap \exists$payment.EPayment $\sqcap \exists$to.$\{$bari$\} \sqcap$
$\qquad \sqcap \exists$from.$\{$cologne,hahn$\} \sqcap\ \leq 1$ hasAlliance $\sqcap$
$\qquad \sqcap \forall$hasFidelityCard.$\{$milesAndMore$\}$;
$\qquad \{$cologne,hahn$\} \sqsubseteq \exists$ from$^-.S_r \qquad\qquad\qquad \}$
$KB = \{$cologne:Germany, hahn:Germany, bari:Italy, milesAndMore:Card$\}$
As defined with framework, $D_r$ is described as a set of axioms that impose restrictions on $S_r$ which is the service that has to be performed. The requester asks for flight companies that fly from Cologne and Hahn to Bari and accept electronic payment when selling tickets. Then it is required that a company has at most one alliance with another flight company and, if it has a fidelity program, it is "Miles and More". In the description, different several kinds of constraints are reported. *Variety* constraints are used with the properties to, from and hasFidelityCard, indeed these properties are restricted to a fixed value. The *at-most* number restriction ($\leq 1$) for the property hasAlliance is a *Multiplicity* constraint with which the property hasAlliance is declared to be single-value. A *Coverage* constraint is expressed by the last axiom in $D_r$ which makes explicit the range covered by the property from. Namely, this axiom asserts that $\{$cologne,hahn$\}$ is the range coverage of the property from.

If we require that, for all air companies, the payment method is specified and that the unique method allowed is electronic payment, the service description has to be:
$D_r = \{\ S_r \equiv$ Company $\sqcap \exists$payment.EPayment $\sqcap \forall$payment.EPayment $\sqcap$
$\qquad \sqcap \exists$from.$\{$cologne,hahn$\} \sqcap \exists$to.$\{$bari$\} \sqcap\ \leq 1$ hasAlliance $\sqcap$
$\qquad \sqcap \forall$hasFidelityCard.$\{$milesAndMore$\}$;
$\qquad \{$cologne,hahn$\} \sqsubseteq \exists$ from$^-.S_r \qquad\qquad\qquad\qquad \}$
In this way we force the existence of a payment method and oblige that all payment methods have to be electronic payments. $\qquad\qquad\qquad\qquad\qquad\qquad\qquad\qquad \Box$

The services presented in the example represent simple descriptions. In real scenarios a service request is typically characterized by some needs that *must* be necessarily satisfied and others that *should* be satisfied (expressing a preference). Then, the former will be considered as *Hard Constraints (HC)* and the latter as *Soft Constraints (SC)*. Taking this difference into account makes the service description and management more complex. The new descriptions have to be defined by the user/requester through an *HC* set and an *SC* set, whose elements are expressed in DL as seen above.

More formally, let $D_r^{HC} = \{S_r^{HC}, \sigma_1^{HC}, ..., \sigma_n^{HC}\}$ be the set of *HC* for a requested service description $D_r$ and let $D_r^{SC} = \{S_r^{SC}, \sigma_1^{SC}, ..., \sigma_m^{SC}\}$ be the set of *SC* for $D_r$. Every element in $D_r^{HC}$ and in $D_r^{SC}$ is expressed as previously seen. The complete description of $D_r$ is given by $D_r = \{S_r \equiv S_r^{HC} \sqcup S_r^{SC}, \sigma_1^{HC}, ..., \sigma_n^{HC}, \sigma_1^{SC}, ..., \sigma_m^{SC}\}$. Note that, in this description, new information on constraint hardness has been added.

*Example 2.2.* Let us consider a slightly modified version of the previous example distinguishing between *HC* and *SC*:

$$D_r = \{\ S_r \equiv \text{Flight} \sqcap \exists\text{from.}\{\text{Cologne, Hahn, Frankfurt}\} \sqcap \exists\text{to.}\{\text{Bari}\} \sqcap$$
$$\sqcap \forall\text{hasFidelityCard.}\{\text{MilesAndMore}\};$$
$$\{\text{Cologne, Hahn, Frankfurt}\} \sqsubseteq \exists\text{from}^-.S_r; \quad \{\text{Bari}\} \sqsubseteq \exists\text{to}^-.S_r \quad \}$$

where

$$HC_r = \{\ \text{Flight} \sqcap \exists\text{to.}\{\text{Bari}\} \sqcap \exists\text{from.}\{\text{Cologne, Hahn, Frankfurt}\};$$
$$\{\text{Cologne, Hahn, Frankfurt}\} \sqsubseteq \exists\text{from}^-.S_r; \quad \{\text{Bari}\} \sqsubseteq \exists\text{to}^-.S_r \ \}$$
$$SC_r = \{\ \text{Flight} \sqcap \forall\text{hasFidelityCard.}\{\text{MilesAndMore}\}\};$$

$$KB = \{\ \text{cologne,hahn,cologne:Germany, bari:Italy, MilesAndMore:Card}\}$$

With this service description a requester asks for flights starting from Frankfurt or Cologne or Hahn and arriving at Bari. The use of "Miles And More" card would be preferred. Departure and arrival places are expressed as *HC*. This means that provided services must fulfil these constraints. This is understandable thinking, for instance, to a requester that want to go from Koblenz to Bari. He/she is interested in Cologne, Hahn and Frankfurt airports because they have the same distance from Koblenz, while he/she is not interested in other airports because much more distance. Instead the use of "Miles And More" card is expressed as *SC*, namely flights that allow the use of this card are preferred, but the requester accepts also flights that do not allow the use of this card. This is because the use of *Miles and More* card is advantageous for the requester but it is not his primary need; his/her primary need is to have a flight for reaching Bari.    □

This new representation can better model the requester's needs, allowing to express real-life preferences, feature not considered in the original framework [6]. Moreover expressing *SC* allows to have service instances satisfying a request even if part of it is ignored, thus augmenting the possibility of having response for a request.

## 3    Service Discovery and Ranking

*Service Discovery* is the task of locating service providers that can satisfy the requester's needs. In this scenario, semantic service descriptions can be used to automate the task. Discovery is performed by matching a requested service description to the service descriptions of potential providers, in order to detect relevant ones. Two service descriptions match if there is an acceptable instance for both descriptions [14, 12, 6, 7].

Considering the framework presented in Sect. 2, let $D_r$ and $D_p$ respectively a requested service description and a provided service description, expressed as a set of axioms imposing restrictions on the services that have to be performed that are called $S_r$ and $S_p$ respectively. The matching process (w.r.t. a $KB$) can be defined as a boolean function $match(KB, D_r, D_p)$ which specifies how to apply DL inferences to perform matching. Various matching procedure, based on DL inferences, have been proposed [7, 14, 12]. We fix our attention to those proposed in [6]. Differently from the others, this procedure is able to treat *variance* (particularly variance due to incomplete knowledge) without being too weak or too strong. Indeed, the other matching procedures [13, 14, 5] consider a match valid if there exists a common instance service at least in *one possible world*. This match, called *Satisfiability of Concept Conjunction*, is the weakest check w.r.t. both kinds of variance. Indeed, along the dimension of intended diversity, it is sufficient to find one common service instance. Along the dimension of incomplete knowledge, it is sufficient to find one possible world in which such a service instance exists, regardless of all other possible worlds.

Another type of matching procedure [7, 10, 9] executes match by checking for subsumption, either of the requestor's description by the provider's or vice versa. It is called *Entailment of Concept Subsumption*. This check is very strong, since it requires one of the service descriptions to be more specific than the other, for all service instances in all possible worlds. Conversely, a valid match for the procedure in [6] occurs when there exists a common instance service between a provider's service description $D_p$ and a requestor's service description $D_r$ w.r.t. $KB$, in *every possible world*. It can be formalized as:

$$KB \cup D_r \cup D_p \models \exists x S_r(x) \wedge S_p(x) \Leftrightarrow KB \cup D_r \cup D_p \cup \{S_r \sqcap S_p \sqsubseteq \bot\} \text{unsatisfiable}$$

This check is called *Entailment of Concept Non-Disjointness*. It is stronger than *Satisfiability of Concept Conjunction* because checks for an intersection in every possible world, but it is not as strong as *Entailment of Concept Subsumption*, because it does not require one of the sets of acceptable service instances to be fully contained in the other set. This match increases (w.r.t *Entailment of Concept Subsumption*) the possibility to find interesting provided services, decreasing the error due to variety (more present in *Satisfiability of Concept Conjunction*).

The provided services, selected by the matching process, have to be ranked w.r.t. certain criteria and then returned to the requestor, in order to start the negotiation process between the requested service and provided services. We focus our attention on the ranking services process and propose a ranking procedure based on the use of a semantic similarity measure for DL. This procedure ranks in higher positions, provided services that are most similar to the requested service and that satisfy both $HC$ and $SC$ of the requested service. Instead, services that are less similar and/or satisfy only $HC$ are ranked in lower positions. This is because services that satisfy both $HC$ and $SC$ can satisfy more needs of the requested service than services that satisfy only $HC$. In the following, the measure used for determining the similarity value between service descriptions is presented, then the ranking services process is explained.

## 3.1 The Semantic Similarity Measure

The semantic similarity measure used for ranking services is presented in [4], in which a semantic similarity measure for DL concept definitions, asserted in the same ontology, is defined. Considering Sect. 2, service descriptions can be viewed as DL concept descriptions asserted in a *T-Box* and their instances can be regarded as concept assertions in an *A-Box* and the *Canonical Interpretation* can be considered (see [1] for details about *T-Box, A-Box* and *Canonical Interpretation*). So the following similarity measure can be applied to the service descriptions.

**Definition 3.1 (Semantic Similarity Measure).** *Let $\mathcal{L}$ be the set of all service descriptions and let $\mathcal{I}$ be the canonical interpretation which maps every service description to its instances. The Semantic Similarity Measure s is a function $s : \mathcal{L} \times \mathcal{L} \mapsto [0,1]$ defined as follows:*

$$s(S_r, S_p) = \frac{|(S_r \sqcap S_p)^{\mathcal{I}}|}{|(S_r \sqcup S_p)^{\mathcal{I}}|} \cdot \max\left(\frac{|(S_r \sqcap S_p)^{\mathcal{I}}|}{|S_r^{\mathcal{I}}|}, \frac{|(S_r \sqcap S_p)^{\mathcal{I}}|}{|S_p^{\mathcal{I}}|}\right)$$

*where $(\cdot)^{\mathcal{I}}$ computes the concept extension w.r.t. $\mathcal{I}$, $|\cdot|$ returns the cardinality of a set.*

This function assigns the maximum value in case of semantic equivalence of the service descriptions. Otherwise it assigns a value in the range $[0,1[$. This value grows with the increasing size of the set of service instances in common (given by the first factor) and it is weighted by a factor which represents the incidence of the intersection with respect to either concept. Particularly, the increase of this factor implies that the concepts are closer to subsume one the other (or even to be equivalent). This means to consider similarity not as an absolute value, but weighted with respect to the degree of non-similarity. The function $s$ is really a similarity measure, (according to the formal definition [2]) and its complexity mainly depends on the complexity of the instance checking operator (for the chosen DL) used to define the extension of concept descriptions (see [4] and Sect.3.3 for details). Similarity value is computed between a requested service description $S_r$ and a provided service description $S_p$, so the instance checking operator has to define the set of instances for them. For every provided service, the set of instances is known. We need to define the extension of $S_r$. Note that the measure is applied after the matching process and that the chosen matching procedure (see Sect.3) selects all provided services $S_p$ that have at least one instance satisfying $S_r$. So it is straightforward to understand that the set of instances for $S_r$ is given by the union of the provided service instances that satisfy $S_r$. Namely:

$$S_r^I = \bigcup_{j=1}^{n} \{x | S_r(x) \wedge S_p^j(x)\}$$

where $n$ is the number of provided services selected by the matching process.

## 3.2 Ranking Procedure

The rationale of the procedure consists in measuring the similarity between the requested and the provided services, selected by the matching phase: a higher similarity will result in higher rankings.

The presented measure assigns highest values to services that share most of the instances with $S_r$ so, as in [6], the criterion used is based on *variance*, namely, a provider is better than another if the variance it provides is greater than the other. However, differently from [6], we are able to supply a total order of the provided services (rather than a partial order). Anyway this is not enough for ensuring that provided services satisfying both $HC$ and $SC$ of $S_r$ will be in the higher positions, while services satisfying only $HC$ will be in the lower positions. Let us consider the following scenario: let $S_r$ be the requested service and let $S_p^l$ and $S_p^k$ two provided services, selected by the matching procedure. As said in Sect.2, a service is mainly described by the set of $HC$ and $SC$. Particularly, a service can also be described only by $HC$ [4]. Let us suppose that $S_r$ is described by both $HC$ and $SC$, that $S_p^l$ is a provided service whose instances all satisfy only the $HC$ of $S_r$ and that $S_p^k$ is a provided service whose instances all satisfy both $HC$ and $SC$ of $S_r$. So let us consider the canonical interpretation, it is straightforward to see that $\forall x : S_p^k(x) \rightarrow S_p^l(x) \Leftrightarrow (S_p^k)^I \subseteq (S_p^l)^I \Rightarrow |(S_p^k)^I| \leq |(S_p^l)^I| \Rightarrow s(S_r, S_p^k) \leq s(S_r, S_p^l)$. This is the opposite result w.r.t. our criterion. Indeed we want that provided services satisfying both $HC$ and $SC$ of $S_r$ and more similar to $S_r$ are on top of the ranking. For achieving this goal, the ranking procedure is:

**given** $S_r = \{S_r^{HC}, S_r^{SC}\}$ service request; $S_p^i (i = 1, .., n)$ provided services selected by $match(KB, D_r, D_p^i)$;
**for** $i = 1, \ldots, n$ **do** compute $\bar{s}_i := s(S_r^{HC}, S_p^i)$
**let be** $S_r^{new} \equiv S_r^{HC} \sqcap S_r^{SC}$
**for** $i = 1, \ldots, n$ **do**
    compute $\bar{\bar{s}}_i := s(S_r^{new}, S_p^i)$
    $s_i := (\bar{s}_i + \bar{\bar{s}}_i)/2$

Let us call $S_r^{HC}$ the requested service description relative to $HC$ and $S_r^{SC}$ those relative to $SC$. For all $S_p^i$, the similarity values $\bar{s} := s(S_r^{HC}, S_p^i)$ are computed. Hence, let us consider a new service description $S_r^{new} \equiv S_r^{HC} \sqcap S_r^{SC}$ defined as the conjunction of $HC$ and $SC$ of $S_r$. The instances of $S_r^{new}$ satisfy both $HC$ and $SC$ of $S_r$. So, for all $S_p^i$ the similarity values $\bar{\bar{s}} := s(S_r^{new}, S_p^i)$ are computed. It is straightforward to understand that a $S_p^i$ satisfying only $HC$ of $S_r$ will has $\bar{\bar{s}} = 0$. For all $S_p^i$, the final similarity value $s_i$ is given by the average between $\bar{s}$ and $\bar{\bar{s}}$. This last value $s_i$ is used for setting the rank of the services.

Let clarify this process considering the following example. $D_r$ is a requested service description, $D_p^l$ and $D_p^k$ are two provided service description, selected by the matching process. $KB$ is the used knowledge base. We rank $D_p^l$ and $D_p^k$. Let note that here $D_p^l$ and $D_p^k$ are described specifying their $HC$ and $SC$. This is in order to show how the ranking process work in this case. However, it is straightforward to see that the procedure can rank provided services even if they are described without any specification about their constraint hardness.

$D_r = \{ \ S_r \equiv$ Flight $\sqcap \forall$operatedBy.LowCostCompany $\sqcap \exists$to.$\{$bari$\} \sqcap$
              $\sqcap \exists$ from.$\{$cologne,hahn$\} \sqcap \forall$applicableToFlight.Card;
        $\{$cologne,hahn$\} \sqsubseteq \exists$ from$^-$.$S_r$                                  $\}$

---

[4] A service can not be described only by $SC$ because it means ask for a service that contains only optional constraints and this does not make sense.

where

$$HC_r = \{ \text{Flight} \sqcap \exists \text{to}.\{\text{bari}\} \sqcap \exists \text{from}.\{\text{cologne,hahn}\}$$
$$\{\text{cologne,hahn}\} \sqsubseteq \exists \text{from}^-.S_r \qquad \}$$
$$SC_r = \{ \text{Flight} \sqcap \forall \text{operatedBy.LowCostCompany} \sqcap \forall \text{applicableToFlight.Card}\};$$

$$D_p^l = \{ S_p^l \equiv \text{Flight} \sqcap \exists \text{to.Italy} \sqcap \exists \text{from.Germany};$$
$$\text{Germany} \sqsubseteq \exists \text{from}^-.S_p^l; \quad \text{Italy} \sqsubseteq \exists \text{to}^-.S_p^l \}$$
where

$$HC_p^l = \{ \text{Flight} \sqcap \exists \text{to.Italy} \sqcap \exists \text{from.Germany};$$
$$\text{Germany} \sqsubseteq \exists \text{from}^-.S_p^l; \quad \text{Italy} \sqsubseteq \exists \text{to}^-.S_p^l \}$$
$$SC_p^l = \{\}$$

$$D_p^k = \{ S_p^k \equiv \text{Flight} \sqcap \forall \text{operatedBy.LowCostCompany} \sqcap \exists \text{to.Italy} \sqcap$$
$$\sqcap \exists \text{from.Germany};$$
$$\text{Germany} \sqsubseteq \exists \text{from}^-.S_p^k; \quad \text{Italy} \sqsubseteq \exists \text{to}^-.S_p^k \qquad \}$$
where

$$HC_p^k = \{ \text{Flight} \sqcap \exists \text{to.Italy} \sqcap \exists \text{from.Germany};$$
$$\text{Germany} \sqsubseteq \exists \text{from}^-.S_p^k; \quad \text{Italy} \sqsubseteq \exists \text{to}^-.S_p^k \}$$
$$SC_p^k = \{ \text{Flight} \sqcap \forall \text{operatedBy.LowCostCompany}\};$$

$$KB = \{ \text{cologne,hahn:Germany, bari:Italy, LowCostCompany} \sqsubseteq \text{Company} \}$$

Let us consider $S_r$, $S_p^l$ and $S_p^k$. Let note that $S_p^l$ satisfies only $HC$ of $S_r$ while $S_p^k$ satisfies both $HC$ and $SC$ of $S_r$. Let us suppose that the extensions of $S_p^l$ and $S_p^k$ are: $|(S_p^l)^{\mathcal{I}}| = 8$ and $|(S_p^k)^{\mathcal{I}}| = 5$ and all instances satisfy $S_r$. Note that $S_p^k \sqsubseteq S_p^l$ then $(S_p^k)^{\mathcal{I}} \subseteq (S_p^l)^{\mathcal{I}}$. So $|(S_r)^{\mathcal{I}}| = 8$. Furthermore, $S_r \not\equiv S_p^l$ and $S_r \not\equiv S_p^k$. Let us consider $S_r^{HC}$ given by: $S_r^{HC} \equiv \text{Flight} \sqcap \exists \text{from}.\{\text{cologne,hahn}\} \sqcap \exists \text{to}.\{\text{bari}\}$ and $S_r^{SC}$ given by $S_r^{SC} \equiv \text{Flight} \sqcap \forall \text{operatedBy.LowCostCompany} \sqcap \forall \text{applicableToFlight.Card}$. Known that all the instances of $S_p^l$ and $S_p^k$ satisfy $S_r$ and particularly that $S_p^l$ satisfies only $HC$ of $S_r$ while $S_p^k$ satisfies both $HC$ and $SC$ of $S_r$, it is straightforward to understand that $|(S_r^{HC} \sqcap S_p^l)^{I}| = 8$ and that $|((S_r^{HC} \sqcap S_r^{SC}) \sqcap S_p^l)^{I}| = |(S_r^{new} \sqcap S_p^l)^{I}| = 0$, consequently $\overline{s_l} = 0$. In the other case, we know that $|(S_p^k)^{\mathcal{I}}| = 5$ and that $S_p^k$ satisfies both $HC$ and $SC$ of $S_r$. So, some instances of $S_p^k$ can satisfy only $HC$ of $S_r$ and others satisfy both $HC$ and $SC$ (in the better case we could have that all instances of $S_p^k$ satisfy both $HC$ and $SC$). Let us suppose that instances of $S_p^k$ that satisfy both $HC$ and $SC$ of $S_r$, namely that satisfy $S_r^{new} \equiv S_r^{HC} \sqcap S_r^{SC}$ are 3. Let applying the procedure:

$$\bar{s}_l := s(S_r^{HC}, S_p^l) = \frac{|(S_r^{HC} \sqcap S_p^l)^{\mathcal{I}}|}{|(S_r^{HC} \sqcup S_p^l)^{\mathcal{I}}|} \cdot \max\left(\frac{|(S_r^{HC} \sqcap S_p^l)^{\mathcal{I}}|}{|(S_r^{HC})^{\mathcal{I}}|}, \frac{|(S_r^{HC} \sqcap S_p^l)^{\mathcal{I}}|}{|(S_p^l)^{\mathcal{I}}|}\right) = \frac{8}{8} \cdot \max\left(\frac{8}{8}, \frac{8}{8}\right) = 1$$

$$\bar{s}_k := s(S_r^{HC}, S_p^k) = \frac{|(S_r \sqcap S_p^k)^{\mathcal{I}}|}{|(S_r \sqcup S_p^k)^{\mathcal{I}}|} \cdot \max\left(\frac{|(S_r \sqcap S_p^k)^{\mathcal{I}}|}{|S_r^{\mathcal{I}}|}, \frac{|(S_r \sqcap S_p^k)^{\mathcal{I}}|}{|(S_p^k)^{\mathcal{I}}|}\right) = \frac{5}{8} \cdot \max\left(\frac{5}{5}, \frac{5}{5}\right) = 0.625$$

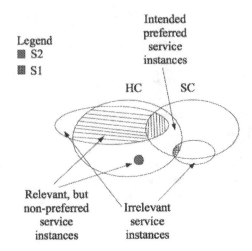

**Fig. 1.** Common instances between requested service and provided services for their ranking

The next step is computing $\overline{\overline{s_l}}$ and $\overline{\overline{s_k}}$, that, considering the observation above are given by:

$$\overline{\overline{s_l}} := s(S_r^{new}, S_p^l) = 0$$
$$\overline{\overline{s_k}} := \frac{|(S_r^{new} \sqcap S_p^k)^{\mathcal{I}}|}{|(S_r^{new} \sqcup S_p^k)^{\mathcal{I}}|} \cdot \max(\frac{|(S_r^{SC} \sqcap S_p^k)^{\mathcal{I}}|}{|(S_r^{new})^{\mathcal{I}}|}, \frac{|(S_r^{new} \sqcap S_p^k)^{\mathcal{I}}|}{|(S_p^k)^{\mathcal{I}}|}) = \frac{3}{5} \cdot \max(\frac{3}{3}, \frac{3}{5}) = \frac{3}{5} = 0.6$$

Hence the final similarity values are: $s_l = 0.5$, $s_k = 0.6125$ and so the ranking of the provided services is:

1.  $S_p^k$    *Similarity Value*  0.6125
2.  $S_p^l$    *Similarity Value*  0.5

This result is consistent with the goal. Namely, using this procedure, provided services are ranked w.r.t. both variance and satisfaction of $S_r$'s SC.

More in general, the rational of the ranking procedure is showed in Fig. 1. As seen in Sec. 3.1, due to the chosen matching procedure, all the services that have to be ranked have at least one instance satisfying $S_r$. In the figure, HC and SC represent the Hard and Soft Constraints of the requested service and $S_1$ and $S_2$ represent services to rank. All the instances of $S_1$ or $S_2$ that are in HC are relevant instance service for $S_r$, because they satisfy its HC. However they are not the preferred instance services for $S_r$ because they do not satisfy also SC of $S_r$. For example if the HC of $S_r$ ask for flights from Cologne to Bari and the SC of $S_r$ ask for flights that allow the use of Miles and More card then all the instances of $S_1$ and $S_2$ that are in HC are all flights from Cologne to Bari held by two different company. This instances are relevant because they satisfy the main need, however flights from Cologne to Bari that allow the use of Miles and More card will be preferred w.r.t. flights that do not allow the use of this card. Thus the preferred instance services for $S_r$ are all the instances of $S_1$ and $S_2$ that are in the intersection between HC and SC. These instances are all the flights from Cologne to Bari of $S_1$ and $S_2$ that allow the use of Miles and More Card.

The parts of $S_1$ and $S_2$ outside $HC$ represents all the instances that do not satisfy $HC$ and thus irrelevant service instances for $S_r$; for example flights having a departure and/or arrival place different from those requested. In the same way the part of $S_2$ outside $HC$ but in $SC$ represents irrelevant service instances for $S_r$ because these instances satisfy $SC$ without satisfying $HC$; for example represents flights that allow the use of Miles and More card but that do not arrive in Bari and so these are not interesting for the request.

At the first time, the procedure ranks provided services that satisfy $HC$ w.r.t. variance criteria, indeed provided services that share most of service instances with $S_r$ have higher similarity value. Hence $SC$ are considered. The procedure assigns an additional similarity value to provided services that satisfy also $SC$. This similarity value is assigned, again using the variance criteria. Let note that in computing the additional similarity value are not considered all the service instances satisfying $SC$ of $S_r$ but only the service instances satisfying both $HC$ and $SC$ of $S_r$. This avoid to have in higher ranking position provided services that are very similar to $SC$ but dissimilar from $HC$, whose instances are obviously not preferred w.r.t. to services mostly similar to $HC$. Indeed the latter can have a lot of instances satisfying $SC$ but that are not relevant at all for the main request.

### 3.3 Discussion

In this section the complexity of the proposed algorithms is analyzed. Both matching and ranking procedure use reasoning services. Indeed for the matching process, two service descriptions match if their conjunction is not subsumed by the *bottom* concept. So the complexity of the matching procedure depends from the complexity of the subsumption operator for the chosen DL. For the ranking process, the dominant operation is the computation of the similarity value, for which the $s$ measure is called twice for every matched provided service that has to be ranked. The complexity of $s$ mainly depends from the complexity of the *instance checking* operator (for the chosen DL), used for computing the extensions of the service descriptions and the extension of their conjunction and disjunction. However the complexity of the ranking procedure could be decreased by reducing the number of calls to the instance checking operator. Indeed, the extensions of all available services can be computed beforehand, so at request-time, only the extension of the requested service description has to be computed. The extensions of the conjunctive and disjunctive service descriptions can be computed by the use of set theory applied to the extensions already determined.

## 4   Conclusion and Future Work

This paper proposes a framework based on DL for describing services. Differently from [6], to which it is inspired, our framework allows to express hard and soft constraints in a service description, thus obtaining a more flexible framework for service modeling.

Moreover, these new kind of constraints can be useful for supplying to the requester the most appropriate provided services among those selected from the matching phase. Indeed a new ranking procedure was presented in order to rank services selected by the discovery process. The aim of this ranking procedure was to help during the choice in the list of eligible provided services discovered in the previous phase. To this purpose, the procedure can take into account the presence of *HC* and *SC*, the *variance* exploiting a measure that can assess the semantic similarity between service descriptions. This yields a total order among the selected services, differently from [6] where the ranking procedure provides only a partial order and is not able to manage *HC* and *SC*.

For the future, an experimentation involving the framework, the matching and ranking procedures is necessary, in order to show the improvement of the quality of the results supplied to the requester. Moreover, a new matching process could be useful for further increasing the quality of the discovery process and reduce the noise in the selection of services.

# References

[1] F. Baader, D. Calvanese, D. McGuinness, D. Nardi, and P. Patel-Schneider, editors. *The Description Logic Handbook.* Cambridge University Press, 2003.

[2] H.H. Bock. *Analysis of Symbolic Data: Exploratory Methods for Extracting Statistical Information from Complex Data.* Springer-Verlag, 1999.

[3] Andrea Calì, Diego Calvanese, Simona Colucci, Tommaso Di Noia, and Francesco M. Donini. A description logic based approach for matching user profiles. In *Description Logics*, 2004.

[4] C. d'Amato, N. Fanizzi, and F. Esposito. A semantic similarity measure for expressive description logics. In A. Pettorossi, editor, *Proceedings of Convegno Italiano di Logica Computazionale, CILC05*, Rome, Italy, 2005.

[5] J. Gonzales-Castillo, D. Trastour, and C. Bartolini. Description logics for matchmaking of services. In *Proc. of KI-2001 Workshop on Applications of Description Logics*, page vol. 44, 2001.

[6] S. Grimm, B. Motik, and C. Preist. Variance in e-business service discovery. In *Proceedings of the ISWC Workshop on Semantic Web Services*, 2004.

[7] L. Li and I. Horrocks. A software framework for matchmaking based on semantic web technology. In *WWW '03: Proceedings of the 12th international conference on World Wide Web*, pages 331–339, New York, NY, USA, 2003. ACM Press.

[8] Sheila A. McIlraith and David L. Martin. Bringing semantics to web services. *IEEE Intelligent Systems*, 18(1):90–93, 2003.

[9] T. Di Noia, E. Di Sciascio, F.M. Donini, and M. Mongiello. A system for principled matchmaking in an electronic marketplace. In *WWW*, pages 321–330, 2003.

[10] M. Paolucci, T. Kawamura, T.R. Payne, and K.P. Sycara. Semantic matching of web services capabilities. In *International Semantic Web Conference*, pages 333–347, 2002.

[11] Massimo Paolucci and Katia P. Sycara. Autonomous semantic web services. *IEEE Internet Computing*, 7(5):34–41, 2003.

[12] Chris Preist. A conceptual architecture for semantic web services. In *Proceeding of International Semantic Web Conference*, pages 395–409, 2004.

[13] D. Trastour, C. Bartolini, and J. Gonzalez-Castillo. A semantic web approach to service description for matchmaking of services. In *SWWS*, pages 447–461, 2001.

[14] D. Trastour, C. Bartolini, and C. Preist. Semantic web support for the business-to-business e-commerce lifecycle. In *WWW '02: Proceedings of the 11th international conference on World Wide Web*, pages 89–98, New York, NY, USA, 2002. ACM Press.

# Version Management in Semantic Web Services Using OWL-S*

Maria Cecilia Bastarrica, Carlos Hurtado, and Alejandro Vaisman

Department of Computer Science, Universidad de Chile
{cecilia, churtado, avaisman}@dcc.uchile.cl

**Abstract.** In the last few years there has been an increasing interest in studying ontology evolution and versioning for the World Wide Web, in particular, applied to OWL. However, little attention has been given to the problem of Web services evolution, with a focus on OWL-S, an ontology of services recently proposed. In this paper, we show that recent work on Temporal RDF can be extended to support versioning of an ontology of services. We introduce a formal model and a query language that allow accessing different versions of an OWL-S specification. We present the language semantics and discuss complexity issues. We show how our proposal can be implemented within the OWL-S framework.

## 1 Introduction

OWL [19] is an ontology language for the Semantic Web, developed by the World Wide Web Consortium (W3C). It allows the representation of information about categories of objects, and how these objects interrelate. This information, in a Semantic Web scenario, can help to develop efficient automated processes in order to access information on the Web. OWL is built on top of the Resource Description Framework (RDF) [1,11], and extends RDF and RDFS, adding restrictions on properties, and operations like disjunction and negation.

Web services are software applications that interact using Web standards. Although Web service technology is rapidly gaining popularity, it still requires more human involvement than may be wanted. Avoiding this would imply the ability of automatically discovering and invoking Web services. Semantic Web technology has helped to solve this problem by means of *ontologies of services* that are used for representing a *service profile* (for describing services offered by a Web site). These ontologies can be used by service-seeking agents. The efforts for defining a standard for ontologies of services led to OWL-S [17], a language that allows to describe what a service provides, what a service requires from the users, how the service works, and how the service is used. OWL-S is aimed at enabling efficient automatic Web service discovery, invocation, interoperation, and execution monitoring.

---

* Partially supported by Millennium Nucleus Center for Web Research, Grant P04-67-F, Mideplan, Chile, and Project Fondecyt No. 1050642.

J. Eder, S. Dustdar et al. (Eds.): BPM 2006 Workshops, LNCS 4103, pp. 483–494, 2006.

## 1.1   Motivation

Today's business systems must be able to adapt to changes and so does the Semantic Web. Most of the change management tasks are still being performed manually [20], which is time-consuming and error prone. It would be desirable to add change management capabilities to the Semantic Web. An example of an evolving ontology is *MeSH*, a medical ontology used by MEDLINE, a huge source of medical information on the Web. *MeSH* is frequently updated in order to stay in line with the state-of-the-art in medical research. The changes that *MeSH* goes through consist of the addition of new terms, and also reclassification of such terms. It seems clear that there is need for ontology evolution support on the Web, as it has been pointed out in [5,10,13,14], among other works.

Another real-life example that illustrates the need for Web services versioning, is the area of mobile phones. Phone companies need to incorporate new services continuously in order to keep competitive in the market. To achieve the required flexibility and evolvability many of them are currently migrating their platforms towards service oriented architectures [4] where each service is implemented as a Web service. Each Web service may then provide a particular service with as many diverse operations as different cell phone platforms need to access the service. For example, the monotone ringtone service is different depending on the phone model. As the cell phone technology advances rapidly, new phone devices appear continuously and there is a need to provide support for them. Also, it may be necessary to keep the service version history in order to provide the service if holders of older phone models require it. Another typical use of this version history keeping is to determine the time interval in which the cell phone company supported the service for a certain phone model so that it can charge the phone vendor for providing support for its devices.

There are many ways to address ontology changes. Stojanovic [20] classifies ontology changes in four categories: (a) ontology management; (b) ontology modification; (c) ontology evolution, and (d) ontology versioning. There is limited work on ontology evolution, but little has been done on ontology versioning [13]. In this paper we address a topic still more unexplored: versioning of Web services ontologies. Versioning has been recognized as a relevant problem in Web service development [2,3]. However, no formal study has been attempted. Developers devise ad-hoc solutions when they need to deal with the problem of maintaining different versions of their applications. A proper mechanism for version management would allow easy access to different versions of a Web service ontology as of any point in time. Moreover, it would add flexibility, allowing to access simultaneously multiple versions of a service [3].

## 1.2   Problem Statement and Contributions

We address the problem of Web service versioning and we show that OWL-S, as a language for describing Web service ontologies, can be extended in order to support versioning. In this way, we are able to query and use past states of a service ontology. For this purpose, we use the approach in [6,7] for RDF.

A proper version management mechanism requires a temporal data model to support it. Thus, this paper proposes a temporal data model supporting versioning of Web services. We define an abstract model for OWL-S, and extend its components with temporal labels that indicate their intervals of validity, leading to a temporal OWL-S graph. This temporal model, denoted OWL-S(T), allows to manage versioning at two levels: version and state (i.e., within a version different states can be supported). We then define a notion of OWL-S(T) consistency, based on the framework proposed in [9], and we show how consistency can be checked in a temporal setting, ensuring that a document is consistent at any point in time. We propose a query language that supports typical temporal queries, and allows to retrieve versions of an OWL-S(T) document as of any instant in time. We give the semantics an complexity of the language. Finally, we sketch how our proposal can be implemented in the OWL-S framework.

Section 2 discusses related work. Section 3 gives an overview of temporal concepts and the OWL-S notions used in the paper; we also introduce the abstract model for OWL-S. Section 4 presents the model for introducing time in OWL-S and Section 5 a proposal for a query language. Section 6 discusses how the introduced concepts could be implemented within the OWL-S framework. We conclude in Section 7.

# 2  Related Work

The Ontology Web Language (OWL) [19] was developed by the W3C Web Ontology Working Group. Many of its features come from its predecessor DAML+OIL, and from the fields of Description Logic and Knowledge Representation. Horrocks et al [12] detail the evolution of OWL. OWL is built on top of RDF [16], a metadata language for the Semantic Web. Several languages for querying ontologies have been proposed and implemented, some of them in the lines of traditional database query languages, others based on logic and rule languages [8,15].

Although temporal management has been recently studied for semistructured, XML, and RDF data, little has been done to this respect in the Semantic Web setting. Among the four categories in which Stojanovic [20] classified ontology changes, we are particularly interested in *evolution* and *versioning*. Stojanovic addressed the first problem, and defined the requirements for an efficient ontology evolution system. This approach was implemented in the so-called KAON framework. The problem of preserving consistency upon an evolving ontology was studied by Haase et al [9]. This work provides a comprehensive overview of the state-of-the-art in ontology evolution [10]. Finally, Flouris et al [5] claim that the current approaches for ontology evolution lack formality, and propose a model that generalizes and applies the AGM postulates.

In the field of ontology versioning, Klein et al [13] present a system, called Onto View, that helps specifying relations between different versions of an ontology (but does not keep track of the history). Visser et al [22] propose a temporal reasoning framework for the Semantic Web, applied in BUSTER, an ontology-based prototype supporting the so-called *concept@location in time* type of query.

Huang *et al* propose a reasoning framework for ontology versioning, based on temporal logic; they claim that ontology evolution is well-understood, although ontology integrity is still an open research field. Their multi-version reasoning framework is aimed at discovering inconsistencies caused by ontology evolution. It is defined as an extension of linear temporal logic (LTL), denoted LTLm.

There is a clear need for version management in the design of Web services [2,3]. Brown *et al* [2] classified changes in Web services in two broad classes: *backward-compatible* and *non-backward-compatible*. In the former, we have the addition of new WSDL operations and new XML schema types. In the latter, they include: removing/renaming operations, changing the parameters of an operation, and changing the structure of a complex data type. In spite of this there is still no study of temporality issues in OWL-S ontologies and query languages.

## 3   Preliminaries

### 3.1   Temporal Issues

The existing approaches to ontology versioning are based on developing a new physical version of the ontology each time a change occurs. In [6], they propose a different approach for the evolution of RDF specifications, which can be seen as a logical theory. They timestamp the RDF triples with their interval of validity. In order to introduce the time dimension into OWL-S, we are faced with the same question: should we maintain a snapshot of each state of the graph or, should we label the elements of the OWL-S specification that are subject to changes? Although both models are equivalent, the first one appears to be not suitable for queries of the form: "all time instants where some condition $\Phi$ holds in the specification". It is well-known [21] that there are at least two temporal dimensions to consider: *valid* and *transaction* times. *Valid* time is the time when data is valid in the modeled world; *transaction* time is the time when data is actually stored in the database. The snapshot approach captures transaction time, while labeling is mostly used when representing valid time. The approach we present in this paper can support both time dimensions.

For evolving OWL-S specifications, labeling may do better in scenarios where changes are frequent and only affecting a few elements. In this situation, creating a new *physical* version of the graph each time an update occurs may lead to large overheads when processing temporal queries that span multiple versions. Thus, labeling will be our approach. We work with the point-based temporal domain for defining our data model and query language, but we encode time-points in intervals whenever possible, for the sake of clarity. We consider time as a discrete, linearly ordered domain, as usual in virtually all temporal database applications. As usual in temporal databases, the (moving) current instant is denoted *Now*.

### 3.2   OWL-S Overview

Software agents that access Web services need a description of the available services to perform an efficient service lookup. This description is provided by OWL-S [17]. At a high level of abstraction, OWL-S can be seen as an ontology structure

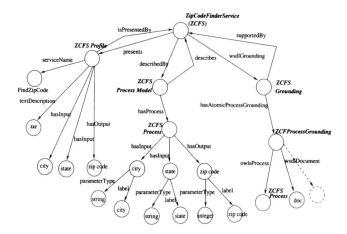

**Fig. 1.** Running example

whose instances are the OWL-S specifications. This structure or schema is composed of three classes: *ServiceProfile*, *ServiceModel* and *ServiceGrounding*. These classes are related to the *Service* class by the properties *presents*, *describedby*, and *supports*, respectively. These properties have also their inverse. For simplicity we focus on the properties `serviceName`, `textDescription`, `has parameter`, `has input`, `has output` for the class *Profile*; from the *Process* class (a subclass of *ServiceModel*), we use the `has input`, `has output`, `parameterType` and `label` properties; from *ServiceGrounding* we use the `wsdlDocument` property, which is the URI of the WSDL operation corresponding to an atomic process. We have chosen these properties because they give a good intuition of the problem, and their instances are likely to change over time.

Throughout the paper we use the service ontology depicted in Figure 1, adapted from [18]. This is an abstract representation of an OWL-S specification for a Web service that receives a pair city-state, and returns the corresponding zip code (for brevity, we only partially show the *Grounding* part). The service *Profile* tells what the service does, the *Process Model* tells the service clients how to use the service, and the *Grounding* specifies how an agent can access the service. WSDL operations bind the ontology to the implementation of the Web service. In the example of Figure 1, we have included the types and names of the service input and output parameters. The following fragment corresponds to the abstract graph in Figure 1.

```
...
<grounding:WsdlAtomicProcessGrounding rdf:ID=''ZCFProcessGrounding''>
 <grounding:owlProcess rdf:resource=''#ZipCodeFinderProcess''/>
 <grounding:wsdlDocument>
 ''http://www.dcc.uchile.cl/2005/ws/docum/ZipCode-v1.0.asmx?WDSL''
 </grounding:wsdlDocument>
 .... >
```

### 3.3   Abstract Model of OWL-S

In what follows, we adopt an abstract model for an instance of an OWL-S specification and we describe it as a graph (from now on, an *OWL-S graph*). We are
not interested in the OWL-S structure, given that we will consider this structure
*static*. Thus, we do not need our model to represent relations like *subpropertyOf*,
*subclassOf*, and so on. Figure 2 (a) shows an abstract model for an OWL-S instance. The nodes represent resources (domain and range of each property). The
edges represent OWL-S properties, which include properties provided by the
OWL-S ontology such as `presents`, `serviceName`, `hasInput`, and `hasOutput`.
Although we have denoted the properties $p_i$ with different names, this may not
always be the case. Edges denoted $inv(p_i)$ represent the inverse property of $p_i$,
like in the case of *describes* and *describedBy* in Figure 1. Note that this graph is
analogous to an RDF graph.

**Definition 1 (OWL-S graph).** *An OWL-S graph is a set of RDF triples*
$(a, p, b)$*, where p is an OWL-S property.*

We next incorporate OWL-S constraints and consistency in our model. We denote $\Sigma$ the set of OWL constraints given in the OWL-S specification. As an
example, we have in $\Sigma$ a constraint that states that all property $p$ is equivalent
to $inv(p)$, and a constraint that `isDescribedBy` has max cardinality 1.

**Definition 2 (OWL-S Consistency).** *An OWL-S graph is consistent if an
only if it satisfies the set of OWL-S constraints $\Sigma$.*

## 4   Introducing Time into OWL-S

As mentioned in Section 3, we consider the schema (i.e., OWL-S ontology) as
fixed. Thus, the instances of the ontology are the only elements subject to
change. We extend the graph in Definition 1 with temporal labels, yielding a
*temporal OWL-S graph*, and we state consistency conditions these graph must
satisfy.

   We assume the existence of three finite sets: intervals $\mathcal{I}$, timestamps $T$, and
versions $\mathcal{V}$, and two functions: $\text{init} : \mathcal{I} \to T$ and $\text{end} : \mathcal{I} \to T$, which return the
starting and ending timestamps of an interval, respectively.

**Definition 3 (Temporal OWL-S graph).** *A temporal OWL-S graph H is a
tuple $(G, V, \rho)$, where G is an OWL-S graph whose triples are annotated with
intervals in $\mathcal{I}$, $V \subseteq \mathcal{V}$ is a set of versions, and $\rho : V \to \mathcal{I}$ is a function that
assigns to each version an interval (lifespan of the version). The intervals in
$ran(\rho)$ do not appear in G.*

Note that the model only supports single intervals. This introduces some limitations on the model's expressive power. However, the model can be extended
to support sets of intervals. Figure 2 (b) shows a temporal OWL-S graph.

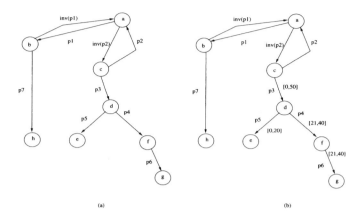

**Fig. 2.** (a) An abstract OWL-S graph. (b)The corresponding $t$-OWL-S graph.

**Definition 4 (Lifespan of a node).** *Given a temporal graph $H$, the lifespan of a node $n$ of it, denoted $lifespan(n)$ is the interval $i$ such that $\text{init}(i) = Min(\{\text{init}(i') : (a, p, n)[i'] \in G\} \cup \{\text{init}(i') : (n, p, b)[i'] \in G\})$ and $\text{end}(i) = Max(\{\text{end}(i') : (a, p, n)[i'] \in G\} \cup \{\text{end}(i')(n, p, b)[i'] \in G\}).$*

**Definition 5 (Snapshot).** *Given a temporal OWL-S graph $G$, a snapshot of $G$ at time $t$, denoted $G(t)$, is an OWL-S graph, with triples $(a, p, b)$ such that $(a, p, b)[t]$ is in $G$.*

Definition 5 provides the link between OWL-S with versioning, and temporal OWL-S. A specification has as many *versions* as different snapshots can be obtained at different instants. Thus, all versions of an OWL-S specification are embedded in a single document.

## 4.1   Updates

We consider the following subset of the changes proposed in [2]: (a) add a new WSDL operation; (b) remove an WSDL operation; (c) change the parameters of an operation. However, note that the abstract model defined above hides most of the non-temporal semantics of OWL-S. In this way, the update operations can be implemented as operations over the graph, as follows: (1) adding a new operation at time $t$ is the insertion of a new edge (and the corresponding node), with temporal label $[t, Now]$; (2) removing (at time $t$) an existing WSDL operation (indicated by and edge with label $[t_s, Now]$) is implemented replacing the label by $[t_s, t]$ (thus, the history is retained); (3) changing some parameter implies the following operations over the graph: (a) remove, at time $t - 1$, the edge to be modified; (b) add an edge with the new parameter, at time $t$. For example, suppose we want to update property $p_7$, at time $t = 100$, replacing the range URI $h$, by $r$, in the graph in Figure 2. The edge $(b, p_7, h)[0, Now]$ is replaced by $(b, p_7, h)[0, 99]$, and a new edge $(b, p_7, g)[100, Now]$ is inserted.

This definition of updates shows that we can partition the time line (i.e. the temporal document's lifespan) in a set of intervals such that, within these intervals, all the snapshots remain the same.

**Definition 6 (Interval Partition).** *The interval partition $P$ of a set of intervals $i_1, \ldots, i_n$, is the smallest set of intervals $\mathcal{P} = P_1, \ldots, P_n$, such that all the $P_i$'s in $\mathcal{P}$ are pairwise disjoint and $\mathcal{P}$ contains a partition of every interval $i_j$.*

### 4.2  Consistency

Hasse *et al* [9] studied the problem of keeping an evolving ontology consistent through its different states. They defined three different notions of consistency, respectively denoted $\kappa_S$, $\kappa_L$, and $\kappa_U$: (a) structural; (b) logical; (c) user-defined. We are interested in extending OWL-S consistency for the temporal model. Therefore we show how the set of OWL-S constraints $\Sigma$, which captures structural and logical consistency, can be applied in the temporal setting.

**Definition 7 (Consistency).** *A temporal OWL-S graph $G$ is consistent if and only if every snapshot $G(t)$ is consistent.*

Given a temporal OWL-S graph $G$ and an interval $i$, we denote $G(i)$, the (non-temporal) OWL-S graph with triples $(a, b, c)$ such that $(a, b, c) : i \in G$.

**Theorem 1.** *A temporal OWL-S graph $G$ is consistent if and only if for every interval $i$ in the partition of the intervals of $G$, $G(i)$ is consistent.*

*Proof.* (sketch) Follows from defining the partition of the sets of intervals in the graph. The document is consistent within the set of timestamps defined by each interval in the partition.

The theorem yields an algorithm to verify consistency, which consists of two steps: (i) compute the partition of the intervals of $G$; (ii) compute $G(i)$ for each interval $i$ in the partition and check satisfiability of the constraints in $G(i)$. Step (i) can be done by building intervals from consecutive timestamps mentioned in the intervals of $G$. Satisfiability can be checked using any OWL reasoner.

## 5   Querying Temporal OWL-S

The temporal OWL-S graph can be fully queried using the notion of temporal RDF [6,7]. Here we sketch a query language that allows to query different versions of OWL-S(T) specifications, along with changes inside versions themselves.

In order to capture changes inside versions, we introduce the notion of a state. Therefore, our query language augment standard RDF querying with the notions of version and state. Intuitively, a state is a maximal interval inside a version for which the OWL-S specification does not change.

**Definition 8 (State).** *Given an OWL-S(T) graph $H = (G, V, \rho)$, the set $S$ of states of $H$ is the smallest interval partition of the intervals in $\rho(V)$ such that for each interval $i \in S$ and for every pair of timestamps $t_1, t_2$, where* $\mathtt{init}(i) \leq t_1, t_2 \leq \mathtt{end}(i)$, *we have $H(t_1) = H(t_2)$.*

## 5.1  Queries by Example

Both, states and versions have "init" and "end" timestamps. We use the functions init and end to refer respectively to them. As an example, $\text{init}(s_2) = \text{end}(s_1)$, says that $s_2$ is a successor of $s_1$, and by $\text{end}(v) = \text{end}(s)$ we restrict $s$ to be the last state of version $v$. We also include standard arithmetic built-in predicates $(<, \leq, =, \geq, >)$ to compare timestamps. For instance, $\text{init}(s_2) < 2$ tells that $s_2$ started before timestamp 2.

Now, let us begin with a simple query: "Find the inputs of the Web service *ZipCodeFinderService* in the last state of version v1".

$$(ZipCodeFinderService, hasInput, ?U)[?S] \leftarrow$$
$$(?X, hasInput, U?)[?S][v1], \text{end}(?S) = \text{end}(v1)$$
$$(ZipCodeFinderService, presents, ?X)[?S][v1].$$

Annotations inside brackets in the queries represent variables that range over states and versions. The following query returns "the profiles and states of version v1 of Web service *ZipCodeFinderService*".

$$(ZipCodeFinderService, presents, ?Z)[?S] \leftarrow$$
$$(ZipCodeFinderService, presents, ?Z)[?S][v1].$$

Now consider the query "Find the versions of Web services that output a Zip code". We express it as the following query:

$$(?V, \text{versionOf}, ?Y) \leftarrow (?Y, hasOutput, zipcode)[?S][?V], (?S, presents, ?Y)[?S][?V].$$

## 5.2  Semantics

We consider the following disjoint sets of variables: a set $V_r$ of RDF variables, a set $V_v$ containing version variables, and a set $V_s$ of state variables. Individual variables are denoted $?X, ?Y, ?Z$, etc.

A query is a tableau, which is a pair $(H, B \cup A)$, where $H$ and $B$ are graph patterns, and the set $A$ has the usual arithmetic predicates over timestamps and applications of the functions init and end. A graph pattern is a set of expressions of the form $(a, b, c)[s][v]$, where $(a, b, c)$ is an RDF triple where some elements may be variables in $V_r$, $s \in V_s$ is a state variable, and $v$ may be a version variable in $V_v$ or a constant for a version name.

We adopt a notion of *safe rule* similarly to Datalog to prevent operations on infinite predicates. A rule is *safe* if each of its variables appear as an argument in a non-built-in predicate of the body.

In order to give the semantics of a query we transform a temporal OWL-S graph $H = (G, V, \rho)$ into an RDF graph whose triples are annotated with versions and states. This annotated graph, denoted $\text{VS}(H)$, is a set containing triples $(a, b, c)[s][v]$, which establishes that $(a, b, c)$ holds in a state $s$ of $H$, and $s$ arises within a version $v \in V$ (i.e., $\text{init}(s) \leq \text{init}(v)$ and $\text{end}(v) \leq \text{end}(s)$).

Given an interval $i$ and a set of intervals $S$, we denote $\mathtt{CoverSet}(i, S)$ the set containing the intervals $i' \in S$ such that $\mathtt{init}(i') \leq \mathtt{init}(i)$ and $\mathtt{end}(i) \leq \mathtt{end}(i')$. Then, the set $\mathtt{VS}(H)$ is obtained as follows. Let $S$ be the set of states of $H$, and let $U$ be the set of intervals in $G$. For each interval $i \in S$, and version $v$ that contains $i$, we annotate with $[i][v]$ all the triples in $\bigcup_{i' \in \mathtt{CoverSet}(i, U)} H(i')$, and add them to $\mathtt{VS}(H)$.

The semantics is similar to temporal RDF [6]. Given a query $(H, B \cup A)$ and a OWL-S(T) graph $H$, for each matching of the graph pattern $B$ in $\mathtt{VS}(H)$, pick the values of the variables for versions and states, and check if they satisfy the built-in predicates in $A$. If this is the case, construct a pre-answer, which is the graph resulting by substituting the values of the variables in the head. The answer of the query is the union of all pre-answers.

## 5.3  Complexity

We now show that the query language proposed does not increase the complexity of temporal RDF.

**Lemma 1.** *Given an OWL-S(T) graph $H = (G, V, \rho)$, for each state $s$ of $H$, there are intervals $i, i'$ in $H$ such that $\mathtt{init}(i) = \mathtt{init}(s)$ and $\mathtt{end}(i') = \mathtt{end}(s)$.*

This lemma gives a simple procedure to compute states. We need to order all the timestamps that limit the intervals in $H$, and search for maximal intervals that have these timestamps as limits, within which the temporal OWL-S graph does not change. This procedure takes $O(N^2 M)$, where $N$ is the size of $H$, and $M$ is the number of intervals in $H$. It also shows that $\mathtt{VS}(H)$ has size in $O(NM)$.

To get the complexity of query processing, we consider the problem of testing emptiness of the query answer set in the following forms: (1) Query complexity version: for a fixed database $D$, given a query $q$, is $q(D)$ non-empty? (2) Data complexity version: for a fixed query $q$, given a database $D$, is $q(D)$ non-empty?

**Theorem 2.** *The evaluation problem is NP-complete for the query complexity version, and polynomial for the data complexity version.*

The proof is similar to temporal RDF and is based on the fact that the graph $\mathtt{VS}(H)$ over which the search for matching is done is of polysize in $H$.

## 6    Temporal OWL-S Implementation

Now we sketch how the concepts introduced in the paper can be embedded in an actual OWL-S specification. For this, we propose two mechanisms: (1) slightly extend the OWL-S vocabulary, specifying a new profile; (2) timestamp the elements of the OWL-S specification.

*Versioning Profiles.* The first extension we need is a small OWL-S vocabulary in order to define a fourth component of a OWL-S(T) specification (along with profile, process model, and grounding), that we will call a *versioning profile*. The vocabulary of this new profile includes the classes `versioningprofile`, `version`, `interval`, `date`, and the properties `hasVersion`, `spans` (and its inverse `isSpannedBy`), `lifeSpan`, `init` and `end`. The constraints for the versioning profile are: (a) the domain of `lifeSpan` is `version`, and its range is `interval`; (b) the domain and range of `init` and `end` are `interval` and `date`, respectively; (c) the domain and range of `hasVersion` are `versioningprofile` and `version`, respectively; (d) the domain and range of `spans` are *Service* and `versioningprofile`, respectively;(b) the cardinality of the `lifeSpan` property is 1-1.

In our running example, for instance, we would have the following triples stating that $v1$ is a version of the OWL-S(T) specification and its lifespan lies within the interval $i$, whose limits are 1 and 2:

$(ZCFS, \texttt{isSpannedBy}, ZCFSVersioningProfile)$, $(ZCFSVersioningProfile,$ $\texttt{hasVersion}, v_1)$, $(v1, \texttt{lifeSpan}, i)$, $(i\texttt{init}, 1)$, $(i, \texttt{end}, 3)$.

*OWL-S Timestamping.* Assume that from 2005 on, a new version of the process which implements the service of our running example was released. The corresponding timestamped OWL-S specification would look as follows:

```
<rdf:RDF xmlns:owl=''http://www.w3c.org/2002/07/owl#''?>
  xmlns:Time=''http://www.dcc.uchile.cl/db/time''
  ...
<grounding:WsdlAtomicProcessGrounding rdf:ID=''ZCFProcessGrounding''>
 <grounding:owlProcess Time:FROM='1999-01-01' Time:TO='Now'
  rdf:resource=''#ZipCodeFinderProcess''/>
 <grounding:wsdlDocument Time:FROM='1999-01-01' Time:TO='2004-12-31'>
''http://www.dcc.uchile.cl/2005/ws/docum/ZipCode-v1.0.asmx?WDSL''
 </grounding:wsdlDocument>
 <grounding:wsdlDocument Time:FROM='1999-01-01' Time:TO='2004-12-31'>
''http://www.dcc.uchile.cl/2005/ws/docum/ZipCode-v2.0.asmx?WDSL''
 </grounding:wsdlDocument>
  ....
```

# 7 Conclusion

Versioning of Web services ontologies has not yet been studied by the Semantic Web community. We introduced OWL-S(T), a formal model for OWL-S, along with a query language supporting a two-level versioning scheme for OWL-S specifications. Our model and query language allow, for instance, simultaneously accessing different versions of the same specification.

A lot of research and practical issues remain open. Among these problems, the development of efficient algorithms for checking consistency, and fixing inconsistent specifications is required. Future work also includes the implementation of our proposal.

# References

1. D. Brickley and R.V.(Eds.) Guha. RDF vocabulary description language 1.0: RDF schema. *W3C Recommendation, 10 February 2004.*
2. K. Brown and M. Ellis. Best practices for web services versioning. 2004. http://www-128.ibm.com/developerworks/webservices/library/ws-version.
3. C. Chris Peltz and A. Anagol-Subbarao. Design strategies for web services versioning. *Web Services Journal, SYS-CON Media,* 2004. http://webservices.syscop.com/read/44356.htm.
4. Thomas Erl. *Service-Oriented Architecture : Concepts, Technology, and Design.* Prentice Hall, August 2005.
5. Giorgos Flouris, Dimitris Plexousakis, and Grigoris Antoniou. Evolving ontology evolution. In *SOFSEM*, pages 14–29, 2006.
6. C. Gutiérrez, C. Hurtado, and A. Vaisman. Temporal RDF. In *European Conference on the Semantic Web (ECSW'05) (Best paper award)*, pages 93–107, 2005.
7. C. Gutiérrez, C. Hurtado, and A. Vaisman. Introducing time into RDF. *IEEE-TKDE Special Issue on the Semantic Web (in press)*, 2006.
8. P. Haase, J. Broekstra, A. Eberhart, and R. Volz. A Comparison of RDF Query Languages. In *International Semantic Web Conference*, 2004.
9. P. Haase and L. Stojanovic. Consistent Evolution of OWL Ontologies. In *Proceedings of the 2nd. European Semantic Web Conference*, pages 182–197, 2005.
10. P. Haase and Y. Sure. State-of-the-Art on Ontology Evolution. *SEKT/2004/D3.1.1.b/v0.5*, 2004.
11. Patrick Hayes(Ed.). RDF semantics. *W3C Recommendation, 10 February 2004.*
12. I. Horrocks, P. Patel-Schneider, and F. Van Harmelen. From SHIQ and RDF to OWL: the making of a Web Ontology Language. *Journal of Web Semantics,* 1(1):7–26, 2003.
13. M. Klein, D. Fensel, A. Kiryakov, and D. Ognyanov. Ontology Versioning and Change Detection on the Web. In *EKAW*, pages 197–212, 2002.
14. A. Maedche, B. Motik, L. Stojanovic, R. Studer, and R. Volz. Establishing the Semantic Web 11: An infrastructure for searching, reusing, and evolving distributed ontologies. In *Proceedings of the 12th. International Conference on World Wide Web*, pages 439–448, 2003.
15. A. Magkanaraki, G. Karvounarakis, T.T. Anh, V. Christophides, and D. Plexousakis. Ontology Storage and Querying. Technical Report 308, Foundation for Research and Technology Hellas, Institute of CS, Information System Lab, 2002.
16. F. Mannola and E. Miller. RDF Primer. *W3C Recommendation,* Feb. 2004.
17. David Martin(Ed.). OWL-S: Semantic Markup for Web Services. *OWL-S 1.1 Release.* http://www.daml.org/services/owl-s/1.1.
18. The Mindswap Project. http://www.mindswap.org.
19. M. Smith, C. Welty, and D.L. (Eds.) McGuiness. OWL Web Ontology Language Guide. *W3C Recommendation,* February 2004.
20. L. Stojanovic. *Methods and Tools for Ontology Evolution.* PhD thesis, University of Karlsrhue, 2004.
21. A. Tansel, J. Clifford, and S. Gadia (eds.). *Temporal Databases: Theory, Design and Implementation.* Benjamin/Cummings, 1993.
22. U. Visser. Intelligent Information Integration for the Semantic web. *Lecture Notes in Computer Science (3159)*, 2004.

# BPEL Behavioral Abstraction and Matching

Nomane Ould Ahmed M'bareck and Samir Tata

GET/INT, Institut National des Télécommunications
9 rue Charles Fourier 91011 Evry, France
{Nomane.Ould_ahmed_mbarek, Samir.Tata}@int-evry.fr

**Abstract.** *BPEL* is the most popular language for describing business process and business interaction based on Web services for inter-organizational cooperation. Nevertheless, *BPEL* requires a static binding of services to the flows. We propose in this paper a new approach enabling dynamic binding. This approach consists of, first, providing a high-level description of process, second, abstracting the process behavior using symbolic observation graphs and third providing an efficient algorithm for symbolic observation graphs matching which is used for binding dynamically business processes.

## 1 Introduction

In context of globalization, organizations are increasingly using process-aware information systems to perform automatically their business processes. Based on such systems, organizations focus on their core competencies and access other competencies through cooperation. In order to manage the cooperation between organization, Business Process Execution Language for Web Services (*BPEL* for short) was introduced for specifying business processes behavior based on Web services and business interaction protocols. A *BPEL* process allows can be abstract or executable. The first type defines the business protocol role and describes its public aspects. The second one defines the logic and state of the process by providing sequence of Web service interactions conducted at each business partner. Moreover, *BPEL* defines a set of primitive activities, such as *invoke*, to invoke Web service operations. These primitive activities can be combined into more complex primitives using any of the structure activities provided such as *sequence* and *flow*. One of the main drawbacks of *BPEL* is that it requires that the process details are known at the design time. Indeed, *BPEL* requires static binding of services to the flows [Verma et al., 2004]. Nevertheless it turns out that sometimes some parts of *BPEL* are not known at the design time. To overcome this lack we propose here a new approach to represent, abstract and match *BPEL* processes.

The idea of *dynamic BPEL* is not new. Ideed, in [Karastoyanova et al., 2005], the authors propose to extend *BPEL* by the "find and bind" mechanism. By adding a new construct ¡find_bind¿ to BPEL, they enable users to choose explicitly web services at run time. Users have only to specify the selection criteria within ¡find_bind¿ construct and they do not care about how the matching is performed. However, this work deals mainly with matching of two web services according to criteria like QoS or semantics. It does not care about the matching of control flow between web services which is important as we will show in this paper.

J. Eder, S. Dustdar et al. (Eds.): BPM 2006 Workshops, LNCS 4103, pp. 495–506, 2006.

Our approach allows a dynamic binding of services to the flows and it consists, first, providing a high-level description of process, second, abstracting the process behavior using symbolic observation graphs (SOG for short) [Haddad et al., 2004] and third providing an efficient algorithm for SOG matching used for binding dynamically business processes. The rest of this paper is organized as follows. Section 2 presents our running example. Section 3 introduce the *dynamic BPEL* notion. In Section 4 we show how process behaviors are abstracted using SOG. Section 5 is devoted to a matching algorithm. Conclusion and perspectives are given in Section 6.

## 2    Our Motivating Scenarios

The example we present here involves two business partners: a client and a product provider. Figure 1 presents a specification of the client's *BPEL* behavior using Petri net notation [van der Aalst, 1998]. First, the client sends an order for a product. Then it receives a notification. If the notification is negative (*i.e.* the product is unavailable), then the client looks for an alternative. Otherwise, first, the client receives the delivery. Then, it sends the payment and uses its product. Finally, it evaluates the product.

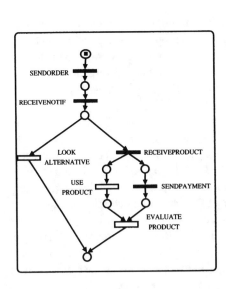

**Fig. 1.** The client's workflow

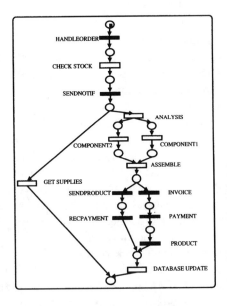

**Fig. 2.** The provider's workflow

Figure 2 presents the provider's *BPEL* behavior. First, the provider waits for an order request. Then it checks the stock. After that, it notifies the client whether its order has been taken into account. If the order was refused then the provider gets supplies. Otherwise, it analyzes the order components and then it gets the components and assembles them. After that, according to the type of the client, the provider can have two different behaviors. If the client is faithful the provider sends the product and the invoice together and waits for the payment. Otherwise the provider sends the invoice, waits for the payment and then sends the product. Finally, the provider updates its database according to the performed activities. Cooperative activities, represented by filled transitions in Figure 1 and Figure 2, are the ones that send and/or receive data to/from partners that are not known at the design time.

We assume that at the design time, the client and the provider do not know each other. Indeed, the client does not know which provider will offer the required service and the provider as well does not know who will use his services. Consequently, they cannot describe their processes using *BPEL* and deploy them because *BPEL* requires a static binding of services to the flows. In our example, we want to enable the client and the provider to discover each other at the run time and then generate automatically a traditional *BPEL* descriptions for each and deploy them.

## 3   Dynamic BPEL

Our objective is to enablepartners to describe their processes at the design time, even if some parts of them are not known, and at the run time they bind the unknown parts to discovered services. To reach this end, each business process must be abstracted, published in certain registry. In addition a matching mechanism must be used to identify partners and bind them at run time. For illustration, let us look at the previous example. At the design time the client describes its *BPEL* process in which some parts are not known (*i.e.* information about the actual provider). At the execution time he wants to discover a provider and bind the unknown parts of his process to the discovered services. As provider, the client means a process that receives an order, notifies, sends a product and afterward receives the payment. The execution of these activities in this order is important from the client point of view. Consequently, the he looks for a process that satisfies these conditions. Indeed, in several cases the required partner is composed of more than one activity. Also in several cases at the design time, the client does not know which provider will use and the provider as well does not know who will use his service. Therefore, these processes cannot be represented in *BPEL* because *BPEL* requires that all partners are known and described at the design time. By dynamic *BPEL*, we mean a *BPEL* document in which some partners are not known i.e. certain activities are not associated to concrete web services. To do that, we propose here to describe processes using *dynamic BPEL*, abstract *dynamic BPEL* using symbolic observation graphs (*SOG* and finally perform the matching between *SOGs* to bind dynamically processes.

Figure 3 summarizes our approach. Given two *dynamic BPEL* we build, tanks to our *SOGConstructor*, a *SOG* representation for each *dynamic BPEL*. Then the matchmaker compares *SOGs* representation. Finally if the result is positive, our *BPELGenerator* takes as input the *dynamic BPELs* description and constructs for each *dynamic BPELs* a traditional *BPEL* that later can be executed by any *BPEL* engine.

Dynamic *BPEL* processes are described using traditional *BPEL* except the unknown parts. To distinguish between these parts and the known ones, we add an element *Partner* which is specified for each unknown *portType*. The name of this element is the same as the name of the unknown *portType* and initially its value is *unknown*. This acts like a formal parameter. Its actual value will be provided only after the matching process.

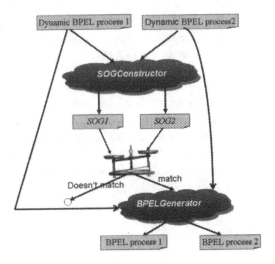

**Fig. 3.** Steps for BPEL generation

In our example the client does not know all parts of his workflow and so he describes it as a *dynamic BPEL*. This description is given bellow. First the client sends an order (*SendOrder* operation) but he does not know who will receive this order (*ReceiveOrder* operation is not known). Then he waits for a notification (*ReceiveNotif* operation) but he does not know who will send this notification (*SendNotif* operation is not known too). Also, the client waits for a product reception and then he sends the payment (*ReceiveProduct* and *SendPayment* are known). However, the client does not know who will send the product and receives the payment (resp. the operation *SendProduct* and *ReceivePayment* are not known).

```
<portType name="purchaseOrderPT">
 <operation name="SendOrder">
  <output message= "Order" />
 </operation>
 <operation name="ReceiveNotif">
  <input message= "Notification" />
 </operation>
 <operation name= "ReceiveProduct">
  <input message= "ProductDetail" />
 </operation>
 <operation name= "SendPayment">
  <output message= "AccountInfo" />
 </operation>
</portType>
<!-- The unknown operations -->
 <portType name="ProviderPT_1" >
  <partner name="ProviderPT_1" value="unknown" />
  <operation name= "ReceiveOrder">
```

```
  <input name= "Order" />
 </operation>
 <operation name= "SendNotif">
  <output name= "Notification" />
 </operation>
 <operation name= "SendProduct">
  <output name= "ProductDetail" />
 </operation>
 <operation name= "ReceivePayment">
  <input name= "AccountInfo" />
 </operation>
</portType>
```

Once the *portType*s (the known and the unknown ones) are described, we can use them in the process description. The rest of *dynamic BPEL* description is the same manner as for traditional *BPEL*. Bellow we give how the client *dynamic BPEL* looks like. Note that we describe here only the operation that interact with external partners.

```
<process>
 <variables> ... </variables>
 <partnerLinks> ...   </partnerLinks>
 <sequence>
  <invoke partnerLink = "purchasing"
   portType = "purchaseOrderPT" operation= "SendOrder"
   outputVariable= "POrder" />
  <receive partnerLink = "purchasing"
   portType = "ProviderPT_1" operation= "ReceiveOrder"
   inputVariable= "POrder" />
  <invoke partnerLink = "purchasing"
   portType = "ProviderPT_1" operation= "SendNotif"
   inputVariable= "Notification" />
  <flow>
    <receive partnerLink = "purchasing"
     portType = "purchaseOrderPT" operation = "ReceiveNotif"
     variable = "Notification" />
    <invoke partnerLink = "purchasing"
     portType = "ProviderPT_1" operation= "SendProduct"
     outputVariable= "Product" />
  </flow>
  <receive partnerLink = "purchasing"
   portType = "purchaseOrderPT" operation = "ReceiveProduct"
   variable = "Product" />
  <invoke partnerLink = "purchasing"
   portType = "purchaseOrderPT" operation = "SendPayment"
   variable = "AccountInfo" />
  <receive partnerLink = "purchasing"
   portType = "ProviderPT_1" operation = "ReceivePayment"
   inputVariable= "AccountInfo" />
 </sequence>
</process>
```

A client who wish to cooperate with the provider must support *PlaceOrder* (send an order), *RecNotif* (receive a notification), *RecOrder* (receive the ordered product), *SendPayment* (send payment) operations and sometimes it must support the *RecInvoice* (receive the invoice) operation. For sake of space we do not give the description of all these operations.

```
<!-- portType for the known operation -->
 <portType name="OrderingPT">
  <operation name= "HandleOrder">
   <input name= "Order" />
  </operation>
  ... ...
 </portType>
<!-- portType for th unknown operation -->
 <portType name="ClientPT_1" State="unknown">
  <partner name="ClientPT_1" value="unknown" />
  <operation name= "PlaceOrder">
   <output name= "Order" />
  </operation>
  ... ...
 </portType>
```

The provider *dynamic BPEL* should looks like the description given bellow.

```
<process>
 <sequence>
  <invoke partnerLink = "purchasing"
   portType = "ClientPT_1" operation= "PlaceOrder" />
  <receive partnerLink = "purchasing"
   portType = "OrderingPT" operation= "HandleOrder" />
  <invoke partnerLink = "purchasing"
   portType = "OrderingPT" operation= "SendNotif" />
  <flow>
    <receive partnerLink = "purchasing"
     portType = "ClientPT_1" operation = "ReceiveNotif" />
    <switch isFaithful>
     <case "isFaithful=true">
      <sequence>
       <invoke partnerLink = "purchasing"
        portType = "OrderingPT" operation= "SendProduct" />
       <receive partnerLink = "purchasing"
        portType = "ClientPT_1" operation = "ReceiveProduct" />
       <invoke partnerLink = "purchasing"
        portType = "ClientPT_1" operation= "SendPayment" />
       <receive partnerLink = "purchasing"
        portType = "OrderingPT" operation= "RecPayment" />
      </sequence>
     </case>
     <case "isFaithful=false">
       <invoke partnerLink = "purchasing"
        portType = "OrderingPT" operation= "SendInvoice" />
       ...
```

```
      </case>
     </switch>
   </flow>
  </sequence>
</process>
```

In the follow we give how we abstract and advertise *BPEL* behavior.

# 4   BPEL Behavior Abstraction and Advertisement

In this section we propose to abstract the behavior of a given *dynamic BPEL* with *the symbolic observation graph* (*SOG* for short) [Haddad et al., 2004] and we present how Ordered Binary Decision Diagram (OBDD) techniques [Bryant, 1986, Wegener, 2000] can be used to advertise *dynamic BPEL* abstractions into registries. Before we go through the abstraction details, let us give these definitions.

**Definition 4.1 (Wf-net).** To model *dynamic BPEL* behavior, we use workflow nets (Wf-nets) [van der Aalst, 1998] which is a specific form of Petri nets. In WF-nets, activities (operations) are modeled by transitions, and dependencies (control flow) are modeled by places and arcs. A WF-net has one source place and one sink place and all its nodes should be on some path from source to sink. Let $P$ and $T$ be disjoint sets of places and transitions respectively, the elements of $P \cup T$ are called nodes. A Petri net W(P,T,Pre,Post) is a Wf-net if and only if :

- Pre $\subseteq$ (P×T) is a finite set of arcs connecting places to transitions,
- Post $\subseteq$ (T×P) is a finite set of arcs connecting transitions to places,
- there is one source place $i \in$ P s.t. $\bullet i = \emptyset$ and one sink place $o \in$ P s.t. $o \bullet = \emptyset$, and
- every node $x \in P \cup T$ is on a path from $i$ to $o$.

The set of input (resp. output) places for a transition t is noted $\bullet t$ (resp. $t\bullet$). The set of transitions sharing a place p as output (resp. input) place is noted $\bullet p$ (resp. $p\bullet$).

**Definition 4.2 (*dynamic BPEL* behavioral language).** Let $\sigma$ be a sequence of transitions ($\sigma \in T^*$). The projection of $\sigma$ on a set of transitions $X \subseteq T$ (denoted by $\sigma_{\lfloor X}$) is the sequence obtained by removing from $\sigma$ all transitions that do not belong to $X$. A sequence $\sigma = t_1 t_2 \dots t_n$ over transitions is said to be accepted if $i \in \bullet t_1$, $o \in t_n \bullet$ and $\sigma$ can be executed by the *BPEL* engine. The language $L(B)$ of a *dynamic BPEL* behavior $B$ is the set of all accepted sequences and the projection function is extended to $L$ as follows: $L_{\lfloor X} = \{\sigma_{\lfloor X}, \sigma \in L\}$.

In [Haddad et al., 2004], the authors have introduced the *SOG* as an abstraction of the *reachability marking graph* of a given Petri net and showed that the verification of an event-based formula of $LTL \setminus X$ ($LTL$ minus the next operator) on the *SOG* is equivalent to the verification on the original reachability graph. To summarize, the building of the *SOG* is guided by the set of the actions occurring in the formula. Such actions are called *observed* while the other actions of the system are *unobserved*. Then, the *SOG* is defined as a deterministic graph where each node is a set of markings linked by unobserved sequences of actions and each arc is labeled with an observed transition.

Nodes of the *SOG* are called *meta-states* and may be represented and managed efficiently by using OBDD techniques. Each marking of a meta-state is viewed as a vector of boolean variables by choosing the appropriate variables describing the system (in our case each place of the Wf-net will be represented by a boolean variable). Then the set of marking in the meta-state is equivalent to the boolean function which returns true iff the input vector corresponds to a reachable state (via the firing of a sequence of unobserved transitions). The boolean expression associated with the function can now be represented in a compact way by factorizing the multiple occurrences of the subexpression. Hence the final structure is a rooted directed acyclic graph (DAG) where the subgraph rooted at each node corresponds to a subexpression and the root corresponds to the function to be represented.

The benefit of OBDDs comes from the fact that a small OBDD can often represent a huge set of states, and the "symbolic" operations like the set operations (union, inclusion...) and the membership test are cheap as long as the OBDD is small. Equally important are the operations associated to an event of the system and a set of states: the subset of states for which this event is enable, the "image" of this set obtained by the occurrence of the event and the "preimage" of the set i.e. the set of states where the occurrence of this event leads to a state of the specified set. Generally, these latter algorithms have a time complexity proportional to the size of the OBDD on which they are applied. Thanks to the efficiency of OBDDs and the symbolic operations they supply, the SOG approach allow to handle huge systems (more than $10^{30}$ reachable states) in a reasonable time. In practice, this efficiency is optimal whenever the number of the observed transitions is small with respect to the total number of transitions [Haddad et al., 2004, van Noord, 2000].

We think that the *SOG* technique is suitable for abstracting *dynamic BPEL* behavior for many reasons: First, by considering that the observed transitions are the cooperative activities and the unobserved are the local ones, the *SOG* allows one to represent the *dynamic BPEL* projected on the cooperative transitions i.e. the local behaviors are hidden. The second reason is that such an abstraction is suitable for checking whether two *dynamic BPELs* represented by their *SOG* can be interconnected. Moreover, given an *dynamic BPEL*, its *SOG* is built once and it may still unchanged as long as the changes on the model do not lead to a potential additional occurrence of a new activity. Finally, the reduced size of the *SOG* (in general) could be an advantage when one plans to store and manage a big number of *dynamic BPELs* abstractions in the same registry.

For sake of space, we do not give the *SOG* building algorithm, we refer the reader to [Haddad et al., 2004] for more details about the *SOG* technique. Here, we use such algorithm to construct the *SOG* of the client (Figure 1) and the *SOG* of the provider (Figure 2). Figure 4 and Figure 5 illustrates these graphs respectively. Hence, the advertisement of *BPEL* will be done via its *SOG*. Even if, the size of the *SOG* is generally small, one can represent this structure more compactly using again OBDD. In fact, OBDD are quite often used to represent structures of graph viewed as matrices. The following section will be devoted to the detail of the matching

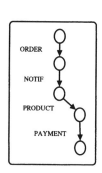

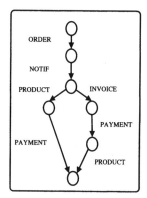

**Fig. 4.** The client's observation graph          **Fig. 5.** The provider's observation graph

## 5  Dynamic BPEL Behavior Matching

As it can be seen from the example above, matching between two dynamic *BPEL* is a real need. Indeed, in several cases the required partner is composed of more than one service. The algorithm that we propose here deal with the matching of control flow. This algorithm compares the structure of two *dynamic BPEL*

Figure 3 summarizes the matching procedure. In the beginning we suppose that we have two dynamic *BPEL*. Thanks to our *SOGConstructor* we build *SOG* representation for each dynamic *BPEL*. Then the matchmaker compares *SOGs* representation. Finally if the result given by the matchmaker is positive, our *BPELGenerator* takes as input dynamic *BPELs* description and constructs two new standard *BPELs*. The later can be executed by *BPEL* engine like Orchestra or other.

Given a Wf-net $W_1$ and a registry of potential partners for $W_1$, we discuss in this section the selection criteria making a choice of a Wf-net $W_2$ in the registry as a partner of $W_1$ be an effective one. Such criteria are based on the behavior of $W_1$ i.e. its behavior on the cooperative transitions, which must match with the observable behavior of $W_2$. Before presenting the matching conditions, let us introduce some definitions.

**Definition 5.1 (Transition).** Each transition $t$ of Wf-net $W$ is represented by a tuple $t = \langle name, guard, type, msg \rangle$ s.t.
- the *name* attribute of $t$, denoted by $t.name$, is the label associated to $t$,
- the *guard* attribute is boolean expression. The transition is enable iff the input places are sufficiently marked and $t.guard = true$,
- the *type* attribute of $t$, denoted by $t.type$, indicates that $t$ is supposed to receive a message ($type = 1$), to send a message ($type = 0$), to receive and after it sends a message ($type = 10$) or to send and after it receives a message ($01$).
- the *msg* attribute of $t$, denoted by $t.msg$, represents the semantic description of the message (using a common ontology) $t$ has to send or to receive.

This section is organized in two parts. The first one deals with checking the possibility of cooperation between two *SOGs* of two dynamic *BPELs*. In the second one we treat the question of constructing a *BPEL* description from dynamic *BPEL* and the result of matching.

## 5.2  Checking Cooperation Possibility

In order to check whether there exists a correspondence between two cooperative transitions $t_1$ and $t_2$ belonging to two different Wf-nets, we need to compare these transitions with respect to their attributes. Two attributes are taken in account: $type$ and $msg$. For instance, if $t_1$ is a reception transition then $t_2$ must be a sending transition and both transitions have to match on the semantic of the exchanged message. We denote by $t_1.msg \equiv t_2.msg$ the fact that messages of $t_1$ and $t_2$ deal with the same data type and semantics. Now, if $t_1.type = \neg(t_2.type)$ and $t_1.msg \equiv t_2.msg$, then we say that $t_1$ matches with $t_2$ (and vice versa) and denote this relation by $t_1 \sim t_2$.

The following hypothesis is important for the remaining part of the paper. It says that, within the same Wf-net $W_1$, if a cooperative transition occur in a Wf-net more than once then these occurrences are executed in an exclusive way (c.f. transitions PRODUCT and PAYMENT of Figure 2). In this case we denote by $\{t\}$ the set of occurrences of a cooperative transition $t$ in a Wf-net. Let $\langle W_1, m_1 \rangle$ be a marked Wf-net and let $T_1$ be its set of cooperative transitions. Then $\forall t_1 \in T_1$, $\forall \sigma = \alpha t_1 \alpha' t_1$, where $\alpha$ and $\alpha' \in T_1^*$, then $\sigma \notin L(W_1, m_1)$. (H)

**The Cooperation Candidate Property.** In this section, we define the *cooperation candidate property*: an asymmetric property to be checked between two given marked Wf-nets. This property will help us to define formally the fact that a Wf-net $W_1$ can cooperate with a given Wf-net $W_2$. For this issue, we need to introduce a renaming procedure $\mathcal{L}_{W_1}$ which operates on $W_2$ via a possible renaming of its cooperative transitions.

**Definition 5.2  (Renaming procedure).** Let $W_1$ and $W_2$ be two Wf-nets and let $T_1$ and $T_2$ be their sets of cooperative transitions. The renaming procedure $\mathcal{L}_{W_1}$ associated to $W_1$ is defined as follows:

$$\mathcal{L}_{W_1}(W_2) = \forall t_2 \in T_2 \text{ if } \exists t_1 \in T_1 \text{ s.t. } t_1 \sim t_2 \text{ then } t_2.name := t_1.name.$$

Now, $\langle W_2, m_2 \rangle$, a marked workflow, is said to be a cooperation candidate for $\langle W_1, m_1 \rangle$ if for any firing sequence enabled from $\langle W_1, m_1 \rangle$, there exists a firing sequence enabled from $\langle \mathcal{L}_{W_1}(W_2), m_2 \rangle$, which both have the same projection on the cooperative transitions (of $W_1$). In the following, we define such a property in terms of inclusion of projected languages.

**Definition 5.3  (cooperation candidate property).** Let $\langle W_1, m_1 \rangle$ and $\langle W_2, m_2 \rangle$ be two marked Wf-nets: $\langle W_2, m_2 \rangle$ is said to be a candidate for cooperation with $\langle W_1, m_1 \rangle$ iff $L_{\lfloor T_1}(\langle W_1, m_1 \rangle) \subseteq L_{\lfloor T_2}(\langle \mathcal{L}_{W_1}(W_2), m_2 \rangle)$.

Note that if $\langle W_1, m_1 \rangle$ and $\langle W_2, m_2 \rangle$ have the same observable language then the cooperation candidate property holds mutually.

**An Algorithm for Checking the Cooperation Candidate Property.** The cooperation candidate property is expressed as an inclusion relation between the languages of two Wf-nets once projected on the cooperative transitions. Checking such property represents the main difficulty of our approach. A naive test of this relation could drastically limit the interest of our approach. Here, we propose to use the *SOG* for this purpose. In fact, the local moves induced by the non cooperative transitions are hence abstracted (unobserved) since they are not directly involved in the inclusion test. The Wf-net $W_2$ would be an effective candidate to cooperate with $W_1$ if the language induced by the *SOG* of $W_1$ is included in that induced by *SOG* of $\mathcal{L}_{W_1}(W_2)$. To check such an inclusion, the *SOG* of $(W_1, m_1)$ is synchronized against the *SOG* of $(\mathcal{L}_{W_1}(W_2), m_2)$.

The inclusion test Algorithm 1 works on the fly i.e. the building of the synchronized product can be stopped at any moment as soon as the inclusion is proved unsatisfied. When the synchronized product is entirely built, one deduce that the inclusion holds (as long as the guards of the cooperative transitions are satisfied). The parameters of this algorithm are the *SOGs* $SoG_1 = \langle s_0, S_1, E_1 \rangle$ and $SoG_2 = \langle s'_0, S'_1, E'_1 \rangle$ of $(W_1, m_1)$ and $(\mathcal{L}_{W_1}(W_2), m_2)$ respectively. $s_0$ (resp. $s'_0$) is the initial meta-state of $SoG_1$ (resp. $SoG_2$), $S_1$ (resp. $S_2$) its set of meta-states and $E_1$ (resp. $E_2$) its set of arcs.

---

**Algorithm 1.** $(L(\langle s_0, S_1, E_1 \rangle) \subseteq L(\langle s'_0, S_2, E_2 \rangle))$?

1: **State** $s_1, s_2, s'_1, s'_2$;
2: **Set of transition** $f_1, f_2$;
3: **stack** $st(\langle State, State, Transitions \rangle)$;
4: $s_1 = s_0$;
5: $s_2 = s'_0$;
6: $f_1 = Out(s_0)$,
7: $f_2 = Out(s'_0)$;
8: **if** $f_1 \neq \emptyset$ and $f_2 \neq \emptyset$ **then**
9:    **if** $(Names(f_1) \not\subseteq Names(f_2))$ **then**
10:      **return false**;
11:    **end if**
12: **end if**
13: $Synch = \{\langle s_1, s_2 \rangle\}$;
14: $st.\textbf{Push}(\langle s_1, s_2, f_1 \rangle)$;
15: **repeat**
16:    $st.\textbf{Pop}(\langle s_1, s_2, f_1 \rangle)$;
17:    **for** $t \in f_1$ **do**
18:      $s'_1 = Img(s_1, t)$; $s'_2 = Img(s_2, t)$;
19:      **if** $\langle s'_1, s'_2 \rangle \notin Synch$ **then**
20:        $f_1 = Out(s'_1)$; $f_2 = Out(s'_2)$;
21:        **if** $f_1 \neq \emptyset$ and $f_2 \neq \emptyset$ **then**
22:          **if** $(Names(f_1) \not\subseteq Names(f_2))$
         **then**
23:            **return false**;
24:          **end if**
25:          $Synch = Synch \cup \{\langle s'_1, s'_2 \rangle\}$;
26:          $st.\textbf{Push}(\langle s'_1, s'_2, f_1 \rangle)$;
27:        **end if**
28:      **end if**
29:    **end for**
30: **until** $st$ *is empty*;
31: **return true**;

---

The data structures used by Algorithm 1 are a table *Synch* and a stack *st*. *Synch* is used to store the visited states of the synchronized product. An item of *st* is a tuple $\langle s_1, s_2, f_1 \rangle$ composed of a reachable meta-state of $(W_1, m_1)$, a reachable meta-state of $(\mathcal{L}_{W_1}(W_2), m_2)$ and a set of cooperative transitions enabled from both nodes.

Moreover, three functions are used in this algorithm. The two first ones, *Out()* and *Img()*, collect information associated to the *SOG* structure. The first one is applied to a node of the *SOG* and return the set transitions labeling its output edges. The second function is applied to a state $s_1$ and a transition $t$ (enabled in this node) and returns the reached state. The third function is *Names()* whose parameters are a set of transitions $f$ returns the set of their names.

## 5.4 BPEL Generation

Once the matching is done, we can generate a *BPEL* standard description for each *SOG*, of course if the result of the matching is positive . For instance, in our example the matching between the client *SOG* and the provider one is positive and consequently we can fill the values of the unknown *portType* in both of them.

```
<partner name="ClientPT_1" value="purchaseOrderPT">
<partner name="ProviderPT_1" value="OrderingPT">
```

In the generated *BPEL* description for the client we will have the *OrderingPT* instead of *ProviderPT_1*. Consequently, *HandleOrder, SendNotif, SendProduct* and *RecPayment* operations of *OrderingPT* will respectively replace *ReceiveOrder, SendNotif, SendProduct* and *ReceivePayment* of *ProviderPT_1*. Also, in the generated *BPEL* description for the provider the *ClientPT_1* will be replaced by *purchaseOrderPT*. For sake of space do not give the whole client and provider *BPEL* descriptions.

## 6   Conclusion and Perspectives

In this paper, we have presented an approach that enable dynamic binding for *BPEL process* that is done in three steps. First, we provide a high-level description for the process that we called *dynamic BPEL* description. In this description some parts of the process might not be known at the design time. Then the *Business process* behaviors are abstracted into symbolic observation graph using the ordered binary decision diagram technique. Finally, we have presented an efficient algorithm for symbolic observation graph matching. If the result of the matching is positive, we generate a traditional *BPEL* description for each dynamic *BPEL* process.

Since the matching is currently based on the process behavior, we are going to work on adding semantic facilities in order to enhance the matching. This ongoing work will lead to the development of a semantic registry for dynamic *BPEL* processes.

## References

[Bryant, 1986] Bryant, R. E. (1986). Graph-based algorithms for boolean function manipulation. *IEEE Transactions on Computers*, 35(8):677–691.

[Haddad et al., 2004] Haddad, S., Ilié, J.-M., and Klai, K. (2004). Design and evaluation of a symbolic and abstraction-based model checker. In Wang, F., editor, *ATVA*, volume 3299 of *LNCS*. Springer.

[Karastoyanova et al., 2005] Karastoyanova, D., Houspanossian, A., Cilia, M., Leymann, F., and Buchmann, A. (2005). Extending bpel for run time adaptability. *edoc*, 0:15–26.

[van der Aalst, 1998] van der Aalst, W. M. P. (1998). The application of petri nets to workflow management. *Journal of Circuits, Systems, and Computers*, 8(1):21–66.

[van Noord, 2000] van Noord, G. (2000). Treatment of epsilon moves in subset construction. *Computational Linguistics*, 26(1):61–76.

[Verma et al., 2004] Verma, K., Akkiraju, R., Goodwin, R., Doshi, P., and Lee, J. (2004). On accommodating inter service dependencies in web process flow composition. *AAAI Spring*, pages 37–43.

[Wegener, 2000] Wegener, I. (2000). *Branching programs and binary decision diagrams: theory and applications*. Society for Industrial and Applied Mathematics, Philadelphia, PA, USA.

# Author Index

# Lecture Notes in Computer Science

For information about Vols. 1–4074

please contact your bookseller or Springer

Vol. 4128: W.E. Nagel, W.V. Walter, W. Lehner (Eds.), Euro-Par 2006 Parallel Processing. XXXIII, 1221 pages. 2006.

Vol. 4127: E. Damiani, P. Liu (Eds.), Data and Applications Security XX. X, 319 pages. 2006.

Vol. 4126: P. Barahona, F. Bry, E. Franconi, N. Henze, U. Sattler, Reasoning Web. X, 269 pages. 2006.

Vol. 4124: H. de Meer, J.P. G. Sterbenz (Eds.), Self-Organizing Systems. XIV, 261 pages. 2006.

Vol. 4121: A. Biere, C.P. Gomes (Eds.), Theory and Applications of Satisfiability Testing - SAT 2006. XII, 438 pages. 2006.

Vol. 4119: C. Dony, J.L. Knudsen, A. Romanovsky, A. Tripathi (Eds.), Advanced Topics in Exception Handling Components. X, 302 pages. 2006.

Vol. 4117: C. Dwork (Ed.), Advances in Cryptology - CRYPTO 2006. XIII, 621 pages. 2006.

Vol. 4116: R. De Prisco, M. Yung (Eds.), Security and Cryptography for Networks. XI, 366 pages. 2006.

Vol. 4115: D.-S. Huang, K. Li, G.W. Irwin (Eds.), Computational Intelligence and Bioinformatics, Part III. XXI, 803 pages. 2006. (Sublibrary LNBI).

Vol. 4114: D.-S. Huang, K. Li, G.W. Irwin (Eds.), Computational Intelligence, Part II. XXVII, 1337 pages. 2006. (Sublibrary LNAI).

Vol. 4113: D.-S. Huang, K. Li, G.W. Irwin (Eds.), Intelligent Computing, Part I. XXVII, 1331 pages. 2006.

Vol. 4112: D.Z. Chen, D. T. Lee (Eds.), Computing and Combinatorics. XIV, 528 pages. 2006.

Vol. 4111: F.S. de Boer, M.M. Bonsangue, S. Graf, W.-P. de Roever (Eds.), Formal Methods for Components and Objects. VIII, 447 pages. 2006.

Vol. 4110: J. Díaz, K. Jansen, J.D.P. Rolim, U. Zwick (Eds.), Approximation, Randomization, and Combinatorial Optimization. XII, 522 pages. 2006.

Vol. 4109: D.-Y. Yeung, J.T. Kwok, A. Fred, F. Roli, D. de Ridder (Eds.), Structural, Syntactic, and Statistical Pattern Recognition. XXI, 939 pages. 2006.

Vol. 4108: J.M. Borwein, W.M. Farmer (Eds.), Mathematical Knowledge Management. VIII, 295 pages. 2006. (Sublibrary LNAI).

Vol. 4106: T.R. Roth-Berghofer, M.H. Göker, H. A. Güvenir (Eds.), Advances in Case-Based Reasoning. XIV, 566 pages. 2006. (Sublibrary LNAI).

Vol. 4105: B. Gunsel, A.K. Jain, A. M. Tekalp, B. Sankur (Eds.), Multimedia, Content Representation, Classification and Security. XIX, 804 pages. 2006.

Vol. 4104: T. Kunz, S.S. Ravi (Eds.), Ad-Hoc, Mobile, and Wireless Networks. XII, 474 pages. 2006.

Vol. 4103: J. Eder, S. Dustdar (Eds.), Business Process Management Workshops. XI, 508 pages. 2006.

Vol. 4102: S. Dustdar, J.L. Fiadeiro, A. Sheth (Eds.), Business Process Management. XV, 486 pages. 2006.

Vol. 4099: Q. Yang, G. Webb (Eds.), PRICAI 2006: Trends in Artificial Intelligence. XXVIII, 1263 pages. 2006. (Sublibrary LNAI).

Vol. 4098: F. Pfenning (Ed.), Term Rewriting and Applications. XIII, 415 pages. 2006.

Vol. 4097: X. Zhou, O. Sokolsky, L. Yan, E.-S. Jung, Z. Shao, Y. Mu, D.C. Lee, D. Kim, Y.-S. Jeong, C.-Z. Xu (Eds.), Emerging Directions in Embedded and Ubiquitous Computing. XXVII, 1034 pages. 2006.

Vol. 4096: E. Sha, S.-K. Han, C.-Z. Xu, M.H. Kim, L.T. Yang, B. Xiao (Eds.), Embedded and Ubiquitous Computing. XXIV, 1170 pages. 2006.

Vol. 4095: S. Nolfi, G. Baldassare, R. Calabretta, D. Marocco, D. Parisi, J.C. T. Hallam, O. Miglino, J.-A. Meyer (Eds.), From Animals to Animats 9. XV, 869 pages. 2006. (Sublibrary LNAI).

Vol. 4094: O. H. Ibarra, H.-C. Yen (Eds.), Implementation and Application of Automata. XIII, 291 pages. 2006.

Vol. 4093: X. Li, O.R. Zaïane, Z. Li (Eds.), Advanced Data Mining and Applications. XXI, 1110 pages. 2006. (Sublibrary LNAI).

Vol. 4092: J. Lang, F. Lin, J. Wang (Eds.), Knowledge Science, Engineering and Management. XV, 664 pages. 2006. (Sublibrary LNAI).

Vol. 4091: G.-Z. Yang, T. Jiang, D. Shen, L. Gu, J. Yang (Eds.), Medical Imaging and Augmented Reality. XIII, 399 pages. 2006.

Vol. 4090: S. Spaccapietra, K. Aberer, P. Cudré-Mauroux (Eds.), Journal on Data Semantics VI. XI, 211 pages. 2006.

Vol. 4089: W. Löwe, M. Südholt (Eds.), Software Composition. X, 339 pages. 2006.

Vol. 4088: Z.-Z. Shi, R. Sadananda (Eds.), Agent Computing and Multi-Agent Systems. XVII, 827 pages. 2006. (Sublibrary LNAI).

Vol. 4087: F. Schwenker, S. Marinai (Eds.), Artificial Neural Networks in Pattern Recognition. IX, 299 pages. 2006. (Sublibrary LNAI).

Vol. 4085: J. Misra, T. Nipkow, E. Sekerinski (Eds.), FM 2006: Formal Methods. XV, 620 pages. 2006.

Vol. 4084: M.A. Wimmer, H.J. Scholl, Å. Grönlund, K.V. Andersen (Eds.), Electronic Government. XV, 353 pages. 2006.

Vol. 4083: S. Fischer-Hübner, S. Furnell, C. Lambrinoudakis (Eds.), Trust and Privacy in Digital Business. XIII, 243 pages. 2006.

Vol. 4082: K. Bauknecht, B. Pröll, H. Werthner (Eds.), E-Commerce and Web Technologies. XIII, 243 pages. 2006.

Vol. 4081: A. M. Tjoa, J. Trujillo (Eds.), Data Warehousing and Knowledge Discovery. XVII, 578 pages. 2006.

Vol. 4080: S. Bressan, J. Küng, R. Wagner (Eds.), Database and Expert Systems Applications. XXI, 959 pages. 2006.

Vol. 4079: S. Etalle, M. Truszczyński (Eds.), Logic Programming. XIV, 474 pages. 2006.

Vol. 4077: M.-S. Kim, K. Shimada (Eds.), Geometric Modeling and Processing - GMP 2006. XVI, 696 pages. 2006.

Vol. 4076: F. Hess, S. Pauli, M. Pohst (Eds.), Algorithmic Number Theory. X, 599 pages. 2006.

Vol. 4075: U. Leser, F. Naumann, B. Eckman (Eds.), Data Integration in the Life Sciences. XI, 298 pages. 2006. (Sublibrary LNBI).